UNDERSTANDING SECURED TRANSACTIONS

LexisNexis Law School Publishing Advisory Board

UNDERSTANDING SECURED TRANSACTIONS

FOURTH EDITION

William H. Lawrence
*University of San Diego
School of Law*

William H. Henning
*University of Alabama
School of Law*

R. Wilson Freyermuth
*University of Missouri-Columbia
School of Law*

ISBN#: 1-4224-1750-6

Library of Congress Cataloging-in-Publication Data

Lawrence, William H.
  Understanding secured transactions / William H. Lawrence, William H. Henning, R.
  Wilson Freyermuth. --4th ed.
    p. cm.
  Includes index.
  ISBN 1-4224-1750-6 (softbound)
    1. Security (Law)--United States. I. Henning, William H., 1947-II. Freyermuth, R.
  Wilson, 1962-III. Title.
  KF1050.L39 2007
  346.7307'4--dc22

                                                              2007028341

NOTE TO USERS
**To ensure that you are using the latest materials available in this area, please
be sure to periodically check the LexisNexis Law School web site for
downloadable updates and supplements at www.lexisnexis.com/lawschool**

Editorial Offices
744 Broad Street, Newark, NJ 07102 (973) 820-2000
201 Mission St., San Francisco, CA 94105-1831 (415) 908-3200
701 East Water Street, Charlottesville, VA 22902-7587 (434) 972-7600
www.lexis.com

For my son, Marcus, with love
W.H.L.

For my wife, Jeannie,
who is still my sweetheart after all these
years
W.H.H.

For my wife, Shari, with love and gratitude
R.W.F.

PREFACE

Like the other books in the *Understanding* series, this book is designed as a student text. Our approach is to aid students' understanding of secured transactions by informing them about both the law and the nature of the transactions to which the law applies.

The primary sources of law are Article 9 of the Uniform Commercial Code and selected provisions of the Bankruptcy Reform Act. Beyond a focus on the text of the statutes, an analysis of their underlying rationales is critical to an in-depth understanding of the codified provisions. The Official Comments to the U.C.C. and the Historical and Revision Notes to the Bankruptcy Reform Act are helpful but often lack sufficient insights or clarity to provide adequate guidance. Learning the essence of each statutory section in isolation is difficult and insufficient; students must learn to interrelate multiple sections in a sophisticated manner in order to solve problems in this complex area of the law.

When the first edition of this book was published, the 1972 text of Article 9, as amended from time to time, was in effect. In 1998, the U.C.C.'s sponsoring bodies, the National Conference of Commissioners on Uniform State Laws and the American Law Institute, adopted a revised version of Article 9.[1] The revision represented a comprehensive modernization and reformulation of the law governing secured transactions. It was not in effect in any state as of the publication date of the second edition of this book, which was designed as a transitional work. The primary emphasis of the second edition was the 1972 Official Text, but it also provided a discussion of the revision and explained how its provisions would change existing law.

Revised Article 9 was a remarkable success! It was promulgated with a delayed effective date of July 1, 2001,[2] and by that date it was in effect in virtually every state, with the other states coming along within a few months thereafter. This universal adoption compelled the third edition, which focused on revised Article 9 and discussed former law only to the extent necessary to shed light on particular provisions of the revision.

This fourth edition was necessitated by significant revisions to bankruptcy law resulting from the Bankruptcy Abuse Prevention and Consumer Protection Act of 2005. It comes at an opportune time, however, as the first wave of reported cases under revised Article 9 has now been published. It is still true that most of the cases cited in this edition were decided under former law, but many of the cited cases interpret and apply the revision.

---

[1] The sponsors approved minor amendments to revised Article 9 in 1999, 2000, and 2001.

[2] This was done to avoid the "horrendous complications" that would have arisen had part of the country remained subject to former law while another part adopted revised Article 9. U.C.C. § 9-701, Comment 1.

The law of secured transactions reflects business practices with which many students are unfamiliar. An understanding of the essential aspects of the transactions themselves is crucial for any student who seeks to comprehend the law that governs them. This book explains different types of secured transactions. For example, it describes the structure and use of financing arrangements that are made possible through such techniques as asset-based securitization, mortgage warehouse lending, terminal and field warehousing, financing of accounts, factoring of accounts, and floor planning, as well as other methods of transacting business. The discussion of each financing arrangement is integrated into the place in the text in which the relevant substantive concepts are covered.

Much of the practice in the area of secured transactions involves preventative law, in which the practitioner advises the client on alternative methods of structuring transactions and the risks associated with each option. The book integrates and develops significant aspects of these considerations, going beyond the text of the U.C.C. by explaining the practical constraints that ultimately shape decision-making in this field.

The organization of the subject matter of the text is largely based upon the traditional five-part approach to the law of secured transactions: (1) scope of the article, (2) attachment (creation) of security interests, (3) perfection of security interests, (4) priorities among competing claimants to collateral (*i.e.*, the effects of perfection or nonperfection), and (5) enforcement of security interests. This organizational scheme is emphasized by designating each of these five concepts as a separate Part of the book.

Entries in the Table of Contents include a descriptive word or phrase, along with relevant section numbers of the U.C.C. and the Bankruptcy Reform Act. The Table of Contents does not cite all the provisions that might be relevant, but only the most fundamental provisions relating to the particular topic. This approach should aid students using the book as a supplemental text by enabling them to find the relevant discussion based on either the subject or the basic statutory section numbers. The Index and the Table of Statutes and Authorities enable a more detailed search.

ACKNOWLEDGMENTS

Professor Lawrence gratefully acknowledges the support provided by a summer research grant from the University of San Diego.

Professor Henning gratefully acknowledges the generosity of the University of Alabama Law School Foundation, which supports his scholarship.

Professor Freyermuth gratefully acknowledges the generosity of John K. Hulston, W. Dudley and Elizabeth McCarter, Charles H. Rehm, Edgar Mayfield, John W. Cowden, and the law firm of Thompson Coburn LLP, whose financial support facilitated his contributions to this book.

June 2007
William H. Lawrence
William H. Henning
R. Wilson Freyermuth

TABLE OF CONTENTS

Part I

SCOPE

SYNOPSIS

[A] The Security Concept

The concept of a secured obligation arose to encourage lending, and thus promote commercial activity, by reducing the risk borne by lenders. Absent security, a borrower's mere promise to repay money, albeit legally enforceable, might not suffice to induce a prospective lender to proceed with a transaction — and even if the lender agreed to proceed, the interest rate would inevitably reflect the level of risk. Similarly, a seller might be reluctant to give a prospective buyer current possession of property based solely on the buyer's promise to make installment payments. Lenders and credit sellers inevitably, whether secured or not, run the risk that an obligor will prove unable or unwilling to make the agreed payments. An unsecured creditor of either type that wishes to enforce its rights following a breach must proceed by judicial action. The process can be long and expensive, requiring a lawsuit to reduce the claim to judgment and then, perhaps, an execution on the judgment. To execute on a judgment, the successful litigant must procure a writ of execution, which the sheriff will attempt to execute by levying on property of the debtor. Exemption provisions will likely shield some or all of the debtor's property from the execution process. For property that is reached, the sheriff will conduct an auction sale, which generally yields low prices, and distribute the proceeds to the judgment creditor in full or partial satisfaction of the judgment. The expense and delay associated with these procedures leaves lenders and sellers reluctant to rely solely upon their rights under debt or sales law.

Lenders and credit sellers can enhance their positions in two major ways. They can insist that their obligor obtain a promise from a third person to act as surety and pay the obligation in the event of default. They can also insist that their obligor grant them an interest in real or personal property as security. The latter technique gives the creditor a special property interest in the identified property. One of the great advantages of this enhanced position is that, in the event of default, the creditor can proceed directly against the security without having first to reduce its claim to judgment. Secured creditors thus can reduce significantly the costs and delays associated with enforcement of their rights.

Although mortgage financing and secured financing are analogous with regard to real and personal property respectively, they are governed by separate bodies of law. The focus of this book is on secured personal-property financing, with Article 9 of the Uniform Commercial Code (U.C.C.)

as the predominant applicable law. Some overlaps between the bodies of law will be discussed in this book, the most important being the treatment of fixtures. [1]

In Article 9 terminology, the creditor's special property interest is called a "security interest," [2] and it is created through the consent of the debtor. Absent a security interest, a creditor has no property interest in any particular asset of its debtor. An unsecured seller of goods does not retain a property interest even in the goods sold; [3] in the event of a breach, the seller's basic remedy is its Article 2 claim for the unpaid balance of the purchase price. [4] Acquiring a consensual security interest adds the rights available to secured parties under Article 9.

Although a security interest gives a secured party a property interest in identified assets of the debtor, the interest is unique, with two primary features defining its essential nature. First, a secured party does not have any right to foreclose on collateral unless a default occurs. [5] Because the secured party's property interest does not allow it to proceed against the property absent default, such action would constitute conversion. Second, even following a default, the secured party's disposition of the collateral is only for the purpose of satisfying the outstanding indebtedness. Generally, the secured party will dispose of the collateral by sale and apply the proceeds of the sale to the amount of the debt still owed. [6] A security interest thus allows a creditor to proceed, after default and without judicial process, directly against specific assets of the debtor to satisfy the outstanding indebtedness.

[B] An Organizational Overview of Article 9

The content of Article 9 is organized around five major concepts: the scope of the article; attachment of security interests; perfection of security interests; priorities among competing claimants to collateral; and enforcement of security interests. These concepts are so logical and basic that the

---

[1] Fixtures are discussed in Chapter 15. *See also* the discussion of secondary financing transactions involving real estate in § 1.07[C] *infra*.

[2] U.C.C. § 1-201(b)(35).

[3] A "sale" involves the passage of title to goods for a price. U.C.C. § 2-106(1). Unless the seller and buyer agree otherwise, the goods belong to the buyer and the seller receives in exchange only a legally enforceable right to the purchase price. U.C.C. §§ 2-607(1), 2-709(1).

[4] A credit seller may also have a right to reclaim the goods themselves from the buyer, but such rights are extremely limited. The seller must ascertain that the buyer received the goods while insolvent, and even then the seller generally must notify the buyer of its intent to reclaim them within ten days following their receipt. *See* U.C.C. § 2-702.

[5] "*After default*, a secured party has the rights provided in this [Part 6 governing enforcement of security interest]. . . ." U.C.C. § 9-601(a) (emphasis supplied). For a discussion of this provision, *see* § 17.02 *infra*.

[6] U.C.C. §§ 9-615(a). The secured party cannot retain any surplus realized upon the sale, but rather must account for it to the debtor. U.C.C. § 9-615(d). For discussion of the disposition of collateral after default, see § 18.02 *infra*.

text of this book is structured around them; they constitute the subjects of the five Parts of the book.

Scope questions focus on identification of the transactions to which Article 9 applies. Although, generally, the applicability of Article 9 is eminently apparent, the issue has proved to be one of the most litigated areas under the U.C.C. Certain transactions may be labeled as something other than a security interest by the parties (*e.g.*, a lease or consignment) yet be the functional equivalent of an Article 9 secured transaction and thus within its scope.[7] In addition, certain outright sales transactions also fall within the scope of the article.[8]

Attachment of a security interest addresses how security interests are created. The process is contractual because Article 9 security interests are consensual in nature. The essential requirements are quite simple, although troublesome questions inevitably arise in some specific contexts. Enforceability of the agreement may also be an issue because of the inclusion in Article 9 of a statute-of-frauds provision.

The relationship between a secured party and a debtor is established by agreement. A secured party must also be concerned, however, about the possibility of competing third-party claims to the collateral. In particular, courts are sympathetic with third parties that enter into relationships with the debtor on the mistaken belief that the debtor holds unencumbered ownership of assets in its possession. This problem is sometimes referred to as an "ostensible ownership" problem. To enhance its position against such claimants, a secured party must ordinarily "perfect" its security interest, generally by taking steps designed to give public notice of the interest. The most effective mechanism for overcoming the ostensible-ownership problem is for the secured party to take possession of the collateral, and thus possession is an accepted method of perfection for assets capable of being physically possessed. Possession is impossible with certain forms of collateral and often impractical with others, and the most commonly used method of perfection is the public filing of a financing statement.[9] Several additional methods of perfection are available in limited circumstances. The discussion of perfection in this book focuses on the applicable methods of giving public notice and the policy choices that the drafters made in devising the perfection process.

If the interests of claimants conflict with respect to particular property, the law must have rules by which it can prioritize the competing interests. If one of the competing claimants is a secured party, most of the priority rules are contained in Article 9. Federal bankruptcy law is also important with respect to secured claims that are asserted in a bankruptcy proceeding. Some of the third-party claimants with which a secured party might have

---

[7] *See* § 1.03[B] *infra.*

[8] *See* § 1.06 *infra.*

[9] Indeed, filing is the default rule for perfection under Article 9. U.C.C. § 9-310(a). An overview of the various methods of perfection is provided in Chapter 4 *infra.*

to compete include a bankruptcy trustee, another secured party, an unsecured creditor that causes the sheriff to levy on the collateral, a person that buys, leases, or licenses the collateral from the debtor, a person that stores or repairs the collateral and thereby acquires a claim to it based on state law other than Article 9, and a person with an interest in real estate to which a fixture that is collateral is affixed. This list by no means exhausts the potential claimants.

Default is a pivotal concept because it permits the secured party to enforce its security interest against the collateral. The enforcement phase of a transaction is sometimes referred to as the "foreclosure process." The issues associated with default include a determination of the events that constitute a default, the rights and duties of the parties following a default, the method chosen for the disposition of the collateral, and the provisions dealing with misbehavior by the secured party.

[C] The Revised Uniform Commercial Code

The Uniform Commercial Code is the product of a partnership between two organizations: the National Conference of Commissioners on Uniform State Laws and the American Law Institute. After an Official Text has been approved by the sponsors, it is introduced in the legislatures of the various states[10] and only becomes law to the extent it is adopted by a particular legislature. The 1962 Official Text of the Uniform Commercial Code was the first to be widely enacted, and the version of Article 9 contained in that text was a radical departure from antecedent security devices.[11] It was extensively revised in 1972, and again in 1998. The 1998 Official Text was amended by the Code's sponsors in 1999, 2000, and 2001. It was amended again in 2003 by a set of conforming amendments promulgated as part of a revision of Article 7. Thus, a cite to Article 9 in this book that does not designate an official text is to the 2003 Official Text. When the book makes a reference to the intent of the original drafters, it cites the 1962 Official Text even though there were antecedent versions of the Code. When it discusses former law, it generally means the law that immediately preceded the 1998 revision and cites the 1972 Official Text, even though that text was amended from time to time. Citations to the 1962 or 1972 Official Texts are so noted within the citation.

Article 9 is, of course, part of the broader Uniform Commercial Code, and it interrelates with provisions of the other articles in a variety of ways.[12] Beginning in 1987, there was an extensive effort by the Code's sponsors to update and modernize it, beginning with a new Article 2A on leases of goods. The process included a revision of Article 1 that was approved in

---

[10] As used in Article 9 (and the U.C.C. generally), the term "state" means "a State of the United States, the District of Columbia, Puerto Rico, the United States Virgin Islands, or any territory or insular possession subject to the jurisdiction of the United States." U.C.C. § 9-102(a)(76).

[11] *See* § 1.02 *infra.*

[12] *See* the discussion in § 1.08 *infra.*

2001 and culminated in 2003 with revisions of, or amendments to, Articles 2, 2A, and 7. Unless otherwise stated, all citations in this book to another article are to the latest Official Text of the article.

Chapter 1

TRANSACTIONS WITHIN ARTICLE 9

SYNOPSIS

§ 1.01   THE PRE-CODE DISARRAY OF SECURED TRANSACTIONS LAW

The law governing the use of personal property as collateral prior to the promulgation of the U.C.C. was inefficient, unduly complicated, and inadequate. It consisted of a patchwork quilt of common-law rules and statutes governing each of the security devices that states chose to recognize. Some of the traditional security devices included the pledge (in which the lender took possession of the collateral pending default or repayment), chattel mortgage (in which the debtor retained possession pending default), conditional sale (in which the seller delivered goods to the buyer but retained title pending payment), trust receipt (a three-party arrangement by which a lender financed a dealer's acquisition of new inventory from a supplier), and factor's lien (in which the debtor obtained financing on the strength of its existing inventory).[13]

Because each security device was the subject of a separate rule or statute, differences in formal requirements were common. For example, failure to file public notice of a chattel mortgage generally voided the mortgage against all third parties, whereas filing was not needed for a conditional sale or at most was required only in order for the seller to prevail over lien creditors. States maintained multiple filing systems to accommodate the different security devices, and inconsistencies in formalities, rights, and filing requirements abounded. Most of the differences could not be traced to functional justifications. Errors attributable to the undue complexity of the overall system were frequent and had a serious impact on affected parties.

---

[13] Other devices, usually authorized by statute, permitted the use of accounts receivable as collateral, facilitated the establishment of corporate trust indentures, authorized the use of field warehouses, etc. A laundry list of pre-Code security devices was originally provided in U.C.C. § 9-102(2) (1962 Official Text). By the time of the most recent revision of the article, the list was no longer considered necessary.

Despite the multiplicity of security devices, the overall system was inadequate. The economy constantly evolves, thereby necessitating the creation of new types of transactions that are responsive to unique business conditions. Some desirable secured financing transactions could not go forward because they did not fall squarely within the parameters of any of the existing security devices. For example, despite increased interest in using inventory and intangibles as collateral, lenders struggled for years to develop devices that would be effective for these kinds of assets. These problems were eventually solved in some states by the addition of new, statutorily-sanctioned security devices, but ultimately this approach proved unpalatable as each device added new wrinkles to an already overly complex system. The state of the law imposed unacceptable delay, cost, and uncertainty.

§ 1.02   THE UNITARY APPROACH OF ARTICLE 9; TERMINOLOGY DESCRIBING PARTIES

The promulgation of Article 9 of the U.C.C. represented a significant milestone in the law of secured financing. Article 9 provides the basis for a single, comprehensive statutory framework for the governance of secured transactions in personal property and fixtures. The objective of the original drafters was stated succinctly in the Comments: "The aim of this Article is to provide a simple and unified structure within which the immense variety of present-day secured financing transactions can go forward with less cost and with greater certainty."[14]

Article 9 achieved this objective by adopting a unitary approach to secured transactions. It did not abolish the previously existing security devices.[15] Even today, the use of terms like "pledge" and "conditional sale" is common. Prior statutes governing these devices were repealed, however, and Article 9 replaced them. Unless specifically excluded,[16] Article 9 applies to all transactions that create security interests in personal property or fixtures by contract. Neither the form of the transaction nor the terminology used by the parties is controlling. In other words, all consensual transactions that created security interests in personal property or fixtures were swept into the article.[17]

In addition to overcoming the disarray associated with prior secured financing law, the enactment of Article 9 with its comprehensive, unitary approach facilitated the use of new financing methods. The benefits of such flexibility were touted as among the basic objectives of the article. The original Comments stated:

---

[14] U.C.C. § 9-101, Comment (1962 Official Text). Although Official Texts were promulgated earlier, it was not until the promulgation of the 1962 Official Text that the U.C.C. achieved widespread adoption.

[15] U.C.C. § 9-102(2) and Comment 1 (1962 Official Text).

[16] *See* § 1.07 *infra.*

[17] U.C.C. § 9-109(a).

The Article's flexibility and simplified formalities should make it possible for new forms of secured financing, as they develop, to fit comfortably under its provisions, thus avoiding the necessity, so apparent in recent years, of year by year passing new statutes and tinkering with the old ones to allow legitimate business transactions to go forward.[18]

The simplification achieved by Article 9's unitary approach is readily demonstrated through the terms used to describe secured transactions and their participants. Irrespective of the nature of the transaction or the terminology employed by the parties, Article 9 applies a consistent set of terms. The underlying "security agreement"[19] creates a "security interest"[20] in favor of a "secured party."[21] The property that is subject to the security interest is the "collateral."[22] The person that provides the collateral is the "debtor."[23] The term "obligor" describes the person that owes payment or performance of the secured obligation.[24] If the transaction is a consumer transaction,[25] the terms "consumer debtor"[26] and "consumer obligor"[27] are used.

Article 9 also contains certain provisions that apply to parties that are secondarily obligated[28] (such as sureties) and such parties are known as "secondary obligors."[29] For example, suppose A needs to borrow money but

---

[18] U.C.C. § 9-101, Comment (1962 Official Text).

[19] U.C.C. § 9-102(a)(73). Security agreements are discussed extensively in Chapter 2.

[20] U.C.C. § 1-201(b)(35). This term is discussed extensively in the next subsection of the text.

[21] U.C.C. § 9-102(a)(72).

[22] U.C.C. § 9-102(a)(12). For a discussion of the different classifications of collateral, see § 1.04 infra.

[23] U.C.C. § 9-102(a)(28). In the original article, the person that owed payment or other performance of the secured obligation was also a "debtor," but use of the same term to describe parties with different functions caused confusion. U.C.C. § 9-105(1)(d) (1962 Official Text).

[24] U.C.C. § 9-102(a)(59). In a transaction in which one person incurs an obligation and provides collateral to secure it, that person is both a debtor and an obligor, meaning that a Code provision applicable to either a debtor or to an obligor applies to the person. However, if one person incurs the obligation and another provides the collateral, the former person will be an obligor and the latter a debtor. A provision applying to obligors applies to the former person but not the latter; a provision applying to debtors applies to the latter person but not the former.

[25] See U.C.C. § 9-102(a)(26) and the discussion in § 1.04[A][1] infra. Article 9 contains a number of protective provisions applicable to consumer transactions.

[26] U.C.C. § 9-102(a)(22).

[27] U.C.C. § 9-102(a)(25).

[28] For example, most of the rights and duties with regard to the foreclosure process affect secondary obligors but not other obligors. See, e.g., U.C.C. § 9-611(c) (requiring secured party to send notice of disposition to secondary obligors but not other obligors). The major exception to this is U.C.C. § 9-616(b), which gives any consumer obligor, whether secondary or otherwise, a right in some circumstances to an explanation of the method by which a surplus or deficiency was calculated.

[29] U.C.C. § 9-102(a)(71). "Secondary obligor" is a subset of "obligor," and a provision applicable to obligors is also applicable to secondary obligors. A provision applicable to secondary obligors is not applicable to an obligor that is not a secondary obligor.

has insufficient collateral. A's friend, B, allows A to use her car as collateral but refuses to become personally obligated, meaning that she will not be liable if A defaults and foreclosure on the car yields less than the amount of the secured obligation. Even this is not enough for the secured party, and another friend, C, incurs personal liability for the debt, either by co-signing A's promissory note for accommodation[30] or by signing a separate guaranty agreement.[31] On these facts, A is an obligor, B is a debtor, and C is an obligor and a secondary obligor. For another example, assume A borrows money and uses his car as collateral. To accommodate A, B co-signs A's note for accommodation and grants a security interest in her car as collateral for her obligation as co-signer. If the secured party enforces its security interest in A's car, A is both a debtor and an obligor and B is an obligor and a secondary obligor. If the secured party enforces its security interest in B's car, A is an obligor but not a debtor; B is a debtor, an obligor, and a secondary obligor.

The definition of "debtor" includes any person, other than a secured party or lienholder, with an interest in the collateral.[32] This can be the person that created the security interest, another person with an interest in the collateral at the time the security interest is created (*e.g.*, a joint tenant), or a subsequent transferee of the collateral or of an interest in the collateral. The person being referred to in a particular provision is generally clear from the context. Subject to exceptions discussed elsewhere in this book, an ordinary transferee will take the collateral subject to the secured party's security interest but beyond that will not be bound by the terms of the security agreement that created the interest. There are certain situations, however, in which a transferee does become so bound,[33] and, to differentiate that transferee from others, the term "new debtor"[34] is used.

---

[30] *See* U.C.C. § 3-419(a) (accommodation party is a person that, without benefitting directly, signs a negotiable instrument in order to accommodate another party to the instrument). An accommodation party's obligation might be stated in primary (*i.e.*, unconditional) terms, but such a party would have a right of recourse against the accommodated party and thus would qualify as a secondary obligor. U.C.C. § 3-419(e).

[31] Unlike an accommodation party, whose obligations are governed by Article 3, the obligations of a surety that does not sign a negotiable instrument are governed by law other than the U.C.C.

[32] U.C.C. § 9-102(a)(28)(A).

[33] *See* U.C.C. §§ 9-203(d), (e) (when person becomes bound by security agreement and effect of becoming bound); 9-508 (effectiveness of financing statement filed in the name of the original debtor after new debtor becomes bound).

[34] U.C.C. § 9-102(a)(56) (new debtor is "a person that becomes bound as debtor under Section 9-203(d) by a security agreement previously entered into by another person."). The person that previously entered into the security agreement is the "original debtor." U.C.C. § 9-102(a)(60). "New debtors" are discussed in § 5.02[C][2] *infra*.

§ 1.03 GENERAL APPLICABILITY OF ARTICLE 9

[A] Consensual Security Interests — § 9-109(a)(1)

Article 9 applies to "a transaction, regardless of its form, that creates a security interest in personal property or fixtures by contract."[35] Article 1 defines "security interest" broadly, the key part of the definition for current purposes being "an interest in personal property or fixtures which secures payment or performance of an obligation."[36] Article 9 thus applies to consensual encumbrances, as distinct from encumbrances that arise by operation of law (such as judicial, common-law, or statutory liens). Excluding for now certain designated exceptions from its scope,[37] Article 9 governs all consensual transactions that create security interests in personal property and fixtures.

The scope of Article 9 is based on substance rather than form. With parties sometimes disposed to disguise the true nature of their transactions, courts cannot simply accept their expressions of intention as controlling. As will be demonstrated below,[38] parties sometimes characterize a transaction as a consignment or lease when, at a functional level, the transaction operates like a secured transaction. Thus, the basic scope provision of the 1998 revision does not refer, as did former law,[39] to contracts that are intended to create security interests, but rather to contracts that actually create such interests.[40]

[B] Leases and Consignments

[1] Disguised Leases

One of the primary areas of difficulty with the scope of Article 9 has been distinguishing secured transactions involving goods as collateral from leases of goods. With the promulgation of Article 2A on leases of personal property, the drafters made corresponding amendments to Article 1 to address the problem. The previous test, which relied on intent,[41] was replaced with a test that focuses on a transaction's economic nature.[42]

---

[35] U.C.C. § 9-109(a)(1). The article also governs sales of certain rights to payment. *See* § 1.06 *infra*.

[36] U.C.C. § 1-201(b)(35).

[37] *See* § 1.07 *infra*.

[38] *See* § 1.03[B] *infra*.

[39] U.C.C. § 9-102(a)(1) (1972 Official Text). The use of the word "intended" led to undue confusion.

[40] U.C.C. § 9-109, Comment 1, states that the article applies "regardless of the form of the transaction or the name that parties have given to it."

[41] U.C.C. § 1-201(37) (1962 Official Text).

[42] The provision was initially part of a revised definition of security interest but was moved as part of the 2001 revision of Article 1 to a separate section — U.C.C. § 1-203.

The essential characteristics of secured transactions and leases are easy to distinguish. A credit seller that retains a security interest in goods delivered to a buyer passes title to the goods.[43] The retained security interest gives the seller the right to repossess the goods in the event of default by the buyer.[44] Upon repossession, the seller/secured party must dispose of the goods[45] and apply the proceeds to the outstanding indebtedness.[46] Any surplus proceeds belong to the buyer/debtor.[47]

A lessor also retains an interest in goods delivered to another, in this case the lessee. Like a secured party, a lessor can repossess the goods following a default.[48] Unlike the secured party, however, the lessor is not required to dispose of the goods following repossession.[49] The lessor at all times retained title and thus owns the residual interest.

Distinguishing leases and secured transactions in actual practice has proved difficult and has led to some of the most pervasive litigation under the Code.[50] The similarity of some of the attributes of the transactions contributes to the problem. An even more significant factor is that, for a variety of reasons related to taxes, accounting, or bankruptcy, parties sometimes disguise a secured transaction by calling it a lease. For example, suppose a dealer delivers a piece of equipment to a user pursuant to a written contract binding the user to make 24 equal monthly payments of $1,000 each. The writing, which refers to the transaction as a "lease," the installments as "lease payments," and the parties as "lessor" and "lessee," provides that the user will have the option to purchase the equipment for $10 at the end of the "lease term" even though the parties anticipate that it will have significantly more value at that time. Because any rational economic actor will exercise the option and become the owner, the transaction is the economic equivalent of a sale. Further, the "lessor's" right to repossess the "leased property" in the event of default operates as a security device. The Code directs the courts to look through the parties' terminology and sweeps the security aspects of the transaction into Article 9.[51] This means that the "lessor" will have to follow Article 9's disposition rules after repossession and will have to perfect its interest under Article 9 (usually

---

[43] A sale by definition involves the passage of title. U.C.C. § 2-106(1). Even if the seller and buyer agree that the seller will retain title to the goods pending full payment (sometimes called a "conditional sale"), the seller's interest is limited to a reservation of a security interest. U.C.C. §§ 1-201(b)(35), 2-401(1). *See also* U.C.C. § 9-110.

[44] U.C.C. § 9-609(a).

[45] U.C.C. § 9-610(a).

[46] U.C.C. § 9-615(a). This assumes that strict foreclosure is not used. The different methods for disposing of collateral after default are discussed in Chapter 18 *infra*.

[47] U.C.C. § 9-615(d)(1).

[48] U.C.C. § 2A-525(2).

[49] U.C.C. § 2A-527.

[50] *See* the extensive case law citations in W. Lawrence & J. Minan, The Law of Personal Property Leasing 2-6 to 2-21 (1993).

[51] U.C.C. § 9-109(a)(1).

by a public filing)[52] to obtain priority against third parties that might acquire a competing interest in the goods.[53]

Inadequate legal standards have played a significant role in blurring the boundaries. The original definition of "security interest" included a sentence directed toward distinguishing leases and secured transactions[54] which proved woefully inadequate.[55] The revised test is extremely long and complex, but it does provide an effective standard based on functional considerations. Rather than continuing the original test's unworkable central standard relying on the parties' intent, the current test focuses on the economics of the transaction. The basic economic reality of a lease is that the lessor has retained a meaningful residual interest. The test thus is directed toward determining whether the terms of the transaction actually compensate the purported lessor for the residual interest, as well as for the use of the goods during the lease term.

Whether a transaction called a lease by the parties creates a true lease or a security interest is generally determined by the facts of the case.[56] However, a transaction creates a security interest as a matter of law if: (1) the lessee does not have a right to terminate the lease before its stated expiration date, and (2) any one of several enumerated factors is present.[57] If the lessee has a right to terminate the lease, the lessor retains a meaningful residual interest unless the right cannot be exercised until the lessor has been fully compensated for the economic value of the goods. Accordingly, if the lease contains a right of termination, whether it creates a security interest must be determined under a facts-and-circumstances test.

Assuming no right of termination, a transaction creates a security interest as a matter of law if any of the enumerated factors is present. One of these factors is that the original term of the lease equals or exceeds the

---

[52] Article 9 provides that a lessor, concerned that a court might conclude that a transaction called a lease in fact creates a disguised security interest, may make a protective filing, using the terms "lessor" and "lessee" instead of "secured party" and "debtor." U.C.C. § 9-505(a). Such a filing, standing alone, is not an admission that the transaction is not a true lease. U.C.C. § 9-505(b). This provision also applies to certain consignment and consignment-like transactions, a related topic that is discussed in the next subsection.

[53] With one optional provision for leased goods that become fixtures, U.C.C. § 2A-309, a true lessor need not make a public filing to protect its residual interest. U.C.C. § 2A-301.

[54] U.C.C. § 1-201(37) (1962 Official Text).

[55] For a critique of the inadequacies of the original definition, see W. Lawrence & J. Minan, The Law of Personal Property Leasing 2-15 to 2-21 (1993).

[56] U.C.C. § 1-203(a). Subsection (c) provides that a transaction in the form of a lease does not create a security interest merely because certain factors may be present. For example, a full payout lease does not create a security interest as a matter of law, nor does a typical net lease. In a full payout lease, the lessor receives rent equaling or exceeding the full cost of its investment in the leased goods. In a net lease, the lessee assumes responsibilities normally associated with ownership, such as the responsibilities to pay for insurance, taxes, or maintenance.

[57] U.C.C. § 1-203(b).

remaining economic life of the goods.[58] The economic reality of such a transaction is that the purported lessor has not retained a meaningful residual interest in the goods but rather has sold the goods and retained a security interest in them against the outstanding obligation. The practical effect is precisely the same if a lessee that cannot terminate the lease is bound to renew it to the end of the economic life of the goods, or is bound to become the owner of the goods. The lessee is contractually obligated to pay for the remaining economic life of the goods, leaving no meaningful residual interest in the lessor.

The remaining factors address the role of options. They cover the circumstances in which a lessee, upon compliance with the terms of the lease, has the option to become the owner of the goods or to renew the lease for the remaining economic life of the goods. If the lessee can exercise either option for no additional consideration or for only nominal consideration,[59] the transaction is not a true lease but is rather a security interest. The purported rental payments in such a transaction obviously compensate the lessor not only for the lessee's use of the goods during the lease term but also for the residual value that remains in the goods following the lease term. Despite the labels applied by the parties, the economic reality is that a lessor willing to allow a lessee to retain the goods for nominal or even no additional consideration has not retained a meaningful residual interest. Conversely, a lessor has retained the requisite interest for a true lease if the lessee must pay more than nominal additional consideration in order to exercise an option to purchase the goods or to renew the lease until the end of the economic life of the goods.

[2] Disguised Consignments

In some trades, it is common for a supplier to send goods to a retailer on consignment, with the understanding that the retailer will make an effort to sell the goods. If successful, the retailer retains a percentage of the sales price and remits the remainder to the supplier. Until and unless the consigned goods are sold, title remains with the supplier/consignor and does not pass to the retailer/consignee. Goods that the retailer cannot sell are returned to the supplier, with no further obligation on the part of the retailer. The consignment approach — which has the legal characteristics of a bailment with an authority in the bailee to sell — serves to entice the retailer to attempt sales of merchandise that the retailer would not purchase outright. It can also serve as a type of inventory financing because the retailer's inventory is maintained through the capital of the consignor.

---

[58] The remaining economic life of the goods must be determined based on the facts and circumstances that exist at the time the transaction is entered into. U.C.C. § 1-203(e).

[59] Additional consideration is deemed to be nominal "if it is less than the lessee's reasonably predictable cost of performing under the lease agreement if the option is not exercised." U.C.C. § 1-203(d). It is not nominal if, at the time the option to renew or become the owner is granted, the agreed rent or price is to be based on fair market values for rent or price. *Id.* The various components of the test (reasonably predictable cost of performing, fair market rent or price) are to be determined based on the facts and circumstances that exist at the time the transaction is entered into. U.C.C. § 1-203(e).

At common law, consignors could reacquire consigned goods free of the interests of creditors of the consignee, even if the consignor did nothing to provide public notice of its interest in the consigned goods. This created an ostensible-ownership problem in that a dishonest consignee could hold itself out as the true owner of the consigned goods and thereby deceive a lender into advancing funds against their value.[60]

The key feature of a true consignment is that the risk of nonsale falls on the consignor. By contrast, in a sales transaction, the buyer must pay for the goods whether or not they are successfully resold. Under Article 2, an agreement reserving title in a seller until the buyer fully pays for delivered goods in a sale transaction is reduced in effect to the creation of a security interest.[61] If the parties call their transaction a consignment but the economic reality is that the risk of nonsale falls on the "consignee" (*e.g.*, the consignee must pay for the goods even if it cannot sell them), the economic reality is that the transaction is the equivalent of a credit sale with a title-retention agreement that is reduced in effect to a security interest. There should be no difference merely because the parties have used the label "consignment" rather than "sale."

Consignments that function as security devices are within the scope of Article 9 in the same manner as leases that function in that manner.[62] In such cases, a repossessing "consignor" must follow Article 9's disposition rules. Further, public filing of an Article 9 financing statement is required to protect the "consignor's" interest against third parties that assert competing claims to goods in the possession of the "consignee."[63]

[3] True Consignments

Although disguised consignments are within the scope of Article 9 for the reasons discussed in the preceding subsection, Article 9 also brings within

---

[60] Ostensible-ownership problems arise when goods in one party's possession are subject to a property interest of another. Third parties, believing from appearances that the party in possession has unencumbered title, may acquire an interest in the goods, thereby creating a priority contest. Sometimes, the outcome turns on whether the third party has the attributes of a bona fide purchaser for value. *See, e.g.*, U.C.C. § 2-403(1). Statutes requiring public filing alleviate ostensible-ownership problems by giving notice of interests that would otherwise be hidden.

A consignment is a type of bailment, meaning a transaction in which goods are placed in the rightful possession of one who is not their owner. R. Brown, The Law of Personal Property § 10.1 (W. Raushenbush 3d ed. 1975). There are numerous types of bailments, and the rules governing the rights of third parties who are misled by the bailee's ostensible ownership vary with the context. As a rule, though, the common law of bailment has not generally provided protection for such parties. *See* § 2.02[C] *infra*.

[61] U.C.C. § 2-401(1).

[62] *See* § 1.03[B][1] for a discussion of the attributes of a disguised lease transaction.

[63] As with leases, in case of doubt a consignor can make a protective filing using the terms "consignor" and "consignee" rather than "secured party" and "debtor" and the filing, standing alone, is not an admission that the transaction is not a true consignment. U.C.C. § 9-505(a), (b). Unlike the lease situation, however, and for reasons to be discussed in the next subsection, a filing under Article 9 is generally necessary to protect the interest of even a true consignor.

its scope most commercially valuable true consignments.[64] The term "consignment" for Article 9 purposes is defined[65] as a transaction in which goods are delivered to a merchant for the purpose of sale and the merchant "(i) deals in goods of that kind under a name other than that of the person making delivery; (ii) is not an auctioneer; and (iii) is not generally known by its creditors to be substantially engaged in selling the goods of others." Further limiting the definition are requirements that, for a transaction to qualify as a consignment, each delivery must have an aggregate value of $1,000 or more and, without regard to value, the goods must not be consumer goods immediately before delivery to the merchant.

Article 9 defines a "consignor"[66] as the person that delivers the goods to the merchant, or the "consignee,"[67] and the consignor's retained interest in the goods is a security interest[68] in inventory that is deemed to be purchase-money in nature.[69] The consignor's interest is subject to the claims of creditors of the consignee,[70] but it can protect that interest by using the methods available to any other Article 9 secured party.[71] These methods include filing a financing statement in order to defeat the consignee's creditors generally, and making certain that the filing occurs and appropriate notice is provided before the goods are delivered to the consignee in order to defeat a prior-perfected inventory financer with an after-acquired property clause.[72]

Although true consignments are within the scope of Article 9, they have features that are inconsistent with an ordinary Article 9 security interest — most notably the fact that, once returned by the consignee due to nonsale, the goods belong to the consignor. Accordingly, the consignor need not go through a foreclosure.[73] By contrast, an ordinary Article 9 foreclosure is necessary for a consignment that is a disguised security interest.

Consignment-like transactions exceed the scope of Article 9 in four situations: (1) consumer goods consigned to a merchant for sale; (2) a delivery to a merchant for sale that in the aggregate has a value of less than $1,000; (3) a delivery to an auctioneer; and (4) goods delivered to a merchant that is generally known by its creditors to be substantially engaged in selling the goods of others. Each of these transactions is governed by the common law of bailment rather than by Article 9, and, as a general proposition, that law insulates the goods from the claims of the bailee's creditors.[74]

---

[64] U.C.C. § 9-109(a)(4).

[65] U.C.C. § 9-102(a)(20).

[66] U.C.C. § 9-102(a)(21).

[67] U.C.C. § 9-102(a)(19).

[68] U.C.C. § 1-201(b)(35).

[69] U.C.C. § 9-103(d). Purchase-money security interests are discussed generally in § 1.05 *infra*.

[70] U.C.C. § 9-319(a).

[71] U.C.C. § 9-319(b).

[72] Purchase-money priorities in inventory are discussed in § 10.04[B] *infra*.

[73] U.C.C. § 9-601(g) (exempting consignments from Part 6 of Article 9).

[74] A person that is in doubt about whether a transaction is within an excluded category can make a precautionary filing under U.C.C. § 9-505.

§ 1.04 CLASSIFICATIONS OF COLLATERAL

Any form of personal property can be used to secure an obligation, provided the creditor is willing to accept it as collateral. Different forms of personal property, however, pose distinct issues within the context of secured financing. The functional distinctions within Article 9 are most often based on the type of personal property involved. The classification of the collateral is thus frequently critical with respect to the application of a particular provision.

Most personal property fits, sometimes uncomfortably, into one of three distinct, broad categories: goods, indispensable records, and intangibles. Goods and intangibles represent opposite ends of a scale based on the property's characteristics. The term "goods" refers generally to assets which are movable at the time the security interest attaches to them, with the specific exclusion of any of the property belonging in the indispensable records or intangibles categories.[75] Essentially, goods are a form of personal property in which value is a function of physical (tangible) characteristics.

The value of intangibles is not based on anything physical. The category consists of assets that are sometimes called choses in action, like accounts and general intangibles. Although records of these rights may be maintained in various forms, the business and legal communities do not recognize such records as the physical embodiment of the underlying rights. Intangibility means that the rights may effectively be assigned even if the assignee does not obtain possession of whatever records happen to exist.

The category of indispensable records[76] fits between the other two categories, reflecting aspects of each. The category includes instruments, negotiable documents, and chattel paper.[77] These forms of personal property consist of rights that are reified, meaning that they are embodied (made real) in a record. If the record is a writing, it is tangible and movable, but its value is not based on the value of the paper itself. Its value is instead based on the reified rights that are tied to the paper. A promissory note or a check, for example, has value because it evidences a right to enforce an obligation to pay money. Because the writing is recognized as the single embodiment of the right, physically transferring the paper is the accepted mechanism for transferring the enforcement right. For this reason, the paper is referred to as "indispensable."[78] Similarly, certain electronic

---

[75] U.C.C. § 9-102(a)(44).

[76] The term "record," used in Article 9 to achieve medium neutrality, means "information that is inscribed on a tangible medium or which is stored in an electronic or other medium and is retrievable in perceivable form." U.C.C. § 9-102(a)(69). The term thus includes traditional writings as well as their electronic equivalents (*e.g.*, electronic mail messages, voice mail messages, and other forms of electronic data capable of storage and retrieval).

[77] Chattel paper actually fits somewhere between the indispensable-records and intangibles categories. Enforcement rights can be transferred by assignment without transfer of the record itself, but the record has certain characteristics of negotiability. Chattel paper is sufficiently similar to other types of indispensable records that it is placed in that category for purposes of this discussion.

[78] *See* U.C.C. § 9-106, Comment.

records, although lacking a physical dimension, perform the same function as would a writing containing the same information (*e.g.*, electronic chattel paper and electronic negotiable documents).[79]

The forms of personal property that comprise the indispensable records category also possess another important attribute — negotiability (or quasi-negotiability). As a rule, rights are derivative in nature, meaning that the rights of a transferee of property in a voluntary transaction are generally coextensive with the rights of the transferor. This rule finds expression in the law governing assignments, where the assignee is said to "stand in the shoes" of the assignor.[80] This means that the assignee cannot enforce the assigned rights if the assignor could not have done so. The significance of an asset's negotiability is that its transfer can invoke an exception to the derivative-rights rule. Under the right circumstances, a bona-fide purchaser for value of negotiable property can receive rights greater than those of the transferor. The classic illustration with regard to indispensable records is found in Article 3, which provides that if a transferee of a negotiable instrument qualifies as a holder in due course (a specialized type of bona-fide purchaser for value), it takes the instrument free from all property claims and most defenses that could be asserted against its transferor. The negotiability of personal property is most significant in secured financing with respect to prioritizing competing claims to the property.

Classifying collateral has numerous consequences, one of the most important of which relates to the use of generic descriptions. For example, if a generic description like "all farm products" is used in a security agreement, the security interest will attach to all assets that are within that category at the moment the security interest first attaches to any asset.[81] Subsequently-acquired assets that fall within the category will also be covered if the security agreement contains an after-acquired property clause, as will existing assets in other categories whose classification later changes to farm products.[82] Assets that are farm products at the time of attachment continue to be subject to the security interest if their classification later changes,[83] but an asset that is not a farm product at the time of attachment and does not fall into that category at a later date cannot be subject to the

---

[79] Electronic negotiable documents were introduced into the Code with the 2003 revision of Article 7 and conforming amendments to the definition of "document of title" in Article 1. See U.C.C. § 1-201(b)(16).

[80] It also underlies the common-law rule that precludes a thief of goods from transferring good title to anyone, even a bona-fide purchaser for value. Of course, there are exceptions to this rule where the owner voluntarily gives a bad actor possession of the goods, thereby creating an ostensible-ownership problem. In such cases, the law often clothes the bad actor with voidable title, meaning that good title can be passed to a bona-fide purchaser for value. *See, e.g.,* U.C.C. § 2-403(1). The voidable-title doctrine can best be understood as a rule of negotiability applicable to goods.

[81] Attachment is discussed in Chapter 2 *infra*.

[82] After-acquired property clauses are discussed in § 3.02 *infra*.

[83] The new category would be a proceed of the old category. Attachment to proceeds is discussed in § 2.03[B] *infra*.

security interest. Coverage of such an asset requires an expanded description. Classification also drives many issues related to perfection, although less so than under former law.

The following material describes some of the kinds of assets that fall within the Code's various classifications.[84] Most of the discussion concerning the effect of classification on foreclosure, perfection, and priorities appears in other chapters.

[A]   Goods — § 9-102(a)(44)

Article 9 establishes four basic classifications of goods: consumer goods, farm products, inventory, and equipment. The proper classification of goods may change over time, depending upon changes in their use.[85] For example, goods held as inventory by a dealer might be sold and used as consumer goods in the buyer's home and then later used as equipment in the buyer's office.[86] The classifications are mutually exclusive, however, so that at any given point in time the goods can fit into only one of them.[87]

There is an important distinction between mixed usage and permanent changes in use. The drafters recognized that sometimes a use (or intended use) of the goods will not be exclusive. In cases of mixed use, the primary use predominates for classification purposes. For example, if the goods are used most of the time for personal reasons and only occasionally in the owner's business, the goods are continuously classified as consumer goods.[88] As indicated above, though, a permanent change in the pattern of usage throws the goods into another category.

The definition of goods includes "(i) fixtures, (ii) standing timber that is to be cut and removed under a conveyance or contract for sale, (iii) the unborn young of animals, (iv) crops grown, growing, or to be grown, even if the crops are produced on trees, vines, or bushes, and (v) manufactured homes."[89] The term also includes an "embedded" computer program.[90] A computer program is embedded if "(i) the program is associated with the

---

[84] Other kinds of assets are discussed elsewhere in this chapter. *See* §§ 1.05 (investment property), 1.07[F][2] (commercial tort claims), 1.07[H] (deposit accounts), and 1.08 (letter-of-credit rights).

[85] *In re* Elie, 11 B.R. 24, 31 U.C.C. Rep. Serv. 687 (Bankr. D. Mass. 1981) (primary factor is principal use to which goods are put). *See also* U.C.C. § 9-102, Comment 4a.

[86] First Nat'l Bank of Thomasboro v. Lachenmyer, 146 Ill. App. 3d 1035, 497 N.E.2d 844, 2 U.C.C. Rep. Serv. 2d 703 (1986) (airplane originally purchased in pursuit of hobby was later used for business purposes).

[87] North Ridge Farms, Inc. v. Trimble, 37 U.C.C. Rep. Serv. 1280 (Ky. Ct. App. 1983). *See also* U.C.C. § 9-102, Comment 4a.

[88] Commercial Credit Equip. Corp. v. Carter, 83 Wash. 2d 136, 516 P.2d 767, 13 U.C.C. Rep. Serv. 1212 (1973) (occasional use of airplane in new employment did not affect its classification as consumer goods). *See also* U.C.C. § 9-102, Comment 4a.

[89] U.C.C. § 9-102(a)(44).

[90] If a computer program is not embedded, it is classified as "software," a subset of general intangibles. U.C.C. § 9-102(a)(75).

goods in such a manner that it customarily is considered part of the goods, or (ii) by becoming the owner of the goods, a person acquires the right to use the program in connection with the goods."[91] For example, suppose Bank takes a security interest in goods that consist of Debtor's car. Bank's security interest attaches to Debtor's rights in the computer program that runs the anti-lock brakes because the program is embedded in the goods. The security interest in the software need not be separately described in the security agreement or separately perfected. By contrast, suppose Bank takes a security interest in Debtor's computer. The operating system that Debtor uses to run the computer is separately licensed, and thus Debtor does not acquire the right to use the program in connection with the goods by becoming the owner of the goods. Whether the program is associated with the goods in such a manner that it customarily is considered part of the goods is an issue of fact, although as a matter of policy it should not be so considered. If the program is embedded, Bank need only describe and perfect as to the computer; otherwise, it must also describe and perfect as to the software.

[1] Consumer Goods and Manufactured Homes — § 9-102(a)(23), (24), (53), (54)

Goods are classified as consumer goods if they are "used or bought for use primarily for personal, family, or household purposes."[92] Actual use for these purposes is generally controlling. Note, however, that goods that are intended at the time of purchase for a personal, family, or household use qualify initially as consumer goods even though they may not actually be used for that purpose. If their predominant use is actually for a nonconsumer purpose, the classification will ordinarily change to another appropriate category, although some courts have declined to change the category when doing so would be disadvantageous to a secured party that relied in good faith upon a statement by the debtor regarding the use to which the goods would be put.[93]

Article 9's definitional scheme creates some complexities if the collateral is consumer goods or the purpose of the transaction is to create consumer debt. A "consumer transaction" is a transaction in which an individual

---

[91] U.C.C. § 9-102(a)(44).

[92] U.C.C. § 9-102(a)(23). *In re* Elia, 18 B.R. 89, 33 U.C.C. Rep. Serv. 750 (Bankr. W.D.Pa. 1982) (hospital beds purchased for personal use); *In re* Nicolosi, 4 U.C.C. Rep. Serv. 111 (Bankr. S.D. Ohio 1966) (purchase of engagement ring as gift to fiancee does not mean it was not for purchaser's own "personal, family, or household purposes").

[93] *In re* Pettit, 18 B.R. 8, 33 U.C.C. Rep. Serv. 1762 (Bankr. E.D. Ark. 1981) (even though goods were actually used in debtor's business, seller/secured party held to have an automatically perfected purchase-money security interest in consumer goods where debtor unambiguously represented to seller/secured party that goods were purchased for personal, family, or household purposes); *In re* Troupe, 59 U.C.C. Rep. Serv. 2d 23 (W.D. Okla. 2006) (statements of debtors at time of purchase that they would use tractor for consumer purposes, coupled with provision in security agreement specifying that it would be so used, held to protect seller/secured party even if tractor used predominately for ranching-business purposes).

incurs an obligation for personal, family, or household purposes and holds the collateral for personal, family, or household use.[94] In most cases, a consumer transaction is also a "consumer-goods transaction" — a transaction in which an individual incurs an obligation for personal, family, or household purposes and secures that obligation by granting a security interest in consumer goods.[95] At first blush, these definitions may seem identical, but the difference reflects the limit on the definition of the term "goods." For example, consider a transaction in which an individual borrows money to pay her personal medical expenses. If she secures the obligation by granting a security interest in her personal automobile, the transaction is both a consumer-goods transaction and a consumer transaction. However, if she secures the obligation by granting a security interest in 1,000 shares of stock in a corporation — which is investment property rather than goods — and she has been holding the stock for the purpose of someday paying for her children's education, the transaction is a consumer transaction but not a consumer-goods transaction. In other words, consumer-goods transactions are a subset of the broader category of consumer transactions. By contrast, if an individual secures a business loan with consumer goods or with investment property held for a personal, family, or household purpose, the transaction is neither a consumer-goods transaction (even if the collateral is consumer goods) nor a consumer transaction. The same is true of a consumer loan secured by business assets.

Article 9 contains a number of protective rules that apply if the collateral is consumer goods even if the transaction is not a consumer-goods transaction.[96] Other rules apply only if the transaction is a consumer transaction[97] or a consumer-goods transaction.[98] In addition, many states have enacted consumer protection laws that either preempt or supplement the Code's provisions,[99] and the Federal Trade Commission has adopted a rule that makes it a deceptive trade practice for a lender to take a nonpossessory, nonpurchase-money security interest in many types of consumer goods.[100]

---

[94] U.C.C. § 9-102(a)(23).

[95] U.C.C. § 9-102(a)(24).

[96] For example, U.C.C. § 9-204(b)(1) limits the effectiveness of an after-acquired property clause to the extent that it would otherwise apply to consumer goods. See § 3.02[B] infra. Likewise, U.C.C. § 9-625(c)(2) provides that a secured party that fails to comply with its obligation to dispose of consumer goods in a commercially reasonable manner following default is liable for minimum statutory damages even if the debtor suffers no actual harm as a result of the secured party's conduct. See § 19.03 infra.

[97] For example, as explained in Chapter 18, the "safe-harbor" rule pursuant to which a notice of disposition sent at least ten days before the disposition is deemed timely as a matter of law does not apply to consumer transactions. U.C.C. § 9-612(b).

[98] For example, as explained in Chapter 19, a court in a case involving a consumer-goods transaction could conclude that a secured party that failed to satisfy its obligation to conduct a commercially reasonable disposition of the collateral following default would be barred from recovering a deficiency judgment. See U.C.C. § 9-626(b). Such an "absolute bar" rule would not apply to transactions other than consumer-goods transactions.

[99] See U.C.C. § 9-201(b), (c) (Article 9 defers to other law protecting consumers).

[100] 16 C.F.R. Pt. 444. A parallel rule, Regulation AA, has been adopted by the Federal Reserve Board. 12 C.F.R. Pt. 227. See discussion in §§ 3.02[B] and 7.01[B] infra.

Article 9 also provides for a category of collateral called "manufactured homes."[101] Manufactured homes are usually consumer goods, and if a manufactured home that is consumer goods is used as collateral for an Article 9 transaction, the transaction is subject to applicable rules governing consumer goods, consumer transactions, and consumer-goods transactions. The transaction might also constitute a "manufactured-home transaction," meaning either a transaction that creates a purchase-money security interest in a manufactured home that is not inventory or a transaction in which a manufactured home that is not inventory serves as the primary collateral.[102] The fact that goods are a manufactured home has no relevance unless the transaction is a manufactured-home transaction. Manufactured-home transactions are relevant for a limited set of perfection and priority issues. Regarding perfection, a financing statement covering a manufactured-home transaction can be made effective for thirty years.[103] Regarding priority, there is a special rule for a manufactured home that has become a fixture and as to which a security interest has been perfected under a state certificate-of-title law.[104]

[2] Farm Products — § 9-102(a)(34)

Farm products consist of goods, other than standing timber, with respect to which the debtor is engaged in a farming operation and which consist of

(A) crops grown, growing, or to be grown, including: (i) crops produced on trees, vines, and bushes; and (ii) aquatic goods produced in aquacultural operations;

(B) livestock, born or unborn, including aquatic goods produced in aquacultural operations;

(C) supplies used or produced in a farming operation; or

(D) products of crops or livestock in their unmanufactured states.[105]

The term "farming operation" means "raising, cultivating, propagating, fattening, grazing, or any other farming, livestock, or aquacultural operation."[106]

Goods that constitute crops, livestock, and supplies can be readily determined, but an issue can arise as to whether the debtor was engaged

---

[101] U.C.C. § 9-102(a)(53). Comment 4b to section 9-102 states that "the definition borrows from the federal Manufactured Housing Act, 42 U.S.C. §§ 5401 et seq., and is intended to have the same meaning."

[102] U.C.C. § 9-102(a)(54).

[103] U.C.C. § 9-515(b). Many states subject manufactured homes to their certificate-of-title laws and perfection by filing is not effective. Methods of perfection are discussed generally in Chapter 4 and specifically in other chapters.

[104] U.C.C. § 9-334(e)(4).

[105] U.C.C. § 9-102(a)(34).

[106] U.C.C. § 9-102(a)(35).

in a farming operation with respect to them.[107] Vegetables grown in a family garden by a farmer are unlikely to qualify, as are horses ridden for pleasure or used for teaching equestrian skills. Farming operations can, however, be undertaken by someone who has a separate career or livelihood.[108] Seed and fertilizer held in stock to produce a farm crop are examples of goods that would qualify as supplies, as is gasoline held in an underground tank installed on a farm and used to run farm machinery.[109]

A potentially difficult line-drawing problem arises because crops and livestock often are processed, and the farm products category includes the products of crops or livestock in their unmanufactured states.[110] The courts must determine whether the goods have been subjected to a manufacturing operation or whether they simply have been processed in a way that falls short of manufacturing.[111] To illustrate, grapes harvested from a vintner's land would be farm products, but bottled wine would be inventory.[112] Once farm products are subjected to a manufacturing process, they become inventory.[113] Obviously, this particular characterization can present close questions on which reasonable persons might differ — questions that will be of critical importance depending upon how a security agreement describes the collateral. If goods are farm products and later become inventory, the description "farm products" in the security agreement and financing statement will be adequate to cause the security interest to attach and become perfected, and neither description needs to be amended to account for the new category;[114] if, on the other hand, the goods were inventory at the time the security interest attached, the description "farm products" will not be sufficient. An attorney advising a secured party in a borderline case will suggest that the description refer to both farm products and inventory. The same is true in the many other instances in which assets sit on the borderline between classifications.

---

[107] Morgan County Feeders, Inc. v. McCormick, 836 P.2d 1051, 18 U.C.C. Rep. Serv. 2d 632 (Colo. Ct. App. 1992) (stipulating that longhorn cattle used for recreational cattle drives were not farm products); In re Creel, 118 B.R. 372, 13 U.C.C. Rep. Serv. 2d 943 (Bankr. D. S.C. 1988) (commercial logging not considered farming operation). "Animals in a herd of livestock are covered whether the debtor acquires them by purchase or as a result of natural increase." U.C.C. § 9-102, Comment 4a.

[108] In re Blease, 24 U.C.C. Rep. Serv. 450 (Bankr. D.N.J. 1978) (veterinarian who owned and operated two farms qualified).

[109] The tank itself would be a fixture, and the machinery would be equipment.

[110] U.C.C. § 9-102(a)(34)(D).

[111] In re K.L. Smith Enterprises, Ltd., 2 B.R. 280, 28 U.C.C. Rep. Serv. 534 (Bankr. D. Colo. 1980) (highly mechanized process of washing, candling, spraying with oil, and packing eggs for shipment did not constitute manufacturing process).

[112] The 1972 text gave as examples of manufactured goods "ginned cotton, wool-clip, maple syrup, milk, and eggs." U.C.C. § 9-109(3). U.C.C. § 9-102, Comment 4a, provides the following explanation: "At one end of the spectrum, some processes are so closely connected with farming — such as pasteurizing milk or boiling sap to produce maple syrup or sugar — that they would not constitute manufacturing. On the other hand an extensive canning operation would be manufacturing."

[113] U.C.C. § 9-102, Comment 4a.

[114] The inventory is proceeds of the farm products.

Former law explicitly required that, for goods to qualify as farm products, they had to be "in the possession of a debtor engaged in raising, fattening, grazing, or other farming operations."[115] Once the goods left the possession of the farming debtor, they lost their characterization as farm products,[116] and their subsequent characterization depended upon the use to which they were then applied.[117] For example, cattle on a rancher's land are farm products, but the same cattle held for sale in a commission merchant's barn are inventory. Revised Article 9 does not expressly require that the goods be in a farmer's possession but the phrase "with respect to which the debtor is engaged in a farming operation" leads to the same result.[118]

[3]   Inventory — § 9-102(a)(48)

Goods are inventory if they are held by a person for sale or lease or to be furnished under a contract of service.[119] This part of the definition is the principal test of inventory, and it is implicit that these transactions occur within the ordinary course of business.[120] Thus, if a company occasionally sells its used machinery when it needs to be replaced, such sales are insufficient to characterize the machinery as inventory.[121]

Goods actually leased by a lessor or furnished under a contract of service are also inventory. Thus, for example, a secured party that takes a security interest in "all inventory" acquires an interest in leased goods — or more accurately, the merchant's residual interest in the leased goods as lessor — even though, at the time of attachment, the goods are not available to the merchant for lease.

Raw materials, work in process, or materials used or consumed in a business are also inventory.[122] Thus, a stockpile of packaging material used by a company to ship its manufactured goods and the coal used to fire its generators qualify as inventory. These types of goods are inventory even though they are not held for sale, lease, or any other type of transfer. The

---

[115] U.C.C. § 9-109(3) (1972 Official Text). *In re* Charolais Breeding Ranches, Ltd., 20 U.C.C. Rep. Serv. 193 (Bankr. W.D. Wis. 1976) (operator of breeding ranch which dealt with cattle under programs to provide tax benefits to investors was engaged in farming operations); Baker Production Credit Ass'n v. Long Creek Meat Co., 266 Or. 643, 513 P.2d 1129, 13 U.C.C. Rep. Serv. 531 (1973) (debtor who bought cattle, fed and fattened them, and sold them for slaughter was engaged in farming operations).

[116] U.C.C. § 9-109, Comment 4 (1972 Official Text).

[117] First Nat'l Bank of Elkhart County v. Smoker, 153 Ind. App. 71, 286 N.E.2d 203, 11 U.C.C. Rep. Serv. 10 (1972) (cattle became inventory upon transfer of possession from farmer to packer).

[118] U.C.C. § 9-102, Comment 4a.

[119] U.C.C. § 9-102(a)(48)(B), (C).

[120] U.C.C. § 9-102, Comment 4a. Nichols Motorcycle Supply, Inc. v. Regency Kawasaki, Inc., 295 S.C. 138, 367 S.E.2d 438, 6 U.C.C. Rep. Serv. 2d 823 (Ct. App. 1988) (bulk transfer of goods is transfer not in ordinary course of business).

[121] The machinery is equipment under U.C.C. § 9-102(a)(33). *See* § 1.04[A][4] *infra. In re* Benton Trucking Service, Inc., 21 B.R. 574, 34 U.C.C. Rep. Serv. 332 (Bankr. E.D. Mich. 1982).

[122] U.C.C. § 9-102(a)(48)(A), (C), (D).

concept is similar to supplies used or consumed in a farming operation, which are part of the definition of farm products. In a sense, farm products are the inventory of a farmer, but the definitions are entirely discrete; if goods are within the definition of farm products, they cannot be inventory.[123]

[4] Equipment — § 9-102(a)(33)

The category "equipment" is entirely residual in nature; that is, goods are equipment if they are not consumer goods, farm products, or inventory.[124] This can lead to some interesting results. For example, standing timber that is to be cut and removed under a conveyance or contract of sale is goods under the Code,[125] is excluded from the definition of farm products,[126] and is highly unlikely to qualify as consumer goods. If it is held for sale or lease, it will be inventory; otherwise it will be classified as equipment.

The category includes assets that are used in a business, but it cannot overlap with the definition of inventory, which refers to materials used or consumed in a business.[127] The borderline is not entirely clear and the Comments provide the following guidance: "In general, goods used in a business are equipment if they are fixed assets or have, as identifiable units, a relatively long period of use, but are inventory, even though not held for sale or lease, if they are used up or consumed in a short period of time in producing a product or providing a service."[128] As a rule of thumb, goods that are used up are inventory while goods that are used again are equipment.

The category must be considered in any borderline case involving goods. Suppose, for example, that an individual who is the sole proprietor of a business buys a pick-up truck to make deliveries. The truck is also used as a family vehicle. If the business use predominates, the truck is equipment because it does not come within the definition of consumer goods. If the family use predominates, it is within the consumer-goods category. If a court finds that the buyer's mixed business and family motives are evenly balanced, there is no primary use and the truck is equipment, again because it does not come within the definition of consumer goods.

---

[123] U.C.C. § 9-102(a)(48).

[124] *In re* Estate of Silver, 2003 WL 21362809, 50 U.C.C. Rep. Serv. 2d 1196 (Mich. Ct. App. 2003) (paintings that were displayed in model homes and in various offices of the debtor's company were properly characterized as equipment rather than consumer goods).

[125] U.C.C. § 9-102(a)(44).

[126] U.C.C. § 9-102(a)(34).

[127] *See* the discussion in the preceding subsection.

[128] U.C.C. § 9-102, Comment 4a.

[B] Indispensable Records

[1] Documents — § 9-102(a)(30)

Article 9 defines "document" to mean either a document of title (a term defined in the general definitions of Article 1) or a receipt of the kind described in Section 7-201(2).[129] The essence of this form of property is set forth in the Article 1 definition: "[A] record . . . that in the regular course of business or financing is treated as adequately evidencing that the person in possession or control of the record is entitled to receive, control, hold, and dispose of the record and the goods the record covers."[130] To qualify, the record must purport "to be issued by or addressed to a bailee and to cover goods in the bailee's possession which are either identified or are fungible portions of an identified mass."[131] The most common forms of documents are bills of lading issued by a carrier upon shipment of goods and warehouse receipts issued by a warehouse upon storage of goods.[132]

A document of title operates as a receipt for goods placed in the custody of a bailee[133] and also controls access to the goods. In other words, the bailee will not release the goods to anyone that cannot present a document in proper form. A negotiable document also represents title to the covered goods; *i.e.*, an interest in the goods can be created by transferring the document to the party acquiring the interest even though the goods remain in the custody of the bailee.[134] Even though an interest has been conveyed by transfer, the bailee need not (and should not) release the goods unless the transferee is a "person entitled under the document."[135] Both negotiable

---

[129] U.C.C. § 9-102(a)(30). The reference to U.C.C. § 7-201(2) (§ 7-201(b) in the 2003 Official Text) is to receipts in the nature of warehouse receipts issued under other statutes governing distilled spirits or agricultural commodities.

[130] U.C.C. § 1-201(b)(16). The use of the term "record" in the definition signifies that documents may either be in tangible or electronic form. *See* various provisions of Article 7 (2003 Official Text) that provide for electronic documents, and the use of the terms "tangible negotiable documents" and "electronic negotiable documents" in Article 9. U.C.C. §§ 9-313(a) (perfection by possession of tangible negotiable documents), 9-314(a) (perfection by control of electronic negotiable documents).

[131] U.C.C. § 1-201(b)(16)(ii).

[132] *Id. See also,* U.C.C. §§ 1-201(b)(42) (warehouse receipt defined) and (b)(6) (bill of lading defined). Article 7 of the Code provides substantive rules governing the use of warehouse receipts and bills of lading.

[133] "Bailee" means "a person that by a warehouse receipt, bill of lading, or other document of title acknowledges possession of goods and contracts to deliver them." U.C.C. § 7-102(a)(1).

[134] A transferee to whom a negotiable document is "duly negotiated" acquires title to both the document and the underlying goods. U.C.C. § 7-502(a)(1), (2). Due negotiation is defined in § 7-501. At the core of the concept is a requirement that the transferee have the characteristics of a bona-fide purchaser for value.

A transferee of a nonnegotiable document acquires the title and rights that his transferor had or had actual authority to convey (as does a transferee of a negotiable document that does not take by due negotiation). U.C.C. § 7-504(a). In other words, the transferee derivatively acquires the transferor's title (with whatever defects may exist), but the document does not represent complete title.

[135] A "person entitled under the document" means the holder of a negotiable document or

and nonnegotiable documents play important roles in secured financing, and those roles are discussed later in this book.[136]

[2] Instruments — § 9-102(a)(47), (65)

An instrument is either a negotiable instrument[137] or any other writing evidencing a right to be paid money which is of a type that is, in the ordinary course of business, transferred by delivery with any necessary indorsement or assignment.[138] The definition thus recognizes two basic categories of instruments — those that are negotiable, and those that are technically nonnegotiable but that the market imbues with some of the key attributes of negotiability. Instruments in the latter category are sometimes called "quasi-negotiable."

A negotiable instrument, governed by Article 3, is a written promise or order to pay a fixed amount of money that is in negotiable form.[139] The most common forms of negotiable instruments are checks, promissory notes, and certificates of deposit.[140] The value of a negotiable instrument is based on the obligation to pay money that the instrument represents. This form of indispensable record thus can be referred to as "money paper."[141]

The category of nonnegotiable instrument has created difficult line-drawing issues.[142] Conceptually, these instruments could have been

---

the named consignee under a nonnegotiable document (or delivery order issued pursuant to a nonnegotiable document). U.C.C. § 7-102(a)(9). A person becomes a holder of a negotiable document when it is issued or negotiated to that person. The process for negotiation of tangible and electronic documents is governed by U.C.C. §§ 7-501(a) (tangible) and (b) (electronic). A nonnegotiable document will inevitably name a consignee (without additional words indicating that the document runs to the order of the named person). That consignee is entitled under the document. If the named consignee wants another person to obtain possession, the nonnegotiable document can be surrendered to the bailee in exchange for a new document running to the other person, or the named consignee can issue a delivery order (defined in U.C.C. § 7-102(a)(5)) directing the bailee to release all or a portion of the goods to the other person. Once accepted by the bailee, a delivery order functions like an ordinary document in that the bailee's obligation to deliver the goods runs to the person named in the order. U.C.C. § 7-502(a)(4).

[136] *See* §§ 6.02[B][1] (terminal warehousing), 6.02[C] (goods in transit), and 6.02[B][2] (field warehousing) *infra*.

[137] *See* U.C.C. § 3-104.

[138] U.C.C. § 9-102(a)(47). The definition excludes investment property (*e.g.*, bonds), letters of credit, or rights arising out of the use of credit or charge cards. If an instrument is part of chattel paper, it falls within that definition. U.C.C. § 9-102(a)(11). *See* § 1.04[B][3] *infra*.

[139] U.C.C. § 3-104(a). To be negotiable, an instrument must be payable to bearer or order. U.C.C. § 3-104(a)(1).

[140] Certificates of deposit are discussed in § 1.07[H] *infra*.

[141] The term "paper" is appropriate as Article 3 has not been amended to accommodate electronic negotiable instruments and the definition of instrument refers to a negotiable instrument under Article 3 or any other "writing." U.C.C. § 9-102(a)(47).

[142] Cases in which nonnegotiable writings were held not to be instruments include Capitran Inc. v. Great Western Bank, 872 P.2d 1370, 22 U.C.C. Rep. Serv. 2d 1191 (Colo. Ct. App. 1994) ("vacation membership" contracts); *In re* Newman, 993 F.2d 90, 20 U.C.C. Rep. Serv. 2d 1377 (5th Cir. 1993) (annuity contract); *In re* Brendle's Stores, Inc., 22 U.C.C. Rep. Serv. 2d 450

categorized as intangibles because the right to payment is not reified. Nevertheless, the market treats some nonnegotiable instruments as if they were negotiable for certain purposes, including transferring rights to payment through delivery of the writings. Because of these functional similarities, Article 9 groups such writings with negotiable instruments.[143]

Article 9 recognizes "promissory notes" as a subset of instruments.[144] In essence, a promissory note is an instrument that is neither a draft nor a certificate of deposit. The primary significance of the category is that Article 9 governs sales of promissory notes but does not govern sales of instruments that are not promissory notes.[145]

[3] Chattel Paper — § 9-102(a)(11), (31), (78)

The basic definition of chattel paper is as follows:

> Chattel paper means a record or records that evidence both a monetary obligation and a security interest in specific goods, a security interest in specific goods and software used in the goods, a security interest in specific goods and license of software used in the goods, a lease of specific goods, or a lease of specific goods and license of software used in the goods.[146]

Chattel paper is thus a record or group of records that include a monetary obligation either as part of or together with a security agreement or a lease.[147]

(M.D.N.C. 1993) (credit card receivables); *In re* Air Florida System Inc., 49 B.R. 321, 41 U.C.C. Rep. Serv. 197 (Bankr. S.D. Fla. 1985) (airline tickets); *In re* Blankinship-Cooper, Inc., 43 B.R. 231, 39 U.C.C. Rep. Serv. 1008 (Bankr. N.D. Tex. 1984) (quarter horse's registration certificate).

Cases in which nonnegotiable writings have qualified as instruments include Army Nat'l Bank v. Equity Developers, Inc., 245 Kan. 3, 774 P.2d 919, 9 U.C.C. Rep. Serv. 2d 722 (1989) (nonnegotiable mortgage note); Berkowitz v. Chavo Int'l, Inc., 74 N.Y.2d 144, 544 N.Y.S.2d 569, 542 N.E.2d 1086, 9 U.C.C. Rep. Serv. 2d 4 (1989) (nonnegotiable promissory note); First Nat'l Bank in Grand Prairie v. Lone Star Life Ins. Co., 524 S.W.2d 525, 17 U.C.C. Rep. Serv. 835 (Tex. Civ. Ct. App. 1975) (nonnegotiable certificate of deposit).

[143] This characterization does not mean that these nonnegotiable instruments will be treated like negotiable instruments for all aspects of Article 9. The major difference will be in priorities because holder-in-due-course status is available only with negotiable instruments. *See* § 11.03[C] *infra*.

[144] U.C.C. § 9-102(a)(65).

[145] *See* discussion in § 1.06 *infra*.

[146] U.C.C. § 9-102(a)(11).

[147] The definition makes clear that "monetary obligation" includes an obligation with respect to software used in the goods, and the Comments explain the concept as follows:

> The monetary obligation with respect to the software need not be owed under a license from the secured party or lessor, and the secured party or lessor need not be a party to the license transaction itself. Among the types of monetary obligations that are included in "chattel paper" are amounts that have been advanced by the secured party or lessor to enable the debtor or lessee to acquire or obtain financing for a license of the software used in the goods.

U.C.C. § 9-102, Comment 5b.

One common pattern involving chattel paper arises when a merchant sells goods on a secured basis, retaining a purchase-money security interest. Typically, this transaction will be accomplished with one record,[148] usually called a "retail installment contract," which combines features of a promissory note and of a security agreement.[149] In these cases, the buyer's payment obligation and the merchant's security interest are both covered in the record. Title to the goods passes to the buyer as part of the sale,[150] but the merchant retains an Article 9 security interest that it can foreclose if the buyer defaults. In effect, the merchant has traded the goods for a set of intangible rights — the right to enforce the buyer's payment obligation (through litigation, if necessary), and the right to use Article 9's mechanisms to foreclose on the goods if the buyer defaults.

The record authenticated by the buyer is chattel paper, but this term has no significance if the merchant does not make use of the chattel paper in a secondary financing arrangement. In other words, if no third party acquires an interest in the chattel paper, the merchant simply has a garden-variety security interest in the buyer's goods. If, however, the merchant uses the chattel paper as collateral for a loan from a bank,[151] the bank's collateral is the chattel paper itself rather than the goods sold by the merchant. The easiest way to understand this is to visualize a two-tier arrangement in which one security agreement (the merchant/buyer agreement) serves as collateral for another security agreement (the merchant/bank agreement). The collateral in the merchant/buyer transaction is consumer goods; the collateral in the merchant/bank transaction is chattel paper. If the merchant defaults, the bank will foreclose on the chattel paper. Foreclosure entitles the bank to enforce the rights that, absent default, could have been enforced by the merchant. The Code has a provision that allows the bank to require the buyer to begin making the installment

---

Chattel paper with respect to which there is a monetary obligation relating to software is sometimes referred to as "hybrid" chattel paper. A secured party (including a seller) financing the sale of a computer that is loaded with software should take a security interest in both the computer (the goods) and the software (a general intangible). When used in a secondary financing transaction, the total secured obligation qualifies as chattel paper. *See also* the discussion of embedded software in § 1.04[A] *supra* and the discussion of a purchase-money security interest in software that is part of an integrated transaction in § 1.05 *infra*.

[148] The buyer need not be a consumer, nor do the payment and security aspects of the transaction have to be in one writing. Two writings consisting of a promissory note and a security agreement will be taken together and treated as chattel paper. U.C.C. § 9-102(a)(11).

[149] It is possible for a writing that includes both a monetary obligation and a security interest to qualify as a negotiable instrument under Article 3 (although most retail installment contracts contain provisions that render them nonnegotiable). U.C.C. § 3-104(a)(3). Such a writing would not qualify as an instrument for Article 9 purposes, however. U.C.C. § 9-102(a)(47) specifies that an instrument cannot be a writing that itself qualifies as a security agreement or lease.

[150] U.C.C. § 2-106(1). Even if the record states that the seller is to retain title pending final payment, its interest is limited to a security interest. U.C.C. §§ 1-201(b)(35), 2-401(1).

[151] Article 9 is also triggered if the merchant sells the chattel paper outright. Article 9's treatment of sales of chattel paper is discussed in § 1.06 *infra*.

payments to it.[152] That provision permits an assignee[153] of chattel paper to notify the account debtor[154] (the buyer) and thereby divert the payments from the merchant to itself. The bank is in the same position with regard to the buyer's goods as the merchant, however, and cannot foreclose on them unless the buyer defaults.

Chattel paper also arises when goods are leased. A lease agreement in record form almost invariably includes the payment obligation of the lessee in the record.[155] If the lessor borrows money from a bank on the security of the lease, the lease is chattel paper.[156] If the lessor defaults, the bank can enforce the payment obligation created by the lease using the mechanism discussed in the preceding paragraph. If the lessee in turn defaults, the bank can recover the leased goods under the self-help provisions of Article 2A,[157] which governs the relationship between lessor and lessee. If the bank also has a security interest in the lessor's inventory, it can then foreclose on the formerly leased assets using Article 9's normal foreclosure rules.[158]

Note that transactions using chattel paper based on an underlying lease or an underlying security agreement are comparable because the record in both instances includes a payment obligation that is tied to specific goods.[159] The rights that the chattel paper represents with respect to the goods are the feature distinguishing chattel paper from other forms of personal property that include an obligation to pay money (*i.e.*, instruments, accounts, and payment intangibles).[160] These goods-oriented rights pose

---

[152] U.C.C. § 9-406(a).

[153] The merchant/bank security agreement operates as a conditional assignment to the bank of the merchant's rights. It is conditional in that, unless otherwise agreed, the bank cannot enforce its rights as assignee unless the merchant defaults.

[154] The term includes a person obligated on an account, chattel paper, or a general intangible. U.C.C. § 9-102(a)(3). It does not include a person obligated on a negotiable instrument, even if the instrument is part of chattel paper. *Id.*

[155] *In re* ICS Cybernetics, Inc., 123 B.R. 467, 17 U.C.C. Rep. Serv. 2d 609, *aff'd w.o. op.*, 123 B.R. 480 (N.D.N.Y. 1990), dealt with multiple writings. Because the master agreement provided for payment of "the monthly rent set forth in [the] equipment schedules" and did not specify the basic lease terms, the court held that the equipment schedules alone constituted chattel paper. *Compare* this case *with In re* Funding Sys. Asset Mgmt. Corp., 111 B.R. 500, 11 U.C.C. Rep. Serv. 2d 205 (Bankr. W.D. Pa. 1990) (chattel paper consisted of twelve equipment schedules, which contained monetary obligations, and master leases, which contained lease terms).

[156] *In re* Keneco Fin. Group, Inc., 131 B.R. 90, 16 U.C.C. Rep. Serv. 2d 219 (Bankr. N.D. Ill. 1991) (equipment leases). Charters of vessels are excluded because they constitute accounts. U.C.C. § 9-102(a)(2).

[157] U.C.C. § 2A-525(2).

[158] The term "inventory" includes goods that are actually leased as well as those held for sale or lease. U.C.C. § 9-102(a)(48). *See also* the discussion in § 1.04[A][3] *supra*.

[159] Note that the problems that can arise in determining whether an agreement is a true lease or a security interest in the form of a disguised lease, discussed in § 1.03[B][1] *supra*, are not important in this context because both leases and security agreements are included within the meaning of chattel paper.

[160] Berkowitz v. Chavo Int'l, Inc., 74 N.Y.2d 144, 544 N.Y.2d 569, 542 N.E.2d 1086, 9 U.C.C.

unique issues that justify identifying chattel paper as a separate category for Article 9 purposes. Thus, even if the monetary obligation is evidenced by a separate writing that, standing alone, qualifies as an instrument, it is treated as part of the chattel paper.[161]

Chattel paper can be further broken down into "tangible chattel paper"[162] and "electronic chattel paper."[163] The latter term adapts Article 9 to the growing practice among some secured lenders of representing such interests in a purely electronic form. The main distinction between the forms of chattel paper is that perfection by possession is available for tangible chattel paper while the electronic counterpart of possession — control — is available for electronic chattel paper.[164]

[C] Intangibles

Rights that do not qualify as "indispensable records" (*e.g.*, instruments, documents, or chattel paper) are treated separately, either because they are not in record form or, even if they are, the effectiveness of an assignment of the rights does not require transfer of possession or control of the record. These distinctions have practical ramifications for secured financing that make separate categories necessary for purposes of Article 9.

[1] Accounts — § 9-102(a)(2), (46)

An "account" is a right to payment, whether or not earned by performance, arising in one of a number of specific contexts. Because payment rights may fall into one of many Code categories, it is as important to understand what is not an account as it is to know what is within the category. Accounts include rights to payment:

(i) for property that has been or is to be sold, leased, licensed, assigned, or otherwise disposed of, (ii) for services rendered or to be rendered, (iii) for a policy of insurance issued or to be issued, (iv) for a secondary obligation incurred or to be incurred, (v) for energy provided or to be provided, (vi) for the use or hire of a vessel under a charter or other contract, (vii) arising out of the use of a credit or charge card or information contained on or for use with the card, or (viii) as winnings in a lottery or other game of chance operated or sponsored by a State, governmental unit of a State, or person licensed or authorized to operate the game by a State or

Rep. Serv. 2d 4 (1989) (written purchase agreement was not chattel paper because it did not create a security interest in the goods sold under it); *In re* Padgett, 49 B.R. 212, 41 U.C.C. Rep. Serv. 1020 (Bankr. W.D. Ky. 1985) (monetary obligation alone not sufficient to create chattel paper).

[161] U.C.C. § 9-102(a)(11).

[162] U.C.C. § 9-102(a)(78).

[163] U.C.C. § 9-102(a)(31).

[164] U.C.C. § 9-313(a) (possession of tangible chattel paper); §§ 9-314(a), 9-105 (control of electronic chattel paper). Security interests in both forms of chattel paper may also be perfected by filing. § 9-312(a).

governmental unit of a State. The term includes health-care-insurance receivables.[165]

The effect of the phrase "whether or not earned by performance" can be illustrated by the following example. Suppose a painting contractor needing a loan is owed $5,000 for a completed job and has a contract to paint a building the next week for another $5,000. The right to payment from each job is an account.[166]

The term account does not include the following types of payment rights:

(i) rights to payment evidenced by chattel paper or an instrument, (ii) commercial tort claims, (iii) deposit accounts, (iv) investment property, (v) letter-of-credit rights or letters of credit, or (vi) rights to payment for money or funds advanced or sold, other than rights arising out of the use of a credit or charge card or information contained on or for use with the card.[167]

To illustrate the last category, suppose Lender owns the right to be paid on a number of loans which are not represented by instruments. If it packages the loans and sells fractional shares in the payment rights associated with the package to various participants,[168] the rights represent funds advanced and do not qualify as accounts.[169]

---

[165] U.C.C. § 9-102(a)(2). Under prior versions of Article 9, many of these rights were classified as general intangibles, but they have been shifted to the account category primarily to facilitate securitizations. Sales of accounts are governed by Article 9 which provides clear rules protecting parties participating in the securitization; sales of general intangibles that are not also payment intangibles are governed by other law under which the rules are not so clear. *See, e.g., In re* Nittolo Land Dev. Ass'n, 58 U.C.C. Rep. Serv. 2d 313 (Bankr. S.D. N.Y. 2005) (right to payment under contract to sell real estate held to be an account under revised Article 9 even though it would have been a general intangible prior to the revision). The subset of accounts called health-care-insurance receivables is defined in U.C.C. § 9-102(a)(46) and discussed in note 160 infra.

[166] The mechanics of assigning accounts, including the vulnerability of the assignee to defenses such as might arise if the contractor does not perform under the second contract, are discussed elsewhere in this chapter. *See* § 1.04[D] *infra.*

[167] U.C.C. § 9-102(a)(2).

[168] There is debate about whether the assignment of a fractional share of a promissory note should still be characterized as an assignment of a promissory note or recharacterized as an assignment of a payment intangible. In *In re* Commercial Money Ctr., Inc., 350 B.R. 465, 60 U.C.C. Rep. Serv. 2d 584 (BAP 9th Cir. 2006), the court came down on the side of recharacterization by holding that an assignment of the payment stream generated by equipment leases without an assignment of the underlying leases constituted an assignment of payment intangibles even though the records that evidenced the payment rights were chattel paper. The case has unleashed a flood of reactions from commercial law scholars and practitioners, most of them negative. The problem with the recharacterization is that it may cause certain priority rules for chattel paper upon which commercial entities rely to be inoperative.

[169] The rights do not fall directly into any other defined category and thus, by default, are general intangibles. They are also within the subset of general intangibles called "payment intangibles" and thus their sale is governed by Article 9. U.C.C. §§ 9-102(a)(61) (payment intangible defined), 9-109(3) (sales of payment intangibles within scope of Article 9). Sales of general intangibles that are not payment intangibles are not governed by Article 9. Payment intangibles are discussed further in the next subsection.

There is a subset of accounts called health-care-insurance receivables.[170] Article 9 excludes from its scope most assignments of rights under policies of insurance,[171] but it governs assignments under private health-care insurance policies. This facilitates commerce by making it easier for health-care providers to sell or borrow against their rights to the proceeds of their patients' health-care-insurance policies.[172]

[2] General Intangibles — § 9-102(a)(42), (61)

Article 9 defines "general intangibles" in residual terms, meaning any personal property that does not fall within one of the other categories.[173] General intangibles thus include any form of personal property that might be used as collateral and that is not covered by the definition of any other Article 9 category nor specifically excluded from the scope of the article. Just a few examples of personal property that have been categorized by the courts as general intangibles include patent rights,[174] trademark rights,[175] rights to tax refunds,[176] rights to refunds for overpayments to an employee pension plan,[177] claims for breach of contract,[178] liquor licenses,[179] FCC licenses,[180] state water permits,[181] and refunds from

---

[170] U.C.C. § 9-102(a)(46). A health-care-insurance receivable is "an interest in or claim under a policy of insurance which is a right to payment of a monetary obligation for health-care goods or services provided."

[171] U.C.C. § 9-109(d)(8). *See* § 1.07[G] *infra.*

[172] There are some differences between the treatment of accounts generally and the treatment of health-care-insurance receivables. U.C.C. § 9-404(e), for example, excludes health-care-insurance receivables from the general rules governing the rights of account debtors to assert claims and defenses against assignees. The rationale is that the obligation of an insurer (the account debtor in this context) is governed by other law. For similar reasons, U.C.C. § 9-405(d) excludes health-care-insurance receivables from the general rules governing the effects of modifications against assignees, and U.C.C. § 9-406(e) excludes health-care-insurance receivables from other aspects of the assignment rules, such as the obligation to pay an assignee after receiving notification.

Health-care-insurance receivables are subject to U.C.C. § 9-408(a), which invalidates an anti-assignment clause in a health-care-insurance policy to the extent that it prohibits assignment or makes assignment an event of default between the account debtor (insurer) and the debtor (insured), but that section specifies that the account debtor need not honor the assignment if the anti-assignment clause would be effective under other law. U.C.C. § 9-408(d). *See also* the discussion of Article 9's treatment of anti-assignment provisions in note 172 *infra.*

[173] U.C.C. § 9-102(a)(42).

[174] *In re* Emergency Beacon Corp., 23 U.C.C. Rep. Serv. 766 (S.D.N.Y. 1977).

[175] *In re* Roman Cleanser Co., 43 B.R. 940, 39 U.C.C. Rep. Serv. 1770 (Bankr. E.D. Mich. 1984), *aff'd* 802 F.2d 207, 2 U.C.C. Rep. Serv. 2d 269 (6th Cir. 1986).

[176] *In re* Metric Metals Int'l, Inc., 20 B.R. 633, 33 U.C.C. Rep. Serv. 1495 (S.D.N.Y. 1981).

[177] *In re* Long Chevrolet, Inc., 79 B.R. 759, 5 U.C.C. Rep. Serv. 2d 462 (N.D. Ill. 1987).

[178] Merchants Nat'l Bank of Mobile v. Ching, 681 F.2d 1383, 34 U.C.C. Rep. Serv. 270 (11th Cir. 1982).

[179] Queen of the North, Inc. v. LeGrue, 582 P.2d 144, 24 U.C.C. Rep. Serv. 1301 (Alaska 1978).

[180] *In re* Ridgely Communications, Inc., 139 B.R. 374, 17 U.C.C. Rep. Serv. 2d 877 (Bankr. Md. 1992).

security retainers.[182]

Why is a general intangible of value as collateral? To illustrate, a patent represents a federally guaranteed right to exclusive exploitation of an invention for seventeen years.[183] The patent holder can produce and sell the invention, or license another to do so. A secured party with a security interest in the patent can sell the patent, including the patent-holder's exploitation rights, at foreclosure in the event of default. Likewise, a secured party with a security interest in a government-issued license can sell the license at foreclosure in the event of default.[184] Often the license is the single most valuable asset owned by a business.

Although one would not ordinarily anticipate any difficulties in characterizing property as either goods or general intangibles, courts occasionally have faced the necessity of distinguishing the two. For example, in one case, a court appropriately held that blueprints, drawings, and technical data produced by a company's engineering staff constituted general intangibles rather than goods.[185] It reasoned that, even though reduced to tangible form, the value was in the concepts and ideas represented by the paper. Similarly, the court found that the written bids, proposals, and cost estimates that various departments of the company had preserved so that they could be drawn upon in preparing future bids were general intangibles.

---

[181] Lake Region Credit Union v. Crystal Pure Water, Inc., 502 N.W.2d 524, 21 U.C.C. Rep. Serv. 2d 774 (N.D. 1993).

[182] *In re* E-Z Serve Convenience Stores, Inc., 299 B.R. 126, 51 U.C.C. Rep. Serv. 2d 858 (Bankr. M.D. N.C. 2003) (debtor's right to receive refund on unearned portion of retainer paid to a law firm constituted general intangible).

[183] 35 U.S.C. § 261.

[184] Some government licenses are regulated by statutes or rules that make them nontransferable. *See, e.g.,* Brown v. Baker, 688 P.2d 943, 39 U.C.C. Rep. Serv. 1105 (Alaska 1984) (state statute invalidated security interest in limited-entry fishing permits); *In re* Chris-Don, Inc., 367 F. Supp.2d 696, 57 U.C.C. Rep. Serv. 2d 496 (D. N.J. 2005) (state statute precluded licensee from using liquor license to secure loan). Other licenses are transferable, although typically the issuing governmental agency must approve of the transferee. This simply means that the foreclosing secured party must locate a qualifying buyer. A similar problem arises with certain contracts rights. For example, some franchise agreements can be assigned if the franchisor approves of the transferee while others are by their terms nonassignable.

Article 9 contains a provision that makes any legal rule or contract term ineffective to the extent that it either impairs the creation, attachment, or perfection of a security interest in a general intangible or causes any of those events to constitute a default. U.C.C. §§ 9-408(a), (c). However, to the extent that such limitations are generally effective under law other than Article 9, the affected governmental agency or franchisor need not recognize the security interest or the rights of a foreclosure-sale transferee. U.C.C. § 9-408(d). Put another way, a debtor can grant a valid security interest in an otherwise nontransferable license without suffering any penalties, but that does not mean that it will have value in the event of default. A secured party with an interest in a franchise agreement can do no more than ask the franchisor to waive the anti-assignment clause. Perhaps the most important effect of these provisions is that they may provide a basis for increasing the value of secured claims in bankruptcy. *See* discussion in § 16.02[C] *infra.*

[185] United States v. Antenna Systems, Inc., 251 F. Supp. 1013, 3 U.C.C. Rep. Serv. 258 (D.N.H. 1966).

The category of general intangibles contains two discrete subsets — software and payment intangibles. Software means "a computer program and any supporting information provided in connection with a transaction relating to the program."[186] A secured party may take a security interest in software as part of an integrated transaction in which it also takes a security interest in the goods for which the software is being acquired, in which case the security interest in the software qualifies for purchase-money status to the same extent as the security interest in the goods.[187] The term is also relevant to the definition of chattel paper.[188] Note that software does not include embedded computer programs that are part of goods under the definition of that term.[189]

A payment intangible is "a general intangible under which the account debtor's principal obligation is a monetary obligation."[190] Sales of payment intangibles are within the scope of Article 9[191] but sales of general intangibles that are not payment intangibles are not within the article's scope. Thus, the payment intangible subset of general intangibles is similar to the promissory note subset of instruments.[192]

[D] A Comparison of Accounts, Instruments, and Chattel Paper

Assume that a farm-implement dealer sells a tractor to a farmer. The farmer might pay cash for the tractor but may prefer to buy on credit, and the dealer may feel compelled to provide credit in order to close the deal. The dealer will then receive one of three forms of personal property that are typically created in a noncash sale — an account, an instrument (most likely in the form of a negotiable promissory note), or chattel paper. Distinctions among these three forms of property can be explained by comparing them in the context of this simple hypothetical.

If the dealer sells the tractor to the farmer on an open account, the dealer acquires an Article 2 contract right to payment by the buyer.[193] If the buyer

---

[186] U.C.C. § 9-102(a)(75).

[187] U.C.C. § 9-103(b). *See also* the discussion in § 1.05 *infra*.

[188] *See* the discussion in § 1.04[B][3] *supra*.

[189] Goods are defined in U.C.C. § 9-102(a)(44). *See also* the discussion in § 1.04[A] *supra*.

[190] U.C.C. § 9-102(a)(61). An example of a payment intangible (payment rights that are a fractional share of a package of loans not represented by instruments) is provided in the discussion of accounts in § 1.04[C][1] *supra*. *See also, In re* Wiersma, 324 B.R. 92, 106-07 (BAP 9th Cir. 2005) (discussing why definition of payment intangibles includes assignment of rights under settlement agreement); *cf. In re* Cohen, 305 B.R. 886, 53 U.C.C. Rep. Serv. 2d 148 (Bankr. 9th Cir. 2004) (security interest in potential settlement proceeds of tort claim prior to judgment or settlement did not create a payment intangible because alleged tortfeasors' liability had not been established and thus they were not obligated to pay debtors anything).

[191] U.C.C. § 9-109(a)(3).

[192] Promissory notes and other instruments are discussed in § 1.04[B][2] *supra*.

[193] U.C.C. § 2-301.

breaches, the dealer does not have a right to repossess the tractor.[194] The dealer must instead sue the farmer for breach.[195] If the suit is successful and the farmer does not pay the judgment, the dealer may then have the sheriff execute on the judgment by seizing available assets of the farmer, selling them, and remitting the proceeds to satisfy the judgment in whole or in part. In the suit for breach, however, the farmer may assert any applicable defenses, such as breach of a warranty of quality with respect to the tractor.

If the dealer takes a negotiable promissory note for the farmer's payment obligation, the dealer will acquire Article 3 rights in the note, in addition to the Article 2 rights arising from the sale. The major significance of the additional Article 3 rights of a dealer/payee that retains the note are procedural in nature. The dealer may still have to sue to enforce the payment obligation, but Article 3 has provisions that make the case easier to prove when there is a negotiable instrument.[196] The farmer may still assert any available contract defenses.

If the dealer sells the tractor on secured credit and takes back chattel paper from the farmer, the dealer will acquire both Article 2 rights arising from the sales contract and Article 9 rights on the security agreement that is part of the chattel paper.[197] If the farmer defaults on the payment obligation, the dealer can repossess the tractor, hold a foreclosure sale, and use the sale proceeds to satisfy the outstanding indebtedness. The dealer thus can protect its interests without having to reduce its claim to judgment. Once again, the farmer may assert any available defenses.

Selling the tractor on any of these noncash bases creates a problem for the dealer. The dealer must replenish its inventory of tractors, and if its supplier will not sell to the dealer on credit or deliver on consignment, the dealer must pay for replacement inventory on delivery. Payment for the tractor sold to the farmer, however, will be made over time. Confronted with this cash-flow problem, the dealer is likely to seek inventory financing and will probably secure the financing with its rights against the farmer. Thus the dealer might borrow from a bank, granting the bank a security interest in the account, the note, or the chattel paper, or it might sell them to the

[194] The sale passes title to the buyer, U.C.C. §§ 2-106(1) and 2-401, and the dealer receives an enforceable promise in exchange. U.C.C. § 2-702 provides a limited right to reclaim goods delivered pursuant to a credit transaction if the buyer is insolvent at the time of receipt.

[195] The dealer's cause of action in this context is predicated on U.C.C. § 2-607(1), which makes the buyer liable for the contract price once the tractor has been accepted. *See also* U.C.C. § 2-709(1)(a) (seller's action for the price of accepted goods). If the buyer breaches without accepting the goods, the dealer's damages will be predicated on other provisions of Article 2.

[196] U.C.C. § 3-308.

[197] If the chattel paper consists of two writings, a negotiable promissory note and a security agreement, the dealer will also have Article 3 rights, meaning that it can use the procedural advantages of Article 3 if it brings an action to enforce the payment obligation. However, the writings together comprise chattel paper. U.C.C. § 9-102(a)(11). Because the dealer sold the tractor to the farmer, the lease aspect of chattel paper is not applicable to this hypothetical.

bank. Article 9 governs both the sale of each of these assets and their use as collateral for an obligation.[198]

Further aspects of the three types of property can be illustrated by comparing their use in a loan transaction between the dealer and a bank. Note carefully, however, that the hypothetical now involves the dealer offering as collateral the rights created in the dealer's favor by the sale to the farmer. In Article 9 terminology, the bank will be the secured party, the dealer will be the debtor, and the dealer's rights against the farmer will be the collateral.

Assume the bank accepts the account as collateral and the dealer later defaults. The bank can then either require that the account debtor[199] (the farmer) make future payments directly to the bank[200] or it can sell the account at foreclosure. In either event, the money it receives will go to reduce the indebtedness of the dealer. Because the enforcement rights of the bank and any foreclosure-sale purchaser are predicated on the farmer's Article 2 obligation, they are subject to most contract defenses that the farmer could have asserted against the dealer had the account not been assigned (the merchandise risk). This risk can be avoided if the contract between the dealer and the farmer contains a waiver-of-defenses clause and if the bank has certain characteristics normally associated with a bona-fide purchaser for value.[201] The bank and a foreclosure-sale purchaser also run the risk that the farmer might become insolvent (the credit risk). Lenders discount the value of accounts when lending against them based on the level of risk they are assuming.

The position of the bank will be significantly improved if the dealer acquired the farmer's payment obligation in the form of a negotiable promissory note. The bank will then be much less concerned about the underlying transaction between the dealer and the farmer because of the enhanced rights that it will obtain under Article 3. As with the account, if the dealer defaults the bank can either apply the farmer's payments on the note to the dealer's debt or it can sell the note, in either event using

---

[198] U.C.C. § 9-109(a)(1), (3).

[199] The term means "a person obligated on an account, chattel paper, or general intangible. The term does not include persons obligated to pay a negotiable instrument, even if the instrument constitutes part of chattel paper." U.C.C. § 9-102(a)(3).

[200] *See* § 1.04[C][1] for a discussion of the mechanics by which the bank will assert its collection rights.

[201] U.C.C. §§ 9-404(a), 9-403. In effect, the waiver-of-defenses clause permits the bank to acquire rights that are indistinguishable from those of a holder in due course of a negotiable instrument, discussed *infra* this subsection. The characteristics required of the bank are set forth in U.C.C. § 9-403(b).

In consumer purchases of goods, a Federal Trade Commission rule makes it an unfair or deceptive act for certain sellers to take a contract that does not contain a notice preserving the consumer's defenses against assignees. The FTC rule applies whether the consumer buyer's payment obligation takes the form of an account, an instrument, or chattel paper. Trade Regulation Rule Concerning Preservation of Consumer Claims and Defenses, 16 C.F.R. § 433. U.C.C. §§ 9-403(d) and 9-404(d) provide that, in a consumer transaction, a record that *should* contain the required FTC notice will be treated as if it *did* contain the notice.

the money it receives to reduce the dealer's debt. The enhanced position of the bank or the foreclosure-sale purchaser becomes relevant only if the farmer stops paying on the note. Unlike the dealer, the bank did not deal with the farmer. Provided the bank qualifies under Article 3 as a holder in due course, a particular type of bona-fide purchaser for value, the bank and any foreclosure-sale purchaser will take free of most contract defenses of the farmer.[202] In effect, a holder in due course gets the benefit of a waiver of defenses without such a waiver having to be spelled out in the instrument. The elimination of the risk that the obligor on the note[203] may have an effective defense, combined with the procedural advantages discussed *supra*, render a payment obligation in the form of a negotiable instrument more marketable than payment obligations in other forms.

If chattel paper is created in the underlying sales transaction, the bank will again have a form of property that represents the farmer's Article 2 payment obligation.[204] Further, with the inclusion of the security interest in the tractor, if both the dealer and the farmer default on their payment obligations, the bank as assignee or a foreclosure-sale purchaser from the bank will be able to enforce the dealer's right to foreclose on the tractor. Whether the bank is subject to the farmer's contract defenses turns on whether the contract between the dealer and the farmer contains either an effective waiver-of-defenses clause or an obligation in the form of a negotiable promissory note.[205] If so, and if the bank has the requisite characteristics under either Article 9 (waiver-of defenses clause) or Article 3 (negotiable promissory note), it will take free of most such defenses.

As this hypothetical demonstrates, the greatest bundle of property rights in a credit sale is created when the seller takes chattel paper that contains an effective waiver-of-defenses clause or a negotiable promissory note. Legal rights alone, however, do not drive all business transactions. Transaction costs are higher with notes and chattel paper, and these costs may outweigh the enhanced rights provided, particularly when relatively small amounts of debt are involved. Alternative methods of risk assessment may also lessen the need for additional rights, and the rights themselves may not be particularly valuable in some transactions. For example, the right to foreclose on the underlying collateral when chattel paper is involved may not be viable if the property is difficult to resell or if an entity like a bank is not well-suited to undertake its sale. Practical aspects of structuring a

---

[202] U.C.C. §§ 3-302(a)(2), 3-305(b).

[203] Recall that the term "account debtor" is inapplicable in the context of a negotiable instrument. U.C.C. § 9-102(a)(3).

[204] If the chattel paper is a package that includes both a negotiable instrument and a security agreement, the bank's rights and duties are governed by Articles 3 and 9 to the extent they are consistent. In case of a conflict, Article 9 governs. U.C.C. § 3-102(b).

[205] If the chattel paper consisted of two writings, a negotiable instrument and a security agreement, the package of writings would still be chattel paper but the bank would have the benefit of the Article 3 rules associated with negotiable instruments, including both the procedural advantages and the rights of a holder in due course.

transaction with respect to accounts, notes, or chattel paper are developed in subsequent parts of this book.[206]

[E] Investment Property — § 9-102(a)(49)

"Investment property" is a broad category of intangible assets within one or more of the following subsets: securities (both certificated and uncertificated), security entitlements, securities accounts, commodity contracts, and commodity accounts.[207] Certain of these assets function like indispensable records while others do not. Accordingly, it is best to deal with investment property as a separate category altogether.

Although investment property is an Article 9 term, it relies to a large extent on terminology and concepts developed in Article 8. As will be explained below, Article 8 deals with securities held directly by an investor and with financial assets, including securities, held indirectly through a securities intermediary (e.g., a broker). Investments in commodities are beyond the scope of Article 8, and Article 9 is self-contained with respect to security interests in such investments.

A security is an obligation of an issuer or a share or other interest in an issuer or its property that is, or is of a type, commonly dealt with in the securities markets, or that is a medium for investment that by its terms expressly provides that it is within the scope of Article 8.[208] A certificated security is a security that is represented by a physical certificate.[209] The most common forms of certificated securities are stock and bond certificates.[210] The represented rights are commonly transferred by delivery of the certificate,[211] and thus a certificated security is a form of indispensable record.

An uncertificated security, sometimes called a book-entry security, is a security for which there is no certificate.[212] The security holder's interest is represented by a notation in books or records maintained by or on behalf of the issuer. Uncertificated securities are typically transferred by making appropriate changes in these records.[213] For example, mutual funds do not

---

[206] See, e.g., § 3.04 infra.

[207] U.C.C. § 9-102(a)(49).

[208] U.C.C. § 8-102(a)(15). An asset need not actually be dealt with in the securities markets as long as it is of a type that is traded. Thus, a stock certificate representing an ownership interest in a closely held corporation is a security even though the stock is not publicly traded.

[209] U.C.C. § 8-102(a)(4).

[210] In re H.J. Otten Co., Inc., 8 B.R. 781, 31 U.C.C. Rep. Serv. 702 (W.D.N.Y. 1981) (municipal bonds included); Traverse v. Liberty Bank & Trust Co, 5 U.C.C. Rep. Serv. 535 (Mass. Super. Ct. 1967) (convertible debentures included).

[211] See U.C.C. §§ 8-104(a)(1) (describing how a person acquires an interest in a security), 8-302 (describing the rights acquired by a purchaser of a security), and 8-301(a) (defining delivery in the context of certificated securities).

[212] U.C.C. § 8-102(a)(18).

[213] See U.C.C. §§ 8-104(a)(1) (describing how a person acquires an interest in a security), 8-302 (describing the rights acquired by a purchaser of a security), and 8-301(b) (defining delivery in the context of uncertificated securities).

ordinarily issue certificates to their shareholders but instead show share-holder interests as notations in their records. An uncertificated security cannot function as an indispensable record.

The term "security" includes both certificated and uncertificated securi-ties,[214] and it is primarily used when there is a direct relationship between the investor and the issuer. Most assets held indirectly through a broker are called "security entitlements,"[215] which are defined in terms of "finan-cial assets." A financial asset may be a security, but the term also includes investment vehicles that are not securities but that are either of a type commonly traded on financial markets or are a recognized medium for investment.[216] Article 8 contains a section that further differentiates between financial assets that are securities and those that are not.[217] A financial asset that is not a security and is held directly by the debtor is not investment property and is almost certainly a general intangible. A financial asset held by a broker is almost always a security entitlement whether or not it qualifies as a security, and is therefore investment property.[218]

Assume, for example, that an investor owns 100 shares of ABC Corp. If the investor is in possession of a certificate showing this interest, the asset is a certificated security. If there is no certificate but the books of ABC Corp. reflect the investor's interest, the asset is an uncertificated security. If the investor indirectly holds 100 shares of ABC Corp. through a broker, the asset is a security entitlement. A securities account consists of all security entitlements held in a particular account by a securities intermediary.[219]

Now assume that the same investor directly owns a membership interest in a limited liability company. Unless the terms that define the interest specify that it is a security governed by Article 8, the interest is a financial asset but not a security.[220] It does not qualify as investment property and is instead a general intangible; moreover, since the principal right associ-ated with the interest is not the payment of money, it is not a payment intangible (a subset of general intangibles). If, however, a broker holds the financial asset for the investor, it is a security entitlement and therefore qualifies as investment property.

---

[214] U.C.C. § 8-102(a)(15)(i).

[215] U.C.C. § 8-102(a)(17). The investor is called an "entitlement holder." § 8-102(a)(7).

[216] U.C.C. § 8-102(a)(9). The term also includes any other asset that is held in a securities account and that the broker and customer have agreed will be treated as a financial asset.

[217] U.C.C. § 8-103.

[218] It is possible for a financial asset held through a broker to be treated as if it were held directly by the debtor. See § 8-501(d) (financial asset registered in the name of, payable to the order of, or specially indorsed to the debtor and not indorsed by the debtor to the broker or in blank). If such a financial asset is a security, it is investment property. If it is not a security, it is a general intangible.

[219] U.C.C. § 8-501(a). Attachment of a security interest to a securities account carries with it automatic attachment to each security entitlement within the account. § 9-203(h).

[220] U.C.C. § 8-103(c). Partnership interests are treated similarly.

The treatment of investments in commodity contracts is similar to that for security entitlements and securities accounts. A commodity account is an account maintained by a commodity intermediary (dealer) on behalf of an investor.[221] A commodity contract is a commodity futures contract or option that is traded on a commodities market.[222] Commodity contracts are functionally identical to security entitlements. A commodity account includes all the commodity contracts in an account maintained by a dealer and is functionally identical to a securities account.[223]

A security agreement that describes the collateral as "all investment property" will cover every asset within each category. The parties can also carve up the assets: The security agreement might, for example, cover "all securities," giving the secured party an interest in all certificated and uncertificated securities held directly by the debtor and all financial assets that are securities held through a broker. The secured party would not have a security interest in other financial assets held through a broker, nor would its interest attach to any commodity contract or commodity account. On the other hand, a security agreement that covers "all security entitlements" will reach each financial asset held through a broker but will not reach securities held directly by the debtor, nor will it reach commodity contracts or commodity accounts. A security agreement that describes the collateral as a particular securities account attaches to all security entitlements within the account, and a security agreement that describes the collateral as a particular commodity account attaches to all commodity contracts within the account.[224] Of course, the parties need not select a generic category. If the debtor holds a stock certificate representing an interest in a closely held corporation, the description in the agreement can be tailored to that asset. Likewise, if the parties want to use a particular security entitlement without using all the assets in a particular account they are free to do so.[225]

---

[221] U.C.C. § 9-102(a)(14). The investor is called a "commodity customer." U.C.C. § 9-102(a)(16).

[222] U.C.C. § 9-102(a)(15).

[223] As is true with securities accounts, attachment of a security interest to a commodity account carries with it automatic attachment to each commodity contract within the account. U.C.C. § 9-203(i).

[224] U.C.C.§§ 9-203(h), (i).

[225] U.C.C. § 9-108(d) validates generic descriptions that use investment property or any of its subcategories, as well as specific descriptions of the underlying asset. Further, U.C.C. § 9-108(b) permits the description to identify the collateral by category or type, by quantity, by a computational or allocational formula or procedure, or by any other method that renders the identity of the collateral objectively determinable. In a consumer transaction, however, a description of a security entitlement, securities account, or commodity account only by one of the defined types is insufficient as a matter of law. U.C.C. § 9-108(d).

§ 1.05 PURCHASE-MONEY SECURITY INTERESTS — § 9-103

[A] General

Although many distinctions in Article 9 are based on the classification of the collateral involved in a transaction, the nature of the transaction itself can also be relevant.[226] One form of secured transaction does not involve the acquisition of the collateral; the debtor simply grants a security interest in assets in which the debtor already has an interest. For example, a consumer debtor might grant a security interest in a car she already owns or a business debtor might grant a security interest in its existing equipment.

Secured transactions also frequently play a significant role in the acquisition of goods. Many buyers cannot afford to pay the full purchase price at the time they enter into a sales contract, or they choose for a variety of reasons not to do so. One solution that facilitates these transactions is an unsecured installment sales contract. The buyer is allowed to take immediate possession of the goods upon making a down payment and agreeing to pay the balance, plus interest and other charges, in installments. The seller, however, faces a risk that may make the transaction unpalatable. If the seller does not receive the promised installments, its options are generally limited to bringing an action for the unpaid balance.[227] A seller that has not reserved a security interest in the goods can only recover them *in specie* in limited circumstances.[228]

An alternative is for the seller and the buyer to enter into a secured installment sales contract, sometimes called a conditional sales contract. In this type of contract, the seller sells the goods on credit terms but retains an Article 9 security interest in them. The term "conditional sale" originated with a pre-Code security device pursuant to which a seller retained title to the goods until the purchase price was fully paid. Under the Code, in a contract for sale the title to the goods passes to the buyer notwithstanding a term reserving it to the seller until payment is received. The term is reduced in effect to the creation of an Article 9 security interest.[229]

---

[226] For example, a purchase-money security interest, which is described in this section, can enable a creditor to acquire special rights in priority contests.

[227] "Unless otherwise explicitly agreed title passes to the buyer at the time and place at which the seller completes his performance with reference to the physical delivery of the goods . . . ." U.C.C. § 2-401(2). Although the seller in Evans Products Co. v. Jorgensen, 245 Ore. 362, 421 P.2d 978, 3 U.C.C. Rep. Serv. 1099 (1966), had intended to reserve title until it was paid for the veneer that it delivered to a plywood manufacturer, the delivery passed title.

[228] The seller must ascertain that the buyer received the goods on credit while insolvent and, even then, the seller generally must give notice of its intent to reclaim them within ten days of their receipt. *See* U.C.C. § 2-702.

[229] U.C.C. § 2-401(1).

In the case of a conditional sale, the seller's reserved security interest qualifies as a type of "purchase-money" security interest.[230] The Code provides that a security interest is purchase money in nature if the obligation was "incurred as all or part of the price of the collateral."[231] In effect, the seller has loaned the buyer the purchase price, and the collateral is the goods acquired with the loan.[232]

Many merchants, particularly those that sell and lease on credit, do not have sufficient capital to finance the acquisition of inventory. They must continually replenish their inventory, and, if their suppliers require payment on delivery, they cannot afford to wait for installment payments from their buyers and lessees. Their business depends upon turning over inventory, not upon earning the interest that is added to an installment-payment obligation. These credit-sale transactions can nevertheless go forward through the involvement of a bank or other financing entity. If strategic planning necessitates purchase-money secured financing, a transaction can be structured to qualify as another type of purchase-money secured transaction. A purchase-money security interest is created if it is taken by a person that gives value "to enable the debtor to acquire rights in or the use of the collateral if the value is in fact so used."[233] Loans of this nature are commonly referred to as "enabling loans" because the lender provides the financing that enables the debtor to acquire the collateral.[234]

A purchase-money lender must take care that the value provided in fact be used by the debtor to acquire rights in or the use of the collateral.[235] A lender will find itself unsecured if the debtor squanders the loan proceeds and never acquires the collateral described in the security agreement. Even if the debtor acquires the collateral so that a security interest attaches, it will not be purchase-money in nature if the lender is unable to bear the burden of tracing its loan proceeds into the collateral. The lender can protect itself by making payment directly to the seller of the collateral or by issuing a check naming the seller and the debtor as joint payees.

---

[230] Burlington Nat'l Bank v. Strauss, 50 Wis. 2d 270, 184 N.W.2d 122, 8 U.C.C. Rep. Serv. 944 (1971) (defendant retained purchase-money security interest in cattle sold to debtor under conditional sales contract taken by defendant to secure sales price).

[231] U.C.C. § 9-103(a)(2) (part of definition of "purchase-money obligation").

[232] A merchant selling inventory can also enter into a consignment arrangement with a supplier under which the supplier delivers the goods but reserves title. The reservation of title is effective because the transaction is not a sale in that the goods can be returned if the merchant is unable to sell them. The interest of a consignor (the supplier), like the interest of a secured credit seller, is a purchase-money security interest. U.C.C. § 9-103(d). Consignments are discussed generally in § 1.03[B][3] *supra*.

[233] U.C.C. § 9-103(a)(2).

[234] Chrysler Credit Corp. v. B.J.M., Jr., Inc., 834 F. Supp. 813, 22 U.C.C. Rep. Serv. 2d 379 (E.D. Pa. 1993), *aff'd* 30 F.3d 1485 (3d Cir. 1994) (lender's financing was intended to permit dealer to acquire its inventory); Nauman v. First Nat'l Bank of Allen Park, 50 Mich. App. 41, 212 N.W.2d 760, 13 U.C.C. Rep. Serv. 1191 (1973) (bank made advances to customers to enable them to acquire rights in trailers).

[235] *See* Mays v. Brighton Bank, 832 S.W.2d 347, 18 U.C.C. Rep. Serv. 2d 621 (Tenn. Ct. App. 1992) (question of fact as to whether loan given by bank was used to purchase trailer).

Under former law, there was no explicit limitation on the types of assets that could serve as purchase-money collateral. By contrast, revised Article 9 explicitly limits purchase-money collateral to goods and, in limited situations, software. [236] To be purchase-money collateral, software must be acquired in an integrated transaction in which goods are also acquired and the software must be acquired for the principal purpose of being used with the goods. If the test is met, a security interest in the software is purchase-money in nature to the same extent that the security interest in the goods is purchase-money in nature. [237]

[B]   Adoption of "Dual-Status" Rule

Purchase-money secured parties operating under former law sometimes ran into difficulties when they refinanced the original obligation. Refinancing can take many forms. For example, a financially troubled debtor might ask that a purchase-money loan be restructured to reduce the monthly payments. If the secured party canceled the old agreement and substituted a new agreement reflecting new payment terms, some courts held there had been a new loan and that its proceeds were used to pay off the old loan — and thus that the refinanced loan did not enable the debtor to acquire the collateral. [238] The secured party did not lose its security interest or its perfected status, but its security interest was no longer purchase-money in nature. [239]

A related problem occurred if the security interest in acquired goods secured more than their purchase price. For example, a seller with a purchase-money security interest in one item might sell a second item to the debtor, also on a purchase-money basis. If the two loans were consolidated into a single loan for which both items served as collateral, [240] some courts applied a "transformation rule" and held that the seller's combined security interest was not purchase-money as applied to either item. The rationale was that the security interest, as applied to each item, was not retained solely to secure all or part of its price. [241] Problems also arose when a purchase-money lender made a later advance to the debtor for a purpose other than the acquisition of collateral and combined the obligations, thus mixing purchase money and nonpurchase money.

Some courts under former law rejected the transformation rule and held that a secured party's interest was purchase money if it could prove the

---

[236] U.C.C. § 9-103(a)(1).

[237] U.C.C. § 9-103(c). *See also* U.C.C. § 9-324(f) (providing purchase-money priority in the software to the same extent such priority is provided for the associated goods).

[238] *See In re* Matthews, 724 F.2d 798, 37 U.C.C. Rep. Serv. 1332 (9th Cir. 1984). *But see In re* Billings, 838 F.2d 405, 5 U.C.C. Rep. Serv. 1259 (10th Cir. 1988) (refinancing did not amount to new loan).

[239] As a result, such a secured party may have lost priority that it otherwise would have held as a purchase-money secured party. *See* §§ 10.04, 14.02[B] *infra*.

[240] This approach is called "cross-collateralization."

[241] *See In re* Manuel, 507 F.2d 990, 16 U.C.C. Rep. Serv. 493 (5th Cir. 1975).

extent to which the outstanding balance at any given point in time retained its purchase-money character. Revised Article 9 adopted this approach, called the "dual-status" approach, for transactions that are not consumer transactions.[242] Article 9 rejects the transformation rule by providing that a purchase-money security interest does not lose its status as such even if "(1) the purchase-money collateral also secures an obligation that is not a purchase-money obligation; (2) collateral that is not purchase-money collateral also secures the purchase money obligation; or (3) the purchase-money obligation has been renewed, refinanced, consolidated, or restructured."[243] It also adopts the dual-status rule by providing as follows:

> A security interest in goods is a purchase-money security interest:
>
> (1) *to the extent* that the goods are purchase-money collateral[244] with respect to that security interest;
>
> (2) if the security interest is in inventory that is or was purchase-money collateral, also *to the extent* that the security interest secures a purchase-money obligation[245] incurred with respect to other inventory in which the secured party holds or held a purchase-money security interest; and
>
> (3) also *to the extent* that the security interest secures a purchase-money obligation incurred with respect to software in which the secured party holds or held a purchase-money security interest.[246]

The "to the extent" language makes it clear that a transaction can be part purchase-money and part nonpurchase-money in nature. The burden of establishing the extent to which a security interest is purchase-money in nature is on the party claiming that status,[247] and to aid the secured party in sustaining its burden there is guidance as to how payments are to be allocated. Payments must be allocated in accordance with any reasonable method agreed to by the parties,[248] and the secured party will

---

[242] The appropriate approach in consumer transactions is left to the courts, and the fact that the dual-status rule is adopted for other transactions does not create an inference that the transformation rule should be adopted by the courts for consumer transactions. U.C.C. § 9-103(h). Consumers prefer the transformation rule because, in bankruptcy, a nonpossessory, nonpurchase-money security interest can be invalidated to the extent the interest impairs a debtor's ability to claim an exemption in certain specified categories. 11 U.S.C. § 522(f)(1)(B). "Lien stripping" in bankruptcy is discussed in § 16.07[B] *infra*.

[243] U.C.C. § 9-103(f).

[244] "Purchase-money collateral" means the goods or software that secure a purchase-money obligation. U.C.C. § 9-103(a)(1).

[245] "Purchase-money obligation" means a seller's retention of collateral to secure all or part of the purchase price or a lender's retention of collateral to secure an enabling loan. U.C.C. § 9-103(a)(2). Comment 3 to that section states that the "price" or "value given to enable" includes "obligations for expenses incurred in connection with acquiring rights in the collateral, sales taxes, duties, finance charges, interest, freight charges, costs of storage in transit, demurrage, administrative charges, expenses of collection and enforcement, attorney's fees, and other similar obligations."

[246] U.C.C. § 9-103(b) (emphasis supplied).

[247] U.C.C. § 9-103(g).

[248] U.C.C. § 9-103(e)(1).

want a term in its security agreement providing that payments will be allocated first to any unsecured obligations, next to any nonpurchase-money secured obligations, and finally to any purchase-money secured obligations.[249] If the parties do not agree, payments are to be allocated in accordance with any intent manifested by the obligor at or before the time payment is made.[250] Failing agreement or obligor manifestation, a default rule provides that payments are to be allocated first to any obligations that are unsecured, next to any purchase-money secured obligations, and finally to any nonpurchase-money secured obligations.[251]

Section 9-103(b)(2), which adopts the dual-status rule regarding transactions involving inventory,[252] overrules a case that had sent shock waves through the secured lending industry.[253] That case held that a purchase-money inventory financier that relied on an after-acquired property clause to cover multiple transactions lost its purchase-money status entirely. Revised Article 9's solution might be called a "dual-status-plus" rule. To illustrate its application, suppose Manufacturer retains a purchase-money security interest in an item that will be inventory in the hands of Retailer as collateral for the item's price, and that the security agreement also grants Manufacturer a security interest to secure the price of any other items that it might later sell to Retailer. Manufacturer later sells another item to Retailer on a purchase-money basis, and Retailer resells the second item to a buyer in ordinary course of business that takes it free from the security interest.[254] Under revised Article 9, Manufacturer's security interest in the first item is still entirely purchase-money in nature even though it now secures the price of both items. Without this special provision, the dual status approach would apply and Manufacturer's security interest would only be partially purchase-money in nature.

§ 1.06 SALES OF ACCOUNTS, CHATTEL PAPER, PAYMENT INTANGIBLES AND PROMISSORY NOTES — § 9-109(a)(3)

Many Article 9 transactions are loan transactions and the security interest is a device that serves the function of providing collateral in the event of default. An ostensible-ownership problem arises if the secured

---

[249] *See, e.g., In re* Cersey, 321 B.R. 352, 56 U.C.C. Rep. Serv. 2d 772 (Bankr. M.D. Ga. 2004) (the contracts provided the following allocation for each payment: "all sales taxes, all finance charges, all insurance charges, all delinquency charges, all court costs, all dishonored payment fees, all delivery charges, all set-up or installation fees, and then to the purchase price of each item in order of earlier items paid for first, and in the case of multiple items purchased on the same day, in order of lesser value items paid for first").

[250] U.C.C. § 9-103(e)(2).

[251] U.C.C. § 9-103(e)(3).

[252] U.C.C. § 9-103(b)(2).

[253] Southtrust Bank of Alabama v. Borg-Warner Acceptance Corp., 760 F.2d 1240, 40 U.C.C. Rep. Serv. 1601 (11th Cir. 1985).

[254] The rights of a buyer in ordinary course are discussed in § 11.03[A][1] *infra.*

party lacks possession of the collateral, but the public filing of a financing statement resolves that problem. The filing protects the secured party from most adverse claims to its collateral.

In real estate recording systems, any person with an interest in land, including mortgagees and buyers, must record that interest in order to gain protection against adverse claimants. A buyer, for example, will record a deed so that the seller cannot fraudulently reconvey an interest in the property to a third party whose claim might defeat the buyer's interest. Buyers of most goods need not record their interests since the mere fact of possession is sufficient to put third parties on notice. Public recording is required, however, for certain types of goods. We are accustomed, for example, to title certificates evidencing ownership of motor vehicles, and buyers of aircraft must register with the Federal Aviation Administration to gain protection from adverse claimants.[255]

Recall that an account is a pure intangible, meaning that there is no indispensable record that must be transferred in order to assign the right to payment represented by the account.[256] If the owner of an account wants to realize upon it before payment is due from the account debtor, it can either conditionally assign the account as collateral for a loan or sell it via an unconditional assignment. In either case, the underlying mechanism by which the right to payment is transferred is assignment.

Assignment of accounts is important in the context of merchants that sell some of their inventory on an installment plan.[257] Because of the need to replenish inventory and the desire to free the capital represented by the account, many merchants seek to finance against the value of their accounts. Various dynamics of the marketplace, which will be explained later,[258] tend to dictate whether the merchant can borrow against the accounts or must sell them outright. The driving force in both circumstances, however, is the need of the merchant to finance the acquisition of additional inventory.

In a loan transaction, the assignment is effectuated by an Article 9 security agreement, and the secured party (assignee) must file a financing statement to protect its security interest in the event the owner fraudulently assigns the account a second time. The intangible nature of the collateral facilitates fraudulent reassignment, and the filing puts third parties on notice of the secured party's interest and establishes priority should a third party take an assignment anyway. The same problems may arise when an account is sold by an unconditional assignment. The drafters of the original article wanted a mechanism that would encourage the buyer of an account to make a public filing in order to warn third parties that might either buy or lend against the same account. Their resolution was

---

[255] 49 U.S.C. § 1403.

[256] *See* the discussion in §§ 1.04[C][1] and [D] *supra.*

[257] *See* the discussion in § 1.04[D] *supra.*

[258] *See* § 3.04 *infra.*

to expand the scope of Article 9 to cover "any sale of accounts or chattel paper."[259] Revised Article 9 adds sales of payment intangibles (a subset of general intangibles) and promissory notes (a subset of instruments) to its scope.[260]

The rationale for bringing sales of accounts and chattel paper into Article 9 was to encourage assignees to give public notice by filing financing statements.[261] The mechanism employed by the drafters to achieve their goal is awkward and confusing. The Code defines a "security interest" to include the interest of a buyer of accounts or chattel paper (or, in revised Article 9, also payment intangibles or promissory notes),[262] "secured party" to include a buyer of such assets,[263] and "debtor" to include a seller of such assets.[264] Because a buyer of accounts or chattel paper is a secured party with a security interest, it needs to file a financing statement to protect that interest. Under the normal Code priority rule governing contests among secured parties,[265] a buyer of accounts that fails to file will lose to a subsequent buyer or secured lender that does file.[266]

This mechanism accomplished the drafters' goal, but calling a buyer's interest a security interest when there is no loan (and therefore the security interest does not function as a security device) inevitably has consequences. For example, the sales agreement between the buyer and seller is a "security agreement"[267] and to be enforceable must meet the formalities required of any security agreement.[268] Also, because the security interest does not operate as a security device, the Code's foreclosure procedures do not apply to covered sales.[269] For example, if a lender acquires a security interest in accounts to secure a loan, following default it must adhere to Article 9's provisions governing foreclosure. Most importantly, it is subject to a standard of commercial reasonableness in either collecting the accounts[270] or selling (reassigning) them at a foreclosure sale.[271] If the collection or foreclosure brings a surplus, it belongs to the debtor, and if proper procedures have been followed, the obligor is liable for any remaining deficiency.[272] By contrast, if a buyer of accounts acquires a security

---

[259] U.C.C. § 9-102(1)(b) (1962 Official Text).

[260] U.C.C. § 9-109(a)(3).

[261] The rationale for expanding the article's scope to cover sales of payment intangibles and promissory notes is different as the interest of the buyer is automatically perfected. U.C.C. § 9-309(3), (4). The rationale is explained *infra* this section.

[262] U.C.C. § 1-201(b)(35).

[263] U.C.C. § 9-102(a)(72)(D).

[264] U.C.C. § 9-102(a)(28)(B).

[265] U.C.C. § 9-322(a)(1).

[266] Priorities among secured parties are discussed in Chapter 10.

[267] U.C.C. § 9-102(a)(73).

[268] U.C.C. § 9-203.

[269] U.C.C. § 9-601(g).

[270] U.C.C. § 9-607(c).

[271] U.C.C. § 9-610(b).

[272] U.C.C. § 9-615(d).

interest that does not secure an indebtedness, these procedures make no sense. The buyer has bought the entire interest and can keep whatever is collected on the accounts or generated by their resale. Because there will typically be neither a surplus nor a deficiency,[273] it should not matter whether the buyer's collection or resale efforts are commercially reasonable.

At least one court applying former law was thoroughly fooled by Article 9's terminology. It concluded that, since an account buyer's interest was limited to a security interest, Article 9 precluded the seller from transferring outright ownership of the account. Accordingly, it held that the account was still owned by the seller and was part of the seller's bankruptcy estate.[274] Of course, the decision was wrong,[275] but using "security interest" to describe a buyer's interest invites confusion. The decision is overruled by revised Article 9, which provides that "[a] debtor that has sold an account, chattel paper, payment intangible, or promissory note does not retain a legal or equitable interest in the collateral sold."[276]

The public-notice rationale did not drive the decision to expand the scope of the revision to cover sales of payment intangibles and promissory notes. Instead, the primary rationale was to facilitate a financing device called an "asset-based securitization." For example, a company that needs immediate funds can create an "SPV," or special-purpose vehicle (often a business trust) and then sell (i.e., unconditionally assign) a package of receivables to the SPV.[277] Capital is then raised through the sale to investors of shares in the SPV, sometimes called "asset-backed securities." Investors in the SPV must be certain that the SPV's interest in the receivables is protected against adverse claimants, primarily a trustee in the event the company

---

[273] The parties sometimes agree that the seller of accounts or chattel paper will make up any deficiency if collections do not bring a projected amount and/or the seller will be liable for any surplus if they exceed a projected amount. These consensual risk-allocation mechanisms are enforceable. U.C.C. § 9-607(c)(2).

[274] Octagon Gas Sys., Inc. v. Rimmer, 995 F.2d 948, 20 U.C.C. Rep. Serv. 2d 1330 (10th Cir. 1993), cert. denied, 510 U.S. 993, 114 S.Ct. 554, 126 L.Ed.2d 455 (1993).

[275] P.E.B. Commentary No. 14 (June 10, 1994) disapproved of Octagon Gas and cited with approval Major's Furniture Mart v. Castle Credit Corp., 602 F.2d 538, 26 U.C.C. Rep. Serv. 1319 (3d Cir. 1979). The Permanent Editorial Board (P.E.B.) is a joint committee of the National Conference of Commissioners on Uniform State Laws and the American Law Institute that oversees the development of the Uniform Commercial Code. One of the responsibilities of the P.E.B. is to provide commentaries that clarify issues that have troubled the courts.

[276] U.C.C. § 9-318(a). It would have been best for the drafters to say no more because subsection (b), which was intended to reinforce the rule of subsection (a), is subject to being misconstrued. The subsection provides that "[f]or purposes of determining the rights of creditors of, and purchasers for value of an account or chattel paper from, a debtor that has sold an account or chattel paper, while the buyer's security interest is unperfected, the debtor is deemed to have rights and title to the account or chattel paper identical to those the debtor sold." The deeming rule only means that, while the debtor does not have the right to reassign the assets, it has the power to do so. The subsection should not be construed to mean that, as between the debtor and the buyer, the debtor retains any interest that might become part of its bankruptcy estate.

[277] The transaction can also be structured as a secured loan from the SPV with the receivables serving as collateral.

seeks protection in bankruptcy. If the sale to the SPV is within the scope of Article 9, this simply means that the SPV must perfect its interest using one of the ordinary Article 9 methods. In the case of accounts or chattel paper, this can be accomplished by the filing of a financing statement. Most of the assets used for securitization purposes will fall within the expanded definition of accounts or chattel paper, but the line between accounts and general intangibles is quite thin. Because of the variety of assets that may qualify as general intangibles, the sale of such assets is not generally within the scope of Article 9. However, the subset of general intangibles that comprise payment intangibles — meaning that the principal value of the intangible is the account debtor's[278] obligation to pay money — is particularly attractive for securitization purposes, and thus sales of payment intangibles were brought within the article's scope. Unlike accounts and chattel paper, the interest of a buyer of payment intangibles is automatically perfected,[279] so no action to perfect will be required of the SPV. Sales of general intangibles that are not payment intangibles are not within the scope of Article 9.

Similar reasoning underlies the decision to cover sales of promissory notes. As new forms of financing evolve, a court might some day decide that the asset backing a securitized offering is an instrument rather than an account or general intangible. To guard against this risk, the "promissory note" subset of instrument was created. Sales of promissory notes are governed by Article 9 and, as with payment intangibles, the buyer's interest is automatically perfected.[280] Sales of instruments that are not promissory notes are not governed by the article.

---

[278] The term "account debtor" refers to an obligor on an account, chattel paper, or a general intangible, but not to an obligor on a negotiable instrument. U.C.C. § 9-102(a)(3).

[279] U.C.C. § 9-309(a)(3). The automatic perfection approach was adopted in part because of problems arising from loan participation arrangements. Mortgage lenders often sell fractional interests in packages of their notes and mortgages, and these should be characterized as interests in promissory notes although there is some authority for recharacterizing them as payment intangibles. The recharacterization issue is discussed in note 156 *supra*. Filing of financing statements is not customary in such arrangements, and the rationale for adopting automatic perfection is to prevent the necessity of such filings. Buyers of loan participations should be wary, however. Some courts have held that participation arrangements characterized as "sales" by the parties are in fact disguised security transactions. *See, e.g., In re* Coronet Capital Co., 142 B.R. 78 (Bankr. S.D.N.Y. 1992) (discussing factors indicative of disguised security transaction). Automatic perfection applies to outright sales of payment intangibles but not to their use as collateral for loans. A precautionary filing is suggested to protect against a court holding that the "buyer" is really a lender.

[280] U.C.C. § 9-309(4). Notwithstanding automatic perfection, which will suffice in bankruptcy (as will perfection by filing and temporary automatic perfection), to be completely protected the buyer would have to take possession of the instrument to preclude the seller from fraudulently reconveying the instrument to a holder in due course or a good faith purchaser for value. *See* discussion in § 11.03[D], [C] *infra*. Further, if the instrument is negotiable, the buyer should have it indorsed by the seller so that the buyer can become a holder in due course, discussed in § 1.04[D] *supra*. Article 3 governs the rights of a holder in due course.

§ 1.07   EXCLUSIONS FROM ARTICLE 9 — § 9-109(c), (d)

Some types of transactions fit the definition of a security interest and would otherwise clearly be within the general scope of Article 9 except that the drafters chose to exclude them. A variety of policies supports the exclusions, which are summarized below.

[A]   Federal Statutes

Based on the principle of federal preemption, Article 9 does not apply to a security interest that is subject to a federal statute to the extent that the statute governs the rights of the parties.[281] A number of federal statutes govern aspects of security interests in a variety of kinds of personal property.[282] None of these statutes, however, are comprehensive in their regulation of secured financing. Because the exclusion applies only "to the extent" of federal preemption, Article 9 applies to any aspect of a transaction not covered by the statute.[283] For example, the Federal Aviation Act of 1958 establishes a federal recording system for interests, including security interests, in aircraft, but most courts have determined that priority issues are to be decided under Article 9 because the Aviation Act does not address them.[284]

Some of the most complex issues of federal preemption occur in the area of intellectual property. For example, copyrights are general intangibles under Article 9 but assignments of such rights are the subject of federal law. The scope of federal recording systems vary, and a lawyer must carefully consider the relevant statutes and cases in determining the extent to which Article 9 is preempted.[285]

---

[281] U.C.C. § 9-109(c)(1).

[282] *See, e.g.,* 17 U.S.C. § 205 (copyrights); 46 U.S.C. §§ 911–961 (ship mortgages); 49 U.S.C. § 1403 (aircraft); 49 U.S.C. § 11304 (railroad rolling stock).

[283] Despite the clear intent of the drafters, not every court under former law understood that preemption is only partial. *See, e.g., In re* Peregrine Entertainment, Ltd., 116 B.R. 194, 11 U.C.C. Rep. Serv. 2d 1025 (C.D. Cal. 1990) (copyrights). Revised Article 9 makes clear that it defers to federal law only when, and to the limited extent that, it must. U.C.C. § 9-109(c)(1) and § 9-109, Comment 8.

[284] *Cf.* Carolina Aircraft Corp. v. Commerce Trust Co., 289 So. 2d 37, 14 U.C.C. Rep. Serv. 505 (Fla. Dist. Ct. App. 1974) (repairman's lien priority); Suburban Trust & Sav. Bank v. Campbell, 250 N.E.2d 118, 6 U.C.C. Rep. Serv. 964 (Ohio Ct. App. 1969) (buyer of aircraft in ordinary course of business prevails).

[285] To perfect a security interest in a registered copyright, the security agreement must be recorded with the U.S. Copyright Office. *In re* Peregrine Entertainment, Ltd., 116 B.R. 194 (C.D. Cal. 1990); *In re* AEG Acquisition Corp., 127 B.R. 34 (Bankr. C.D. Cal. 1991), *aff'd*, 161 B.R. 50 (BAP 9th Cir. 1993). Recordation with the Copyright Office is not required for an unregistered copyright; rather, filing of an Article 9 financing statement perfects such security interests. *In re* Auxiliary Power Co., 2002 WL 31017352 (9th Cir.). Perfection is also accomplished by filing a financing statement if the collateral is a trademark (Trimarchi v. Together Dev. Corp., 255 B.R. 606 (D. Mass. 2000)) or a patent (*In re* Cybernetic Services, Inc., 252 F.3d 1039 (9th Cir. 2001)).

[B] Landlord and Statutory Liens

Article 9 does not apply to a landlord's lien[286] or to a lien provided for by statute or common-law rule for the provider of services or materials.[287] These exclusions simply reiterate the intention generally to limit the scope of Article 9 to consensual security interests.[288] Article 9, however, generally applies to security interests created by contract.[289] The article thus does not apply to liens that arise by operation of law.[290] This means that no security agreement is necessary for the creation of such a lien and that the lienor need not follow Article 9's rules for giving public notice or for foreclosing on assets subject to the lien.

Even though Article 9 generally does not apply to liens that arise by operation of law, section 9-333 nevertheless governs the priority of certain of these lien interests as against a security interest in the property to which the lien has attached.[291] This section generally grants priority to a lienor that, in the ordinary course of business, furnishes services or materials with respect to goods.[292] For example, an auto-body repair shop might be granted a statutory lien covering body restoration work performed on an automobile that had been in a collision. The section applies only to liens on goods in the lienholder's possession. Article 9 does not provide a rule that governs priority between a secured party and a nonpossessory lien that arises by operation of law. Article 9 also does not provide a rule that governs priority between a secured party and a landlord's lien[293] (even if the landlord is in possession of the goods) because a landlord by definition provides land rather than services or materials.

The following is an example of a court that understood the proper application of the exception with respect to liens for services and materials.[294] The court held that the predecessor to section 9-333[295] did not provide a pig feeder with priority over a prior-perfected Article 9 security interest in the pigs because the feeder did not have possession of them at

[286] U.C.C. § 9-109(d)(1) (except agricultural liens, discussed *infra* this subsection).

[287] U.C.C. § 9-109(d)(2) (except agricultural liens).

[288] Article 9 does apply to security interests arising under other articles of the U.C.C., and these security interests are not consensual in nature. U.C.C. § 9-109(a)(5), (6). Thus, the term "security interest" is defined in Article 1, and the definiton does not contain a requirement that the interest arise consensually. U.C.C. § 1-201(b)(35). *See generally* the discussion in § 1.08 *infra*.

[289] U.C.C. § 9-109(a)(1).

[290] *In re* Tacoma Aviation Ctr., Inc., 23 B.R. 326, 35 U.C.C. Rep. Serv. 298 (Bankr. W.D. Wash. 1982) (statutory mechanic's lien excluded); Universal C.I.T. Credit Corp. v. Congressional Motors, Inc., 228 A.2d 463, 4 U.C.C. Rep. Serv. 152 (Md. 1967) (common-law landlord's lien excluded).

[291] U.C.C. § 9-109(d)(2).

[292] This priority is discussed in § 13.01 *infra*.

[293] This is true unless the landlord's lien is an agricultural lien, in which case Article 9 applies to all issues other than creation of the lien.

[294] Leger Mill Co. v. Kleen-Leen, Inc., 563 P.2d 132, 21 U.C.C. Rep. Serv. 896 (Okla. 1977).

[295] U.C.C. § 9-310 (1972 Official Text).

the time it attempted to enforce its lien. The court did not conclude by negative implication, however, that the secured party prevailed. Rather, it concluded that the nonpossessory lien fell within the Article 9 exclusion and therefore the priority determination was outside the scope of the article.[296]

Article 9 does govern a type of nonconsensual lien called an "agricultural lien."[297] An agricultural lien is by definition a nonpossessory lien, and it must arise under a statute other than Article 9 and not under the common law. Agricultural liens are, as the term suggests, limited to assets that are within the Article 9 definition of farm products, and the farm products subject to the lien must secure payment to a person that in the ordinary course of business furnishes goods or services, or a person that leases real property, to assist with a debtor's farming operation. An example of an agricultural lien would be the pig feeder's lien in the case described in the preceding paragraph. Revised Article 9 would not cover the creation of the lien, which would arise as a result of the statute without the need for a security agreement. Article 9 would, however, apply to the priority of the pig feeder's lien; to obtain priority, the pig feeder would have to file a financing statement.[298] In other words, agricultural liens arise outside Article 9 but, once in existence, are swept into the article for other purposes as if they were consensual security interests.

[C] Real Estate Interests

Article 9 does not apply to the creation or transfer of real estate interests, including liens on real estate and leases or the rents due thereunder.[299] This exclusion reiterates the general scope provision that Article 9 applies to transactions creating security interests in personal property or fixtures.[300] Mortgages are governed by real estate law. Fixtures are governed by both real estate law and by Article 9.[301]

---

[296] The court ultimately found priority for the secured party, but it reached that result by shaping a common-law rule. The court might alternatively have granted priority to the secured party under Article 9's "default" priority provision found in U.C.C. § 9-201. *See* § 14.04 *infra*.

[297] U.C.C. § 9-109(a)(5). *See* § 13.02 *infra*.

[298] *See* U.C.C. § 9-308(a) (agricultural lien perfected when it becomes effective and proper step has been taken); § 9-310(a) (proper step for perfecting agricultural lien is filing financing statement); § 9-509(a)(2) (person holding agricultural lien entitled to file financing statement); and § 9-322 (agricultural lienor treated like secured party for priority purposes, except that statute creating agricultural lien can provide that it takes priority over all secured parties if it is perfected (§ 9-322(g)).

[299] U.C.C. § 9-109(d)(11). *See* Wells Fargo Home Mortgage, Inc. v. McCarthy, 51 U.C.C. Rep. Serv. 2d 853 (Minn. Ct. App. 2003)(unpublished) (agreement purporting to grant security interest in parcel of land did not create Article 9 security interest); *In re* Moukalled, 59 U.C.C. Rep. Serv. 2d 301 (Mich. Ct. App. 2006) (even though entitled "security agreement," document did not create Article 9 security interest in two parcels of real estate).

[300] U.C.C. § 9-109(a)(1).

[301] The nature of fixtures and the relationship between real estate law and Article 9 are covered in Chapter 15 *infra*.

Article 9 explicitly applies to a security interest in a promissory note secured by a mortgage on land. The relevant provision states as follows: "The application of this article to a security interest in a secured obligation is not affected by the fact that the obligation is itself secured by a transaction or interest to which this article does not apply."[302] In other words, even though the creation of a mortgage on land is beyond its scope, Article 9 applies to a security interest in a mortgage-backed debt. If a credit buyer of land executes a note that embodies the payment obligation and secures it with a mortgage, the entire transaction is beyond the scope of Article 9.[303] If the mortgagee subsequently uses the note and mortgage to secure a loan or sells them, Article 9 governs the transaction. The primary collateral is the note, which qualifies as a promissory note.[304] The lender or buyer will also take an assignment of the mortgage, giving it foreclosure rights in the event both its borrower and the note's maker (the buyer of the land) default on their payment obligations.

A related problem arises when a vendor sells land pursuant to an installment land contract, sometimes called a contract for deed. Instead of taking back a note and mortgage, the vendor retains title to the land until the last installment is paid. This transaction is entirely outside the scope of Article 9, but what if the vendor sells the right to the stream of payments or uses it as collateral for a loan? The secondary financing transaction is within the scope of the article[305] and the collateral is an account.[306] Along with the assignment of the account, there will be an assignment of the vendor's interest in the land.

Article 9 addresses the secured party's relationship with the underlying land by providing that a security interest in a secured obligation automatically attaches to the interest that secures the obligation.[307] In other words,

---

[302] U.C.C. § 9-109(b).

[303] If the note is negotiable, it is governed by Article 3. The mortgage is governed by real estate law.

[304] *See* U.C.C. § 9-109, Comment 7, Example 1. A promissory note is a subset of the larger class of instruments. *See* the discussion in § 1.04[B][2] *supra.*

[305] Not all courts have so held. *See, e.g., In re* Shuster, 784 F.2d 883, 42 U.C.C. Rep. Serv. 1433 (8th Cir. 1986) (third party tracing title to land would not check U.C.C. filings). The decision is wrong. The vendor's title-retention scheme is a security device, rendering the underlying transaction a secured obligation within the meaning of U.C.C. § 9-109(b).

[306] U.C.C. § 9-102(a)(2). *See In re* Tops Appliance City, Inc., 372 F.3d 510, 54 U.C.C. Rep. Serv. 2d 68 (3d Cir. 2004) (secured party's interest in right to payment arising from a contract to sell leasehold interest qualified as account for purposes of Article 9).

[307] U.C.C. § 9-203(g). Article 9 uses a similar approach with what it calls a "supporting obligation," meaning a letter-of-credit right or other secondary obligation (such as a guaranty) that supports payment or performance under an account, chattel paper, document, general intangible, instrument or investment property. U.C.C. § 9-102(a)(77). A security interest in a supported obligation automatically attaches to the supporting obligation, and perfection of the security interest in the supported obligation also perfects the security interest in the supporting obligation. U.C.C. §§ 9-203(f) (attachment), 9-308(d) (perfection). If, for example, a secured party has a perfected security interest in a negotiable promissory note (an instrument) that is supported by a standby letter of credit, it automatically has a perfected security interest in the underlying letter-of-credit rights.

attachment of a security interest to a note secured by a mortgage automatically causes the security interest to attach to the mortgagee's interest in the mortgage; and attachment of a security interest to an installment-contract vendor's account automatically causes the security interest to attach to the vendor's interest in the underlying land. Further, perfection of the security interest in the note or account perfects the security interest in the underlying land.[308] These rules bring the entire transaction within the scope of Article 9.

The intent is to make it unnecessary to record anything in the real estate records in order to defeat a lien creditor (including a bankruptcy trustee) or a subsequent assignee of the payment rights. Nothing in Article 9, however, preempts the real estate recording acts to the extent that they protect a bona fide purchaser of an interest in the land. For example, if the developer in one of the prior examples colludes with a buyer to place a fraudulent deed of release in the real estate records and the secured party fails to record an assignment of the mortgage or the vendor's interest, a purchaser protected by the recording act will acquire its interest in the land free of the secured party's security interest.

[D] Wage Claim Assignments

Article 9 does not apply to a transfer of a claim for wages, salary, or other employee compensation.[309] These assignments are excluded because their assignment presents "important social problems whose solution should be a matter of local regulation."[310] Many states have enacted laws that either prohibit or significantly limit wage assignments. The laws are designed to protect wage earners from financially overburdening themselves and their families.[311]

[E] Government Transfers

Transfers by a government or governmental agency were excluded entirely under former law. For example, a governmental agency might have borrowed money and provided collateral in the form of a revenue stream based on its charges for water, electricity, or sewer service. Government transfers were excluded because they generally are governed by other law.[312]

---

[308] U.C.C. § 9-308(e).

[309] U.C.C. § 9-109(d)(3). *See* Massachusetts Mutual Life Ins. Co. v. Central Penn Nat'l Bank, 372 F. Supp. 1027, 14 U.C.C. Rep. Serv. 212 (E.D. Pa. 1974), *aff'd mem.*, 510 F.2d 970 (3d Cir. 1975) (agent for insurance company held to be more like independent contractor than employee, so that renewal commissions were not employee compensation).

[310] U.C.C. § 9-109, Comment 11.

[311] *See In re* Gwynn, 82 B.R. 121, 5 U.C.C. Rep. Serv. 2d 1136 (Bankr. S.D. Cal. 1988) (California statutory prohibition against wage assignments absent permission of wage earner's spouse).

[312] U.C.C. § 9-104, Comment 5 (1972 Official Text).

Revised Article 9 significantly narrows the exception. It applies to a government-created security interest unless preempted by a state statute that expressly governs the creation, perfection, priority, or enforcement of the interest.[313] In other words, government transfers are now within the scope of Article 9 unless another state statute expressly takes them out.[314]

Article 9 also creates a new category of transactions called "public-finance transactions."[315] A public-finance transaction is a secured transaction in which the secured obligation is represented by debt securities (e.g., bonds, indentures, certificates of participation) issued by a state or governmental unit of a state with an initial stated maturity of at least twenty years. The only importance of the category is that a financing statement perfecting a security interest in the collateral securing the debt securities in a public-finance transaction can be made effective for a period of thirty years.[316]

[F] Transfers Irrelevant to Commercial Finance

Article 9 was drafted to facilitate commercial financing. The paradigmatic transactions involve a person using personal property or fixtures as collateral to secure a debt and a person selling accounts, chattel paper, payment intangibles, or promissory notes. It is assumed that these transactions are motivated primarily by commercial financial considerations, although it is recognized that the rules can sweep in some noncommercial transactions. There are, however, certain categories of transactions that fit within the transactional models but have little or nothing to do with commercial financing. Article 9 thus excludes these transactions.

[1] Specified Transfers of Rights to Payment

Several types of transfers of accounts, chattel paper, payment intangibles, or promissory notes are irrelevant to commercial financing interests and, thus, are excluded from Article 9.[317] These transfers are: (1) the sale of any of the listed assets as part of a sale of the business out of which the asset arose; (2) the assignment of any of the listed assets for the purpose of collection; (3) a transfer of any right to payment under a contract to an assignee that is also to render the performance due under the contract; and (4) a transfer of a single account, payment intangible, or promissory note to an assignee in whole or partial satisfaction of a preexisting debt.[318] These exclusions enable transferees like collection agencies and delegates

---

[313] U.C.C. § 9-109(c)(2).

[314] In enacting revised Article 9, many states retained the original, broader exception for all governmental transfers.

[315] U.C.C. § 9-102(a)(67).

[316] U.C.C. § 9-515(b).

[317] U.C.C. § 9-109(d)(4)–(7).

[318] *See* Bramble Transp., Inc. v. Sam Senter Sales, Inc., 294 A.2d 97, 10 U.C.C. Rep. Serv. 939 (Del. Super. Ct. 1971), *aff'd*, 294 A.2d 104, 10 U.C.C. Rep. Serv. 939 (Del. 1972) (transfer under collection-only exclusion requires transfer after accounts are in default).

to take assignments without having to comply with the Article 9 perfection provisions in order to protect their interests against other parties that deal with the assignor.

[2] Judgment Rights and Tort Claims

Article 9 does not apply to "a right represented by a judgment."[319] Thus, if a party obtains a judgment and then assigns the right to collect on it as collateral to secure a loan, the assignee will not be required to file a financing statement with respect to the assignment because the assignment is expressly exempt from the application of Article 9.[320] An assignee should be cautious, however. Except for claims arising in tort that are not commercial tort claims, for which there is a separate exclusion discussed *infra* this subsection, an assignment covering rights which might arise from litigation that has not yet commenced or has not yet reached the judgment stage will be within the scope of Article 9.[321]

The exclusion from Article 9 does not include "a judgment taken on a right to payment that was collateral."[322] A security interest, for example, might attach to an instrument or an account. If the obligation to pay that is represented by the collateral is reduced to judgment, an assignment of that judgment right is not excluded from Article 9.

With the exception of commercial tort claims, Article 9 does not apply to a transfer of all or part of a claim arising in tort.[323] This treatment stands in stark contrast to the assignment of contract claims as collateral, which are central to the Article 9 scheme. Once a claim is reduced to judgment without a security interest having attached to the pre-judgment rights, whether a claim in tort or contract or otherwise, the exclusion with respect to judgments applies. By contrast, if a tort claim is settled, the settlement agreement is a payment intangible and its assignment is within the scope of the article.

As indicated, the exclusion for claims arising in tort does not apply to commercial tort claims,[324] meaning claims sounding in tort that arise out of the debtor's business or profession. If the debtor is an individual rather than an organization, the tort claim must not include a claim for death or personal injury. Commercial tort claims may not be described generically by type (*i.e.*, "all commercial tort claims") in the security agreement,[325]

---

[319] U.C.C. § 9-109(d)(9).

[320] Sun Bank, N.A. v. Parkland Design and Dev. Corp., 466 So. 2d 1089, 40 U.C.C. Rep. Serv. 636 (Fla. Dist. Ct. App. 1985).

[321] Estate of Hill, 557 P.2d 1367, 20 U.C.C. Rep. Serv. 1319 (Or. Ct. App. 1976).

[322] U.C.C. § 9-109(d)(9).

[323] U.C.C. § 9-109(d)(12).

[324] U.C.C. § 9-102(a)(12).

[325] U.C.C. § 9-108(e)(1). Complete specificity is not required. U.C.C. § 9-108, Comment 5 states that "a description such as 'all tort claims arising out of the explosion of debtor's factory' would suffice, even if the exact amount of the claim, the theory on which it may be based, and the identity of the tortfeasor(s) are not described. (Indeed, those facts may not be known at the time.)"

which means that a security interest cannot attach to a commercial tort claim pursuant to an after-acquired property clause.[326]

[3] Rights of Set-off

Another exclusion from Article 9 includes any right of recoupment or set-off.[327] The exclusion exempts banks from having to obtain security agreements or perfect their interests in order to preserve their set-off rights. Subject to certain limitations that are beyond the scope of this book, a bank that is not paid money that is due and owing to it by a depositor has a common-law right to set-off the money owed, which it will accomplish by reducing the depositor's account balance.

There are two exceptions to the exclusion. Article 9 governs, except in consumer transactions,[328] the use of deposit accounts as collateral. If the bank at which the account is maintained exercises a set-off right against a deposit account in which a secured party has a security interest, the resolution of the priority issue that arises is governed by Article 9. The bank exercising set-off will have priority unless the secured party has perfected its security interest by becoming the customer with respect to the account (*i.e.*, by having its name shown as the customer on the records of the maintaining bank).[329]

The other exception to the exclusion of rights of recoupment or set-off is that, if the person obligated (the account debtor) has a defense or claim that could be asserted against an assignee under Article 9,[330] the defense or claim can be asserted against the party exercising recoupment or set-off.

[G] Insurance Assignments

Subject to an exception for health-care-insurance receivables,[331] Article 9 does not govern the transfer of an interest in, or the assignment of a claim under, a policy of insurance.[332] It thus does not apply to a security assignment of the cash surrender value of a life insurance policy or the assignment of an insured's right to recover unearned premiums following cancellation.[333]

---

[326] U.C.C. § 9-204(b)(2).

[327] U.C.C. § 9-109(d)(10).

[328] Consumer transactions are discussed in § 1.04[A][1] *supra*.

[329] U.C.C. §§ 9-340(c) (priority rule), 9-104(a)(3) (perfection by becoming customer). The secured party can also perfect by obtaining a control agreement authenticated by itself, the debtor, and the maintaining bank; however, this will not provide it with priority in the event of set-off (although nothing prevents the maintaining bank from agreeing to subordinate its interest).

[330] U.C.C. § 9-404 governs the effectiveness of an account debtor's claims and defenses as against an assignee. *See* the discussion in § 1.04[D] *supra*.

[331] Health-care-insurance receivables are discussed in § 1.04[C][1] *supra*.

[332] U.C.C. § 9-109(d)(8).

[333] *In re* Duke Roofing Co., 47 B.R. 990, 40 U.C.C. Rep. Serv. 1431 (E.D. Mich. 1985).

The exclusion does not encompass all transactions related to insurance. An assignment of renewal commissions earned by an insurance agent is covered by Article 9.[334] The exclusion also specifically indicates that it does not extend to proceeds or to priorities in proceeds. Proceeds includes, "insurance payable by reason of the loss or nonconformity of, defects or infringement of rights in, or damage to, the collateral."[335]

The reasons given by the original drafters for the insurance exclusion were that "[s]uch transactions are often quite special, do not fit easily under a general commercial statute and are adequately covered by existing law."[336] The exclusion does not mean that insurance interests are not transferable, just as the other exclusions do not prohibit parties from entering into the excluded transactions.[337] Most states allow parties to assign insurance rights as long as the policy does not prohibit assignment.

[H] Deposit Accounts

Under former law, interests in deposit accounts[338] were entirely excluded, although a secured party could trace proceeds of its collateral into such an account. Under revised Article 9, the exclusion is limited to consumer transactions.[339] This approach for the most part eliminates the confusing state laws governing common-law pledges and provides lenders with clear rules for creating and perfecting security interests in, and resolving priority disputes regarding, these assets. Security interests can be created in deposit accounts maintained at any bank, including a bank that is not the secured party,[340] and they are not invalidated merely

---

[334] The right to payment is an account. U.C.C. § 9-102(a)(2)(iii).

[335] U.C.C. § 9-102(a)(64)(E).

[336] U.C.C. § 9-104, Comment 7 (1962 Official Text).

[337] Whether an excluded transaction can be entered into — and, if so, its effect on third parties — is governed by other law.

[338] A deposit account is "a demand, time, savings, passbook, or similar account maintained with a bank." U.C.C. § 9-102(a)(29). The term does not include investment property or an account evidenced by an instrument. In other words, an account in which deposited funds are invested in money-market securities and an account represented by a certificate of deposit are, respectively, investment property and an instrument for purposes of Article 9. Lawyers must look beyond the labels used by banks in determining the appropriate category. For example, banks sometimes call accounts "money-market" but do not invest the deposited funds in money-market securities. Such an account is a deposit account, not investment property. Also, not every account represented by what a bank calls a "certificate of deposit" involves an instrument. For example, banks sometimes label accounts "book-entry certificates of deposit." When funds are deposited to a book-entry certificate, the depositor is given a receipt for the deposit, but there is no writing issued by the bank that comes within the definition of instrument. Deposited funds represented by book-entry certificates are in fact deposit accounts.

[339] U.C.C. § 9-109(d)(13). Consumer transactions are discussed in § 1.04[D] *supra*.

[340] If the secured party is the bank with which the deposit account is maintained, the fact that it takes a security interest in the account under Article 9 does not affect any set-off or recoupment rights that it may have under other law. U.C.C. § 9-340(b).

because the debtor has access to the funds in the account pending default.[341]

§ 1.08   RELATIONSHIP BETWEEN ARTICLE 9 AND OTHER ARTICLES

Although Article 9 is the primary source for determining the existence and effect of security interests, it is by no means the only source. It is just one article of the U.C.C., and it must be viewed in relation to the other articles.

Article 2 has a number of rules that intersect with Article 9. If a seller and buyer of goods agree that the seller will retain title pending full payment of the purchase price, Article 2 limits the effect of the term to the reservation of a security interest.[342] If a lender extends funds on the strength of goods being bought by an Article 9 debtor, Article 2 determines when the debtor has sufficient rights in the goods for a security interest to attach to them.[343] If a buyer in possession of goods rightfully rejects or justifiably revokes acceptance of them, Article 2 grants the buyer a security interest in the goods as collateral for any payments made on the price and for certain expenses.[344] Article 2 even contains priority rules protecting good faith purchasers for value that can be utilized by secured parties.[345]

Article 2A also contains provisions that intersect with Article 9. For example, a lessee in possession of goods that rightfully rejects or justifiably revokes acceptance of them has a security interest in them for any lease payments made and for certain expenses.[346] The article also contains provisions governing the priority rights of secured parties with interests in both the lessor's and lessee's interest in the goods.[347]

---

[341] U.C.C. § 9-104(b). Although the debtor's access does not invalidate the security interest, it may create a choateness problem that would subordinate the interest to the federal government making a claim under the Tax Lien Act (26 U.S.C. § 6321 et seq.) or the federal claims priority statute (31 U.S.C. § 3713(a), usually referred to by its Revised Statute designation, R.S. § 3466). Choateness is discussed in § 13.03 *infra*.

[342] U.C.C. § 2-401(1).

[343] The buyer acquires a special property interest in the goods when they are identified to the contract for sale. U.C.C. § 2-501(1). Issues involving rights in the collateral are discussed in § 2.02[C] *infra*.

[344] U.C.C. § 2-711(3). U.C.C. § 9-110 intersects with security interests arising solely by force of Article 2 or Article 2A. It states that the provisions of Article 9 govern such security interests generally, but so long as the debtor does not obtain possession of the goods no security agreement is necessary to make the interest enforceable, no filing is necessary to perfect it, and the rights of the secured party upon default are governed by the rules of Article 2 or Article 2A.

[345] U.C.C. § 2-403(1). *See also*, U.C.C. §§ 1-201(b)(30), (b)(29) (defining "purchaser" to include party with consensual lien). For an example of the operation of the priority rule, *see In re* Samuels & Co., 510 F.2d 139, 16 U.C.C. Rep. Serv. 577 (5th Cir. 1975), *rev'd*, 526 F.2d 1238 (5th Cir. 1975), *cert. denied*, 429 U.S. 834 (1976) (secured party with security interest in debtor's inventory qualified as good faith purchaser for value under U.C.C. § 2-403(1), thereby defeating reclamation rights of unpaid seller).

[346] U.C.C. § 2A-508(5).

[347] U.C.C. § 2A-307.

Security interests arising under Article 2 or 2A are subject to special Article 9 rules.[348] Specifically, the security interest is enforceable even though there is not a security agreement complying with Article 9's attachment rules,[349] a filing is not required to perfect the security interest, the rights of the secured party after default are governed by Article 2 or 2A,[350] and the security interest has priority over a conflicting security interest created by the debtor. With regard to priority, suppose Seller owns equipment subject to a perfected security interest in favor of Bank and sells the equipment to Buyer, who justifiably rejects it. Buyer's Article 2 security interest is senior to Bank's Article 9 security interest.[351]

Article 4, which deals with bank deposits and collections, provides that a collecting bank (usually a depositary bank) that has given its customer access to funds represented by a deposited item such as a check before the item clears the payor bank has a security interest in the item and its proceeds.[352] The security interest is subject to Article 9 but no security agreement is necessary to make it enforceable, no filing is necessary to perfect it, and it has priority over conflicting security interests.[353]

Under Article 5, the beneficiary of a letter of credit can assign its right to the proceeds[354] of the letter, either outright or as collateral for a loan.[355] That article differentiates between an assignment of a beneficiary's right to the proceeds of a letter of credit and a transfer of the beneficiary's right to draw or demand performance under the letter. Transactions in the latter category are analogous to novations in which a new beneficiary is substituted for the original beneficiary.[356] Because of this distinction, Article 5 provides that an issuer (or nominated person) need not recognize an assignment of the proceeds of the letter until it consents to the assignment. In other words, a secured party with a security interest in the proceeds cannot enforce the beneficiary's rights as against a nonconsenting issuer.[357] Article 9 calls the right of a beneficiary under a letter of credit to assign its right to the proceeds a "letter-of-credit right,"[358] meaning "a right to payment and performance under any letter, written or otherwise, but the term does not include the right of a beneficiary to demand payment or

---

[348] U.C.C. § 9-110.

[349] The rules are set forth in U.C.C. § 9-203(b)(3).

[350] See U.C.C. §§ 2-711(3) and 2-706; 2A-508(5) and 2A-527(5).

[351] U.C.C. § 9-110, Comment 4.

[352] U.C.C. § 4-210(a). Receipt of a final settlement for the item is a realization upon the security interest. § 4-210(c). The statutory grant of a security interest has ramifications for Article 3 as well as Article 9 because the collecting bank is deemed to have given value for holder-in-due-course purposes to the extent that it has a security interest. U.C.C. § 4-211.

[353] U.C.C. § 4-210(c).

[354] U.C.C. § 5-114(a) defines the term "proceeds of a letter of credit" to mean value given by the issuer or any nominated person under the letter.

[355] U.C.C. § 5-114(b).

[356] See U.C.C. § 5-112 and Comment 2 to that section.

[357] U.C.C. § 5-114(c).

[358] U.C.C. § 9-102(a)(51).

performance." This definition maintains the Article 5 distinction between the right to the proceeds of a letter of credit and the right of a beneficiary to demand payment or performance.

Article 7 contains rules that govern warehouse receipts and bills of lading, including, as of the most recent revision in 2003, electronic warehouse receipts and bills of lading. Article 9 deals extensively with security interests in such documents and the goods they represent.[359]

Article 8 governs transfers of securities held directly by investors and certain financial assets held indirectly through financial intermediaries. Security interests in such assets are governed in part by Article 8 and in part by Article 9 and are discussed elsewhere in this chapter.[360]

In sum, understanding secured-transactions law requires more than understanding Article 9. It requires that Article 9's rules be placed in the context of a unified code. Moreover, the Uniform Commercial Code itself must be placed in the context of the broader world of commercial law. It is, in effect, a "common-law code" because of the extent to which its provisions interface with, and depend upon, principles developed at common law (and in equity). Indeed, Article 1 specifically provides that, unless displaced by a particular Code provision, "the principles of law and equity, including the law merchant and the law relative to capacity to contract, principal and agent, estoppel, fraud, misrepresentation, duress, coercion, mistake, bankruptcy, and other validating or invalidating cause supplement its provisions."[361]

§ 1.09   NONUNIFORM ADOPTIONS

As part of the Uniform Commercial Code, Article 9 is a statutory model that has no force of law until it is enacted by an appropriate legislative body. Congress has never enacted any of the Code as federal law. State legislatures[362] generally have been the enacting bodies.[363]

Although one of the underlying objectives of the Uniform Commercial Code is to promote uniformity of law among the various jurisdictions,[364] state legislatures can and frequently do deviate from the Code model. As a result, readers of this book should be mindful of the fact that the book discusses the uniform provisions found in the Official Text of Article 9 as

---

[359] *See* § 1.04[B] *infra.*

[360] *See* § 1.04[E] *infra.*

[361] U.C.C. § 1-103(b).

[362] The Uniform Commercial Code defines "state" to include "the District of Columbia, Puerto Rico, the United States Virgin Islands, or any territory or insular possession subject to the jurisdiction of the United States." U.C.C. § 9-102(a)(76).

[363] Article 9 has been adopted by certain Native American tribes, and there is reason to expect that this will occur more frequently in the future since the National Conference of Commissioners on Uniform State Laws has drafted a version of revised Article 9 entitled the Model Tribal Secured Transactions Act that is specifically adapted to tribal needs.

[364] U.C.C. § 1-103(a)(3).

promulgated by its sponsors and that a particular jurisdiction may have adopted a variation of a uniform provision.

Part II

ATTACHMENT OF SECURITY
INTERESTS

Chapter 2

CREATION AND ENFORCEABILITY
OF SECURITY INTERESTS

SYNOPSIS

§ 2.01   OVERVIEW: THE CONCEPT OF ATTACHMENT

A security agreement is a specialized type of contract entered into between a secured party and a debtor. Through this contract, the debtor creates a security interest in personal property or fixtures that runs in favor of the secured party. The requirement that an Article 9 security interest be consensual in nature is satisfied through the voluntary association of the parties that underlies any contract.[1]

There are three prerequisites to the creation of an enforceable security interest: a security agreement, value given by the secured party, and the debtor having rights, or the power to transfer rights, in the collateral.[2] In addition, Article 9 contains a statute-of-frauds provision, but this should be considered part of the security-agreement requirement and not a

---

[1] U.C.C. § 9-109(a)(1). *See* § 1.03[A] *supra.*

[2] U.C.C. § 9-203(b).

69

separate element.[3] When each of these elements has been satisfied, in whatever order, the security interest "attaches."[4]

The term "attachment" goes to the essence of contracts of this type. An Article 9 security interest cannot exist as an abstract or generalized concept. Rather, it creates a property interest in specific collateral that has been identified by the parties. There is no such thing as an Article 9 security interest in just any of the property owned by the debtor that might be sufficient to satisfy the outstanding indebtedness.

Unless another provision of Article 9 yields a contrary result, the terms of a security agreement are effective between the parties to the agreement, against purchasers of the collateral,[5] and against creditors that assert a claim to the collateral.[6] If a third party is involved, there are many exceptions to this general rule. With respect to the secured party and the debtor, there are but a few exceptions. Certain clauses in their agreement might be unenforceable,[7] and a secured party's failure to comply with the foreclosure procedures dictated in Article 9 might cause it to suffer a loss of rights.[8] The relationship between the secured party and the debtor is, however, established through their security agreement, which is subject to the general principle of freedom of contract.

It is important at the outset to differentiate between the concepts of attachment and perfection. Once a security interest attaches, it is enforceable against the debtor.[9] This means that the secured party may proceed to foreclose upon the collateral in the event of default. Perfection is irrelevant to a dispute between the secured party and the debtor. Perfection, which is best understood as a method for giving public notice of a security interest, becomes important only in the context of a dispute between a secured party and a third party asserting a claim to the collateral.[10]

§ 2.02   CREATION OF AN ENFORCEABLE SECURITY INTEREST — § 9-203

An Article 9 security interest attaches only if the parties enter into a security agreement.[11] Unless the secured party takes possession or control

---

[3] U.C.C. § 9-203(b)(3).

[4] U.C.C. § 9-203(a).

[5] The term "purchaser" is broadly defined to include any person that acquires an interest in the collateral through a voluntary transaction (*e.g.*, buyer, lessee, licensee, etc.). U.C.C. § 1-201(b)(30), (29).

[6] U.C.C. § 9-201(a).

[7] *See, e.g.*, U.C.C. §§ 9-204(b), 9-602.

[8] The consequences of creditor misbehavior are discussed generally in Chapter 19 *infra*.

[9] U.C.C. § 9-203(a).

[10] Perfection is discussed generally in Chapter 4 *infra*.

[11] U.C.C. § 9-203(b)(3).

of the collateral, the debtor must authenticate[12] the agreement, and it must provide a description of the collateral.[13] The agreement must be in record[14] form for the debtor to be able to authenticate it.

The requirement that a debtor authenticate a security agreement serves as a statute of frauds,[15] providing probative evidence that an asserted security interest rests on a real transaction between the parties. The agreement must be authenticated by the party against whom the security interest is to be enforced — the debtor. The general rule is that a security interest may not be enforced unless Article 9's statute of frauds has been satisfied.[16]

Consistent with the approach to the statute of frauds in Article 2,[17] Article 9 provides an exception to the authentication requirement. A security agreement is enforceable, even in the absence of an authenticated record, if the secured party has possession or control of the collateral pursuant to agreement.[18] The secured party's possession or control provides

---

[12] The term "authenticate" means "(A) to sign; or (B) to execute or otherwise adopt a symbol, or encrypt or similarly process a record in whole or in part, with the present intent of the authenticating person to identify the person and adopt or accept a record." U.C.C. § 9-102(a)(7). The first part of the definition — sign — is defined in Article 1 with reference to writings only and includes the use of "any symbol executed or adopted with present intention to adopt or accept" the writing. U.C.C. § 1-201(b)(37). The second part of the definition validates electronic signatures. Although most of the Code is now medium-neutral, the definition in revised Article 1 does not refer to electronic signatures. The Article 1 definition was not made medium-neutral primarily because negotiable instruments under Article 3 must still be in writing.

There is a problem with the definition of "authenticate." Note that the definition of "sign" requires only that the signer of a writing have present intention to adopt or accept the writing. The part of the definition dealing with signatures on electronic records adds a requirement that the electronic signature identify the signer. This is a mistake. It is a generally accepted principle that a person that forges another's signature has in fact signed his or her own name. Cf. U.C.C. § 3-403(a). As drafted, a forger would be bound by the terms of a written security agreement but not by the terms of a security agreement contained in an electronic record. The courts should simply ignore the mistake. Later revisions to the Code have gone back to the term "sign" and defined it to include both manual and electronic signatures, omitting any indication that a signature must identify the signer. See U.C.C. §§ 2-103(1)(p), 2A-103(1)(dd), 7-102(a)(11).

[13] The agreement must also describe the land concerned if the collateral is timber to be cut. U.C.C. § 9-203(b)(3)(A).

[14] The term "record" means "information that is inscribed on a tangible medium or which is stored in an electronic or other medium and is retrievable in perceivable form." U.C.C. § 9-102(a)(69).

[15] "[E]nforceability requires the debtor's security agreement and compliance with an evidentiary requirement in the nature of a Statute of Frauds." U.C.C. § 9-203, Comment 3. Tate v. Gallagher, 116 N.H. 165, 355 A.2d 417, 19 U.C.C. Rep. Serv. 281 (1976).

[16] In re R. & L. Cartage & Sons, Inc., 118 B.R. 646, 13 U.C.C. Rep. Serv. 2d 543 (Bankr. N.D. Ind. 1990) (oral agreement with debtor not sufficient for enforceable security interest).

[17] U.C.C. § 2-201(3).

[18] U.C.C. § 9-203(b)(3)(B)–(D). See In re Miller, 320 B.R. 911, 56 U.C.C. Rep. Serv. 2d 499 (Bankr. E.D. Mo. 2005) (no security interest can attach based on a purely oral agreement if the debtor remains in possession of the purported collateral); In re Timothy Dean Restaurant & Bar, 2006 WL 1206021, 59 U.C.C. Rep. Serv. 2d 485 (D. D.C. 2006) (lessor both created and perfected security interest in security deposit by taking possession of money provided by tenant).

corroborative evidence to support its assertion that the parties entered into a security agreement.

In addition to the requirement that there be a security agreement and that a statute-of-frauds provision be satisfied, attachment requires that value be given by the secured party and that the debtor have rights, or the power to transfer rights, in the collateral. The requirements for attachment can occur in any order. When the last of the requirements occurs, the security interest attaches unless the parties explicitly postpone the time for attachment.[19] Each requirement is discussed in detail below.

[A] Security Agreement — § 9-203(b)(3)

Article 9 defines "security agreement" as an agreement that "creates or provides for a security interest."[20] The term "agreement" is itself defined as "the bargain of the parties in fact, as found in their language or inferred from other circumstances, including course of performance, course of dealing, or usage of trade as provided in Section 1-303."[21] All that is required is that the parties enter into a contractual relationship that falls within the scope of Article 9; it is not necessary that they contract with reference to Article 9.[22] A legally operative record might describe particular goods yet evidence a transaction for their sale, lease, or bailment, or it might be completely ambiguous with respect to the type of transaction intended. A record in the latter category cannot operate as a security agreement absent a finding that it creates a security interest.

Some courts have been too rigid in construing the agreement require-ment. They have injected into the Article 9 realm a degree of formalism generally associated with real estate conveyances by requiring that the parties use formal granting language (*e.g.*, "I hereby grant to the secured party a security interest").[23] A security agreement is not a formal convey-ancing document. Although the prerequisites for attachment are sometimes referred to as the "formalities" for the creation of a security interest, they

---

[19] U.C.C. § 9-203(a).

[20] U.C.C. § 9-102(a)(73).

[21] U.C.C. § 1-201(b)(3).

[22] It is not necessary that the parties intend for their transaction to be a security arrange-ment. The 1972 text was misleading on this point, providing that Article 9 applied "to any transaction (regardless of its form) which is intended to create a security interest." U.C.C. § 9-102(1)(a) (1972 Official Text). The parties must intend a contractual relationship, but they need not intend that it create a security interest. For example, a transaction intended by the parties as a lease of goods may come within the scope of Article 9 by operation of law. *See* § 1-203. *See also* § 1.03[B][1] *supra*. Revised Article 9 resolves the problem by providing that it applies to "a transaction, regardless of its form, that creates a security interest." § 9-109(a)(1).

[23] *In re* Modafferi, 45 B.R. 370, 40 U.C.C. Rep. Serv. 268 (Bankr. S.D. N.Y. 1985); Mitchell v. Shepherd Mall State Bank, 458 F.2d 700, 10 U.C.C. Rep. Serv. 737 (10th Cir. 1972).

are both simple in nature and easily satisfied. No formalistic or magic words are required.[24]

A comparison of the bankruptcy referee's[25] findings and the appellate court's decision in *In re Amex-Protein Development Corp.*[26] is illustrative. The parties intended to create a security interest in property sold as collateral for an obligation evidenced by a promissory note signed by the buyer. The note contained the following language: "This note is secured by a Security Interest in subject personal property as per invoices."[27] The referee held that the note was insufficient to constitute a security agreement because the quoted language was passive and informative, not active or creative. The Ninth Circuit properly found the referee's construction too restrictive and held that the language was sufficient in that it demonstrated that the parties had agreed that the note would be secured.[28]

Article 9 does not require the existence of a record designated "Security Agreement." In a nonpossessory arrangement, it does require that the debtor authenticate a security agreement that contains a description of the collateral, but a number of courts have been willing to consider multiple sources to locate these elements. In *Amex-Protein*, for example, the requisite intent to contract and signature[29] were found in the note, and the collateral description was found in the invoices.[30] In *In re Bollinger Corp.*,[31] a promissory note indicated that it was secured by a security agreement to be delivered by the debtor to the secured party, but the referenced agreement was never in fact delivered.[32] By itself, the note did not suffice as

---

[24] *In re* Thompson, 315 B.R. 94, 54 U.C.C. Rep .Serv. 2d 1017 (Bankr. W.D. Mo. 2004) (language in installment sales agreement for cattle providing that, if any payment was ten days late, the personal property listed in the agreement became the property of the seller until the debt and incurred expenses were paid in full was sufficient to show intent to create security interest).

[25] Today, the presiding judicial officer in bankruptcy proceedings is referred to as a "bankruptcy judge." Bankruptcy is discussed generally in Chapter 16 *infra*.

[26] 504 F.2d 1056, 15 U.C.C. Rep. Serv. 286 (9th Cir. 1974).

[27] 504 F.2d at 1057, 15 U.C.C. Rep. Serv. at 287. *See also* Fantry v. Medical Capital Corp., 2002 WL 172708, 47 U.C.C. Rep. Serv. 2d 354 (Conn. Super. Ct. 2002) (recital in security agreement to the effect that property had been attached and was to be secured held to create security interest).

[28] *See also* Simplot v. William C. Owens, MD, PA, 119 Ida. 243, 805 P.2d 449, 14 U.C.C. Rep. Serv. 2d 896 (1990) (note stating "SECURITY: 1956 GMC bus" sufficient when accompanied by debtor's indorsement and delivery of certificate of title to bus).

[29] When referring to a security agreement or financing statement executed under former law, the terms "writing" and "sign" are retained. Financing statements are not authenticated under revised Article 9. *See* § 5.02 *infra*.

[30] *But see In re* Yantz, 55 U.C.C. Rep. Serv. 2d 19 (Bankr. D. Vt. 2004) (parties did not create security interest in snow blower to secure debtor's obligation to pay attorney's fees where notes taken by attorney's paralegal containing description of collateral were not signed by debtor and retainer agreement, which was signed by debtor, did not refer to collateral).

[31] 614 F.2d 924 (3d Cir. 1980).

[32] Reference to a nonexistent record can be fatal. *See, e.g.,* Wilmot v. Central Oklahoma Gravel Corp., 629 P.2d 1350, 29 U.C.C. Rep. Serv. 1650 (Okla. Ct. App. 1980) (note stated that it was secured by a security agreement bearing the same date but no such agreement existed).

a security agreement because it did not show present intent to create a security interest. Likewise, although there was a financing statement describing the collateral and signed by the debtor, the financing statement by itself did not constitute a security agreement.[33] The court, however, read the note and financing statement in conjunction with a series of correspondence between the parties (subsequent to the execution of the note) in which they clarified whether the debtor could substitute or replace collateral in the ordinary course of its business. Although the court never even found the type of passive language relied upon by the *Amex-Protein* court, it concluded that the correspondence made no sense if the parties had not intended that their transaction be secured. Summarizing *Bollinger*, the signature was found on both the note and the financing statement, the description was found in the financing statement, and the present intent to create a security interest was found in an inference based on correspondence exchanged during a course of performance.[34]

Occasionally, parties adopt a record that categorizes their transaction as something other than a secured transaction and one of the parties later attempts to prove that their real intent was to create a security interest. For example, a record might indicate that one party has delivered goods to another as part of a credit sales transaction. After paying the stipulated "price," the "seller" may argue that the goods were actually delivered to the "buyer" as security for an obligation (*i.e.*, a loan) that has now been satisfied. In other words, the argument is that the seller is in reality an Article 9 debtor and the buyer is a secured party with a possessory security interest in the goods. Traditionally, parties have been allowed to introduce extrinsic evidence to the effect that a bill of sale that is absolute on its face was actually given as security. The Code provisions are not intended to change this right.[35] Establishing that the transaction was in fact for security entitles the "seller" (debtor) to a return of the asset upon complete satisfaction of the obligation.

By contrast, Article 9 rejects the principle of equitable mortgage, under which a creditor can enforce a real estate security arrangement that does not comply with the requisite formalities by presenting clear and convincing

---

[33] A financing statement may be filed before a security agreement is made. U.C.C. § 9-502(d). There are numerous decisions holding that a financing statement standing alone does not constitute a security agreement. *See, e.g.,* American Card Co. v. HMH Co., 196 A.2d 150, 1 U.C.C. Rep. Serv. 447 (R.I. 1963). *But see* Gibson Cty. Farm Bureau Co-op Ass'n. v. Greer, 643 N.E.2d 313, 25 U.C.C. Rep. Serv.2d 954 (Ind. 1994) (extrinsic evidence admissible to show that debtor intended to grant a security interest to secured party whose only record was a signed financing statement). *See also* § 5.03[D] *infra*.

[34] *See* Sears, Roebuck & Co. v. Conry, 321 Ill. App.3d 997, 748 N.E.2d 1248, 46 U.C.C. Rep. Serv. 2d 859 (2001) (customer signed credit card receipts granting retailer a security interest in items purchased and incorporating by reference a security agreement included in the credit-card application). *Compare In re* Shirel, 251 B.R. 157, 42 U.C.C. Rep. Serv. 2d 604 (Bankr. W.D. Okla. 2000) (description of collateral in credit card agreement as all merchandise purchased using the card was too vague to satisfy description requirement; signed purchase receipt describing refrigerator did not contain cross-reference to security agreement).

[35] U.C.C. § 9-203, Comment 3.

evidence of intent.[36] Even courts that are willing to find an Article 9 security agreement in a collage of documents must locate a record that is authenticated by the debtor, a description of the collateral in record form, and evidence of present intent to create a security interest. A lender that is unable to satisfy these minimal formalities may not use extrinsic evidence to establish its secured status.

[1] **Authenticated by the Debtor**

As indicated above, unless a secured party has taken possession or control of the collateral, a debtor must authenticate a record describing the collateral in order for attachment to occur.[37] In this regard, the Comments to the definition of "sign" in Article 1 are relevant:

> This provision also makes it clear that, as the term "signed" is used in the Uniform Commercial Code, a complete signature is not necessary. The symbol may be printed, stamped or written; it may be by initials or by thumbprint. It may be on any part of the document and in appropriate cases may be found in a billhead or letterhead. No catalog of possible situations can be complete and the court must use common sense and commercial experience in passing upon these matters. The question always is whether the symbol was executed or adopted by the party with present intention to adopt or accept the writing.[38]

The critical issue is not the form of the authentication but whether the requisite intent is present.

The term "debtor" refers to a person with an interest in the collateral.[39] A debtor may or may not be an obligor.[40] Suppose A needs to borrow money but has insufficient collateral. A's friend, B, allows A to use her car as collateral but refuses to become personally obligated for the debt. Because A has permission to use B's car, A has sufficient rights in the collateral to grant the security interest.[41] Thus, A should qualify as a "debtor" whose authentication will satisfy the statutory requirement. B also qualifies as a "debtor" because she owns the car. If the secured party obtains only A's authentication, it must prove that B authorized the use of the car as collateral. If it obtains B's authentication, it needs no other proof of authorization. A prudent secured party will obtain the authentication of

---

[36] U.C.C. § 9-203, Comment 5 (1962 Official Text).

[37] *See supra* notes 12 and 14. *See* Meade v. Richardson Fuel, Inc., 58 U.C.C. Rep. Serv. 2d 501 (Ky. Ct. App. 2005) (agreement between seller and buyer that title to goods would pass only as buyer paid for them did not create a security interest because buyer did not authenticate a security agreement).

[38] U.C.C. § 1-201, Comment 37.

[39] U.C.C. § 9-102(a)(28)(A). The term also includes a seller of accounts, chattel paper, payment intangibles, or promissory notes as well as a consignee. U.C.C. § 9-102(a)(28)(B), (C).

[40] U.C.C. § 9-102(a)(28)(A). "Obligor" is defined in U.C.C. § 9-102(a)(59). *See* § 1.02 *supra.*

[41] *See* § 2.02[C] *infra.*

each party with an interest in the collateral because doing so provides proof that the party authorized the creation of the security interest.[42]

If a debtor is an organization (*e.g.*, a corporation, a limited liability company, or a general partnership), the authentication must be made by a representative acting with actual or apparent authority. Extrinsic evidence of actual or apparent authority may be used to bind an organization not identified in a security agreement authenticated by an agent.[43]

[2] Description of the Collateral — § 9-108

If an authenticated security agreement is required, it must provide a description of the collateral and, in the case of timber to be cut, a description of the land concerned.[44] The description is the means by which the property to which the security interest attaches is identified. Because a security interest cannot attach indiscriminately to a debtor's assets,[45] the affected property must be identified. A description is not necessary if the secured party takes possession or control of the collateral pursuant to agreement because the possession or control provides the identification.[46]

The description in a security agreement delineates the assets of the debtor that are subject to the security interest.[47] If the debtor defaults and the secured party ascertains that it is under-collateralized (meaning that the value of the collateral is not sufficient to satisfy the balance of the outstanding indebtedness), the secured party might be tempted to try to extend the reach of its security interest. The description requirement protects the debtor against such overreaching — the collateral consists only of the property that is encompassed within the description.[48]

---

[42] It is common practice for a debtor that is an obligor to authenticate a security agreement and for a debtor that is not an obligor to authenticate a separate agreement — commonly called either an hypothecation agreement or a waiver — evidencing the debtor's consent to attachment of the security interest.

[43] *In re* Mid-Atlantic Piping Prods. of Charlotte, Inc., 24 B.R. 314, 35 U.C.C. Rep. Serv. 618 (Bankr. W.D.N.C. 1982).

[44] U.C.C. § 9-203(b)(3)(A).

[45] *See* § 2.01 *supra*.

[46] U.C.C. § 9-203(b)(3)(B)–(D). *See In re* Airwest Int'l, 70 B.R. 914, 3 U.C.C. Rep. Serv. 2d 1936 (Bankr. D. Haw. 1987) (sufficiency of description of two certificates of deposit in written security agreement was irrelevant because certificates had been pledged and were in possession of secured party). *See also In re* Midland Transp. Co., 292 B.R. 181, 50 U.C.C. Rep. Serv. 2d 579 (Bankr. N.D. Iowa 2003) (security interest intended by parties did not attach to trucks because secured party did not take possession of the trucks and debtor did not authenticate security agreement).

[47] Personal Thrift Plan of Perry, Inc. v. Georgia Power Co., 242 Ga. 388, 249 S.E.2d 72, 25 U.C.C. Rep. Serv. 310 (1978) (descriptions in security agreement have purpose of avoiding disputes over identity of collateral); *In re* S.M. Acquisition Co., 296 B.R. 452, 51 U.C.C. Rep. Serv. 2d 867 (Bankr. N.D. Ill. 2003) (provision in security agreement consisting of the debtor's promise to keep collateral at designated locations did not alter description that clearly showed the intent to create a security interest in debtor's assets located anywhere).

[48] *In re* Levitz Ins. Agency, Inc., 152 B.R. 693, 19 U.C.C. Rep. Serv. 2d 1177 (Bankr. Mass. 1992) (description in security agreement as "customer list" did not extend to cover accounts).

With certain exceptions discussed below, "a description of personal or real property is sufficient, whether or not it is specific, if it reasonably identifies what is described."[49] This standard is an explicit direction to analyze descriptions under a functional test. The objective is to be able to identify the property that comprises the collateral with a reasonable degree of certainty.

The court's opinion in *In re Drane*[50] provides valuable insight into the proper application of the standard. The secured party filed a proof of claim in a bankruptcy proceeding in which it claimed a perfected security interest in specified furniture. A part of the description of the collateral was as follows: "1–2 pc. Living room suite, wine."[51] The bankruptcy referee determined that the description was insufficient because the two-piece suite could consist of any of a variety of combinations of furniture commonly used in a living room, such as two chairs, a chair and a couch, or a chair and a couch that could converted into a bed. The referee's position was essentially that a description must be sufficient on its face to identify the property that is subject to the security interest.

The United States District Court appropriately rejected this position and held that extrinsic evidence was admissible to aid in resolving the ambiguity in the description. The relevant evidence in *Drane* was that the debtor owned only one living-room suite and it consisted of two pieces that were wine-colored. Because of the extrinsic evidence, the description reasonably identified the collateral.[52]

The court in *In re* Quisenberry, 295 B.R. 855, 51 U.C.C. Rep. Serv. 2d 548 (Bankr. N.D. Tex. 2003), held that a bank did not have a security interest in a checking account that the debtor maintained with the bank because the description in the security agreement did not include the checking account. A section of the agreement that reserved the bank's right to exercise setoff against the account did not create a security interest because it was not part of the collateral description. The bank had a right of setoff by virtue of its deposit agreement with the debtor irrespective of the security agreement. The court noted that a right to setoff is neither a security interest nor a lien.

[49] U.C.C. § 9-108(a). U.C.C. § 9-108(b) provides that a description reasonably identifies the collateral if it describes the collateral by specific listing, category, Code type, quantity, or computational or allocational formula or procedure. Any other method may be used if it renders the identity of the collateral objectively determinable. *Id.*

U.C.C. § 9-108(d) contains a special rule for investment property. Much of the terminology in this area comes from Article 8 and is unfamiliar to many lenders, and the special rule is designed to minimize the damage if the wrong term is selected. With certain exceptions for consumer transactions that are discussed in the next paragraph of the text, a description of a security entitlement, securities account, or commodity account is sufficient if it uses those terms, the term "investment property," or if it describes the underlying financial asset or commodity contract. The special rule invites courts to accept extrinsic evidence to ascertain the intent of the parties even though their description uses a term that appears facially to be unambiguous. Investment property is discussed in § 1.04[E] *supra.*

[50] 202 F. Supp. 221, 1 U.C.C. Rep. Serv. 436 (W.D. Ky. 1962).

[51] 202 F. Supp. at 221, 1 U.C.C. Rep. Serv. at 436.

[52] *See also In re* Simplified Data Processing Sys., 55 B.R. 77, 42 U.C.C. Rep. Serv. 1441 (Bankr. E.D. N.Y. 1985) (description of collateral as "Prime 550" and "Prime 650" computer was upheld because the debtor had only one Prime 550 and one Prime 650 system).

Drane by no means stands for the proposition that a nonspecific description will always pass muster. The description could very well have failed if the debtor had owned two separate living room suites consisting of two wine-colored pieces each, or if the debtor had owned a single, wine-colored living-room suite consisting of three pieces. In either case, evidence of the living room furniture owned by the debtor would not have facilitated the identification of the two pieces of furniture that were intended to serve as collateral.[53]

The parol evidence rule was successfully (although incorrectly) invoked to defeat a secured party's claim in *In re Martin Grinding & Machine Works, Inc.*[54] In that case, the parties apparently intended that a loan be secured by equipment, fixtures, inventory, and accounts. The security agreement inadvertently omitted inventory and accounts, but they were included in descriptions in an SBA authorization, in the debtor's corporate resolution authorizing the transaction, and in the financing statement signed by the debtor. The description in the security agreement was unambiguous, and the court held that this precluded the introduction of extrinsic evidence. The court's analysis of the parol evidence rule is not convincing. The court did not discuss whether the security agreement was intended as a complete integration of the parties' agreement;[55] a record that is merely a partial integration may be supplemented by evidence of consistent additional terms, although in the case of a security agreement any additional descriptive terms would have to be in record form to satisfy the statute-of-frauds requirement. Nothing in the security agreement was inconsistent with the addition of inventory and accounts as collateral categories. Moreover, the court failed to consider the fact that evidence from contemporaneous records — and the financing statement was contemporaneous with the security agreement — is not excluded by the parol evidence rule at all.[56] Contemporaneous records should be read together to determine the intent of the parties.[57] The court's policy rationale, which was that third parties would be misled by the description in the security agreement, cannot withstand scrutiny. The primary function of the security agreement is to identify the assets that the parties have agreed will serve as collateral, and it is a financing statement or another method of perfection that provides notice

---

[53] *See* Raash v. Tri-County Trust Co., 712 S.W.2d 5, 2 U.C.C. Rep. Serv. 2d 294 (Mo. Ct. App. 1986) (description of hogs only by number and breed is insufficient if debtor owns other hogs of the same breed); Pontchartrain State Bank v. Poulson, 684 F.2d 704, 34 U.C.C. Rep. Serv. 693 (10th Cir. 1982) ("various equipment totaling $158,600.00 located at Haskel County, Oklahoma" failed as description because it did not enable identification of specific equipment covered).

[54] 793 F.2d 592, 1 U.C.C. Rep. Serv. 2d 1329 (7th Cir. 1986).

[55] *See In re* Maddox, 92 B.R. 707, 9 U.C.C. Rep. Serv. 2d 333 (Bankr. W.D. Tex. 1988) (*Martin Grinding* analysis not applicable because security agreement not completely integrated record).

[56] *Cf.* U.C.C. § 2-202.

[57] Dickason v. Marine Nat'l Bank of Naples, N.A., 898 So.2d 1170, 57 U.C.C. Rep. Serv. 2d 127 (Fla. Dist. Ct. App. 2005) (provision in promissory note stating that note was secured by a financing statement on all business assets of the maker held to incorporate the collateral description included on the financing statement, including the after-acquired property clause).

to third parties. Nevertheless, *Martin Grinding* sounds a cautionary note for lenders.

Although not required, a detailed description can often help identify collateral with great precision, lessening the problems that flow from ambiguities. Increased specificity can also, however, lead to errors. Including a serial number, for example, enhances the specificity of the description[58] but increases the chances of a mistake by misstating the numbers. The measure of acceptable error depends on the reasonableness of the description in light of the error and the total circumstances of the case. The transposition of two digits in a serial number is not likely to be fatal to the description,[59] whereas a number that does not correspond at all with the number on the collateral poses a greater problem. Even a description containing a noncorresponding serial number was upheld, however, when the court determined that the rest of the description of a tractor and its make and model corresponded to the only tractor that the debtor owned.[60] Other courts have not been as lenient.[61]

Increased specificity also increases the risk of debtor deceit. For example, specificity is enhanced by indicating the location of the collateral or features like its color. Identification issues can arise, however, if the collateral is relocated or painted a different color.[62] For example, the secured party in *American Indian Agricultural Credit Consortium, Inc. v. Fort Pierre Livestock, Inc.*[63] was fortunate that the court upheld its description even though

---

[58] *In re* Richman, 181 B.R. 260, 26 U.C.C. Rep. Serv. 2d 506 (Bankr. D. Md. 1995) (description as "all amounts on deposit in brokerage firm account no. 6282588026038 upheld); Personal Thrift Plan of Perry, Inc. v. Georgia Power Co., 242 Ga. 388, 249 S.E.2d 72, 25 U.C.C. Rep. Serv. 310 (1978) (use of model and serial numbers to identify consumer appliances).

[59] Dick Hatfield Chevrolet, Inc. v. Bob Watson Motors, Inc., 10 Kan. App. 2d 350, 699 P.2d 566, 40 U.C.C. Rep. Serv. 1876 (1985) (inadvertent addition of extra digit to serial number of pickup truck held not to affect sufficiency of description).

[60] Appleway Leasing, Inc. v. Wilkin, 39 Or. App. 43, 26 U.C.C. Rep. Serv. 209 (1979). *See also In re* Vintage Press, Inc., 552 F.2d 1145, 21 U.C.C. Rep. Serv. 1197 (5th Cir. 1977) (erroneous serial number of offset press not fatal because rest of description sufficient to identify collateral). *But see In re* Pickle Logging, Inc., 286 B.R. 181, 49 U.C.C. Rep. Serv. 2d 971 (Bankr. M.D. Ga. 2002) (description of collateral as a 648G skidder serial number DW648GX568154 when it was actually a 548G skidder serial number DW548GX568154 was inadequate because there was a substantial difference between the two types of skidders and the debtor owned at least two of each type).

[61] *In re* Eldridge, 10 B.R. 835, 36 U.C.C. Rep. Serv. 1422 (Bankr. E.D. Mich. 1981) (mistake in last four digits of vehicle information number fatal to description); *In re* Bolinger, 3 B.R. 186, 28 U.C.C. Rep. Serv. 1119 (Bankr. E.D. Mich. 1980) (correct serial number listed but the Pontiac automobile was described as a Chevrolet).

[62] *In re* Freeman, 33 B.R. 234, 37 U.C.C. Rep. Serv. 268 (Bankr. C.D. Cal. 1983) (description of collateral as "all furniture and fixtures and inventory of debtor now or at any time located or installed" at a specified location held inadequate to cover inventory kept at a different location). *But see* Baldwin v. Castro Cty. Feeders I, Ltd., 678 N.W.2d 796, 53 U.C.C. Rep. Serv. 2d 1 (S.D. 2004) (description of collateral as the livestock debtor delivered to secured party's feedlot in a stated community held to be sufficient even though it did not specify a particular lot or lots).

[63] 379 N.W.2d 318, 42 U.C.C. Rep. Serv. 1443 (S.D. 1985).

the collateral did not fit part of the description. The cattle subject to the security interest were described as being branded and tagged as follows: "-W on their right ribs, with an orange ear tag right ear." The court upheld the description with respect to the cattle with the "-W" brand alone, contending that the reference to the ear tag was surplusage that could not be relied upon because of the ease with which ear tags could be removed. All courts would not be this liberal, which suggests the importance of devising descriptions that can withstand the tests of time, debtor manipulation, and judicial vagaries.

Although broad, generic descriptions might be perceived as potentially more vulnerable to attack on grounds of sufficiency, such descriptions are often the most precise. A description reading "all of the equipment and fixtures" of the debtor has the virtues of being both inclusive and precise.[64] It is certainly more efficient, and ultimately likely to be more accurate, than using a description that attempts to state each separate item of the debtor's equipment and fixtures. Generic descriptions are the only means by which after-acquired property clauses can be drafted.[65]

Broad descriptions pose a concern that differs from reasonable identification of the collateral. The broadest possible description would be "all personal property and fixtures" of the debtor. Although some courts upheld such "supergeneric" descriptions under former law,[66] other courts refused to do so.[67] These latter courts maintained an attitude that a single creditor should not be able to encumber all of the assets of a debtor and struck such broad descriptions as "dragnet clauses" that were unconscionable or violative of public policy. Although the policy justifications are debatable, the drafters of revised Article 9 sided with the latter courts and provided that a supergeneric description is insufficient as a matter of law.[68] Nevertheless, a secured party can achieve virtually the same result by separately listing each Code type. The result is not precisely the same because there are a

---

[64] With certain exceptions discussed below, a description by a generic "type" of collateral defined in the U.C.C. (*e.g.,* inventory, accounts) is expressly approved. U.C.C. § 9-108(b)(3). The parties are also permitted to create their own generic "category" (*e.g., machinery, cattle*). U.C.C. § 9-108(b)(2). *See* Credit Alliance Corp. v. Trigg, 41 U.C.C. Rep. Serv. 208 (S.D. Miss. 1985) (description of collateral as "all . . . equipment" belonging to debtor sufficient to include a bulldozer used in debtor's business).

[65] After-acquired property clauses are discussed in § 3.02 *infra.*

[66] *In re* Legal Data Systems, Inc., 135 B.R. 199, 16 U.C.C. Rep. Serv. 2d 519 (Bankr. Mass. 1991) (all of debtor's "properties, assets, and rights of every kind and nature" sufficient); Federal Deposit Ins. Corp. v. Hill, 13 Mass. App. 514, 434 N.E.2d 1029, 33 U.C.C. Rep. Serv. 1510 (1982) (description as "all personal property" upheld).

[67] *In re* Wolsky, 68 B.R. 526, 2 U.C.C. Rep. Serv. 2d 1689 (Bankr. D. N.D. 1986) ("all property of every kind and description in which the Debtor has or may acquire any interest" held insufficient).

[68] U.C.C. § 9-108(c). By contrast, a financing statement must contain either a description of the collateral that complies with the requirements of section 9-108 or an indication of the collateral that can be in the form of "all assets" or "all personal property." U.C.C. § 9-504(2). This is appropriate because the function of a financing statement is to provide notice, not to identify the collateral subject to a security agreement. *See* § 5.02[A] *infra.*

few situations in which a description by type will not suffice. Commercial tort claims[69] must be separately described;[70] and in a consumer transaction, the same is true for consumer goods, security entitlements, securities accounts and commodity accounts.[71]

The use of generic categories can raise ambiguity issues. One concern is whether the parties to a transaction intended to use a term in accordance with its Article 9 meaning.[72] For example, a creditor of a manufacturing concern with a large stockpile of finished gymnasium apparatuses might describe the collateral as "all of the debtor's equipment," whereas Article 9 would characterize the finished products as inventory. The courts should seek to ascertain the intentions of the parties;[73] the risk, however, is that a court will simply apply the Code classifications to terms of the description that echo the categories included in Article 9.[74] For this reason, secured parties often describe their collateral in multiple, overlapping categories.

[B] Value — §§ 9-203(b)(1), 1-204

A security interest does not attach until the secured party gives value.[75] One way that a secured party can give value is to provide consideration. The U.C.C. provides that "a person gives value for rights if the person acquires them . . . in return for any consideration sufficient to support a simple contract."[76]

The common-law's bargain theory of consideration, particularly as manifested by the preexisting duty rule, is too restrictive for many commercial transactions. The U.C.C. thus expands the concept of value to include the acquisition of rights "as security for, or in total or partial satisfaction of, a preexisting claim."[77] Thus, a secured party may give value by taking a

---

[69] U.C.C. § 9-102(a)(13), discussed in § 1.07[F][2] *supra*.

[70] U.C.C. § 9-108(e)(1). Comment 5 to that section indicates that "a description such as 'all tort claims arising out of the explosion of debtor's factory' would suffice, even if the exact amount of the claim, the theory on which it may be based, and the identity of the tortfeasor(s) are not described."

[71] U.C.C. § 9-108(e)(2). Consumer transactions are discussed in § 1.04[A][1] *supra*. *See also* the discussion of descriptions of consumer goods in the context of after-acquired property clauses in § 3.02[B] *infra*.

[72] A prudent secured party will make it clear in the security agreement that a description by type is based on the relevant Article 9 definition if that is what is intended.

[73] Fifth Third Bank v. Comark, Inc., 794 N.E.2d 433, 51 U.C.C. Rep. Serv. 2d 533 (Ind. Ct. App. 2003) (security agreement incorrectly described collateral as inventory rather than equipment but description held adequate because remainder of description language clearly showed intent to include computer products bearing the name Comark).

[74] K.L. Smith Enterprises v. United Bank, 2 B.R. 280, 28 U.C.C. Rep. Serv. 534 (Bankr. D. Colo. 1980) (description of inventory of debtor farmer's egg business held not to include eggs).

[75] U.C.C. § 9-203(b)(1).

[76] U.C.C. § 1-204(4); Trinity Holdings, Inc. v. Firestone Bank, 24 U.C.C. Rep. Serv. 2d 1263 (W.D. Pa. 1994) (forbearance to commence collection on two delinquent loans).

[77] U.C.C. § 1-204(2). The more restrictive meaning of value in section 3-303(a) is adopted

security interest to collateralize an existing, legally enforceable obligation.[78] For example, the court in *Hillman's Equipment, Inc. v. Central Realty, Inc.*[79] recognized that the debt incurred for the purchase price of restaurant equipment constituted value even though the security agreement with respect to the equipment was not executed until after the purchase. In *Ford Motor Credit Co. v. State Bank & Trust Co.*,[80] a finance company gave value by taking a security interest in all of a car dealer's inventory only after the dealer failed to pay for the new cars that it had financed.

The preexisting-claim aspect of value is particularly important with after-acquired property clauses.[81] For example, suppose a debtor authenticates a security agreement granting a secured party a security interest in all equipment, including after-acquired equipment, in exchange for a loan. Later, the debtor acquires a new item of equipment. For the security interest to attach to that item, all the prerequisites for attachment must be met. The requirement that there be agreement is satisfied by the after-acquired property clause, which the debtor has accepted by its authentication, and the description requirement is satisfied by the reference to after-acquired equipment. The value requirement is satisfied because the security interest in the new item of equipment is taken as security for a preexisting claim; thus, the security interest attaches at the moment the debtor acquires rights in the new item.

The definition of value includes another alternative that is directly relevant to secured financing. It provides that "a person gives value for rights if the person acquires them . . . in return for a binding commitment to extend credit or for the extension of immediately available credit, whether or not drawn upon and whether or not a charge-back is provided for in the event of difficulties in collection."[82] Under this provision, value is given when an executory promise to extend credit becomes binding.[83] For example, a merchant and a bank might agree to a revolving line of credit pursuant to which the merchant is entitled on demand to draw up to a prescribed amount of money, and the merchant might authenticate a

---

if the issue involves the right of an assignee to enforce an account debtor's agreement not to assert defenses. U.C.C. § 9-403(a). This puts the assignee on an equal footing with a holder in due course under Article 3.

[78] Chicago Limousine Service, Inc. v. Hartigan Cadillac, Inc., 191 Ill. App. 3d 886, 548 N.E.2d 386, 10 U.C.C. Rep. Serv. 2d 1418 (1989) (preexisting indebtedness owed to lender by debtor constituted value with respect to subsequently-acquired limousines).

[79] 144 Ind. App. 18, 242 N.E.2d 522, 5 U.C.C. Rep. Serv. 1160 (1968), *rev'd on other grounds*, 253 Ind. 48, 246 N.E.2d 383 (1969).

[80] 571 So. 2d 937, 13 U.C.C. Rep. Serv. 2d 548 (Miss. 1990).

[81] After-acquired property clauses are discussed in § 3.02 *infra*.

[82] U.C.C. § 1-204(1). Pittsburgh Tube Co. v. Tri-Bend, Inc., 185 Mich. App. 581, 463 N.W.2d 161, 14 U.C.C. Rep. Serv. 2d 230 (1990) (extension of credit by agreeing to receive payment over five years).

[83] *In re* Air Vermont, Inc., 45 B.R. 817, 39 U.C.C. Rep. Serv. 1534 (D. Vt. 1984) (value given by binding commitment to extend credit even though money not transferred to debtor until six days later).

security agreement granting the bank a security interest in its inventory. Even though no funds have yet been requested, value has been given and the security interest attaches as soon as the other requirements are met. Of course, the merchant will not have any repayment obligation until it draws against the line of credit, and until that occurs there will be no occasion for the secured party to foreclose on the inventory.[84] Nevertheless, it is in the secured party's interest for attachment to occur at the earliest possible moment.

Article 9 requires that the secured party give value but does not require that the party providing the collateral receive it. In *In re Valle Feed of Farmington, Inc.*,[85] the assets of a corporation were used as security for a loan from a bank to the corporation's sole shareholders. The security interest was supported by value even though that value did not flow to the corporation.

[C] Rights or the Power to Transfer Rights in the Collateral — § 9-203(b)(2)

The debtor must have rights in the collateral, or the power to transfer rights in the collateral, before a security interest can attach.[86] This requirement is obvious because, in an enforceable secured transaction, the debtor must transfer a property interest to the secured party and must itself have a property interest in order to be able to do so. The interest that the secured party receives is generally controlled by the extent to which the debtor has transferable rights in the asset. Put another way, a security interest does not attach to the described asset; it attaches to the debtor's rights in the asset.

The common conceptualization of property rights as consisting of a bundle of sticks is helpful in understanding when a debtor has sufficient rights in an asset to grant an enforceable Article 9 security interest. Full owner-ship of an asset includes, *inter alia*, the rights to possess and use the asset. Moreover, with full ownership comes the right to transfer all or some of the owner's rights by way of sale, lease, or license. A person with transfer-able rights may grant an enforceable security interest in those rights. In the full-ownership situation, the security interest attaches to the full pano-ply of rights, and upon default the secured party may take possession of the asset[87] if it is capable of being possessed and, in any event, convey full ownership to a transferee through a foreclosure disposition, most often a

---

[84] It is possible (but unlikely) for the merchant to breach the agreement with the bank before drawing against the credit line, and any obligation to pay damages to the bank would be secured by the inventory.

[85] 80 B.R. 150, 5 U.C.C. Rep. Serv. 2d 1499 (Bankr. E.D. Mo. 1987). *Cf.* Restatement (Second) of Contracts § 71(4) (performance or return promise constituting consideration may be given to the promisor or to some other person).

[86] U.C.C. § 9-203(b)(2).

[87] U.C.C. § 9-609.

sale.[88] At the other extreme, a thief with mere possession of goods does not have transferable rights and thus cannot create an enforceable security interest in them.[89] Cases can fall between these two extremes: A debtor may have transferable rights that amount to something less than the full panoply of rights represented by full ownership.[90]

The foregoing analysis is nothing more than a particularized application of the doctrine of derivative title. Under that doctrine, a transferee's interest in property is derived from, and coextensive with, the interest of the transferor.[91] A debtor with limited rights in an asset generally lacks either the right or the power effectively to transfer more than its own bundle of rights.[92] The limitations on the debtor's rights also constitute limitations on the interest taken by the secured party and on the interest that can be transferred to a buyer through a post-default disposition. Recall that the "collateral" to which the security interest attaches is not the asset itself; it is the sum total of the debtor's transferable rights with respect to the asset.

The limits on a debtor's ability to create a security interest in goods leased by it provide a good illustration.[93] A lessee does not acquire any of the residual interest in the leased goods and therefore may not create a security interest that will effectively encumber that interest.[94] The lessee does,

---

[88] U.C.C. § 9-617(a) (disposition after default transfers all debtor's rights in collateral).

[89] *See, e.g.,* First Southern Ins. Co. v. Ocean State Bank, 562 So. 2d 798, 11 U.C.C. Rep. Serv. 2d 1255 (Fla. Ct. App. 1990). A thief of a negotiable instrument that qualifies as bearer paper is a holder, U.C.C. § 1-201(b)(21)(A), and has the power to transfer the instrument free of the claim of the true owner to a secured party that qualifies as a holder in due course. U.C.C. § 3-306.

[90] State Bank of Young Am. v. Vidmar Iron Works, Inc., 292 N.W.2d 244, 28 U.C.C. Rep. Serv. 1133 (Minn. 1980) (debtor's rights consisted of statutory lien for services provided on goods owned by third party).

[91] The doctrine of derivative title underlies the common expression that an assignee "stands in the shoes" of the assignor. *See* U.C.C. § 9-404(a) for a statement of this doctrine in the context of Article 9. *See* Delacy Investments, Inc. v. Thurman, 693 N.W.2d 479, 56 U.C.C. Rep. Serv. 2d 84 (Minn. Ct. App. 2005) (assignee of accounts receivable subject to account debtor's right of setoff for past-due overhead fees that assignor owed under an independent-contractor agreement with the account debtor); Magill v. Schwartz, 197 Or. App. 334, 105 P.3d 867, 55 U.C.C. Rep. Serv. 2d 1002 (Or. Ct. App. 2005) (because a member of a limited liability company (LLC) does not have any interest in specific LLC property under Washington law, a debtor with an interest in the LLC did not have rights in the company's anticipated proceeds from settlement of litigation and its lender's security interest did not attach to those proceeds).

[92] National City Bank, N.W. v. Columbian Mut. Life Ins. Co., 282 F.3d 407, 47 U.C.C. Rep. Serv. 2d 361 (6th Cir. 2002) is illustrative. An insurance company advanced substantial amounts of unearned commissions to an agent and retained a right to recoup payments for policies that were not taken or that lapsed. The court held that the secured party's perfected security interest in the agent's accounts receivable was subject to the recoupment provision because it was part of the underlying contract that gave rise to the accounts.

[93] Provisions on the transferability of leasehold interests in goods are included in Article 2A. *See* U.C.C. § 2A-303. For assistance in working through the thicket posed by this section, *see* W. Lawrence & J. Minan, The Law of Personal Property Leasing 8-4 to 8-13 (1993).

[94] *In re* Holiday Airlines Corp., 647 F.2d 977, 31 U.C.C. Rep. Serv. 1172 (9th Cir. 1981).

however, acquire the right to the exclusive use and enjoyment of the goods for the duration of the lease term, and those property rights may be used as the basis for a security interest.[95] If the debtor (lessee) were to default, the secured party could not dislodge the lessor's residual interest in the goods but could proceed against the debtor's remaining leasehold interest.[96] In practical terms, this means that, through foreclosure, the secured party may convey to a transferee the right to the exclusive use and enjoyment of the goods for the remainder of the lease term (subject, of course, to any obligation to pay rent under the terms of the lease contract).[97]

Similarly, a secured party that takes a security interest in a joint tenant's interest in an asset cannot thereby dislodge the interest of the other joint tenant. At foreclosure, the secured party may convey only the rights to which its security interest attached, and the buyer at foreclosure becomes a tenant-in-common[98] with the nondebtor co-owner.

A buyer of goods often will grant a security interest in the purchased goods — to the seller in a credit sale, or to a lender that provides the financing used to acquire the goods.[99] Under Article 2, the buyer acquires an insurable interest and a special property interest when the goods are "identified" to the contract. Identification is an Article 2 concept that essentially signifies the earliest point in time at which the actual goods that the seller will deliver to the buyer are designated.[100] For example, if a seller with a contract to deliver 100 units of a specific model of television has 1,000 of the units in its warehouse, identification occurs at the moment 100 of the units are selected as those that will be delivered. The buyer's special property interest provides a sufficient quantum of rights for attachment to occur.[101]

The significance of attachment upon identification can easily be overstated. Because identification creates an insurable interest, a secured party

---

[95] A term in a lease agreement is ineffective to the extent that it invalidates an assignment or transfer of an interest of either the lessor or the lessee under the lease, including a transfer that creates an enforceable security interest, and it is also ineffective to the extent that it provides that an assignment or transfer constitutes an event of default. U.C.C. § 9-407(a). This provision preserves for a secured party the value of a lessee's interest in leased goods.

[96] Towe Farms, Inc. v. Central Iowa Prod. Credit Ass'n, 528 F. Supp. 500, 32 U.C.C. Rep. Serv. 1431 (S.D. Iowa 1981).

[97] United States v. PS Hotel Corp., 404 F. Supp. 1188, 18 U.C.C. Rep. Serv. 770 (E.D. Mo. 1975), aff'd, 527 F.2d 500, 18 U.C.C. Rep. Serv. 775 (8th Cir. 1975). The transferee at the post-default disposition is not personally obligated to pay rent, but a failure to pay will give the lessor the right to cancel the lease and repossess the goods. U.C.C. § 2A-523(1). Other events of default under the lease agreement may also give the lessor the right to cancel and repossess.

[98] It is a tenancy in common because the unity of title has been severed. As a tenant in common, the disposition buyer may sue for partition, in which event the asset will be sold and the proceeds distributed according to the interests of the co-tenants.

[99] These transactions typically create purchase-money security interests. U.C.C. § 9-103. See § 1.05 supra.

[100] U.C.C. §§ 2-401(1), 2-501(1).

[101] Kendrick v. Headwaters Prod. Credit Ass'n, 523 A.2d 395, 3 U.C.C. Rep. Serv. 2d 1551 (Pa. Super. Ct. 1987).

might reach insurance proceeds[102] if the buyer's interest was insured and the goods were lost or damaged. The secured party could not defeat the seller, however, if the buyer were to repudiate the contract before taking delivery of the goods. Such a breach would entitle the seller to cancel the contract, thereby ending the debtor's rights in the goods.[103] Because the rights of the secured party are coextensive with the rights of the debtor, they would also be extinguished.[104]

A secured party's rights expand as additional parties with rights in the collateral consent to having their rights encumbered. For example, if both a lessee and a lessor consent to a security interest, the secured party's interest attaches cumulatively to the full ownership interest. The same result obtains if each joint tenant consents to a security interest. Consent to use a person's property rights as collateral does not automatically render that person liable for the underlying indebtedness. Consistent with suretyship principles, the value given by a secured party may run to an obligor even though another person provides part or all of the collateral.[105]

A person that has not consented to a security interest may nevertheless be estopped to deny its effectiveness. The effect of estoppel is equivalent to that of consent in that the estopped person may not contest the secured party's claim that the security interest attached to the person's rights in the collateral. Estoppel can result from either a common-law rule or a statute and is inevitably based on the estopped person's actions in clothing the debtor with indicia of ownership.[106] In this regard, the analysis is similar to that which underlies the doctrine of voidable title.[107] Estoppel provides a debtor with the power, if not the right, to grant a secured interest that has the effect of encumbering the estopped person's property rights.[108]

---

[102] The insurance would have to be payable to the buyer or to the secured party. U.C.C. § 9-102(a)(64)(D). Proceeds are discussed in § 2.03 *infra*.

[103] U.C.C. § 2-703(2)(f).

[104] These limitations generally should not be a problem for purchase-money secured parties. If the seller retains the security interest in the goods sold, the seller will simply retain title to those goods following a default by the buyer/debtor. If the purchase-money secured party is a lender that loans the money for the buyer/debtor to obtain the goods, the lender should protect itself by loaning the money in a form that will go directly to the seller of the goods. A seller that is paid will lack the grounds to retain title to the goods.

[105] *In re* Terminal Moving & Storage Co., 631 F.2d 547, 28 U.C.C. Rep. Serv. 1146, *rev'd on rehearing en banc*, 631 F.2d 547, 29 U.C.C. Rep. Serv. 679 (8th Cir. 1980).

[106] First Nat'l Bank v. Kisaare, 22 Okla. 545, 98 P. 433 (1908).

[107] Indeed, the doctrine of voidable title, which is predicated on estoppel principles, can be directly relevant. Under U.C.C. § 2-403(1), a person with voidable title has power to transfer full title to a good faith purchaser for value. The term "purchaser" includes, *inter alia*, a secured party. U.C.C. § 1-201(b)(30), (29). Thus, a person with voidable title has the power to grant a security interest that attaches to the true owner's rights to a secured party that gives value and lacks notice of the true owner's interest. Section 2-403(1) not only gives a person with voidable title the power to grant an enforceable security interest, it functions as a priority rule in favor of the secured party. *See, e.g., In re* Samuels & Co., 526 F.2d 1238, 18 U.C.C. Rep. Serv. 545 (5th Cir.), *cert. denied*, 429 U.S. 834 (1976) (secured financer of cattle buyer prevailed as good-faith purchaser for value over cash seller of cattle's reclamation rights when buyer's checks to seller bounced).

[108] U.C.C. § 9-203(b)(2) (debtor must have rights or power to transfer rights in collateral).

Many of the estoppel cases arise in the context of a bailment, meaning a transaction in which an owner of goods (a bailor) places them in the rightful possession of another (a bailee).[109] In giving up possession, the bailor clothes the bailee with the appearance of ownership, and the question arises whether the grant of a security interest by the bailee will cause the security interest to attach by estoppel to the bailor's rights.

Perhaps the simplest type of bailment is one in which a bailor turns goods over to a bailee for storage or carriage but does not give the bailee permission to use the goods while they are in its possession. At common law, such a bailee lacks the power to alienate the bailor's rights, even to a good-faith purchaser for value.[110] Because the bailee cannot alienate the bailor's rights, a security agreement authenticated by the bailee will not suffice to cause a security interest to attach to the bailor's rights. There are numerous cases holding that such a bailee lacks sufficient rights to grant a security interest in the bailed goods.[111]

At the other extreme lies a "consignment," a type of bailment in which a consignor delivers goods to a consignee and authorizes the consignee to sell them. For example, suppose a manufacturer of goods consigns them to a merchant in the business of selling such goods with the understanding that they can be returned if they are not sold. Because a third party would naturally believe that the goods were part of the consignee's inventory and could be misled more easily than a third party dealing with a bailee for storage or carriage, the case for estoppel is especially strong. Indeed, Article 9 explicitly governs most commercially valuable consignments and provides that the consigned goods are subject to the claims of the consignee's creditors.[112] Accordingly, the consignee has the power to cause a security interest to attach to the consignor's rights in the goods.

A consignment of goods to a merchant for the purpose of sale also qualifies as an "entrustment," and the entrustment aspect of the transaction is governed by Article 2.[113] In an entrustment, a person delivers (or acquiesces in the delivery of) goods to a merchant that deals in goods of the kind, and this gives the merchant the power to convey the entruster's rights in the goods to a buyer in ordinary course of business.[114] The classic example is a watch owner who delivers a watch to a jeweler for repair and the jeweler negligently or fraudulently places the watch in its inventory and sells it to an ordinary-course buyer. The sale transfers the owner's title to the

---

[109] R. Brown, The Law of Personal Property § 10.1 (W. Raushenbush 3d ed. 1975). Unlike a sale, title to the goods does not pass in a bailment and thus the doctrine of voidable title is inapt.

[110] E. Goddard, The Law of Bailments and Carriers § 29 (2d ed. 1908); Smith v. Clews, 114 N.Y. 190, 21 N.E. 160 (1889).

[111] See, e.g., Evergreen Marine Corp. v. Six Consignments of Frozen Scallops, 4 F.3d 90, 21 U.C.C. Rep. Serv. 2d 502 (1st Cir. 1993).

[112] Consignments governed by Article 9 are discussed in § 1.03[B][2] supra.

[113] See U.C.C. §§ 2-403(3), (2).

[114] Buyers in ordinary course of business are discussed in § 11.03[A][1] infra.

buyer. Because the entrustment statute protects only buyers in ordinary course of business, it cannot be used by a secured party to which the jeweler has granted a security interest. Under the common-law rules governing bailments generally, the jeweler lacks the power to grant an enforceable security interest in the watch. The fact that a secured party cannot prevail over the owner under either Article 2 or the common law does not end the analysis. In any bailment situation, including an entrustment, the bailor may, in addition to placing the goods in the hands of the bailee, have used language or engaged in conduct that led the secured party to believe that the bailee had the power to transfer full ownership. In such a case, general estoppel principles may cause the security interest to attach to the bailor's interest.[115]

Kinetics Technology International Corp. v. Fourth National Bank[116] is an example of general estoppel in a bailment context. In that case, the plaintiff delivered certain goods that it owned to a manufacturer, whose job was to add components to the goods — thereby creating finished products — and to deliver the finished products back to the plaintiff. The court ultimately invoked estoppel principles to subject the plaintiff's ownership interest in the goods still in the manufacturer's hands to a security interest that the manufacturer granted to the defendant. The court's rationale was that the plaintiff was, in effect, a type of lender — one that loaned goods rather than money to enable the manufacturer to produce the finished product. Had the plaintiff loaned money to enable the manufacturer to acquire the goods, it could have taken a security interest in the goods and filed a financing statement to protect its interest. The financing statement would have warned the defendant of the plaintiff's interest. Even though it supplied the goods rather than the money to acquire them, the court concluded that the plaintiff should have used the mechanisms of Article 9 to take and perfect a security interest in the goods. Courts in similar circumstances have reached the same result by holding that the goods in question were actually sold to the manufacturer and that the attempt to retain title amounted to nothing more than a security interest.[117] As owner of the goods, the manufacturer would clearly have sufficient rights to grant a security interest in them; as secured party, the supplier would need to file a financing statement to assure itself of priority over third-party claims.[118]

---

[115] U.C.C. § 1-103(b) (unless displaced, principles of law and equity supplement the Code). *Cf.* Tumber v. Automation Design and Mfg. Corp., 130 N.J. Super. 5, 324 A.2d 602 (1974) (a person that does not qualify as a buyer in ordinary course of business may nevertheless prevail under estoppel principles).

[116] 705 F.2d 396, 36 U.C.C. Rep. Serv. 292 (10th Cir. 1983). *See also In re* Pubs, Inc., 618 F.2d 432, 28 U.C.C. Rep. Serv. 297 (7th Cir. 1980) (closely held corporation estopped when two key officers used its assets as collateral for a personal loan).

[117] *See* U.C.C. §§ 2-106(1) (sale is passing of title from seller to buyer for a price), 2-403(1) (contract term providing for title to remain in seller until buyer pays for goods reduced in effect to retention by seller of a security interest).

[118] *See, e.g.,* Morton Booth Co. v. Tiara Furniture, Inc., 564 P.2d 210 (Okla. 1977).

In *Fifth Third Bank v. Comark, Inc.,* [119] the bank entered into a security agreement with Vertica, Inc. for assets owned by Vertica, LLC, a separate but related entity. The bank argued that Vertica, LLC should be estopped from asserting that Vertica, Inc. did not have rights in the collateral but the court disagreed. The bank could not prove that (a) Vertica, LLC had consented to Vertica, Inc. encumbering its assets, (b) Vertica, Inc. had ever been in possession of the assets, (c) Vertica, Inc. had allowed Vertica, LLC to appear as the owner of the collateral, or (d) Vertica, Inc. had notice of the secured transaction.

§ 2.03 PROCEEDS

Debtors sometimes dispose of collateral in their possession or control. The disposal might be authorized by the secured party, as commonly occurs when the secured party expects the debtor to sell financed inventory in order to acquire the money to repay the loan, or it might be without the awareness of the secured party and in violation of a prohibition in the security agreement. Either way, the secured party is likely to be interested in pursuing the proceeds that the debtor receives from its disposition of the collateral. The discussion below explains the concept and classification of proceeds, and describes how a security interest attaches to proceeds. Problems involving perfection and priority of a security interest in proceeds are discussed elsewhere in the text. [120]

[A] Defined — § 9-102(a)(64)

The term "proceeds" means:

   (A) whatever is acquired upon the sale, lease, license, exchange, or other disposition of collateral;

   (B) whatever is collected on, or distributed on account of, collateral;

   (C) rights arising out of collateral;

   (D) to the extent of the value of collateral, claims arising out of the loss, nonconformity, or interference with the use of, defects or infringement of rights in, or damage to the collateral; and

   (E) to the extent of the value of collateral and to the extent payable to the debtor or the secured party, insurance payable by reason of the loss or nonconformity of, defects or infringement of rights in, or damage to, the collateral. [121]

In effect, virtually anything that replaces the economic value of collateral constitutes a proceed.

---

[119] 794 N.E.2d 433, 51 U.C.C. Rep. Serv. 2d 533 (Ind. Ct. App. 2003).

[120] *See* discussions in §§ 8.02 (perfection) and 10.05 (priority) *infra.*

[121] U.C.C. § 9-102(a)(64).

Proceeds can take almost any form. Cases have found proceeds to consist of cash,[122] checks,[123] promissory notes,[124] payments of principal and interest on promissory notes,[125] used cars accepted as trade-ins on sales of automobile inventory,[126] shares of stock received in the sale of partnership assets,[127] and a new certificate of deposit resulting from rolling over two other certificates.[128] By contrast, calves are not proceeds of the cattle that give birth to them because they do not in any sense replace those cattle.[129]

Under original Article 9, a majority of courts applied a misguided "passage-of-title" theory and held that casualty insurance payments arising out of damage to insured collateral did not qualify as proceeds because there was no disposition of the original collateral.[130] The passage-of-title theory was predicated on the then-current definition of proceeds as assets acquired upon the "sale, exchange, collection or other disposition" of collateral. The terms "sale," "exchange," and "collection" refer to types of transactions in which title is surrendered or payment rights are satisfied.[131] The 1972 Official Text expressly overruled the insurance cases but did not amend the language that gave rise to the passage-of-title theory.[132] Revised Article

---

[122] Bank of Kansas v. Hutchinson Health Servs., Inc., 12 Kan. App. 2d 87, 735 P.2d 256, 3 U.C.C. Rep. Serv. 2d 1537 (1987).

[123] Farms Associates, Inc. v. South Side Bank, 93 Ill. App. 3d 766, 417 N.E.2d 818, 30 U.C.C. Rep. Serv. 1729 (1981).

[124] In re Guil-Park Farms, Inc. v. South Side Bank, 90 B.R. 180, 7 U.C.C. Rep. Serv. 2d 1675 (Bankr. W.D. N.C. 1988).

[125] In re Charter First Mortgage, Inc., 56 B.R. 838, 2 U.C.C. Rep. Serv. 2d 1409 (Bankr. D. Or. 1985).

[126] Chrysler Credit Corp. v. Knebel Chevrolet-Buick, Inc., 976 F.2d 1012, 20 U.C.C. Rep. Serv. 2d 645 (7th Cir. 1992).

[127] In re Guaranteed Muffler Supply Co., Inc., 1 B.R. 324, 27 U.C.C. Rep. Serv. 1217 (Bankr. N.D. Ga. 1979).

[128] In re Airwest Int'l, 70 B.R. 914, 3 U.C.C. Rep. Serv. 2d 1936 (Bankr. D. Haw. 1987).

[129] Citizens Sav. Bank, Hawkeye, Iowa v. Miller, 515 N.W.2d 7, 24 U.C.C. Rep. Serv. 2d 1032 (Iowa 1994). See also PNC Bank v. Marty's Mobile Homes, Inc., 45 U.C.C. Rep. Serv. 2d 659 (Del. Ct. Ch. 2001) (sales tax receipts not proceeds from sale of mobile home because they were never intended to be part of seller's assets and were regularly forwarded to state agency in the normal course of business); Western Farm Serv., Inc. v. Olsen, 114 Wash. App. 508, 59 P.3d 93, 49 U.C.C. Rep. Serv. 2d 936 (2002) (cash received as separate allowance to reimburse grower/debtor for expenses incurred in delivering potatoes to processing site not a proceed because it did not result from the sale, exchange, lease, license or other disposition of the potato crop).

[130] See, e.g., Universal C.I.T. Credit Corp. v. Prudential Inv. Corp., 222 A.2d 571, 3 U.C.C. Rep. Serv. 696 (R.I. 1966).

[131] U.C.C. § 9-306(1) (1962 Official text). The passage-of-title theory was inconsistent with Article 9's basic approach, which is that the location of title to collateral is immaterial. See U.C.C. § 9-202 (1962 and 2003 Official Texts). See also R. Wilson Freyermuth, Rethinking Proceeds: The History, Misinterpretation and Revision of U.C.C. Section 9-306, 69 Tulane L. Rev. 645 (1995).

[132] U.C.C. §§ 9-306(1) (defining proceeds), 9-104(g) (1972 Official Text) (narrowing the exclusion from Article 9 so that transfers of insurance interests that constitute proceeds are within its scope).

9 continues the 1972 approach for insurance payments and, indeed, extends it to insurance payments for lost economic value of, as well as physical damage to, collateral.[133] It also amends the definition of proceeds to include "whatever is acquired upon the sale, *lease, license,* exchange, or other disposition of collateral" (emphasis supplied). Lease and license transactions do not involve passage of title.[134]

Revised Article 9 also continues a rule first adopted in a conforming amendment to Article 9 that was part of the 1994 revision of Article 8 — proceeds includes "whatever is distributed on account of" collateral.[135] The rule was adopted for the express purpose of overruling the decision in *In re Hastie,*[136] a case in which the court, relying on the passage-of-title theory, held that cash dividends paid on account of stock were not proceeds because the debtor did not give up title to the stock in order to obtain them.

Although revised Article 9 extends the definition of proceeds to cover any rights arising out of collateral or claims predicated on a loss of the economic value of collateral,[137] it does not deal directly with "nonexistent collateral." Suppose, for example, that a secured party acquires a security interest in a debtor's crops. The parties anticipate at the time that the debtor will plant crops annually, but subsequently the debtor enrolls in a federal program that pays a subsidy to farmers who permit their land to go fallow. The subsidy is a direct economic substitute for a crop that never existed and therefore ought to qualify as a proceed, but most courts facing this issue have held otherwise.[138] Revised Article 9's textual treatment of proceeds reflects a value-based approach to proceeds that honors the *ex ante*

---

[133] U.C.C. § 9-102(a)(64)(E). *In re* Wiersma, 283 B.R. 294, 49 U.C.C. Rep. Serv. 2d 309 (Bankr. D. Ida. 2002) (settlement payments by insurance company represented compensation to debtors for the loss of and damage to secured party's collateral).

[134] Some courts applying the passage-of-title theory held that lease payments did not constitute proceeds. *See, e.g., In re* Cleary Bros. Constr. Co., 9 B.R. 40, 30 U.C.C. Rep. Serv. 1444 (Bankr. S.D. Fla. 1980). Such decisions defied economic reality. Leased property depreciates in value as it ages and is used, and the rental payments, which reflect that depreciation, are direct economic substitutes for the collateral's lost value. Prior to the promulgation of revised Article 9, the Comments were amended to disapprove of these holdings. U.C.C. § 9-306, Comment 6, *authorized by* P.E.B. Commentary No. 9 (June 25, 1992).

[135] U.C.C. § 9-102(a)(64)(B).

[136] 2 F.3d 1042, 21 U.C.C. Rep. Serv. 2d 212 (10th Cir. 1993).

[137] U.C.C. § 9-102(a)(64)(C), (D). A claim might consist of a debtor's right to recover against its seller or lessor for a breach of warranty, a claim against an economic competitor for infringement of an intellectual property right, or even a tort claim, such as a right to payment for the negligent destruction of collateral. The extension of the definition corresponds with a narrowing of the exclusion from Article 9 for claims arising in tort. In addition to a proceeds interest, a secured party may also take an original security interest in a commercial tort claim. *See* § 1.07[F][2] *supra.*

[138] *See, e.g., In re* Schmaling, 783 F.2d 680, 42 U.C.C. Rep. Serv. 1074 (7th Cir. 1986) (federal Payment-in-Kind, or PIK, program). *Contra* Sweetwater Production Credit Ass'n v. O'Briant, 764 S.W.2d 230, 7 U.C.C. Rep. Serv. 2d 1247 (Tex. 1988).

expectations of the parties. Courts considering nonexistent collateral cases[139] should carefully consider the implications of this approach.

After the landlord in *U.S. Bank Trust National Association v. Venice MD LLC*[140] had not been paid, it wrongfully took possession of the debtor's inn and operated it using assets that were subject to the bank's security interest. The bank argued that the landlord's conduct constituted an unauthorized disposition of its collateral and sought to recover the gross revenues generated during the landlord's operation as proceeds of that disposition. Because most of the collateral remained intact after the landlord relinquished possession, it had not been disposed of and thus there were no proceeds under section 9-315(a). Although the landlord did dispose of food and beverage inventory during its operation of the inn, the court held that the gross revenues could not be traced to the dispositions. Unlike the direct sale of inventory from a grocery store, the gross proceeds from the restaurant and bar operation reflected preparation, atmosphere, and service.

Article 9 distinguishes (for some perfection and priority purposes) between cash and noncash proceeds. Cash proceeds[141] include assets like money, checks, and deposit accounts. The definition is open-ended so that an asset that is a cash equivalent, like a money-market account that is a financial asset in a securities account, is covered.[142] All other proceeds are noncash proceeds.[143] For example, suppose a secured party has a security interest in a debtor's inventory. If the debtor sells the inventory for cash or a check, the proceeds are cash proceeds. If the debtor takes a used item in trade or sells the inventory on credit, the proceeds are noncash proceeds.[144] If the debtor takes a check for the inventory and later deposits it to a bank account, the bank's obligation to repay the deposited funds is a proceed of a proceed (and therefore qualifies as a proceed)[145], and because it is a deposit account it is a cash proceed. If money is later withdrawn from the account and used to buy a piano, the money is a cash proceed and the piano is a noncash proceed.

---

[139] Another example of "nonexistent collateral" arises in the context of business interruption insurance. A secured creditor may claim that a debtor's insurance claim is a proceed of accounts or general intangibles that would have existed but for the interruption of the business. Cases dealing with this issue include *In re* Investment and Tax Servs., 148 B.R. 571, 19 U.C.C. Rep. Serv. 2d 905 (Bankr. D. Minn. 1992) (business interruption insurance not proceeds); and MNC Commercial Corp. v. Rouse, No. 91-0615-CV-W-2, 1992 U.S. Dist. Lexis 22166 (W.D. Mo. 1992) (business interruption insurance qualifies as proceeds).

[140] 53 U.C.C. Rep. Serv. 2d 394 (4th Cir. 2004) (unpublished).

[141] U.C.C. § 9-102(a)(9).

[142] U.C.C. § 9-102, Comment 13(e).

[143] U.C.C. § 9-102(a)(58).

[144] The buyer's payment obligation is an account. U.C.C. § 9-102(a)(2). An account is a noncash proceed, while a deposit account is a cash proceed.

[145] U.C.C. § 9-102(a)(12)(A).

[B]   Attachment — §§ 9-203(f), 9-315(a)(2), (b)

The attachment concept applies automatically to proceeds. The section on attachment provides that a security interest in collateral attaches automatically to proceeds as soon as they come into existence, even if the security agreement is silent on the matter.[146] A corresponding provision then limits attachment to proceeds that are identifiable.[147] Identification means that the proceeds can be traced back to the collateral from which they sprang, and the cases place the burden of tracing on the secured party.[148] The fact that the secured party may look to the proceeds to satisfy the indebtedness does not mean that its interest in the original collateral was severed by the disposition. A secured party that consents to disposition of the collateral free from its security interest is limited to the identifiable proceeds from the disposition.[149] If, however, the disposition occurs without such consent, the secured party's interest attaches to the identifiable proceeds and, unless a provision of Article 9 or section 2-403 provides to the contrary, also continues in the original collateral.[150] This allows the secured party to look to two sources for satisfaction.

What is the impact on identification if cash proceeds are deposited to a deposit account? Depositing proceeds into a deposit account that contains only proceeds permits easy identification[151] but is not required for a

---

[146] U.C.C. § 9-203(f).

[147] U.C.C. § 9-315(a)(2). If goods, including goods that are proceeds, are commingled in such a way that their separate identity is lost, a security interest ceases to attach to them and instead attaches to the product or mass into which they have been subsumed. U.C.C. §§ 9-315(b)(1), 9-336. Commingled goods are discussed in § 15.06 *infra*.

A different sort of commingling was present in *U.S. Bank Trust National Association v. Venice MD LLC,* 53 U.C.C. Rep. Serv. 2d 394 (4th Cir. 2004) (unpublished). A landlord that had not been paid rent wrongfully took possession of the debtor's inn and operated it — in the process using food and beverage assets that were subject to the bank's security interest in operating the inn's restaurant. The bank argued that the landlord's conduct constituted an unauthorized disposition of its collateral and sought to recover the gross revenues generated during the landlord's operation as proceeds of that disposition. The court ruled in favor of the landlord, holding that the bank's security interest did not extend to the sums generated from the restaurant and bar operation. This result is defensible, because a security interest only extends to "identifiable" proceeds of the secured party's collateral. Unlike the direct sale of inventory from a grocery store, the gross revenues from the debtor's restaurant and bar operation reflected not only the food and beverage inventory but also the labor involved in preparing and serving it to customers. Thus, the gross revenues could not be traced solely to the food and beverage inventory.

[148] *See, e.g.,* Universal C.I.T. v. Farmers Bank, 358 F. Supp. 317, 13 U.C.C. Rep. Serv. 109 (E.D. Mo. 1973); *In re* Superior Used Cars, Inc., 258 B.R. 680, 44 U.C.C. Rep. Serv. 2d 293 (Bankr. W.D. Mich. 2001) (secured party could not meet its burden in tracing cash proceeds).

[149] U.C.C. § 9-315(a).

[150] U.C.C. § 9-315(a). Dry Canyon Farms, Inc. v. United State Nat'l Bank of Oregon, 84 Or. App. 686, 735 P.2d 620, 4 U.C.C. Rep. Serv. 2d 277 (1987) (security interest continues in proceeds, whether or not secured party authorizes disposition). For a discussion of a secured party's continuing interest in the collateral disposed of by a debtor, see §§ 11.01, 11.02 *infra*.

[151] *In re* Cullen, 71 B.R. 274, 3 U.C.C. Rep. Serv. 2d 815 (Bankr. W.D. Wis. 1987).

security interest in the deposited proceeds to remain valid.[152] Commingling funds in a deposit account, by contrast, raises serious identification problems. Because former law did not specifically provide for the identification of commingled cash proceeds, courts turned to equitable tracing concepts developed in the law of trusts.[153] Revised Article 9 adopts this approach.[154] The applicable equitable tracing rule is the "lowest intermediate balance" rule, and it is based the following assumptions: (1) as a debtor spends funds from a deposit account, it spends the proceeds of a security interest last;[155] and (2) the amount that constitutes identifiable proceeds is not increased by a later deposit of nonproceed funds unless the debtor intends that the later deposit restore, or partially restore, the proceeds balance.[156] For example, suppose a secured party has a security interest in a debtor's inventory and permits the debtor to deposit cash proceeds into its general checking account. On Day 1, the debtor has a balance of $10,000 in the account, none of which represents proceeds. On Day 2, the debtor deposits $5,000 in cash proceeds, resulting in an overall balance of $15,000 and a proceeds balance of $5,000. The next day, the debtor withdraws and dissipates $4,000.[157] This reduces the overall balance to $11,000, but

---

[152] A security interest is not invalid or fraudulent merely because the debtor has the right or the ability to use, commingle, or dispose of all or part of the collateral. U.C.C. § 9-205(a)(1). "Collateral" includes proceeds. U.C.C. § 9-102(a)(12)(A). *See* § 3.01 *infra.*

[153] Bank of Kansas v. Hutchinson Health Serv., Inc., 12 Kan. App. 2d 87, 735 P.2d 256, 3 U.C.C. Rep. Serv. 2d 1537 (1987). The tracing concept is not limited to deposits into a debtor's deposit account. Frike v. Valley Prod. Credit Ass'n, 778 S.W.2d 829, 10 U.C.C. Rep. Serv. 2d 1454 (Mo. Ct. App. 1989) (secured party traced deposit of cash proceeds into business account of debtor's business partner); Farns Associates, Inc. v. South Side Bank, 93 Ill. App. 3d 766, 417 N.E.2d 818 (1981) (secured party traced proceeds by showing that bank received checks representing the proceeds directly from the account debtor and then cashed the checks).

[154] U.C.C. § 9-315(b)(2).

[155] *Ex parte* Alabama Mobile Homes, Inc., 468 So. 2d 156, 40 U.C.C. Rep. Serv. 1898 (Ala. 1985).

[156] The deposit of new proceeds is distinguishable. In *Central Prod. Credit Ass'n v. Hans*, 189 Ill. App. 3d 889, 545 N.E.2d 1063, 11 U.C.C. Rep. Serv. 2d 696 (1989), identifiable proceeds that had been deposited in a deposit account were withdrawn to purchase investments. When those investments were sold, their proceeds were deposited into the same account. Because the second deposit also constituted identifiable proceeds, it increased the balance of proceeds in the account.

[157] U.C.C. § 9-332(b) provides that a transferee of funds from a deposit account, even a transferee that does not give value, takes the funds free of even a perfected security interest in the account unless the transferee acts in collusion with the debtor to violate the rights of the secured party. U.C.C. § 9-332(a) provides a similar rule for transferees of money. U.C.C. § 9-332, Comment 3 explains the rule as follows:

> Broad protection for transferees helps to ensure that security interests in deposit accounts do not impair the free flow of funds. It also minimizes the likelihood that a secured party will enjoy a claim to whatever the transferee purchases with the funds. Rules concerning recovery of payments traditionally have placed a high value on finality. The opportunity to upset a completed transaction, or even to place a completed transaction in jeopardy by bringing suit against the transferee of funds, should be severely limited. Although the giving of value usually is a prerequisite for receiving the ability to take free from third-party claims, where payments are concerned the law is even more protective.

applying the first assumption leaves the proceeds balance at $5,000. On Day 3, the debtor withdraws an additional $7,000 and buys an item of equipment. The overall balance is $4,000, all of which is proceeds. In addition, the secured party has an interest in the equipment to the extent of $1,000 (the amount of proceeds that went towards the purchase). On Day 4, the debtor deposits $15,000, none of which is proceeds. The overall balance is $19,000, but applying the second assumption leaves the proceeds balance at $4,000. In other words, the proceeds balance is the lowest balance between the time proceeds are first withdrawn and the time the account balance later rises as a result of nonproceed deposits — *i.e.,* the lowest intermediate balance. If the debtor deposits $6,000 in new proceeds on Day 5, the overall balance will rise to $25,000 and the proceeds balance will rise to $10,000.

Former law provided that a security interest continued in identifiable proceeds "received by the debtor."[158] Revised Article 9 eliminates the phrase, thereby making it clear that a security interest attaches to proceeds even if they are acquired by a person that did not create the original security interest. The Comments state that "[t]his Article contains no requirement that property be 'received' by the debtor for the property to qualify as proceeds. It is necessary only that the property be traceable, directly or indirectly, to the original collateral."[159]

§ 2.04 ATTACHMENT TO UNDERLYING OBLIGATIONS — § 9-203(f), (g)

Article 9 contains special attachment rules that apply to: (1) obligations that support payment or performance of collateral; and (2) property, including real estate, that secures a right to payment or performance that is within the scope of Article 9.

Section 9-203(f) provides that attachment of a security interest to collateral causes the security interest also to attach to any "supporting obligation" for the collateral. A supporting obligation is a letter-of-credit right or other type of secondary obligation, such as a guaranty, that supports payment or performance under a supported obligation that is itself within the scope of Article 9.[160] A supported obligation might be an account,

---

See Keybank Nat'l Ass'n v. Ruiz Food Products, Inc., 59 U.C.C. Rep. Serv. 2d 870 (D. Ida. 2005) (§ 9-332 protects innocent transferee of funds wrongfully paid by the debtor from a perfected security interest in the funds as identifiable proceeds from the sale of debtor's inventory).

[158] U.C.C. § 9-306(2) (1972 Official Text).

[159] U.C.C. § 9-102, Comment 13(d). *See* Case Corp. v. Gehrke, 208 Ariz. 140, 91 P.3d 362, 55 U.C.C. Rep. Serv. 2d 1 (Ariz. Ct. App.2004) (because security interest extended to proceeds and security agreement required debtor to transfer proceeds from sale of inventory to secured party within seven days, secured party had a viable claim for conversion against debtor because the proceeds could be identified even though they had been commingled with other funds in the debtor's general operating account).

[160] U.C.C. § 9-102(a)(77).

chattel paper, document, general intangible, instrument, or investment property. A security interest that attaches to a supported obligation automatically attaches to any supporting obligation.[161] For example, suppose a secured party has a security interest in a negotiable promissory note (an instrument) that is supported by a standby letter of credit. The security interest automatically attaches to the letter-of-credit right[162] even though there is no reference to the right in the security agreement.

Section 9-203(g) contains a similar attachment rule for property that secures a right to payment or performance. For example, suppose a secured party lends money and takes a security interest in a note that is secured by a mortgage on real estate. Even though the initial acquisition of the mortgage by the payee of the note was outside the scope of Article 9, the secondary financing transaction in which the note and mortgage are used as collateral is within its scope. The security interest automatically attaches to the mortgage when it attaches to the note.[163] This area presents complex issues that overlap with aspects of real-estate law and is discussed in more detail in connection with Article 9's scope provisions.[164]

---

[161] U.C.C. § 9-203(f). Moreover, perfection of the security interest in the supported obligation also perfects the security interest in the supporting obligation. U.C.C. § 9-308(d). This is true even though a security interest in a letter-of-credit right that is not a supporting obligation must be perfected by control. U.C.C. §§ 9-312(b)(2), 9-107.

[162] U.C.C. § 9-102(a)(51) defines "letter-of-credit right." *See* § 1.08 *supra.*

[163] U.C.C. § 9-308(e). Perfection of the interest in the note automatically perfects the interest in the mortgage. Although the drafters' intent in adopting these provisions was to preempt real estate law, a legislative note appended to § 9-308 suggests that each state legislature should provide further clarification by enacting an amendment to the state's real estate recording act expressly providing that perfection under Article 9 is sufficient for all purposes.

[164] *See* § 1.07[C] *supra.*

Chapter 3
ONGOING FINANCING RELATIONSHIPS

§ 3.01   FACILITATING CLAUSES GENERALLY

The parties to some financing arrangements do not view their initial security agreement as representing a static, one-shot transaction. Rather, they anticipate at least the potential for a dynamic, ongoing financing relationship in which additional funds will be advanced by the secured party, further property of the debtor will become collateral, or both will occur.

The parties to such a transaction would be burdened considerably if they had to formalize all subsequent modifications and additions to their agreement. The transaction costs associated with a requirement that they enter into a new security agreement each time the secured party advances additional funds, or each time the debtor acquires additional collateral, would be significant. Requiring new agreements would also slow the processing of some transactions, as well as increase the chances of overlooking some necessary formality. The parties would be better served if they could incorporate their long-term intent into their initial security agreement.

Consider the following hypothetical. D is the owner of a retail furniture outlet. SP provides D with financing for the acquisition of inventory and takes as collateral a security interest in all of D's inventory. The parties anticipate that D will repay SP with the proceeds derived from inventory sales and envision a long-term financing arrangement under which SP will finance D's acquisitions of inventory for many years to come. They want each future extension of credit to be secured by D's entire stock of inventory, and accordingly they want SP's security interest to attach to new inventory as D acquires it.

Article 9 includes provisions that greatly facilitate such transactions. It enables parties to include terms in their security agreement that will implement their intentions with respect to the continuing nature of their financing arrangement. The use of an after-acquired property clause or a future-advances clause, or both, enables parties to craft their transaction with efficiency.

Although both an after-acquired property clause and a future-advances clause refer to events that are to transpire in the future, they cover distinct concepts and should not be confused. An after-acquired property clause concerns future assets that will serve as collateral for an obligation. It reflects the parties' understanding that the security interest will attach to property within the security agreement's description of the collateral which the debtor acquires subsequent to the agreement's effective date. In the hypothetical stated above, if the security agreement provides for after-acquired inventory, SP will acquire a security interest not only in all of D's existing inventory but also in additional inventory as D acquires rights in it.

A future-advances clause, on the other hand, concerns the money or other value that is advanced by the secured party. In the hypothetical, if the security agreement contains a future-advances clause, D's inventory will be encumbered as collateral to the extent of the initial loan and all future loans.

Article 9 thus validates "floating liens" — that is, liens that expand the pool of collateral as new assets are acquired and expand the obligation as new value is advanced.[1] Historically, this approach generated considerable judicial hostility.[2] The original drafters concluded that this aversion was premised "on a feeling, often inarticulate in the opinions, that a commercial borrower should not be allowed to encumber all his assets present and future, and that for the protection not only of the borrower but of his other creditors a cushion of free assets should be preserved."[3] Judicial resistance reached its zenith with the United States Supreme Court opinion of *Benedict v. Ratner*.[4] The Court there struck down as a fraudulent conveyance an assignment of present and future accounts receivable. It reasoned that the debtor's unfettered dominion and control over the collateral and

---

[1] Article 9 security interests also "float" in the sense that they attach automatically to proceeds. *See* § 2.03[B] *supra*.

[2] *See generally* 1 G. Gilmore, Security Interests in Personal Property §§ 2.2–2.5, 11.6–11.7 (1965).

[3] U.C.C. § 9-204, Comment 2 (1962 Official Text).

[4] 268 U.S. 353, 45 S. Ct. 566, 69 L. Ed. 991 (1925).

its proceeds created such an ostensible-ownership problem that the entire transaction was void as a matter of law.

The effect of rulings like *Benedict* was to impose expensive formalities on the ongoing financing of accounts and inventory. For example, "it was thought necessary for the debtor to make daily remittances to the lender of all collections received, even though the amount remitted is immediately returned to the debtor in order to keep the loan at an agreed level."[5] Many states overcame the policing requirements that constituted the substance of the *Benedict* rule by enacting laws that countered its effect.[6] Section 9-205(a) repeals the *Benedict* rule:

> A security interest is not invalid or fraudulent against creditors solely because:
>
> (1) the debtor has the right or ability to:
>
>> (A) use, commingle, or dispose of all or part of the collateral, including returned or repossessed goods;
>>
>> (B) collect, compromise, enforce, or otherwise deal with collateral;
>>
>> (C) accept the return of collateral or make repossessions; or
>>
>> (D) use, commingle, or dispose of proceeds; or
>
> (2) the secured party fails to require the debtor to account for proceeds or replace collateral.[7]

A lender with a nonpossessory[8] security interest might, as a practical matter, be quite concerned with policing the activities of its debtor with respect to collateral and its proceeds. The extent of policing measures now, however, is determined by business rather than legal considerations.[9]

§ 3.02   AFTER-ACQUIRED PROPERTY — § 9-204(a), (b)

[A]   General Applicability

Article 9 explicitly validates the use of terms providing for a security interest in after-acquired property.[10] Such terms are common with regard to all types of commercial loans, but they are most important with "revolving" forms of collateral like inventory and accounts. By their nature, these forms of collateral will dissipate over a period of time. Inventory will be

---

[5] U.C.C. § 9-205, Comment 1 (1962 Official Text).

[6] U.C.C. § 9-205, Comment 1. *Benedict v. Ratner* was based on New York law, rather than the federal law of bankruptcy.

[7] U.C.C. § 9-205(a).

[8] U.C.C § 9-205(b) makes it clear that nothing in the section relaxes the requirements for possession if attachment, perfection, or enforcement depends on a secured party's possession. Possession is discussed in Chapter 6 *infra*.

[9] U.C.C. § 9-205, Comment 2.

[10] U.C.C. § 9-204(a).

sold to buyers in ordinary course of business that will take it free from the security interest,[11] and the obligations that constitute accounts will be satisfied as the accounts are paid.

If a secured party continues to loan money against inventory or accounts, it must have its interest attach to additional inventory or accounts as they are acquired by the debtor or its collateral will ultimately disappear. An after-acquired property clause extends the scope of the security interest to cover the property as it is acquired by the debtor.[12] Without such a clause, a secured party would have to enter into a new security agreement with respect to each of the debtor's new acquisitions of inventory or accounts. In the absence of both an after-acquired property clause and a new security agreement, the secured party would be effectively unsecured with respect to new acquisitions.[13]

An after-acquired property clause is, in essence, part of the description of the collateral in the security agreement. Rather than covering only property like the debtor's existing inventory or accounts, the collateral is described to include any property of the type specified that is subsequently acquired by the debtor.[14] This arrangement creates a floating lien on a shifting pool of collateral.[15]

What is the mechanism by which a security interest attaches to after-acquired property? When the parties initially enter into their security agreement, the debtor does not yet have rights in such property. Indeed, the property may not even exist. Because of the debtor's lack of rights, the security interest cannot attach.[16] Attachment occurs immediately upon the debtor's acquisition of rights in the collateral, however.[17] The

---

[11] *See* § 11.03[A][1] *infra.*

[12] The case of *In re* Travelers Petroleum, Inc., 86 B.R. 246, 6 U.C.C. Rep. Serv. 2d 911 (Bankr. W.D. Okla. 1987), shows how an after-acquired property clause also can later bring some of the debtor's existing property within the scope of the security agreement. Trucks that were being used by the debtor as equipment later became inventory, and subject to the after-acquired property clause, when they were leased.

[13] New assets might qualify as proceeds, but tracing requirements would make their identification as such problematic. *See* § 2.03[B] *supra.*

[14] Parker Roofing Co. v. Pacific First Fed. Sav. Bank, 59 Wash. App. 151, 796 P.2d 732, 13 U.C.C. Rep. Serv. 2d 501 (1990) ("general intangibles . . . now or hereafter owned"); In the Matter of Penn Housing Corp., 367 F. Supp. 661, 13 U.C.C. Rep. Serv. 947 (W.D. Pa. 1973) ("inventory present and after-acquired" and "all present and future accounts receivable submitted, including new accounts receivable whenever acquired"); South Cty. Sand & Gravel Co., Inc. v. Bituminous Pavers Co., 256 A.2d 514, 6 U.C.C. Rep. Serv. 901 (R.I. 1969) (all of debtor's accounts receivable "now existing and hereafter arising").

[15] U.C.C. § 9-204, Comment 2.

[16] *See* U.C.C. § 9-203(b)(2) and § 2.02[C] *supra.* Valley Nat'l Bank of Arizona v. Flagstaff Dairy, 116 Ariz. 513, 570 P.2d 200, 22 U.C.C. Rep. Serv. 787 (Ariz. Ct. App. 1977) (security interest cannot attach in after-acquired property until debtor acquires rights in it).

[17] Babson Credit Plan, Inc. v. Cordele Prod. Credit Ass'n, 146 Ga. App. 266, 246 S.E.2d 354, 24 U.C.C. Rep. Serv. 437 (1978). With respect to accounts, the interest in after-acquired property attaches when the accounts are created. Shaw Mudge & Co. v. Sher-Mart Mfg. Co., Inc., 132 N.J. Super. 517, 334 A.2d 357, 16 U.C.C. Rep. Serv. 847 (1975).

after-acquired property clause provides the necessary agreement in advance,[18] and the value initially given by the secured party is sufficient to support extension of the security interest to the newly acquired assets.[19]

A question that has been litigated several times is whether, in the absence of an explicit clause, a security agreement covering all of a particular category extends to after-acquired property within the category. For example, suppose a security agreement describes the collateral as "inventory" or "all inventory." Do these descriptions mean "existing inventory" or "existing and future" inventory? A judicial finding that the term is ambiguous opens the door to extrinsic evidence to explain the parties' intent. If a bank lends against a revolving type of asset like inventory or accounts, it can introduce evidence of a course of performance, course of dealing, or usage of trade[20] to support its argument for an expansive interpretation. Suppose, however, an individual sells a business enterprise to another on credit and retains a security interest in "all inventory." Because the secured party is not providing ongoing financing, it is less likely that there will be convincing extrinsic evidence supporting an expansive interpretation.[21] The most plausible meaning is that the parties intended that the security interest attach only to the inventory delivered to the buyer as part of the sale of the business.

Although the courts generally have been permissive with ordinary-course financers of inventory and accounts,[22] there are decisions to the contrary.[23] The secured party's argument for implicit coverage of after-acquired assets is much weaker if the collateral is not of a revolving type.[24] The ease of avoiding the issue in litigation should provide ample motivation to use

---

[18] "This section follows Section 9-203, the section requiring a written security agreement, and its purpose is to make clear that confirmatory agreements are not necessary where the basic agreement has the clauses mentioned." U.C.C. § 9-204, Comment 5 (1972 Official Text).

[19] "[A] person gives 'value' for rights if the person acquires them . . . as security for, or in total or partial satisfaction of, a preexisting claim." U.C.C. § 1-204(2). *See also* Barry v. Bank of New Hampshire, N.A., 113 N.H. 158, 304 A.2d 879, 12 U.C.C. Rep. Serv. 732 (1973); In the Matter of King-Porter Co., Inc., 446 F.2d 722, 9 U.C.C. Rep. Serv. 339 (5th Cir. 1971).

[20] U.C.C. § 1-303(a)–(c). *Cf.* U.C.C. § 2-202 and Comment 1(c) (extrinsic evidence based on course of performance, course of dealing, or usage of trade admissible for purposes of interpretation without a showing of ambiguity).

[21] *See* Stoumbos v. Kilimnik, 988 F.2d 949, 20 U.C.C. Rep. Serv. 2d 333 (9th Cir. 1993).

[22] Kubota Tractor Corp. v. Citizens & S. Nat'l Bank, 198 Ga. App. 830, 403 S.E.2d 218, 14 U.C.C. Rep. Serv. 2d 1247 (1991); *In re* Shenandoah Warehouse Co., 202 B.R. 871, 32 U.C.C. Rep. Serv. 2d 573 (W.D. Va. 1996).

[23] Wollenberg v. Phoenix Leasing Inc., 182 Ariz. 4, 893 P.2d 4, 24 U.C.C. Rep. Serv. 2d 770 (Ct. App. 1994) (accounts); *In re* Balcain Equip. Co., Inc., 80 B.R. 461, 5 U.C.C. Rep. Serv. 2d 766 (Bankr. C.D. Ill. 1987) (inventory).

[24] *See, e.g.,* Dowell v. D.R. Kincaid Chair Co., 125 N.C. App. 557, 481 S.E.2d 670, 31 U.C.C. Rep. Serv. 2d 987 (1997) (court refused to imply after-acquired property clause for security agreement covering equipment).

specific language referring to after-acquired property in any security agreement that contemplates the inclusion of such assets.[25]

[B] Exceptions

Article 9 limits the reach of after-acquired property clauses in the context of consumer goods.[26] The limitation precludes a security interest created by such a clause from attaching to consumer goods, other than an accession, given as additional collateral unless the debtor acquires rights in the goods within ten days after the secured party gives value.[27] For example, suppose a secured party makes a loan and takes a security interest in a consumer's computer pursuant to a security agreement that includes an after-acquired property clause covering all computers and computer peripherals. The security interest will not attach to a new printer that the debtor acquires two weeks later unless the secured party extends additional value.[28]

A secured party needs to be careful with respect to after-acquired property clauses covering consumer goods, and perhaps the best advice is not to use such a clause at all. Assume that the secured party in the illustration in the prior paragraph forecloses upon what it considers to be its collateral. If it repossesses the printer in addition to the computer, it could incur conversion liability.[29]

A secured party must also be concerned about compliance with applicable state and federal consumer protection laws.[30] For example, a Federal Trade

---

[25] U.C.C. § 9-204, Comment 7 indicates states that "[t]he references to after-acquired property clauses and future advance clauses in this section are limited to security agreements. There is no need to refer to after-acquired property or future advances or other obligations secured in a financing statement."

[26] If the transaction is a consumer transaction, a description using the generic type "consumer goods" is insufficient as a matter of law. U.C.C. § 9-108(b)(3), (e)(2). Thus, in a consumer transaction a security agreement covering "all present or after-acquired consumer goods" would not attach to any collateral, including consumer goods owned by the debtor at the time of attachment and those acquired within ten days after value is given. Article 9 leaves open the possibility that a description using a category not defined in the Code might suffice. Even though such a description is not *per se* insufficient under the Code, it might be invalidated under other law, and even if valid the reach of its after-acquired aspect would be limited by the ten-day rule. Consumer transactions are discussed in § 1.04[A][1] *supra*.

Similarly, a description using the generic types "security entitlement," "securities account," or "commodity account" is ineffective. *Id.* There are no explicit limitations on descriptions using categorical groupings not defined in Article 9. U.C.C. § 9-108(b)(2). *See* discussion of investment property generally in § 1.04[E] *supra*.

Article 9 also contains limitations that preclude the use of "all commercial tort claims" to describe existing or after-acquired collateral of that type. U.C.C. §§ 9-108(e)(1), 9-204(b)(2). *See* discussion of commercial tort claims generally in § 1.07[F][2] *supra*.

[27] U.C.C. § 9-204(b)(1).

[28] *In re* Harris, 23 U.C.C. Rep. Serv. 220 (Bankr. N.D. Ga. 1977) (clause giving secured party security interest in replacement household consumer goods was ineffective to give security interest in such goods acquired more than ten days after the loan).

[29] For a discussion of conversion liability, see § 19.01 *infra*.

[30] Article 9's rules are explicitly subordinated to such laws. U.C.C. § 9-201(b).

Commission rule makes it an unfair trade practice for a lender or a retail installment seller to take from a consumer a nonpossessory security interest in household goods other than a purchase-money security interest.[31] The Federal Reserve Board has adopted a parallel rule that applies the same constraint on financial institutions.[32] Under the rules, "household goods" are defined to include clothing, furniture, appliances, one radio and one television set, linens, china, crockery, kitchenware, and personal effects (including wedding rings).

Another limitation can be found in the federal Truth-in-Lending Act and Regulation Z, which require that the property to which a security interest relates be clearly identified.[33] The Federal Reserve Board has interpreted the statute and regulation to mean that a creditor cannot claim that it has a security interest in all after-acquired property of the debtor in transactions to which the Act applies.[34] That interpretation has been upheld in a number of court opinions.[35]

The limitation on the effectiveness of after-acquired property clauses does not apply to consumer goods that qualify as accessions. An accession is an item of personalty that is attached to another item of personalty but retains its separate identity, meaning that it can be removed and sold separately.[36] If a secured party takes a security interest in a debtor's personal car, a clause in the security agreement extending the security interest to after-acquired accessions is fully enforceable. Thus, the secured party's interest will attach to assets like replacement tires and batteries whenever they are acquired and installed in the car.

§ 3.03 FUTURE ADVANCES — § 9-204(c)

Article 9 validates the use of clauses that provide that the collateral will serve as security for advances or other value that might be extended in the future, whether such advances are obligatory or discretionary.[37] The article uses the phrase "pursuant to commitment" to refer to advances or other value that a secured party is required to extend under the terms of the security agreement or another agreement.[38] An advance can be pursuant

---

[31] 16 C.F.R. § 444.2(a)(4).

[32] 12 C.F.R. 227.13(d) (Regulation AA). The Federal Reserve Board is required to promulgate deceptive trade practice rules that are substantially similar to designated rules prescribed by the FTC. This approach ensures that the limitations imposed by the FTC will also govern banks, savings and loans, and federal credit unions.

[33] 15 U.S.C. § 1638(a)(9) (1994); 12 C.F.R. §§ 226.8(b)(5), 226.18(m) (1995).

[34] Public Loan Co. v. Hyde, 47 N.Y.2d 182, 390 N.E.2d 1162, 4117 N.Y.S.2d 238, 26 U.C.C. Rep. Serv. 781 (N.Y. 1979).

[35] *In re* McCausland, 63 B.R. 665, 1 U.C.C. Rep. Serv. 2d 1372 (Bankr. E.D. Pa. 1986); Smith v. No. 2 Galesburg Crown Fin. Corp., 615 F.2d 407, 53 A.L.R. Fed. 406, 28 U.C.C. Rep. Serv. 212 (7th Cir. 1980).

[36] Accessions are discussed generally in § 15.05 *infra*.

[37] U.C.C. § 9-204(c).

[38] U.C.C. § 9-102(a)(68). In certain circumstances, a secured party's priority rights are enhanced for obligatory advances. *See* §§ 11.03[A][3], 14.02[C] *infra*.

to commitment even though an event of default or other event not within the secured party's control has occurred that would permit the secured party to be relieved of its obligation. [39]

A future-advances clause precludes the necessity of the parties' entering into another security agreement every time the secured party advances more money to the debtor. Through the clause, the debtor in essence agrees to grant a security interest in the designated collateral to the extent not only of the original advance but also of any subsequent advances. [40]

A future-advances clause is an efficient means to extend a secured party's status with each new advance because it obviates the need for a new security agreement at the time of the advance. A secured party that advances additional money under a security agreement that lacks such a clause will find itself unsecured with respect to the new advance unless it obtains a new security agreement to cover the advance. [41] In the absence of either a future-advances clause or a new security agreement, there is no agreement by the debtor to allow a security interest to attach to the collateral to cover the advance. A new security agreement provides the necessary debtor consent at the time of the advance; a future-advances clause provides it at the time of the original agreement.

Issues sometimes arise concerning the scope of a future-advances clause. The parties might include a clause with broad language yet nevertheless intend a much narrower scope. For example, the security agreement in *In re Eshleman* [42] contained a clause providing that the debtor's automobile "shall secure Debtor's obligations to pay the note of the Debtor of even date herewith . . . [and] all other liabilities of Debtor to Lender, now existing or hereinafter incurred . . . ." [43] A year and a half later, the secured party loaned the debtor additional money and obtained a new security agreement covering inventory, equipment, and accounts. The secured party forgot to perfect its security interest under the second security agreement and was therefore subordinated to a bankruptcy trustee with respect to the collateral described in that agreement. [44] The bankruptcy referee refused to allow the

---

[39] U.C.C. § 9-102(a)(68).

[40] Farmers Nat'l Bank v. Shirey, 126 Idaho 63, 878 P.2d 762, 25 U.C.C. Rep. Serv. 2d 566 (1994) (security agreement provided that security interest "is to secure payment and performance of the liabilities and obligations of Debtor to Secured Party of every kind and description . . . due or to become due, now existing or hereafter arising").

[41] Idaho Bank & Trust Co. v. Cargill, Inc., 105 Ida. App. 83, 665 P.2d 1093, 36 U.C.C. Rep. Serv. 691 (1983) (in the absence of future-advances clause, such advances are not within scope of security agreement). The lender can become secured with respect to a subsequent additional advance by entering into a new security agreement with the debtor. Thorp Fin. Corp. of Wisconsin v. Ken Hodgins & Sons, 73 Mich. App. 428, 251 N.W.2d 614, 21 U.C.C. Rep. Serv. 881 (1977). A future-advances clause simply precludes the necessity of entering into the second agreement.

[42] 10 U.C.C. Rep. Serv. 750 (Bankr. E.D. Pa. 1972).

[43] 10 U.C.C. Rep. Serv. at 751.

[44] Perfection was necessary because new collateral outside the original description was taken. A new act of perfection is not necessary merely because a future advance is made.

secured party's claim that the automobile served as security for the second loan. He successfully argued that the second loan "was so unrelated to the earlier loan transaction . . . as to negate the inference that the debtor consented to its inclusion."[45] The *Eshleman* court seems justified in finding that the parties never intended a security interest in consumer goods to cover funds advanced under a separate security agreement for collateral of a commercial nature.

Traditional judicial hostility has continued to assert itself in construing future-advances clauses. At one time, broad clauses were derisively labeled "dragnet clauses" and courts routinely refused to enforce them. Remnants of that judicial attitude, in the guise of the "same-class rule," have survived the adoption of Article 9. Under this rule, a clause describing future advances in general terms is enforceable only if the later advances are of the same class as the initial obligation;[46] otherwise, the advance is not considered to be related to the financing that was contemplated by the parties when they entered into the security agreement.[47] The decision in *In re Eshleman* discussed above reflects the same-class rule.

The drafters of revised Article 9 sought to rein in judicial hostility to dragnet clauses. The Official Comments state a single criteria for assessing the scope of a future-advances clause, and explicitly reject the use of other tests:

> Determining the obligations secured by collateral is solely a matter of construing the parties' agreement under applicable law. This Article rejects the holdings of cases decided under former Article 9 that applied other tests, such as whether a future advance or other subsequently incurred obligation was of the same or a similar type of class as earlier advances and obligations secured by the collateral.[48]

The court in *Pride Hyundai, Inc. v. Chrysler Financial Company, L.L.C.*[49] predicted that the Massachusetts Supreme Judicial Court would follow the direction of the comment if it were faced with the issue and applied the test set forth in the Official Comments. The debtor argued that it had not intended to secure certain debts arising out of an existing retail financing agreement when it authenticated a security agreement containing a future-advances clause. The court, however, concluded that the language used in the clause was clear and unambiguous in securing without exception all future and past obligations.

Notwithstanding the position taken in the Official Comments, courts may continue to apply the same-class rule, and thus secured parties are well

---

[45] 10 U.C.C. Rep. Serv. at 753.

[46] *In re* Smith & West Constr., Inc., 28 B.R. 682, 36 U.C.C. Rep. Serv. 989 (Bankr. D. Or. 1983) (all loans were of a commercial nature related to debtor's construction business).

[47] *In re* Blair, 26 B.R. 228, 36 U.C.C. Rep. Serv. 985 (Bankr. W.D. Tenn. 1982) (two personal loans on vehicles were sufficiently related, but business loan was not).

[48] U.C.C. § 9-204, Comment 5.

[49] 369 F.3d 603, 53 U.C.C. Rep. Serv. 2d 423 (1st Cir. 2004).

advised to draft their future-advances clauses with care.[50] A broad, general clause is simply an invitation for a court to strike the clause with respect to future, unrelated financing. To increase the chances that it will be upheld, the clause should express an intent to include unrelated financing.

The future-advances clause upheld in *In re Dorsey Electric Co.*[51] is illustrative. It provided for the inclusion of "all other indebtedness of every kind and nature, direct and indirect . . . whether or not the same shall be similar or dissimilar or related or unrelated to the primary indebtedness."[52] A clause that shows an intent to include unrelated financing is a good response to the same-class rule because the rule is based on the premise that, if an advance is not of the same class as the initial obligation, the consent of the debtor cannot be inferred.[53]

§ 3.04 FINANCING INVENTORY AND ACCOUNTS

Some of the most sophisticated financing transactions involve inventory, accounts, and their proceeds. These assets are expected to turn over on a regular basis.[54] As a result, they are the most likely candidates for financing transactions that use after-acquired property and future-advances clauses. These transactions thus can be creatively tailored to meet the specific needs of the parties with respect to their ongoing financing relationship.

Three financing patterns have become common: (1) factoring of accounts, (2) general financing of inventory, accounts or both, and (3) floor planning of inventory. Some of the parameters of these common financing patterns are discussed below.

[A] Factoring of Accounts

Factoring of accounts is the outright purchase of accounts from a dealer by a financing agency (typically called a factor). It does not involve a secured loan from the financing agency; rather, the accounts are sold by the dealer. The customers on the accounts (the account debtors)[55] are typically notified that their accounts have been sold and that they are to make payments to the factor when payments are due.[56] The factor typically purchases the

---

[50] *In re* Johnson, 105 B.R. 661, 10 U.C.C. Rep. Serv. 2d 1002 (D. Kan. 1989) (dragnet clauses are to be scrutinized carefully and strictly construed).

[51] 344 F. Supp. 1171 (E.D. Ark. 1972).

[52] 344 F. Supp. at 1175.

[53] Pellegrini v. Nat'l Bank of Washington, 28 U.C.C. Rep. Serv. 209 (D.C. Super. Ct. 1980).

[54] Inventory will be sold to buyers in ordinary course of business, and such a buyer will take inventory free of even a perfected security interest of which the buyer is aware. *See* § 11.03[A][1] *infra*. The obligation to pay money that is at the core of an account is satisfied as the account is paid.

[55] An "account debtor" is a person obligated on an account, chattel paper, or a general intangible. A person obligated on a negotiable instrument is not an account debtor, even if the instrument is part of chattel paper. U.C.C. § 9-102(a)(3).

[56] Although notification of the account debtor is typical, the parties are free to structure

accounts without recourse, meaning that, if an account debtor does not make timely payment, the factor cannot recover from the dealer that sold the account.[57]

Even though factoring of accounts does not involve a secured loan, the transaction nevertheless falls within the scope of Article 9. For reasons that have already been discussed and will be expanded upon in the current discussion, Article 9 applies to outright sales of accounts.[58] A factor's interest is called a security interest even though the accounts do not serve as security for an obligation,[59] and the agreement between the parties is a security agreement. Accordingly, a factor must be certain that the Article 9 formalities are observed. This means that the factor must reduce the agreement with the dealer to a record that describes the accounts and is authenticated by the dealer.[60] In addition, a factor needs to perfect its security interest by filing a financing statement in the appropriate office.[61]

Factoring is a service that enables a dealer to contract separately to have another party conduct the activities related to extending credit to the dealer's customers and assuming the risk that accompanies credit-related activities. A typical factor engages in investigations of the creditworthiness of customers, establishes available credit lines for those customers, does the bookkeeping with respect to accounts, sends the billing statements, and undertakes collection of the accounts. Each account is purchased by the factor at the time the dealer provides its customers with goods or services. Because the accounts are purchased without recourse, the factor also assumes the risk of any credit losses.

In exchange for assuming these duties for the dealer and the risks that they entail, the factor is compensated in accordance with the factoring

the transaction so that the dealer continues to collect the accounts as agent for the factor. If the dealer fails to remit the collections, the factor will be unable to recover from the account debtors for payments made to the dealer. An account debtor is credited for payments made to the assignor prior to receiving notice that the account has been assigned and that payments are to be made to the assignee. The notice must be authenticated by either the assignor (the dealer) or assignee (the factor). U.C.C. § 9-406(a).

[57] A factor is subject to "all terms of the agreement between the account debtor and the assignor and any defense or claim in recoupment arising from the transaction that gave rise to the contract" unless the account debtor entered an enforceable agreement not to assert defenses or claims. U.C.C. § 9-404(a)(1). *See* Systran Fin. Servs. Corp. v. Giant Cement Holding, Inc., 252 F. Supp.2d 500, 50 U.C.C. Rep. Serv. 2d 305 (N.D. Ohio 2003) (factor bound by arbitration clause in agreement between debtor and account debtor). For this reason, many factoring agreements provide for a right of recourse if the account debtor's failure to pay is predicated on a defect in the goods or services, and it is not uncommon for there to be recourse if the account debtor has an unsatisfactory credit rating.

[58] Although the discussion in this section is limited to accounts, Article 9 governs sales of accounts, chattel paper, payment intangibles, and promissory notes. U.C.C. § 9-109(a)(3). The rationale for inclusion of sales of these payment rights and some aspects of the mechanics of such transactions are discussed in § 1.06 *supra*.

[59] U.C.C. § 1-201(b)(35).

[60] U.C.C. § 9-203(b)(3)(A).

[61] Perfection by filing a financing statement is discussed generally in Chapter 5 *infra*.

agreement. The amount is negotiated between the parties and is typically based on a percentage of the value of the accounts purchased, commonly between one and two percent. Whether the account is higher or lower will depend on such factors as the number of accounts that have to be handled, the average value of each account, the projected volume, and the expected losses.

The factoring business is highly specialized and requires careful assessment of all relevant criteria. Keeping compensation low creates a competitive advantage that attracts business, but miscalculations can have disastrous consequences for a factor. Factoring allows the dealer to eliminate a credit department in its business, thereby saving costs that can be used to pay the factor's compensation. Economies of scale and modern credit information networks that use computers enable factors to provide efficient and effective service.

Some dealers will not be able to wait until the accounts become due before they receive their compensation from the factor. These dealers can negotiate an advance from the financing agency against some or all of the sales price of the accounts. These advances are relatively expensive, as in three percent or more over the prime rate.

[B] Financing Against Inventory and Accounts

A dealer that needs money immediately may sell its accounts to a factor or use them as collateral for a loan. If accounts are used as collateral, the dealer commonly collects them and remits the proceeds to the lender to reduce the outstanding indebtedness — *i.e.*, account debtors will not be instructed to pay the lender directly unless the dealer goes into default.[62] The dealer also typically bears the entire risk of nonpayment. The secured party's loan must be repaid, and nonpayment by an account debtor will not discharge any part of the dealer's indebtedness. By way of contrast, account debtors are typically instructed to pay factors directly, and the factor typically bears some or all of the risk of nonpayment.[63]

A dealer's inventory may also be used as collateral. Lenders do not generally consider inventory to be a particularly desirable form of collateral because of certain practical difficulties. With "big-ticket" items, lenders often insist that a percentage of the proceeds of each sale be remitted to reduce the outstanding indebtedness, but desperate dealers can easily sell "out of trust," diverting proceeds for use in their day-to-day operations. Other problems materialize only after repossession. If a dealer defaults because it could not sell its inventory, there is no reason to believe that a secured lender will fare any better. Problems such as obsolescence and

---

[62] A security agreement can provide for account debtors to be instructed to pay the secured party prior to default. Payments received by the secured party reduce the outstanding indebtedness. *See* U.C.C. § 9-607(a) (secured party may notify account debtors to pay it pursuant to agreement and, in any event, on default).

[63] *See* § 3.04[A] *supra*.

erroneous judgment concerning consumer tastes can leave the lender greatly undersecured notwithstanding the high costs associated with the inventory's acquisition. Even if the inventory has good value, the secured lender faces the necessity of making a forced sale of a large volume of merchandise. As a result, the value of the inventory often diminishes considerably following default.

Because of these problems and risks, many secured lenders pursue conservative strategies when lending against inventory. Lenders are usually unwilling to advance more than a small percentage of the value of the dealer's inventory. In other words, lenders typically require very high loan-to-value ratios. For example, a lender may be willing to advance only 25% to 40% of the inventory's value. A 40% loan-to-value ratio means that for every dollar of inventory acquired by the dealer, the lender is willing to advance only 40 cents.

Because the amounts available for financing against inventory are so low, most parties seek alternatives. One approach is to use warehousing arrangements to reduce the risks associated with inventory financing.[64] Another approach is to floor plan inventory when it consists of big-ticket items.[65]

Inventory financing is often used in conjunction with accounts financing or factoring.[66] Accounts are generally more attractive than inventory as collateral. Accounts arise when the dealer's inventory has been sold or leased to a willing buyer or lessee, eliminating concerns about the dealer's ability to sell or lease the goods and the realistic value of those goods. A lender often will be better able to assess the value of a dealer's accounts than to predict the value of its inventory in a forced-sale context. In the event of the dealer's default, the lender generally is better equipped to proceed against a dealer's accounts than against the bulk of the dealer's inventory.

These advantages are reflected in the marketplace. If a dealer produces quality accounts, a secured lender might be willing to advance as much as 85% of their face value. As an accommodation to the nature of a given dealer's business, such as seasonal build-ups of merchandise, a secured lender might be willing to finance the dealer's acquisition of inventory in conjunction with financing the accounts that it generates.

Accounts financing provides a dealer with great flexibility. The dealer can borrow more money against new accounts as they are generated. It can use the proceeds of accounts that it collects to repay the borrowed funds. Most agreements provide a dealer with an assured line of credit upon which it can draw as needed. The limit to the credit is established by the

---

[64] For a discussion of warehousing arrangements, see § 6.02[B] *infra*.

[65] For a discussion of floor planning, see § 3.04[C] *infra*.

[66] Indeed, a security interest in inventory attaches automatically to the accounts that are proceeds of that inventory. Proceeds are discussed generally in § 2.03 *supra*. Priorities in accounts that are proceeds of inventory are discussed in § 10.05[B] *infra*.

percentage of collateralization that is agreed upon in the security agreement. The pricing can be fairly high, as much as six or seven percent over the prime rate. The advantage, however, is that the dealer has to pay that amount only on the outstanding balance. The dealer can reduce its capital costs by keeping its balance low. It has the credit line, however, to take advantage of business opportunities that require liquidity.

Accounts financing poses significant risks of fraud. A dealer that encounters severe cash-flow difficulties may be tempted to use an accounts-financing arrangement as a means to obtain additional money. Because the dealer is entitled to borrow based on the volume of accounts generated in its business, the dealer might be inclined to falsify some accounts in the hope that it can borrow and repay the additional funds without the secured lender's learning of its dishonest activity. Falsification of accounts is tempting because they are so easy to fabricate.

Commercial finance companies that lend against accounts have developed mechanisms to detect fraud in order to minimize losses. They often seek verifications from the identified customers of the dealer to ascertain whether they really ordered and received the stated goods or services. They also typically insist that payments to the dealer be remitted to the lender without a change in form. One example of this practice is a "lock-box" arrangement in which account debtors are instructed to send checks payable to the dealer to a particular post office box. The account debtor believes that the dealer is being paid, but in fact the post office box is controlled by the lender. The security agreement authorizes the lender to collect the checks, thereby reducing the indebtedness. Secured lenders also make unannounced inspections of dealers' books and records, utilizing personnel who are specially trained to detect signs of fraudulent accounts. They must carefully control their personnel in order to minimize the risk of collusion between inspectors and dealers.

Because controls against the risk of fraud impose higher costs on accounts financers, accounts financing is economically feasible only if a dealer has a high volume of accounts. Depending upon the nature of the business and the types of accounts generated, it is not unusual to require a volume of between $500,000 and $1 million in outstanding accounts at any given time. Dealers with smaller volumes that need advances against accounts will be relegated to factoring their accounts and drawing some of the payment price as an advance. The choice between accounts financing and factoring of accounts thus often is not determined by the dealer but rather by the market forces that impose restrictions based on volume of business. Factoring can be a good source of immediate liquidity, but it does not provide the flexibility that is available with accounts financing.

[C] Floor Planning Inventory

One of the most attractive forms of inventory financing is commonly used when a dealer's inventory consists of big-ticket items, such as automobiles, construction equipment, or mobile homes. The suppliers of such items generally do not deliver goods on consignment or even extend much credit to dealers. They tend to insist that dealers pay at least most of the price at the time of delivery. Because most dealers do not have that kind of liquidity, they need to finance the acquisition of their inventories. Floor planning is the predominant method.

Floor planning consists of a two-part transaction. In the first part, the lender provides the funds to pay all or most of the dealer's costs in acquiring big-ticket items and takes back a purchase-money security interest that attaches to each item. [67] The purchase-money status of the lender will enable it to prevail with respect to the goods it finances against any prior secured party with an interest in the dealer's inventory. For example, the dealer might have secured an operating loan from another lender with a blanket lien on all its assets, including inventory. [68]

The second part of floor planning concerns the dealer's retail transactions. Most buyers of big-ticket items cannot afford to pay cash and thus must finance their purchases. The dealer could sell to a buyer on an unsecured basis, thereby generating an account. Given the amounts involved, however, a secured sale that involves the creation of chattel paper is much more likely. In the retail market, chattel paper generally consists of a single record, sometimes called a "retail installment sales contract," that combines the payment obligation and a security interest. Chattel paper can also be created if the buyer issues a promissory note to the dealer for the unpaid purchase price, together with a security agreement granting the dealer a security interest in the item purchased. [69]

The availability of a security interest is valuable for big-ticket items, like automobiles, because the value of the item and the existence of established markets for used goods of the type mean that the item can be readily converted into cash if repossession becomes necessary. Of course, a dealer that was too strapped for cash to purchase its inventory without outside financing is not going to be in a position to carry the paper of its customers, who will be paying on the chattel paper over a period of several years. The solution is to sell the chattel paper to the secured lender. [70]

The retail side can be the most attractive aspect of floor planning to the lender. The finance charge included in the chattel paper often is quite high, which enables the buyer of the chattel paper to realize a good return. As

---

[67] Purchase-money security interests are discussed generally in § 1.05 *supra*.

[68] For a discussion of priority in this context, see § 10.03[B] *infra*.

[69] Chattel paper is discussed in § 1.04[B][3] *supra*.

[70] Sales of chattel paper, like sales of accounts, payment intangibles, and promissory notes, are within the scope of Article 9. *See* generally § 1.06 *supra*. The similar practice of factoring accounts is discussed in § 3.04[A] *supra*.

The parties to a sale of chattel paper often agree that the dealer will buy the paper back if the account debtor (or the obligor if the chattel paper includes a negotiable instrument) goes into default, thereby shifting to the dealer the costs associated with foreclosing on the underlying big-ticket item.

a result, the secured lender often finances the dealer's acquisition of inventory at a relatively attractive rate of interest as the means to assure itself of acquiring the dealer's chattel paper with its high interest rate. The security agreement may link these two transactions so that the dealer is obligated to sell all of its chattel paper to the secured lender.

Part III

PERFECTION OF SECURITY INTERESTS

Chapter 4

PERFECTION IN GENERAL

§ 4.01 PURPOSE

A creditor or seller that retains a security interest in some of a debtor's property may subsequently learn that other parties claim a competing interest in the same property. Competing claims can be asserted by an array of potential claimants — including, *inter alia*, a purchaser (other than a secured party), another secured party, or a lien creditor (*e.g.*, a trustee in bankruptcy). The assertion of competing claims raises issues concerning priorities in rank-ordering the claims, and these issues are covered in Part IV of this book. The concern in this Part of the book is to explain the steps that a secured party can undertake to enhance its position with respect to potential competing claimants.

Taking one of the designated steps results in *perfection* of a security interest. Attachment of a security interest establishes the relationship between the secured party and the debtor and gives the secured party a special property interest in the collateral.[1] Perfection is relevant only to

---

[1] Farmers' State Bank of Palestine v. Yealick, 69 Ill. App. 3d 353, 387 N.E.2d 399, 26 U.C.C. Rep. Serv. 509 (1979) (even unperfected security interest is enforceable against a debtor).

the secured party's position vis-a-vis third-party claims to the collateral. Perfection has no bearing on the relationship between the debtor and the secured party, and an unperfected secured party has the right to enforce its security interest in the event of default.[2] By perfecting the security interest, a secured party reduces the risk that a third-party claimant can successfully assert a superior claim to the collateral.

Although perfection may be accomplished by a variety of methods, the general principle underlying the concept is simple. Because a security interest is created by a contract between the secured party and the debtor, its existence might be known only to the two principals. Perfection generally requires that the secured party take designated steps that are deemed to be sufficient to publicize its interest to other parties that might have an interest in the same property. This notice is intended to overcome, at least in part, problems of "ostensible" ownership.[3] A prospective buyer of the collateral, for example, has an obvious interest in knowing whether the offered property is subject to an outstanding security interest, just as a subsequent lender would want to know of a prior security interest.

Thus, perfection typically entails the steps that are necessary for a secured party to provide adequate public notice of the existence of its security interest. Although perfection will not guarantee priority against all potential competing claimants, it will substantially improve the secured party's chances of achieving priority.

§ 4.02 THE ALTERNATIVE METHODS OF PERFECTION — § 9-310

Article 9 identifies eight different methods by which secured parties can perfect their security interests. The various alternatives are all described, with applicable cross-references to other sections, in section 9-310. The availability of any given method of perfection depends upon the kind of personal property used for the collateral and, sometimes, upon the nature of the transaction. Often, more than one method of perfection is available, with different methods of perfection providing different levels of protection against third-party claimants (although every method will provide protection against lien creditors, including a trustee in bankruptcy). The method chosen by the secured party will reflect an assessment of the practicality of alternative methods — possession will not work for a manufacturer that needs to make use of its equipment but filing a public notice is ideal — and the risks associated with the available methods.

---

[2] Doyle v. Northrop Corp., 455 F. Supp. 1318, 25 U.C.C. Rep. Serv. 932 (D. N.J. 1978) (unnecessary in action between debtor and secured party to determine sufficiency of financing statement to perfect security interest because perfection only determines priority among competing claimants and is irrelevant to validity of security interest). The statement in the text assumes, however, that the obligor has not filed for bankruptcy. If the obligor files for bankruptcy, the Bankruptcy Code will permit the bankruptcy trustee to invalidate an unperfected security interest. *See* § 16.04[B] *infra.*

[3] Ostensible ownership problems are discussed in context throughout the book. For an overview, *see* § 1.02[B][2] *supra.*

[A] Filing a Financing Statement

Article 9's default rule requires that a financing statement be filed to perfect all security interests and agricultural liens.[4] All other methods of perfection are considered to be exceptions to this general rule.[5]

A financing statement is a simple form that is filed in the appropriate public-filing office to enable interested parties to obtain information indicating that there might be a security interest in personal property of the debtor. It is analogous to the public filing of a deed to show a mortgage interest in real property, except that most financing statements are filed in a distinct filing system and are considerably simpler than a real estate filing. Perfection by filing a financing statement is covered extensively in Chapter 5 *infra*.

[B] Possession

A secured party generally can perfect a security interest in goods or in any form of indispensable paper by taking actual or constructive possession of the collateral.[6] With respect to money, perfection by possession is the only method available;[7] with respect to other forms of indispensable paper, filing is available but possession maximizes the secured party's protection from third-party claimants. Perfection by possession is discussed in Chapter 6 *infra*.

[C] Automatic Perfection

In a few circumstances, a security interest becomes automatically perfected upon attachment, even if the secured party takes no other steps to publicize its interest.[8] The policy justifications and implications for exempting the applicable transactions from the normal public-notice requirements are explored in Chapter 7 *infra*.

[D] Temporary Perfection

Article 9 also allows automatic perfection of a limited duration in certain circumstances.[9] Temporary perfection is possible with instruments, certificated securities, negotiable documents, and goods in the possession of a bailee other than one who has issued a negotiable document for them.[10]

---

[4] U.C.C. § 9-310(a).

[5] U.C.C. § 9-310(b) (listing exceptions), and Comment 2 to that section.

[6] U.C.C. §§ 9-310(b)(6), 9-313.

[7] U.C.C. § 9-312(b)(3).

[8] U.C.C. §§ 9-310(b)(2), 9-309.

[9] U.C.C. § 9-310(b)(5), (9).

[10] U.C.C. § 9-312(e), (f), (g).

Temporary perfection is also generally available with respect to proceeds.[11] The details of temporary perfection are spelled out in Chapter 8 *infra*.

[E] Perfection Under Federal Law

Federal law includes some requirements concerning methods of perfecting a security interest.[12] For example, the Federal Aviation Act requires a security interest in an airplane to be perfected by filing with the Federal Aviation Administration.[13] Bowing to inevitable principles of federal preemption, Article 9 recognizes that filing a financing statement is not required and cannot even be effective to perfect a security interest if a federal statute or treaty provides for the use of a national or international registration system, a national or international certificate of title, or otherwise requires a different method of perfection than that specified in Article 9.[14]

[F] State Certificate-of-Title Statute

All states have enacted certificate-of-title statutes that cover motor vehicles and that may cover similar goods, such as trailers, boats, mobile homes, and tractors. In addition to establishing a presumption of ownership of the designated goods in favor of the person shown as title-holder on a certificate issued by the state, these statutes also provide that a security interest in the goods can be noted on the certificate. Generally, the process of obtaining such notation on the certificate of title is the exclusive method of perfecting a security interest in the designated classes of goods.[15]

To achieve consistency with these state statutes, Article 9 provides that the filing of a financing statement is neither necessary nor effective to perfect a security interest in collateral within the scope of a state certificate-of-title statute.[16] The nuances posed by these statutes are detailed in

---

[11] U.C.C. § 9-315(d)(3). When certain conditions are satisfied, the temporary perfection automatically extends beyond the applicable period, thereby constituting a form of indefinite automatic perfection.

[12] Federal preemption is discussed generally in § 1.07[A] *supra*.

[13] 49 U.S.C. § 1403. *In re* AvCentral, Inc., 289 B.R. 170, 49 U.C.C. Rep. Serv. 2d 1336 (Bankr. D. Kan. 2003).

[14] U.C.C. §§ 9-310(b)(3), 9-311(a)(1).

[15] *See, e.g., In re* Morgan, 291 B.R. 795, 50 U.C.C. Rep. Serv. 2d 596 (Bankr. E.D. Tenn. 2003) (the exclusive method in Tennessee to perfect a security interest in automobiles that are not part of inventory is through notation of the interest on the certificate of title in compliance with the state's motor vehicle title and registration laws and the secured party cannot supplement these laws with principles based on the equitable doctrine of subrogation); *In re* Charley's Automotive, Inc., 50 U.C.C. Rep. Serv. 2d 927 (M.D. Ga. 2003) (secured creditor possession of certificates of title signed by the seller of the vehicles insufficient for perfection because the security interest was not noted on the certificates).

[16] U.C.C. §§ 9-310(b)(3); 9-311(a)(2), (3). *But see* Carcorp, Inc. v. Bombadier Capital, Inc., 272 B.R. 365, 47 U.C.C. Rep. Serv. 2d 374 (Bankr. S.D. Fla. 2002) (motor vehicles that are part of a debtor dealer's inventory must be perfected by filing a financing statement rather than under the certificate of title statute).

Chapter 9 *infra.*[17]

[G] Control

The primary method of perfecting a security interest in deposit accounts, letter-of-credit rights, investment property, and electronic chattel paper is control.[18] Control must be used to perfect a security interest in deposit accounts[19] and letter-of-credit rights,[20] and it may be used to perfect an interest in investment property and electronic chattel paper.[21] The specifics on perfection by control are covered in Chapter 6 *infra.*

[H] Delivery

Article 9 permits a security interest in a certificated security in registered form to be perfected by delivery of the security certificate to the secured party even though the indorsement that is necessary for the secured party to take control is missing.[22] Delivery is nothing more than possession of the security certificate, but the term is used in order to conform Article 9 with the terminology of Article 8.[23]

§ 4.03 WHEN PERFECTION OCCURS — § 9-308(a)

A security interest becomes perfected when it has attached and when the applicable steps for perfection have been satisfied.[24] Satisfaction of the steps required for perfection will not of itself achieve perfection; the security interest must also attach to the collateral.[25] It simply makes no sense to talk in terms of perfecting an interest that does not exist.[26] The Code makes it clear that the steps to attachment and to perfection may be completed in any order by providing that if the applicable steps required for perfection are completed prior to attachment, perfection is delayed until the security

---

[17] *See* § 9.06 *infra.*

[18] U.C.C. §§ 9-314(a), 9-106.

[19] U.C.C. §§ 9-312(b)(1), 9-104.

[20] U.C.C. §§ 9-312(b)(2), 9-107.

[21] U.C.C. §§ 9-314(a), 9-105.

[22] U.C.C. § 9-313(a).

[23] U.C.C. § 8-301(a)(1) (delivery requires possession of the security certificate).

[24] U.C.C. § 9-308(a).

[25] In *In re* Browning, 66 B.R. 79, 2 U.C.C. Rep. Serv. 2d 724 (S.D. Ill. 1986), a financing statement filed in 1983 described the collateral as the debtor's crops to be grown during 1983 through 1987. Perfection did not result immediately in the later crops, because perfection requires attachment, and attachment requires the debtor to have rights in the collateral. *See also In re* Lanzatella, 254 B.R. 84, 42 U.C.C. Rep. Serv. 2d 1156 (Bankr. W.D. N.Y. 2000) (although the creditor complied with the perfection requirements, it did not have any written agreement that created a security interest).

[26] Bradley v. K&E Inv., Inc., 847 S.W.2d 915, 22 U.C.C. Rep. Serv. 2d 915 (Mo. Ct. App. 1993) (lender that failed to obtain executed agreement that met U.C.C. § 9-203's requirements for security agreement could not have perfected security interest in cars of debtor).

interest attaches.[27] Perfection occurs at the first point in time at which all of the requirements for both attachment and perfection are satisfied.

Because of practical aspects of achieving priority that will be explained later,[28] a prospective secured party will sometimes want to complete the applicable steps for perfection before the security interest attaches. For example, when it appears that the parties are about to reach a final agreement, a lender might insist that the prospective debtor authorize the filing of a financing statement that will then be filed in the appropriate office. The debtor might not sign the written security agreement or the secured party might not give value, each of which is a requirement for attachment to occur, until after the financing statement is filed. The order of completion of each requirement does not matter,[29] but fulfillment of all of the requirements for both attachment and perfection is required before there can be a perfected security interest.

The opportunity to file a financing statement prior to attachment is also significant in the context of an after-acquired property clause. A security interest in property acquired by the debtor after attachment first occurs cannot attach until the debtor obtains rights in the after-acquired property.[30] The secured party, nevertheless, can file a financing statement with respect to the original collateral and, so long as the description in the financing statement is sufficient to describe the after-acquired collateral, the single filing will be sufficient for both the original and after-acquired collateral.[31] The secured party then will have perfected status as to after-acquired collateral as soon as the debtor obtains rights in that collateral.[32]

§ 4.04 CONTINUITY OF PERFECTION — § 9-308(c)

Article 9 allows a security interest to be perfected by one method and thereafter remain continuously perfected through the process of tacking if there is a shift to another method of perfection. When different but nevertheless appropriate methods of perfection are subsequently used, the security interest is deemed to be continuously perfected from the date of

---

[27] U.C.C. § 9-308(a).

[28] *See* §§ 5.03, 10.01 *infra.*

[29] NBD-Sandusky Bank v. Ritter, 437 Mich. 354, 471 N.W.2d 340, 15 U.C.C. Rep. Serv. 2d 260 (1991) (order of applicable steps is not determinative for perfection).

[30] *See* § 2.02[C] *supra.*

[31] A previously filed financing statement, however, is insufficient to perfect an interest in after-acquired property when there is no security agreement. J.I. Case Credit Corp. v. Foos, 11 Kan. App. 2d 185, 717 P.2d 1064, 1 U.C.C. Rep. Serv. 2d 250 (1986).

[32] Bank of the West v. Commercial Credit Fin. Servs, Inc., 852 F.2d 1162, 6 U.C.C. Rep. Serv. 2d 602 (9th Cir. 1988) (bank acquired perfected security interest in debtor's after-acquired inventory, accounts, and proceeds at time transfer of the assets to debtor took effect because financing statement covering a security interest in such collateral was already on file). An originally filed financing statement will also support future advances against the same collateral, even though the interest does not attach with respect to the future advance until the secured party gives the new value associated with it. Thorp Fin. Corp. of Wis. v. Ken Hodgins & Sons, 73 Mich. App. 428, 251 N.W.2d 614, 21 U.C.C. Rep. Serv. 881 (1977).

the original perfection, *provided* that the interest was not allowed to become unperfected during any interim period.[33] A gap during which the interest was unperfected cannot be bridged by tacking, so that subsequent perfection would date only from the time perfection was accomplished after the gap. Allowing a gap to occur endangers the interests of a secured party because the general rules of priority are based on the principle of first-in-time, first-in-right. A secured party will thus want to be able to establish rights based on the earliest point in time.

A simple example illustrates the application of the continuity-of-perfection provision. Assume that, on March 1, a secured party takes a security interest in the debtor's stamp collection and perfects the interest by taking possession of the collection. On September 1, the parties agree that the collection will be returned to the debtor so that the debtor can remount several of the stamps. The secured party determines to perfect the interest further by filing a financing statement, which it accomplishes on September 1. If the financing statement is filed before the secured party relinquishes possession of the collection, the security interest will be continuously perfected from March 1.[34] If the collection is returned to the debtor prior to the filing, however, an intervening period will result during which the security interest will be unperfected. The perfected status thus will date back only until September 1, the date of filing.[35] The secured party will be vulnerable to any competing interest that arose between March 1 and September 1, a result that could have been avoided by maintaining continuity of perfection.

---

[33] U.C.C. § 9-308(c). *See* Mims v. First Citizens Bank, 913 So.2d 1098, 56 U.C.C. Rep. Serv. 2d 383 (Ala. Ct. App. 2005) (even though the assignor's financing statement lapsed and the assignee filed its statement after the lapse had occurred, the assignee had continuous perfection, initially under the assignor's filing and subsequently through the assignee's possession of the collateral on the date of the assignment and prior to the lapse).

[34] The reverse sequence of perfecting methods was effectively used in First Interstate Bank of Ariz., N.A. v. Interfund Corp., 924 F.2d 588, 14 U.C.C. Rep. Serv. 2d 247 (5th Cir. 1991). A security interest in a horse farm's chattel paper that was perfected originally by filing and subsequently by possession was deemed to be continuously perfected.

[35] *See In re* Stewart, 74 B.R. 350, 4 U.C.C. Rep. Serv. 2d 271 (M.D. Ga. 1987) (secured party became unperfected upon releasing possession of diamond ring back to debtor because execution of document to effect that debtor held ring in trust for secured party was not adequate method of subsequent perfection).

Chapter 5

PERFECTION BY FILING

§ 5.01 GENERAL METHOD—§ 9-310(a)

Filing a financing statement is the Code's default method of perfection. By filing a form that includes certain required information in a designated public office, a secured party publicly announces the possibility that it holds a security interest to any third parties that are concerned enough to search the public files. The filing of a financing statement for purposes of perfecting a security interest is thus analogous to the public recording of a mortgage to indicate an encumbrance on real estate. Third parties considering a transaction with the debtor concerning personal property capable of being perfected by filing should first examine the filing records for a financing statement evidencing someone else's interest in that property.

Article 9 provides, as a general rule, that a financing statement must be filed for perfection to occur.[1] Alternative methods of perfection may be used in numerous situations, but these alternatives are stated as exceptions to the general rule.[2] Part 5 of Article 9 is devoted to the filing process. Its provisions are explained and analyzed in this chapter.

§ 5.02   WHAT CONSTITUTES FILING—§ 9-516

As discussed below, Article 9 envisions the possibility of a number of different filings in the public records, including initial financing statements and various amendments such as continuation statements and termination statements. Article 9 uses the generic term "record" to refer to any of these filings.[3] If the objective of a filing is to perfect a security interest, the record that must be filed is referred to as an initial financing statement. The term "financing statement" means the sum of the filed records, including the initial financing statement and any subsequent filings that relate to it.

Article 9 includes some basic provisions that determine when any record is filed. Filing occurs on the completion of either of two events: (1) "communication of a record to a filing office and tender of the filing fee" or (2) "acceptance of the record by the filing office."[4] Filing does not require completion of the ministerial task of entering the financing statement into its correct location within the files or even of indexing the financing statement in the name of the debtor.[5] Because secured parties cannot complete these tasks, which are the responsibility of the filing office, they are not responsible for either their implementation or the errors made by filing officers.[6]

The first method of filing requires the communication of a record to the filing office and tender of the filing fee. "Communicate" is defined broadly

---

[1] U.C.C. § 9-310(a). Agricultural liens are also perfected by filing. *Id.*

[2] U.C.C. § 9-310(b). *See generally* Chapter 4 *supra.*

[3] "Record" means "information that is inscribed on a tangible medium or which is stored in an electronic or other medium and is retrievable in perceivable form." U.C.C. § 9-102(a)(69).

[4] U.C.C. § 9-516(a).

[5] "The failure of the filing office to index a record correctly does not affect the effectiveness of the filed record." U.C.C. § 9-517.

[6] *In re* Masters, 273 B.R. 773, 47 U.C.C. Rep. Serv. 2d 398 (Bankr. E.D. Ark. 2002) (secured party was properly perfected and did not bear the risk that the filing officer would erroneously terminate the financing statement without the authorization of the secured party); Chattanooga Agricultural Ass'n v. Sapp, 54 U.C.C. Rep. Serv. 2d 114 (Tenn. Ct. App. 2004) (secured party that complied with filing requirements perfected even though financing statement and attached exhibit detailing collateral were never indexed into the records).

to include, in addition to sending a written or other tangible record, transmitting a record by a means prescribed by rules of the filing office.[7] "Send" is defined to mean depositing in the mail or delivering for transmission.[8] This approach is designed to maximize the opportunities for filing officers to authorize the use of any technology to transmit the filing data, including electronic, voice, and optical.

This first method of filing is subject to a significant limitation. Section 9-516(b) includes an extensive list of reasons for a filing officer to reject a communicated record.[9] Refusal to accept for any of these reasons means that filing of the record does not occur.[10] Although the specifics are covered in detail in the discussion below,[11] justifiable reasons to refuse to accept an initial financing statement include the following: communication by a method that is not authorized, failure to tender the filing fee, omission of a required description of the real property to which the initial financing statement relates,[12] omission of required names and addresses, and omission of required information for a debtor that is an organization.[13]

The list in section 9-516(b) serves not only to establish the exclusive grounds for which a filing officer may reject a record for filing; the filing officer is required to reject a record for those reasons.[14] If a filing office fails in this duty and accepts a record that it should have rejected, filing of the record nevertheless occurs.[15] Filing officers who do their jobs properly will reject for any of the enumerated grounds that support rejection and filing will not occur. If the filing officer neither accepts nor rejects, but the filing fee is tendered, filing is deemed to have occurred.

Because a filing may be legally effective before the filing officer has performed the ministerial act of indexing the filing, a gap may exist between the time of perfection and the time a searcher can reasonably learn of the fact of perfection. Anyone who conducts a search during this interim may be misled by the failure of the search to show a recent filing that is nevertheless effective. Contributing further to a searcher's concern is the fact that filings are often backlogged, even though the filing office is

---

[7] U.C.C. § 9-102(a)(18).

[8] U.C.C. § 9-102(a)(74).

[9] U.C.C. §§ 9-516(b), 9-520(a) ("filing officer . . . may refuse to accept a record for filing only for a reason set forth in Section 9-516(b)"). The latter provision was deemed necessary because of problems in some states with filing offices rejecting filings for insufficient reasons. For example, a filing officer might ask for the social security number of an individual debtor, but the officer may not refuse to accept a financing statement that omits the number.

[10] U.C.C. § 9-516(b).

[11] See § 5.02 infra.

[12] Of course, a description of real estate is necessary only for a financing statement that serves as a fixture filing or that covers as-extracted collateral or standing timber. See U.C.C. § 9-502(b).

[13] See also § 5.03[A] infra on the required content for initial financing statements. Many of the grounds for rejection are predicated on the omission of required information.

[14] U.C.C. § 9-520(a).

[15] U.C.C. § 9-516(a).

required to complete the indexing within two business days after filing occurs.[16] A searcher is additionally vulnerable to effective financing statements that are not found because the filing officer has somehow lost or misfiled them.[17]

As between a searcher and a secured party that communicates a financing statement for filing, the latter might appear to be in the better position to initiate action that might alleviate the misleading appearances that can result from filing delays and errors; that is, the filing party could initiate a search for its own financing statement to determine whether it was properly handled by the filing office. Imposition of a search obligation on the filing party would, however, shift a significant risk to that party since the timing of effective filing can be crucial in deciding the outcome of a priority dispute.[18] The drafters chose not to impose this obligation on filers.[19]

Because much of the onus of the practical difficulties in the filing system is borne by parties that conduct searches, those parties should be aware of how to protect their interests as much as possible. For example, they should be aware of the extent of the backlog in filings in the particular jurisdictions in which they conduct searches. A prospective purchaser (*e.g.*, a buyer or a secured party) can then, before consummating a transaction with the debtor, insist upon waiting for that time period to pass. For example, a secured lender could insist on waiting for the time period to pass after making its filing before giving value to the obligor.

Article 9 addresses the backlog problem through two approaches. First, the filing office is required to respond to a search request no later than two business days after receiving it,[20] and the information provided to the searcher must be current based on a date no earlier than three business

---

[16] U.C.C. § 9-519(h).

[17] Cases have held filing officers liable for losses to searchers caused by their errors. *See, e.g.*, Hudleasco, Inc. v. State, 90 Misc. 2d 1057, 396 N.Y.S.2d 1002, 22 U.C.C. Rep. Serv. 545 (Ct. Cl. 1977) (error by filing officer in certifying absence of prior financing statement). The claims lie in negligence, however, and governmental immunity may be available under state tort law. After the Kansas Supreme Court in Borg-Warner Acceptance Corp. v. Secretary of State, 240 Kan. 598, 731 P.2d 301, 2 U.C.C. Rep. Serv. 2d 1725 (1987), upheld negligence liability of the secretary of state for several certifications that failed to disclose a prior filing, the Kansas legislature amended Article 9 to grant immunity to filing officers in conducting searches. A common response in jurisdictions in which filing officers remain potentially subject to claims for loss is for the officers to reduce their risk by offering very little assistance to searchers. In addition to filing officers, abstract companies hired to conduct a search have been sued for negligence. *See, e.g.*, Chemical Bank v. Title Servs., Inc., 708 F. Supp. 245, 9 U.C.C. Rep. Serv. 2d 402 (D. Minn. 1989) (title abstractor found not negligent for failing to conduct search under various misspellings of debtor's name).

[18] Recognizing the critical role of time of filing, Article 9 requires filing officers to mark the time of filing on each financing statement. U.C.C. §§ 9-519(a)(2), 9-523. It does not include a specific requirement on how to determine the time of filing. This determination is to be made by rules adopted by each filing office. U.C.C. § 9-519, Comment 4.

[19] U.C.C. §§ 9-519(a), 9-517.

[20] U.C.C. § 9-523(e).

days before receipt of the request.[21] Because filing offices sometimes cannot or will not comply with such time requirements, the drafters included another provision aimed at surmounting the backlog problem. A filing office or the appropriate official must offer to sell or license to the public on a nonexclusive basis copies of all records filed with it.[22] The copies are to be provided in bulk in every medium available to the filing office, and they must be available at least weekly. This provision facilitates access to the records by private companies that maintain parallel filing systems. If the official filing office fails in meeting its mandate to file financing statements in the time prescribed, searchers can choose to rely on any such privately-maintained systems.

§ 5.03　WHAT TO FILE

[A]　Requirements—§§ 9-502, 9-516(b)

The formal requisites for a filed financing statement to be sufficient to perfect a security interest are stated in section 9-502. To be sufficient, an initial financing statement must include:

- The name of the debtor;

- The name of the secured party or a representative of the secured party;

- An indication of the collateral covered; and

- A real property description if the collateral is as-extracted collateral or timber to be cut, or if the financing statement constitutes a fixture filing.[23]

An initial financing statement that does not contain this minimal information is not sufficient and thus cannot be effective to perfect a security interest,[24] even if the filing office accepts it.[25]

A filing officer should not accept, for the most part, any financing statement that is missing the information required under section 9-502. The filing office is required to reject a record for any of the reasons stipulated in section 9-516(b),[26] and most omissions of information required under section 9-502 are included as a reason for rejection.[27] Section 9-516(b) does

---

[21] U.C.C. § 9-523(c)(1). Section 9-526 imposes requirements on the appropriate official or agency to adopt and publish rules consistent with Article 9. Delays beyond the prescribed time limits are excusable for circumstances beyond the control of the filing office, provided that it exercises reasonable diligence under the circumstances. U.C.C. § 9-524.

[22] U.C.C. § 9-523(f).

[23] U.C.C. § 9-502(a), (b).

[24] U.C.C. § 9-502(a), (b).

[25] U.C.C. § 9-520(c).

[26] U.C.C. § 9-520(a). See § 5.02 supra.

[27] U.C.C. § 9-516(b)(3)(A) (name for the debtor); (b)(4) (name of the secured party); (b)(3)(D) (real property descriptions).

not list the omission of an indication of the collateral as a grounds for rejection; however, a financing statement can only be effective for the indicated collateral and a filed financing statement thus cannot be legally sufficient without an indication of at least some collateral.

Section 9-516(b) lists additional information that should be included in an initial financing statement:[28]

- A mailing address for the debtor;

- A mailing address for the secured party;

- Whether the debtor is an individual or an organization; and

- If the debtor is an organization: (1) the type of organization, (2) the jurisdiction of organization, and (3) either an organizational identification number or an indication that the debtor has no such number.[29]

Although this additional information is not included in section 9-502, it is nevertheless required information because a filing officer may,[30] and in fact must,[31] reject a financing statement that does not include it. The distinction is that the additional, required information is not necessary for the financing statement to be legally sufficient. If the filing office inadvertently accepts an initial financing statement that contains the minimum information required for sufficiency but omits an additional required item, the financing statement is still effective,[32] meaning that the security interest is perfected.[33]

The relationship between the information required by section 9-502 and that required by section 9-516(b) may be summarized as follows: Even though the filing office is required to reject an initial financing statement for the omission of any of the information listed in section 9-516(b), the filing is nevertheless legally sufficient to perfect a security interest if it is accepted for filing and contains the information required by section 9-502.

If a filing officer rejects a record that is communicated for filing, the officer must communicate the reason for the rejection to the person that communicated the record.[34] If the filing officer rejects a record for a reason that is not within the statutory grounds, the filing is effective "except as

---

[28] Requirements for other records presented for filing, and the filing office's responsibilities with regard to such records, are discussed in § 5.06 *infra*.

[29] U.C.C. § 9-516(b)(4), (5). The requirements that relate to the debtor are included to aid the searcher in excluding records that are revealed in a search but do not pertain to the debtor in question, and to aid in identifying the proper jurisdiction for filing.

[30] U.C.C. § 9-516(b).

[31] U.C.C. § 9-520(a).

[32] "A filed financing statement satisfying Section 9-502(a) and (b) is effective, even if the filing office is required to refuse to accept it for filing under subsection (a)." U.C.C. § 9-520(c).

[33] "[A] financing statement must be filed to perfect all security interests and agricultural liens." U.C.C. § 9-310(a).

[34] U.C.C. § 9-520(b) (communication of the reason for rejection must be according to filing-office rules, but in no event more than two days after the filing office receives the record).

against a purchaser of the collateral which gives value in reasonable reliance upon the absence of the record from the files."[35] The rationale for the exception is that rejections for invalid reasons should be rare given the severe restrictions on the filing office's discretion, and in any event the gap in the record caused by an invalid rejection should be short-lived because the reason for the rejection must be promptly communicated to the secured party. Since the rejected filing is ineffective only as to purchasers for value—persons that typically rely on the filing system—a secured party whose initial financing statement is wrongly rejected will be perfected as against a lien creditor, including a trustee in bankruptcy.

The simplicity of the financing statement stands in sharp contrast to the typical security agreement. Terms that are significant in a security agreement—such as the extent of indebtedness, the terms for payment, events of default, and covenants regarding the use of the collateral—have no place in a financing statement. Article 9 includes a statutory form which, if completed properly, will be sufficient to qualify as an initial financing statement.[36] Note that the form contains a space for taxpayer identification or social security numbers. This was included for convenience—the information helps searchers distinguish among persons with similar names—but is not mandatory. For most states, privacy concerns have caused filing offices to request that the information not be provided.

[1]   Names—§ 9-503(a)-(c)

The names of the parties play significant roles in the filing system. The filing officer places financing statements into the public files according to the name of the debtor.[37] The debtor's name is a logical basis upon which to index the files because an individual who searches the files is interested in ascertaining whether a particular person[38] has previously granted a security interest that would conflict with the searcher's proposed transaction. The search, thus, will be based on the debtor's name. If the debtor's name as it appears on the financing statement or as it is indexed is incorrect, a search under the correct name may not reveal the financing statement. The effect of errors and changes in the debtor's name is discussed later.[39]

Article 9 provides explicit guidance on the name of the debtor for a financing statement. If the debtor is a "registered organization," meaning an organization organized solely under the laws of a single state or the United States[40] that requires for the organization's existence the maintenance, in

---

[35] U.C.C. § 9-516(d).

[36] U.C.C. § 9-521(a) (initial financing statement form).

[37] Article 9 requires that filings be indexed in the name of the debtor. U.C.C. § 9-519(c).

[38] "Person" includes an individual or organization. U.C.C. § 1-201(b)(27). "Organization" includes, *inter alia*, corporations, partnerships, associations, governmental entities, trusts and estates.

[39] *See* § 5.03[C] *infra*.

[40] A foreign corporation is not a registered organization; nor is a domestic corporation that has articles filed in more than one state. Such "double domestications" are rare.

the state or the United States, of a public record indicating that the organization was formed, [41] the financing statement must reflect the name shown on the public record. [42] Thus, the name for a corporation is the name shown in the articles of incorporation as filed in the state of organization. [43] Article 9 also has rules for decedents' estates, [44] trusts, [45] and trustees acting with respect to trust property. [46]

The general rule for other debtors, including organizations that are not registered organizations, is that, if the debtor has a name, the financing statement is sufficient "only if it provides the individual or organizational name of the debtor." [47] Article 9 does not include a definition of what constitutes the name of an individual. [48] Section 1-201(b)(25) defines "organization" broadly to include both legal entities and associations that lack entity status. If the debtor does not have a name, as with some informal partnerships and associations, the financing statement is sufficient "only if it provides the names of the partners, members, associates, or other persons comprising the debtor." [49]

Rejecting an alternative approach previously followed in some jurisdictions, revised Article 9 explicitly states that a financing statement that includes only a trade name does not sufficiently name the debtor. [50] It also

---

[41] U.C.C. § 9-102(a)(70).

[42] U.C.C. § 9-503(a)(1) refers to the debtor's name as shown on the public records in the jurisdiction of organization. This means "the jurisdiction under whose law the organization is organized." U.C.C. § 9-102(a)(50).

[43] Among the other organizations that qualify as registered organizations are limited liability companies and limited partnerships. General partnerships and unincorporated non-profit associations depend for their existence on an agreement rather than a public filing and thus do not qualify. The term does not include a limited liability partnership, because the statement of qualification pursuant to which the partnership qualifies for limited liability does not create a new entity — the entity is still the original partnership.

[44] U.C.C. § 9-503(a)(2) (name of decedent and indication that debtor is an estate).

[45] U.C.C. § 9-503(a)(3) (information indicating that debtor is a trust and name as shown in organic documents or, if no name is shown, settlor's name and additional information to distinguish debtor from similar trusts).

[46] U.C.C. § 9-503(a)(3) (name of trustee and information indicating that it is acting with respect to trust property).

[47] U.C.C. § 9-503(a)(4)(A). Thus, if an organization has a name, even though it is not a separate legal entity, the name of the organization is to be used. U.C.C. § 9-503, Comment 2.

[48] See In re Erwin, 2003 Bankr. LEXIS 692, 50 U.C.C. Rep. Serv. 2d 933 (D. Kan. 2003) (because section 9-503 does not require an individual's full name, legal name, or exact full legal name, the use of the debtor's nickname "Mike Erwin" was sufficient to identify "Michael A. Erwin"). But see note 114 infra (discussing why the Erwin case was wrongly decided).

[49] U.C.C. § 9-503(a)(4)(B). Thus, if the organization that is the debtor does not have a name, the names of the individuals or other entities that make up the organization should be used. U.C.C. § 9-503, Comment 2. Of course, a lender could simplify matters by insisting that the organization adopt a name.

[50] U.C.C. § 9-503(c). See Dickason v. Marine Nat'l Bank of Naples, N.A., 898 So.2d 1170, 57 U.C.C. Rep. Serv. 2d 127 (Fla. Dist. Ct. App. 2005) (financing statement in trade name "Patio Plus/Inside Out" instead of the corporate name "The Sawgrass Group, Inc." ineffective).

provides that a financing statement is not rendered ineffective merely because it omits either (1) a trade name, or (2) except as set out above for debtors without a name, the names of partners, members, associates, or the like.[51] Thus, a secured party should state the individual name of a sole proprietor-debtor rather than the trade name under which debtor conducts the business,[52] although the trade name may be added as an additional name.[53]

The reason for this approach is that a sole proprietorship is not considered to be an entity, meaning that it cannot own property in its trade name, nor can it sue or be sued in that name. Moreover, trade names are too uncertain and lack enough common recognition among both secured parties and persons searching the records to form the basis for a filing system. The drafters strove for a degree of certainty in the notice-filing system. Relying on the extent of perceived recognition of a particular trade name as the standard of acceptability for filing injects vagueness that the drafters sought to avoid.

[2] Authorization—§§ 9-509, 9-510

Former Article 9 required a signature of the debtor on the financing statement. This requirement was compelled by two related considerations. First, the mandate of the signature meant that the debtor had to cooperate before an effective filing could be made. This participation guarded against, for example, a secured party that otherwise might overstate the scope of encumbered assets.[54] The signature requirement also served a verification function. Because the debtor had to participate at least to the extent of signing the financing statement, the effective financing statement reflected voluntary dealings between the parties with respect to the described collateral.

The requirement of the debtor's signature on an initial financing statement under revised Article 9 was eliminated to facilitate paperless, electronic filing,[55] and the control and verification objectives are satisfied through alternative methods. The debtor[56] must authorize the filing of an

---

[51] U.C.C. § 9-503(b). *In re* Wisniewski, 265 B.R. 897, 46 U.C.C. Rep. Serv. 2d 1192 (Bankr. N.D. Ohio 2001) (a reference to an incorrect trade name of the debtor did not make the financing statement seriously misleading because the financing statement correctly listed the debtor's name). A financing statement is also not rendered ineffective merely because it fails to indicate the representative capacity of the secured party or a representative of the secured party. U.C.C. § 9-503(d).

[52] *In re* Stanton, 254 B.R. 357, 42 U.C.C. Rep. Serv. 2d 1190 (Bankr. E.D. Tex. 2000) (filing in trade name "Elkhart Pharmacy" was ineffective when the debtor Stanton operated it as a sole proprietorship).

[53] Cross-filing under trade names can be useful because it might enable a searcher who does not know the rules to stumble across the filing, thus preventing a later dispute.

[54] The potential of a tort action for slander of title also operates to control overreaching.

[55] U.C.C. § 9-502, Comment 2.

[56] The term "debtor" means any person with an interest in collateral other than a person with a security interest or lien, and includes transferees of collateral and new debtors. U.C.C. § 9-102(a)(28). In some instances a secured party will want to file in the name of a transferee or new debtor, and it has statutory authority to do so. § 9-509(c), (b).

initial financing statement or of an amendment that adds either collateral or a debtor.[57] Merely by authenticating a security agreement, the debtor authorizes the filing of an initial financing statement that covers collateral described in the security agreement, as well as an amendment that describes proceeds of that collateral.[58] An amendment that indicates collateral not covered in the security agreement or adds a debtor must be authorized in an authenticated record.[59] Any person that files an unauthorized initial financing statement or amendment is liable for actual damages plus a statutory penalty of $500.[60] Furthermore, a filing is effective only to the extent that it is authorized.[61] Thus, if the debtor authorizes filing with respect to inventory but the secured party files for inventory and equipment, the filing is effective only as to inventory.[62]

[3] Addresses

The addresses of the parties are also required,[63] although, as discussed above,[64] they are not necessary for a filed financing statement to be legally sufficient to perfect a security interest.[65] The inclusion of the mailing address of the debtor can aid in determining the identity of the debtor since a searcher should know the debtor's address as well as its name. This information can help in distinguishing between debtors of the same name and in overcoming the misleading effect of filings that contain errors in the debtor's name.

It was initially envisioned that a searcher would contact the secured party to obtain relevant information concerning any transaction between

[57] U.C.C. § 9-509(a).

[58] U.C.C. § 9-509(b). Authentication includes both manual and electronic signatures. U.C.C. § 9-102(a)(7). *See* § 2.02[A][1] *supra*; *In re* Aliquippa Machine Co., Inc., 2006 WL 1121025, 59 U.C.C. Rep. Serv. 2d 773 (Bankr. W.D. Pa. 2006) (authentication of the security agreement constituted debtor's authorization for re-perfection by filing a second financing statement after first statement was allowed to lapse).

[59] U.C.C. § 9-509(a). Only the secured party need authorize the filing of an amendment that releases collateral. U.C.C. § 9-509(c). Releases are described in Section 9-625(b).

[60] U.C.C. § 9-625(e)(3). Damages are described in U.C.C. § 9-625(b).

[61] U.C.C. § 9-510(a).

[62] U.C.C. § 9-510, Comment 2. In this situation, the debtor could demand that the secured party file an amendment deleting "equipment."

[63] U.C.C. § 9-516(b)(4) (secured party), (b)(5)(a) (debtor).

[64] *See* 5.03[A] *supra*.

[65] *Cf.* U.C.C. § 9-502(a) (contents required for sufficient financing statement). *See In re* Hergert, 275 B.R. 58, 47 U.C.C. Rep. Serv. 2d 1 (Bankr. D. Ida. 2002) (errors in the address of the filed financing statement did not adversely affect the sufficiency of the financing statement as the address serves to indicate where required notifications can be sent to the secured party rather than to identify the secured party). *See also In re* Bonds Distrib. Co., Inc., 48 U.C.C. Rep. Serv. 2d 1212 (4th Cir. 2002) (unpublished) (substantial compliance was found despite the omission of the address of the secured party based on the policies underlying the new revision of Article 9, even though the revision was not yet in effect); *In re* Grabowski, 277 B.R. 388, 47 U.C.C. Rep. Serv. 2d 1220 (Bankr. S.D. Ill. 2002) (use of the debtor's separate business address sufficient to perfect a security interest in the debtor's farm equipment).

the secured party and the named debtor. In fact, however, very few secured parties are willing to reveal confidential information to searchers without permission from the debtor. A secured party's address is thus significant primarily as the place to which others can send notifications. If a person required to send a notification to a secured party sends it to the address provided on a financing statement, the sender will have satisfied its notification requirement, even if the address is in error.[66] The secured party will also be deemed to have received a notification delivered to that address.[67] Of course, a searcher will not want to rely exclusively on explanations provided by the debtor, and the Code provides a mechanism by which the debtor can confirm information regarding its transaction with the secured party of record.[68] A prudent searcher will require the debtor to obtain information through the use of this mechanism.

[4] Indication of Collateral

A financing statement is sufficient to perfect a security interest only if it "indicates the collateral covered by the financing statement."[69] "Indication" is broader than description, although a financing statement sufficiently indicates the collateral if it provides a description of the collateral effective under section 9-108.[70] A statement that "all assets" are covered is not sufficient as a description under that section,[71] but it is sufficient as an indication of collateral on a financing statement and therefore will suffice to perfect a security interest in any asset capable of being perfected by filing and within the scope of Article 9.[72]

The basic test for a description of personal or real property is that, whether or not specific, it must reasonably identify the collateral.[73] The drafters of original Article 9, where the test originated, clearly intended

---

[66] U.C.C. § 9-516, Comment 5. *See also* U.C.C. § 9-102(a)(74) (defining "sends").

[67] U.C.C. § 9-516, Comment 5. *See also* U.C.C. 1-202(d) (defining "notifies").

[68] U.C.C. §§ 9-210, 9-102(a)(4). This mechanism is discussed in § 5.03[B][2] *infra*.

[69] U.C.C. § 9-502(a)(3). First Nat'l Bank of Lewisville v. Bank of Bradley, 80 Ark. App. 368, 96 S.W.3d 773, 49 U.C.C. Rep. Serv. 2d 959 (2003) (description of "[a]ll equipment and machinery, including power driven machinery and equipment" in the first secured party's financing statement was sufficient to cover the 113 specific pieces of equipment listed in the second secured party's filing); *In re* Systems Eng'g & Energy Mgmt. Assocs., Inc., 284 B.R. 226, 49 U.C.C. Rep. Serv. 2d 608 (Bankr. E.D. Va. 2002) (description of debtor's accounts, equipment, and other collateral did not include litigation recoveries); *In re* Waldick Aero-Space Devices, Inc., 49 B.R 192, 42 U.C.C. Rep. Serv. 723 (Bankr. D. N.J. 1985) (security interest was unperfected because financing statement referred to collateral "Per the attached Schedule 'A' to be made part hereof," but no schedule was attached to the financing statement).

[70] U.C.C. § 9-504(1).

[71] U.C.C. § 9-108(c).

[72] U.C.C. § 9-504(2).

[73] *See* U.C.C. § 9-108 and the discussion of that section at § 2.02[A][2] *supra*.

a more liberal, functional approach to descriptions than the fanatical "serial number" test that often characterized earlier chattel mortgage cases.[74]

The functional approach to description sufficiency is stressed in the Comments: "The test of sufficiency of a description under this section . . . is that the description do the job assigned to it: make possible the identification of the collateral described."[75] A greater degree of precision is necessary in a security agreement than in a financing statement because the security agreement establishes the intent of the parties regarding the assets that will be subject to the security interest.[76] As in other contractual contexts, ambiguities are often resolved against the drafter.[77] A financing statement, in contrast, serves merely to notify interested third parties that the debtor has dealt with the named secured party concerning at least some property within the description. The financing statement is intended merely to alert the searcher to investigate further before transacting with the debtor.[78]

Descriptions in security agreements and indications in financing statements must, nevertheless, both be sufficient in order to fulfill their respective functions.[79] For example, if a security agreement describes the collateral as "inventory and accounts," but the financing statement indicates only "accounts," perfection does not extend to the security interest in inventory.[80] A third party who reads the financing statement would have notice

---

[74] U.C.C. § 9-108, Comment 2. McGehee v. Exchange Bank & Trust Co., 561 S.W.2d 926, 23 U.C.C. Rep. Serv. 816 (Tex. Civ. Ct. App. 1978) (description upheld despite errors of one digit in model year, engine number and license number of boat); In re Delta Molded Products, Inc., 416 F. Supp. 938, 20 U.C.C. Rep. Serv. 795 (N.D. Ala. 1976) (upholding description that stated model number, type of machine, factory modifications, and list of attached auxiliary equipment despite inclusion of incorrect serial number).

[75] U.C.C. § 9-108, Comment 2. See Planned Furniture Promotions, Inc. v. Benjamin S. Youngblood, Inc., 57 U.C.C. Rep. Serv. 2d 678 (M.D. Ga. 2005) (although financing statement described collateral as the assets of "Old Salem Furniture" and did not mention assets held under two other company names subsequently used by debtors, the court pointed to the inclusion of the address where the collateral was located as being sufficient to enable a prudent searcher to identify the described property).

[76] World Wide Tracers, Inc. v. Metropolitan Protection, Inc., 384 N.W.2d 442, 42 U.C.C. Rep. Serv. 1573 (Minn. 1986).

[77] Shelby Cty. State Bank v. Van Diest Supply Co., 303 F.3d 832, 48 U.C.C. Rep. Serv. 2d 790 (7th Cir. 2002) (court construed security-agreement description of "all inventory, including but not limited to . . . materials sold to Debtor by [Creditor]" against the secured party that drafted it).

[78] U.C.C.§ 9-504, Comment 2. See § 5.03[B] infra. Kubota Tractor Corp. v. Citizens & Southern Nat'l Bank, 198 Ga. App. 830, 403 S.E.2d 218, 14 U.C.C. Rep. Serv. 2d 1247 (1991).

[79] In re Lynch, 313 B.R. 798, 54 U.C.C. Rep. Serv. 2d 849 (Bankr. W.D. Wis. 2004) (financing statement describing collateral as "general business security agreement now owned or hereafter acquired" described the financial transaction under which the bank claimed its security interest but it did not indicate any of the collateral that was described in the referenced security agreement).

[80] In re Katz, 563 F.2d 766, 22 U.C.C. Rep. Serv. 1282 (5th Cir. 1977). See also In re American Home Furnishings Corp., 48 B.R. 905, 4 U.C.C. Rep. Serv. 631 (Bankr. W.D. Wash. 1985) (inclusion in security agreement of intangibles held broad enough to cover tax refund, but omission from financing statement left the interest unperfected).

of only the narrower description.[81] Conversely, had the security agreement stated only "accounts" and the financing statement indicated "inventory and accounts," the security interest would probably be construed as covering only the accounts.[82] The security agreement, of course, is the contract that creates the security interest.[83]

As mentioned above, Article 9 recognizes the use of the broadest-possible indication in a financing statement: "A financing statement sufficiently indicates the collateral that it covers if the financing statement provides . . . an indication that the financing statement covers all assets or all personal property."[84] The provision was in response to some court decisions under former laws that had been unwilling to uphold broad descriptions in financing statements.[85] The notice function that financing statements are intended to serve discredits these holdings.[86] Such a supergeneric indication will not suffice as a description for purposes of a security agreement, however.[87]

An interest in after-acquired property need not be indicated in the financing statement's description of the collateral. An after-acquired property clause may be included in a security agreement to eliminate the necessity for the debtor and secured party to enter subsequent security agreements each time the debtor acquires additional property that fits the description of the collateral.[88] For as long as a financing statement is effective, however, it functions without regard to the time at which the debtor acquires the collateral. The financing statement may be filed even before any security agreement has been entered into,[89] which means that it may be filed even before the debtor has rights or the power to transfer rights

---

[81] *In re* Marta Cooperative, Inc., 344 N.Y.S.2d 676, 12 U.C.C. Rep. Serv. 955 (N.Y. Cty. Ct. 1973).

[82] The issue turns on whether the court will admit extrinsic evidence to supplement the description in the security agreement. *See* discussion in § 2.02[A][2] *supra* of *In re* Martin Grinding & Machine Works, Inc., 793 F.2d 592, 1 U.C.C. Rep. Serv. 2d 1329 (7th Cir. 1986) (inclusion of inventory and accounts receivable in the financing statement description does not expand scope of security interest when those categories of property were inadvertently omitted from the security agreement's description of collateral). *See also* Landen v. Production Credit Ass'n of the Midlands, 737 P.2d 1325, 4 U.C.C. Rep Serv. 2d 240 (Wyo. 1987) (narrower description of "cattle" in the security agreement controlled over the description in the financing statement of "livestock" to exclude a security interest in the debtor's horses).

[83] *In re* Marta Cooperative, Inc., 344 N.Y.S.2d 676, 12 U.C.C. Rep. Serv. 955 (N.Y. Cty. Ct. 1973).

[84] U.C.C. § 9-504(2).

[85] *See, e.g., In re* Boogie Enterprises, Inc., 866 F.2d 1172, 7 U.C.C. Rep. Serv. 2d 1662 (9th Cir. 1989) (description of "personal property" lacks required specificity); *In re* Grey, 29 B.R. 286, 36 U.C.C. Rep. Serv. 724 (Bankr. D. Kan. 1983) (description "all personal property" held insufficient to perfect an interest in grain).

[86] *See* § 5.03[B] *infra*.

[87] U.C.C. § 9-108(c).

[88] U.C.C. § 9-204(1). "The references to after-acquired property clauses and future advance clauses in this section are limited to security agreements." U.C.C. § 9-204, Comment 7.

[89] U.C.C. § 9-502(d). *See* § 5.04 *infra*.

in the initial collateral. A prudent searcher who encounters a filed financing statement will inquire to determine the exact property that is subject to an effective security agreement. Nevertheless, despite unequivocally clear drafters' statements to the contrary[90] and the vast bulk of conforming case law,[91] an occasional court decision under former law refused to recognize perfection with respect to after-acquired property because the description in the financing statement did not include an after-acquired property clause.[92] The clear distinction between indication and description makes such decisions less likely under the revision.

A description of the affected real property is required if the collateral is as-extracted collateral, timber to be cut, or is fixtures and the filing is to be a fixture filing.[93] In these situations, the financing statement must also indicate that it is to be filed in the real property records and, if the debtor does not have an interest of record in the real property, provide the name of at least one record owner, thereby permitting the filing to be incorporated into the real estate recording system.[94] A security interest in these types of collateral may also be perfected from the date of recording of a real property mortgage if the mortgage indicates the assets covered and satisfies the requirements for a financing statement.[95]

[B] Notice Filing

[1] The Function of Notice

The filing of an effective financing statement does not indicate as much as an uninitiated searcher is likely to assume. For example, it does not even show that the parties have entered into a security agreement. Article 9 specifically provides that "[a] financing statement may be filed before a security agreement is made or a security interest otherwise attaches."[96] For reasons that will developed in a later chapter,[97] prudent secured parties in large transactions commonly insist upon "pre-filing;" that is, filing a completed financing statement before making a commitment to give the value necessary for the creation of a security interest. At most, therefore, a filed financing statement indicates only that there might be a security interest affecting the indicated collateral. The function that the filing system is designed to serve is strikingly modest.

---

[90] "There is no need to refer to after-acquired property or future advances or other obligations secured in a financing statement." U.C.C. § 9-204, Comment 7.

[91] *In re* Brace, 163 B.R. 274, 22 U.C.C. Rep. Serv. 2d 1184 (Bankr. W.D. Pa. 1994); American Nat'l Bank & Trust Co. of Sapula v. National Cash Register Co., 473 P.2d 234, 7 U.C.C. Rep. Serv. 1097 (Okla. 1970).

[92] *In re* Young, 42 B.R. 939, 39 U.C.C. Rep. Serv. 1041 (Bankr. E.D. Pa. 1984).

[93] U.C.C. §§ 9-516(b)(3)(D), 9-502(b).

[94] U.C.C. § 9-502(b).

[95] U.C.C. § 9-502(c).

[96] U.C.C. § 9-502(d). For discussion of the desirability of pursuing this option, *see* §§ 5.04, 10.01 *infra*.

[97] *See* § 10.01 *infra*.

The drafters of the original article adopted a system of "notice filing" that had been utilized previously in the Uniform Trust Receipts Act. The function of notice filing is described quite ably in the Comments:

> What is required to be filed is not, as under pre-UCC chattel mortgage and conditional sales acts, the security agreement itself, but only a simple record providing a limited amount of information (financing statement). The financing statement may be filed before the security interest attaches or thereafter. . . . The notice itself indicates merely that a person may have a security interest in the collateral indicated. Further inquiry from the parties concerned will be necessary to disclose the complete state of affairs. [98]

Once placed on notice of the possible existence of a security interest, the searcher can protect itself through further inquiry. [99] A financing statement simply cannot be relied upon to reveal all of the information needed by a prudent searcher.

[2] Requests for Information—§§ 9-210, 9-625(f), (g)

A searcher should not, of course, rely totally upon the debtor's explanation of the secured party's interest. The searcher who contacts the secured party for information directly, however, is likely to be rebuffed. [100] Accordingly, the searcher should ask the debtor to employ a Code mechanism that enables the debtor to verify its position vis-a-vis the secured party. The debtor is entitled to submit an authenticated record requesting a list of the collateral, [101] a statement of account, [102] or an "accounting." [103] A secured party must respond to the request within fourteen days after its receipt. [104]

---

[98] U.C.C. § 9-502, Comment 2.

[99] *In re* Wak Ltd., Inc., 147 B.R. 607, 19 U.C.C. Rep. Serv. 2d 915 (Bankr. S.D. Fla. 1992) (description directed reader to specific lease). The requirement that the financing statement include at least a statement indicating the types of collateral is designed to spare every prospective creditor from the need to make further inquiry of every party who has filed a financing statement against the debtor. *In re* Kirk Kabinets, Inc., 15 U.C.C. Rep. Serv. 746 (Bankr. D. M.D. Ga. 1974).

[100] Secured lenders, particularly banks, are often subject to confidentiality requirements. Comment 3 to U.C.C. § 9-210, reflecting this fact, states that "the secured party should not be under a duty to disclose any details of the debtor's financing affairs to any casual inquirer or competitor who may inquire."

[101] U.C.C. § 9-210(a)(3) (request to approve or correct a list stating collateral and reasonably identifying the transaction or relationship that is the subject of the request).

[102] U.C.C. § 9-210(a)(4) (request to approve or correct a statement of the aggregate unpaid balance as of a specified date and reasonably identifying the transaction or relationship that is the subject of the request).

[103] U.C.C. § 9-210(a)(2) (request must reasonably identify the transaction or relationship that is the subject of the request). An accounting is a record authenticated by the secured party that indicates the aggregate unpaid secured obligations (as of a date not more than 35 days before or after the date of the record) and identifies the components of the obligation in reasonable detail. U.C.C. § 9-102(a)(4).

[104] U.C.C.§ 9-210(b). A secured party who is a consignor or a buyer of accounts, chattel paper, payment intangibles, or promissory notes need not respond. *Id.*

A secured party that fails to comply with its duty to respond is liable to the debtor for $500 and for any actual damages caused by its failure.[105] As against a party misled by its failure to respond to a request for a list of collateral, the secured party may claim an interest only as shown in the debtor's list.[106] Although the utilization of these mechanisms appears to protect a searcher by providing information directly from the secured party, an understanding of the Article 9 priority rules will caution the searcher against transacting with the debtor with respect to collateral described in an effective filed financing statement even if the secured party disclaims any current interest in the described collateral.[107]

[C] Effect of Errors and Changes

[1] Errors—§ 9-506(a)

[a] Information Required for Sufficiency

Even when parties prepare the simplest of records, errors occur. Article 9 provides a standard for resolving the effect of errors that appear on filed financing statements: "[a] financing statement substantially satisfying the requirements of this part is effective, even if it has minor errors or omissions, unless the errors or omissions make the financing statement seriously misleading."[108] The objective of the drafters is clear from the accompanying Comments: "[The provision] is in line with the policy of this Article to simplify formal requisites and filing requirements [and] . . . is designed to discourage the fanatical and impossibly refined reading of statutory requirements in which courts occasionally have indulged themselves."[109] Bear in mind that if the issue is the sufficiency of a filed financing statement to perfect a security interest, the only items the court may consider are those listed in section 9-502.[110]

The effect of errors essentially is a matter of degree. The purpose of a filed financing statement is to provide notice that informs interested parties that a particular person might have granted a security interest in particular property. If the filing, despite some error, is reasonably sufficient to place such parties on notice, the error should not affect the filing's effectiveness.[111] The savings provision that permits effectiveness for financing

---

[105] U.C.C. § 9-625(f).

[106] U.C.C. § 9-625(g).

[107] See § 10.02 infra.

[108] U.C.C. § 9-506(a).

[109] U.C.C. § 9-506, Comment 2.

[110] See 5.03[A] supra.

[111] The financing statement in Fifth Third Bank v. Comark, Inc., 794 N.E.2d 433, 51 U.C.C. Rep. Serv. 2d 533 (Ind. Ct. App. 2003), incorrectly described the collateral as inventory rather than equipment. The appellate court nevertheless affirmed the trial court decision that the description was adequate because additional language in the description referring to computer products bearing the name Comark was sufficient to place searchers on notice.

statements that contain minor errors places a greater degree of responsibility on searchers. While even minor errors might tend to mislead, searchers have grounds to complain only if they have been seriously misled. For example, the Comments suggest that searchers will rarely be seriously misled by an error in the secured party's name.[112]

There is less tolerance for error if the information at issue is the debtor's name. Although the standard remains the same—whether the error is seriously misleading—there is a statutory presumption than *any* error is seriously misleading.[113] The presumption is rebutted if a search under the correct name using the standard search logic of the filing office would nevertheless disclose the erroneous financing statement.[114] This rule properly allocates to the filer the risk of a mistake in the debtor's name. However, the rule will result in considerable differences among jurisdictions in the near-term, particularly as the search standard still varies considerably among filing offices with computerized systems. Even a slight error will be seriously misleading if the computerized search logic utilized by the filing office can make only an exact match.

Article 9 provides a nonjudicial method for a debtor to complain on the record about a financing statement that contains errors or that was wrongfully filed.[115] The debtor can file a record that indicates that it is a correction statement and states the debtor's basis for believing that there is an error or a wrongful filing. The correction statement must also indicate any way in which the financing statement can be amended to eliminate the error. The correction statement becomes part of the financing statement[116] but does not negate its effectiveness.[117] In other words, a

---

[112] U.C.C. § 9-506, Comment 2. *In re* Hergert, 275 B.R. 58, 47 U.C.C. Rep. Serv. 2d 1 (Bankr. D. Ida. 2002) (name of secured creditor that was incorrect at the time of the effective date of the new revision to Article 9 was not seriously misleading).

[113] U.C.C. § 9-506(b).

[114] U.C.C. § 9-506(c). The search logic standards adopted in Kansas apply only standardized search logic to each name presented to the filing officer, with each search request processed using the name in the exact form it is submitted. Kan. Admin. Reg. § 7-17-22 & 21(b) (2002 Supp.). These regulations also provide that "[h]uman judgment shall not play a role in determining the results of the search, except with respect to supplemental responses regarding individual debtor names that are not automated." *Id.* at § 7-17-22(a). The court in *In re* Erwin, 2003 Bankr. LEXIS 692, 50 U.C.C. Rep. Serv. 2d 933 (D. Kan. 2003), based on these regulations, held that searchers must use reasonable diligence in formulating their requests, and using only the exact name of an individual debtor was not diligent. The decision is clearly wrong. *Compare In re* Kinderknecht, 308 B.R. 71, 53 U.C.C. Rep. Serv. 2d 167 (Bankr. 10th Cir. 2004) (reversing Kansas bankruptcy court decision holding that financing statement using debtor's nickname is not seriously misleading when a search under the debtor's legal name using the filing office's standard search logic would not produce the filed financing statement); Pankratz Implement Co. v. Citizens Nat'l Bank, 55 U.C.C. Rep. Serv. 2d 245 (Kan. Ct. App. 2004), *aff'd* 59 U.C.C. Rep. Serv. 2d 53 (Kan. 2006) (lower court erred in failing to find seriously misleading a financing statement that spelled the debtor's name as "House, Roger" rather than "House, Rodger" because a search using the standard search logic would not produce the filed financing statement).

[115] U.C.C. § 9-518.

[116] U.C.C. § 9-102(a)(39).

[117] U.C.C. § 9-518(c).

correction statement provides searchers with additional information but has no legal effect.

The term "financing statement" includes "any filed record relating to the initial financing statement"[118] and the first record filed is referred to as the initial financing statement. Through this mechanism, the seriously-misleading standard is made applicable to initial financing statements, amendments, continuation statements, termination statements and the like.

[b] Other Required Information

If the error relates to information other than that required by section 9-502 (*i.e.*, information not necessary for a filed financing statement to be sufficient to perfect a security interest), the "seriously misleading" standard does not apply. Thus, the issue is not whether the secured party is perfected but whether it can claim that status against a specific searcher who was misled.[119] Section 9-338 contains rules that in effect estop a secured party from taking advantage of even a sufficient financing statement if a subsequent purchaser of the collateral (*e.g.*, a buyer or a secured party) reasonably relies on the erroneous information to its detriment. For example, suppose the debtor's name is Jane Smith and she lives at 323 Apple Street. By coincidence, another Jane Smith lives at 323 Peach Street. If the secured party correctly provides the information required by section 9-502 but erroneously lists 323 Peach Street as the debtor's address, the error will have no effect on its perfected status. However, the secured party will be subordinated to a searcher who is misled into thinking that the financing statement refers to the wrong Jane Smith.

This approach properly balances the equities. As against a lien creditor, including a trustee in bankruptcy, the other required information is irrelevant. Those who give value in reliance on the appearances created by the erroneous record gain appropriate protection.

[2] Changes—§§ 9-507, 9-508

Even if a financing statement does not contain any errors, changes might occur after filing that can mislead subsequent searchers. The general rule under Article 9 is that such changes do not render a properly completed, properly filed financing statement ineffective.[120] There is an exception, however, for changes in the debtor's name. Section 9-507(c) provides:

> If a debtor so changes its name that a filed financing statement becomes seriously misleading under Section 9-506:

---

[118] U.C.C. § 9-102(a)(39).

[119] U.C.C. § 9-520(c) (cross-referencing § 9-338).

[120] U.C.C. § 9-507(b). *In re* Hergert, 275 B.R. 58, 47 U.C.C. Rep. Serv. 2d 1 (Bankr. D. Ida. 2002) (change in secured party's name after an effective filed financing statement did not render the original filing ineffective under section 9-504). For the consequences of filing a financing statement that contains incorrect information at the time that it is filed, *see* U.C.C. § 9-338 and the discussion at § 5.03[C][1] *supra*.

(1) the financing statement is effective to perfect a security interest in collateral acquired by the debtor before, or within four months after, the change; and

(2) the financing statement is not effective to perfect a security interest in collateral acquired by the debtor more than four months after the change, unless an amendment to the financing statement which renders the financing statement not seriously misleading is filed within four months after the change.[121]

A seriously misleading change in the name of the debtor has a limited impact on the effectiveness of a properly prepared financing statement.[122] The original filing continues to perfect the security interest with respect to the original collateral. Thus, a secured party not relying on after-acquired collateral need not worry about name changes. In addition, the original filing remains effective as to any collateral acquired by the debtor prior to the name change if the security agreement has an after-acquired property clause.[123] It also remains effective to perfect the security interest in collateral acquired during the four months following the change, even if the secured party never files an amendment to the financing statement to reflect the debtor's new name.[124] Thus, the secured party needs to file an amendment to the financing statement only to perfect its security interest in collateral acquired by the debtor more than four months after the change,[125] and then only if the name change has rendered the original financing statement "seriously misleading."[126] The amendment will be

---

[121] U.C.C. § 9-507(c). In Planned Furniture Promotions, Inc. v. Benjamin S. Youngblood, Inc., 57 U.C.C. Rep. Serv. 2d 678 (M.D. Ga. 2005), a name change from "Benjamin Scott Youngblood and Laura B. Youngblood" to "Benjamin S. Youngblood, Inc." was held to be not seriously misleading, because a search under the changed name would almost assuredly produce the filed financing statement. The result may be correct, but the court should have insisted that the secured party prove that a search under the corporate name, with the "Inc.," would have produced the financing statement in the individual name.

[122] The change in the debtor's name refers to the name of the individual, the partnership, or the corporation, as required in Article 9. A change in the trade name of a debtor will not bring into play the name-change provision when the debtor has filed under the proper name. In re Miraglia, 11 B.R. 77, 31 U.C.C. Rep. Serv. 1196 (Bankr. W.D.N.Y. 1991) (debtor's change of trade name from "Louie's Deli" to "Pizza Pit" held irrelevant because financing statement was in name of individual proprietor).

[123] In re Custom Coals Laurel, 258 B.R. 597, 44 U.C.C. Rep. Serv. 2d 1 (Bankr. W.D. Pa. 2001) (amendment to the financing statement is not required with respect to collateral acquired prior to the name change).

[124] Fleet Factors Corp. v. Bandolene Indus. Corp., 27 U.C.C. Rep. Serv. 2d 1105 (N.Y. 1995) (amended financing statement not required with respect to assets acquired by debtor six weeks after changing its name).

[125] In re Motrobility Optical Sys., Inc., 279 B.R. 37, 48 U.C.C. Rep. Serv. 2d 727 (Bankr. D. N.H. 2002) (filing made six months after name change from "Lancast, Inc." to "Aura Networks, Inc." held ineffective with respect to collateral acquired more than four months after the name change); In re Cohuta Mills, Inc., 108 B.R. 815, 11 U.C.C. Rep. Serv. 2d 338 (N.D. Ga. 1989) (failure to file in name of new corporation within four months of its creation left secured party unperfected with respect to all collateral acquired after the grace period).

[126] U.C.C. § 9-507(c). This standard is identical to the standard for determination of the

sufficient if it either provides the debtor's new correct name or comes close enough that the financing statement is no longer seriously misleading. The four-month grace period allows the secured party to check on the debtor's name on a periodic basis without having to monitor the debtor constantly.

Assume, for example, that a bank has a perfected security interest in all the debtor's present and after-acquired inventory. On May 1, the debtor's name changes in a manner that renders the bank's financing statement seriously misleading. The bank does not refile under the new name during the four-month grace period. On December 1, a finance company takes a competing security interest in the debtor's inventory. Despite its failure to refile, the bank will be perfected, and will thus have priority over the finance company,[127] as to all inventory on hand at the time of the name change and all inventory acquired through the end of August. It will be unperfected and subordinate to the finance company as to all inventory acquired thereafter. If the bank files its amendment reflecting the new name *after* the expiration of the grace period, but before December 1, it will have priority over the finance company as to all collateral, including that acquired more than four months after the name change.[128] There will have been a gap, but no harm will have befallen the bank.

The practical implication for searchers is that it behooves them to know any prior names the debtor may have used. Otherwise, a search under the debtor's current name may not reveal an effective financing statement. As indicated above, because many secured parties do not look to after-acquired property for their collateralization, their interests will be unaffected by changes in the debtor's name. This is true even though their financing statements may seriously mislead subsequent searchers. The secured parties that most commonly look to after-acquired property, and thus should be the most concerned with the refiling requirement, are financers against inventory or accounts.

Rather than simply a change in the debtor's name, a change might be made in the debtor's business structure. For example, a debtor operating its business as a sole proprietorship might incorporate, or a corporate debtor might merge with another corporation.[129] When collateral subject to a perfected security interest is transferred from the debtor to the new entity, does the security interest remain perfected? The general rule on continuation, expressed in section 9-507(a), is that a filed financing statement

---

effect of errors in the initial preparation of financing statements. *See, e.g.,* Union Nat'l Bank of Chandler v. Bancfirst (Seminole), 22 U.C.C. Rep. Serv. 2d 347 (Okla. 1993) (change from "Webb Metals, Inc." to "Webb Expanded, Inc." in corporate restructuring held not seriously misleading because names are linguistically similar); First Agri Servs., Inc., 42 U.C.C. Rep. Serv. 1583 (Wis. Ct. App. 1986) (financing statement listing debtor as "Gary and Dale Kahl" held seriously misleading when debtors began operating their farm as a partnership under the name "Kahl Farms" and filing officer had separate indexes for individual and organizational debtors).

[127] Priority contests between secured parties are discussed in detail in Chapter 10.

[128] U.C.C. § 9-507, Comment 4.

[129] U.C.C. § 9-508, Comment 2.

remains effective with respect to any collateral that is disposed of and in which a security interest continues, "even if the secured party knows of or consents to the disposition." This must be read in connection with section 9-315(a)(1), which provides that a security interest continues in collateral notwithstanding its disposition, "unless the secured party authorized the disposition free of the security interest." Thus, as to the transferred collateral, the secured party continues to have an enforceable, perfected security interest.[130]

Whether the transferee is bound by the terms, especially the after-acquired property clause, if any, of the existing security agreement turns on whether it is a "new debtor." A new debtor is a person that is bound by the terms of the security agreement entered into by the original debtor.[131] Whether a transferee is a "new debtor" is determined by section 9-203(d), which states:

A person becomes bound as debtor by a security agreement entered into by another person if, by operation of law other than this article or by contract:

(1) the security agreement becomes effective to create a security interest in the person's property; or

(2) the person becomes generally obligated for the obligations of the other person, including the obligation secured under the security agreement, and acquires or succeeds to all or substantially all of the assets of the other person.

Whether a person becomes bound as a new debtor is thus determined in most instances by law other than Article 9, primarily the law of contracts and business organizations. For example, if a corporation created by the debtor/sole proprietorship agreed to assume the business-related contractual obligations of the debtor, it would be a new debtor. The same result sometimes obtains under the laws governing the merger of corporate entities. If a person becomes bound as a new debtor, a new security agreement is not necessary to make the terms of the original agreement enforceable against it. Finally, if the difference between the name of the original debtor and the name of the new debtor is sufficient to render the filing under the original debtor's name seriously misleading, the filing is effective only as to the collateral transferred[132] and any new collateral acquired during the four months after the new debtor becomes bound[133] unless the

---

[130] If the transferee is located in a jurisdiction other than that of the transferor, the secured party will become unperfected if it fails to file in the transferee's name and in its jurisdiction within a year after the transfer (or earlier if the financing statement lapses in the transferor's jurisdiction) or otherwise perfect its security interest, as by possession. See U.C.C. § 9-316(a) and § 9.04 infra. The secured party has statutory authority to make such a filing. U.C.C. § 9-509(c).

[131] U.C.C. § 9-102(a)(56). The "original debtor" is a person that, as the debtor, entered into the security agreement to which the "new debtor" has become bound. U.C.C. § 9-102(a)(60).

[132] U.C.C. §§ 9-508(c), 9-507(a).

[133] U.C.C. § 9-508(b)(1).

secured party files an initial financing statement in the name of the new debtor before the expiration of the four-month period.[134]

Note that a new debtor is bound by all the terms of the original debtor's security agreement. Thus, if Corporation A buys all the assets of Corporation B and the owners of Corporation B then dissolve their corporation, and assuming that Corporation A is a new debtor, a secured creditor of Corporation B with an interest in all its present and after-acquired equipment will have a security interest in all the equipment owned by Corporation A prior to the acquisition, all the equipment sold by Corporation B, and all the equipment later acquired by Corporation A.[135]

[D] May Financing Statement Function as Security Agreement?

When perfection is accomplished by filing, a typical secured transaction will involve at least two separate records: (1) a security agreement that meets the requirements of section 9-203 for attachment and enforceability, and (2) a financing statement that complies with sections 9-502 and 9-516(b). A security agreement is often lengthy because it includes provisions that go far beyond the minimum requirements for attachment. A financing statement, in contrast, is generally a simple form that follows the model provided in section 9-521(a). The use of the simple form is efficient. The limited basic information that is required facilitates the practice of filing even before creation of the security interest. Filing fees based on the number of pages and whether or not the financing statement is in a standard form also create an incentive to keep filings simple.

The question sometimes arises whether a financing statement can serve both functions.[136] In this regard, the court's decision in *Evans v. Everett*[137] is instructive. The *Evans* court stated that "[a] financing statement which does no more than meet the [statutory] requirements . . . will *not* create

---

[134] U.C.C. § 9-508(b)(2). The secured party has statutory authority to make such a filing. U.C.C. § 9-509(b). As with name changes, a secured party that files its initial financing statement in the name of the new debtor after the four-month period expires will have a gap in its perfection but will still be perfected as to a third party whose interest arises after the secured party belatedly files.

[135] U.C.C. § 9-203(e)(1). Section 9-326 governs priority contests between the original debtor's secured party and a secured party that has dealt directly with the new debtor.

[136] Under prior law, a copy of the security agreement was sufficient to constitute a valid financing statement if it was filed and included all of the information required for a valid financing statement. U.C.C. § 9-402(1) (1972 Official Text). This provision created problems for filing officers, because a typical security agreement is much more detailed than a financing statement and is formatted quite differently. As a result, if a secured party filed a security agreement as its financing statement, it created more work for the filing officer in indexing the filing correctly (and, correspondingly, increased the likelihood of a filing or indexing error). Revised Article 9 no longer expressly authorizes the use of a security agreement as a financing statement, and many filing offices have established filing rules that would discourage or prohibit a party from filing a copy of a typical security agreement (which would look nothing like the approved financing statement form in U.C.C. § 9-521(a)).

[137] 279 N.C. 352, 183 S.E.2d 109, 9 U.C.C. Rep. Serv. 769 (1971).

a security interest in the debtor's property."[138] The court considered a basic financing statement to be insufficient because it does not create or provide for a security interest; that is, it does not contain language indicating an intent that there be a security interest. The financing statement before the court, however, contained more than the basic statutory requirements, stating that it *"covers the following type of collateral: (all crops now growing or to be planted on 5 specified farms) same securing note for advanced money to produce crops for the year 1969."*[139] This additional language was held sufficient to show that the debtor granted a security interest to the plaintiff.[140] Thus, a financing statement that satisfies the formal requirements for an enforceable security agreement can serve both functions.

§ 5.04 WHEN TO FILE—§ 9-502(d)

One caveat on the timing of filing is readily apparent. A secured party perfects to enhance its position vis-a-vis other potential competing claimants against the debtor's property. It is, therefore, in the secured party's interest to file sooner rather than later because, as a general proposition, the secured party will defeat most claimants whose interests arise after perfection but will be subordinate to most preceding claims. This ranking of competing claimants is the concept of priorities, which is covered in detail in subsequent chapters. Nevertheless, the basic importance of perfecting promptly is easy to grasp. Delay in perfection leaves the secured party vulnerable to competing interests.

A logical assumption is that parties will first create a security interest through the execution of a security agreement and the secured party will then perfect that interest by filing. The logic stems from the realization that you cannot perfect an interest that has not yet attached and therefore does not exist.[141] In this case, however, that logic is not reliable because Article

---

[138] 183 S.E.2d at 113, 9 U.C.C. Rep. Serv. at 774 (emphasis supplied).

[139] 183 S.E.2d at 114, 9 U.C.C. Rep. Serv. at 775 (emphasis supplied). The debtor had also signed a promissory note that contained a statement that it "is *secured by* Uniform Commercial Code financing statement of North Carolina." *Id.* (emphasis provided). *See In re* Outboard Marine Corp., 300 B.R. 308, 52 U.C.C. Rep. Serv. 2d 488 (Bankr. N.D. Ill. 2003) (additional documents were invoices that included a reservation of a security interest by the seller as part of the terms and conditions of the sales of pieces of machinery; court declined to grant summary judgment because, although the writings clearly showed the seller's intent to create security interest, there was a genuine issue as to whether the buyer had the same intention).

[140] The courts have been virtually unanimous in holding that a financing statement that does not create or provide for a security interest cannot qualify as a security agreement. *See,* e.g., *In re* Arctic Air, Inc., 202 B.R. 533, 31 U.C.C. Rep. Serv. 2d 233 (Bankr. D. R.I. 1996). Professor Grant Gilmore, a principal drafter of the original version of Article 9, disagreed, arguing that "nothing in § 9-203 requires that the 'security agreement' contain a granting clause." 1 G. Gilmore, *Security Interests in Personal Property,* § 11.4, at 347 (1965). For a case that relies on Prof. Gilmore's analysis to conclude that a financing statement qualifies as a security agreement if extrinsic evidence shows that the parties so intended, *see* Gibson Cty. Farm Bureau Co-op Ass'n v. Greer, 643 N.E.2d 313, 25 U.C.C. Rep. Serv. 2d 954 (Ind. 1994). *See also* § 2.02[A] *supra.*

[141] U.C.C. § 9-308(a). *See* § 4.03 *supra.*

9 specifically authorizes early filing: "A financing statement may be filed before a security agreement is made or a security interest otherwise attaches."[142] This provision allows a secured party to "pre-file," thereby "staking out" priority against possible competing claimants while making a decision whether to make a secured loan to the debtor.[143] Knowing about the priority advantage and the risks that it can help eliminate, lenders often require a prospective debtor to authenticate a record authorizing the filing of a financing statement[144] as a condition to continuing the negotiations on the secured transaction.

There is another consequence to the pre-filing rule. If a secured party files to perfect a security interest and then the secured obligation is fully satisfied, the filing, unless it is terminated or lapses first, will still be effective to perfect a security interest created much later and not originally anticipated as long as the description in the financing statement covers the collateral in the later transaction.[145]

§ 5.05 WHERE TO FILE—§ 9-501

A financing statement must be filed in the appropriate office to be effective. Interested parties are likely to search the files only in the office designated in Article 9 as the proper place for filing. A filing in any other office cannot meet the notice function which the filing system is intended to advance.[146]

Because Article 9 is state law, its provisions designating the office in which to file refer to offices within the borders of the enacting state.[147] Many secured transactions involve contacts with more than one state, however, as when a debtor moves from one state to another or has a physical presence in more than one state. Multiple-state contacts raise choice-of-law issues that are addressed by provisions that determine the state in which to file initially and the effect on filing of subsequent moves to another state.[148] The choice-of-law provisions are explained in a subsequent chapter.[149] The focus now is on the choices that confront a secured party that wants to file an initial financing statement once the appropriate state has been determined.

---

[142] U.C.C. § 9-502(d).

[143] U.C.C. § 9-322(a). *See* § 10.01 *infra* for a more detailed discussion of Article 9's "first-to-file-or-perfect" rule for governing priority between conflicting security interests in the same collateral.

[144] U.C.C. § 9-509(a)(1).

[145] *In re* Payless Cashways, Inc., 273 B.R. 789, 47 U.C.C. Rep. Serv. 2d 366 (Bankr. W.D. Mo. 2002) (filing of a financing statement three years prior to the debtor granting a security interest led to a perfected security interest).

[146] *See* § 5.03[B] *supra*.

[147] This point is made clear in the Code: "if the local law of this State governs perfection of a security interest or agricultural lien." U.C.C. § 9-501(a).

[148] *See* U.C.C. Part 3, Subpart 1.

[149] *See* §§ 9.01, 9.02 *infra*.

The vast bulk of filings under Article 9 are now made centrally, at the state level.[150] The exceptions are for (1) timber to be cut, (2) as-extracted collateral,[151] and (3) fixture filings for goods that are or are to become fixtures. Filings for transactions involving these situations are made locally in "the office designated for the filing or recording of a record of a mortgage on the related real property,"[152] *i.e.*, the office where interests in real estate are recorded. That office is most likely to be in the county in which the affected real property is located. A separate filing system for personal property is no longer maintained locally. Because of concerns about competing real-estate-based claimants with respect to a secured transaction using real-estate-related collateral, the filing with respect to such collateral is consolidated in the real estate filing system to provide effective notice to parties interested in the real estate.

§ 5.06 LAPSE AND TERMINATION OF FILING

[A] Lapse of Initial Financing Statement—§ 9-515(a)

The general rule under Article 9 is that a financing statement is effective for five years after filing.[153] Unless continued through the mechanisms discussed below, the effectiveness of the financing statement lapses at the end of this five-year period.[154] Lapse provides a means to keep the filing system from being cluttered with financing statements that are unlikely to have further commercial relevance. Note that the five-year period runs

---

[150] U.C.C. § 9-501(a)(1). Historically, the states required that certain designated categories of Article 9 filings be made at the local level. It was assumed that the local availability of the files facilitated searches. With the advent of computerized systems capable of handling massive quantities of information, it was inevitable that there would be movement toward centralized filing. The trend ultimately may culminate with a single national (or international) system in which searchers can search a single data bank from their desks and filers can make effective filings with the push of a button.

[151] "As-extracted collateral" is a defined term with two basic applications. First, the term applies to "oil, gas, or other minerals that are subject to a security interest that (i) is created by a debtor having an interest in the minerals before extraction; and (ii) attaches to the minerals as extracted." U.C.C. § 9-102(a)(6)(A). Second, the term refers to "accounts arising out of the sale at the wellhead or minehead of oil, gas, or other minerals in which the debtor had an interest before extraction." U.C.C. § 9-102(a)(6)(B).

[152] U.C.C. § 9-501(a)(1).

[153] U.C.C. § 9-515(a). A mortgage can be effective as a fixture filing if it contains all the information required of a fixture filing, and in such cases the mortgage is effective until it "is released or satisfied of record or its effectiveness otherwise terminates as to the real property." U.C.C. § 9-515(g). The Code also permits a filing as to the assets of a transmitting utility to be made centrally even though the filing covers fixtures. The rationale is that the fixtures are typically located in numerous counties, rendering local filings impractical. A filing as to a transmitting utility is effective until a termination statement is filed. § 9-515(f). A special 30-year period is available for public-finance transactions and manufactured-home transactions. § 9-515(b).

[154] U.C.C. § 9-515(c). *See In re* Hurst, 308 B.R. 298, 53 U.C.C. Rep. Serv. 2d 342 (Bankr. S.D. Ohio 2004) (perfection lapsed when five years expired because secured party had not undertaken any measures to continue its perfected status).

from the date of filing of the financing statement, not the date of attachment of the security interest. Even though a filing made before attachment does not result in perfection,[155] the effective period during which the filing perfects a subsequently attached security interest is measured from the date of filing. Note also that since the filing is effective for five years after filing, it lapses at the end of the anniversary date, not the day before.

The filing office can destroy any written record immediately upon lapse.[156] It must, however, maintain a record of the information destroyed for at least one year thereafter.[157]

[B] Continuation Statements—§ 9-515(c)-(e)

Obviously, some secured transactions will extend beyond five years, and the secured parties in these transactions will be concerned about remaining continuously perfected beyond the initial five-year period. The solution is the filing of a continuation statement. A timely continuation statement prevents a filed financing statement from lapsing.[158]

A continuation statement is a type of amendment that provides notice that the lapse date is being extended. It must identify the initial financing statement to which it relates by its file number and indicate that it is filed as a continuation statement or to continue the effectiveness of the identified financing statement.[159] A filing fee also must be paid.[160] The filing office is required to index all filed records that relate to an initial financing statement, including continuation statements, in a way that associates the

---

[155] U.C.C. § 9-308(a).

[156] U.C.C. § 9-522(b).

[157] U.C.C. § 9-522(a). The record must be maintained for one year after the financing statement would have lapsed even if it is terminated earlier. Thus, information will always be available for at least six years after initial filing.

[158] U.C.C. § 9-515(c). The courts have disagreed on the necessity of filing a continuation statement after a secured party has commenced litigation. *Compare* Hassell v. First Pa. Bank, N.A., 41 N.C. App. 296, 254 S.E.2d 768, 26 U.C.C. Rep. Serv. 1380 (1979) (secured party held to be unperfected despite having obtained judgment against debtor prior to expiration of five-year period), *with* Chrysler Credit Corp. v. United States, 24 U.C.C. Rep. Serv. 794 (E.D. Va. 1978) (filing of litigation tolled any obligation of plaintiff to file continuation statement because defendant was clearly aware of plaintiff's security interest). However, a prudent secured party should simply file a continuation statement in a timely manner rather than rely upon questionable case authority (such as *Chrysler Credit Corp.*) that a continuation statement is unnecessary.

[159] U.C.C. § 9-102(a)(27). Nat'l Bank of Fulton City. v. Haupricht Bros., Inc., 55 Ohio App. 3d 249, 564 N.E.2d 101, 14 U.C.C. Rep. Serv. 2d 215 (1988) (nonconforming filings not effective as continuation statement). If a security interest is assigned, it makes sense to file a record of the assignment. Otherwise, the assignor will continue as the secured party of record, and a continuation statement signed by the assignee will have to be accompanied by a separate statement of assignment authenticated by the secured party of record. The assignment of a security interest of record can be made in two ways: naming the assignee in the initial financing statement or making a subsequent amendatory filing. U.C.C. § 9-514.

[160] U.C.C. § 9-525.

related records to the initial financing statement.[161] The sum of the related records is the "financing statement."[162]

A continuation statement may be filed at any time during the six months that precede lapse of the financing statement.[163] A timely filing that contains the correct information extends the effectiveness of the financing statement for an additional period of five years.[164] The additional five years are measured not from the date of filing of the continuation statement, but rather from the date that the five-year period under the original filing ends.[165] A secured party that desires to extend the effectiveness of a financing statement even further may file additional continuation statements during the six-month periods that precede lapse *ad infinitum*.[166]

Unless it is perfected through some means other than filing,[167] a security interest becomes unperfected prospectively upon lapse.[168] The security interest is also "deemed never to have been perfected as against a purchaser of the collateral for value."[169] Even though the filing is effective and the security interest is thus perfected when the interest of a purchaser arises, this "retroactive invalidation" provision will cause the unperfected status of the secured party to relate back *ab initio* in the case of a later priority dispute with the purchaser.[170] In other words, a secured party that allows its filing to lapse will be treated, as against a purchaser for value, as if

---

[161] U.C.C. § 9-519(c).

[162] U.C.C. § 9-102(a)(39).

[163] U.C.C. § 9-515(d). A filing office is required to reject a continuation statement that is not filed within this six-month period. U.C.C. §§ 9-520(a), 9-516(b)(7). Any continuation statement that nevertheless is accepted for filing outside of this time frame is ineffective. U.C.C. § 9-510(c). In *re* Quality Seafoods, Inc., 104 B.R. 560, 9 U.C.C. Rep. Serv. 2d 1156 (Bankr. D. Mass. 1989) (filing continuation statement five years and one day after filing of financing statement caused security interest to be unperfected because financing statement had lapsed before filing of continuation statement).

[164] U.C.C. § 9-515(e); Bank of Holden v. Bank of Warrensburg, 15 S.W.3d 758, 41 U.C.C. Rep. Serv. 2d 708 (Mo. Ct. App. 2000) (filing a continuation statement on January 30, 1997 with respect to a financing statement with effectiveness running from January 30, 1992 through January 30, 1997 was sufficient to prevent perfection in the collateral from lapsing).

[165] U.C.C. § 9-515(e). *See also In re* Davison, 29 B.R. 987, 36 U.C.C. Rep. Serv. 717 (Bankr. W.D. Mo. 1983).

[166] U.C.C. § 9-515(e). *See also* United States v. Branch Banking & Trust Co., 11 U.C.C. Rep. Serv. 2d 351 (E.D. N.C. 1990).

[167] *See* Chapter 4 *supra*.

[168] U.C.C. § 9-515(c). *See also* State Bank of Harland v. Arndt, 129 Wisc.2d 411, 385 N.W.2d 219, 42 U.C.C. Rep. Serv. 1850 (Ct. App. 1986).

[169] U.C.C. § 9-515(c). The latest revision to Article 9 eliminates vulnerability of a secured party to invalidation of the prior perfected security interest as against lien creditors. The primary effect of this change is to protect the secured party from the bankruptcy trustee when the debtor files for bankruptcy prior to lapse. Priority contests between secured parties and lien creditors, including bankruptcy trustees, are discussed in § 14.02 *infra*.

[170] *In re* Hilyard Drilling Co., Inc., 60 B.R. 500, 2 U.C.C. Rep. Serv. 2d 370 (Bankr. W.D. Ark. 1986) (upon lapse, prior-perfected secured company became junior to competing security interest that had been perfected during five-year period of effective filing of prior-perfected secured party).

it had never filed at all.[171] This approach is followed to reduce the likelihood of circular priority. Note that there is no retroactive invalidation against nonpurchasers, notably lien creditors, including a trustee in bankruptcy. The trustee will lose to a secured party that was perfected on the date of the debtor's bankruptcy filing (and whose interest was not otherwise avoidable under bankruptcy law)[172] even if lapse later occurs.

The array of competing claimants that fall within the scope of the retroactive-invalidation rule is broader than initially appears. The term "purchaser" is defined to include a buyer, secured party, and any other party who acquires an interest in property through a voluntary transfer.[173] For example, suppose SP-1 takes and perfects by filing a security interest in Debtor's equipment. A year later, SP-2 does likewise. If a priority dispute comes to trial before SP-1's financing statement lapses, SP-1 will have priority.[174] If SP-1 permits its filing to lapse, however, SP-2 will gain priority over SP-1. Even if SP-1 files a new financing statement after lapse, it cannot repair the gap in perfection caused by lapse. The new filing will only operate to perfect SP-1 prospectively for five years.

[C] Termination Statements and Releases of Collateral— §§ 9-513, 9-509

A debtor will encounter significant difficulty in obtaining secured financing against any property that is described as collateral on a filed financing statement. The reasons for this reluctance on the part of prudent lenders are covered in a subsequent chapter.[175] The mere existence of this potential difficulty is sufficient for present purposes, however, to suggest that a debtor that pays off the debt and does not have an on-going financing relationship with a secured party will desire to terminate the effectiveness of the secured party's filed financing statement without waiting for lapse.

The solution for such a debtor is a termination statement.[176] A

---

[171] Federal Fin. Co. v. Grady Cty., Okla., 988 P.2d 908, 40 U.C.C. Rep. Serv. 2d 574 (Okla. Ct. Civ. App. 1999) (once creditor with priority allowed its financing statement to lapse, it lost its position of priority); Charles Ligeti Co., Inc. v. Ernie Goldberger & Co., 51 U.C.C. Rep. Serv. 2d 822 (Cal. Ct. App. 2003) (unpublished) (senior secured party that allowed perfection to lapse treated as unperfected at all times against perfected junior secured party even though junior secured party at all relevant times had actual knowledge of the senior's perfected status and the lapse of its financing statement).

[172] For discussion of applicable bankruptcy law, see Chapter 16 infra.

[173] "Purchaser" is defined to mean "a person who takes by purchase." U.C.C. § 1-201(b)(30). The term "purchase" is, in turn, defined to include "taking by sale, discount, negotiation, mortgage, pledge, lien, issue or re-issue, gift or any other voluntary transaction creating an interest in property." U.C.C. § 1-201(b)(29).

[174] Priority rules governing competing security interests are discussed in detail in Chapter 10 infra.

[175] See § 10.02 infra. For a case in which a subsequent creditor did not concern itself with a prior-filed financing statement on a debt that had been paid in full but found itself ultimately in a subordinate position, see Provident Fin. Co. v. Beneficial Fin. Co., 36 N.C. App. 401, 245 S.E.2d 510, 24 U.C.C. Rep. Serv. 1332 (1978).

[176] "[U]pon the filing of a termination statement with the filing office, the financing statement to which the termination statement relates ceases to be effective." U.C.C. § 9-513(d).

termination statement is an amendment to a financing statement which identifies the initial financing statement to which it refers by its file number and either indicates that it is a termination statement or that the identified financing statement is no longer effective.[177] As with continuation statements and all other records that relate to an initial financing statement, the filing office must index a termination statement in a way that associates it with the initial financing statement.[178]

A debtor may make an authenticated demand on the secured party to provide the debtor with a termination statement if "there is no obligation secured by the collateral covered by the financing statement and no commitment to make an advance, incur an obligation or otherwise give value."[179] A debtor may also demand a termination statement with respect to the filing of an initial financing statement that the debtor did not authorize.[180] Subject to an exception for consumer goods discussed below, the secured party may file the termination statement itself and pay the statutory fee or deliver the statement to the debtor, who may then present it with the fee to the filing officer.[181] A filed termination statement ends the effectiveness of a financing statement earlier than would occur through lapse.[182]

If a secured party fails to file or deliver a termination statement within twenty days after a proper demand,[183] it incurs the same liability as that imposed for filing an unauthorized initial financing statement or amendment. First, a civil penalty of $500 automatically applies in favor of the debtor.[184] Second, the secured party is liable for any losses to the debtor caused by the secured party's failure to comply.[185]

Although a secured party does not ordinarily have a duty to provide a termination statement absent a demand from the debtor,[186] an exception

---

[177] U.C.C. § 9-102(a)(79).

[178] U.C.C. § 9-519(c).

[179] U.C.C. § 9-513(c)(1).

[180] U.C.C. § 9-513(c)(4). Article 9 also includes other grounds for which a debtor can make an authenticated demand on a secured party for a termination statement: the financing statement covers accounts or chattel paper on which the person obligated has been discharged, § 9-513(c)(2), and the financing statement covers goods that were on consignment but are not in the debtor's possession, § 9-513(c)(3).

[181] U.C.C. § 9-525.

[182] J.I. Case Credit Corp. v. Foos, 11 Kan. App. 2d 185, 717 P.2d 1064, 1 U.C.C. Rep. 2d 250 (1986) (filing of termination statement under erroneous belief that debtor had paid in full was nevertheless effective to terminate perfection).

[183] U.C.C. § 9-513(c).

[184] U.C.C. § 9-625(e)(4). Household Fin. Corp. of Atlanta v. Raven, 136 Ga. App. 424, 221 S.E.2d 488, 18 U.C.C. Rep. Serv. 540 (1975).

[185] U.C.C. § 625(b). For example, the secured party's failure to file a timely termination statement could cause the debtor to be unable to borrow money from another secured party on favorable terms. In such a case, the debtor's foreseeable consequential damages could include the additional cost of obtaining substitute financing on less favorable terms (such as a higher interest rate).

[186] Full payment of all outstanding indebtedness does not terminate the effectiveness of

applies if the financing statement covers consumer goods. Under this exception, the secured party must file a termination statement within one month after the outstanding secured obligation is extinguished, even without a demand from the debtor.[187] The secured party does not have the option of delivering the termination statement to the debtor.[188] If the secured party receives an authenticated demand from the debtor, it must file a termination statement with respect to consumer goods within the earlier of twenty days after the demand or one month after the secured obligation is satisfied.[189]

If the secured party fails to file (in the case of consumer goods) or file or deliver (in other cases) a required termination statement, a termination statement may be filed without the secured party's authorization.[190] The filed termination statement is effective, however, "only if the debtor authorizes the filing and the termination statement indicates that the debtor authorized it to be filed."[191]

Instead of filing a termination statement, a secured party may release some or all of the collateral described in its financing statement. A release is accomplished by an amendment to the financing statement. As with other amendments, including termination statements and continuation statements, a release must identify the initial financing statement by file number[192] and must be filed in a manner that relates it to the initial financing statement.[193] An amendment that adds collateral or adds a debtor must be authorized by the debtor in an authenticated record,[194] but an amendment that operates as a release of collateral or a debtor need only be authorized by the secured party.[195] For records authorized by the secured party, there is obviously no authentication requirement.

As the case law demonstrates, secured parties that intend a partial release of collateral should be careful that they do not inadvertently create a termination statement instead. For example, in one case a bank erroneously checked a box on the form that it filed which indicated that the filing was a "termination statement" rather than a "partial release of collateral."[196] The description portion of the form showed that the bank intended

---

a filed financing statement. *In re* Bishop, 52 B.R. 470, 41 U.C.C. Rep. Serv. 1491 (Bankr. N.D. 1985). Absent the required demand from the debtor, a secured party is not under a duty to prepare or file a termination statement. Texas Kenworth Corp. v. First Nat'l Bank of Bethany, 564 P.2d 222, 21 U.C.C. Rep. Serv. 1512 (Okla. 1977).

[187] U.C.C. § 9-513(a).

[188] *Id.*

[189] U.C.C. § 9-513(b).

[190] U.C.C. § 9-509(d)(2).

[191] *Id.*

[192] U.C.C. § 9-512(a)(1).

[193] U.C.C. § 519(c).

[194] U.C.C. § 9-509(a)(1).

[195] U.C.C. § 9-509(d)(1).

[196] *In re* Kitchin Equip. Co. of Va., Inc., 960 F.2d 1242, 17 U.C.C. Rep. Serv. 2d 322 (4th

to release only two specific items of collateral, whereas its security interest was in nearly all of the debtor's assets. The court, nevertheless, held that, by checking the box, the bank created an effective termination statement. To hold otherwise would be to permit a filing to be effective even though it would mislead subsequent searchers.

Cir. 1992). *See also, In re* Silvernail Mirror & Glass, Inc., 142 B.R. 987, 18 U.C.C. Rep. Serv. 2d 322 (Bankr. M.D. Fla. 1992); *In re* Pacific Trencher & Equip., Inc., 735 F.2d 362, 38 U.C.C. Rep. Serv. 1121 (9th Cir. 1984).

Chapter 6

PERFECTION BY POSSESSION AND CONTROL

§ 6.01　POSSESSION GENERALLY

[A]　History

The Code's approach to perfection by possession is illuminated by the problems surrounding nineteenth-century secured financing. Common-law judges in the first half of that century refused to enforce "chattel mortgages" in which the debtor retained possession of the collateral. The perceived problem was ostensible ownership—the arrangement could mislead third parties into believing that the debtor had unfettered ownership of the

155

collateral. Courts were concerned that another creditor might be induced to make an ill-advised loan because the debtor's apparent ownership of the collateral would lead the creditor to miscalculate the debtor's net worth. As a result, courts routinely voided nonpossessory security arrangements, classifying them as fraudulent conveyances.[1] Because the arrangements were void *ab initio*, creditors were precluded from foreclosing even if no third party was misled.

An ostensible-ownership problem did not exist if a debtor surrendered possession of collateral to a creditor.[2] This arrangement, called a "pledge" at common law,[3] provided sufficient notice to third parties to overcome judicial concerns about fraud.[4] The pledge, however, was not sufficient to meet the needs of the marketplace because it was impractical for borrowers to surrender possession of assets used in the ordinary course of their business affairs.

Responding to these needs, state legislatures began to enact chattel mortgage recording acts that permitted nonpossessory security interests conditioned on creditors placing notices describing their interests in the public records. The legislatures saw filing as a satisfactory substitute for possession, but the courts remained hostile. They required the description of the collateral in the filing to be very specific, and any mistake, such as transposing digits within a serial number, could lead to judicial invalidation of the arrangement as fraudulent. Of course, a failure to file at all led to the same result.

The Code's approach to filing and possession is radically at odds with this history. Filing is the default method of perfection,[5] with possession one of several substitutes.[6] The Code facilitates filing by dramatically reducing the formal requirements for an effective financing statement. Serial number specificity is no longer necessary; all that is required is an indication of the collateral sufficient to place a searcher on notice.[7] The Code also specifies that a security interest is not fraudulent merely because the debtor retains

---

[1] *See, e.g.*, Clow v. Woods, 5 Sergeant & Rawle 275, 9 Am. Dec. 346 (Pa. 1819). This line of cases can be traced to *Twyne's Case*, 76 Eng. Rep. 809, 3 Coke 80 (Star Ch. 1601).

[2] Although pledges were routinely enforced at common law, it is worth noting that the pledge does not entirely remove the ostensible-ownership problem. Third parties can still be misled about the nature of a creditor's interest in pledged assets, *e.g.*, the debtor could advise a prospective third-party lender that the creditor in possession of a pledged asset is merely a bailee of that asset.

[3] *See* Restatement of Security § 1 (1941) (a pledge constitutes a bailment to secure an obligation). The origins of the pledge can be traced to all of the ancient nations. A. Dobie, *Handbook on the Law of Bailments and Carriers* § 70 at 173-74 (1914).

[4] For an extensive array of citations to pre-Code authorities on the law of the pledge, see R. Hillman, J. McDonnell, & S. Nickles, *Common Law and Equity Under the Uniform Commercial Code* ¶ 23.01 (1985).

[5] U.C.C. § 9-310(a) (filing mandatory absent provision to the contrary).

[6] U.C.C. § 9-310(b)(6) (possession available if permitted by U.C.C. § 9-313).

[7] *See* § 5.03[A][4] *supra*.

control of the collateral.[8] Thus, even an unperfected nonpossessory security interest can be enforced against the debtor.[9]

The provisions authorizing (or, in the case of money, mandating)[10] possession as a method of perfection are the modern counterpart of the pledge. Although the term "pledge" is still commonly used, reference to the arrangement as a "possessory Article 9 security interest" is more precise.

[B] Possession Under Article 9—§ 9-313

Section 9-313 provides that possession is an appropriate method of perfection for tangible negotiable documents,[11] goods, instruments, money, and tangible chattel paper. In addition, a secured party may perfect a security interest in a certificated security by taking delivery of the certificate as provided in section 8-301.[12] The listing includes goods and virtually all the kinds of personal property that can be reduced to the form of an indispensable paper.[13]

The intangible categories, such as accounts and general intangibles, are omitted.[14] With minor exceptions,[15] security interests in intangible assets may be perfected only by filing a financing statement. For collateral other than goods, perfection by possession requires a writing that is the physical embodiment of underlying rights in such a form that the rights may be transferred by transfer of the writing. The right to payment created by an account, for example, does not satisfy this requirement.[16] Tangible writings that indicate the existence of an account—ledger entries, invoices, written contracts, *etc.*—are not recognized as the physical embodiment of the right to be paid. They have evidentiary value, but the right to be paid can be enforced by an assignee that does not acquire possession of them.

---

[8] U.C.C. § 9-205(a)(1)(A). *See* § 3.01 *supra*.

[9] The adverse consequence of failing to perfect is the potential loss of priority to competing third-party interests in the collateral.

[10] U.C.C. § 9-312(b)(3). Money is defined in U.C.C. § 1-201(b)(24). The court in State of Minnesota v. 14,000 Dollars, 345 N.W.2d 277, 38 U.C.C. Rep. Serv. 1007 (Minn. Ct. App. 1984) erred by holding that a security interest cannot attach to money, because U.C.C. § 9-313 explicitly recognizes such an interest.

[11] Revised Article 7 (2003 Official Text) provides for both tangible and electronic documents, and conforming changes have been made to Article 9 to accommodate the distinction.

[12] Delivery is nothing more than possession, but the term is used to conform to the usage of Article 8, which governs investment securities. Certificated securities are a subset of investment property, and perfection in such property is discussed generally in § 6.04 *infra*.

[13] The concept of indispensable records, of which indispensable paper is a subset, is discussed in § 1.04[B] *supra*. Indispensable records in electronic form are not capable of being possessed but may be perfected by the analogous method of control. Control is discussed generally in § 6.04 *infra*.

[14] The concept of intangibles is discussed in § 1.04[C] *supra*.

[15] Automatic perfection is occasionally available. *See* § 7.02 *infra*.

[16] *In re* Sanelco, 7 U.C.C. Rep. Serv. 65 (Bankr. M.D. Fla. 1969) (account not capable of being possessed); First Bethany Bank & Trust, N.A. v. Arvest United Bank, 56 U.C.C. Rep. Serv. 2d 1209 (Okla. 2003) (security interest in account may not be perfected by possession).

Instruments[17] and tangible negotiable documents, by contrast, are the exclusive representation of the rights indicated thereon. Thus, the right to enforce payment of an obligation represented by an instrument is normally transferred by delivering the writing to the transferee,[18] and title to goods covered by a tangible negotiable document is normally transferred by delivery of the document.[19] Possession serves as a reliable means of perfection only if it provides notice comparable to that achieved by filing.[20] If a debtor seeks to induce subsequent parties to enter into a transaction with respect to pledged property, those parties should be alert enough to inquire as to the reason the debtor does not have possession of the property. Adequate notice through possession only works with goods and with property that the legal and business communities recognize as being comprised of a physical embodiment of represented rights.

Failure to take possession of the physical embodiment of the collateral cost a bank perfection of its security interest, worth more than $5 million, in *In re Funding Systems Asset Management Corp.*[21] The collateral consisted of chattel paper made up of a note and leases of underlying equipment. The leases had been prepared in duplicate originals (original ink signatures without any designation of one as the original). The secured party took possession of one set of originals but left another set in the possession of the debtor. The court properly noted that a subsequent lender would not be placed on notice if the debtor decided to offer the duplicate originals as collateral.[22]

§ 6.02 POSSESSORY SECURITY ARRANGEMENTS IN SPECIFIC TYPES OF PERSONAL PROPERTY

Even though possession is a permitted method of perfection for security interests in a wide array of collateral, practical considerations narrow considerably the circumstances in which a secured party realistically can take delivery of the debtor's property. For example, a manufacturer that

---

[17] To fall within the definition of "instrument," nonnegotiable writings must be treated by the market as a tangible embodiment of a right to be paid and sometimes are referred to as "quasi-negotiable." U.C.C. § 9-102(a)(47). *See* § 1.04[B][2] *supra.*

[18] U.C.C. §§ 3-203(b) (transfer requires delivery); 1-201(b)(15) (delivery requires voluntary transfer of possession); 3-203(b) (transfer vests in the transferee any enforcement rights of the transferor).

[19] U.C.C. § 7-502(a)(2). The use of negotiable documents in commercial financing transactions is discussed in §§ 6.02[B][1] and 6.02[C] *infra.*

[20] The court in Hutchison v. C.I.T. Corp., 726 F.2d 300, 37 U.C.C. Rep. Serv. 1760 (6th Cir. 1984), stressed that for the purpose of notice to third parties, possession must be unequivocal, absolute, and notorious. A night watchman on the property where collateral was located indicated that he would keep an eye on it for the secured party. The court appropriately concluded that the arrangement was insufficient to provide notice to third parties and thus did not constitute perfection.

[21] 11 U.C.C. Rep. Serv. 2d 205 (Bankr. W.D. Pa. 1990).

[22] The problem could easily have been solved by having the chattel paper indicate that it had been assigned to a named assignee, *i.e.*, the bank. *See* § 11.03[C] *infra.*

delivers its equipment to a creditor will not be able to produce its products. The same problem exists for a consumer who needs to make home use of collateral consisting of appliances or furniture. Any collateral that the debtor must make use of is ill-suited to a possessory security interest.

Another practical problem results if the collateral has great bulk. A bank simply cannot store a debtor's pile of coal or its stockpiled inventory of finished goods in the lobby or the vault. Although more appropriate facilities could be arranged, the transactional costs associated with transport and storage are generally prohibitive. In addition to the other problems associated with taking delivery, a secured party in possession of collateral incurs an obligation to "use reasonable care in the custody and preservation of collateral" in its possession.[23]

The secured-lending community has responded to these practical problems in two distinct ways. One approach is to confine possessory secured lending to transactions in which the lender can easily manage receipt and custody of the collateral. The other approach is to use documents as a means to facilitate possessory security interests in goods. The basic patterns of the two approaches are explained below.

[A] Pledges of Valuables and Indispensable Paper

Secured lenders realistically can take delivery and maintain a possessory security interest in a relatively narrow range of goods. For an entity like a bank, this typically includes valuables, like jewelry or a coin collection, that the bank can store in its vault. Pawnbrokers have more expanded facilities for dealing with goods, but they also generally limit their transactions to items that are not bulky. Some of the items against which loans are extended become the inventory of the pawnbroker's shop.

Much possessory secured financing involves the use of indispensable paper as the collateral. Financing institutions can easily take a pledge of paper—like a promissory note or tangible chattel paper—that represents an obligation to pay money. Although perfection may be achieved by filing,[24] a debtor that lacks possession also lacks the power to create a bona-fide-purchaser type of status in a subsequent transferee.[25] Possession also facilitates collection or disposition in the event of default.[26] By taking

---

[23] U.C.C. § 9-207(a); First Nat'l Bank of Thomasboro v. Lachenmyer, 131 Ill. App. 3d 914, 476 N.E.2d 755, 41 U.C.C. Rep. Serv. 234 (1985) (debtor allowed to set off damages to property in bank's possession). The duty of reasonable care applies to possessory security interests and to collateral repossessed following default. For a discussion of the duty of reasonable care in the context of default, *see* Chapter 17 *infra*.

[24] U.C.C. § 9-312(a). Filing is sufficient to obtain priority over a lien creditor, including a trustee in bankruptcy. U.C.C. § 9-201(a).

[25] Article 9 contains a series of rules that protect good-faith purchasers for value that acquire possession of negotiable and quasi-negotiable collateral that is subject to a perfected security interest. To qualify, a purchaser must satisfy slightly different requirements depending upon the circumstances. *See* § 11.03[C], [D] *infra*.

[26] For example, only a "person entitled to enforce" a negotiable instrument can collect it. That status typically requires physical possession of the instrument. U.C.C. § 3-301.

possession of an instrument or chattel paper, a secured party does incur an obligation of "taking necessary steps to preserve rights against prior parties unless otherwise agreed."[27] The rights and responsibilities with respect to these kinds of paper are well within the expertise of most financial institutions, however, and do not constitute barriers to the effective use of possession as a method of perfection.

Tangible negotiable documents are another form of indispensable paper that is ideal for a possessory security interest. The document controls access and title to specified goods, thereby facilitating a possessory security interest without the secured party having to deal with the covered goods directly. Possession is preferable to filing[28] as a method of perfection because it eliminates the risk that the document will be "duly negotiated" to a person that will thereby gain priority over the secured party,[29] and it facilitates disposition of the goods in the event of default by the obligor. The role of the pledge of negotiable documents in possessory secured financing is discussed below in the contexts of terminal warehousing and goods in transit.[30]

A secured party cannot perfect a security interest in an asset subject to a state certificate-of-title law by taking possession of the certificate.[31] A certificate of title is issued by a state as a fraud-prevention mechanism, and while the certificate represents the best evidence of title to the covered goods, title is not merged into it. Thus, it does not qualify as a document under Article 9.[32]

It should be noted that these materials and the materials that follow focus on possession of paper assets. The Code also provides for electronic chattel paper and electronic negotiable documents, although it does not yet contemplate electronic instruments.[33] Any of the advantages that can be achieved

---

[27] U.C.C. § 9-207(a). For example, a person that indorses a negotiable instrument may be discharged from liability by lack of timely notice of dishonor. U.C.C. § 3-503(a). Courts generally have found secured parties liable for failure to make a favorable conversion of pledged debentures into common stock. Traverse v. Liberty Bank & Trust Co., 5 U.C.C. Rep. Serv. 535 (Mass. Super. Ct. 1967). Although secured parties are responsible for the physical care of pledged stock, they have, almost without exception, not been held liable for failing to sell the stock in a declining market. Tepper v. Chase Manhattan Bank, NA, 376 So. 2d 35, 27 U.C.C. Rep. Serv. 1104 (Fla. Dist. Ct. App. 1979); Layne v. Bank One, Ky., N.A., 395 F.3d 271, 55 UCC Rep. Serv. 2d 704 (6th Cir. 2005).

[28] U.C.C. § 9-312(a) permits perfection of a security interest in a negotiable document by filing. As with instruments and chattel paper, filing is sufficient to obtain priority over a lien creditor, including a bankruptcy trustee. U.C.C. § 9-201(a).

[29] U.C.C. § 9-331(a). A holder to whom a negotiable document is duly negotiated is the Article 7 equivalent of a bona-fide purchaser for value. U.C.C. § 7-501(b)(3).

[30] *See* §§ 6.02[B][1] and 6.02[C] *infra.*

[31] McDonald v. Peoples Automobile Loan & Fin. Corp. of Athens, Inc., 115 Ga. App. 483, 154 S.E.2d 886, 4 U.C.C. Rep. Serv. 49 (1967); *In re* Global Environ. Serv. Group, LLC, 2006 WL 980582, 59 UCC Rep. Serv. 2d 655 (Bankr. D. Haw. 2006) (the secured party taking possession of the certificates of title of vehicles titled in California and Louisiana did not perfect a security interest in those vehicles).

[32] Nationwide Mut. Ins. Co. v. Hayes, 276 N.C. 620, 174 S.E.2d 511, 7 U.C.C. Rep. Serv. 1105 (1970).

[33] *See* § 1.04[B] *supra.*

by possession of paper can also be achieved by obtaining control of the electronic equivalent of the paper.

[B] Goods in Storage or Manufacture

Raw materials or finished goods that are either being stored by a manufacturer or used in a manufacturing process typically represent a considerable capital investment by the manufacturer. Consequently, many manufacturers are interested in using these goods as collateral to facilitate the financing of their operations. A prospective secured lender may balk at relying upon perfection by filing because it does not provide the same level of protection against debtor dishonesty as perfection by possession. The financing community has developed mechanisms by which a secured party may attain protection comparable to possession without having to take delivery of the goods.

[1] Terminal Warehousing—§ 9-312(c)

Terminal warehousing is used to store goods. The name derives from the fact that many such warehouses are located at railroad terminals in order to facilitate shipment of the stored goods. The warehouse company is responsible for the care and custody of the goods placed in its charge.[34] It usually issues a negotiable document to a party that deposits goods for storage.

Tangible negotiable documents can be envisioned as "goods paper." The Comments stress that Article 9, like Article 7, "takes the position that, so long as a negotiable document covering goods is outstanding, title to the goods is, so to say, locked up in the document" and "[a]ccordingly, a security interest in goods covered by a negotiable document may be perfected by perfecting a security interest in the document."[35]

To illustrate, a farmer who harvests wheat might transport it to a grain elevator so that it can be properly dried and stored. The elevator operator will give the farmer a negotiable document for the quantity of the grade of wheat the farmer delivered. The farmer then can sell the wheat by delivering the document to the buyer. In fact, the document might pass through the hands of several buyers until, ultimately, a buyer like a cereal manufacturer takes delivery of the wheat. This can be accomplished only by surrendering the document to the elevator operator.[36] Until this occurs, the document facilitates the marketing of the wheat without it having to be moved from the elevator.

---

[34] U.C.C. § 7-204.

[35] U.C.C. § 9-312, Comment 7. *See* U.C.C. § 7-502(a) (holder to which negotiable document of title is duly negotiated receives title to the document, title to the goods, and the obligation of the issuer to hold or deliver the goods).

[36] The issuer of the negotiable document must deliver the goods to the holder of the document. U.C.C. §§ 7-403(a); 7-102(a)(9).

A negotiable document can also be used to facilitate secured financing. The relevant provision in Article 9 provides that, while goods are in the possession of a bailee that has issued a negotiable document for them, a security interest in the goods is perfected by perfecting a security interest in the document.[37] The motivating interest of the creditor is the goods, of course, because they are the source of the collateral's value. If goods have been warehoused under a negotiable document, however, a prudent secured party will deal with the goods only through the document. The merger of title to the goods into the document facilitates secured lending because the lender can confidently control access to the goods by taking a security interest in, and possession of, the document.

The pledge of a negotiable document perfects the lender's security interest.[38] The lender controls access to the goods because the warehouse will not release them without surrender of the document. If the obligor pays the outstanding indebtedness, the lender will return the document to the debtor so that the debtor can either sell it or acquire possession of the goods for use in its own operations. In the event of default by the obligor, the secured party can sell the document in satisfaction of the outstanding indebtedness.[39]

Most goods will have an existence both prior to and after being warehoused. During these prior and subsequent periods, the goods obviously are not in the possession of a person that has issued a negotiable document for them. Accordingly, buyers or lenders that wish to deal with the goods during these periods cannot deal with them through a document but rather must deal with the goods themselves.

Assume that goods are in the debtor's possession during Year 1, in the possession of a warehouse that issues a negotiable document for them during Year 2, and back in the debtor's possession during Year 3. Any security interest taken and perfected in the goods during Years 1 and 3 must be in the goods themselves. A secured party that takes a security interest in the goods during Year 1 and perfects by filing a financing statement describing the goods need not reperfect as to the document in order to protect its security interest during Year 2.[40]

A secured party that takes a security interest during Year 2, however, should deal with the goods through the negotiable document. In other words, the security agreement should describe the document for attachment purposes, and the security interest should be perfected by filing a financing statement describing the document or, preferably, by taking possession of the document. What is the consequence to a lender that takes a security

---

[37] U.C.C. § 9-312(c)(1).

[38] U.C.C. § 9-313(a).

[39] After default, the secured party can proceed against either the documents or the goods covered thereby. U.C.C. § 9-601(a)(2).

[40] Article 7 is consistent. Absent specified entrustment or acquiescence, "[a] document of title confers no right in goods against a person that before issuance of the document had a legal interest or a perfected security interest in the goods." U.C.C. § 7-503(1).

interest in the goods rather than the document during Year 2 and perfects by filing a financing statement covering the goods? The Code subordinates such a lender's interest to that of another secured party, either earlier or later in time, that takes and perfects a security interest in the document.[41] This result is an exception to the general rule that rank-orders perfected security interests on the principle of first-to-file-or-perfect.[42] The lender would, however, have a perfected security interest in the goods that would defeat any subsequent secured party that dealt with the goods rather than the document. It would also defeat lien creditors, including a bankruptcy trustee.

When Year 2 ends, the document will have to be surrendered in order to facilitate the debtor's reacquisition of the goods.[43] Once the document is surrendered to the bailee in exchange for possession of the goods, it ceases to exist. If the secured party has, in addition to taking and perfecting its security interest in the document, previously filed a financing statement describing the goods, it will continue its perfected status without interruption. If it filed a financing statement covering the document but not the goods, the goods are a proceed of the document and the secured party's interest will remain continuously perfected.[44] Relying on its proceeds interest is dangerous, however, because the secured party will have to identify the proceeds if it wishes to foreclose on them. Identification is difficult under any circumstances, and particularly so with fungible goods.[45] If the secured party perfected its security interest in the document by possession and did not file as to the goods, the goods still qualify as proceeds (if they can be identified), but the secured party's interest in them becomes unperfected 20 days after their receipt by the debtor unless the secured party files a financing statement describing them.[46] Accordingly, the best practical advice to a secured party acquiring a security interest during the period when goods are subject to a negotiable document is not only to take a possessory security interest in the document but also to file a financing statement describing both the document and the goods.[47]

---

[41] U.C.C. § 9-312(c)(2).

[42] For a discussion of the general rule of priority, *see* § 10.01 *infra*.

[43] A secured party that has perfected by possession of a negotiable document and has not filed a financing statement describing either the documents or the goods will be temporarily perfected for a maximum of 20 days after it returns the document to the debtor, but not later than the time the debtor surrenders the document to the bailee. U.C.C. § 9-312(f) (temporary perfection for collateral made available to debtor if certain conditions satisfied). As long as the temporary perfection does not lapse, it will continue for at least 20 days after surrender of the document, and perhaps longer, because the goods are proceeds of the document. The text provides further explanation of perfection as to proceeds.

[44] *See* § 8.01[B] *infra*.

[45] A secured party's interest and priority in commingled goods is governed by U.C.C. § 9-336, discussed *infra* § 15.06.

[46] *See* §§ 8.02[A], 8.02[B][4] *infra*. The secured party could also remain perfected beyond the 20-day grace period by taking possession of the goods before the period expires.

[47] The description of the document might seem superfluous, but it will provide continuous perfection if the document is surrendered to the debtor and the debtor retains possession of it beyond the 20-day period of temporary perfection provided for by U.C.C. § 9-312(f).

[2] Field Warehousing—§ 9-312(d)

Whereas a terminal warehouse is used to store goods, a field warehouse is not created for storage and is simply a method of facilitating secured financing. It facilitates a possessory secured interest by placing the goods in the actual possession and control of the secured party's agent, who acts as a warehouseman on the premises of the debtor. The transactional costs associated with a possessory security interest in bulky goods are reduced sharply because the warehouse is created around the goods while they are located on the debtor's premises, eliminating any need to move them back and forth between the secured party and the debtor.

A field warehouse can be a very simple creation. [48] Assume that a debtor has a large stock of finished inventory, like Christmas ornaments, that will be delivered to retail merchants for resale during the holiday season. A secured party would like to take possession of the inventory until the debtor needs it but does not want to pay transportation and storage costs. A field warehouse is an ideal solution. The key to the creation of the field warehouse is to exclude the debtor's access to the goods, both physically and legally. The warehouse can be created physically merely by enclosing the area around the finished goods with temporary walls of chicken wire, with access through a padlocked door. The debtor and secured party will enter into a simple lease whereby the portion of the debtor's premises that comprises the warehouse is leased to the secured party.

The secured party is likely to be too busy to be bothered with actually operating the field warehouse and will appoint an agent to perform that task. [49] The agent often will issue nonnegotiable warehouse receipts to the secured party for the goods that are located within the warehouse. These nonnegotiable documents, unlike the negotiable variety, do not represent title to the goods. [50] Like their negotiable counterparts, however, they serve as a receipt for goods that have been delivered to the bailee and stored in the warehouse, and they establish a contractual relationship between the bailor and the warehouse agent.

Nonnegotiable warehouse receipts play a role in satisfying the notice requirement for perfection of a security interest in the underlying goods. Article 9 provides three perfection alternatives for a security interest in goods covered by a nonnegotiable document: (1) issuance of a document in the name of the secured party; (2) the bailee's receipt of notification of the secured party's interest; and (3) filing as to the goods. [51] The

---

[48] For a description of a typical field warehouse, *see* Scott v. Lawrence Warehouse Co., 227 Or. 78, 360 P.2d 610 (1961).

[49] The agent, while frequently an employee of the debtor, must be made responsible to the secured party and not to the debtor. U.C.C. § 9-313, Comment 3.

[50] A transferee of a nonnegotiable document acquires only whatever title and rights the transferor has or has power to transfer, not complete title. U.C.C. § 7-504(a). Thus, there is no practice by secured parties of taking security interests in nonnegotiable documents (as opposed to the goods they represent), and Article 9's perfection rules (discussed *infra* this subsection) focus on the goods rather than the document.

[51] U.C.C. § 9-312(d).

field-warehouse agent will typically use the first alternative, issuing warehouse receipts for the goods in the name of the secured party. This makes the secured party the "person entitled under the document,"[52] giving it control over the disposition of the goods.[53]

If the debtor seeks to enter into subsequent transactions concerning the goods with other parties, those parties will be alerted to the prior interest upon finding that the debtor cannot open the lock on the field warehouse to gain access to the goods. Upon consulting with the only person who can gain access, the field-warehouse agent, an interested party will learn of the secured party's security interest. Although it is not an act of perfection, notice of the security interest is often provided by placing signs outside the warehouse indicating that the goods contained within are subject to a security interest and providing the name and telephone number of the agent for purposes of any inquiries.

Secured lenders using a field warehouse are well-advised to take the additional step of filing with respect to the goods. Then, if any aspect of the field-warehousing arrangement is challenged for the purpose of defeating perfection by possession, the secured party can easily prove perfection by filing. The advantage of the field warehousing arrangement, however, is that it facilitates a secured financing agreement if the lender is unwilling to finance against goods that remain within the control and custody of the debtor.[54]

Sometimes, a field warehouse can be incredibly simple and not require much from the field-warehouse agent. For example, a large cask of whiskey might need to age for several years without being disturbed. Debtor access can be denied by having the field-warehouse agent padlock the spigot. Notice to interested parties can be facilitated by posting signs on the cask indicating that the goods have been pledged to the secured party and providing the name and address of the field-warehouse agent from whom further information can be obtained. The agent need not be on the premises very often, but visits should be frequent enough to determine that the posted signs have not been removed and that the padlocked access has not been tampered with.

More sophisticated field warehouses can also be established. Rather than locking up a completed seasonal inventory for several months, the parties might create a more fluid arrangement whereby the debtor can remove some of the finished goods as sales of those goods are executed and can store additional finished goods as they are manufactured. The field-warehouse agent will issue nonnegotiable documents in the name of the secured party

---

[52] "Person entitled under the document" in the case of a nonnegotiable document means "the person to whom which delivery of the goods is to be made by the terms of, or pursuant to instructions in a record under" the document. U.C.C. § 7-102(a)(9).

[53] U.C.C. § 7-403(a) (bailee must deliver the goods to a person entitled under the document).

[54] An article that focuses extensively on the control aspects of field warehousing and on the requirement of possession in this context is Skilton, *Field Warehousing as a Financing Device*, 1961 Wisc. L. Rev. 221 (Part I), 403 (Part II).

as goods are received into the warehouse and the secured party can prepare delivery instructions to the agent concerning the release of collateral to the debtor.[55] The precise arrangements will depend upon the terms negotiated between the secured party and the debtor. One possibility is that the agent will be instructed to release any goods requested by the debtor but always to retain within the warehouse finished goods whose value totals a particular amount (called in the industry a "loan-to-collateral ratio").[56] The field-warehouse agent's compliance with such instructions will leave the lender with a perfected security interest in goods whose value is considered sufficient to cover the outstanding indebtedness. If the obligor borrows more money against an established credit line or makes payments that reduce the extent of indebtedness, new delivery instructions from the secured party to the field-warehouse agent can change the amount of collateral required to be maintained within the warehouse.

Another possibility is to create two field warehouses, one for raw materials used in the debtor's manufacturing operations and the other for finished goods, and to prepare delivery instructions that tie the two warehouses together. The field-warehouse agent could be instructed, for example, that for every ten units of raw materials released to the debtor, three units of finished goods must be received. Extending field warehouses to the raw materials facilitates secured financing of those goods as well, allowing an enhanced borrowing position for the obligor.

Whitney National Bank of New Orleans v. Sandoz demonstrates the consequences of becoming too lax in establishing a field warehouse.[57] The bank took a security interest in the debtor canning company's inventory of canned goods and purportedly perfected by possession through a field-warehouse arrangement. Parts of the debtor's plants were leased to a warehouse company, which issued warehouse receipts for the goods. The debtor, however, retained possession of the leased spaces and had unfettered access to its inventory.[58] The appellate court found that the transaction was a sham and that the bankruptcy court had held properly that the warehouse receipts were invalid. The warehouse agent filled the function in name only, because the goods were not actually warehoused. The obvious lesson is that a field warehouse must exist in more than name only to

---

[55] The debtor becomes the person entitled under the document to the extent of the secured party's written instructions, U.C.C. § 7-102(a)(9), and the bailee is then obligated to deliver the designated goods to the debtor. U.C.C. § 7-403(a).

[56] Ribaudo v. Citizens Nat'l Bank of Orlando, 261 F.2d 929 (5th Cir. 1958) (warehousing company instructed by bank to retain in its custody warehoused merchandise worth 133-1/3% of $50,000 loaned, or $66,666.67).

[57] 362 F.2d 605 (1966).

[58] The potential risk exposure associated with poorly-maintained field warehouses is illustrated in the extreme by one of the biggest business-fraud cases ever. Several banks in the United States and Britain extended loans for $150 million based on warehouse receipts for vegetable oils supposedly located in Bayonne, New Jersey. The contents that were actually located there were over a billion pounds short. *See* Proctor & Gamble Distrib. Co. v. Lawrence American Field Warehousing Corp., 16 N.Y.2d 344, 266 N.Y.S.2d 785, 213 N.E.2d 873, 21 A.L.R.3d 1320, 3 U.C.C. Rep. Serv. 157 (1965); N. Miller, *The Great Salad Oil Swindle* (1965).

provide perfection by possession. It must be operated in a manner sufficient to satisfy the notice function that underlies perfection of security interests.[59] Another lesson is that a proper filing as to the goods, while insufficient to protect against debtor defalcations, would have defeated the bankruptcy trustee.

An alternative method of protecting a secured lender against a debtor's improper use of collateral has developed. Rather than creating a field warehouse and issuing warehouse receipts to the secured party, a bonded warehousing company may issue a certification in record form of the value of the collateral on the debtor's premises. The company also contracts to comply with the secured party's delivery instructions concerning the collateral and to assume liability for any losses that result from not fulfilling its duties. A three-way agreement among the debtor, the secured party, and the warehouse company authorizes policing and control by the warehouse company, and the secured party simply perfects by filing as to the goods. This approach to certified inventory control protects the secured party by passing the risk of debtor defalcation to the warehousing company.[60]

[C] Goods in Transit

Sometimes a person will wish to arrange financing to be secured by goods that are in transit. Assume a transaction in which an importer in the United States is purchasing several hundred tons of copper from Chile. The goods might take up to three weeks to arrive by ocean carrier at a U.S. port. The importer will then break down the shipment into domestic shipments that it will route to each of its pre-arranged buyers. An importer that must pay the seller shortly after the goods are shipped but that will not be paid on its resale transactions until the copper is delivered to domestic buyers may need financing to cover the interim period.

The importer can enter into a transaction with a bank in this country under which the bank will issue a letter of credit to the exporter.[61] The bank will require that the importer execute a security agreement granting a security interest in the copper and in any documents covering the copper,

---

[59] Article 9 stresses the importance of proper maintenance of a field warehouse. U.C.C. § 9-205(a)(1)(A) allows the debtor to use and dispose of collateral without impairing the security interest's validity. *See* § 3.01 *supra*. U.C.C. § 9-205(b) provides that the section "does not relax the requirements of possession if attachment, perfection, or enforcement of a security interest depends upon possession of the collateral by the secured party."

[60] Descriptions of certified inventory control arrangements are provided in McGuire, *The Impact of the UCC on Field Warehousing*, 6 U.C.C. L.J. 267, 280-82 (1974). The article further explains that warehouse companies also enter into accounts-receivable programs in which they guarantee the validity of accounts and protect against debtor diversion of funds received on accounts.

[61] A letter of credit is "a definite undertaking that satisfies the requirements of Section 5-104 by an issuer to a beneficiary at the request or for the account of an applicant or, in the case of a financial institution, to itself or for its own account, to honor a documentary presentation by payment or delivery of an item of value." U.C.C. § 5-102(a)(10).

and it will file a financing statement perfecting its security interest in the goods and documents. The letter of credit will require the bank to pay the exporter's drafts, provided that the appropriate records accompany the drafts.[62] One of the required records will be a negotiable bill of lading, which will be issued by the carrier when the goods are shipped.[63] After shipment, the exporter will prepare a draft drawn on the bank demanding payment in the amount of the purchase price. It will then forward the draft and the negotiable bill of lading (together with other required records)[64] through banking channels to the bank. The bank will receive possession or control of the bill of lading when it pays the draft.[65] Although the secured party's interest was perfected by its financing statement, possession or control of the bill of lading enhances its position.[66]

This type of transaction can be desirable from the perspectives of all the parties. The exporter need not relinquish ownership or control of the goods until it is paid, because it will not deliver the bill of lading to the bank until its draft is paid. The bank acquires control over the goods when it pays the draft. The importer is able to use the copper in transit as security to facilitate the transaction.

The bank, of course, will have to relinquish possession or control of the bill of lading for the goods to be released by the ocean carrier. It will then have a perfected nonpossessory security interest in the importer's copper. The bank can further enhance its position by insisting that each buyer of copper provide the importer with a letter of credit.[67] As the copper is delivered to domestic shippers, new negotiable bills of lading will be issued. These documents can be negotiated to the secured party, which will then forward them to the issuing banks with drafts ordering payment to itself.

---

[62] A draft is a negotiable instrument that includes an order to pay money. U.C.C. § 3-104(e).

[63] A bill of lading is "a document of title evidencing the receipt of goods for shipment issued by a person engaged in the business of directly or indirectly transporting or forwarding goods" U.C.C. § 1-201(b)(6). The U.C.C. provisions on bills of lading are provided in Article 7 on documents. For interstate shipments and exports, however, bills of lading are governed by the Federal Bills of Lading Act, 49 U.S.C. App. §§ 81-124 (1988), rather than the U.C.C.

[64] To assure itself that conforming goods have been shipped, the bank's letter of credit will probably require the seller to deliver certificates related to inspection of the goods. It will also require evidence of insurance, and records demonstrating compliance with the laws of the exporting and importing countries.

[65] The named consignee on the bill of lading, the exporter, will "negotiate" it to the bank by indorsing and delivering it. U.C.C. § 7-501(a)(1). This gives the bank the status of holder, making it the person entitled under the document. U.C.C. § 7-102(a)(9). The carrier will only release the goods to a person entitled to enforce the document. U.C.C. § 7-403(a).

[66] See § 6.02[B][1] supra.

[67] The bank's security agreement can cover the importer's rights to the proceeds of the letters of credit as additional collateral. The term "letter-of-credit rights" means the right to payment or performance under a letter of credit. U.C.C. § 9-102(a)(51). Except when the letter of credit represents a supporting obligation, a security interest in letter-of-credit rights must be perfected by control. U.C.C. §§ 9-312(b)(2), 9-107. Control requires that the issuer or its nominee consent to the security assignment. Without this consent, the secured party is not only unperfected but cannot require that the issuing bank honor the letter. See § 1.08 supra. Supporting obligations are discussed in § 1.07[C] supra.

Payments under the drafts will be applied to reduce the importer's indebtedness.

§ 6.03   THE CONCEPT OF POSSESSION—§ 9-313

[A]   Possession by the Secured Party

Article 9 provides that "perfection occurs no earlier than the time the secured party takes possession and continues only while the secured party retains possession."[68] The first part of this sentence rejects the common-law theory of the "equitable pledge."[69] Under this theory, the taking of possession could relate back to the date of an original security agreement that included an agreement for future possession. Taking possession shortly before bankruptcy, however, may create a voidable preference under federal bankruptcy law.[70] To achieve consistency with this federal policy, relation-back is eliminated for possessory security interests.[71] Perfection by possession applies only during the time that the secured party takes and retains possession of the collateral.[72] Perfection either prior to or after the period of possession must be attained through tacking with other applicable methods of perfection.[73]

In *Transport Equipment Co. v. Guaranty State Bank*,[74] perfection by possession of the debtor's machinery occurred too late to protect the secured party against a second secured party that perfected by filing. Although representatives of the first secured party arrived on the debtor's premises in the morning, they did not load the collateral onto their trucks until the afternoon. The court held that possession occurred only upon the loading, and thus the filing by the second secured party earlier in the afternoon afforded it priority. A purchase-money seller in *In re Automated Bookbinding Services, Inc.*[75] lost perfection when it shipped the goods by carrier

---

[68] U.C.C. § 9-313(d).

[69] *See* U.C.C. § 9-313, Comment 5. If a security interest in instruments, certificated securities, or negotiable documents is granted in exchange for new value, the Code provides for a 20-day period of temporary perfection without possession or filing. U.C.C. § 9-312(e). This period of automatic perfection can be seen as a limited relation-back rule. There can also be automatic perfection for a short time after possession is relinquished if the collateral consists of negotiable documents, goods in the possession of a bailee other than one that has issued a negotiable document, instruments, and certificated securities. U.C.C. § 9-312(f), (g). Temporary perfection is discussed in § 8.01 *infra*.

[70] 11 U.S.C. § 547. *See* § 16.04[E] *infra*.

[71] *In re* Granite City Coop. Creamery Ass'n, Inc., 7 U.C.C. Rep. Serv. 1083 (Bankr. Vt. 1970).

[72] An otherwise unperfected secured party that takes possession of collateral following a default by the obligor thereby perfects its security interest. *In re* Osborn, 389 F. Supp. 1137, 16 U.C.C. Rep. Serv. 827 (N.D. N.Y. 1975); Walter E. Heller & Co. v. Salerno, 168 Conn. 152, 362 A.2d 904, 16 U.C.C. Rep. Serv. 840 (1975). Obtaining a default judgment against the defendant in a replevin action is not sufficient to perfect by possession because the right to take possession of the collateral is not the same as having actual possession of it. *In re* Walter Neilly & Co., Inc., 1 U.C.C. Rep. Serv. 364 (Bankr. W.D. Pa. 1961).

[73] U.C.C. § 9-308(c). *See also* § 4.04 *supra*.

[74] 518 F.2d 377, 17 U.C.C. Rep. Serv. 1 (10th Cir. 1975).

[75] 471 F.2d 546, 11 U.C.C. Rep. Serv. 897 (4th Cir. 1972).

under a nonnegotiable bill of lading showing the buyer as the consignee. Possession terminated because the seller lost control of the goods in transit.

[B] Possession by Agents and Bailees

A secured party may use an agent for purposes of possession.[76] In accordance with the principles of agency law, the agent acts on behalf of the principal, and thus possession by the agent serves as possession by the secured party.[77] The key is to exclude the debtor from both possession and control of the collateral.[78] The Comments succinctly state the necessary relationship as follows:

> The debtor cannot qualify as an agent for the secured party for purposes of the secured party's taking possession. And, under appropriate circumstances, a court may determine that a person in possession is so closely connected to or controlled by the debtor that the debtor has retained effective possession, even though the person may have agreed to take possession on behalf of the secured party. If so, the person's taking possession would not constitute the secured party's taking possession and would not be sufficient for perfection.[79]

Retention of possession or control by the debtor facilitates the possibility that the debtor might use its access to the collateral to deceive a subsequent party. Possession by the secured party or by an agent controlled by the secured party advances the notice function that lies at the core of the concept of perfection.

Possession by the secured party or its agent is actual possession. With collateral other than certificated securities and goods covered by a negotiable document, the secured party can also perfect by obtaining what is sometimes called "constructive possession." Under former law, constructive possession commenced when a bailee (a person in possession of the collateral other than the debtor) received notification of the secured party's interest. Revised Article 9 restricts the receipt-of-notification method for obtaining constructive possession to bailees that have issued nonnegotiable documents covering the goods.[80] In other situations, constructive possession requires that the bailee authenticate a record acknowledging that it holds, or as to future assets will hold, the collateral for the secured party's benefit.[81] This technique cannot be used if the bailee is a lessee of the

---

[76] U.C.C. § 9-313, Comment 3. *See also In re* Bruce Farley Corp., 26 B.R. 164, 35 U.C.C. Rep. Serv. 1304 (Bankr. S.D. Cal. 1981).

[77] Restatement (Second) of Agency § 17, Comment a (1958) (delegated act done by representative has same legal effect as if done personally by the principal).

[78] *In re* Maryville Sav. & Loan Corp., 27 B.R. 701, 35 U.C.C. Rep. Serv. 983 (Bankr. E.D. Tenn. 1983) (collateral that remained in debtor's possession was not constructively delivered for purposes of perfection by possession).

[79] U.C.C. § 9-313, Comment 3.

[80] U.C.C. §§ 9-312(d)(2) and 9-313, Comment 7.

[81] U.C.C. § 9-313(c).

collateral from a debtor that leased the goods in the ordinary course of its business.[82] The limitation represents a policy judgment that the lessee's possession of the goods in such circumstances is insufficient to provide adequate public notice of the secured party's interest.

A bailee is under no legal obligation to sign an acknowledgment,[83] and unless the bailee otherwise agrees or law outside Article 9 otherwise provides, the fact that the bailee has chosen to do so does not subject the bailee to any duty to the secured party or to any third party.[84] Because of the risk that the bailee will refuse to sign an acknowledgment, a secured party should take the precautionary step of filing a financing statement in order to ensure perfected status.

Determining whether a third person is an agent or a bailee can occasionally be difficult. For example, in *In re Rolain*,[85] the collateral consisted of a promissory note issued to the debtor by a third party. The promissory note contained confidential information which the debtor had agreed not to release, and the secured party and debtor agreed that the debtor's attorney would hold the note pursuant to an escrow agreement. The attorney was agent for both the debtor and the secured party, and it was unclear for purposes of perfection by possession whether the attorney was acting as an agent of the secured party or as an independent bailee. Under former law it did not really matter, and the court ruled for the secured party without deciding the issue. If the attorney was a bailee, he had received notification of the secured party's interest, which sufficed for constructive possession under former law. As the secured party's agent, he was sufficiently independent of the debtor for the secured party to have actual possession—an appropriate result given that attorneys are capable of understanding situations involving divided loyalties and are bound by rules of professional conduct. The lesson of *Rolain* for lawyers practicing under revised Article 9 is clear: If there is any ambiguity regarding the status of the person in possession, the secured party should obtain from that person a signed acknowledgment.[86]

The drafters of revised Article 9 were concerned that the acknowledgment rule might interfere with mortgage warehouse lending, and so they provided a special rule for situations in which collateral already in the possession of the secured party is delivered by the secured party to a bailee. In that case, the secured party is not deemed to have relinquished possession if it instructs the bailee, either before or contemporaneously with the

---

[82] U.C.C. § 2A-103(1)(u).

[83] U.C.C. § 9-313(f).

[84] U.C.C. § 9-313(g)(2). Section 9-313(g)(1) makes a signed acknowledgment effective to perfect a security interest even if it violates the debtor's rights.

[85] 823 F.2d 198, 4 U.C.C. Rep. Serv. 2d 5 (8th Cir. 1987).

[86] U.C.C. § 9-313, Comment 3 supports the decision in *Rolain* by stating that "[i]n a typical escrow arrangement, where the escrowee has possession of collateral as agent for both the secured party and the debtor, the debtor's relationship to the escrowee is not such as to constitute retention of possession by the debtor." The Comment implies but does not flatly state that an escrowee is an agent rather than a bailee.

delivery, to hold the collateral for the secured party's benefit or to redeliver it to the secured party.[87] For example, assume Mortgage Lender pledges its notes and mortgages as collateral for a series of short-term loans from Bank. As each transaction is closed, the note and mortgage are physically delivered to Bank, which is a mortgage warehouse lender. The loans provide operating capital to Mortgage Lender while it accumulates a sufficient pool of such assets to justify selling them as a package on the secondary mortgage market. A potential buyer may wish to inspect the documentation, and the common practice is for the warehouse lender (Bank) to forward a package of notes and mortgages under a cover letter advising the potential buyer of its security interest. The letter provides the notification that permits the mortgage warehouse lender to maintain its perfected status.

Although designed for mortgage warehouse lending, the notification-to-bailee rule also facilitates "repledges" of other kinds of collateral. An example may be found in section 9-207(c)(3), which expressly authorizes a secured party to create a security interest in collateral in its possession. To illustrate, suppose Finance Co. acquires a possessory security interest in Debtor's instruments. To obtain financing of its own, Finance Company repledges the instruments to Bank as collateral for a loan. Finance Co. retains its perfected status vis-a-vis Debtor by instructing Bank to redeliver the collateral to Finance Co. upon repayment of Bank's loan to Finance Co.[88]

[C] Symbolic or Constructive Delivery

Possession is a concept that arises in numerous legal contexts and has varied meanings within those contexts. The popular saying that "possession is nine points in the law" reflects the fundamental significance that possession historically has enjoyed in our legal culture. In numerous contexts, possession has evolved to encompass symbolic or constructive delivery.[89] Although such delivery is appropriate in some contexts, it will not be appropriate for the purpose of perfecting an Article 9 security interest unless it provides sufficient notice to potential third parties.

The case of *In re Bialk*[90] is illustrative. The secured party sought to take a pledge of medals and coins that the debtor had placed in a bank safe-deposit box. The debtor gave his only keys to the box to the secured party, which argued that delivery of the keys constituted symbolic delivery of the contents sufficient to constitute perfection by possession. The bankruptcy court disagreed because the bank had not also been notified of the secured party's interest. The debtor could have gained access to the locked goods

---

[87] U.C.C. § 9-313(h).

[88] A repledge will not excuse a secured party from its duty of reasonable care. U.C.C. § 9-207(a). *See* § 6.02 *supra*.

[89] It is important to differentiate between constructive delivery of an asset to a secured party and constructive possession by a secured party. Constructive possession is discussed in the preceding subsection.

[90] 16 U.C.C. Rep. Serv. 519 (Bankr. W.D. Mich. 1974).

by advising the bank that the keys were lost. Consequently, delivery of the keys to the secured party did not provide the required level of notice to potential third parties.

§ 6.04   PERFECTION BY CONTROL

Control was first introduced as a method of perfection when Article 9 was amended to conform to the 1994 revision of Article 8. At that time, it applied only to investment property. Revised Article 9 extended perfection by control to deposit accounts, electronic chattel paper, and letter-of-credit rights. To conform with the 2003 revision of Article 7, perfection by control has also been extended to electronic documents.

[A]   Investment Property—§§ 9-314(a), 9-106

The Code's treatment of securities has evolved significantly over the past quarter-century. Prior to a revision of Article 8 and conforming amendments to Article 9 in 1977, the assumption was that physical certificates would be issued for investment securities. The owner of a certificated stock or bond could create a perfected secured interest by entering into a security agreement and giving the secured party possession of the certificate. This type of asset was thus treated as indispensable paper, like an instrument.[91] Any interest that a debtor might have in an investment vehicle for which no certificate existed qualified as a general tangible.

The number of securities transactions increased so drastically during the 1960s that the industry looked for ways to reduce the amount of paperwork. One practice that developed was the issuance of certificates in "street name." Rather than issuing certificates to each individual investor, an issuing entity would issue only a few certificates in large amounts to stockbrokers. The certificates represented the ownership interests of each of a broker's customers.

Today, it is unlikely that even a broker will hold a certificate. Under the indirect holding system that has developed in recent years, it is more common for a "jumbo certificate" to be held by a clearing corporation of which the broker is a member. Thus, the broker may own, for all its customers, 100,000 shares of a particular stock, and the books of the broker will reflect the ownership interests of each of the broker's customers. The certificate itself will be held by a clearing corporation and may represent hundreds of thousand of shares. The books of the clearing corporation will show that the broker owns 100,000 of these shares.

Another practice is the issuance of uncertificated securities, which are sometimes referred to as "book entry" securities. The issuing entity does not issue a physical certificate; rather, ownership and transfer are recorded

---

[91] Indeed, what are now called certificated securities were defined as instruments for Article 9 purposes until the 1994 revision of Article 8 and the conforming changes to Article 9. *See* U.C.C. § 9-105(1)(i) (1972 Official Text).

by the issuer or its agent through book or computer entries. If uncertificated securities are held through a broker, a customer's interest will be shown on the broker's records and confirmations of purchase. Many government securities are issued in uncertificated form.

Perfection of a security interest in certificated securities held indirectly by a broker created problems under former law. Filing was ineffectual,[92] and for a pledge to work, a debtor would have to obtain a certificate from a broker (which, in turn, would typically have to obtain one from a clearing corporation). Perfecting an interest in uncertificated securities was also problematic. Such securities were classified as general intangibles, and the only means of perfection was to file a financing statement. The securities industry, however, was not in the practice of searching for financing statements because securities previously had all been certificated and filing was excluded as a method of perfection. Although the use of uncertificated securities might have forced a change in industry practices, the objective of lessening transaction costs that was a leading motivation for the introduction of uncertificated securities would have been undercut with the imposition of a requirement for searching the U.C.C. filing system.

In an attempt to accommodate the changes in the securities industry, Article 8 was revised in 1977. These amendments, however, proved unsatisfactory, and the article was revised again in 1994. The latter revision created, through conforming amendments to Article 9, "investment property" as an umbrella category for most interests in investment vehicles.[93] Investment property consists of securities (whether held directly or indirectly and whether certificated or uncertificated), security entitlements, securities accounts, commodity contracts, and commodity accounts. Many of the key provisions governing noncommodity-related investment property were (and still are) found in Article 8. Commodity-related assets have always been beyond the scope of Article 8, and provisions governing security interests in commodity contracts and commodity accounts were placed exclusively in Article 9. Revised Article 9 did some reorganizing of the relevant provisions but left the law essentially unchanged.

Control is the primary method for perfecting a security interest in investment property.[94] A secured party has control if it has the power to control the disposition of the collateral. Filing is permitted as an alternative means of perfection.[95] Filing, however, is irrelevant when the security interest is created by a broker,[96] a securities intermediary,[97] or a commodity

---

[92] Until the promulgation of revised Article 9, filing was unavailable as a method of perfection for security interests in instruments, the category to which certificated securities belonged until 1994. Permissive filing became available for certificated securities with the 1994 revision of Article 8 and conforming changes to Article 9.

[93] The definitions and basic structure for investment property are discussed in detail in § 1.04[E] *supra*.

[94] U.C.C. §§ 9-314, 9-106.

[95] U.C.C. § 9-312(a).

[96] A "broker" is a person defined as a broker or dealer under federal securities laws, including a bank acting in that capacity. U.C.C. § 8-102(a)(3).

intermediary,[98] because these security interests in investment property are perfected automatically.[99] As will be shown below, filing is a decidedly inferior method of perfection.

As applied to a certificated security, uncertificated security, or security entitlement, control has the meaning specified in Article 8.[100] For a certificated security held directly by the debtor, control requires that the certificate be delivered to the secured party.[101] If the certificate is in bearer form, the secured party need only gain actual or constructive possession.[102] If it is in registered form, meaning that it specifies the debtor as the person entitled under it,[103] the secured party must gain actual or constructive possession and must also either obtain the debtor's indorsement[104] or have the certificate registered with the issuer in the secured party's name.[105] This might occur, for example, if the certificate is surrendered by the debtor to the issuer and it is reissued showing the secured party as the entitled person.

Uncertificated securities held directly by a debtor can also be controlled through delivery,[106] but delivery has an unusual meaning in this context. It means that the issuer has registered the secured party (or another person acting on the secured party's behalf) on its books as the owner of the security.[107] Control can also be obtained without delivery, but only if the issuer agrees to comply with the secured party's orders without the further consent of the debtor.[108]

Security entitlements[109] are by definition held indirectly through a securities intermediary,[110] usually a broker, and a secured party can acquire control either by becoming the entitlement holder (meaning that

---

[97] The term "securities intermediary" includes brokers and clearing corporations. U.C.C. § 8-102(a)(14).

[98] The term "commodity intermediary" includes persons registered under federal law as futures commission merchants and others who perform clearance or settlement services for certain boards of trade. U.C.C. § 9-102(a)(17).

[99] U.C.C. § 9-309(10),(11).

[100] U.C.C. § 9-106(a).

[101] U.C.C. § 8-106(a), (b). "Delivery" as applied to certificated securities is defined in § 8-301(a).

[102] U.C.C. §§ 8-106(a), 8-301(a).

[103] U.C.C. § 8-102(a)(13)(i).

[104] U.C.C. §§ 8-106(b)(1), 8-301(a). Indorsements are governed by § 8-304.

[105] U.C.C. §§ 8-106(b)(2), 8-301(a). If the secured party takes possession of the certificate but does not obtain control, it is nevertheless perfected by the delivery. U.C.C. § 9-313(a). A security interest perfected by this method has priority over a security interest perfected by a method other than control (e.g., by filing). U.C.C. § 9-328(5).

[106] U.C.C. § 8-106(c)(1).

[107] U.C.C. § 8-301(b).

[108] U.C.C. § 8-106(c)(2).

[109] A "security entitlement" is defined in terms of financial assets, which may or may not be securities. U.C.C. § 8-102(a)(17). See discussion in § 1.04[E] supra.

[110] U.C.C. § 8-102(a)(14), (7).

the books of the broker are changed to reflect ownership by the secured party)[111] or by having the broker agree to comply with the secured party's orders without the further consent of the debtor.[112] With a commodity contract, control requires that the secured party, the debtor, and the commodity intermediary (*e.g.*, dealer) agree that any value on account of the contract will be distributed as directed by the secured party without the further consent of the debtor.[113] Securities and commodity accounts are controlled if the secured party has control respectively of all security entitlements or commodity contracts.[114] Conversely, perfection as to a securities or commodity account carries with it perfection as to each security entitlement or commodity contract held in the account.[115]

Investors often obtain purchase-money financing from their brokers, which take security interests in the purchased financial assets.[116] A secured party that takes control of a financial asset held indirectly through a broker or other securities intermediary should obtain an agreement subordinating any security interest that the intermediary may have to that of the secured party. Otherwise, the intermediary will have priority over the secured party.[117]

As an alternative to control, Article 9 permits secured parties to perfect by filing an ordinary Article 9 financing statement. Permissive filing is sufficient to defeat lien creditors, including a bankruptcy trustee, but it exposes the secured party to significant risks. For example, a secured party that perfects by control takes priority over another secured party that perfects by filing, even if the filing predates control and the secured party with control knows of the other secured party's interest.[118] In addition, a security interest perfected by filing may be severed by a person that acquires protected-purchaser status.[119] The rule subordinating security interests perfected by filing to those perfected by control and to protected purchasers stems from the realities of the securities market, where it would be impractical for investors to check the Article 9 filing system.

---

[111] U.C.C. § 8-106(d)(1).

[112] U.C.C. § 8-106(d)(2).

[113] U.C.C. § 9-106(b)(2).

[114] U.C.C. § 9-106(c).

[115] U.C.C. §§ 9-308(f) (security entitlements), 9-308(g) (commodity contracts).

[116] An intermediary has control of all security entitlements or commodity contracts entrusted to it. *See* U.C.C. §§ 9-106(b)(1) (commodity intermediary), 8-106(e) (securities intermediary).

[117] U.C.C. § 9-328(3), (4) (securities intermediary and commodity intermediary respectively).

[118] U.C.C. § 9-328(1). If both secured parties perfect by filing, the normal first-to-file rule applies. U.C.C. § 9-328(7).

[119] U.C.C. § 9-331(a), (b), deferring to Article 8 for a description of protected purchasers. *See* U.C.C. § 8-303.

[B]   Deposit Accounts, Electronic Chattel Paper, Electronic Documents, and Letter-of-Credit Rights— §§ 9-314(a), 9-104, 9-105, 9-107

As indicated above, revised Article 9 extended the concept of control beyond investment property. Security interests in deposit accounts, electronic chattel paper, electronic documents, and letter-of-credit rights may also be perfected by control. Indeed, with certain limited exceptions, control is the exclusive method for deposit accounts[120] and letter-of-credit rights.[121] Filing is an alternative for electronic chattel paper and electronic documents.[122]

With deposit accounts, control is automatic (meaning it occurs upon attachment) if the secured party is the bank[123] with which the account is maintained.[124] If the account is maintained with a bank that is not the secured party, control requires either that the secured party become the customer with respect to the account[125] or that the secured party, the debtor, and the bank with which the account is maintained agree that the maintaining bank will follow the secured party's orders without the further consent of the debtor.[126] A secured party that has satisfied one of the above requirements has control even if the debtor retains the right to direct the disposition of the deposited funds.[127] For example, suppose the secured party takes a security interest in a deposit account maintained at a bank that is not the secured party and enters into a control agreement with the debtor and the maintaining bank. This means that the maintaining bank must follow the secured party's orders. The parties also agree, however, that the maintaining bank must also follow the debtor's instructions until it is ordered to stop doing so by the secured party.[128] What the secured party obtains is a perfected security interest in whatever remains in the account at the time it issues the stop order. This flexibility permits a lending bank to take a security interest in a deposit account maintained with

---

[120] U.C.C. § 9-312(b)(1).

[121] U.C.C. § 9-312(b)(2).

[122] U.C.C. § 9-312(a).

[123] "Bank" is broadly defined to include, *inter alia*, savings and loan associations, credit unions and trust companies. U.C.C. § 9-102(a)(8).

[124] U.C.C. § 9-104(a)(1).

[125] U.C.C. § 9-104(a)(3). This method may also be used with a deposit account maintained with the secured party. Control by becoming the customer with respect to the account, whether maintained with the secured party or another bank, provides a secured party with priority over another secured party that has obtained control by another method. U.C.C. § 9-327. *See* § 10.03[A] *infra*. Also, a secured party that becomes the customer with respect to a deposit account maintained at a bank that is not the secured party has priority to the funds in the account in the event the maintaining bank exercises its common-law right of set-off. U.C.C. § 9-340(c). *See* § 11.03[E] *infra*.

[126] U.C.C. § 9-104(a)(2). The agreement must be authenticated by each party. *Id.* A maintaining bank is not under a duty to enter into a control agreement. U.C.C. § 9-342.

[127] U.C.C. § 9-104(b).

[128] Either the security agreement or the control agreement can establish the grounds (typically default by the obligor) for issuance of such an order by the secured party.

other another bank,[129] leaves the debtor free to use the funds, and allows the lending bank to take priority over a trustee if the debtor subsequently files for bankruptcy protection. Article 8 contains a similar provision for uncertificated securities and security entitlements that are controlled through an agreement by which the issuer or securities intermediary agrees to comply with the secured party's orders.[130]

With letter-of-credit rights, control requires that the issuer or a nominated person consent to the security assignment of the proceeds of the letter.[131] This approach can be traced to the distinction in the letter-of-credit area between a right to the proceeds of the letter and a right to draw against it.[132] Control of electronic chattel paper requires that the electronic record be stored in such a way that a single authoritative copy identifies the secured party and cannot be changed in any way without the secured party's participation.[133] Article 7 contains a similar rule for control of an electronic document.[134]

---

[129] The mechanism may also be used with an account maintained with the secured party, in which case it augments the bank's common-law right of set-off. Set-off rights are discussed in § 11.03[E] *infra.*

[130] U.C.C. § 8-106(f).

[131] U.C.C. § 9-107. Consent may be pursuant to U.C.C. § 5-114(c) or any other applicable law or practice.

[132] *See* § 1.08 *supra.*

[133] U.C.C. § 9-105.

[134] U.C.C. §§ 9-314(a), 7-106. There is a subtle problem in the rules governing perfection when a bailee has issued a nonnegotiable electronic document. U.C.C. § 9-312(d) provides that perfection of a security interest in goods in the hands of a bailee that has issued a nonnegotiable document for them requires that the document be issued in the name of the secured party, that the bailee receive notification of the secured party's interest, or that the secured party ignore the document and file as to the goods. Unlike the situation with a negotiable document, neither filing with respect to, nor possession of, a nonnegotiable document is an appropriate means of perfection as to the goods because title to the goods is not reified in the document. U.C.C. § 9-313(a), which governs perfection by possession, is appropriately limited to negotiable documents. However, U.C.C. § 9-314(a), which governs perfection by control (the counterpart of possession in the electronic world), is not so limited. Because of this, a lawyer might be misled into thinking that obtaining control of an electronic nonnegotiable document accomplishes something worthwhile when, in fact, it does not protect a secured party's interest in the bailed goods. Accordingly, control should not be used as a method of perfection for electronic nonnegotiable documents.

Chapter 7

AUTOMATIC PERFECTION

SYNOPSIS

In some transactions, the security interest is perfected as soon as it attaches. The secured party is not required to take any further action to perfect because perfection occurs automatically with attachment.[1] Parties dealing with types of personal property that are eligible for automatic perfection need to be aware that a perfected security interest might exist despite the secret nature of the encumbrance. This chapter discusses the policies that led the drafters to permit automatic perfection and some practical consequences of this decision.

---

[1] U.C.C. § 9-309 (identifying security interests that are perfected "when they attach").

§ 7.01 PURCHASE-MONEY SECURITY INTERESTS IN CONSUMER GOODS—§ 9-309(1)

[A] Application of the Provision

The most important automatic perfection provision applies to purchase-money security interests in consumer goods.[2] This situation is the only permanent exception to the general filing requirement when a secured party leaves goods subject to a security interest in a debtor's possession.[3] Thus, a seller of goods that are (or are bought to be) used for a personal, family or household purpose is automatically perfected with respect to a security interest retained in the goods to secure the unpaid purchase price. Similarly, a lender that provides an enabling loan to facilitate a debtor's acquisition of consumer goods retains an automatically perfected security interest in the goods after the borrower buys them from a seller.

To qualify for automatic perfection, obviously, the goods must be consumer goods[4] and the transaction must create a purchase-money security interest.[5] An issue that has received considerable attention is the effect on automatic perfection of a secured party's reliance upon erroneous representations by the debtor concerning the projected use of the purchased goods.[6] Some courts have upheld automatic perfection when the debtor has unequivocally indicated to the secured party that the goods will be used for a consumer purpose.[7] A bankruptcy court in Pennsylvania approved this result but added the qualification that the secured party not have reason to believe that the debtor would actually use the goods differently.[8] That

---

[2] U.C.C. § 9-309(1); *In re* Haus, 18 B.R. 413, 33 U.C.C. Rep. Serv. 694 (Bankr. D. S.C. 1982) (household appliances); Meskell v. Bertone, 2004 WL 2451354, 55 UCC Rep. Serv.2d 179 (Mass. Super. Ct. 2004) (boat). Although perfection is automatic with respect to purchase-money security interests in consumer goods, secured parties that rely on automatic perfection incur a unique risk with respect to certain competing claimants. *See* U.C.C. § 9-320(b). For a discussion of this priority issue, *see* § 11.03[A][2] *infra*.

[3] Although automatic perfection may extend indefinitely with respect to goods that constitute proceeds, appropriate filing or possession with respect to the original collateral is required. U.C.C. § 9-315(d)(1). *See* § 8.02 *infra*.

[4] For a general discussion of consumer goods, *see* § 1.04[A][1] *supra*.

[5] For discussion of the requirements for a purchase-money security interest, *see* § 1.05 *supra*.

[6] Article 9 does not address the issue, but it does have a provision that insulates a secured party from liability or a reduction in its right to a deficiency if it reasonably believes that a transaction is not a consumer or consumer-goods transaction. U.C.C. § 9-628(c). Because the interests of third parties are involved when perfection is at stake, the provision sheds no real light on the appropriate resolution of the problem.

[7] *In re* Pettit, 18 B.R. 8, 33 U.C.C. Rep. Serv. 1762 (Bankr. E.D. Ark. 1981); Franklin Inv. Co. v. Homburg, 252 A. 2d 95, 6 U.C.C. Rep. Serv. 60 (D.C. Cir. 1969).

[8] *In re* Fiscante, 141 B.R. 303, 19 U.C.C. Rep. Serv. 2d 1188 (Bankr. W.D. Pa. 1992).

court denied automatic perfection to the seller of a lawn tractor because the seller should have known that the buyer intended to use the tractor in its business after the buyer initially tried to obtain the tractor in its business name. The seller's designation of the loan application as "personal" and its insistence that the buyer use a personal charge card were irrelevant.

[B] Policy

A provision permitting automatic perfection authorizes the creation of a secret lien—a circumstance that Article 9 generally avoids. Although several policy considerations underlie this departure from the norm, the Comments are not very helpful in explaining them. The Comments to revised Article 9 merely indicate that the prior approach is being continued,[9] and the Comments to the prior version of Article 9 only indicate that automatic perfection for purchase-money security interests in consumer goods follows the policy of jurisdictions that, under pre-Code law, did not impose filing requirements in connection with security interests in consumer goods under conditional sales or bailment leases.[10]

One reason for treating these transactions differently is the undesirable consequences that would result from requiring perfection by filing. Consumer transactions are so common that filing might overburden the filing system, although this is less so with modern electronic information storage capacity. No one is well-served if the volume of filings renders use of the system unwieldy. A related consideration is that most consumer transactions involve a relatively low value.[11] The transaction costs associated with preparing and filing financing statements would thus be proportionately higher than in most other types of transactions, and the consumer would invariably bear those costs. Thus, automatic perfection might be seen as a form of consumer protection.

The nature of the collateral provides another justification for automatic perfection. Consumer goods tend to depreciate rapidly and are difficult to deal with following a default by the debtor. As a consequence, many creditors do not favor using consumer goods as collateral to secure a loan. Merchants that sell goods to consumers under installment sales contracts, on the other hand, sometimes retain purchase-money security interests. In the event of a default, the merchant (because it deals in goods of that kind) is in a somewhat better position to repossess and sell them than would be a lender with a similar security interest. The prospect of repossession in the event of default can be used as leverage to motivate a consumer to fulfill the obligation to pay the purchase price. Moreover, sellers have an incentive to sell to consumers on credit, and taking a security interest somewhat reduces their risk (and therefore the consumer's cost of credit).

---

[9] U.C.C. § 9-309, Comment 3.

[10] U.C.C. § 9-302, Comment 4 (1972).

[11] Some states had adopted a nonuniform provision that eliminated the option of automatic perfection when the value of the goods exceeded a specified dollar threshold. Adoption of revised Article 9 eliminated most of these provisions. *See* note 22 *infra*.

In the past, secured lenders in nonpurchase-money secured transactions in consumer goods often sought to improve their positions in dealing with this unfavored form of collateral by extending their net over most or all of a debtor's consumer goods. This approach significantly enhanced their leverage by positioning them to threaten defaulting debtors with the loss of all or many of their worldly possessions. However, because this practice was perceived as abusive, the Federal Trade Commission promulgated a rule making it an unfair practice under federal law for a lender or a retail installment seller[12] to receive a consumer obligation that "[c]onstitutes or contains a nonpossessory security interest in household goods other than a purchase-money security interest."[13] Purchase-money security interests and possessory security interests are the only security interests that this rule permits in consumer goods.[14]

Astute lenders to, and buyers from, a consumer should be aware of the potential for automatic perfection with regard to relatively new goods in the consumer's possession. These parties can protect themselves by requiring satisfactory documentation from the consumer showing that the seller of the goods has been paid and that the source of the funds used for payment was not a lender whose obligation has not been satisfied.

A buyer who purchases goods from a consumer and who also qualifies as a consumer is not expected to have the same degree of sophistication. Reflecting this assessment, a special priority provision enables such a buyer to attain priority over a purchase-money secured party that relies upon automatic perfection.[15] Secured parties can avoid the risk posed by consumer buyers by taking the additional step of filing with respect to the goods.[16]

[C] Exceptions

The automatic perfection provision with respect to consumer goods is subject to two exceptions. If the consumer goods become fixtures, a fixture filing is needed to attain the priority that Article 9 provides with respect to most other realty interests, although automatic perfection will defeat lien creditors like a trustee in bankruptcy.[17] Article 9 also precludes automatic

---

[12] A retail installment seller is defined in the rule as "[a] man who sells goods or services to consumers on a deferred payment basis or pursuant to a lease-purchase arrangement within the jurisdiction of the Federal Trade Commission." 16 C.F.R. § 444.1(b).

[13] FTC Rule on Credit Practices, Regulation AA, 16 C.F.R. § 444.2(a)(4)(1994). *See also* Bankruptcy Reform Act § 522(f) (nonpossessory nonpurchase security money interests can be avoided in bankruptcy in stipulated consumer transactions).

[14] A further reason for secured parties to avoid nonpossessory, nonpurchase-money security interests in consumer goods is that such an interest can be invalidated to the extent it impairs a debtor's ability to claim an exemption in certain specified categories. 11 U.S.C. § 522(f)(1)(B). "Lien stripping" in bankruptcy is discussed in § 16.07[B] *infra*.

[15] U.C.C. § 9-320(b). For discussion of this provision, *see* § 11.03[A][2] *infra*.

[16] U.C.C. § 9-320(b).

[17] *In re* Hinson, 77 B.R. 34, 5 U.C.C. Rep. Serv. 2d 233 (Bankr. M.D.N.C. 1987) (fixture

perfection for goods subject to state certificate-of-title laws, as well as for goods subject to a federal statute, regulation, or treaty that preempts the general filing requirements of Article 9.[18] Thus, if a security interest in a motor vehicle can be perfected only by notation on a certificate of title, a purchase-money security interest in the vehicle cannot be automatically perfected, even if the vehicle is used for a consumer purpose.[19]

An occasional decision has created nonstatutory exceptions to automatic perfection for certain types of consumer goods. In *In re Sprague*,[20] the bankruptcy referee in New York refused to characterize a mobile home as consumer goods even though it had been purchased for household purposes. The referee reasoned that automatic perfection was not intended to apply to goods as large and expensive as mobile homes. Similarly, the court in *Union National Bank of Pittsburgh v. Northwest Marine, Inc.*[21] held that a 33-foot motorboat purchased for family purposes for $8,000 was not consumer goods for purposes of automatic perfection. The court reasoned that the concept of consumer goods envisions a "using up" or "wasting away" of the asset to the extent that a second institution would not be inclined to loan money against it. It thus found that the motorboat constituted goods of substantial magnitude compared to the "ordinary" concept of consumer goods and concluded that the secured lender that provided the enabling loan was not automatically perfected. These decisions are wrong, as the drafters did not include any limiting criteria based on the size or value of the consumer goods. Even if the results achieved by the courts are desirable, the standard articulated by them is far too vague for practical application.[22]

§ 7.02   CERTAIN TYPES OF ASSIGNMENTS

Article 9 recognizes automatic perfection for assignments of specified types of assets in certain limited circumstances. Among the circumstances in which automatic perfection is available are isolated assignments of accounts or payment intangibles, sales of payment intangibles and promissory notes, assignment of a health-care-insurance receivable to a provider

---

filing required for windows and gutters attached to house); *In re* Weaver, 69 B.R. 554, 3 U.C.C. Rep. Serv. 2d 1231 (Bankr. W.D. Ky. 1987) (no automatic perfection for mobile home situated on permanent foundation). For discussion of the concepts of fixtures and fixture filings, *see* Chapter 15 *infra*.

[18] U.C.C. §§ 9-309(1); 9-311(a)(1) (federal law), (a)(2) (state certificate-of-title law).

[19] United States v. One 1987 Cadillac DeVille, VIN 1G6CD5184H4348815, 774 F. Supp. 221, 16 U.C.C. Rep. Serv. 2d 1194 (D.Del. 1991) (automobile); *In re* Radny, 12 U.C.C. Rep. Serv. 583 (Bankr. W.D. Mich. 1973) (mobile home). Compare In re Lance, 2006 WL 1586745, 59 UCC Rep. Serv. 2d 632 (Bankr. W.D. Mo. 2006) (because Missouri law does not require snowmobiles to be covered by a certificate of title, a purchase money security interest in a snowmobile used for consumer purposes became perfected upon attachment).

[20] 4 U.C.C. Rep. Serv. 702 (Bankr. N.D.N.Y. 1966).

[21] 27 U.C.C. Rep. Serv. 563 (Pa. Ct. Comm. Pl. 1979).

[22] Maine has narrowed the availability of automatic perfection for consumer goods by including a monetary limitation on the value of the affected goods. Me. Rev. Stat. Ann. § 9-1309(1) ($10,000 or less). Colorado, Kansas, and Wisconsin eliminated prior monetary limitations when they enacted revised Article 9.

of health-care goods or services, certain interests in investment property, an assignment for the benefit of all creditors, an assignment of a beneficial interest in a decedent's estate, and an assignment involving a sale of lottery winnings.

The foregoing circumstances must be considered in conjunction with the Code's scope provision, which excludes certain transfers from the reach of Article 9 entirely.[23] Excluded transactions include a sale of accounts, chattel paper, payment intangibles, or promissory notes as part of a sale of the business out of which they arose;[24] the assignment of any such asset for the purpose of collection;[25] a transfer of any right to payment under a contract to an assignee that is also to render the performance due under the contract;[26] and a transfer of a single account, payment intangible, or promissory note to an assignee in whole or partial satisfaction of a preexisting debt.[27]

Article 9 also recognizes automatic perfection for security interests created under other articles of the Code, specifically security interests arising under Article 2 on sales or Article 2A on leases, and the security interest of a collecting bank under Article 4.[28] These security interests are unique to the transactions covered in those articles and thus are largely beyond the scope of this book.[29]

[A] Isolated Assignment of Account or Payment Intangible—§ 9-309(2)

Filing is not required for perfection with respect to an assignment of accounts or of payment intangibles which, by itself or together with other assignments to the same assignee, does not transfer a significant part of the outstanding accounts of the assignor.[30] The Comments indicate that this exception is designed to save "casual or isolated" assignments from invalidation.[31] The original drafters included the exception in response to accounts receivable statutes that were commonly enacted prior to the Code and which encompassed "assignments which no one would think of filing."[32] The Comments caution, however, that a person that regularly takes assignments of debtor accounts or payment intangibles (except in the

---

[23] U.C.C. § 9-109(d)(4)-(7). *See* § 1.07[F] *supra*.

[24] U.C.C. § 9-109(d)(4).

[25] U.C.C. § 9-109(d)(5).

[26] U.C.C. § 9-109(d)(6).

[27] U.C.C. § 9-109(d)(7).

[28] U.C.C. § 9-309(6), (7). Article 9 also provides for automatic perfection of a security interest of an issuer of a letter of credit (or that of a nominated person) arising under Article 5. U.C.C. § 9-309(8). *See also* U.C.C. § 9-110.

[29] There is a limited discussion, particularly of the Article 2 and 2A provisions, in § 1.08 *supra*.

[30] U.C.C. § 9-309(2).

[31] U.C.C. § 9-309, Comment 4.

[32] *Id.*

context of a sale of payment intangibles, in which case there is automatic perfection under another provision)[33] should file.[34] The Comments thus strongly suggest that this automatic-perfection provision should be construed narrowly. The safest conclusion to draw from the cases is that no prudent secured party should ever rely on the provision. The courts have been inconsistent both in the criteria they have considered relevant and in the application of the criteria.

Some courts apply the "casual-or-isolated" test suggested by the Comments.[35] Sometimes the focal point has been the extent of business transacted between the assignor and assignee so that a one-shot transaction, even though for a considerable amount, is automatically perfected.[36] For other courts, the status of the assignee has served as the central feature of the casual-or-isolated test.[37] Under this view, automatic perfection is not available if the assignee regularly engages in commercial financing transactions, thereby precluding use of the exception by professional creditors.[38] Some courts applying the test have disqualified a transaction if it fails under either standard.[39]

Other courts have ignored the casual-or-isolated test suggested by the Comments in favor of a percentage test. Some courts evaluate whether the assignor has assigned a significant percentage of its accounts by reference to the number of outstanding accounts assigned,[40] while others refer to the dollar value of those accounts.[41] Courts focusing on the latter percentage have also been influenced by the amount involved.[42] Yet other courts have

---

[33] U.C.C. § 9-309(3), discussed in the next subsection.

[34] U.C.C. § 9-309, Comment 4.

[35] *Id.*

[36] Architectural Woods, Inc. v. State of Wash., 88 Wash. 2d 406, 562 P.2d 248, 21 U.C.C. Rep. Serv. 1181 (1977) (assignment of $100,000, of an account for $144,953, held to be isolated). *See also In re* Fort Dodge Roofing Co., 50 B.R. 666, 41 U.C.C. Rep. Serv. 1839 (Bankr. N.D. Iowa 1985) (one-shot assignment).

[37] Daly v. Shrimplin, 610 P.2d 397, 29 U.C.C. Rep. Serv. 237 (Wyo. 1980) (no automatic perfection because assignees each regularly took assignments of accounts from this assignor).

[38] K.A.O.P. Co. v. Midway Nat'l Bank of St. Paul, 372 N.W.2d 774, 41 U.C.C. Rep. Serv. 1045 (Minn. Ct. App. 1985) (exception applicable only to assignee not regularly engaged in financing as a business).

[39] M.D. Hodges Enterprises, Inc. v. First Georgia Bank, 243 Ga. 664, 256 S.E.2d 350, 26 U.C.C. Rep. Serv. 1333 (1979) (exception not available because, as part of its business, plaintiff bank regularly loaned money and accepted accounts as security).

[40] *In re* Bougher, 8 U.C.C. Rep. Serv. 144 (Bankr. W.D. Mich. 1979) (no exception when assignor assigned all accounts due from his company, even though assignee was not a professional and did not regularly take assignments of accounts); *In re* Rankin, 102 B.R. 439, 9 U.C.C. Rep. Serv. 2d 301 (Bankr. W.D. Pa. 1989) (exception not applicable because entire account was assigned and it was debtor's only account of substance).

[41] *In re* Crabtree Constr. Co., Inc., 87 B.R. 212, 6 U.C.C. Rep. Serv. 2d 1322 (Bankr. S.D. Fla. 1988) (transfer of 14% of debtor's overall accounts was not significant portion, even though transfer actually covered 25% of collectible accounts); *In re* Munro Builders, Inc., 20 U.C.C. Rep. Serv. 739 (Bankr. W.D. Mich. 1976) (40% of total accounts of bankrupt was significant part).

[42] Consolidated Film Indus. v. U.S., 547 F.2d 533, 20 U.C.C. Rep. Serv. 1360 (10th Cir. 1977)

required that both a percentage test and the casual-or-isolated test be satisfied in order for automatic perfection to apply.[43]

[B] Sales of Payment Intangibles and Promissory Notes—§ 9-309(3), (4)

Article 9 provides for automatic perfection of the security interest acquired by the buyer of payment intangibles[44] or promissory notes.[45] Payment intangibles is a subset of general intangibles, and promissory notes is a subset of instruments. The categories are new to revised Article 9 and were created so that sales of such property could be brought within the scope of the article while sales of other general intangibles and instruments remained outside its scope. The rationale for both the expansion in scope and the automatic-perfection rule is the protection of specialized financing arrangements like loan participations and securitizations, topics that are discussed elsewhere in this book.[46] Persons dealing with payment intangibles and promissory notes should be aware that automatic perfection applies only to the interest of a buyer. If the security interest is granted to provide collateral for an obligation, automatic perfection is generally not available, although it would apply to a casual or isolated assignment of a payment intangible.[47]

[C] Assignment of Health-Care-Insurance Receivables to a Provider—§ 9-309(5)

A health-care-insurance receivable is "an interest in or claim under a policy of insurance which is a right to payment of a monetary obligation for health-care goods or services provided."[48] The category is a subset of account,[49] and unless otherwise stated, rules applicable to accounts are applicable to health-care-insurance receivables.[50] Inclusion in the account

---

(size of transaction did not suggest casual transaction that would ordinarily be exempt); Miller v. Wells Fargo Bank Int'l Corp., 406 F. Supp. 452, 18 U.C.C. Rep. Serv. 489 (S.D.N.Y. 1975) (no exemption for assignment of just under 20% of debtor's total outstanding accounts, particularly in view of $1,000,000 absolute value of transaction).

[43] *In re* Tri-County Materials, Inc., 114 B.R. 160, 12 U.C.C. Rep Serv. 2d 869 (Bankr. C.D. Ill. 1990) (12% of outstanding accounts met percentage test, but formality and notice to account debtor meant it was not a casual transaction); H. & Val J. Rothschild, Inc. v. Northwestern Nat'l Bank of St. Paul, 309 Minn. 35, 242 N.W.2d 844, 19 U.C.C. Rep. Serv. 673 (1976) (assigned percentage exceeded one-third and bank was involved in business of interim financing, although it had not previously taken assignments of contract rights as security).

[44] U.C.C. § 9-309(3).

[45] U.C.C. § 9-309(4).

[46] *See* § 1.06 *supra*.

[47] U.C.C. § 9-309(2). *See* § 7.02[A] *supra*.

[48] U.C.C. § 9-102(a)(46).

[49] U.C.C. § 9-102(a)(2).

[50] Some of the distinctions between health-care-insurance receivables and other accounts are discussed in § 1.04[C][1] *supra*.

category means that sales of health-care-insurance receivables are within the scope of Article 9.[51] As with any account, the interest of an assignee in the case of an isolated assignment is automatically perfected.[52] Also, an assignment to the provider of the health-care goods or services is automatically perfected. For example, suppose that to pay for services rendered, Patient assigns to Doctor his rights under a private health-insurance policy. The transaction is governed by Article 9 and the Doctor's interest is automatically perfected. If Doctor assigns all of her accounts, including health-care-insurance receivables, to Bank as collateral for a loan, Bank must file in order to perfect its interest.

[D] Investment Property—§ 9-309(9), (10), (11)

Article 9 provides special rules on security interests in investment property in order to provide certainty in the securities settlement system. One set of rules[53] applies to the rights of a seller that delivers, before receiving the agreed-upon payment, a certificated security or other financial asset represented by a writing of a kind that in ordinary course of business is transferred by delivery (with any necessary indorsement or assignment), if both persons are in the business of dealing with such assets. This often occurs when the seller's securities custodian delivers physical certificates to the buyer's securities custodian pursuant to an agreement that the buyer's custodian will remit payment. In accordance with the custom in the trade, the security is to be returned to the seller's custodian if payment is not forthcoming. Under the rules, the seller has an attached security interest in the asset even if there is not an authenticated security agreement, and that interest is automatically perfected.[54] The rules promote efficiency in that they permit high volumes of assets to be delivered with minimal documentation.

Article 9 is also coordinated with Article 8 to facilitate secured financing arrangements for securities firms. In some transactions, a lender requires that securities maintained on a clearing corporation's books be transferred to the lender's account, resulting in perfection by control.[55] In other transactions, the lender allows the debtor to retain the positions in its own accounts under an agreement-to-deliver arrangement. The debtor's books reflect the security and the debtor promises that the security will be transferred to the secured party's account upon demand. Perfection in these latter transactions occurs automatically if the debtor is a broker or securities intermediary.[56] Comparable automatic perfection is provided for a security interest in a commodity contract or a commodity account created

---

[51] U.C.C. § 9-109(a)(3).

[52] *See* § 7.02[A] *supra.*

[53] U.C.C. § 9-206(c), (d).

[54] U.C.C. § 9-309(9).

[55] Perfection of investment property by control is discussed in § 6.04[A] *supra.*

[56] U.C.C. § 9-309(10).

by a commodity intermediary.[57] The availability of automatic perfection precludes the necessity for the parties to engage in their prior practice of indefinitely rolling over a new loan agreement every 21 days (20 days under revised Article 9) in order to qualify continually for temporary automatic perfection.[58]

[E] Assignment for the Benefit of All Creditors—§ 9-309(12)

Another exception from the filing requirement for perfection applies to "an assignment for the benefit of all the creditors of the transferor and subsequent transfers by the assignee thereunder."[59] The Comments state that these assignments need not be filed because they "are not financing transactions, and the debtor ordinarily will not be engaging in further credit transactions."[60] This policy justification suggests that, rather than providing for automatic perfection of these assignments, the transactions should be excluded in their entirety from the scope of Article 9.[61]

[F] Assignment of a Beneficial Interest in a Decedent's Estate—§ 9-309(13)

Automatic perfection is available for "a security interest created by an assignment of a beneficial interest in a decedent's estate." Such an interest is a general intangible, and perhaps a payment intangible.[62] Article 9 governs the sale of payment intangibles but not the sale of other general intangibles.[63] Thus, a lender against a beneficial interest always gets the benefit of automatic perfection; a buyer of a beneficial interest gets the same benefit if the interest is a payment intangible and, therefor, the transaction is governed by Article 9.

Prior law provided the same treatment for an assignment of a beneficial interest in a trust. Revised Article 9 eliminated automatic perfection in this context because of the more prevalent use of interests in trusts in commercial financing transactions.[64]

[G] Sales of Lottery Winnings—§ 9-309(14)

A right to payment of winnings in a lottery or other game of chance is an account,[65] and the interest of a buyer of such an account is automatically

---

[57] U.C.C. § 9-309(11).

[58] U.C.C. § 9-309, Comment 6.

[59] U.C.C. § 9-309(12).

[60] U.C.C. § 9-309, Comment 8.

[61] *See* U.C.C. § 9-109, Comment 6 (transfers of accounts that are excluded from Article 9 because, by their nature, they have nothing to do with commercial financing transactions).

[62] U.C.C. § 9-102(a)(42), (61).

[63] U.C.C. § 9-109(a)(3).

[64] U.C.C. § 9-309, Comment 7.

[65] U.C.C. § 9-102(a)(2)

perfected. The reason is that the payments are typically made over an extended period of time and, without this rule, the buyer would have to reperfect within one year each time the seller changed its location.[66] Curiously, the same protection was not provided to a lender that takes an assignment of the right to payment, perhaps because the loan might be paid back over a shorter period of time.

---

[66] U.C.C. § 9-316(a), (b). *See* § 9.04 *infra*.

Chapter 8

TEMPORARY PERFECTION AND PERFECTION OF PROCEEDS

SYNOPSIS

In addition to the normal methods of perfection, Article 9 includes some circumstances in which a secured party can either acquire or retain perfected status on a temporary basis. Although temporary perfection is a form of automatic perfection, it is distinguishable from the continuous automatic perfection discussed in Chapter 7. Temporary perfection is limited to periods of only twenty days.

§ 8.01 INSTRUMENTS, CERTIFICATED SECURITIES, DOCUMENTS AND BAILED GOODS— § 9-312(e)-(h)

[A] Initial Perfection

Perfection with respect to instruments, certificated securities, and negotiable documents can be automatically attained by a secured party for a

191

period of twenty days after attachment if the secured party gives "new value" for the security interest.[1] Prior to expiration of the twenty-day grace period, the secured party must comply with another appropriate method of perfection in order to remain continuously perfected without a gap.[2]

The new-value requirement means that the secured party cannot gain the protection of temporary perfection if it acquires its interest to secure an antecedent debt. New value means "(i) money, (ii) money's worth in property, services, or new credit, or (iii) release by a transferee of an interest in property previously transferred to the transferee." The definition excludes the substitution of one obligation for another obligation.[3]

Under original Article 9, perfection by filing was not available for security interests in instruments. At that time, what are now called "certificated securities" were within the "instrument" category. Perfection by filing became available for all types of investment property—which now is the category that includes certificated securities—when Article 8 was revised in 1994. Moreover, perfection by filing became available for instruments with revised Article 9. Thus, there is no category for which temporary perfection is really necessary, although it remains important in that it facilitates truly short-term transactions. For example, a bank might make a two-day loan to a mortgage lender secured by the lender's stockpile of instruments, or make "day loans" to stockbrokers secured by certificated securities. Temporary perfection obviates the need for the bank either to file or take possession of the collateral.

Notwithstanding the convenience of the temporary perfection and permissive filing rules, there are risks inherent in relying upon these types of perfection when the collateral is negotiable or quasi-negotiable.[4] Of course, any lender that agrees to a security interest based on collateral that the debtor claims to own always runs the risk that the property does not exist or that the debtor either does not own it or has already encumbered it. In the case of instruments, certificated securities, and negotiable documents, however, a significant risk persists even after the security interest attaches and filing occurs or temporary perfection is attained. Leaving this type of collateral in the debtor's hands permits a wrongful transfer to a third party that might take priority over the secured party. The prudent secured party should consider the following priority rules:

---

[1] U.C.C. § 9-312(e).

[2] U.C.C. § 9-312(h).

[3] U.C.C. § 9-102(a)(57). The requirement of new value eliminates temporary perfection for any collateral of these types to which a security interest attaches by virtue of an after-acquired property clause, unless the secured party extends additional value to the debtor for this new collateral. *See In re* Reliance Equities, Inc., 966 F.2d 1338, 17 U.C.C. Rep. Serv. 2d 1316 (10th Cir. 1992) (automatic perfection with respect to each promissory note in issue because the secured party gave new value with respect to each note).

[4] The risk also applies in the case of a buyer of a promissory note that fails to obtain possession of the note. The buyer is a secured party for purposes of Article 9, U.C.C. § 9-102(a)(72)(D), and its security interest in the note is automatically perfected. U.C.C. § 9-309(4).

- Nothing in Article 9 limits the rights of a holder in due course of a negotiable instrument, a holder to which a negotiable document has been duly negotiated, or a protected purchaser of a security. Furthermore, filing does not constitute notice to such persons.[5] This rule must be read in conjunction with provisions in Articles 3, 7, and 8 that permit certain holders and purchasers to take free of adverse claims.

- A purchaser of an instrument (whether negotiable or not) has priority over a secured party that perfects by a method other than possession if the purchaser gives value and takes possession in good faith and without knowledge that the purchase violates the secured party's rights.[6] If, however, there is an indication on an instrument that it has been assigned to an identified assignee, any purchaser is deemed to have knowledge that the purchase violates the assignee's rights.[7] Accordingly, a secured party can insist that its debtor only take notes that contain a notation indicating that they have been assigned to the secured party, using the name of the secured party in the notation.

Bear in mind that "purchaser" means a person that acquires an interest in property as a result of a voluntary transaction;[8] thus, a secured party relying on filing or temporary perfection is at risk from buyers and other secured parties.

The advantage of permissive filing can be illustrated with reference to negotiable documents. The filing will not be sufficient to overcome the loss of priority if the debtor, left in possession or control of the document, wrongfully transfers it to a bona-fide purchaser for value.[9] Filing addresses a different risk. A negotiable document represents title to goods and, during the period of temporary perfection, the debtor might surrender the document and obtain the goods from a carrier or a warehouse. In fact, the very purpose of relying upon temporary perfection might be to enable the debtor to acquire the goods for resale or other use. The advantage of filing is that it provides continuous perfection of the collateral, whether in the form of the document or the underlying goods.

---

[5] U.C.C. § 9-331. *In re* Kontaratos, 10 B.R. 956, 31 U.C.C. Rep. Serv. 1124 (Bankr. D. Me. 1981) (temporarily perfected security interest in shares of stock held subordinate to subsequent security interest of bank to whom stock certificates were delivered as collateral). For further discussion of § 9-331, *see* § 11.03[D] *infra*.

[6] U.C.C. § 9-330(d).

[7] U.C.C. § 9-330(f). For further discussion of § 9-330 in the context of instruments, *see* § 11.03[C][2] *infra*.

[8] U.C.C. § 1-201(b)(30), (29).

[9] The only adequate protection against this risk is for the secured party to perfect by taking possession or control of the document, leaving the debtor unable to pass the possession or control that a subsequent transferee needs in order to attain priority. The risk of wrongful transfer explains why most secured lenders rely on possession or control of documents for perfection rather than on the filing of a financing statement. *See* U.C.C. §§ 9-331(a), 7-501, 7-502, 1-201(b)(20). The same analysis applies with respect to certificated securities and instruments.

[B]   Continuing Perfection for Collateral Made Available to Debtor

A temporary perfection period is also provided for certain circumstances in which collateral is made available to a debtor. If the collateral is a negotiable document or goods in the possession of a bailee that has not issued a negotiable document (including a bailee that has issued a nonnegotiable document), a perfected security interest remains perfected for 20 days without filing if the secured party makes available to the debtor either the goods or the document for the following limited purposes: "(1) ultimate sale or exchange; or (2) loading, unloading, storing, shipping, transshipping, manufacturing, processing, or otherwise dealing with them in a manner preliminary to their sale or exchange."[10] In addition, comparable continuing temporary perfection is provided upon the delivery to the debtor of a certificated security or instrument for the purpose of: "(1) ultimate sale or exchange; or (2) presentation, collection, enforcement, renewal, or registration of transfer."[11]

The foregoing rule on negotiable documents and goods in the possession of a bailee that has not issued such a document must be understood in the context of the following rules, which generally govern perfection in those categories of collateral:

- While goods are in the possession of a bailee that has issued a negotiable document, a security interest in the goods may be perfected by perfecting as to the document, and a security interest perfected in the document has priority over a security interest perfected in the goods by any other method during that time.[12]

- While goods are in the possession of a bailee that has issued a nonnegotiable document, a security interest must be perfected as to the goods and not as to the document. Perfection may be accomplished by issuance of a document in the name of the secured party, thereby giving the secured party control over access to the goods, by the bailee's receipt of notification of the secured party's interest, or by filing as to the goods.[13]

- While goods are in the possession of a bailee that has not issued either a negotiable or nonnegotiable document, perfection may accomplished by filing or by obtaining from the bailee an authenticated record acknowledging that it holds, or will hold, the collateral for the secured party's benefit.[14]

The temporary perfection period runs from the date the secured party makes the document or goods available, or delivers the instrument or

---

[10] U.C.C. § 9-312(f).

[11] U.C.C. § 9-312(g).

[12] U.C.C. § 9-312(c). For further discussion, see § 6.02[B][1] supra.

[13] U.C.C. § 9-312(d). For further discussion, see § 6.02[B][2] supra.

[14] U.C.C. § 9-313(c). For further discussion, see § 6.03[B] supra.

certificated security, to the debtor. Perfection by a different method is required prior to expiration of the 20-day temporary-perfection period if the secured party wishes to remain perfected beyond the end of that period.[15] Continuing temporary perfection is not necessary if the secured party has perfected by filing.[16]

Unlike initial temporary perfection, new value is not required, but the collateral must be returned to advance one of the stated purposes. This requirement actually is not very limiting because it covers nearly all of the legitimate purposes for returning such collateral. Case law has recognized the legitimacy of the return of a certificate of deposit so that it could be renewed by issuance of a new certificate,[17] the return of a negotiable bill of lading to acquire the goods from a carrier and store them,[18] and the return of a promissory note for purposes of collection.[19] Even the return of the collateral for purpose of sale is recognized as legitimate, based on the rationale that the parties may envision debtor sale of the collateral as the means by which the debtor will acquire the assets to pay the secured debt.

The convenience associated with temporary perfection must be balanced against the enhanced risk that accompanies debtor reacquisition of collateral in the form of a negotiable document. The debtor will then have the means to transfer the collateral to a party who can achieve priority against even a perfected security interest.[20] The risks are described in more detail in the prior subsection dealing with initial temporary perfection.[21]

§ 8.02   PROCEEDS—§ 9-315(c)-(e)

[A]   The Grace Period of Temporary Perfection

Article 9 provides that a secured party's interest in collateral attaches automatically to identifiable proceeds received by a debtor upon disposition of that collateral.[22] It also determines whether the secured party's interest

---

[15] U.C.C. § 9-312(h). *See In re* Schwinn Cycling & Fitness, Inc., 313 B.R. 473, 54 UCC Rep. Serv. 2d 645 (D. Colo. 2004) (because the common carrier with the security interest did not file a financing statement after releasing possession of the goods and the negotiable document to the debtor for purpose of sale of the goods, the carrier did not have a continuously perfected security interest).

[16] Priority in a security interest in goods after a document that covers them is surrendered is not governed by the provisions on temporary perfection.

[17] Wrightman v. American Nat'l Bank of Riverton, 610 P.2d 1001, 29 U.C.C. Rep. Serv. 251 (Wyo. 1980).

[18] Scallop Petroleum Co. v. Banque Trad-Credit Lyonnais S.A., 690 F. Supp. 184, 6 U.C.C. Rep. Serv. 2d 1573 (S.D.N.Y. 1988).

[19] McIlroy Bank v. First Nat'l Bank of Fayetteville, 252 Ark. 558, 480 S.W.2d 127, 10 U.C.C. Rep. Serv. 1111 (1972).

[20] *See* U.C.C. § 9-331 and § 11.03[D] *infra*.

[21] *See* § 8.01[A] *supra*.

[22] U.C.C. §§ 9-203(f), 9-315(a)(2). For a discussion of automatic attachment of security interests to identifiable proceeds, *see* § 2.03[B] *supra*.

in the proceeds is perfected.[23] "Proceeds" includes, *inter alia*, whatever the debtor receives upon any kind of disposition of collateral.[24] Irrespective of whether the disposition is authorized or is instead in violation of the security agreement, the security interest continues automatically in the proceeds, so long as they can be identified.

In some types of financing, proceeds are expected. In inventory financing, for example, a secured party is virtually certain to authorize sale or lease of the inventory. Its security interest is extinguished by an authorized disposition[25] and even by an unauthorized disposition to a buyer or lessee in ordinary course of business.[26] For continuing security, the secured party will look to proceeds, which are likely to be in the form of cash, checks, notes, accounts, or chattel paper. Similarly, an accounts financier will claim the proceeds received from payments on accounts, which are likely to be in the form of checks.

Although a security interest attaches automatically to identifiable proceeds, perfection is generally necessary to protect the secured party's interest against other claimants. Perfection continues automatically if the security interest in the original collateral was perfected by any method,[27] but it lapses on the 21st day after attachment of the security interest to the proceeds unless one of the conditions discussed in the ensuing subsections is satisfied.[28]

The secured party's goal is to have its security interest in proceeds continuously perfected so that its priority relates back to its initial perfection.[29] In every case, the Code grants temporary automatic perfection for the duration of the 20-day grace period. If one of the statutory conditions that does not require any further action by the secured party is satisfied, perfection continues automatically beyond that period. If not, and if the secured party is not perfected *as to the proceeds* before the grace period expires, its interest in the proceeds becomes unperfected.[30]

---

[23] U.C.C. § 9-315(c)-(e).

[24] U.C.C. § 9-102(a)(64)(A). For a discussion of the concept of proceeds, *see* § 2.03[A] *supra*.

[25] U.C.C. § 9-315(a)(1). For a discussion of these provisions, *see* §§ 11.01, 11.02 *infra*.

[26] U.C.C. §§ 9-320(a) (buyer), 9-321(c) (lessee). For further discussion of these provisions, *see* § 11.03[A][1] *infra*.

[27] "A security interest in proceeds is a perfected security interest if the security interest in the original collateral was perfected." U.C.C. § 9-315(c).

[28] U.C.C. § 9-315(d).

[29] Article 9 does not provide for continuous perfection with respect to proceeds if the secured party was not perfected in the original collateral. *In re* Beacon Light Marina Yacht Club, Inc., 125 B.R. 154, 14 U.C.C. Rep. Serv. 2d 1230 (Bankr. W.D. Va. 1990) (secured party, which did not perfect its interest in boat by noting its interest on boat's certificate of title, did not have perfected security interest in proceeds from sale of boat).

[30] U.C.C. § 9-315(e).

[B] Continuous Perfection

Automatic temporary perfection in proceeds will extended into continuous perfection if one of several conditions is satisfied.[31] The nature of these conditions is discussed below.

[1] Identifiable Cash Proceeds

Perfection does not lapse at the end of the grace period if the proceeds are identifiable cash proceeds.[32] "Cash proceeds," defined to include only "money, checks, deposit accounts, or the like," are essentially cash or cash equivalents.[33] Cash proceeds most commonly arise when the debtor receives cash or a check in full or partial payment for collateral comprised of accounts or inventory in which the secured party has a perfected security interest.

Cash proceeds are easily dissipated, and a secured party relying on such proceeds must be aware of the following risks:

- If the proceeds become commingled with other funds, the secured party may lose its security interest in them entirely because of an inability to identify them. Article 9 codifies the result of cases permitting a secured party to use equitable tracing principles, notably the lowest-intermediate-balance rule, to identify the amount of commingled proceeds to which its security interest attaches.[34]

- A transferee of a check that qualifies as a holder in due course under Article 3 takes the check free of a perfected security interest.[35]

- A transferee of a check may take it free of a perfected security interest even if the transferee does not qualify as a holder in due course.[36] To take advantage of the rule, the transferee must give value and take possession of the check in good faith and without knowledge that the transfer violates the rights of the secured party.[37]

- A transferee of funds from a deposit account takes the funds free of a perfected security interest in the deposit account if the transferee does not act in collusion with the debtor to violate the

---

[31] U.C.C. § 9-315(d).

[32] U.C.C. § 9-315(d)(2).

[33] U.C.C. § 9-102(a)(9). *See* § 2.03[A] *supra.*

[34] U.C.C. § 9-315(b)(2). For further discussion, *see* § 2.03[B] *supra.* If goods that are proceeds are commingled, U.C.C. § 9-315(b)(1) provides that identification is to be determined under U.C.C. § 9-336.

[35] U.C.C. § 9-331(a). For further discussion, *see* § 11.03[D] *infra.*

[36] U.C.C. § 9-330(d).

[37] For further discussion, *see* § 11.03[C][2] *infra.*

secured party's rights.[38] There is a similar rule for a transferee of money.[39]

Continuous perfection for identifiable cash proceeds most commonly applies when the secured party has a perfected security interest in accounts or chattel paper and the cash proceeds are paid in full or partial satisfaction thereof,[40] and when the perfected security interest is in inventory and the cash proceeds are received on its sale.[41] One bankruptcy opinion correctly indicates that perfection was continuous and automatic with respect to traceable cash proceeds from the sale of inventory in which the secured party had a perfected security interest, but not with respect to the proceeds of inventory in which the secured party did not have a perfected interest.[42] Another bankruptcy decision held that a filing for national registration with the FAA, which is required to perfect a security interest in an airplane,[43] led to continuous automatic perfection in the identifiable cash proceeds received upon the debtor's sale of the airplane.[44]

The cash and cash-like nature of the property that constitutes "cash proceeds" suggests that great care is advisable in structuring transactions in which a secured party desires continuous automatic perfection. Cash proceeds are easily dissipated or commingled with other funds, which may jeopardize the secured party's interest on the grounds that the cash proceeds are no longer identifiable.[45] A secured lender may be wise to require the debtor to segregate all cash proceeds it receives and deposit them into a special account to which the secured party can control access. The secured party can then make unannounced spot-checks to monitor the debtor's compliance.

The secured party in *In re Schwinn Cycling and Fitness, Inc.*[46] had temporary perfection under section 9-312(f) in goods that it made available to the debtor for ultimate sale. The secured party did not take steps to re-perfect its interest in the goods, which were sold by the debtor within the 20-day temporary-perfection period. The secured party then claimed its interest in the proceeds of the sale. The bankruptcy court held that the secured party's failure to maintain continuous perfection of its security interest in the goods meant that its security interest in the proceeds was

---

[38] U.C.C. § 9-332(b). For further discussion, *see* § 11.03[E] *infra*.

[39] U.C.C. § 9-332(a).

[40] *In re* John Deskins Pic Pac, Inc., 59 B.R. 809, 1 U.C.C. Rep. Serv. 2d 1696 (Bankr. W.D. Va. 1986); Farns Assocs., Inc. v. South Side Bank, 93 Ill. App. 3d 766, 417 N.E.2d 818, 30 U.C.C. Rep. Serv. 1729 (1981).

[41] Dixie Production Credit Assn. v. Kent, 167 Ga. 714, 307 S.E.2d 277, 37 U.C.C. Rep. Serv. 595 (1983).

[42] *In re* Critiques, Inc., 29 B.R. 941, 36 U.C.C. Rep. Serv. 1778 (Bankr. D. Kan. 1983).

[43] Article 9's perfection rules are preempted by the Federal Aviation Act of 1958, 49 U.S.C. § 1403. *See* § 1.07[A] *supra*.

[44] *In re* Turner, 13 B.R. 15, 32 U.C.C. Rep. Serv. 1240 (Bankr. D. Neb. 1981).

[45] *See* § 2.03[B] *supra*.

[46] 313 B.R. 473, 54 UCC Rep. Serv.2d 645 (D. Colo. 2004).

unperfected. On appeal, the district court held that the secured party should prevail under section 9-315(d)(2) if the proceeds were in fact identifiable cash proceeds, and remanded the case to the bankruptcy court for a determination of this issue. In reaching this result, the court specifically referred to Comment 7 of section 9-315, which provides that "if the security interest in the original collateral was perfected, a security interest in identifiable cash proceeds will remain perfected indefinitely, regardless of whether the security interest in the original collateral remains perfected."

[2] Same Filing Office: The Basic Rule

Continuous perfection beyond the grace period is sometimes recognized with respect to noncash proceeds, but only if the secured party has perfected its security interest in the original collateral by filing and other conditions are met.[47] The other conditions are that the office in which a financing statement would be filed with respect to the proceeds is the same as the office in which the secured party actually filed to perfect its security interest in the original collateral,[48] and that the debtor did not receive cash proceeds in exchange for the original collateral. The prime example occurs when a secured party has a perfected-by-filing security interest in inventory and the debtor generates accounts or chattel paper upon disposition of the inventory. Because the secured party would have filed as to the accounts or chattel paper (had they been the original collateral) in the same office as it filed with respect to the inventory, perfection does not lapse at the end of the 20-day grace period. Perfection is predicated on the initial financing statement, and the secured party will become unperfected if the financing statement lapses.[49]

This approach represents a compromise between the need to reduce transaction costs and the need for adequate notice to searchers. The basic idea is that, in certain common financing transactions, a searcher should be able to recognize that a particular type of described collateral will yield a particular type or types of undescribed proceeds. The classic example is inventory sold to produce accounts or chattel paper. A searcher that is interested in lending against, or buying, a dealer's accounts or chattel paper should be aware that such assets typically arise when inventory is sold on credit or leased. If a financing statement covering inventory is found, the searcher is on notice that the secured party will also claim the accounts and chattel paper. This explains why it is so important that the filing as to the original collateral be in the same office as that in which a filing would be made as to the proceeds. A searcher that looks in the proper office for

---

[47] U.C.C. § 9-315(d)(1).

[48] The proper office for purposes of Article 9 filings is determined by sections 9-501 (selection of the office within a given state) and 9-301 through 9-307 and 9-316 (selection of the state whose law governs perfection). *See* § 5.05 *supra* and Chapter 9 *infra*.

[49] Following the passage of the grace period of 20 days, a security interest in the proceeds that is perfected continuously will become unperfected if the effectiveness of the financing statement covering the original collateral lapses or is terminated. U.C.C. § 9-315(e).

accounts and does not find a financing statement describing inventory cannot draw the proper inference.

Because the same-filing-office rule is based on the predictability of certain types of proceeds in common financing transactions, it tends to break down in less common situations. For example, suppose Secured Party files to perfect a security interest in Farmer's tractor, using a specific description rather than a category or type of collateral. Farmer later trades the tractor in on a new tractor. Secured party's interest in the new tractor will remain perfected beyond the grace period, meaning that it will have priority over a person that buys or lends against the tractor even though the buyer or lender will not be on notice in any real sense.

Another, and more exotic example, involves Farmer trading the original tractor to Neighbor for a valuable painting. Filings as to equipment and consumer goods are made in the same office. Thus, if Farmer later sells the painting to another neighbor, the secured party's security interest will be continuously perfected and can be enforced against the neighbor. Such situations are, of course, relatively rare.[50]

[3] Same Filing Office: The "Cash-Phase" Rule

Continuous perfection with respect to noncash proceeds is more restricted when there is a "cash phase"—*i.e.*, when original collateral is disposed of to produce cash proceeds that are in turn used to acquire noncash proceeds.[51] Cash proceeds may be used to purchase assets of any type, and thus the predictability upon which the same-filing-office rule is predicated vanishes. If there is a cash phase, perfection in the noncash proceeds will lapse at the end of the grace period unless (1) the secured party originally perfected by filing a financing statement containing a description broad enough to cover the proceeds, or (2) perfection occurs by any appropriate method before the grace period expires.

For example, suppose Secured Party files as to all of Rancher's "cattle" and Rancher later sells some cattle in exchange for a check, which Rancher deposits in a bank account. If Rancher later uses the proceeds in the account to purchase additional cattle, the secured party's perfected status will not lapse at the end of the grace period. A purchase of a tractor with the cash proceeds, however, would result in lapse of perfection unless the secured party filed as to the tractor or took possession of it before the grace period expired. Similarly, a financing statement that describes the collateral as "accounts" is inadequate to perfect a security interest in inventory acquired with cash proceeds of the accounts. The result would be otherwise if the financing statement also listed "inventory."

---

[50] *But see In re* Wiersma, 283 B.R. 294, 49 U.C.C. Rep. Serv.2d 309 (Bankr. D. Ida. 2002), *aff'd*, 324 B.R. 92, 56 UCC Rep. Serv. 2d 452 (Bankr. 9th Cir. 2005) (security interest in cows and milk was properly perfected in the office of the Secretary of State, which is the same office where a secured creditor would file to perfect an interest in an insurance settlement).

[51] U.C.C. § 9-315(d)(1).

The facts of *Citicorp (USA), Inc. v. Davidson Lumber Co.*[52] demonstrate the rules for perfection in noncash proceeds that are acquired with cash proceeds. Two banks had security interests in present and after-acquired general intangibles, and each had perfected by filing. The debtor later received a federal tax refund of approximately $1.3 million, which it used (without the knowledge of the banks) to purchase a certificate of deposit payable at a future date. The right to a tax refund is a general intangible, and the refund check was a cash proceed of that right. Transfer of the check in exchange for the certificate of deposit generated noncash proceeds from the cash proceeds.[53] The banks could have attained continuous perfection of their interests in the CD by taking the necessary steps for perfection of a security interest in the CD within the 20-day grace period.[54] The court properly rejected the policy argument of the banks that such a requirement was "preposterous" because it left them vulnerable to the actions of a debtor that secretly converted the collateral into a type of proceeds that necessitated action by them to attain continuous perfection. The court noted that this argument simply raises concerns regarding a secured party's need to implement adequate measures to police the actions of its debtor. It further noted that the banks could have protected themselves with respect to the expected tax refund by using the federal Assignment of Claims Act.[55]

[4] Timely General Perfection

As indicated above, if neither the identifiable-cash-proceeds option nor the same-filing-office option is available, perfection will lapse at the end of the grace period unless the secured party takes appropriate steps to perfect as to the proceeds. In other words, the secured party must take a step that would have been appropriate had the proceeds been the original collateral. This might involve, *inter alia*, the filing of a financing statement describing the proceeds, taking possession or control of them, or complying with a relevant certificate-of-title statute or federal law. A secured party that allows the grace period to expire becomes unperfected, and even though it can later perfect its interest in the proceeds, its priority date cannot relate back to the date on which it perfected as to the original collateral.

An occasional case involves a secured party that has succeeded in taking the timely action necessary to achieve continuous perfection in proceeds. In *In re Airwest International,*[56] a bank used possession to perfect its interest in two certificates of deposit and, when the bank "rolled over" the certificates upon their maturity, to perfect its interest continuously in the

[52] 718 F.2d 1030, 37 U.C.C. Rep. Serv. 324 (11th Cir. 1983).

[53] The characterization of the certificate of deposit was one of the primary issues litigated. The appellate court properly held that the CD was non-cash proceeds, thus precluding continuous perfection based on the filing with respect to the original collateral. The court followed prior decisions in holding that an instrument in the form of a certificate of deposit is more like a promissory note than a check.

[54] *See* U.C.C. § 9-315[d][3] and § 8.02[B][4] *infra*.

[55] 31 U.S.C. § 203 (1976), *amended by* 31 U.S.C. § 3727 (1983).

[56] 70 B.R. 914, 3 U.C.C. Rep. Serv. 2d 1936 (Bankr. D. Haw. 1987).

resulting single new certificate. In *Wrightman v. American National Bank of Riverton*,[57] a bank, initially perfected by possession of an instrument in the form of a certificate of deposit, continued perfected by temporary perfection when it returned the certificate to its owner for the purpose of renewal by issuance of a new certificate.[58] The replacement certificate constituted proceeds of the first certificate, and the bank's interest in the proceeds continued perfected because the bank obtained possession of the new certificate before expiration of the grace period.[59]

Secured parties more often become unperfected with respect to proceeds by reason of their failure to take timely steps to perfect their interests in proceeds. An example is *Citicorp (USA), Inc. v. Davidson Lumber Co.*,[60] discussed in the preceding subsection. In *Security Savings Bank of Marshalltown, Iowa v. United States*,[61] the bank had a security interest in a Chevrolet truck which it had properly perfected by notation on a certificate of title. The bank agreed that the debtor could substitute a Ford truck for the Chevy; however, because the bank did not provide for notation of its security interest on a certificate of title covering the Ford within the grace period, continuous perfection was lost. Another case in which continuous perfection in a vehicle as proceeds was lost is *In re Charles E. Sutphin, Inc.*[62] The secured party properly perfected by filing with respect to farm vehicles that were part of the debtor's inventory. In exchange for two of the vehicles, the debtor received a tractor. The tractor was not added to the debtor's inventory, but rather was placed in over-the-road service and thus was subject to a certificate-of-title requirement. Because the secured party failed to perfect under the certificate-of-title law within the grace period, its security interest in the tractor became unperfected.

---

[57] 610 P.2d 1001, 29 U.C.C. Rep. Serv. 251 (Wyo. 1980).

[58] *See* U.C.C. § 9-312(g).

[59] *See* U.C.C. § 9-315(d)(3).

[60] 718 F.2d 1030, 37 U.C.C. Rep. Serv. 324 (11th Cir. 1983).

[61] 440 F. Supp. 444, 22 U.C.C. Rep. Serv. 1260 (S.D. Iowa 1977).

[62] 44 B.R. 533, 39 U.C.C. Rep. Serv. 1499 (Bankr. W.D. Va. 1984).

Chapter 9

MULTISTATE TRANSACTIONS

SYNOPSIS

§ 9.01 THE CODE'S BASIC CHOICE-OF-LAW PROVISION

The Code's basic choice-of-law provision, which is contained in Article 1 and is therefore applicable throughout the U.C.C., permits the parties to select the state whose laws will govern their transaction, so long as there is a reasonable relationship between the transaction and the selected state. Prior to the revision of Article 1, the Code provided as follows:

> Except as provided hereafter in this section, when a transaction bears a reasonable relation to this state and also to another state or nation the parties may agree that the law either of this state or of such other state or nation shall govern their rights and duties. Failing such agreement this Act applies to transactions bearing an appropriate relation to this state.[1]

---

[1] U.C.C. § 1-105(1) (2000 Official Text).

203

The official text of revised Article 1 provides a different, but controversial rule.[2] Because of significant opposition to this provision, states adopting the revision have chosen to retain the original rule. Because of this, the authors have chosen to deviate in this single instance from the exclusive use of the revised text of Article 1.

The parties' right to choose the applicable law is consistent with the Code's basic freedom-of-contract philosophy, but it is not unlimited. The basic choice-of-law provision requires that the transaction bear a reasonable relationship to the selected state. More importantly, Article 9 contains mandatory choice-of-law provisions that govern perfection of security interests, the effects of perfection or nonperfection, and the priority of security interests.[3] Article 1 permits the parties to choose the law that will govern other relevant issues concerning secured transactions, including attachment, validity, characterization, and enforcement.[4] The discussion below addresses the choice-of-law provisions of Articles 1 and 9.

[A] The Reasonable Relationship Test

The Comments[5] indicate that the Code's "reasonable relationship" test is similar to the test created by the United States Supreme Court in *Seeman v. Philadelphia Warehouse Co.*,[6] but this reference is not particularly helpful. In *Seeman,* the Court upheld a choice-of-law clause designating Pennsylvania law because the lender was a Pennsylvania corporation that regularly conducted business within the state. The courts have routinely acceded to the parties' wishes when one of them (usually the creditor) resides or conducts business in the selected state.[7]

Even when neither party resides in the chosen state, the courts may find a sufficient nexus between the transaction and the state to uphold the choice. For example, in *Key Bank of Maine v. Dunbar,*[8] a choice-of-law clause selecting Maryland law was held to be reasonable because the collateral, a boat, was to be kept in that state. The courts have not required that the parties select the state that has the most significant contacts with the transaction, only that they select a state that has some legitimate contact with the transaction.

---

[2] "[A]n agreement by parties to a domestic transaction that any or all of their rights and obligations are to be determined by the law of this State or of another State is effective, whether or not the transaction bears a relation to the State designated." U.C.C. § 1-301(c)(1).

[3] *See* Article 9, Part 3, Subpart 1.

[4] *See* Prefatory Comment, Part 3, Article 9.

[5] U.C.C. § 1-105, Comment 1 (2000 Official Text). The Comments to the revision of Article 1 drop this reference, of course, as irrelevant under the new test.

[6] 274 U.S. 403, 47 S. Ct. 626, 71 L. Ed. 1123 (1927).

[7] *See, e.g., In re* Keene Corp., 188 B.R. 881, 28 U.C.C. Rep. Serv. 2d 651 (Bankr. S.D.N.Y. 1995) (selection of Illinois law upheld where debtor, a New York resident, granted secured party, an Illinois corporation, a security interest in book-entry Treasury securities).

[8] 28 U.C.C. Rep. Serv. 2d 398 (E.D. Pa. 1995), *aff'd,* 91 F.3d 124 (3d Cir. 1996).

Courts only rarely have invalidated a choice-of-law agreement,[9] and when this occurs, the result is obvious. In *Woco v. Benjamin Franklin Corp.*,[10] for example, the parties to a lease agreement selected California law, but the testimony failed to establish that either party resided or did business there, that the collateral was kept there, or that the contract had been formed there. The court properly applied New Hampshire law to resolve the dispute.

The fact that revised Article 9 is universally in effect significantly dilutes the importance of the choice-of-law issue. Nevertheless, some significant differences among the states persist. Virtually every state has nonuniform amendments that make its version of Article 9 unique, and even the uniform provisions have been subjected to varying judicial interpretations. In most cases, a court will apply the parties' choice-of-law provision routinely, but in certain situations one party (usually the debtor) may argue that a compelling state policy requires the courts of the forum state to ignore an otherwise valid choice. Suppose, for example, that the forum state has an anti-deficiency rule in consumer transactions that penalizes secured parties that fail to follow the proper procedures for foreclosure, but the law of the chosen state allows the secured party to overcome a negative presumption and recover a deficiency.[11] Courts faced with such arguments should defer to the parties' choice and resist the temptation to apply local law and, for the most part, they have done so.[12]

It is generally understood that a court that applies the substantive law of another state will nevertheless apply the procedural law of the forum state. In *Nez v. Forney*,[13] for example, the parties selected the law of Texas. The court held, however, that New Mexico's statute of limitations was procedural in nature and applied it.

[B] The Appropriate Relationship Test

If the parties fail to designate the controlling law (or if their choice-of-law clause is not enforced), the forum state's version of the Code "applies to

---

[9] Section 1-105(1) (2000 Official Text) requires that the parties "agree" on the law of a particular state, and "agreement," as defined in section 1-201(b)(3), includes both the expressions of the parties and implications drawn from the surrounding facts. While most choice-of-law agreements are memorialized in a record (and it is dangerous not to do so), a record is not required. *See, e.g.,* Neville Chem. Co. v. Union Carbide Corp., 422 F.2d 1205 (3d Cir. 1970), *cert. denied*, 400 U.S. 826, 91 S. Ct. 51, 27 L. Ed. 2d 55 (1970) (court relies on fact that parties assumed Pennsylvania law would apply).

[10] 20 U.C.C. Rep. Serv. 1015 (D. N.H. 1976), *aff'd on other grounds*, 562 F.2d 1339 (1st Cir. 1977).

[11] For discussion of the general rules regarding a secured party's ability to obtain a deficiency judgment following a commercially unreasonable disposition, *see* § 19.02.

[12] *See, e.g.,* Interfirst Bank Clifton v. Fernandez, 853 F.2d 292, 6 U.C.C. Rep. Serv. 2d 1275 (5th Cir. 1988) (court refused to apply Louisiana anti-deficiency statute to protect Louisiana resident); *see contra*, Lewis v. First Nat'l Bank of Miami, 216 S.E.2d 347, 17 U.C.C. Rep. Serv. 197 (Ga. Ct. App. 1975) (case decided under 1962 Official Text applying Georgia law to repossession, notwithstanding choice of Florida law).

[13] 109 N.M. 161, 783 P.2d 471, 10 U.C.C. Rep. Serv. 2d 289 (1989).

transactions bearing an appropriate relation to this state."[14] The fact that the drafters chose a different verbal formula suggests that the "appropriate relationship" test is more stringent than the "reasonable relationship" test that governs choice-of-law agreements. Suppose, for example, that the parties litigate a case in State A, which has a sufficient relationship to the transaction to support *in personam* jurisdiction and bears a sufficient relationship to the transaction that an agreement choosing its law would be effective, but State B has the most significant relationship with the transaction. Most courts have concluded that the courts in State A should apply the substantive law of State B,[15] although a minority have equated the "reasonable relationship" and "appropriate relationship" tests in order to apply the law of the forum state.[16]

While the Comments leave interpretation of the term "appropriate relationship" to the courts,[17] equating the two tests runs counter to the normal rules of statutory construction. It should be presumed that the drafters intended different tests since they used differing language. The courts that have taken the "most significant contacts" approach appear to have the better of the argument.

Even if the parties have selected a state that satisfies the reasonable relationship test, the courts should apply the appropriate relationship test if one of the disputants is a third party that did not participate in the agreement process.[18] Of course, many issues involving the rights of third parties will turn on perfection and the effects of perfection or nonperfection, and will be governed by Article 9 rather than section 1-105(1).

§ 9.02 THE ARTICLE 9 CHOICE-OF-LAW RULES

The Article 9 choice-of-law provisions, which govern perfection, the effects of perfection or nonperfection, and the priority of a security interest, significantly limit the operation of the Code's basic choice-of-law provision.[19] The

---

[14] U.C.C. § 1-105(1) (2000 Official Text). The Official Text of revised Article 1 eliminates this test, and provides instead that in the absence of an effective agreement between the parties, "the rights and obligations of the parties are determined by the law that would be selected by application of this State's [the forum State's] conflict of laws principles." U.C.C. § 1-301(d) (2003 Official Text). Interpreting "appropriate relationship" in the original Article to mean that a court should apply the forum state's conflict-of-law rules is entirely appropriate.

[15] *See, e.g., In re* Nantahala Village, Inc., 976 F.2d 876, 18 U.C.C. Rep. Serv. 2d 1027 (4th Cir. 1992) (Florida law, rather than law of forum state, North Carolina, governed).

[16] *See, e.g.,* Bos Material Handling, Inc. v. Crown Controls Corp., 137 Cal. App. 3d 99, 186 Cal. Rptr. 740 (1982) (applying law of forum state even though it did not have most significant contacts with transaction).

[17] U.C.C. § 1-105, Comment 3.

[18] *See, e.g.,* Hong Kong & Shanghai Banking Corp. v. HFH USA Corp., 805 F. Supp. 133, 19 U.C.C. Rep. Serv. 2d 885 (W.D.N.Y. 1992).

[19] Section 1-105(2) (2000 Official Text) expressly subjects section 1-105(1) to sections 9-301 through 9-307 with respect to the law governing perfection, the effect of perfection or nonperfection, and the priority of security interests and agricultural liens. The Official Text of revised Article 1 is comparable. U.C.C. § 1-301(g)(8) (2003 Official Text).

reason for the limitation should be clear: Perfection issues invariably involve the rights of third parties, and, as indicated in the preceding subsection, such parties ought not be bound by agreements to which they are not privy. Furthermore, leaving the decision to the courts under the appropriate relationship test would not provide third parties with the clear guidance they require regarding the filing and other perfection systems that need to be searched.

Dissatisfaction with the Article 9 choice-of-law rules was one of the primary motivations that impelled the latest revision of Article 9. Subpart I of Part 3 of the revision includes the new choice-of-law provisions that are now enacted in all of the states.[20] These provisions are explained in the discussion provided below.

[A] General Rule: Location of the Debtor—§ 9-301(1)

Article 9 provides different choice-of-law rules for possessory and non-possessory security interests. The default rule, which is the one that governs nonpossessory security interests, is that perfection, the effect of perfection, and, with an important exception discussed below,[21] priority are governed by the local law of the jurisdiction in which the debtor is located.[22] Because most secured transactions are nonpossessory, the law of the jurisdiction of the debtor's location will govern most frequently.[23]

This approach substantially simplifies the choice-of-law rules, which under former law most commonly turned on the location of the collateral. One of the greatest advantages over former law is the reduction in the circumstances under which the governing law will change once a financing statement has been properly filed.[24] Because debtors are likely to change their location less frequently than the location of their assets, the change to determining choice of law based on debtor location reduces the instances in which reperfection will be required in another jurisdiction. Moreover, debtor location for a registered organization is deemed to be the jurisdiction under whose laws the debtor is organized,[25] reducing further the chance

---

[20] Part 3 is entitled "Perfection and Priority." Subpart I, entitled "Law Governing Perfection and Priority," contains seven sections.

[21] *See* § 9.02[c] *infra*.

[22] U.C.C. § 9-301(1). Priority and perfection of possessory security interests are governed by the local law of the jurisdiction in which the collateral is located. U.C.C. § 9-301(2). *See* § 9.02[B] *infra*. A situs-of-collateral rule applies to certain types of collateral that are closely related to real property. It applies to a security interest in goods perfected by fixture filing, U.C.C. § 9-301(3)(A), and a security interest in timber to be cut, U.C.C. § 9-301(3)(B). It also applies to an agricultural lien on farm products, U.C.C. § 9-302, as well as to a security interest in as-extracted collateral, U.C.C. § 9-301(4). For discussion of these provisions *see* § 9.02[D][1],[2] *infra*.

[23] *See In re* Lance, 59 U.C.C. Rep. Serv. 2d 632 (Bankr. W.D. Mo. 2006) (Missouri law applied to perfection of security interest in snowmobile because debtor resided in Missouri even though he used the snowmobile exclusively at his brother's house in Minnesota).

[24] U.C.C. § 9-301, Comment 4.

[25] U.C.C. § 9-307(e). *See* discussion below and the discussion of registered organizations in connection with the appropriate name for a financing statement in § 5.03[A][1] *supra*.

that reperfection will become necessary. Even if reperfection is required, the chances for compliance are enhanced because secured parties should be able to detect changes in debtor location more easily than changes in collateral location.

Determining the applicable law based on the debtor's location in the case of a nonpossessory security interest promotes additional efficiencies as well. A nonpossessory secured lender that has pre-filed its financing statement prior to completing its agreement with the debtor does not have to worry that the collateral may have been moved to another state prior to attachment because its perfection and priority will be determined by the law of the state of the debtor's location. Consider furthermore a debtor that is a multinational corporation incorporated under the law of an American state and with offices and assets located all over the world. Even though the debtor has assets subject to the security interest in several states and nations, the secured party needs to file, and searchers need to search, only in the state in which the debtor is incorporated.

Article 9 includes a very precise set of rules that establish the location of the debtor.[26] Several baseline rules are provided in section 9-307(b). An individual is located at the individual's principal residence.[27] An organization that is not a registered organization is located at its place of business, and, if it has more than one place of business, at its chief executive office.[28] A registered organization[29] that is organized under the law of a state is located in that state.[30] Thus, a debtor corporation is located in the state in which its articles of incorporation are filed.

The rule with respect to registered organizations represents a significant advantage over the prior rule applicable to intangible assets and mobile equipment, which was based on the chief executive office of a debtor with places of business in multiple states. For example, a corporation is ordinarily organized under the law of the United States or a single state,[31] and

---

[26] U.C.C. § 9-307.

[27] U.C.C. § 9-307(b)(1).

[28] U.C.C. § 9-307(b)(2), (3). "Place of business" is defined to mean "a place where a debtor conducts its affairs." U.C.C. § 9-307(a). This broad definition is included to encompass organizations that do not engage in "for profit" business activities. U.C.C. § 9-307, Comment 2. Multiple filings may be necessary if the organization has a decentralized management structure and there is doubt about the location of its chief executive office. *See* discussion *infra* this subsection.

[29] "Registered organization" means "an organization organized solely under the law of a single State or the United States and as to which the State or the United States must maintain a public record showing the organization to have been organized." U.C.C. § 9-102(a)(70). The term includes, *inter alia*, corporations, limited partnerships and limited liability companies. It does not include a general partnership, which is an entity created by contract.

[30] U.C.C. § 9-307(e). Events like dissolution of a corporation or suspension or revocation of its charter that affect its corporate status do not affect its location for purposes of this rule. U.C.C. § 9-307(g).

[31] There are examples of corporations that have articles on file in more than one state. Such a corporation is not a registered organization, and this can lead to a tricky choice-of-law problem. The proper place to file would be the location of the chief executive office, which is not necessarily any of the places where articles are filed.

the necessary information is readily available through public records, typically computer files. Comparable information is not available to determine a debtor's chief executive office. Reliance on the incorporation records should also lead to a substantial reduction in errors with respect to the debtor's name, as both filers and searchers need to consult those records to determine the proper jurisdiction in which to file or search. The Comments point out that a jurisdiction could even program its filing system to reject any filing that designates an incorrect debtor name for a registered organization.[32]

The shift from either the location-of-the-collateral or the location-of-the-chief-executive-office rule to the state of organization for a registered organization is one of the most beneficial aspects of the revision's treatment of this complex area. Of course, some organizations are not registered organizations. If a non-registered organization has more than one place of business, it is deemed to be located at its chief executive office.[33] "Place of business" is defined as the place where the debtor conducts its affairs,[34] but the definition does not provide a test for determining a multistate organization's chief executive office. The Comments, however, focus on the place from which the debtor conducts the main part of its business and indicate that this is the place where creditors would most likely conduct a search.[35]

Article 9 also provides rules for determining the location of non-U.S. debtors. The general location-of-debtor rules of section 9-307(b) apply even though they result in the location being deemed to be a foreign jurisdiction if that jurisdiction is one whose laws generally require "information concerning the existence of a nonpossessory security interest to be made generally available in a filing, recording, or registration system as a condition or result of the security interest's obtaining priority over the rights of a lien creditor with respect to the collateral."[36] That is, the law of the foreign jurisdiction will apply, but only if it provides a means for public notice and obtaining priority over lien creditors. Without a qualifying public-notice system, the advantages of applying the location-of-debtor test would be lost. Accordingly, in such cases Article 9 establishes the debtor's location as Washington, D.C.[37] For example, suppose a German multinational corporation has offices all over the world, with its chief executive office in London. Because it is an organization but not a registered organization, it is deemed to be located in London and thus a filing should be made in England. The filing would be made in the District of Columbia if the chief executive office was located in a nation without a qualifying public-notice system.

---

[32] U.C.C. § 9-307, Comment 4.

[33] U.C.C. § 9-307(b)(3).

[34] U.C.C. § 9-307(a).

[35] U.C.C. § 9-307, Comment 2.

[36] U.C.C. § 9-307(c).

[37] U.C.C. § 9-307(c). The same location is designated for the United States as a debtor. U.C.C. § 9-307(h).

[B] Possessory Security Interest Exception—§ 9-301(2)

Possessory security interests fall under a situs-of-collateral rule,[38] and the efficiency of such an approach is obvious. Because the secured party, its representative, or a bailee obligated to follow the secured party's instructions is in possession of the collateral, movement of the collateral to another jurisdiction can be readily controlled. Moreover, since revised Article 9 has been universally adopted, possession will result in perfection under the law of the new jurisdiction at the moment the goods are moved there.[39] The situs rule applies only to perfection, the effects of perfection or nonperfection, and priority of possessory security interests and non-possessory security interests in certain land-related collateral; subject to an important exception for priority discussed in the next subsection, the general rule based on location of the debtor governs perfection, the effects of perfection or nonperfection, and priority of all other nonpossessory security interests.

[C] Tangible Property Partial Exception—§ 9-301(3)(c)

Although most of the advantages of revised Article 9 over former law articulated above relate specifically to *perfection,* the drafters recognized a problem with respect to the *effects of perfection or nonperfection* and *priority* that could result from applying the location-of-debtor rule to nonpossessory security interests when the debtor and the collateral are located in different jurisdictions. The Comments explain the problem through the following example:

> For example, assume a security interest in equipment located in Pennsylvania is perfected by filing in Illinois, where the debtor is located. If the law of the jurisdiction in which the debtor is located were to govern priority, then the priority of an execution lien on goods located in Pennsylvania would be governed by rules enacted by the Illinois legislature.[40]

To address the problem, there is a significant exception to the general rule that the law governing the perfection, the effects of perfection or nonperfection, and priority of nonpossessory security interests is the law of the jurisdiction in which the debtor is located. With respect to the *effect of perfection or nonperfection and the priority of* a nonpossessory security interest, the law of the situs of the collateral governs for collateral consisting of goods, instruments, negotiable documents, money, or tangible chattel paper.[41] The affected collateral thus consists of goods and indispensable

---

[38] "While collateral is located in a jurisdiction, the local law of that jurisdiction governs perfection, the effect of perfection or nonperfection, and the priority of a possessory security interest in that collateral." U.C.C. § 9-301(2).

[39] *See* § 9-316(c) and § 9.03 *infra.*

[40] U.C.C. § 9-301, Comment 7.

[41] U.C.C. § 9-301(3).

paper—the types of collateral that have a tangible form and thus can be located within a particular jurisdiction. The law governing *where to perfect* security interests in these types of collateral is determined under the general rule, which is the local law of the jurisdiction in which the debtor is located.[42] In other words, Article 9 bifurcates the selection of the applicable law for these types of collateral according to issues of perfection and issues of priority. Although this bifurcated approach adds an element of complexity, it preserves the benefit associated with a location-of-the-debtor rule while avoiding the problems that would arise in allowing distant jurisdictions to control issues related to priorities.

The exception will not have any effect on the result of any particular priority dispute if the priority rules of the situs state and the state of the debtor's location are the same—which they will be in nearly every case. The result will differ only if the situs state has a nonuniform priority rule, which can be illustrated with the following example. On February 1, Bank takes a security interest in the equipment of ABC, Inc., a Nevada corporation doing business at two locations—Las Vegas, Nevada and San Diego, California. That same day, Bank files a financing statement covering the equipment with the central filing office in Nevada. Bank does not make a filing in California. Unknown to Bank, on January 1 Victim had obtained a tort judgment in a California court against ABC, Inc., and Victim had filed a notice of judgment lien against ABC, Inc. with the California Secretary of State under Cal. Civ. Pro. Code §§ 697.510 to 697.530. On February 30, Victim levies upon ABC's equipment located at its San Diego facility.

Even though the relevant equipment is located in California, Bank's security interest in the equipment unquestionably is perfected properly. Section 9-301(1) requires Bank to file a financing statement in Nevada in order to perfect its security interest because Nevada is ABC, Inc.'s location under section 9-307(e). Under the uniform version of Article 9 in effect in Nevada, Victim could not acquire a judgment lien on the equipment until February 30, when levy occurs.[43] As a result, if Nevada priority rules controlled, Bank's security interest would take priority over Victim's judgment lien because it was perfected prior to February 30.[44]

Section 9-301(3)(C), however, provides that, while Nevada law controls whether Bank's security interest is perfected, California law governs the relative priority of Bank and Victim because the levied-upon equipment is located in California. Because California has nonuniform provisions that allow a judgment lien on personal property to arise by public filing (rather than actual levy), California law gives priority to Victim in this case based upon Victim having filed its notice of judgment lien before Bank filed its financing statement. Thus, under California's version of section 9-317(a)(2), Bank's security interest is subordinate to Victim's prior judgment lien on the equipment.

---

[42] U.C.C. § 9-301(1). *See* § 9.02[A] *supra*.

[43] *See* U.C.C. § 9-102(a)(52)(A).

[44] U.C.C. §§ 9-201, 9-317(a)(2) (converse reading).

The ultimate effect of the choice-of-law rules for nonpossessory security interests can be easily summarized. The location of the debtor controls both perfection, the effects of perfection or nonperfection, and priority with respect to collateral that consists of intangibles.[45] The location of the debtor also controls perfection with respect to tangible collateral (goods and indispensable paper).[46] A situs rule, however, governs the effects of perfection and priority with respect to tangible collateral.[47] In other words, if goods are located in State A and the debtor is located in State B, a nonpossessory security interest will be perfected by filing in State B, but priority contests will be resolved under the law of State A. The law of State A will govern every aspect of a possessory security interest.[48] This summary is subject to certain additional exceptions that are discussed below.

[D] Additional Exceptions

[1] Land-Related Collateral—§ 9-301(3), (4)

Article 9 includes several special rules that involve collateral that has a close relationship to specific land. A situs rule applies to goods that are fixtures and are to be perfected by a fixture-filing, and to timber that is yet to be cut.[49] The difference from the tangible property partial exception is that the situs rule for fixtures and standing timber extends to the law that governs perfection in addition to the effects of perfection or nonperfection and priority. If fixtures or standing timber are located in a different state from the debtor, the state where the collateral is located is the place for filing.[50] This is because the law of the debtor's state would not take into account any special local filing and recording requirements that the state where the collateral is located might require.[51] The drafters, therefore, applied the law of the situs of the collateral to govern perfection as well as the effects of perfection and priority in these cases. Precisely the same reasoning supports the comparable treatment provided for security interests in as-extracted collateral.[52]

[2] Agricultural Liens—§ 9-302

A situs rule governs perfection and priority with respect to agricultural liens on farm products. Perfection, the effects of perfection or nonperfection, and priority are all governed by the law of the jurisdiction in which the

---

[45] U.C.C. § 9-301(1).

[46] *Id.*

[47] U.C.C. § 9-301(3)(c).

[48] U.C.C. § 9-301(2).

[49] U.C.C. § 9-301(3)(A), (B).

[50] *See* U.C.C. § 9-501(a)(1) & § 5.05 *supra.*

[51] U.C.C. § 9-301, Comment 5(b), (c).

[52] U.C.C. § 9-301(4) & Comment 5(d). *See* § 5.05 *supra.*

farm products are located.[53] This provision also accommodates any local filing and recording requirements.

[3] Deposit Accounts—§ 9-304

Perfection, the effects of perfection and nonperfection, and priority of security interests in deposit accounts are governed by the local law of the jurisdiction of the bank with which the account is maintained.[54] Rules that determine a bank's jurisdiction for purposes of this section are provided by the Code.[55] By express agreement, the bank and its customer (the debtor) may choose the law that will govern for purposes of the priority rules of Part 3 of Article 9, for purposes of all of Article 9, or for purposes of the entire U.C.C., even if there is no relationship between the chosen jurisdiction and either the parties or the transaction.[56] If the parties do not make a choice expressly referencing part or all of Article 9 or the U.C.C. but their agreement contains a general choice-of-law clause, the law of the chosen jurisdiction governs. If there is no party agreement as to choice of law, the governing law will be that of the jurisdiction in which the bank office that maintains the deposit account is located if the parties' agreement expressly identifies that location. Otherwise, the jurisdiction will be the location of the bank office identified in an account statement as the office serving the customer's account, or, if the account statement does not identify an office, the location of the bank's chief executive office.

[4] Investment Property—§ 9-305

Article 9 includes choice-of-law rules for perfection, the effects or perfection or nonperfection, and priority of security interests in investment property.[57] If perfection is accomplished by control, the law of the jurisdiction where the certificate is located governs in the case of a certificated security; the law of the issuer's jurisdiction as specified in section 8-110(d) governs in the case of an uncertificated security; the law of the security intermediary's jurisdiction as specified in section 8-110(e) governs in the case of a security entitlement or securities account; and the law of the commodity intermediary's jurisdiction as specified in section 9-305(b) governs in the case of a commodity contract or commodity account. Each of the cross-referenced rules is similar to the rules governing deposit accounts, and the reader is referred to the discussion in the preceding subsection for specifics. The selection of the choice-of-law rule in these cases reflects the principles used in Article 8 to determine other questions on investment property.[58] If perfection is accomplished by filing, or

---

[53] U.C.C. § 9-302. Agricultural liens are discussed in § 13.02 *infra*.

[54] U.C.C. § 9-304(a).

[55] U.C.C. § 9-304(b).

[56] U.C.C. § 9-304, Comment 2. The parties can choose to apply the law of one jurisdiction to perfection and priority and the law of another jurisdiction for other purposes. *Id.*

[57] U.C.C. § 9-305. Investment property is discussed generally in § 1.04[E] *supra*.

[58] U.C.C. § 9-305, Comment 2. *See* U.C.C. § 8-110. Article 9 contains the rules governing commodity intermediaries because commodities are outside the scope of Article 8, but the rules are consistent with those of Article 8. *Compare* U.C.C. § 9-305(b) *with* U.C.C. § 8-110(e).

automatically in certain cases involving a broker, securities intermediary, or commodity intermediary, the law of the debtor's location governs perfection but not the effects of perfection or nonperfection and priority.[59]

[5]　Letter-of-Credit Rights—§ 9-306

A separate provision of Article 9 addresses the law governing perfection, the effects of perfection or nonperfection, and priority with respect to security interests in letter-of-credit rights.[60] The applicable law is the local law of the issuer's jurisdiction (or the local law of a nominated person's jurisdiction), provided that such a jurisdiction is a state. If the jurisdiction is not a state, the general choice-of-law rule applies for such issues, meaning that perfection, the effects of perfection and nonperfection, and priority are governed by the law of the debtor's location.[61] The objective is to prevent foreign law from controlling a transaction that, from the perspective of the debtor-beneficiary, its creditors, and a domestic nominated person, is essentially domestic.[62] The determination of an issuer's or nominated person's jurisdiction is to be made in accordance with provisions in Article 5 on letters of credit.[63]

§ 9.03　CERTIFICATE OF TITLE LAWS—§§ 9-303, 9-337

As was indicated in the material on perfection,[64] the Code does not govern perfection of certain assets that are subject to state certificate-of-title acts.[65] It does, however, govern the effects of perfection or nonperfection as well as priority for goods that are covered by a certificate of title. The relevant choice-of-law rules are found in section 9-303.

The most important assets in this category are motor vehicles. Every state has a statute that requires security interests in motor vehicles to be perfected by a process that results in notation of the secured party's lien on a certificate issued by the state.[66] The idea is quite simple: Everyone

---

[59] Automatic perfection for investment property is discussed in § 7.02[D] *supra*.

[60] U.C.C. § 9-306.

[61] U.C.C. § 9-306, Comment 2. *See* U.C.C. § 9-301(1).

[62] U.C.C. § 9-306, Comment 2.

[63] U.C.C. § 9-306(b) (referencing U.C.C. § 5-116).

[64] *See* § 4.02[F] *supra*.

[65] "Certificate of title" is defined to mean "a certificate of title with respect to which a statute provides for the security interest in question to be indicated on the certificate as a condition or result of the security interest's obtaining priority over the rights of a lien creditor with respect to the collateral." U.C.C. § 9-102(a)(10).

[66] Article 9 defers to such statutes. *See* U.C.C. §§ 9-310(b)(3), 9-311(a)(2),(3). *See In re* Renaud, 302 B.R. 280, 52 U.C.C. Rep. Serv. 2d 761 (E.D. Ark. 2003), *aff'd*, 308 B.R. 347, 53 U.C.C. Rep. Serv. 2d 403 (Bankr. 8th Cir. 2004) (creditor's mortgage on the debtor's real property held to be ineffective to perfect security interest in mobile home permanently affixed to the property because, as the more specific statute, the vehicle titling statute applied to all mobile homes and required notation of the interest on the mobile home's certificate of title and filing with the Department of Finance and Administration); *In re* Gaylord Grain L.L.C., 306 B.R.

should understand the imprudence of buying or lending against a motor vehicle without first seeing the certificate of title, as it is the best evidence of the ownership of the vehicle. If the certificate shows the lien, notice has been given.

A few states have enacted the Uniform Motor Vehicle Certificate of Title and Anti-Theft Act, whereas others have their own systems. Some states have adopted an alternative procedure that allows the secured party to file a notice of its interest with the state department of motor vehicles. The Federal Motor Vehicle Lien Act of 1958,[67] which regulates motor vehicles owned by carriers registered under federal law, defers to state perfection laws, and cases like *In re Paige* [68] permit titling of such vehicles in states that have little or no connection with the secured transaction. Under this approach, for example, a secured party located anywhere would be protected by the notation of its lien upon an Oklahoma certificate of title, even if the debtor did not purchase the vehicle in Oklahoma and had no other connection to the state of Oklahoma. Article 9 directly addresses the issue of connection between the titling state and the secured transaction: It applies the law of the titling state "even if there is no other relationship between the jurisdiction under whose certificate of title the goods are covered and the goods or the debtor."[69] This result is consistent with modern trucking practices.[70]

Motor vehicles are not the only assets subject to state certificate-of-title acts. Assets such as boats, farm tractors, and mobile homes are the subject of certificate legislation in some states, while interests in such assets are perfected by the normal Code methods (filing, possession, or automatic perfection) in other states. As is explained below,[71] the lack of uniformity among state certificate-of-title laws is the source of considerable confusion.

Even in title states, not all security interests in such assets may be perfected using the certificate method. Article 9 makes it clear that "[d]uring any period in which collateral [subject to a certificate of title statute] is inventory held for sale or lease by a person or leased by that person as lessor and that person is in the business of selling goods of that kind, [the certificate of title] does not apply to a security interest in that collateral created by that person."[72] The reason should be obvious. The

624, 53 U.C.C. Rep. Serv. 2d 390 (Bankr. 8th Cir. 2004) (because Missouri certificate-of-title statute requires notation on certificate as exclusive method to perfect a security interest in an automobile, filing financing statement did not perfect bank's security interest).

[67] 49 U.S.C. § 14301.

[68] 679 F.2d 601, 33 U.C.C. Rep. Serv. 1218 (6th Cir. 1982).

[69] U.C.C. § 9-303(a).

[70] U.C.C. § 9-303, Comment 2.

[71] *See* § 9.04 *infra*.

[72] U.C.C. § 9-311(d). *See* Carcorp, Inc. v. Bombadier Capital, Inc., 272 B.R. 365, 47 U.C.C. Rep. Serv. 2d 374 (Bankr. S.D. Fla. 2002) (motor vehicles that are part of a debtor dealer's inventory must be perfected by filing a financing statement rather than under the certificate of title statute). *See also* First Nat'l Bank of the N. V. Automotive Fin. Corp., 50 U.C.C. Rep. Serv. 2d 915 (Minn. Ct. App. 2003) (lender who perfected its interest in a consumer's

titling process is complicated, time-consuming and, if applied to a large volume of vehicles, expensive. If inventory held for sale were covered, the secured party would no sooner apply for a certificate than its interest would be extinguished by the dealer's sale of the vehicle in question to a buyer in ordinary course of business. To avoid the paperwork and expense associated with such a procedure, the Code allows the secured party to perfect its interest by making a single Article 9 filing describing its collateral as all of the debtor's inventory.

The choice-of-law provision for goods "covered" by a certificate of title states that "[t]he local law of the jurisdiction under whose certificate of title the goods are covered governs perfection, the effect of perfection or nonperfection, and the priority of a security interest in goods covered by a certificate of title from the time the goods become covered by the certificate of title until the goods cease to be covered by the certificate of title."[73] Thus, the law of the state that issues a certificate of title governs for so long as the certificate covers the goods.

The choice-of-law provision turns on goods being covered by a certificate of title, and Article 9 specifies when goods become covered and when they cease to be covered. Goods become covered "when a valid application for the certificate of title and the applicable fee are delivered to the appropriate authority."[74] Note that even if the state does not actually issue a certificate following these actions by the applicant, the goods nevertheless are still covered by a certificate of title as that phrase is used in Article 9. The goods cease to be covered when the certificate of title ceases to be effective under the law of the issuing jurisdiction or when the goods subsequently become covered by a certificate of title issued by another jurisdiction, whichever occurs earlier.[75]

The provisions described above are choice-of-law provisions only. They determine the state whose law governs perfection and its effects, but they do not indicate how or when a security interest in goods subject to a state's certificate-of-title act becomes *perfected*. In other words, "coverage" is not the equivalent of "perfection." Perfection is governed by the procedural requirements of the certificate-of-title act. Coverage and perfection will

automobile by notation on the certificate of title had priority under first-to-file or perfect rule of U.C.C. § 9-322(a)(1) over dealership's perfected-by-filing inventory financer when the consumer traded-in its automobile on the purchase of a newer model).

[73] U.C.C. § 9-303(c). *See In re* North, 310 B.R. 152, 53 U.C.C. Rep. Serv. 2d 635 (Bankr. D. Ariz. 2004) (even though Mercedes had been located in California for more than four months, Arizona law continued to govern perfection because no application for certificate had been submitted in California); Keltner v. Resop, 56 U.C.C. Rep. Serv. 2d 663 (W.D. Wis. 2005) (same result for vehicle titled in Minnesota, moved to Wisconsin, but not re-titled in Wisconsin).

[74] U.C.C. § 9-303(b).

[75] *Id. See In re* Baker, 56 U.C.C. Rep. Serv. 2d 256 (W.D. Wis. 2005) (security interest in buyer's vehicle perfected under New Mexico's certificate-of-title act continued to be perfected after buyer moved to Wisconsin because buyer did not apply for Wisconsin title). Due to the differences in state certificate of title laws, Article 9 does not address when a certificate of title ceases to be effective for intrastate purposes.

coincide if the certificate-of-title law provides that perfection occurs when the application and fee are delivered to the proper state official. That is the case in many states, but in others perfection is conditioned upon surrender of any existing certificate of title and/or upon the actual issuance of a certificate of title with the security interest noted thereon.[76] In such a state, a motor vehicle may be covered by a certificate of title even though perfection has not occurred. All being covered means is that issues of perfection, the effects of perfection or nonperfection, and priority will be governed by the covering state's law.

§ 9.04   PERFECTION FOLLOWING CHANGE IN GOVERNING LAW—§ 9-316

With the perfection of security interests governed by the law of the jurisdiction in which the debtor is located, the collateral is located, or the collateral is covered by a certificate of title, complications can arise with a change in the determining factor. What is the effect on a secured party's perfection if the debtor relocates to another state or the collateral is moved to another state? What is the relationship among the certificate-of-title statutes of the various states? Section 9-316 addresses how perfection can be continued in a jurisdiction after it was accomplished under the law of another jurisdiction.

If the determining factor changes, the law chosen to resolve issues of perfection, the effects of perfection and nonperfection, and priority changes as well. Thus, if a debtor located in Alabama relocates to Georgia, Georgia law immediately governs. The same is true if goods are covered by a Missouri certificate of title and the debtor delivers an application for a certificate and the appropriate fee to a Kansas official. Kansas law immediately applies.

A security interest does not become unperfected automatically just because the law of the jurisdiction in which perfection occurred ceases to govern perfection.[77] Section 9-316 provides a grace period during which a security interest perfected in one jurisdiction continues perfected even though the relevant jurisdiction for perfection has changed. The grace period affords the perfected secured party sufficient time to ascertain that the law of the jurisdiction governing perfection has changed and to take the necessary steps for reperfection in the new jurisdiction.[78]

For example, suppose a secured party has properly perfected its security interest according to the law of the jurisdiction in which the debtor is located and the debtor changes its location to another jurisdiction. The

---

[76] See In re Trible, 290 B.R. 838, 50 U.C.C. Rep. Serv. 2d 286 (D. Kan. 2003) (because the exclusive method to perfect a security interest in a mobile home was by notation on the certificate of title, the secured party was not perfected by virtue of its real estate mortgage on the property to which the mobile home was attached).

[77] U.C.C. § 9-316, Comment 2.

[78] Id.

security interest in this situation generally remains perfected for four months after the change.[79] The law of the new state governs, but that law recognizes perfection accomplished in the old state for the first four months after the relocation.

The "four-month" rule for changes in a debtor's location was designed as a compromise between the interests of third parties and perfected secured parties and, as such, it is not totally fair to either group. Because interested parties will naturally search the filing records in the new state, a filing is needed there, but the secured party may not become aware of the change for a significant time. A secured party must check on the location of its debtor somewhat more frequently than every four months to be safe and, if the debtor has changed locations, accomplish perfection in the new state.[80] A third party that has searched the records in the state where the debtor is located and found nothing should make certain that the debtor has been located in that state for more than four months.

The four-month grace period is altered under certain circumstances. If perfection would cease sooner under the law of the jurisdiction of removal, the grace period extends only for the duration that the perfection would have been effective.[81] Thus, if proper perfection by filing would have lapsed in State A within one month of the debtor changing its location to State B, the security interest remains perfected under the filing in State A only for the one-month period. This approach is logical. A security interest for which perfection would have lapsed within one month should not have that perfection extended for three additional months due solely to the fortuity of the debtor having changed its location. The grace period is also altered if collateral is transferred to a new debtor[82] (or to another person that thereby becomes a debtor) who is located in another jurisdiction. The grace period is extended to a period of one year in these circumstances because of the greater difficulty in discerning such events even if the secured party exercises due diligence.[83]

The grace period gives the secured party an opportunity to reperfect in the jurisdiction to which the debtor moves or in which the new debtor or transferee is located. If reperfection is accomplished before the applicable grace period ends, the secured party remains continuously perfected.[84] Failure to reperfect within the grace period leaves the security interest unperfected prospectively. Furthermore, the security interest is deemed to have never been perfected as against a purchaser for value.[85] Only a

---

[79] U.C.C. § 9-316(a)(2).

[80] If the relocation is an event of default, the secured party could take possession, giving it perfected status.

[81] U.C.C. § 9-316(a)(1).

[82] *See* U.C.C. § 9-102(a)(56). There are other consequences in the case of a new debtor. *See* § 5.03[C][2] *supra*.

[83] U.C.C. § 9-316(a)(3) and Comment 2.

[84] U.C.C. § 9-316(b).

[85] *Id.* "Purchaser" means any person with a voluntarily-acquired interest in property and includes a secured party. U.C.C. § 1-201(b)(30), (29).

purchaser for value gains the protection of this retroactive invalidation rule. Thus, for example, a secured party perfected by filing in State A that does not take the necessary step of reperfecting in State B during the applicable grace period will be unperfected against a lien creditor only if the lien creditor's interest arises after the expiration of the grace period.[86] As against a purchaser for value, however, the security interest will be deemed never to have been perfected. With respect to such purchasers, the failure to reperfect during the grace period results in both prospective and retroactive invalidation of the perfection.

Even against purchasers for value, however, the secured party gets the advantage of the full grace period during which to reperfect. For example, assume that a nonpossessory security interest in goods is taken and properly perfected by filing in State A, which is the jurisdiction in which the debtor is located. Three years later, the debtor changes its location to State B, and two months after this change in the debtor's location the goods are purchased by a nonordinary-course buyer that has searched the filing system in State B and found nothing. Shortly before the four-month grace period expires, the secured party discovers what has happened and properly files in State B. In a priority contest between the secured party and the buyer, the secured party will prevail. The filing in State A was effective under the law of State B at the time of purchase, and the rights of a nonordinary-course buyer are subordinate to those of a perfected secured party.[87] Because the secured party filed in State B during the four-month grace period, it never had a gap in its perfection. The result is somewhat harsh because the buyer could only protect itself by inquiring (and getting a truthful answer) about the debtor's location during the four months preceding the purchase, but the buyer is not without a remedy. The debtor will be liable for breach of the Article 2 implied warranty of title.[88]

A grace period is not needed if a secured party has a security interest perfected by possession. The situs rule for perfection applies if the secured party takes a possessory security interest, and in such cases the secured party will control any change in the location of the collateral. If the collateral for a perfected possessory security interest is moved to another jurisdiction, the secured party will continue to be perfected by possession under the law of the new jurisdiction.[89]

---

[86] The fact that the grace period has expired will not undo that perfection, because the lien creditor is not protected by the retroactive invalidation rule. Thus, the secured party could safely repossess the collateral from the lien creditor. In most cases, the collateral will be in the possession of a levying sheriff and, to repossess, the secured party would have to obtain a writ of replevin directing that the sheriff turn the collateral over to it. If the lien creditor is a bankruptcy trustee, the secured party cannot gain possession unless the trustee abandons the collateral or the secured party obtains a turnover order. If the secured party fails to repossess the collateral and it is sold at a sheriff's sale, the buyer would qualify as a purchaser and gain the protection of the retroactive invalidation rule. This conclusion would hold even if the levying creditor bought at its own sheriff's sale.

[87] U.C.C. § 9-317(a)(2).

[88] U.C.C. § 2-312.

[89] U.C.C. § 9-316(c).

As indicated in the preceding section, if goods are covered by a certificate of title, the law of the state that issues the certificate governs for so long as the certificate covers the goods but this provision is a choice-of-law provision only.[90] Section 9-303 determines the state whose law governs perfection, the effects of perfection or nonperfection, and priority, but it does not indicate how or when a security interest in the goods becomes perfected. Perfection is governed by the procedural requirements of the certificate of title law. Coverage and perfection will coincide if the certificate of title law provides that perfection occurs when the application and fee are delivered to the proper state official but not otherwise. Analysis of the movement of goods from one title state to another title state, or from a nontitle state to a title state, requires a clear understanding of this distinction.

For example, assume that a secured party's security interest in a State A resident's boat is perfected by a certificate of title issued by State A and the debtor moves to State B, another title state. State A law governs perfection, the effects of perfection and nonperfection, and priorities until the goods become covered by a certificate of title issued by State B. Coverage will not occur unless and until an application and fee are delivered to the proper official in State B.[91] From that time forward, State B law will govern. Further analysis requires an understanding of section 9-316(d), which of course is part of State B's law.

Section 9-316(d) provides that, under State B law in the hypothetical, perfection by the State A certificate continues until the security interest would have become unperfected under State A law. In other words, the State A certificate continues to perfect the secured party's interest for *general purposes* without special time limitations, but as we shall see, a different rule will apply as against purchasers for value.[92] This means that the secured party will have priority over lien creditors, including bankruptcy trustees, even if it never completes the steps for perfection under State B's certificate of title law. Suppose, though, that the State A certificate of title statute provides that perfection ceases if the certificate is surrendered to authorities in another jurisdiction for the purpose of re-titling the boat.[93] If the secured party surrenders the State A certificate to the authorities in State B, it will no doubt do so as part of a process that will result in perfection under State B's certificate-of-title act, and thus it will have continuous perfection, without an intervening period of nonperfection, by tacking its perfection in State B onto its perfection in State A.[94]

To illustrate, assume that a secured party perfects by having its security interest in a new car that it sells to the debtor noted on the certificate of

---

[90] *See* § 9.03 *supra.*

[91] At the same time, the boat will cease to be covered by the State A statute. U.C.C. § 9-303(b) (goods cease to be covered by a certificate of title when they subsequently become covered under a certificate of title issued by another jurisdiction).

[92] The exceptions with respect to purchasers for value are discussed below.

[93] *See* U.C.C. § 9-316, Comment 5.

[94] U.C.C. § 9-316(d), (e).

title issued by State A. The debtor subsequently moves to State B, and eventually applies for a certificate of title covering the car in that state more than a year later. Until the application is made, State A's law continues to govern all perfection-related issues. Many states will not issue a new title certificate for a pre-owned vehicle unless the outstanding certificate is surrendered. By requiring surrender of the State A certificate, the officials in State B, whose law now governs, will be able to see that the lien on the car is noted thereon, and this should cause them to include a similar notation on the certificate of title that they issue. The secured party thus will have continuous perfection of its interest through the certificates of title issued by States A and B. Secured parties often keep possession of the certificate of title that is issued initially with their liens noted thereon as a means of preventing another state from issuing a new certificate.

Now assume that State A does not have a certificate-of-title act governing boats but that State B does. Assume further that the security interest was perfected in State A by filing a financing statement[95] before the boat became covered by a certificate of title in State B. The law of State B will still recognize the perfection of the security interest in State A for general purposes, even if the steps for perfection in State B are not completed, until the financing statement lapses or is terminated under the law of State A. Consider also the converse situation in which the security interest in the boat was perfected by notation on a State A certificate and moved to State B, a nontitle state. Obviously, the boat will not become covered by a State B certificate. State A's law will continue to govern perfection, therefore, meaning that the State A certificate will continue to perfect the secured party's interest for as long as it remains effective under the State A certificate-of-title act. This policy choice places an enormous burden on searchers in states that do not have certificate-of-title laws for assets like boats and mobile homes.

The rule discussed above pursuant to which State B recognizes perfection achieved under the laws of State A for general purposes until the perfection would have lapsed under the law of State A does not apply if the goods are acquired by a purchaser for value after they become covered by a certificate in State B. In that case, the security interest becomes unperfected as against the purchaser if the secured party does not reperfect under State B's certificate-of-title law or by taking possession pursuant to section 9-313(b)[96] before the earlier of four months after the goods become covered by the State B certificate or the time the security interest would have

---

[95] Perfection might also occur automatically because the secured party has a purchase-money security interest in a boat that qualifies as consumer goods.

[96] Ordinarily, perfection under a state's certificate-of-title law is the exclusive method of perfection for goods covered by the law. U.C.C. § 9-311(a). There is an exception, however, that permits a secured party to reperfect by possession during the four-month grace period provided by section 9-316(e). U.C.C. §§ 9-313(b) and Comment 7; 9-316(d) and Comment 5 (example 9). Thus, if the security agreement permits or the debtor otherwise consents, and in any event if there is a default, the secured party can avoid having to comply with State B's certificate-of-title act.

become unperfected under the laws of State A had the goods not become covered by the State B certificate. [97] Thus, with respect to purchasers for value, the secured party must complete the steps necessary for an effective perfection in State B within a grace period that will never exceed four months. The failure to reperfect within the allowable grace period results not only in the security interest becoming unperfected *prospectively* against a purchaser for value but the interest also "is deemed never to have been perfected as against a purchaser of the goods for value."[98] Thus, the perfected status of the secured party is retroactively invalidated, thereby relegating the secured party to unperfected status even against a purchaser whose interest arose before the expiration of the grace period. By contrast, recall there is no loss of perfection, even prospectively, against a lien creditor. [99]

The same rule applies if goods are moved from a nontitle state to a title state. Assume that State A does not have a certificate of title law governing boats but that State B does, and that the secured party has properly perfected under State A law. State A law continues to govern until the boat becomes covered by certificate issued by State B. Even after that time, State B law makes State A's perfection effective for general purposes until it would have lapsed under State A law.[100] However, the secured party's interest will be unperfected prospectively and retroactively as against a purchaser for value if the secured party fails to take the steps necessary to perfect its interest under State B's law before the earlier of four months after the goods become covered in State B or the time perfection would have lapsed under State A's law.

In addition to the protection for purchasers for value in section 9-316(e), Article 9 also provides a special priority rule in section 9-337 that protects certain buyers of collateral that rely upon the existence of a "clean" certificate of title. [101] The rule is an exception to the ordinary rule subordinating buyers to perfected security interests and thus its application does not depend on whether the secured party reperfects in the issuing state during the four-month grace period. The special priority rule applies only if a state actually issues a certificate of title with respect to goods that are already perfected by any method in another jurisdiction. The certificate must be "clean" in the sense that it neither shows that the goods are subject to the security interest nor contains a statement that the goods may be subject to security interests that are not shown on the certificate. To qualify for priority, the buyer must give value and receive delivery of the goods after the certificate is issued and without knowledge of the security

---

[97] U.C.C. § 9-316(e).

[98] U.C.C. § 9-316(e).

[99] U.C.C. § 9-316(d).

[100] Id.

[101] U.C.C. § 9-337(1).

interest.[102] A buyer in the business of selling goods of the kind at issue does not qualify for protection under the special priority rule.

---

[102] *See* Metzger v. Americredit Fin. Serv., Inc., 273 Ga. App. 453, 615 S.E.2d 120, 56 U.C.C. Rep. Serv. 2d 825 (2005) (buyer met all requirements after car originally titled in New York was re-titled in Georgia with a certificate that did not reflect the security interest due to a data-entry error).

Part IV

PRIORITIES

[A] The Priority Concept

To the extent that it goes beyond the relationship between a debtor and a secured party, the discussion thus far has focused primarily on the means to perfect a security interest. The discussion has chiefly addressed the various mechanisms by which a secured party can attain and retain perfected status. Whether a secured party is perfected has significant consequences in the event of a competing claim to the collateral. The discussion now turns to the rules and policies that determine the outcome of these contests. The focus is on priorities.

A wide variety of different classes of third-party interests, including claims by other secured parties, general creditors, lien creditors, buyers, lessees, licensees, and trustees in bankruptcy, can compete for priority in the secured party's collateral. Perfection generally will enhance a secured party's position against these claimants. As the discussion in the next few chapters will demonstrate, however, a secured party's position, even with perfection, is rarely completely unassailable.

The importance of prevailing in a priority battle can be demonstrated through a simple illustration. Assume that Debtor defaults on its outstanding indebtedness to the following three creditors: Secured Party One (SP-1) for $10,000, Secured Party Two (SP-2) for $20,000, and General Creditor (GC) for $5,000. The only asset of any value owned by Debtor is equipment that is the collateral for both of the secured loans. Sale of this equipment, however, will provide only $14,000.

If these three creditors were asserting unsecured claims in a bankruptcy distribution, a principle of *pro rata* distribution would be applied. All three of the interests would share in the proceeds from the sale of the equipment. The amount received by each claimant would be determined by each party's proportionate share of the total of the three claims. SP-1 would be entitled to two times more than GC, and SP-2 would be entitled to four times more than GC. Accordingly, GC would receive $2,000, SP-1 would receive $4,000, and SP-2 would receive $8,000.

Priority determinations under Article 9 are different. The competing claims are rank-ordered. The claimant with the top priority has the initial claim to payment. If the collateral has enough value to satisfy all of the outstanding indebtedness on that claim, the remaining value is available to the second-ranked claimant. Lower-ranked claimants will realize nothing from the collateral unless it has enough value to satisfy all prior claims in full.

Priority allocations mean that some of the claimants in the illustration will not receive anything from the sale of the equipment. Under priority rules to be explained later, GC will be ranked third and thus will receive nothing. If SP-1 has top priority, the entire $10,000 debt will be satisfied, leaving only $4,000 for SP-2. If, on the other hand, SP-2 has top priority, the entire $14,000 sale proceeds will be applied to its $20,000 claim, leaving nothing for SP-1 or GC.

Priorities can be the ultimate factor that decides the benefit of a security interest. A secured party whose collateral is gobbled up by other claimants with superior priority rankings is effectively relegated to the position of a general creditor. The debt still exists, but the collateral that the secured party initially relied upon is gone. The secured party can only pursue the debt claim against the obligor, and may receive only a portion of its claim if the debtor files for bankruptcy protection.

Priority battles arise whenever two or more parties assert claims to the same specific assets. Many of these conflicts will not involve a secured party, such as competing claims between a buyer and a lessor of the same goods, or between a mortgagee and a trustee in bankruptcy competing for a parcel of real property. All of these conflicts are outside the scope of this book. In contrast, Article 9 governs priority conflicts between secured parties and other classes of claimants. Article 9 priorities thus are a part of a larger area of the law.

[B] Understanding Priorities

An understanding of Article 9 priorities can be furthered by seeing the relationship among the various priority rules, and how they operate together to cover an entire category of cases. Certain themes also run through the priority provisions. The fundamental principle of prioritization is "first-in-time, first-in-right." The party that has taken specified action first will win under this principle. Numerous exceptions to this general rule also follow certain patterns, particularly in cases of purchase-money security interests. Understanding Article 9 priorities requires an understanding of the overall picture, as well as each individual rule. Such understanding inevitably requires an appreciation of the policies that underlie the provisions. The discussion of priorities in this book is designed to advance insight from all of these perspectives.

The Code priority rules are quite precise, and with good reason. Although a security interest is created through a contract between a secured party and a debtor, the secured party's interest can have a competing or adverse effect on the interests of third parties. The broader contracts standards that apply to transactions like sales of goods thus are not workable in the secured transactions context. Other parties must know with certainty what their respective rights are with respect to collateral.

The starting point for priority issues is the Article 9 provision on the general validity of security agreements, which renders a security agreement effective according to its terms "between the parties, against purchasers of the collateral, and against creditors."[1] This provision favors secured parties in priority conflicts with third parties: A security interest prevails even if it is unperfected.

The baseline established by the general validity provision is subject, however, to any exceptions that Article 9 otherwise provides. Those exceptions are numerous. The discussion of priorities in the next few chapters of this book, is technically, a discussion of the exceptions to the general validity provision.

The determination of a priority dispute involves two basic steps. Initially, the status of each of the competing claimants in the conflict must be established; then, the appropriate rule can be applied to decide the outcome of a conflict between any pair of the claimants. Students often overlook the critical importance of the first step. One simply cannot select the correct priority rule without properly characterizing the status of each competing party. Making assumptions about a party's status will often lead to application of the wrong rule, and care must be exercised in ascertaining that status. In the case of some parties, that examination will encompass the issues covered thus far in this book—the determination of whether the claimant is a secured party, and, if so, whether the secured party is perfected.

---

[1] U.C.C. § 9-201. *See* § 14.01 *infra.*

Chapter 10

AMONG SECURED PARTIES

SYNOPSIS

§ 10.01 FIRST-TO-FILE-OR-PERFECT—§ 9-322(a)

If a debtor grants a security interest in the same collateral to two or more secured parties, there will be competing claims to the collateral. Priorities among conflicting security interests in the same collateral are governed by section 9-322. The general rules of that section are stated in subsection (a), which provides:

> Except as otherwise provided in this section, priority among conflicting security interests and agricultural liens in the same collateral is determined according to the following rules:

(1) Conflicting perfected security interests and agricultural liens rank according to priority in time of filing or perfection. Priority dates from the earlier of the time a filing covering the collateral is first made or the security interest or agricultural lien is first perfected, if there is no period thereafter when there is neither filing nor perfection.

(2) A perfected security interest or agricultural lien has priority over a conflicting unperfected security interest or agricultural lien.

(3) The first security interest or agricultural lien to attach or become effective has priority if conflicting security interests and agricultural liens are unperfected.

Because an unperfected secured party that faces a priority dispute with another unperfected secured party can simply perfect to attain priority under subsection (1),[2] recourse to subsection (3) is relatively rare.[3] Consequently, the basic general rule awards priority to the secured party that is the first either to file a financing statement or to perfect its security interest.[4]

The general rule on competing perfected security interests does not simply recognize filing as the predominant method of perfecting a security interest. It affords a special priority advantage to filing that is not available through any alternative method of perfection.[5] A security interest cannot be perfected until all of the applicable steps required for perfection have been taken and the security interest has attached.[6] Nevertheless, a secured party may "pre-file" a financing statement, meaning that it files before the security interest attaches. A secured party that files a financing statement but does not complete the process of attachment until later is not perfected until attachment, but it will achieve priority under the general rule against

---

[2] *See* U.C.C. § 9-322, Comment 4 (Example 2); Engelsma v. Superior Prods. Mfg. Co., 298 Minn. 77, 212 N.W.2d 884, 13 U.C.C. Rep. Serv. 944 (1973).

[3] The provision has been relevant in an occasional case. Milwaukee Mack Sales, Inc. v. First Wis. Nat'l Bank of Milwaukee, 93 Wis. 2d 589, 287 N.W.2d 708, 28 U.C.C. Rep Serv. 540 (1980).

[4] Board of Cty. Commrs., Cty. of Adams v. Berkeley Village, 40 Colo. App. 431, 580 P.2d 1251, 24 U.C.C. Rep Serv. 975 (1978) (first secured party to perfect by filing had priority over both secured party that filed later and creditor that never filed); S. Lotman & Son, Inc. v. Southeastern Fin. Corp., 288 Ala. 547, 263 So.2d 499, 11 U.C.C. Rep. Serv. 218 (1972) (B took security interest; A took competing security interest and filed; B filed later; A won as first to file and first to perfect); St. Paul Mercury Ins. Co. v. Merchants & Marine Bank, 143 S.W.3d 915, 54 U.C.C. Rep. Serv. 2d 671 (Miss. 2004) (second secured party that filed a financing statement had priority over the first secured party that did not perfect, irrespective of whether the second secured party had knowledge of the first secured party's interest prior to extending its own loan).

[5] Priority in favor of the first secured party to file requires the filing to be made properly. Mountain Credit v. Michiana Lumber & Supply, Inc., 31 Colo. App. 112, 498 P.2d 967, 10 U.C.C. Rep. Serv. 1347 (1972) (defendant's financing statement was filed first but in wrong office). *See also* U.C.C. § 9-322, Comment 4.

[6] U.C.C. § 9-308(a). *See* § 4.03 *supra.*

any secured parties that perfect after its filing.[7] The filer has, in effect, staked its claim.

The significance of the priority advantage associated with filing can be illustrated by comparing the position of a secured party that files prior to attachment with what its position would have been had it taken possession of the collateral prior to attachment. Assume that SP-1 files a financing statement before it enters into a security agreement with a prospective debtor. SP-2 afterwards takes and perfects a security interest in the same property described in SP-1's financing statement. SP-1 and the debtor subsequently complete the steps necessary for SP-1 to acquire a security interest. If the debtor later defaults on both loans, SP-1 will have priority in the collateral. Even though SP-2 perfected first, the pre-filing by SP-1 provides it with priority.[8]

In contrast, if SP-1 had merely taken possession of the collateral, it would not have attained priority simply on the basis of possession. For priority, SP-1's perfection would have to have preceded perfection by SP-2, which means that both possession and attachment would have to have predated SP-2's filing.[9] Of course, it would be rare for a debtor to part with possession before entering into a security agreement (which can be oral in the case of possession),[10] and value can consist of an executory promise that constitutes consideration.[11] Thus, it would be rare for a secured party to "pre-possess." Nevertheless, the point remains: The advantage of taking the step necessary for perfection before attachment occurs only gives an advantage under Article 9 to a secured party that files a financing statement.

The reason for affording a special priority protection for filing, even filing done prior to attachment, is stated in the Comments: "The justification for determining priority by order of filing lies in the necessity of protecting the filing system—that is, of allowing the first secured party who has filed to make subsequent advances without each time having to check for subsequent filings as a condition of protection."[12] The existence of this special protection and the reasoning that supports it explain why creditors commonly insist upon authorization from a prospective debtor to file an initial

[7] *In re* McCorhill Pub., Inc., 86 B.R. 783, 8 U.C.C. Rep. Serv. 2d 203 (Bankr. S.D.N.Y. 1988). The priority also extends to after-acquired property within the scope of the secured party's interest. Wade Credit Corp. v. Borg-Warner Acceptance Corp., 83 Or. App. 479, 732 P.2d 76, 3 U.C.C. Rep. Serv. 2d 289 (1987).

[8] Enterprises Now, Inc. v. Citizens & S. Dev. Corp., 135 Ga. App. 603, 218 S.E.2d 309, 17 U.C.C. Rep. Serv. 1114 (1975) (having filed first, appellee had priority over appellant even though appellant perfected first).

[9] Bank of Okla., City Plaza v. Martin, 744 P.2d 218, 5 U.C.C. Rep Serv. 2d 222 (Okla. Ct. App. 1987) (first to record security interest in airplane with FAA); Barry v. Bank of N.H., N.A., 113 N.H. 158, 304 A.2d 879, 12 U.C.C. Rep. Serv. 732 (1973) (plaintiff perfected at the latest when it took possession of collateral).

[10] U.C.C. § 9-203(b)(3)(B).

[11] U.C.C. § 1-204(1), (4).

[12] U.C.C. § 9-322, Comment 4. Enterprises Now, Inc. v. Citizens & S. Dev. Corp., 135 Ga. App. 603, 218 S.E. 2d 309, 17 U.C.C. Rep. Serv. 1114 (1975).

financing statement as a condition to finalization of a secured financing transaction. The creditor can search the filing system and file its financing statement if the search does not show a competing claim. The creditor then can finalize its transaction with the debtor free of concerns that the debtor could be dealing with another lender that might obtain priority. The general rule is a pure-race rule—the first secured party to either file or perfect prevails.[13] Being able to rely upon filing rather than perfection as the required action enables a creditor to establish its priority position before committing itself to any financing.[14]

If a party that pre-files a financing statement later makes a loan but never enters into a security agreement with the debtor, should that party nevertheless prevail against a secured party that files later? Although the general rule awards priority to the secured party that was the first to file, the general rule does not apply in this situation because it only governs priority battles between secured parties. If the first party to file never enters into a security agreement, that party never becomes a secured party and the filing is irrelevant for purposes of the general rule.[15] These facts vividly illustrate the importance of properly characterizing the competing claimants before selecting a rule to govern priority between them.

The characterization of a secured party's status may have to be determined over a period of time. The general rule confers priority on the secured party that was the first to file or perfect, provided that this secured party does not thereafter allow the intervention of a period during which it was neither filed nor perfected.[16] In other words, to retain the advantage of being the first to file or perfect, the secured party's filing or perfection must be continuous.[17] If there is a gap, its perfected status will only date from the time it reperfects.

In applying the first-to-file-or-perfect rule, bear in mind that the term "secured party" includes "a person to which accounts, chattel paper,

---

[13] Knowledge that a prior party has taken a security interest that has not been perfected is irrelevant in the priority determination. U.C.C. § 9-322, Comment 4. State of Alaska, Div. of Agr. v. Fowler, 611 P.2d 58, 29 U.C.C. Rep. Serv. 696 (Alaska 1980). Some priority provisions of Article 9 do refer to knowledge or notice, but not these general rules.

[14] A prospective secured party may also use this approach to protect itself against the delay in placing financing statements into the public record that plagues some states. Upon running a search and finding no competing financing statements, the lender may then wait for the period of time that covers the delay in obtaining any financing statements that have been previously presented into the public records. If another search conducted at the end of this time period reveals no competing financing statements, the lender has strong assurances that its financing statement will be the first to have been filed.

[15] Although it reached the correct result, the Tenth Circuit could have been more accurate by recognizing these principles. Transport Equip. Co. v. Guaranty State Bank, 518 F.2d 377, 17 U.C.C. Rep. Serv. 1 (10th Cir. 1975).

[16] Stearns Mfg. Co., Inc. v. National Bank & Trust Co. of Cent. Pa., 12 U.C.C. Rep. Serv. 189 (Pa. Ct. Com. Pl. 1972) (defendant attained priority when plaintiff's previously filed financing statement lapsed).

[17] See U.C.C. § 9-322, Comment 4 (Example 2).

payment intangibles, or promissory notes have been sold."[18] Thus, if Debtor sells its payment rights to Factor and then fraudulently resells them or uses them as collateral for a loan, Factor and the competing buyer or lender will both be secured parties and priority will be determined under the ordinary rules governing priority between secured parties.[19] The rationale for including sales of payment rights within the definition of "secured party" is discussed elsewhere in this book.[20]

§ 10.02   FUTURE ADVANCES—§§ 9-323, 9-322

Article 9 includes a separate section that deals with future advances.[21] The section does not, however, include the general rule concerning competing security interests when future advances are made; rather "[t]his section collects all of the special rules dealing with the priority of advances made by a secured party after a third party acquires an interest in the collateral."[22] Most cases concerning priority to future advances as between secured parties are governed by the general rule stated in section 9-322.[23] Thus,

---

[18] U.C.C. § 9-102(a)(72)(D). The definition is implicitly limited to buyers of payment rights in transactions that are within the scope of Article 9 because U.C.C. § 1-201(b)(35), which defines "security interest," includes the interest of a buyer of such payment rights only if the buyer acquires the rights in a transaction that is subject to Article 9. Excluded transactions are set forth in U.C.C. § 9-109(d)(4)-(7), discussed in § 1.07[F][1] *supra*. *See also* § 14.03 discussing buyers of payment rights that acquire their interests in transactions excluded from the scope of Article 9.

[19] It bears noting that the security interest of a buyer of payment intangibles or promissory notes is perfected automatically at the time the buyer's interest attaches. *See* § 7.02[B] *supra*.

[20] *See* § 1.06 *supra*.

[21] U.C.C. § 9-323.

[22] U.C.C. § 9-323, Comment 2. For a discussion of a secured party's priority in future advances as against a lien creditor or a buyer or lessee of goods, *see* §§ 14.02[C] and 13.03 *infra* (lien creditors) and §§ 14.03[C] and 11.03[A][3] *infra* (buyers and lessees of goods).

[23] There is a special rule in section 9-323(a) that applies when priority is based on the time an advance is made. The timing of an advance, however, generally is not relevant to a priority conflict between secured parties: "[I]t is abundantly clear that the time when an advance is made plays no role in determining priorities among conflicting security interests except when a financing statement was not filed and the advance is the giving of value as the last step for attachment and perfection." U.C.C. § 9-323, Comment 3. Section 9-323(a) identifies the circumstances in which the timing of an advance will affect priority between secured parties— priority will date from the time an advance is made to the extent that the security interest secures an advance (1) that is made while the interest is perfected automatically or by temporary perfection, and (2) that is not made pursuant to a commitment entered into before or while the security interest was perfected by a method other than automatic or temporary perfection. The emphasis on these forms of perfection should be obvious—while a security interest is perfected by one of these methods, it is a hidden lien and a subsequent secured party should not take subject to an advance. For the definition of "pursuant to commitment," *see* U.C.C. § 9-102(a)(68).

For example, suppose Secured Party has a security interest in a negotiable promissory note executed by Obligor and payable to the order of Debtor. Secured Party has perfected its security interest in the instrument by possession, and the security agreement contains an optional future advances clause. Secured Party later delivers the instrument to Debtor so that Debtor can present it to Obligor for payment, thereby becoming temporarily perfected. U.C.C. § 9-

a security interest with priority under the general rule also gives the secured party priority, as against other secured parties, for all subsequent advances secured by its collateral.

Consider the following hypothetical. On Day 1, SP-1 loans Debtor $50,000, takes a security interest in Debtor's equipment, and files a financing statement. On Day 20, SP-2 takes a security interest in the same equipment, files a financing statement, and loans Debtor $75,000. On Day 30, SP-1 loans Debtor an additional $40,000. Under the provisions of section 9-322(a)(1), SP-1 clearly has priority with respect to its initial loan of $50,000. Does SP-1 also have priority with respect to the additional $40,000 loan?

The question cannot be answered without first characterizing SP-1's status with respect to the second loan, and that status cannot be established based on the facts presented because three relevant scenarios are possible. Under two of them, SP-1 will prevail under the general rule. Under the third scenario, SP-1 will be an unsecured creditor with respect to the second loan and thus will fall, with respect to that loan, outside the scope of the provisions governing priority between secured parties.

One possibility is that SP-1 made the subsequent loan of $40,000 pursuant to a future advances clause in the security agreement between SP-1 and Debtor. The future advances clause would serve as the basis to establish that SP-1 was a secured party in the same collateral with respect to the subsequent loan. Because SP-1 had already filed a financing statement that preceded the filing by SP-2, SP-1 would prevail even with respect to the future advance of $40,000.[24]

A second possibility is that the security agreement did not contain a future advances clause but that SP-1 nevertheless claims secured status for the second loan pursuant to a new security agreement between SP-1 and Debtor that describes the same collateral as that covered in the original security agreement between them. The second security agreement clearly would give SP-1 secured status with respect to the second loan. The issue is whether the interest would be perfected and give priority to SP-1 over SP-2 with respect to the $40,000 advance.

312(f) (20-day period). If Secured Party makes an advance during the period of temporary perfection, its priority for the advance as against another secured party will date only from the time the advance is made. If the security agreement had obligated the secured party to make the advance, however, priority as to the advance would date from the time Secured Party initially took possession. The practical effect of these rules is that very few cases will be governed by the special provision of section 9-323: "Thus, an advance has priority from the date it is made only in the rare case in which it is made without commitment and while the security interest is perfected only temporarily under Section 9-312." U.C.C. § 9-323, Comment 3. Most cases between competing secured parties involving future advances are governed by the first-to-file-or-perfect rule of section 9-322(a).

[24] *In re* Leslie Brock & Sons, 147 B.R. 426, 21 U.C.C. Rep. Serv. 2d 154 (Bankr. S.D. Ohio (1992); Thorp Commercial Corp. v. Northgate Indus., Inc., 654 F.2d 1245, 31 U.C.C. Rep. Serv. 801 (8th Cir. 1981).

This issue proved to be controversial under original Article 9. A minority position that attracted considerable attention was epitomized by the decision in *Coin-O-Matic Service Co. v. Rhode Island Hospital Trust Co.*[25] The original parties in that case entered into a new security agreement at the time of the subsequent loan because, at the time of the first loan, they had not contemplated additional advances by the secured party. The court held that the "first-to-file" rule did not apply if the original security agreement did not provide for future advances, and it concluded that the secured party did not have priority as to the subsequent loan over a conflicting security interest perfected prior to the time of that loan.[26]

Fortunately, most courts refused to follow the erroneous reasoning of the *Coin-O-Matic* case.[27] The drafters of the 1972 revisions to Article 9 rejected the decision and its progeny and, to emphasize this position, added language to the Comments that repudiated the decision.[28] The bankruptcy court in Rhode Island, where *Coin-O-Matic* was decided, later rejected the *Coin-O-Matic* approach based on the changes stressed by the drafters.[29]

Thus, if the second security agreement covers the same collateral as that described in the filed financing statement, SP-1 will have priority for its second loan.[30] Although the subsequent loan is not a future advance at all, but rather a new loan made contemporaneously with the new security agreement, SP-1 will still prevail on the strength of the language and policy of the general rule. The earlier discussion of the general rule[31] demonstrated that, if SP-1 had pre-filed a financing statement and later entered into a security agreement with Debtor after SP-2 perfected its security interest, SP-1 would have attained priority as the first to file or perfect.[32] Conceptually, the relationship between SP-1's filed financing statement and its second security agreement with Debtor is no different merely because SP-1 also entered into an initial security agreement with Debtor that was contemporaneous with its filing.

---

[25] U.C.C. Rep. Serv. 1112 (R.I. Super. Ct. 1966).

[26] A few cases followed the same approach. ITT Indus. Credit Co. v. Union Bank & Trust Co., 615 S.W.2d 2, 30 U.C.C. Rep. Serv. 1701 (Ky. Ct. App. 1981) (future advances clause required in security agreement to cover future advances). Some more recent decisions also suggested that a clause in the security agreement is needed. *In re* Comprehensive Review Tech., Inc., 138 B.R. 195, 17 U.C.C. Rep. Serv. 2d 954 (Bankr. S.D. Ohio 1992).

[27] *See, e.g.,* Provident Fin. Co. v. Beneficial Fin. Co., 36 N.C. App. 401, 245 S.E.2d 510, 24 U.C.C. Rep. Serv. 1332 (1978); *In re* Rivet, 299 F. Supp. 374, 6 U.C.C. Rep. Serv. 460 (E.D. Mich. 1969).

[28] U.C.C. § 9-312, Comment 7 (1972 official text). The same effect is indicated in the current Comments. U.C.C. § 9-323, Comment 3 (Example 1).

[29] *In re* Nason, 13 B.R. 984, 31 U.C.C. Rep. Serv. 1739 (Bankr. D. R.I. 1981). For consistent cases, *see* UNI Imports, Inc. v. Aparacor, Inc., 978 F.2d 984, 18 U.C.C. Rep. Serv. 2d 933 (7th Cir. 1992); State Bank of Sleepy Eye v. Krueger, 405 N.W.2d 491, 3 U.C.C. Rep. Serv. 2d 1145 (Minn. Ct. App. 1987).

[30] Allis-Chalmers Credit Corp. v. Cheney Inv., Inc., 227 Kan. 4, 605 P.2d 525, 28 U.C.C. Rep. Serv. 574 (1980). *See also* U.C.C. § 9-323, Comment 3 (last sentence to Example 1).

[31] *See* § 10.01 *supra.*

[32] U.C.C. § 9-322(a)(1). First Nat'l Bank & Trust Co. of Vinita, Okla. v. Atlas Credit Corp., 417 F.2d 1081, 6 U.C.C. Rep. Serv. 1223 (10th Cir. 1969).

The third possible scenario with respect to the second loan advanced by SP-1 is that the loan was made without a future advances clause and without a subsequent security agreement. In this case, SP-1 would be characterized as an unsecured creditor with respect to the second loan. SP-1 could not establish any way in which Debtor consented to attachment, and thus the collateral described in the original security agreement would not also secure the second loan. The general rule would not apply because, beyond SP-1's initial loan, SP-2 would be the only secured party. A lender in SP-1's position, therefore, must either include a future advances clause in its initial security agreement or remember to enter into another agreement in order to secure any subsequent loans.

The first-to-file-or-perfect rule has enormous practical consequences on the way in which secured financing should be conducted. The practical reality is that there is no real safety in being a subordinate creditor.[33] If a debtor owes only $10,000 to a prior-perfected secured party and the collateral is worth in excess of $100,000, it might initially appear safe to lend several thousand dollars against the equity in the collateral. The debtor's available equity could be wiped out, however, by subsequent advances from the first secured party. The second lender is not safe even if the original security agreement does not include a future advances clause, or, if the first secured party has perfected by filing, even if the outstanding debt to the first secured party has been paid in full. All that must happen to undercut the second lender's position is for the first lender to make a subsequent advance and enter into a new security agreement while the financing statement remains effective.

A prospective lender that wishes to make a loan to the debtor but wants to avoid this risk should follow one of three courses. If the debt to the first lender has been fully paid, the second lender should insist upon a termination statement to end any basis for continuous perfection if the first lender perfected by filing.[34] If money is still owed to the first lender, the second lender could increase the amount of its loan, pay off the first lender, and require an assignment of its financing statement or require a termination statement.[35] The third option would be to negotiate with the first lender[36]

[33] In re Martin Grinding & Machine Works, Inc., 793 F.2d 592, 1 U.C.C. Rep. Serv. 2d 1329 (7th Cir. 1986) (not safe to loan against property described in prior financing statement).

[34] Provident Fin. Co. v. Beneficial Fin. Co., 36 N.C. App. 401, 245 S.E.2d 510, 24 U.C.C. Rep. Serv. 1332 (1978) (defendant could have protected itself by insisting that a termination statement be filed but failed to do so). See § 5.06[C] supra.

[35] In re Bishop, 52 B.R. 470, 41 U.C.C. Rep. Serv. 1491 (Bankr. N.D. Ala. 1985) (bank received correspondence noting its payment of a prior-perfected finance company, but a termination statement was not filed; court held that an enforceable subordination agreement was entered into with respect to the noted inventory but that it did not extend to after-acquired units).

[36] Subordination agreements are generally entered into between two or more creditors. A secondary creditor that was not a party to a subordination agreement between the primary secured party and the debtor has been held to be a beneficiary of that agreement. In re Thorner Mfg. Co., Inc., 4 U.C.C. Rep Serv. 595 (Bankr. E.D. Pa. 1967).

to obtain a subordination agreement[37] by which the first lender would agree to subordinate itself with respect to any further loans that it might advance to the debtor.[38] Although such an agreement is not generally in the interest of the first lender, it might be attainable if the first lender would like to see a new infusion of capital into the debtor's operation, or if the first lender is certain that it will not advance any more money to the debtor.[39]

§ 10.03 EXCEPTIONS FOR NON-FILING COLLATERAL

The Comments to Article 9 draw a distinction between "non-filing collateral" and "filing collateral." The distinction is described as follows:

> As used in these Comments, non-filing collateral is collateral of a type for which perfection may be achieved by a method other than filing (possession or control, mainly) and for which secured parties who so perfect generally do not expect or need to conduct a filing search. More specifically, non-filing collateral is chattel paper, deposit accounts, negotiable documents, instruments, investment property, and letter-of-credit rights. Other collateral—accounts, commercial tort claims, general intangibles, goods, nonnegotiable documents, and payment intangibles—is filing collateral.[40]

The distinction is important because Article 9 provides special priority rules with respect to non-filing collateral that override the first-to-file-or-perfect rule of section 9-322(a).[41] Depending on the specific types of property, these rules on non-filing collateral provide for priority based on the first to perfect by taking control or possession of the collateral.

---

[37] A secured party's priority can also be subordinated through estoppel. Hillman's Equip., Inc. v. Central Realty, Inc., 144 Ind. App. 18, 242 N.E.2d 522, 5 U.C.C. Rep. Serv. 1160 (1968), *rev'd on other grounds,* 246 N.E.2d 383 (1969) (junior secured party changed his position in reliance on senior secured party's statement, prior to sale of collateral, that he would get his equipment).

[38] "This article does not preclude subordination by agreement by a person entitled to priority." U.C.C. § 9-339. *See also In re* Smith, 77 B.R. 624, 5 U.C.C. Rep. Serv. 2d 496 (Bankr. N.D. Ohio 1987) (bank agreed to subordinate its lien on proceeds up to $8000 per year for seven years). *But see* H. & Val J. Rothschild, Inc. v. Northwestern Nat'l Bank of St. Paul, 309 Minn. 35, 242 N.W.2d 844, 19 U.C.C. Rep Serv. 673 (1976) (telephone conversation in which parties assumed mistakenly that plaintiff had a prior claim did not subordinate defendant's claim). The security interest of a person entitled to priority under Article 9's priority rules cannot be subordinated by agreement unless that person is a party to the subordination agreement. One's rights cannot otherwise be adversely affected by an agreement to which it is not a party. U.C.C. § 9-339, Comment 2. First Dakota Nat'l Bank v. Performance Engr. & Mfg., Inc., 676 N.W.2d 395, 53 UCC Rep. Serv.2d 677 (S.D. 2004).

[39] Western Auto Supply Co. v. Bank of Imboden, 17 Ark. App. 4, 701 S.W.2d 394, 42 U.C.C. Rep. Serv. 1506 (1985) (prior-perfected secured party consented because it recognized its own interest in debtor obtaining bank loan). A secured creditor should be careful in agreeing to subordination. *In re* Bar-Cross Farms & Ranches, Inc., 48 B.R. 976, 1 U.C.C. Rep. Serv. 2d 256 (Bankr. D. Colo. 1985) (waiver by secured party did not merely subordinate its interest to another claimant but terminated the interest).

[40] U.C.C. § 9-322, Comment 7.

[41] U.C.C. §§ 9-322(f)(1), 9-327 to 9-330.

[A] Deposit Accounts—§ 9-327

A secured party that has perfected a security interest in a deposit account by control will have priority over a secured party that has a competing interest perfected by any other method.[42] The only alternative method for perfection relevant to a deposit account would be the automatic continuous perfection available for identifiable cash proceeds within the account.[43]

A deposit account might be maintained by a secured party that is a bank or by a bank that is not the secured party. In the former case, control is automatic, although heightened protection may be gained by taking control by having the bank named in its own records as the secured party with respect to the deposit account.[44] In the case of a deposit account maintained at another bank, a secured party may obtain control by entering into a control agreement with the debtor and the maintaining bank or by becoming the customer with respect to the account in the records of the maintaining bank.[45] If the bank with which a deposit account is maintained holds the security interest, that interest takes priority over a conflicting security interest in the deposit account,[46] whether the conflicting interest is as original collateral or as cash proceeds, unless the other secured party obtains control by becoming the customer with respect to the deposit account.[47] This rule leaves banks free to extend credit to their customers without having to consult records to determine whether another security interest has been created in the deposit account.[48] A secured party that wishes to avoid such priority and that does not become the customer with respect to the account[49] can only prevail by obtaining a subordination agreement from the maintaining bank.[50]

[B] Investment Property—§ 9-328

A secured party that has perfected a security interest in investment property by control will have priority over a competing interest perfected by any other means.[51] This rule reflects the unique aspects of the securities markets. It provides a clear mandate that a secured party that wants the greatest level of protection available must obtain control. The availability of filing as an alternative method of perfection for investment property is

---

[42] U.C.C. § 9-327(1). For a discussion of perfection by control in a deposit account, *see* U.C.C. §§ 9-312(b)(1), 9-314, 9-104 and § 6.04[B] *supra*.

[43] *See* U.C.C. §§ 9-312(b)(1), 9-315(c), (d)(2).

[44] U.C.C. § 9-104(a)(1), (3).

[45] U.C.C. § 9-104(a)(2), (3).

[46] U.C.C. § 9-327(3).

[47] U.C.C. § 9-327(4).

[48] U.C.C. § 9-327, Comment 4.

[49] U.C.C. §§ 9-327(4), 9-104(a)(3).

[50] For discussion on priorities in proceeds, *see* § 10.05 *infra*.

[51] U.C.C. § 9-328(1). For discussion of perfection by control in investment paper, *see* U.C.C. §§ 9-314, 9-106 and § 6.04[A] *supra*.

not intended to alter the established practice of not searching the U.C.C. files before entering into securities transactions.[52] Thus, a secured party may obtain control and be unaffected by any prior filings. Filing only provides a secured party with protection against lien creditors (including bankruptcy trustees) and other secured parties that fail to obtain control.

A variety of rules determine priority of conflicting security interests in investment property when each of the interests is perfected by control. A primary advantage is afforded to a securities intermediary that holds a security interest in a security entitlement or in a securities account that is maintained with the intermediary. Such an intermediary has priority over a conflicting security interest held by another secured party.[53] In other cases involving conflicting security interests perfected by control, a rule of temporal priority applies.[54] In other words, the first secured party to obtain control has priority. The occurrence of such dual interests perfected by control is likely to be rare.[55]

A security interest in a certificated security in registered form which is perfected by delivery has priority over a conflicting security interest that is perfected by any method other than control.[56] Thus, a secured party that takes possession of a certificated security in registered form without obtaining the indorsement necessary for control will have priority over a prior secured party that perfected by filing.[57]

[C] Letter-of-Credit Rights—§ 9-329

A secured party having control of a letter-of-credit right will have priority over a conflicting security interest held by a secured party that does not have control.[58] The only alternative methods of perfection in a letter-of-credit right would be automatic perfection in a supporting obligation[59] or temporary perfection if the letter-of-credit right is a proceed of the secured party's original collateral.[60] This allocation of priority is consistent with international practice and promotes finality of payment made to recognized assignees of letter-of-credit proceeds.[61] Multiple secured parties with control rank according to the time of obtaining control.[62]

---

[52] For discussion of practices in the securities markets, see § 6.04[A] supra.

[53] U.C.C. § 9-328(3). Comparable priority is available for a commodity intermediary. U.C.C. § 9-328(4).

[54] U.C.C. § 9-328(2).

[55] U.C.C. § 9-328, Comment 5.

[56] U.C.C. § 9-328(5). The fact that delivery is a half-step short of control justifies the rule. Delivery is discussed in Chapter 4 supra.

[57] Priority between secured parties that both perfect by filing will be governed by the general rule of first-to-file. U.C.C. §§ 9-328(7), 9-322(a)(1).

[58] U.C.C. § 9-329(1). For discussion of perfection by control for letter-of-credit rights, see U.C.C. §§ 9-312(b)(2), 9-314, 9-107 and § 6.04[B] supra.

[59] U.C.C. § 9-308(d).

[60] U.C.C. § 9-315(c).

[61] U.C.C. § 9-329, Comment 2.

[62] U.C.C. § 9-329(2).

[D] Chattel Paper, Instruments, Negotiable Documents, and Securities—§§ 9-330, 9-331

Article 9 includes provisions under which a purchaser may attain priority against even a prior-perfected secured party in chattel paper, instruments, negotiable documents, and securities.[63] These provisions are covered in detail in a subsequent chapter covering other persons (such as buyers) whose interests conflict with a security interest in these types of property.[64] For present purposes, note that "purchaser" is defined broadly to include a secured party.[65] Consistent with the approach taken for other non-filing collateral, priority that is an exception to the first-to-file-or-perfect rule is available under these provisions for secured parties with interests in chattel paper, instruments, negotiable documents, or securities if they take possession of the collateral and satisfy other requirements. Such priority is also available for secured parties that take control of electronic chattel paper.[66]

§ 10.04 PURCHASE-MONEY SECURITY INTERESTS

The first-to-file-or-perfect rule and the rules on priorities with respect to future advances could place a debtor in a difficult position. The debtor's present secured lender might be unwilling to advance additional capital that the debtor needs to acquire more property of the type covered in a filed financing statement, while other financers could refuse to extend credit because they would be vulnerable to any advances that the present secured lender might make. The first-to-file-or-perfect rule and the priority rules governing future advances could practically enable a secured lender to eliminate competing sources of financing and to exert excessive control over the direction of the debtor's business.

This position of excessive control is tempered by other provisions that favor purchase-money secured parties. Under these provisions, a purchase-money secured party can finance the debtor's acquisition of additional goods despite a prior-filed financing statement and attain priority with respect to the goods.[67] Even if the initial secured party's perfected security interest extends to the new goods under an after-acquired property clause in the security agreement, the interest of the initial secured party will be subordinate with respect to the new goods.

---

[63] U.C.C. §§ 9-330, 9-331.

[64] *See* § 11.03[C], [D] *infra.*

[65] U.C.C. § 1-201(b)(30), (29).

[66] U.C.C. § 9-330(a), (b). For discussion of perfection by control for electronic chattel paper, *see* U.C.C. §§ 9-314, 9-105 and § 6.04[B] *supra.*

[67] A purchase-money security interest can only be created in goods and software. U.C.C. § 9-103; First Bethany Bank & Trust, N.A. v. Arvest United Bank, 2003 Okla. LEXIS 70, 50 U.C.C. Rep. Serv. 2d 1209 (Okla. 2003) (cannot take a purchase-money security interest in accounts). *See* § 1.05 *supra.* A purchase-money security interest in software can arise only if the debtor acquires its interest in the software for the purpose of using the software in goods subject to a purchase-money security interest. U.C.C. § 9-103(c). A perfected purchase-money security interest in software is given the same priority as the purchase-money security interest in the goods for which the software was acquired. U.C.C. § 9-324(f).

The prior secured party should have few complaints about the priority granted to later purchase-money secured parties. Because of the secondary source of financing, the debtor acquires additional assets without the prior secured party having to finance the new acquisition. Furthermore, the prior secured party never relied upon the additional collateral in making its original decision to extend financing. The exceptions in favor of purchase-money secured parties are crucial to allow debtors to obtain alternative financing once they have permitted the filing of a financing statement.

[A] Collateral Other Than Inventory—§ 9-324(a)

The general rule on purchase-money priority favors purchase-money secured parties that have interests in goods other than inventory or livestock.

> [A] perfected purchase-money security interest in goods other than inventory or livestock has priority over a conflicting security interest in the same goods . . . if the purchase-money security interest is perfected when the debtor receives possession of the collateral or within 20 days thereafter.[68]

The only requirement imposed on the purchase-money secured party is to perfect in a timely manner, *i.e.*, within the 20-day grace period.[69] The secured party may perfect by filing or by any other available method. This makes automatic perfection potentially relevant (perfection by possession is possible, as is temporary perfection, but both are unlikely given the nature of the typical purchase-money secured transaction). If the collateral is consumer goods, the purchase-money secured party's interest is automatically perfected upon attachment, and no filing is necessary to obtain priority over conflicting security interests.[70] If the collateral is not consumer goods, however, the purchase-money secured party typically must file a financing statement before the expiration of the grace period.[71]

The grace period facilitates the completion of commercial transactions. A supplier thus can sell goods, retain a security interest in them, and conveniently allow the debtor to take possession without having to interrupt this sequence by first filing a financing statement. The supplier can proceed

---

[68] U.C.C. § 9-324(a). The grace period is comparable to the twenty days allowed for a purchase-money secured party to file or take possession of the collateral to achieve priority over an intervening lien creditor. *See* U.C.C. § 9-317(e) and § 14.02[B] *infra*.

[69] State Bank & Trust Co. of Beeville v. First Nat'l Bank of Beeville, 635 S.W.2d 807, 33 U.C.C. Rep. Serv. 1775 (Tex. Ct. App. 1982) (purchase-money secured party filed one day later to qualify under exception).

[70] Nevertheless, the purchase-money secured party may choose to file in order to ensure that it does not lose its priority as against a later consumer that buys the collateral without knowledge of the security interest. *See* § 11.03[A][2] *supra*.

[71] U.C.C. § 9-324(a); Custer v. American Honda Fin. Corp., 2003 Bankr. LEXIS 272, 50 U.C.C. Rep. Serv. 2d 608 (Bankr. N.D. Iowa 2003) (because the purchase-money secured party failed to perfect its interest within the 20-day grace period, the trustee in bankruptcy acquired superior rights in the vehicle).

in its dealings with the debtor, confident that it can achieve priority if it completes the steps for perfection within the allotted grace period. The rationale that underlies pre-filing of financing statements is generally not applicable here.

The grace period begins from the time that the debtor receives possession of the collateral.[72] The provision has generated some controversy in cases in which the debtor acquires possession of goods by a lease containing an option to buy or by a sale on approval. For example, suppose that Debtor leases equipment from Supplier and, thirty days after receiving possession, exercises an option to purchase the equipment. Supplier extends credit to finance payment of the option price, retains a security interest in the equipment, and immediately files a financing statement. Shortly thereafter, Supplier is challenged for priority by Bank, which holds a prior-perfected security interest in the equipment under an after-acquired property clause in its security agreement. Bank will assert that Supplier does not qualify for purchase-money priority because it filed more than twenty days after Debtor acquired possession. Supplier will instead argue that it filed its financing statement within twenty days after the equipment became "collateral," i.e., when Debtor became legally obligated to purchase it.

The Comments now address the issue directly, indicating that "the 20-day period in subsection (a) does not commence until the goods become 'collateral' (defined in Section 9-102), i.e., until they are subject to a security interest."[73] Most courts had already construed the language of Article 9 to support Supplier's position.[74] Even if a financing statement had been filed earlier, it would not have resulted in perfection because no security interest existed until Debtor entered into the security agreement, and the exception in favor of a purchase-money secured party requires perfection within twenty days of the debtor receiving possession of the "collateral."[75] This resolution of the issue obviously perpetuates problems of ostensible ownership.

Article 9 also includes a provision that governs priority between conflicting purchase-money security interests. Priority is given to a security interest that secures the price of the collateral over a security interest acquired through an enabling loan.[76] The general "first-to-file-or-perfect"

---

[72] In re Ivy, 37 B.R. 285, 38 U.C.C. Rep. Serv. 651 (Bankr. E.D. Ky. 1983) (filing financing statement within grace period [then ten days] after debtor received delivery of equipment was adequate even though security agreement was signed more than ten days before filing).

[73] U.C.C. § 9-324, Comment 3.

[74] In re Hooks, 40 B.R. 715, 39 U.C.C. Rep. Serv. 332 (Bankr. M.D. Ga. 1984) (shipment for inspection); Rainier Nat'l Bank v. Inland Mach. Co., 29 Wash. App. 725, 631 P.2d 389, 32 U.C.C. Rep. Serv. 287 (1981) (lease with option to buy).

[75] "Collateral" is defined as "the property subject to a security interest or agricultural lien." U.C.C. § 9-102(a)(12). The analysis in the text applies only to transactions in which a true lease has been created rather than a security interest disguised as a lease. For discussion of the requirements for a true lease, see § 1.03[B][1] supra.

[76] U.C.C. § 9-324(g)(1). This priority allocation reflects the rule adopted in the Restatement (Third) of Property (Mortgages) § 7.2(c) (1997). U.C.C. § 9-324, Comment 13. This allocation is based on a preference for the purchase-money seller, who arguably may not be as well-suited as a purchase-money enabling lender to spread financial losses.

rule governs priority in multiple purchase-money security interests that secure enabling loans.[77]

[B] Inventory—§ 9-324(b), (c)

The exception favoring purchase-money secured parties is more complicated if the collateral is inventory.[78] The text of Article 9 provides:

[A] perfected purchase-money security interest in inventory has priority over a conflicting security interest in the same inventory . . . if:

(1) the purchase-money security interest is perfected when the debtor receives possession of the inventory;

(2) the purchase-money secured party sends an authenticated notification to the holder of the conflicting security interest;

(3) the holder of the conflicting security interest receives the notification within five years before the debtor receives possession of the inventory; and

(4) the notification states that the person sending the notification has or expects to acquire a purchase-money security interest in inventory of the debtor and describes the inventory.[79]

Although these provisions may at first appear quite daunting, they essentially require the purchase-money secured party to do only two things: (a) perfect its security interest at or before the time the debtor receives possession of the inventory, and (b) provide notification in proper form, making sure that it is received prior to the debtor receiving possession of the collateral, to the holder of a conflicting security interest that has filed a financing statement before the purchase-money secured party filed or attained temporary perfection.

The specific requirements of this exception are best understood in the context of the underlying policy concerns. Consider a typical ongoing inventory-financing arrangement in which the secured party advances a specified percentage against invoices for new inventory acquired by the debtor. This type of arrangement is common in inventory financing, and

---

[77] U.C.C. § 9-324(g)(2); Lashua v. La Duke, 707 N.Y.S.2d 542, 41 U.C.C. Rep. Serv. 2d 930 (App. Div. 2000) (although purchase-money secured party failed to perfect within the grace period, it nevertheless prevailed as the first party to perfect).

[78] Article 9 also provides for the priority of purchase-money security interests in livestock that are farm products that is comparable to the purchase-money priority provided for inventory, the main difference being that the purchase-money secured party must renew its notice to prior-perfected secured parties on a six-month rather than a five-year basis. U.C.C. § 9-324(d), (e).

[79] U.C.C. § 9-324(b). "Subsections (b)(2) through (4) apply only if the holder of the conflicting security interest had filed a financing statement covering the same types of inventory: (1) if the purchase-money security interest is perfected by filing, before the date of the filing; or (2) if the purchase-money security interest is temporarily perfected without filing or possession under Section 9-312(f), before the beginning of the 20-day period thereunder." U.C.C. § 9-324(c).

financers often rely upon invoices in deciding whether to advance additional funds. If a purchase-money secured party has financed the debtor's acquisition of inventory covered by a particular invoice, the inventory financer could easily be deceived by a dishonest debtor that presents the invoice with a request for another advance. The purchase-money secured party, therefore, must protect the inventory financer by providing authenticated notification[80] that it has acquired or intends to acquire[81] a purchase-money security interest in specific items or types of inventory.[82] The notice protects the original financer by alerting it to watch out for presentation by the debtor of an invoice that covers any of the inventory described in the notification.[83]

The notification process would be burdensome to a purchase-money secured party that contemplates a series of transactions with the debtor if it had to provide notification prior to each transaction. A manufacturer, for example, may decide to finance all of a retailer's subsequent acquisition of its products. The manufacturer can simply notify the prior inventory financer that it expects to acquire a purchase-money security interest in these items of inventory[84] and that notification will be valid for five years from the date that the inventory financer receives the notification.[85] It will then be incumbent upon the inventory financer to implement a business procedure by which, over the next five years, it can protect itself in light of the information contained in the notification.

Because the notification may describe inventory in which the sender merely expects to acquire a purchase-money security interest,[86] a debtor might acquire some inventory that fits the description but, in fact, is not

---

[80] Elhard v. Prairie Distrib., Inc., 366 N.W.2d 465, 40 U.C.C. Rep. Serv. 1968 (N.D. 1985) (oral notification invalid).

[81] *In re* Daniels, 35 B.R. 247, 37 U.C.C. Rep. Serv. 967 (Bankr. W.D. Okla. 1983) (notification upheld against attack that it should fail because it did not state explicitly that creditor planned to take purchase-money security interest).

[82] U.C.C. § 9-324(b)(2), (4); Guaranty State Bank & Trust Co. v. Van Diest Supply Co., 55 P.3d 357, 48 U.C.C. Rep. Serv. 2d 1197 (Kan. Ct. App. 2002) (held that a notice that does not specifically indicate that a purchase-money security interest is retained or considered is not sufficient because it could mislead the secured party receiving the notice to believe that it retains its priority under the "first to file" rule).

[83] The reason no comparable notification requirement applies to purchase-money security interests for collateral other than inventory is explained in the Comments: "Inasmuch as an arrangement for periodic advances against incoming goods is unusual outside the inventory field, subsection (a) does not contain a notification requirement." U.C.C. § 9-324, Comment 4.

[84] U.C.C. § 9-324(b)(4).

[85] U.C.C. § 9-324(b)(3). The five-year duration of the notification corresponds to the period before a filed financing statement lapses. A purchase-money secured party engaged in ongoing financing of a debtor should provide new notification to all relevant parties when it files a continuation statement.

[86] Fedders Fin. Corp. v. Chiarelli Bros., 289 A.2d 169, 10 U.C.C. Rep. Serv. 880 (Pa. Super. Ct. 1972) (written notification that described variety of types of appliances was valid even though the purchase-money secured party took an interest only in the air conditioners).

financed by the sender of the notification. The inventory financer will have priority as to those items under its after-acquired property clause.[87]

The rules are available to enable any purchase-money secured party[88] to take priority over a prior-perfected secured party. If a purchase-money secured party fails to comply with the procedures required to invoke them, however, it will be subordinate to a prior-perfected secured party that can use an after-acquired property clause to reach the collateral provided by the purchase-money secured party.[89]

§ 10.05 PROCEEDS

A secured party might take its interest in one type of collateral (such as inventory) and another secured party might acquire a security interest from the same debtor in a different type of collateral (such as accounts). What happens if some of the inventory collateral is sold in transactions that create accounts? The accounts are proceeds of the inventory collateral, and a priority dispute might arise between the two secured parties. Before turning to the priority rules, however, it is first necessary to characterize the interests of the competing claimants in the accounts. Because the inventory-based secured party can claim the accounts only as proceeds, the provisions related to attachment and perfection in proceeds must be analyzed.

A security interest attaches automatically to identifiable proceeds received upon the disposition of collateral.[90] Thus, the inventory financer's security interest attaches to accounts created upon the sale of the inventory subject to its security interest. If the inventory financer perfected as to the inventory by filing a financing statement, perfection in the accounts as proceeds will automatically extend beyond the grace period of temporary perfection because the office in which the financing statement was filed would be the same office in which a secured party would file with respect to accounts.[91] Only after determining whether the accounts financer is perfected and whether the inventory financer is perfected as to the accounts as proceeds can the appropriate priority rule be selected.

---

[87] It is a rare inventory financer that does not include such a clause. *See* discussion in § 3.02[A] *supra*.

[88] In this context, note that the term "secured party" includes a consignor, U.C.C. § 9-102(a)(72)(C), and that the interest of a consignor is deemed to be a purchase-money security interest in inventory. U.C.C. § 9-103(d). Consignments are discussed in § 1.03[B][2] *supra*.

[89] U.C.C. § 9-322(a). Zink v. Vanmiddlesworth, 300 B.R. 394, 51 U.C.C. Rep. Serv. 2d 892 (N.D. N.Y. 2003) (because the purchase-money secured party did not perfect its security interest before the debtor received possession of the cattle, and did not notify a prior-perfected secured party with an interest in all of the current and after-acquired debtor's livestock, the purchase-money secured party did not attain priority with respect to the cattle that it sold to the debtor).

[90] U.C.C. § 9-315(a)(2). For discussion of attachment of security interests in proceeds generally, see § 2.03[B] *supra*.

[91] U.C.C. § 9-315(c), (d)(1). For discussion of perfection of security interests in proceeds, see § 8.02 *supra*.

As we have seen, the priority rules governing purchase-money security interests are exceptions to the rules governing priority among ordinary security interests.[92] This same approach is applied to priority with respect to proceeds—different rules govern transactions that involve nonpurchase-money security interests and those that involve purchase-money security interests.

[A] Nonpurchase-Money Security Interests

The Article 9 rules on priority with respect to proceeds include a general rule and special rules. Because the general rule applies the ordinary rule of section 9-322(a)(1) governing priority of competing perfected security interests, it is based on temporal priority ("first-to-file-or-perfect"). The special rules are provided for situations in which this temporal rule is not considered appropriate. The special rules apply only to what is designated as "non-filing collateral," and they encompass both a rule based on non-temporal priority and one based on special temporal priority. The explanation of these provisions and their application is provided below.

[1] General Rule—§ 9-322(b)(1)

The general rule for priority in proceeds makes the time of filing or perfection as to proceeds the same as the time of filing or perfection as to the original collateral, and thus it applies the first-to-file-or-perfect rule governing conflicting perfected security interests in the same collateral.[93] Assume that an inventory financer files on the debtor's present and after-acquired inventory, whereas an accounts financer files on the same debtor's accounts. Some of the inventory is sold, producing accounts as proceeds, and a priority dispute develops between the two secured lenders. The inventory financer would claim a continuously perfected security interest in the accounts as proceeds from the sale of its collateral. As indicated above, each party would have a perfected security interest in the accounts. Priority would depend upon which of the parties was the first to file its financing statement.

[2] Special Rules

The special rules[94] are provided to cover situations in which application

---

[92] *See* § 10.04 *supra.*

[93] "For the purposes of subsection (a)(1), the time of filing or perfection as to a security interest in collateral is also the time of filing or perfection as to a security interest in proceeds." U.C.C. § 9-322(b)(1). *See* § 10.01 *supra. See also In re* Topsy's Shoppes, Inc. of Kan., 118 B.R. 797, 12 U.C.C. Rep. Serv. 2d 1161 (Bankr. D. Kan. 1990) (secured party failed to establish priority in proceeds arising from sales of intangibles when it conceded that another secured party had prior perfection in the same intangibles); *In re* McBee, 20 B.R. 361, 34 U.C.C. Rep. Serv. 1011 (Bankr. W.D. Tex. 1982), *rev'd on other grounds,* 714 F.2d 1316, 36 U.C.C. Rep. Serv. 1473 (5th Cir. 1983) (inventory financers ranked according to time of filing with respect to cash proceeds).

[94] U.C.C. § 9-322(c)-(e).

of the general rule would lead to an inappropriate result.[95] The special rules apply only to what the Comments designate as "non-filing collateral."[96]

[a] Special Rule on Non-Temporal Priority—§ 9-322(c)(2)

Article 9 includes a number of provisions whereby a secured party with a security interest in non-filing collateral may attain non-temporal priority, *i.e.*, priority over a prior-perfected conflicting security interest in the same collateral.[97] This priority may only be obtained through perfection by possession or by control and by compliance with other requirements, and it is an exception to the temporal priority rule (first-to-file-or-perfect) that generally governs when there are conflicting perfected security interests.[98]

If a secured party with a security interest in non-filing collateral has taken the steps necessary for non-temporal priority,[99] section 9-322(c)(2) extends that priority to the proceeds of the non-filing collateral if the security interest in the proceeds is perfected and the proceeds are either cash proceeds or are of the same type as the original collateral.

For example, assume that SP-1 perfects a security interest in all of Debtor's instruments, including after-acquired instruments, by filing.[100] SP-2 later perfects a security interest in a promissory note owned by Debtor by taking possession of the note and acquires priority in the note under section 9-330(d) or section 9-331(a). Debtor subsequently receives an installment payment on the note in the form of cash, and also receives a check for the balance of the note. If applicable, the temporal rule of section 9-322(a)(1) would give priority in the proceeds to SP-1. Section 9-322(c)(2) applies, however, and gives priority to SP-2. The cash and the check are both cash proceeds, and the check is also the same type of collateral as the promissory note, *i.e.*, an instrument.[101]

---

[95] U.C.C. § 9-322, Comment 7.

[96] The distinction between non-filing collateral and filing collateral is provided at § 10.03 *supra*.

[97] U.C.C. §§ 9-327 through 9-331. These provisions are discussed in § 10.03 *supra*.

[98] U.C.C. § 9-322(f)(1).

[99] An actual conflicting security interest in the original non-filing collateral is not necessary. U.C.C. § 9-322(c).

[100] "Non-filing" as used here does not in all instances mean that the secured party cannot file but rather that filing is not the preferred method.

[101] If a secured party perfects in the original non-filing collateral by taking control, the additional step of filing can be beneficial in certain situations. For example, assume that SP-1 perfects a security interest in all of the investment property of Debtor by filing. Afterwards, SP-2 perfects in a certificated security of Debtor by taking control. Debtor subsequently receives a stock dividend on the certificated security controlled by SP-2, in the form of a new certificated security. Even though the proceed is the same type of property as the collateral, if SP-2 does not take delivery or control, or file with respect to the proceeds before the expiration of its 20-day period of temporary perfection, SP-2 will be unperfected as to the proceeds, U.C.C. § 9-315(e)(2), and SP-1 will have priority pursuant to section 9-322(a)(2). In contrast, if SP-2 had filed as to investment property in addition to perfecting in the original certificated security by taking control, SP-2 would be continuously perfected in the certificate constituting proceeds,

The special rule of non-temporal priority in section 9-322(c)(2) also governs if there are proceeds of proceeds. Perfection under the special rule applies only if *all* of the intervening proceeds are cash proceeds, proceeds of the same type as the original collateral, or an account relating to the collateral.[102] If *any* of the intervening proceeds do not comply, priority in the proceeds is governed by the general first-to-file-or-perfect rule of sections 9-322(a) and (b).

[b] Special Rule on Temporal Priority—§ 9-322(d), (e)

Even if a secured party perfects a security interest in non-filing collateral by possession or control and obtains priority over another secured party, it will not achieve priority under section 9-322(c)(2) in proceeds that constitute filing collateral.[103] The first-to-file-or-perfect rule of section 9-322(a) will not apply, but subsections (d) and (e) provide a different temporal rule based on first-to-file to determine priority.[104] This rule is consistent with normal expectations concerning proceeds that are filing collateral.[105]

For example, assume that SP-1 perfects its security interest in Debtor's deposit account by control. SP-2 thereafter files with respect to Debtor's inventory. Debtor subsequently uses funds acquired from the deposit account to purchase additional inventory, and SP-1 promptly files with respect to the inventory, thereby extending its perfected status beyond the twenty-day grace period of automatic perfection for proceeds. SP-1 claims the inventory as proceeds and SP-2 claims it as original collateral by virtue of its after-acquired property clause. SP-2 will have priority under section 9-322(d) as the first party to file. Note that this result, although based on the first filing, is an exception to the first-to-file-or-perfect rule of section 9-322(a). If that subsection applied, SP-1 would prevail as the first party to perfect without any subsequent period during which it was unperfected.

[B] Purchase-Money Security Interests—§ 9-324(a), (b)

An earlier discussion in this chapter explains how Article 9 enables a purchase-money secured party to attain priority over an earlier-perfected

---

U.C.C. § 9-315(d)(1), and would attain priority in the proceeds under section 9-322(c)(2). The extent of benefit achievable through the additional step of filing with respect to original non-filing collateral, however, is limited. For example, if the proceeds received by Debtor took the form of a promissory note covering dividends, the filing by SP-2 in investment property would lead to continuous perfection in the note. SP-2 nevertheless could not prevail under section 9-322(c)(2), however, because the note is neither cash proceeds nor proceeds of the same type as the original collateral (*i.e.*, an instrument as opposed to investment property). SP-1 thus would have priority in the proceeds under sections 9-322(a) and (b).

[102] U.C.C. § 9-322(c)(2)(C).

[103] Filing collateral is not a defined term and, as used here, means any collateral that is not non-filing collateral. Filing collateral could not qualify under subsection (c) as either cash proceeds or proceeds of the same type that constitute the secured party's non-filing collateral.

[104] U.C.C. § 9-322(d), (e).

[105] U.C.C. § 9-322, Comment 9 (Example 12).

competing secured party in the same collateral.[106] As explained, this beneficial treatment varies depending upon whether the purchase-money security interest is taken in inventory or another type of collateral.[107] Those same Article 9 provisions include opportunities for the purchase-money secured party to attain priority with respect to at least some types of proceeds.

If the purchase-money security interest is in collateral other than inventory,[108] the priority for that interest applies to proceeds to the same extent as it does to the original collateral.[109] Thus, if a perfected purchase-money secured party finances the acquisition of equipment for the debtor, priority extends in favor of this secured party against a prior equipment financer that has an after-acquired property clause in its security agreement (assuming that the purchase-money secured party perfects in a timely fashion to obtain purchase-money priority). The priority extends to the equipment subject to the purchase-money security interest and to any proceeds of the equipment in which a continuously perfected security interest is maintained.[110]

In contrast, if the original collateral consists of inventory, the extent of priority for proceeds of purchase-money collateral is narrower. Priority is limited, for the most part, to "identifiable cash proceeds of the inventory to the extent the identifiable cash proceeds are received on or before the delivery of the inventory to a buyer."[111] Any priority under this exception is dependent upon the purchase-money inventory financer's timely compliance with the perfection and notification requirements regarding the collateral it finances.[112] A purchase-money secured party financing a line of inventory may achieve priority over a prior-perfected inventory financer in proceeds like cash or checks,[113] but generally not with respect to non-cash proceeds like promissory notes, chattel paper, or accounts.[114]

---

[106] See § 10.04 supra.

[107] U.C.C. § 9-324(a), (b), (d).

[108] A purchase-money security interest can only be created in goods and related software. U.C.C. § 9-103. See § 1.05 supra.

[109] This result is accomplished through insertion of the language "a perfected security interest in its identifiable proceeds also has priority" in section 9-324(a).

[110] Only disposition of equipment financed by the purchase-money lender could result in proceeds for that lender.

[111] U.C.C. § 9-324(b). This provision also allows purchase-money priority in inventory to carry over to chattel paper and instruments and their proceeds in certain limited circumstances provided in section 9-330.

[112] Bank One, Lima, N.A. v. Duff Warehouses, Inc., 62 Ohio Misc. 2d 481, 601 N.E.2d 678, 19 U.C.C. Rep. Serv. 2d 634 (1992) (failure to comply with notification requirements relegated purchase-money secured party to general rule of priority in time of filing or perfection).

[113] Coachmen Indus., Inc. v. Security Trust & Sav. Bank of Shenandoah, 329 N.W.2d 648, 35 U.C.C. Rep. Serv. 1012 (Iowa 1983) (funds in deposit account).

[114] The purchase-money secured party in inventory also loses on accounts as proceeds to a prior-perfected accounts financer. Mbank Alamo N.A. v. Raytheon Co., 886 F.2d 1149, 10 U.C.C. Rep. Serv. 2d 35 (5th Cir. 1989).

This limitation on the extent of proceeds priority might seem questionable. After all, inventory consists of goods that are held for sale or lease and sales or leases of inventory often produce accounts or chattel paper. Pursuant to the limitation, a secured party with a purchase-money security interest in inventory will lose priority in these proceeds to earlier secured parties with ongoing perfected financing arrangements in such property or in inventory. The significance of the purchase-money priority in the inventory is thus substantially reduced.

The limitation is designed to favor accounts and chattel paper financing. These types of financing are a critical aspect of commercial finance. The danger associated with financing inventory—as compared with the accounts or chattel paper that its sale or lease generates—are obvious and leave many lenders reluctant to lend against inventory.[115] For many lenders, inventory-financing is only one facet of an ongoing financing arrangement that looks predominantly to the accounts or chattel paper proceeds generated by the sales of the inventory. Because accounts and chattel-paper financing plays such a fundamental role in commercial finance, the drafters elected to protect the claims of these financers even against subsequent purchase-money secured parties that claim the accounts as proceeds of their collateral.

Actually, the position of the purchase-money secured party in inventory is not as precarious as it might first appear. The independent financing made available through an accounts or chattel paper financer provides the debtor with funds that can be used to pay the inventory lender.[116] The purchase-money priority in the inventory will serve the inventory lender well in the event the debtor faces financial calamity. The lender then may repossess the unsold inventory free from the claims of other parties.

Although as a rule purchase-money priority does not extend to chattel-paper (or instrument) proceeds, a purchase-money secured party may obtain priority by qualifying as a purchaser entitled to priority under section 9-330.[117] In addition to other requirements for attaining priority, that section requires, in the case of chattel paper, that the purchaser give "new value," and that is generally not the case with proceeds. However, section 9-330(e) provides that the holder of a purchase-money security interest in inventory is deemed to give new value for chattel-paper proceeds, thereby enabling the purchase-money secured party, if it otherwise qualifies under section 9-330, to take the chattel paper free of other claimants, including a prior-perfected secured party with a security interest in the chattel paper.

---

[115] See § 3.04[B] supra.

[116] "In some situations, the party financing the inventory on a purchase-money basis makes contractual arrangements that the proceeds of receivables financing by another be devoted to paying off the inventory security interest." U.C.C. § 9-324, Comment 8.

[117] U.C.C. § 9-324(b). The rights of purchasers of chattel paper subject to a prior-perfected security interest are discussed in § 11.03[C] infra.

Chapter 11

PURCHASERS (OTHER THAN SECURED PARTIES) VERSUS PERFECTED SECURED PARTIES

SYNOPSIS

§ 11.01　GENERAL RULE ON DISPOSITION—§ 9-315(a)

The priority generally enjoyed by a perfected secured party may face a challenge from a person that purchases the collateral from the debtor. As used in the Code, the term "purchaser" means any person that acquires an interest in property through a voluntary transaction and includes, *inter*

253

alia, secured parties, buyers, and lessees.[1] This chapter deals only with purchasers that are not secured parties.[2]

A purchaser of an asset subject to a security interest often seeks to establish that it purchased the asset free of the secured party's interest. By contrast, the secured party may contend that the transfer was subject to its interest, meaning, *inter alia*, that the secured party can foreclose on the asset notwithstanding the transfer[3] if the debtor that created the security interest[4] defaults.[5] This chapter explains the provisions that govern disputes between purchasers (other than secured parties) and secured parties that have perfected their security interests. Priorities between purchasers and unperfected secured parties are discussed elsewhere.[6]

Article 9 contains a residual rule that grants priority to the secured party in the event the debtor disposes of the collateral. Section 9-315(a)(1) provides that "a security interest or agricultural lien continues in collateral notwithstanding sale, lease, license, exchange, or other disposition thereof unless the secured party authorized the disposition free of the security interest or agricultural lien." This rule defeats any argument that mere disposition of the collateral in and of itself terminates a security interest in the collateral; to the contrary, the starting premise is that the security interest remains enforceable despite the disposition.[7] The rule, however, also indicates that continuation of the security interest is subject to three exceptions: 1) cases in which the secured party has authorized the disposition free of the security interest; 2) cases in which a specific rule of Article 9 grants priority to the purchaser; and 3) cases in which section 2-403(2), which deals with entrustments, grants priority to a buyer in ordinary course of business.[8] The discussion in this chapter is directed primarily at these exceptions.

---

[1] U.C.C. § 1-201(b)(30), (29).

[2] The rights of a secured party as a purchaser are discussed in Chapter 10 *supra*.

[3] Alternatively, the purchaser may be liable in conversion for the collateral's fair market value. *See* U.C.C. 9-315, Comment 2; AAA Auto Sales & Rental, Inc. v. Security Fed. Sav. & Loan Ass'n, 114 N.M. 761, 845 P.2d 855, 19 U.C.C. Rep. Serv. 2d 923 (Ct. App. 1992). The mere fact of purchase does not make the purchaser personally liable for the secured obligation.

[4] The term "debtor" includes any person with an interest in the collateral other than a security interest or lien; thus, in the present context, the term encompasses both the person that creates the security interest and the purchaser and it is important in context to differentiate between them. U.C.C. § 9-102(a)(28)(A).

[5] Most security agreements make disposition by the debtor an event of default. *See* § 17.01 *infra*.

[6] *See* § 14.03 *infra*.

[7] The continuation of the security interest had extensive reach in Marine Midland Bank, N.A. v. Smith Boys, Inc., 129 Misc. 2d 37, 492 N.Y.S.2d 355, 41 U.C.C. Rep. Serv. 1843 (1985). The debtor traded in two inboard motors that were subsequently sold three times. The ultimate purchaser took subject to the bank's security interest.

[8] U.C.C. § 2-403 does not operate to cut off the rights of a secured party unless it is an entrustor.

Section 9-315(a) makes clear that, in a typical case, a secured party has dual interests following a disposition of collateral. The security interest remains enforceable against the collateral, which means that the purchaser's rights are subject to the security interest to the extent of the outstanding secured indebtedness. Further, the security interest also attaches automatically[9] to any identifiable proceeds.[10] These dual interests give the secured party the option to pursue the proceeds, the collateral, or both, although it is entitled to only one satisfaction of the secured obligation.[11] Previous chapters have covered the secured party's right to proceeds.[12] This chapter covers the secured party's rights in the collateral following its voluntary transfer to a purchaser.

Another provision of Article 9 that sometimes causes confusion preserves the alienability of the debtor's rights in the collateral. Notwithstanding an agreement between the debtor and the secured party which prohibits transfer or makes transfer an event of default, the debtor's legal and equitable rights in the collateral may be voluntarily or involuntarily transferred.[13] This provision appears at first glance to conflict with the residual rule preserving security interests in transferred collateral, but in fact the two provisions are complementary and must be read together. The provision preserving alienability focuses on the *debtor's rights only*. Those rights can be transferred notwithstanding agreement to the contrary, but the transferee takes the rights subject to an enforceable security interest unless it can take advantage of an exception to the residual rule.

For example, suppose Manufacturer grants a security interest in its equipment to Secured Party and agrees that it will not sell any item of equipment without Secured Party's written consent. In breach of this covenant, Manufacturer sells and delivers an item of equipment to Buyer. The sale is effective to transfer Manufacturer's rights to Buyer,[14] but those rights are encumbered by Secured Party's interest.[15] Unless Buyer can take advantage of an exception to the residual rule, Secured Party may enforce the security interest notwithstanding the sale.[16] In addition, the sale is a

---

[9] U.C.C. § 9-203(f).

[10] U.C.C. § 9-315(a)(2).

[11] *See* U.C.C. 9-315, Comment 2.

[12] *See* §§ 2.03, 8.02, and 10.04 *supra*.

[13] U.C.C. § 9-401(b). An example of an involuntary transfer is a lien creditor's levy on collateral. *See* § 14.02[A] *infra*. *See* Clapp v. Orix Credit Alliance, Inc., 192 Or. App. 320, 84 P.3d 833, 52 U.C.C. Rep. Serv. 2d 1016 (2004) (even though a provision in a sales contract/security agreement prohibited the assignment of the contract note without the written consent of the holder, it did not prevent the assignment to the plaintiff of the vendee's rights under the contract). Voluntary transfers are the focus of this chapter.

[14] Because the transaction is a sale, Buyer acquires Manufacturer's title to the equipment. U.C.C. § 2-106(1) (sale consists of passage of title for a price).

[15] In this situation, Buyer will have, absent an effective disclaimer, a cause of action against Manufacturer for breach of the implied warranty of title that is implied in contracts for sale. U.C.C. § 2-312.

[16] Production Credit Ass'n v. Columbus Mills, 22 U.C.C. Rep. Serv. 228 (Wis. Cir. Ct. 1977).

breach of the security agreement, entitling Secured Party to exercise its remedies under Part 6 of Article 9 as supplemented by the agreement.[17]

§ 11.02 AUTHORIZED DISPOSITION—§ 9-315(a)(1)

If the secured party authorizes the debtor to dispose of all or part of its rights in the collateral free of the security interest, it is obvious that those rights will no longer be encumbered.[18] In that instance, the secured party must rely on its right to proceeds and to any other collateral that has been retained by the debtor. Similarly, if the secured party authorizes the debtor to lease or license the collateral free of the security interest, the lessee or licensee's interest is unencumbered, but the debtor's residual rights remain subject to the security interest. The requisite authorization can be either express or implied.

[A] Express Authorization

Secured parties commonly authorize disposition of collateral free of their security interest in the context of inventory financing. By definition, most inventory consists of goods held for sale or lease,[19] and it would be counterproductive for a secured lender to take a security interest in such inventory and then prohibit its sale or lease. Without such dispositions, the debtor would not generate the income necessary to pay the secured obligation. Consequently, a secured party generally will authorize sales or leases of inventory and look to the proceeds generated by such transactions to protect itself.

Even in inventory financing, however, secured lenders are not likely to give a blanket authorization sufficient to support any disposition. For example, inventory financers typically authorize only sales and leases that are made in the ordinary course of the debtor's business,[20] because other sales and leases may include features that would be disadvantageous to the financer's interests.[21] Even if a sale or lease is made in the ordinary

---

See also Decatur Production Credit Ass'n v. Murphy, 119 Ill. App. 3d 277, 456 N.E.2d 267, 37 U.C.C. Rep. Serv. 1736 (1983) (transferee acquired only rights of debtor and was not free of security interest).

[17] U.C.C. § 9-601.

[18] U.C.C. § 9-315(a)(1).

[19] *See* § 1.04[A][3] *supra.*

[20] Universal C.I.T. Credit Corp. v. Middlesboro Motor Sales, Inc., 424 S.W.2d 409, 4 U.C.C. Rep. Serv. 1126 (Ky. 1968) (sales of automobiles by dealer to owner's wife and employee were in ordinary course of business).

[21] The court in Crocker Nat'l Bank v. Ideco Div. of Dresser Indus., Inc., 889 F.2d 1452, 10 U.C.C. Rep. Serv. 2d 573 (5th Cir. 1989), held that a transfer of goods back to the seller who supplied them was not a sale in the ordinary course of business. The transfer was to cancel the debt owed for their purchase, which would not leave any proceeds to protect the security interest.

The bad faith of the debtor precluded finding a sale in the ordinary course of business in Central Fin. Loan Corp. v. Bank of Illinois, 149 Ill. App. 3d 724, 500 N.E.2d 1066, 3 U.C.C. Rep. Serv. 2d 1178 (1986). A car dealer used false pretenses to obtain a duplicate certificate of title for a sale of an automobile in its inventory.

course of business, the debtor's authorization to dispose of the collateral may be conditioned on determining, through a credit check, that the buyer or lessee is creditworthy. Thus, a particular sale or lease might not be authorized even though made to a buyer or lessee in ordinary course of business. Other provisions of Article 9, to be explained later in this chapter, terminate even an unauthorized security interest in inventory if it is sold or leased to a buyer or lessee in ordinary course of business by the debtor that created the security interest.[22] These provisions are predicated on the fact that the debtor has at least apparent, if not actual, authority to dispose of the inventory free of the security interest.

Another limitation, commonly used with collateral other than inventory, is to condition any authorization to dispose of the collateral free of a security interest on the prior consent of the secured party.[23] This permits the secured party to assess the situation at or near the time of the proposed disposition,[24] and, if it authorizes the disposition, the secured party can insist on a method of payment that will preserve its interest in the proceeds.[25] Thus, the requisite consent is often given on condition that the debtor remit the proceeds of the disposition to the secured party or that the purchaser's check be made jointly payable to the debtor and the secured party.

In cases in which the debtor subsequently failed to account for the proceeds from an otherwise authorized sale, the secured party sometimes has contended that its interest in the collateral continued, arguing that the debtor's failure to satisfy the condition rendered the disposition unauthorized. A few courts have accepted this position.[26] The Ninth Circuit held, for example, that a secured party did not release its security interest in cattle until it actually received the proceeds from the debtor's sales.[27]

Such decisions are unfair in cases in which the purchaser does not know of the condition at the time it pays for the collateral. The authorized-disposition rule is essentially an estoppel rule. Having clothed the debtor with authority to dispose of the collateral, a disappointed secured party

---

[22] See § 11.03[A][1] *infra.*

[23] United States v. E. W. Savage & Son, Inc., 343 F. Supp. 123, 10 U.C.C. Rep. Serv. 1093 (D. S.D. 1972) (cattle sold without written consent as required in security agreement).

[24] First Nat'l Bank & Trust Co. of Oklahoma City v. Atchison Cty. Auction Co., Inc., 10 Kan. App. 2d 382, 699 P.2d 1032, 41 U.C.C. Rep. Serv. 219 (1985) (where secured party waived written consent requirement, but still required prior oral consultation, sale of livestock without consultation was unauthorized).

[25] A secured lender required the debtor to have buyers of hogs issue checks jointly to the lender and debtor, and it informed buyers of this requirement. Sales made without compliance were unauthorized and the buyers were liable for conversion. Lafayette Production Credit Ass'n v. Wilson Foods Corp., 687 F. Supp. 1267, 6 U.C.C. Rep. Serv. 2d 1278 (N.D. Ind. 1987).

[26] See, e.g., Southwest Washington Production Credit Ass'n v. Seattle-First Nat'l Bank, 92 Wash. 2d 30, 593 P.2d 167, 26 U.C.C. Rep. Serv. 1346 (1979); RFC Capital Corp. v. Earthlink, Inc., 2004 WL 2980402, 55 U.C.C. Rep. Serv. 2d 617 (Ohio Ct. App. 2004) (buyer bears the risk that the conditions established by the secured party will be satisfied, even if the buyer lacks control to satisfy the conditions).

[27] In re Ellsworth, 722 F.2d 1448, 37 U.C.C. Rep. Serv. 1376 (9th Cir. 1984).

ought not be allowed to pursue the collateral into the hands of a good-faith purchaser without notice of the condition.[28] Once the purchaser pays the debtor, it cannot control what the debtor does with the proceeds;[29] thus, imposing a condition of debtor compliance makes the purchaser an insurer of acts that are beyond its control.[30] Most courts have correctly recognized that the failure to remit the proceeds constitutes a breach[31] by the debtor but does not retroactively negate the authority to dispose of the collateral free of the security interest.[32] The result should be different, however, if the purchaser knows that authorization for the sale has been conditioned on debtor remittance of the proceeds.[33] The equities in that situation require that the purchaser take steps, such as issuance of a check naming the secured party as joint payee, that will protect the secured party's interest.[34]

Express authorization can be provided by the secured party in the security agreement or otherwise.[35] If disposition is anticipated at the time of attachment, the security agreement itself can include a term giving express authorization.[36] Express authorization can also be provided in another record,[37] or it can even be given orally.[38] Indeed, the authorization

---

[28] Moffat Cty. State Bank v. Producers Livestock Marketing Ass'n, 598 F. Supp. 1562, 40 U.C.C. Rep. Serv. 314 (D. Colo. 1984).

[29] In re Cullen, 71 B.R. 274, 3 U.C.C. Rep. Serv. 2d 815 (Bankr. W.D. Wis. 1987) (condition ineffective unless purchaser can control satisfaction of condition).

[30] Production Credit Ass'n of Baraboo v. Pillsbury Co., 132 Wis. 2d 243, 392 N.W.2d 445, 1 U.C.C. Rep. Serv. 2d 1352 (Ct. App. 1986) (conditions on authorization to sell are effective only if satisfaction of condition is within buyer's control).

[31] Moffat Cty. State Bank v. Producers Livestock Marketing Ass'n, 598 F. Supp. 562, 40 U.C.C. Rep. Serv. 314 (D. Colo. 1984).

[32] Parkersburg State Bank v. Swift Independent Packing Co., 764 F.2d 512, 41 U.C.C. Rep. Serv. 248 (8th Cir. 1985) (sale had been authorized, even though debtor subsequently failed to apply sale proceeds to secured debt).

[33] Lafayette Production Credit Ass'n v. Wilson Foods Corp., 687 F.Supp. 1267, 6 U.C.C. Rep. Serv. 2d 1278 (N.D. Ind. 1987) (secured party notified buyers that checks should be issued jointly to lender and farmer).

[34] The same principle applies when the buyer agrees to the condition on transfer imposed by the secured creditor that the buyer assume the debtor's obligations. In re Hanson Restaurants, Inc., 155 B.R. 758, 21 U.C.C. Rep. Serv. 2d 810 (Bankr. D. Minn. 1993); In re Dawley, 44 B.R. 738, 40 U.C.C. Rep. Serv. 1893 (Bankr. W.D. Pa. 1984).

[35] U.C.C. § 9-315, Comment 2.

[36] Attempts by litigants to stretch common clauses in security agreements to include an authorization to dispose of the collateral have been rebuffed by the courts. Northern Commercial Co. v. Cobb, 778 P.2d 205, 10 U.C.C. Rep. Serv. 2d 197 (Alaska 1989) (inclusion of right to proceeds). The Cobb case also holds that the absence of any restrictions on sale in the security agreement cannot be construed as implying an authorization to sell.

[37] In re Dawley, 44 B.R. 738, 40 U.C.C. Rep. Serv. 1893 (Bankr. W.D. Pa. 1984) (written consent of secured party for debtor to transfer its equity in collateral to another person); Ottumwa Production Credit Ass'n v. Keoco Auction Co., 347 N.W.2d 393, 38 U.C.C. Rep. Serv. 624 (Iowa 1984) (letter instructing debtor to liquidate its hog holdings).

[38] Wright v. Vickaryous, 611 P.2d 20, 28 U.C.C. Rep. Serv. 1177 (Alaska 1980) (secured creditors consented to auction sales of cattle in conversations with owner). See also First Nat'l Bank of Bethany v. Waco-Pacific, Inc., 9 U.C.C. Rep. Serv. 1064 (Okla. Ct. App. 1971) (secured party's promise to release its interest in airplane to facilitate its sale was not subject to statute of frauds).

need not even be express—a secured party may engage in conduct from which it may fairly be inferred that it has authorized sale free of its security interest. Implied waivers are discussed in the ensuing subsection.

[B] Implied Authorization

Even though a secured party says nothing that expressly authorizes a disposition of collateral free of its security interest, consent might nevertheless be implied from its conduct. For example, if a secured party knowingly acquiesces in the debtor's disposition, it may be argued that the disposition is impliedly authorized. Some courts have accepted this argument, holding that a secured party that is aware of a transfer by the debtor and does not object tacitly consents.[39] Other courts have refused to recognize mere acquiescence as a sufficient basis for a finding of implicit authorization.[40]

Another argument sometimes made by purchasers is that a secured party that has accepted the proceeds of a disposition has thereby ratified it—*i.e.*, authorized it after the fact. Mere acceptance of proceeds, however, should not suffice to establish ratification.[41] Article 9 explicitly provides that a security interest continues in identifiable proceeds and, absent authorization or a contrary rule, in the collateral as well. A secured party thus has a right to the proceeds. Indeed, an Official Comment to the 1972 text of Article 9 stated that "[t]he right to proceeds . . . does not in itself constitute an authorization of sale."[42]

A better case for the purchaser can be made if the secured party has engaged in a pattern of accepting proceeds from unauthorized dispositions that is sufficient to establish a course of dealing or course of performance. A course of dealing, which means "a sequence of conduct concerning previous transactions between the parties to a particular transaction that is fairly to be regarded as establishing a common basis of understanding for interpreting their expressions and other conduct,"[43] provides an appropriate basis for supplementing or qualifying the terms of the agreement.[44] For example, a course of dealing might arise between a farmer and a bank that have entered annually into a secured transaction with respect to the farmer's livestock, with each year's security agreement including a prohibition against the farmer's sale of any of the collateral without the bank's

---

[39] Vacura v. Haar's Equip., Inc., 364 N.W.2d 387, 40 U.C.C. Rep. Serv. 1493 (Minn. 1985). *See also* Cessna Fin. Corp. v. Skyways Enterprises, Inc., 580 S.W.2d 491, 26 U.C.C. Rep. Serv. 212 (Ky. 1979) (prior consent requirement waived by secured party's acquiescence in sales of other airplanes subject to same requirement).

[40] *See, e.g.*, Oxford Production Credit Ass'n v. Dye, 368 So. 2d 241, 26 U.C.C. Rep. Serv. 217 (Miss. 1979).

[41] J.I. Case Credit Corp. v. Crites, 851 F.2d 309, 6 U.C.C. Rep. Serv. 2d 551 (10th Cir. 1988). *See also* Brown v. Arkoma Coal Corp., 276 Ark. 322, 634 S.W.2d 390 (1982) (no waiver of security interest in trying to prevent distribution of proceeds from judicial sale after collateral was taken by lien creditor).

[42] U.C.C. § 9-306, Comment 3.

[43] U.C.C. § 1-303(b).

[44] U.C.C. § 1-303(d). The same is true for a course of performance or usage of trade. *Id.*

prior approval.[45] If, in a sequence of annual transactions, the bank had ignored the prior-approval requirement and acquiesced in the debtor's sales, a purchaser could argue that this pattern of conduct created a course of dealing that implicitly authorized the sale to it under the current security agreement.[46]

A course of performance means "a sequence of conduct between the parties to a particular transaction that exists if: (1) the agreement of the parties with respect to the transaction involves repeated occasions for performance by a party; and (2) the other party, with knowledge of the nature of the performance and opportunity for objection to it, accepts the performance or acquiesces in it without objection."[47] A course of performance is comparable to a course of dealing except that, rather than a sequence of repeated conduct within the context of prior transactions between the same two parties, the sequence of conduct transpires under the existing contract. For example, a bank's repeated acquiescence to livestock sales by a debtor with respect to a current security agreement could result in implicit authorization to make additional, similar sales under that agreement.[48]

Although similar in that each is based on a sequence of conduct, the Code makes a functional distinction between a course of dealing and a course of performance. To illustrate the distinction, suppose a security agreement contains an express term prohibiting disposition by the debtor without the prior consent of the secured party. Evidence of a sequence of conduct permitting dispositions without consent, constituting either a course of dealing or course of performance, clearly contradicts the express term. Under the hierarchy established by Article 1, express terms and terms derived from a course of dealing or course of performance are to be construed wherever reasonable as consistent with each other; however, when such construction is unreasonable, express terms control.[49] If this hierarchical provision is applied literally, a course of dealing could not displace an express term prohibiting disposition. Several courts have used this rationale to defeat course-of-dealing arguments advanced by purchasers.[50] By

---

[45] The U.C.C.'s "farm-products rule," discussed in § 12.01 *infra*, continued security interests in farm products notwithstanding their purchase by a buyer in the ordinary course of business. The bulk of the implied-authorization cases arose in the context of such purchases. The rights of most farm-products buyers have now been preempted by the federal Food Security Act of 1985, discussed in §§ 12.02 and 12.03 *infra*.

[46] *See, e.g.*, Producers Cotton Oil Co. v. Amstar Corp., 197 Cal. App. 3d 638, 242 Cal. Rptr. 914, 5 U.C.C. Rep. Serv. 2d 32 (1988).

[47] U.C.C. § 1-303(a).

[48] Farmers State Bank v. Farmland Foods, Inc., 225 Neb. 1, 402 N.W.2d 277, 3 U.C.C. Rep. Serv. 2d 902 (1987), *overruling* Garden City Production Credit Ass'n v. Lannan, 186 Neb. 668, 186 N.W.2d 99, 8 U.C.C. Rep. Serv. 1163 (1971).

[49] U.C.C. § 1-303(e). If there is a conflict between a course of dealing and a course of performance, the course of performance controls. *Id.*

[50] First Bank v. Eastern Livestock Co., 886 F.Supp. 1328, 27 U.C.C. Rep. Serv. 2d 1045 (S.D. Miss. 1995); *In re* Environmental Electronic Systems, Inc., 2 B.R. 583, 29 U.C.C. Rep. Serv. 271 (Bankr. N.D. Ga. 1980); Wabasso State Bank v. Caldwell Packing Co., 251 N.W.2d 321, 19 U.C.C. Rep. Serv. 315 (Minn. 1976).

contrast, a "course of performance" might, subject to the rules of section 2-209 (which are relevant because imported into Article 1), constitute a waiver or modification of an express term.[51] Thus, an argument based on a course of performance might succeed where an argument based on a course of dealing would fail.

§ 11.03 PRIORITIES

As we have seen, a security interest in collateral is terminated if the secured party authorizes its disposition free of the security interest. The termination avoids any priority conflict between the formerly secured party and the purchaser, or a transferee from the purchaser. The situation differs if the disposition is not authorized. Under Article 9's residual rule,[52] the secured party's interest continues in the collateral notwithstanding its disposition. The residual rule is, however, expressly subject to exceptions provided in other sections of Article 9 and to section 2-403.[53] The remainder of this Chapter explains the priority rules that protect purchasers (other than secured parties) of different types of collateral from prior-perfected security interests. The rights of such purchasers against unperfected security interests are discussed in Chapter 14.[54]

[A] Goods

[1] Buyers and Lessees of Goods in Ordinary Course of Business—§§ 9-320(a), 9-321(c)

Article 9 provides that a buyer in ordinary course of business (other than one that buys farm products from a farmer) or a lessee in ordinary course of business takes collateral free of a security interest created by the buyer's immediate seller or the lessee's immediate lessor, even if the security interest is perfected and the buyer or lessee knows of its existence.[55] The rules are primarily designed to protect parties that buy or lease goods in good faith from the inventory stock of a dealer.[56] To the extent the secured party authorizes disposition free of the security interest, which is common with inventory,[57] the rules are superfluous.

---

[51] U.C.C. § 1-303(f).

[52] *See* § 11.01 *supra.*

[53] U.C.C. § 9-315(a).

[54] *See* § 14.03 *infra.*

[55] U.C.C. §§ 9-320(a), 9-321(c). *See* First Nat'l Bank of El Campo, Texas v. Buss, 2004 WL 1908465, 54 U.C.C. Rep. Serv. 2d 706 (Tex. Ct. App. 2004) (buyers of automobiles from a used-car dealer qualified as buyers in ordinary course and took free of the security interest that the bank perfected by filing as to the used-car inventory of the dealer/debtor, despite the fact that the secured party retained the certificates of title for the automobiles).

[56] *See* U.C.C. § 1-201(b)(9) (defining buyer in ordinary course of business) and the discussion in § 11.03[A][1][a] *infra.*

[57] *See* § 11.02 *supra.*

These exceptions to the residual rule continuing the effectiveness of security interests notwithstanding disposition reflect the policy of removing obstacles that would unduly impede the free flow of commerce in goods. Buyers and lessees in ordinary course of business rely on the integrity of the marketplace to pass them good title (buyers) or enjoyment of the leasehold interest without interference (lessees), and transaction costs are reduced if this reliance is well-placed. The exceptions relieve the buyer or lessee from the burdens of checking the filing system for public notices and of negotiating releases from secured parties of whom they are aware.

[a] Defining the Buyer or Lessee—§§ 1-201(b)(9), 2A-103(o)

A buyer must qualify as a "buyer in ordinary course of business" to take free of a perfected security interest. The definition of this term establishes criteria for the buyer, the seller, and the sales transaction.[58] A buyer in ordinary course of business essentially is: (1) a bona-fide purchaser for value of goods, (2) from one that deals in such goods, (3) in the type of transaction by which such dealers normally conduct sales.

To qualify, a buyer must buy from a person, other than a pawnbroker, that is in the business of selling goods of the kind being purchased.[59] This requirement effectively limits the status to buyers from the inventory of a merchant.[60] The primary issue that developed under former law with respect to this part of the definition was whether a buyer could qualify when the transaction at issue fell outside the seller's most common business activity. For example, in *Hempstead Bank v. Andy's Car Rental System, Inc.*,[61] a car rental agency was generally in the business of leasing automobiles but periodically sold an automobile in its inventory in order to keep its fleet modern. The court characterized the sales as merely incidental to the leasing business and therefore held that these sales were not made by a person engaged in the business of selling automobiles.[62]

By contrast, the court in *Tanbro Fabrics Corporation v. Deering Milliken, Inc.*[63] held in favor of a buyer even though the transaction differed from

---

[58] U.C.C. § 1-201(b)(9). The buyer bears the burden of establishing that it qualifies as a buyer in ordinary course. Integrity Bank Plus v. Talking Sales, Inc., 2005 WL 419694, 56 U.C.C. Rep. Serv. 2d 400 (D. Minn. 2005).

[59] U.C.C.§ 1-201(b)(9). Sindone v. Farber, 105 Misc. 2d 634, 432 N.Y.S.2d 778, 31 U.C.C. Rep. Serv. 329 (Sup. Ct. 1980) (goods sold were equipment, not inventory, as debtor did not hold them for purposes of sale). The courts have clarified that sales between dealers can qualify because they frequently sell to one another. Taft v. Jake Kaplan, Ltd., 28 U.C.C. Rep. Serv. 253 (Bankr. D. R.I. 1980); Weidinger Chevrolet, Inc. v. Universal CIT Credit Corp., 501 F.2d 459, 15 U.C.C. Rep. Serv. 197 (8th Cir.), *cert. denied*, 419 U.S. 1003 (1974).

[60] A buyer of farm products from a farmer can qualify as a buyer in the ordinary course of business, but such buyers do not get the benefit of the Article 9 priority rule and, in any event, their rights are determined by preemptive federal law. *See* Chapter 12 *infra*.

[61] 35 A.D.2d 35, 312 N.Y.S.2d 317, 7 U.C.C. Rep. Serv. 932 (Sup. Ct. 1980).

[62] *Accord* O'Neill v. Barnett Bank of Jacksonville, N.A., 360 So. 2d 150, 24 U.C.C. Rep. Serv. 779 (Fla. Dist. Ct. App. 1978) (occasional sale of used airplane by seller in business of airplane rental and service held insufficient to qualify).

[63] 39 N.Y.2d 632, 385 N.Y.S.2d 260, 350 N.E.2d 590, 19 U.C.C. Rep. Serv. 385 (1976).

the seller's most common business practice. Deering sold unfinished fabric to Mill Fabrics, which then finished the fabric and resold it in the course of its business. Mill Fabrics lacked storage capacity, so Deering retained possession of the fabric (even though Mill Fabrics had paid for it) until it was needed. Deering also retained a security interest in the fabric for obligations owed it by Mill Fabrics under an open account. On occasion, Mill Fabric sold unfinished fabric to other fabric converters and ordered Deering to make delivery to the buyer. Tanbro was such a buyer. When Deering refused to make delivery, Tanbro sued it for conversion, arguing that it was a buyer in the ordinary course of business and therefore took free from Deering's security interest, which was perfected by possession. The court held in Tanbro's favor.

The finding that the sale to Tanbro was an ordinary-course transaction was appropriate. Although Mill Fabric more commonly sold finished fabric, its sales of unfinished fabric were consistent with an industry-wide norm and thus reasonably to be expected.[64] As part of the 1998 revision to Article 9, the Article 1 definition of buyer in ordinary course of business was amended to ratify this aspect of *Tanbro*. The revised definition provides that "[a] person buys in the ordinary course if the sale to the person comports with the usual or customary practices in the kind of business in which the seller is engaged or with the seller's own usual or customary practices."[65]

Another aspect of *Tanbro*—its grant of priority to a buyer over a security interest perfected by possession—caused a stir in the marketplace. Nothing in former law restricted the exception favoring such buyers to security interests perfected by a method other than possession. Nevertheless, possession is a common element in rules that protect bona-fide purchasers,[66] and the 1998 revisions reversed this aspect of *Tanbro*. Section 9-320(e) modifies the exception in favor of buyers in ordinary course of business by providing that it does "not affect a security interest in goods in the possession of the secured party under Section 9-313," and the definition of buyer in ordinary course of business states that "[o]nly a buyer that takes possession of the goods or has a right to recover the goods from the seller under Article 2 may be a buyer in the ordinary course of business." The circumstances in which Article 2 provides a buyer with a right of possession are quite limited.[67]

A person must have the requisite bona fides in order to qualify as a buyer in ordinary course of business. The buyer must be in good faith;[68] must

---

[64] *Accord* Sea Harvest, Inc. v. Rig & Crane Equip. Corp., 181 N.J. Super. 41, 436 A.2d 553, 32 U.C.C. Rep. Serv. 1005 (Ch. Div. 1981) (sales of equipment were substantial part of lessor's business).

[65] U.C.C. § 1-201(b)(9).

[66] *See* discussion in § 14.03 *infra*.

[67] *See* U.C.C. §§ 2-502 (pre-paying buyer entitled to possession of consumer goods if seller repudiates or fails to deliver; buyer entitled to possession of any goods if seller becomes insolvent within 10 days after receipt of first installment on the price), 2-716 (buyer's right of replevin).

[68] "Good faith" is defined as "honesty in fact and the observance of reasonable commercial

be without knowledge that the sale violates the rights of another person, including a secured party; and, as indicated above, must buy from a person that is not a pawnbroker and that is in the business of selling goods of the kind. The buyer may give cash, may exchange property for the goods, may buy on secured or unsecured credit, and may buy under a preexisting contract of sale; however, the buyer may not buy in bulk, nor can it take the goods in total or partial satisfaction of a pre-existing money debt.

The requirement that the buyer not know that the sale violates the rights of another person might appear to conflict with that part of section 9-320(a) that allows a buyer in ordinary course of business to take free of a perfected security interest even though the buyer knows of its existence. In fact, the provisions do not conflict. A buyer that knows that a security interest exists qualifies for protection; a buyer that knows that the sale violates the terms of the security agreement does not qualify.[69] The Official Comments reconcile the two provisions as follows:

> The buyer in ordinary course of business is defined as one who buys goods "in good faith, without knowledge that the sale violates the rights of another person and in the ordinary course." Subsection (a) provides that such a buyer takes free of a security interest, even though perfected, and even though the buyer knows the security interest exists. Reading the definition together with the rule of law results in the buyer's taking free if the buyer merely knows that a security interest covers the goods but taking subject if the buyer knows, in addition, that the sale violates a term in an agreement with the secured party.[70]

Suppose, for example, Bank has a perfected security interest in Dealer's inventory of consumer electronics. The security agreement requires Dealer to obtain a check made jointly payable to it and Bank on any cash sale in excess of $3,000. Suppose further that two buyers purchase big-screen TVs on the same day, each paying with a $3,500 check made payable to Dealer alone. Both buyers know of Bank's security interest, but only Buyer 1 knows of the joint-check requirement. If Dealer defaults, Bank can enforce its security interest against Buyer 1, who does not qualify as a buyer in ordinary course of business. Buyer 2 qualifies, assuming all other elements are present, and takes free of Bank's security interest.

An additional requirement is that the buyer purchase the goods in ordinary course. The phrase "of business" is omitted in this context, and

---

standards of fair dealing." U.C.C. § 9-102(a)(43). Revised Article 1 has the same definition, U.C.C. § 1-201(b)(20), and if a state adopts it without revising the definition, the text of the state's version of § 9-102(a)(43) will be deleted and the section will be marked "Reserved" in order to maintain the common numbering scheme.

[69] Quinn v. Scheu, 675 P.2d 1078, 388 U.C.C. Rep. Serv. 367 (Or. Ct. App. 1984) (buyer who paid seller after notification that payment was to be made directly to secured party bought in knowing violation); SK Global Am, Inc. v. John Roberts, Inc., 6 A.D.3d 179, 778 N.Y.S.2d 5, 53 U.C.C. Rep. Serv. 2d 401 (2004) (accord).

[70] U.C.C. § 9-320, Comment 3.

thus the requirement is satisfied by a consumer who, by definition, buys for a personal, family or household purpose. A commercial buyer, however, must do so in the ordinary course of its business to qualify.

The definition of "lessee in ordinary course of business," found in Article 2A,[71] is generally consistent with the Article 1 definition of similarly situated buyers, although it has not been revised to include the requirement that the lessee have possession or the right to possession under Article 2A, nor does it explicitly permit a lessee to qualify if the lease does not comport with the lessor's usual or customary practices but does comport with the usual or customary practices in the kind of business in which the lessor is engaged.[72]

To illustrate the concept, assume that Lessee leases a photocopier from a merchant lessor for a term of one year. Even though Lessee knows that Merchant's inventory[73] is subject to Bank's perfected security interest, a default by Merchant to Bank does not place its leasehold interest at risk. Bank's security interest can be enforced against Merchant's residual interest,[74] but Bank cannot deprive Lessee of its right to possess and use the photocopier during the lease term.

[b] Created by Its Seller or Lessor

A buyer or lessee in ordinary course of business will take free of a perfected security interest only if the security interest was created by the buyer's immediate seller or the lessee's immediate lessor.[75] Put another way, only a person who acquires an interest in goods directly from the Article 9 debtor that granted the security interest can take advantage of the special priority rules protecting ordinary-course buyers and lessees.

For example, assume Bank has a perfected security interest in Retailer's inventory of mainframe computers. If Corporation buys a computer from Retailer for use in its business operations, Corporation will almost certainly take the computer free of Bank's security interest. The sale of the computer was probably authorized by Bank; even if it was not, Corporation probably qualifies as a buyer in ordinary course of business and the security interest was created by its immediate seller, Retailer. For purposes of comparison, assume now that Bank provides an enabling loan for Partnership to acquire

---

[71] U.C.C. § 2A-103(1)(u).

[72] These aspects of the definition of buyer in ordinary course of business are discussed *supra* this subsection. The 2003 amendments to Article 2A make these changes. *See* U.C.C. § 2A-103(1)(u) (2003 Official Text).

[73] Assets that are leased or held for lease are inventory. U.C.C. §§ 9-102(a)(48)(B) (held for lease), 9-102(a)(48)(A) (leased).

[74] U.C.C. § 2A-103(1)(w).

[75] U.C.C. §§ 9-320(a), 9-321(c). Walden v. Mercedes Benz Credit Corp., 2005 WL 995217, 57 U.C.C. Rep. Serv. 2d 182 (Pa. Ct. Com. Pl. 2005) (the original purchaser of an automobile gave a security interest in the car and later sold it to another dealer, but the buyer in ordinary course of the car from the dealer did not take free of the security interest because the interest had not been created by the dealer).

a computer for use in its business, and Bank takes and perfects a security interest in the computer. Partnership, in violation of the terms of the security agreement, sells the computer to Dealer, who specializes in used computers. Dealer will not qualify as a buyer in ordinary course of business (this assumes that Partnership is not in the business of selling computers), and Dealer thus takes the computer subject to Bank's perfected security interest under the Code's residual rule.[76] If Dealer later resells the used computer to Buyer, Buyer will probably qualify as a buyer in the ordinary course. Buyer cannot, however, take free of Bank's security interest under the rule protecting ordinary-course buyers because the security interest was not created by Dealer, Buyer's immediate seller. For priority purposes, Buyer is lumped together with buyers not in ordinary course of business and thus takes the computer subject to security interests that are perfected or of which Buyer is aware.[77]

What explains the differing treatment afforded Corporation, an ordinary-course buyer that takes free of a perfected security interest, and Buyer, an ordinary-course buyer that is subordinated to a perfected security interest? It cannot be explained in terms of the perspectives of the two buyers. Both made good-faith purchases of similar goods from a merchant, and neither expected anything other than clear title.[78] As is explained below, the answer is based on the doctrine of apparent authority,[79] and thus focuses on the actions of the secured party and the business status of the debtor, not on the qualifications of the buyer. If this seems unfair (and perhaps it is), recall that a good-faith purchaser for value from a thief cannot take goods free from the interest of their rightful owner.[80]

As indicated above, inventory financers almost invariably give their debtors authority to sell collateral in ordinary-course transactions, although they sometimes impose conditions that limit the debtor's authority. Buyers and lessees in such transactions do not need a special priority rule to take free of the financer's interest if all conditions imposed by the secured party are satisfied because the debtor has actual authority to conduct the sale.[81] However, suppose that a debtor sells inventory on credit in violation of a requirement that the secured party first determine the creditworthiness of the prospective buyer and approve the sale. Even though the sale is unauthorized, the secured party will, and should, lose to a buyer in ordinary course of business. The rationale for this result is that the secured party has clothed the debtor with the appearance of authority to make the sale.

---

[76] U.C.C. § 9-315(a)(1).

[77] *See* § 14.03 *infra*.

[78] Indeed, both buyers are beneficiaries of the Article 2 implied warranty of title. U.C.C. § 2-312. A similarly situated lessee is entitled to a warranty against interference. U.C.C. § 2A-211(1).

[79] *See generally* William H. Lawrence, *The "Created by His Seller" Limitation of Section 9-307(1) of the UCC: A Provision in Need of an Articulated Policy*, 60 Ind. L.J. 73, 80–83 (1984).

[80] *Cf.* U.C.C. § 2-403(1).

[81] *See* § 11.02 *supra*.

The Article 9 approach for ordinary-course buyers is similar to the Article 2 entrustment rule. Under that rule, a person that delivers goods to, or allows them to be retained by, a merchant that deals in goods of that kind gives the merchant the power (as opposed to the right) to transfer the entruster's rights to a buyer in ordinary course of business.[82] This is contrary to the common law of bailment, which generally protects ownership interests from purchasers from a bailee. The rule is based on the entruster's clothing of the merchant with apparent authority to sell inventory in ordinary-course transactions, just as the similar rule of Article 9 is based on the clothing of the merchant with such apparent authority.[83] By permitting a debtor to be in possession of goods when the debtor is in the business of selling goods of the same kind, a secured party vests the debtor with apparent authority.

The basis for apparent authority is missing if the debtor is in possession of goods other than inventory. A secured party's acquiescence in its debtor's possession of noninventory collateral does not create appearances to third parties that the debtor's primary purpose for holding the goods is to sell them.

Only in rare circumstances would a secured party be responsible for clothing anyone other than its debtor with apparent authority to sell or lease collateral; hence the limitation in Article 9 to persons that buy or lease directly from the person that created the security interest. However, it occasionally occurs that a secured party delivers (or more likely acquiesces in the delivery of) its collateral to a remote party that deals in goods of that kind. In that case, the secured party comes within the Article 2 entrustment rule, which is expressly cross-referenced in Article 9,[84] and the merchant thus has the power to transfer all rights of the secured party to a buyer in ordinary course of business.[85] Suppose, for example, that a financially distressed debtor convinces a secured party to permit the collateral to be placed with a dealer for sale on commission. A buyer in ordinary course of business from the dealer takes free of the rights of both the debtor and the secured party, as both are entrusters.[86]

---

[82] U.C.C. §§ 2-403(3), (2).

[83] Qualification for buyer-in-ordinary-course-of-business status requires, for both Article 2 and Article 9, that the buyer purchase from a person in the business of selling goods of that kind. U.C.C. § 1-201(b)(9).

[84] U.C.C. § 9-315(a)(1). *See* § 2-403(2), (3).

[85] Article 2A does not have a parallel rule for lessees in the ordinary course of business. Nevertheless, if goods are entrusted by a secured party to a merchant who deals in goods of that kind and then leased to an ordinary-course lessee, the lessee should take free of the security interest on estoppel grounds.

[86] By contrast, consider the situation in Conseco Fin. Serv. Corp. v. Lee, 2004 WL 1243417, 54 U.C.C. Rep. Serv. 2d 96 (Tex. Ct. App. 2004). The original buyer of a motor home from a dealer granted a security interest in the motor home which the dealer then assigned to Conseco. A few years later, the motor home ended up back in the hands of the same dealer, for reasons not clearly explained by the court (perhaps because the original buyer did not wish to continue making the payments and turned the motor home back over to the dealer believing the dealer to be Conseco's agent). The dealer resold it to the Lees, who were not aware of

[2] Consumer Buyers of Consumer Goods—§ 9-320(b)

Article 9 includes a provision that allows certain consumer buyers to take free of automatically-perfected security interests. Automatic perfection of purchase-money security interests in consumer goods[87] is a practical necessity given the enormous volume of such transactions, but it does create hidden liens. Enforcement of such liens against nonreliance creditors (*e.g.*, bankruptcy trustees) is fully justified. Enforcement against commercial buyers (*e.g.*, second-hand stores) and other secured lenders is a closer case, but the policy decision has been made to subordinate such buyers and lenders on the ground that they ought to be aware generally of such risks when they deal with used consumer goods and can ask appropriate questions of their seller or borrower. Enforcement against consumer buyers (*i.e.*, persons who buy for their own personal, family or household purposes) goes too far. Accordingly, consumer buyers who give value take free of automatically-perfected security interests unless they know of the security interest.[88]

The priority available through this provision has a narrow range. It applies only if the secured party relies upon automatic perfection in consumer goods, and the buyer must also intend to use the goods for consumer purposes. The section thus governs only consumer-to-consumer sales[89] and is, for that reason, sometimes referred to as the "garage-sale" rule. The secured party can avoid the impact of the rule by filing a financing statement covering the goods prior to the purchase. Although it is far-fetched to believe that an average consumer will know to check the filing system before buying used goods from another consumer, as a practical matter filing is all the secured party can do to stake its claim and thereby ameliorate the problem of ostensible ownership.

[3] Future Advances—§ 9-323(d)–(g)

Article 9 includes provisions that govern priority between a security interest covering future advances and a buyer or lessee not in ordinary course of business.[90] Even a buyer or lessee that takes subject to a security interest will take free of the interest to the extent that it covers future advances made after the earlier of: (1) the time the secured party acquired

---

Conseco's security interest. Conseco sought to repossess the motor home. The Lees were not entitled to protection under the buyer-in-ordinary-course rule, because the security interest was created by the original buyer, not by the dealer. Further, the Lees were not entitled to protection under the entrustment rule, because there was no evidence that Conseco had entrusted the motor home to the dealer.

[87] *See* § 7.01 *supra*.

[88] U.C.C. § 9-320(b).

[89] Security Pac. Nat'l Bank v. Goodman, 24 Cal. App. 3d 131, 100 Cal. Rptr. 763, 10 U.C.C. Rep. Serv. 529 (1972); Meskell v. Bertone, 2004 WL 2451354, 55 U.C.C. Rep. Serv. 2d 179 (Mass. Super. Ct. 2004) (even though a professional agent negotiated the sale of a boat, the agreement between the buyer and the seller qualified as a sale between two consumers and the buyer took free of the security interest of the bank that did not file a financing statement).

[90] U.C.C. §§ 9-323(d), (e) (buyer), 9-323(f), (g) (lessee).

knowledge of the sale or lease, or (2) 45 days after the sale or lease.[91] Notwithstanding these limitations, the secured party has priority if the advance was made pursuant to a commitment entered into without knowledge of the buyer's purchase or the lessee's lease and before the expiration of the 45-day period.[92] The commitment can be made either before or after the sale or lease, as long it is made without knowledge and the 45-day period has not expired. The "45-days-or-less" rule for gaining priority stands in contrast to the "45-days-or-more" rule that applies in priority disputes between a lien creditor and a secured party that made future advances after the lien creditor's lien arose.[93]

A buyer or lessee in ordinary course of business takes free of any security interest created by the immediate seller or lessor and thus does not need protection against future advances.[94] Likewise, a buyer or lessee[95] that takes delivery of the goods for value and without knowledge of an unperfected security interest will take its interest free of that security interest[96] and, accordingly, free from future advances. Thus, the rules regarding future advances only apply if the buyer or lessee is not entitled to priority at the time of purchase.

Obviously, a secured party that knows that its debtor has entered into an unauthorized transaction should not expect to be able to further encumber the collateral in the hands of the buyer or lessee by continuing to advance money to the debtor, unless it has made a commitment to do so. Even in the absence of such knowledge, the secured party's interest will be cut off with respect to any advances that are committed more than forty-five days after the purchase.[97] Secured lenders thus have a grace period during which to extend advances, and they can investigate to make certain the collateral has not been wrongfully disposed of if they want greater security when making a particular advance.

Buyers and lessees will be on notice of perfected security interests and, as a practical matter, should contact the secured party and disclose the intended transaction before completing the sale or lease. This advice serves two functions: (1) it cuts off the secured party's right to make advances that will have priority against the buyer or lessee (absent a commitment, which can be inquired about); and (2) the buyer or lessee can determine whether

---

[91] U.C.C. §§ 9-323(d) (buyer), 9-323(f) (lessee).

[92] U.C.C. §§ 9-323(e) (buyer), 9-323(g) (lessee).

[93] See § 13.03 infra.

[94] See § 11.03[A][1] supra.

[95] This includes a buyer or lessee in ordinary course of business whose seller or lessor did not create the security interest.

[96] See § 14.03 infra.

[97] The court in Spector United Employees Credit Union v. Smith, 263 S.E.2d 319, 28 U.C.C. Rep. Serv. 310 (N.C. Ct. App. 1980), held that a refinancing of the original secured debt, as distinct from a future advance, was not within the scope of § 9-307(3), which was the predecessor of current § 9-323(d). It denied summary judgment and remanded to determine the extent to which a subsequent loan extended to the debtor well beyond 45 days after the sale of the collateral was a refinancing of the original debt.

the secured party intends to treat the sale or lease as a default under the security agreement. If the latter question is answered affirmatively, the buyer or lessee can take steps to avoid negative consequences. For example, the buyer or lessee might negotiate a waiver of the security interest by agreeing to pay all or part of the outstanding balance owed to the secured party by the debtor. If the secured party will not agree to a waiver, the buyer or lessee should (if possible) cancel the transaction.[98]

The following hypothetical demonstrates the application of the future-advances provision. Assume that a secured party took a perfected security interest in the debtor's business assets on June 1. On October 1, the secured party loaned additional funds pursuant to a future advances clause in the security agreement. If the debtor wrongfully sold the collateral on September 1, the buyer would take it subject to the advance, unless the secured party knew of the purchase at the time of the advance. The secured party will lose if it had knowledge of the purchase at the time of the advance, unless it made the advance pursuant to a commitment that was entered into without knowledge of the advance. By contrast, the buyer would prevail with respect to the advance if the purchase had occurred more than 45 days prior to the advance (*e.g.*, on August 1), again provided that the secured party was not committed before lapse of the grace period (*e.g.*, 45 days after August 1) to make the advance.

[B] Licensees of General Intangibles in Ordinary Course of Business—§ 9-321(a), (b)

With regard to general intangibles, Article 9 provides that "[a] licensee in ordinary course of business takes its rights under the license free of a security interest in the general intangible created by its licensor, even if the security interest is perfected and the licensee knows of its existence."[99] The article also provides a definition for "licensee in ordinary course of business" that essentially parallels the definitions of ordinary-course buyers and lessees. The definition eliminates, for obvious reasons, any reference to possession.[100] Curiously, it omits the requirement that present value be given.

A license is a contract that authorizes the use of an asset without an accompanying transfer of ownership. Consider software[101] as an example. A security interest granted by the owner of software covers the owner's right to license authorized persons to use the software and the owner's right to

---

[98] In a sales transaction, the buyer's right to cancel would be predicated on a breach of the implied warranty of title. U.C.C. § 2-312. In a lease transaction, the lessee's right to cancel would be predicated on a breach of the implied warranty against interference. U.C.C. § 2A-211(1).

[99] U.C.C. § 9-321(b).

[100] *Id.*

[101] "Software" is defined in U.C.C. § 9-102(a)(75) and is within the definition of general intangible in § 9-102(a)(42). Users of software generally acquire their rights by license rather than sale.

prohibit unauthorized persons from doing so. If, however, a licensee acquires its rights from the owner in the ordinary course of business, the secured party cannot interfere with the licensee's right to continue using the software in a manner consistent with the license. As in the case of a lessor's residual interest, a secured party can enforce its rights against the owner's interest in the licensed software.

[C] Chattel Paper and Instruments—§ 9-330

[1] Chattel Paper

Article 9 includes two ways in which a purchaser of chattel paper can achieve priority over a perfected security interest in the same property.[102] To prevail under either approach, the purchaser must give new value and take possession of the tangible chattel paper (or control of the electronic chattel paper) in the ordinary course of the purchaser's business.[103] A secured party thus can assure itself of priority against purchasers by perfecting its security interest through possession or control of the chattel paper. As will be discussed below, a secured party can also assure itself of priority by making sure that its debtor's chattel paper is marked so as to indicate that it has been assigned to an identified assignee other than the purchaser. Typically, the identified assignee is the secured party itself.

Chattel paper typically arises from a secured sale or lease of inventory. A secured party may: (1) take a security interest in chattel paper without an accompanying security interest in inventory, (2) take a security interest in both inventory and chattel paper under circumstances in which each serves as an important part of the pool of collateral, or (3) look to the inventory as its primary collateral and claim chattel paper merely as proceeds of that inventory. In the first two situations, a purchaser can take free of a security interest perfected by a method other than possession or control only if the purchaser complies with the requirements set forth in the preceding paragraph and also acts without knowledge that the purchase violates the rights of the secured party.[104] The purchaser is deemed to have knowledge that the purchase violates the rights of the secured party if the paper indicates that it has been assigned to an identified assignee other than the purchaser.[105]

If the secured party claims chattel paper merely as proceeds of inventory,[106] a purchaser can prevail even though the purchaser knows that the

---

[102] U.C.C. §§ 9-330(a) (mere proceeds interest), 9-330(b) (other than mere proceeds interest).

[103] The "ordinary course" requirement in this provision of Article 9 is individualized to the specific purchaser, as distinct from the "buyer in the ordinary course of business" requirement. Blazer Fin. Serv., Inc. v. Harbor Fed. Sav. & Loan Ass'n, 623 So. 2d 580, 23 U.C.C. Rep. Serv. 2d 1241 (Fla. Dist. Ct. App. 1993) (bulk purchase of installment sales contracts was transaction in ordinary course of purchaser's business).

[104] U.C.C. § 9-330(b).

[105] U.C.C. § 9-330(f).

[106] Attachment of a security interest to proceeds is discussed in § 2.03[B] *supra.*

sale violates the rights of the secured party.[107] In this context, the only way for a secured party to prevail, absent possession or control on its part or a failure of the purchaser to comply with one of the general requirements for priority described above, is for the chattel paper to indicate that it has been assigned to an identified assignee other than the purchaser.[108]

Recall that to obtain priority, the purchaser must give "new value" for the chattel paper, whether claimed merely as proceeds or otherwise. The 1972 text did not define what constituted "new value,"[109] but the courts applying it refused to recognize a setoff against a pre-existing debt owed to the purchaser by the Article 9 debtor.[110] The refusal was justified on policy grounds. Although the secured party's interest in the chattel paper could be severed, the new value provided by the purchaser was a proceed of the chattel paper and provided some protection for the secured party. If the purchaser simply set off a prior debt, the purchase transaction did not generate any proceeds that might benefit the secured party. Revised Article 9 provides a definition of "new value" that is consistent with the foregoing analysis. Specifically, "new value" means "(i) money, (ii) money's worth in property, services, or new credit, or (iii) release by a transferee of an interest in property previously transferred to the transferee. The term does not include an obligation substituted for another obligation."[111]

If a security agreement covers inventory alone, the secured party obviously is interested in any resulting chattel paper "merely as proceeds" of its collateral. This conclusion does not change merely because the security agreement also explicitly covers chattel paper. A court can still determine that the secured party's primary interest is in the inventory and that the agreement covers chattel paper to avoid the impact of section 9-330(a).[112] This determination is appropriate if the inventory consists of big-ticket items that are being financed under a floor-plan arrangement.[113] In a typical floor plan, the secured party advances money to enable the debtor to purchase specific items of inventory and expects to be repaid as each item is sold. If the security interest at issue is a general floating lien, however, the typical secured party relies upon a shifting pool of collateral that consists of the inventory and receivables (*i.e.*, accounts, chattel paper,

---

[107] U.C.C. § 9-330(a).

[108] U.C.C. § 9-330(a)(2).

[109] U.C.C. § 9-108 (1972 Official Text) provided that certain persons that took after-acquired collateral for pre-existing claims gave new value. Revised Article 9 omits this provision as "unnecessary, counterintuitive, and ineffective for its original purpose of sheltering after-acquired collateral from attack as a voidable preference in bankruptcy." U.C.C. § 9-102, Comment 21.

[110] General Elec. Capital Corp. v. Deere Credit Serv., Inc., 799 F. Supp. 832, 19 U.C.C. Rep. Serv. 2d 933 (S.D. Ohio 1992); *In re* Dr. C. Huff Co., Inc., 44 B.R. 129, 40 U.C.C. Rep. Serv. 284 (Bankr. W.D. Ky. 1984).

[111] U.C.C. § 9-102(a)(57).

[112] International Harvester Credit Corp. v. Assocs. Fin. Serv. Co., Inc., 133 Ga. App. 488, 211 S.E.2d 430, 16 U.C.C. Rep. Serv. 396 (1974).

[113] Floor planning is discussed in § 3.04[C] *supra*.

and instruments). Indeed, debtors are commonly permitted to borrow up to a pre-set percentage of the cost of the inventory and a different percentage of the face amount of the receivables. With a general floating lien, the secured party's interest in chattel paper can hardly be described as a "mere proceeds" interest.[114]

As indicated above, if a secured party has more than a "mere proceeds" interest, a purchaser of chattel paper can achieve priority only if it lacks knowledge that the purchase violates the rights of the secured party.[115] The lack-of-knowledge requirement does not create a duty for purchasers to check the filing system prior to making their purchase; indeed, the Official Comments make the point that a purchaser that performs a search and finds a financing statement would not thereby acquire the requisite knowledge unless it saw a statement in the financing statement indicating that any purchase would violate the secured party's rights.[116] As also indicated above, if it is desirable for the secured party to leave the chattel paper in the possession or control of the debtor—as is common in the furniture field where the debtor typically collects installment payments directly from account debtors—the secured party can protect itself by making sure that the paper indicates that it has been assigned and identifying itself as the assignee.

[2] Instruments

Article 9 also deals with the rights of purchasers of instruments, both negotiable and nonnegotiable. Except as provided in section 9-331(a) dealing with the rights of a holder in due course of a negotiable instrument under Article 3,[117] a purchaser takes free of a security interest perfected by a method other than possession only if the purchaser gives value and takes possession of the instrument in good faith and without knowledge that the purchase violates the rights of the secured party. Note that a purchaser need not qualify as a holder in due course under Article 3 to take free of a security interest in a negotiable instrument.[118] The purchaser need only have the characteristics described above.

As with chattel paper, former law distinguished between secured parties that claimed instruments merely as proceeds and other secured parties, but revised Article 9 eliminates the distinction for the instrument category. Also, it eliminates the new value requirement, meaning that a purchaser can take free even though it acquires the instrument in total or partial satisfaction of a pre-existing debt. Interestingly, it does not adopt a

---

[114] See P.E.B. Commentary No. 8 (December 10, 1991).

[115] U.C.C. § 9-308(a).

[116] U.C.C. § 9-330, Comment 6.

[117] See § 11.03[D] infra. A purchaser that so qualifies need not comply with the tests set forth in U.C.C. § 9-330(d).

[118] A negotiable instrument payable to the order of a named person must be indorsed by that person for a subsequent transferee to acquire holder-in-due-course status. U.C.C. § 3-201(b).

definition of value consistent with that of Article 3 for a holder in due course, meaning that a purchaser that acquires an instrument in exchange for an executory promise qualifies for protection.[119] As is true of chattel paper claimed as more than mere proceeds, a purchaser is deemed to have knowledge that the purchase violates the rights of the secured party if the instrument indicates that it has been assigned to an identified assignee.

[D] Negotiable Instruments, Negotiable Documents, and Securities—§ 9-331

While the provisions of Article 9 discussed in the preceding subsection provide protection for purchasers of nonnegotiable instruments and for purchasers of negotiable instruments that do not qualify for holder-in-due-course status, another provision[120] covers only purchasers that qualify for the highest status with respect to fully negotiable personal property. That provision states that nothing in Article 9 limits the rights of a holder in due course of a negotiable instrument under Article 3,[121] a holder to whom a negotiable document of title has been duly negotiated under Article 7,[122] or a protected purchaser of a security.[123] Moreover, filing under Article 9 does not constitute notice of the security interest to such holders or purchasers.[124]

The holders and purchasers referred to are types of bona fide purchasers for value that are given priority over adverse claims of ownership under Articles 3 (negotiable instruments), 7 (negotiable documents), and 8 (securities). The provision of Article 9 under discussion provides an interface with those other articles and defers to the results that would follow under those articles.[125] The 1972 text provided that such holders and purchasers took priority over even a perfected security interest,[126] but that statement was overly broad. Revised Article 9 appropriately clarifies that such holders and purchasers take priority only to the extent provided in the other articles.[127] For example, a holder to whom a negotiable document has been duly negotiated takes it subject to any security interest in the covered goods that

---

[119] U.C.C. § 1-204(4). By contrast, a person claiming priority as a holder in due course of a negotiable instrument under U.C.C. § 9-331(a) will not qualify for that status if it merely gives an executory promise. U.C.C. § 3-303(a)(1). *See also* U.C.C. § 9-403(a) (assignee must give value as defined in Article 3 to take free of account debtor's defenses under enforceable waiver-of-defenses term).

[120] U.C.C. § 9-331.

[121] U.C.C. §§ 3-302, 3-305, 3-306.

[122] U.C.C. §§ 7-501, 7-502.

[123] U.C.C. § 8-303. Even though uncertificated securities are not represented by indispensable paper, they are fully negotiable in that Article 8 provides protection for good-faith purchasers who give value, lack notice of adverse claims, and take control. Control is discussed in § 6.04 *supra*.

[124] U.C.C. § 9-331(c).

[125] U.C.C. § 9-331(a).

[126] U.C.C. § 9-309 (1972 Official Text).

[127] U.C.C. § 9-331(a).

attached and was perfected before the document was issued.[128] Nothing in Article 9 changes this result.

This provision shows the risk inherent in leaving fully negotiable collateral in the possession or under the control of the debtor. The security agreement may flatly prohibit any transfer of the property by the debtor absent the secured party's authorization. By retaining possession or control, however, the debtor is nevertheless empowered to transfer the collateral to a qualifying purchaser free from the security interest.[129] Filing and temporary methods of perfection, and the automatic perfection that is provided a buyer of a promissory note,[130] are extremely convenient ways to transact business, but they carry the risk associated with wrongful transfers to protected parties.

[E]   Funds in Deposit Accounts and Money—§§ 9-332, 9-340

Section 9-332(b) provides protection to transferees of funds from deposit accounts and applies without regard to the perfected status of a secured party with a security interest in either the entire account or the specific funds as proceeds. Transfers from deposit accounts normally occur by check, by funds transfer, or by an electronic debit of the account and a corresponding credit of another account.

The priority rule is that the transferee of the funds takes them free of the security interest, even if perfected by any available method, unless the transferee acts in collusion with the debtor in violating the rights of the secured party.[131] The transferee need not give value for the funds, and it does not matter whether the transferee acted with notice, or even knowledge, that the transfer violated the secured party's rights. Rather, the standard is whether the transferee acted in "collusion" with the debtor, a term borrowed from Article 8.[132] The policy rationale for the rule is stated in the Comments as follows:

> Broad protection for transferees helps to ensure that security interests in deposit accounts do not impair the free flow of funds. It also minimizes the likelihood that a secured party will enjoy a claim to whatever the transferee purchases with the funds. Rules concerning recovery of payments traditionally have placed a high

---

[128] U.C.C. § 7-503(1). *See* § 6.02[B][1] *supra.*

[129] Louisiana State School Lunch Employees Retirement Sys. v. Legel Braswell Gov't Securities Corp., 699 F.2d 512, 35 U.C.C. Rep. Serv. 737 (11th Cir. 1983) (priority to bona-fide purchaser of securities); Bowles v. City Nat'l Bank & Trust Co. of Oklahoma City, 537 P.2d 1219, 16 U.C.C. Rep. Serv. 1396 (Okla. Ct. App. 1975) (priority to pledgee of negotiable instrument that qualified as holder-in-due-course).

[130] *See* § 7.02[B] *supra.*

[131] U.C.C. § 9-330(a) provides a similar rule protecting the transferee when a customer withdraws money (currency) subject to a security interest from a deposit account and transfers it.

[132] U.C.C. § 9-330, Comment 4 ("Bad Actors"). *See also* U.C.C. §§ 8-115, 8-503(e).

value on finality. The opportunity to upset a completed transaction, or even to place a completed transaction in jeopardy by bringing suit against the transferee of funds, should be severely limited.[133]

It should be noted that section 9-330(b) applies to a transfer of funds from a deposit account, not to a transfer of the deposit account itself. Competing claims to a deposit account that arise when a debtor grants a security interest in the account to two or more secured parties are governed by other rules.[134]

Section 9-340 contains a related rule that deals with the priority of a bank that maintains a deposit account subject to another person's security interest and exercises set-off (or a right of recoupment) against funds in the account. As a general rule, the bank's set-off rights take priority over the rights of the secured party, even if the secured party has perfected its interest in the account by means of a control agreement.[135] However, if the secured party has perfected its security interest by becoming the customer with respect to the deposit account, its interest has priority over that of the bank exercising set-off or recoupment rights.[136] Interestingly, although the bank may not obtain priority by means of an involuntary transfer of the funds to itself, it can take advantage of the rule of section 9-330(b) that protects voluntary transferees. Thus, if the debtor gives it a check drawn on the account, it will take the funds represented by the check free of a security interest in the account perfected in any manner unless it acts in collusion with the debtor to violate the rights of the secured party.

---

[133] U.C.C. § 9-330, Comment 3.

[134] *See* § 10.03[A] *supra*.

[135] U.C.C. § 9-340(b), 9-104(a)(2). *See* discussion in § 14.04 *infra*.

[136] U.C.C. §§ 9-340(c), 9-104(a)(3).

Chapter 12

THE FARM PRODUCTS RULE

SYNOPSIS

§ 12.01   THE ARTICLE 9 RULE

Article 9 contains an exception to the priority rule that favors a buyer in ordinary course of business over a prior-perfected security interest created by the buyer's seller.[1] The relevant priority provision states an exclusion for "a person buying farm products from a person engaged in farming operations."[2] Even though a debtor's farm products are analogous to a merchant's inventory, and even though a buyer of farm products may qualify as a buyer in ordinary course of business, the Code does not permit such a buyer to prevail over a prior-perfected agricultural lender (or an unperfected lender of which the buyer has knowledge).

The exception dates to the original version of Article 9, and over the years a number of arguments have been advanced in its favor. The buyer-in-ordinary-course rule typically protects consumer buyers that purchase inventory from a seller, and these buyers are often unaware of the need to check for filed financing statements before proceeding with a purchase. By contrast, buyers of farm products generally are merchants that ought to be aware of the need to check for filed financing statements. These buyers are thus in a better position to protect their interests than is the typical inventory buyer. Agricultural lenders are also somewhat more vulnerable than inventory lenders in that farmers often sell all of their farm products at one time.[3] The policing measures that can detect an inventory seller

---

[1] For a discussion of this priority rule, see § 11.03[A][1] *supra*.

[2] U.C.C. § 9-320(1). "Farming operation" is defined in U.C.C. § 9-102(a)(35).

[3] A bulk sale by a nonfarmer would be unlikely to qualify as an ordinary-course transaction. *See* U.C.C. § 1-201(b)(9).

beginning to sell "out of trust"[4] cannot aid a lender once a farmer has wrongfully sold all the crops or livestock. Although the lender's interest extends automatically to the proceeds of the sale,[5] that protection is meaningless if the farmer is dishonest or desperate and the lender is not included as a joint payee on the buyer's check.[6]

The farm-products rule has also had its detractors. The general rule favoring buyers in ordinary course of business protects the free flow of commerce. That principle arguably applies to agricultural commodities as well as to other kinds of goods. Moreover, a search of the filing system may be particularly impractical and costly given that federal laws require prompt payment for certain commodities.[7] The impact of the farm-products rule fell with undue harshness on smaller businesses that buy farm products, who derisively called it the "double-jeopardy" rule.[8]

§ 12.02 THE FEDERAL FOOD SECURITY ACT

In a measure that caught farm lenders by surprise, Congress included a section in the Food Security Act of 1985[9] that is captioned "Protection for Purchasers of Farm Products."[10] The Congressional findings for the provision determined that the possibility of double payment by a buyer of farm products that did not discover the existence of a perfected security interest in farm products constituted a burden on, and an obstruction to, interstate commerce.[11] Congress therefore provided that unless one of two exceptions applies, buyers of farm products in the ordinary course of business are to be treated like other buyers in the ordinary course of business;[12] *i.e.*, they take free of perfected security interests even if they have knowledge of the interests.[13] The federal legislation preempts the farm-products

---

[4] This term is used primarily in floor planning, a type of inventory financing discussed in § 3.04[C] *supra*. It refers to a failure to remit to the lender an agreed percentage of the purchase price of big-ticket inventory items.

[5] *See* § 2.03 *supra*.

[6] The risks to a lender in regard to cash proceeds are discussed in § 8.02[B][1] *supra*.

[7] *See* Packers & Stockyard Act, 7 U.S.C. § 2286 (1994) (full payment before close of next business day following purchase and transfer of livestock).

[8] The term refers to the fact that a buyer could pay a farmer for farm products and then have to pay a secured party a second time in order to avoid foreclosure.

[9] 7 U.S.C. § 1631.

[10] *Id.*

[11] *Id.* § 1631(a).

[12] The protection of the federal legislation also extends to "commission merchants" and "sales agents" that sell farm products in the ordinary course of business, thereby insulating such merchants and agents from conversion liability.

[13] *Id.* § 1631(d). Under Article 9, a person that knows its purchase violates the rights of a secured party does not qualify as a buyer in ordinary course of business. U.C.C. § 1-201(b)(9). There is no similar provision in the federal law. However, like Article 9, a buyer of farm products in ordinary course takes free of a security interest only when the security interest was created by the buyer's seller. The buyer in Fin Ag, Inc. v. Hufnagle, Inc., 720 N.W.2d 579 (Minn. 2006), ran afoul of this limitation. The secured party filed an "effective financing

rule.[14]

As indicated above, the federal law provides two alternative mechanisms by which a perfected secured party's interest can continue in farm products following an unauthorized disposition by the debtor. One approach is for the secured party or the debtor to provide advance notice of the security interest to the buyer. The other approach is to utilize a central registry that a state may create for purposes of providing notification to buyers that request information concerning farm products.[15] The two mechanisms are discussed below.

[A] Advance-Notice Approach

A buyer of farm products that receives, within one year prior to the sale,[16] a written[17] notice containing statutorily prescribed information from either the lender or the debtor advising of the security interest will take subject to it unless the buyer complies with payment instructions included in the notice.[18] The expectation is that the secured party will require that payment be made by way of a jointly payable check so that it can be assured of having control over the sale proceeds.[19] This approach shifts the burden

statement" with the Minnesota central registry on its debtor's corn crop that effectively protected the secured party on purchases made directly from the debtor. The buyer claimed, however, that another party sold some of the debtor's corn to the buyer under the third-party's name. The buyer would still lose to the secured party under this scenario because the security interest was not created by the buyer's seller with respect to this corn.

[14] Lisco State Bank v. McCombs Ranches, Inc., 752 F. Supp. 329, 13 U.C.C. Rep. Serv. 2d 927 (D. Neb. 1990) (federal statute applies retroactively to previously perfected security interests).

[15] First Bank v. Eastern Livestock Co., 837 F. Supp. 792, 23 U.C.C. Rep. Serv. 2d 933 (S.D. Miss. 1993) (because the federal Act provides two exclusive means by which a buyer of farm products in ordinary course can be subject to the perfected security interest, actual knowledge of the buyer through other means would be irrelevant).

[16] Pioneer Hi-Bred Int'l, Inc. v. Keybank Nat'l Ass'n., 742 N.E.2d 967 (Ind. Ct. App. 2001) (buyer held to be subject to the secured party's interest in the seed corn because the buyer received notice from the secured party within one year of the sale).

[17] Although the statute uses the term "written," it is subject to the Electronic Signatures in Global and National Commerce Act (E-Sign), 15 U.S.C. Section 7001 *et seq.* Under E-Sign, a writing requirement imposed by the Food Security Act may, if parties agree, be satisfied by a record in electronic form.

[18] 7 U.S.C. § 1631(e)(1)(A). The perfected secured party in Ag Serv. of Am., Inc. v. DeBruce Grain, Inc., 28 Kan. App. 2d 582, 19 P.3d 188, 45 U.C.C. Rep. Serv. 2d 1193 (Kan. Ct. App. 2001), provided the necessary advance notice to the defendant, which had a contract to buy 30,000 bushels of the debtor's corn crop. After the debtor delivered less than a third of the bushels and repudiated the remainder of the sales contract, the defendant covered on the open market and deducted the amount of its damages from the purchase price for the delivered corn. The majority held that the buyer of farm products in ordinary course could not reduce the secured party's interest through its setoff rights, as the secured party was not liable for claims that the buyer had against the seller. The dissent would have treated the secured party as an account debtor following delivery of the corn and thus would have held that the secured party was subject to the buyer's offset claim under U.C.C.§ 9-318(1)(a).

[19] Farm Credit Bank of St. Paul v. F&A Dairy, 165 Wis. 2d 360, 477 N.W.2d 357, 16 U.C.C.

of checking for adverse interests that the Article 9 filing system imposes on buyers onto the secured party, which must locate and provide direct notice to potential buyers.

The advance notice to buyers must satisfy several requirements.[20] It must be organized by the type of farm product affected and must contain the names and addresses of the secured party and the debtor; the Social Security or taxpayer identification number of the debtor; a description of the farm products subject to the security interest; the amount of the farm products if applicable (*e.g.*, if less than all of a particular category is claimed); the crop year; a reasonable description of the land on which crops are grown, including the county or parish; and any payment obligations imposed on buyers as a condition for release of the security interest.[21] Notices must be amended in writing[22] within three months following any material change in the information provided.[23]

To facilitate effective notification, the act permits the secured party to require that the debtor provide a list of prospective buyers to which the debtor might sell its farm products.[24] Accordingly, a prudent secured party will include covenants in the security agreement under which the debtor promises to provide such a list and to sell only to buyers on the list. A debtor is subject to a fine of the greater of $5,000 or 15% of the value of the farm products sold as a penalty[25] for selling to an unlisted buyer, unless the secured party is notified in writing[26] at least seven days prior to the sale.[27] If the required notice is not given, the debtor can still avoid liability by remitting the proceeds to the secured party within ten days following the

---

Rep. Serv. 2d 885 (Ct. App. 1991) (buyer liable in conversion for failing to comply with advance notice requiring monthly milk payments to be made directly to secured party). *But see* Mercantile Bank of Springfield v. Joplin Regional Stockyards, Inc., 870 F. Supp. 278, 27 U.C.C. Rep. Serv. 2d 269 (W.D. Mo. 1994) (buyer that did not comply with payment instructions still prevailed based on secured party's acquiescence through course of conduct).

[20] Lisco State Bank v. McCombs Ranches, Inc., 752 F. Supp. 329, 13 U.C.C. Rep. Serv. 2d 927 (D. Neb. 1990) (oral notification ineffective).

[21] 7 U.S.C. § 1631(e)(1)(A)(ii). Although the federal Act does not cover the effect of missing information contained in a notice under the advance-notice system, the court in *First Nat'l Bank & Trust v. Miami Cty. Coop. Ass'n*, 257 Kan. 989, 897 P.2d 144 (1995), held that the more probable congressional intent was to avoid making a notice ineffective if it contains minor omissions or errors that are not seriously misleading. It upheld the effectiveness of a secured party's notices to the buyer, even though the notices did not describe the real property or the crop year, because the notices substantially complied and did not mislead the buyer. *Compare* Farm Credit Midsouth, PCA v. Farm Fresh Catfish Co., 371 F.3d 450 (8th Cir. 2004) (because strict compliance is required for the secured party's advance notice, the secured party failed the test by sending a notice that did not include the debtor's taxpayer identification number, the debtor's address, or the counties in which the catfish subject to the security interest were produced).

[22] *See* note 17 *supra.*

[23] 7 U.S.C. § 1631(e)(1)(A)(iii).

[24] *Id.* § 1631(h)(1).

[25] *Id.* § 1631(h)(3).

[26] *See* note 17 *supra.*

[27] *Id.* § 1631(h)(2)(A).

unauthorized sale.[28] The off-list buyer takes the farm products free of the security interest, even if the buyer knows of the security interest's existence.

[B] State Central-Registry Approach

The alternative approach permitted by the federal act requires that a state elect to create a central-filing registry that complies with standards articulated in the act. To qualify, a registry must require that secured lenders seeking priority file with the registry (which must be maintained by the Secretary of State or its designee)[29] a notice referred to in the act as an "effective financing statement" and known to lenders as an "EFS."[30] An EFS must include all of the information mandated under the advance-notice alternative,[31] and, as with that alternative, must be amended within three months following any material change in the information provided.[32] Once filed, an EFS provides constructive notice of the security interest to all potential farm-product buyers.[33] Like an Article 9 financing statement, an EFS is effective for a period of five years.[34]

A central registry must contain several master lists, one of which must be organized according to types of farm products. That list must be arranged alphabetically by the debtors' names, numerically by their Social Security and taxpayer identification numbers, geographically by county, and temporally by crop year. Another master list must indicate all the buyers of farm products that have registered with the system. That list must show the name and address of each registered buyer and the types of farm products in which the buyer is interested. The Secretary of State must, on a regular basis, send registered buyers written[35] notification of the information on file regarding the types of farm products for which they have registered. The Secretary of State must also provide oral confirmation of the existence of an EFS within 24 hours, followed by written confirmation, upon request by an unregistered buyer.[36]

A buyer that does not register with, or make a request of, the Secretary of State prior to purchasing farm products subject to a perfected security interest takes them subject to that interest if the secured party has filed

---

[28] *Id.* § 1631(h)(2)(B).

[29] *Id.* § 1631(d)(11).

[30] If the state permits electronic filings under Article 9, an electronically reproduced copy of the EFS may be filed. *Id.* § 1631(c)(4)(A).

[31] *Id.* § 1631(c)(4)(D).

[32] *Id.* § 1631(c)(4)(E).

[33] Lisco State Bank v. McCombs Ranches, Inc., 752 F. Supp. 329, 13 U.C.C. Rep. Serv. 2d 927 (D. Neb. 1990) (perfected secured party failed to file effective financing statement to take advantage of Nebraska's implementation of central-filing system).

[34] 7 U.S.C. § 1631(c)(4)(F).

[35] The Electronic Signatures in Global and National Commerce Act (E-Sign) permits federal and state regulatory agencies to determine permitted formats. 15 U.S.C. § 7004.

[36] 7 U.S.C. § 1631(c)(2)(F).

an EFS.[37] If the secured party has not done so, even an unregistered buyer in ordinary course prevails.[38] If a registered buyer receives notification from the Secretary of State that an EFS is on file, the buyer can avoid the security interest by obtaining a waiver or release of the interest through compliance with specified payment conditions or otherwise.[39]

§ 12.03 A CRITIQUE

The Food Security Act has significant deficiencies. It was adopted based on a finding that Article 9's farm-products rule was a burden to interstate commerce, but the act's cumbersome mechanisms are poorly designed to overcome such burdens. The act also impedes the important goal of promoting uniformity in commercial law.[40] The very fact that alternative mechanisms are available undercuts uniformity. Moreover, each mechanism as applied undermines uniformity. Under the advance-notice approach, the states may determinate what constitutes "receipt" of a notification;[41] under the central-registry approach, each state is allowed to prescribe what constitutes "regular" distribution of written notices to buyers.[42]

The central-filing approach, in particular, is a source of confusion. It does not in any way replace or operate as a substitute for the Article 9 filing system, meaning that a secured party must still file an Article 9 financing statement in order to obtain priority over other secured parties and lien creditors.[43] The registry has relevance only in determining priority between

---

[37] *Id.* § 1631(e)(2). Ag Serv. of Am., Inc. v. United Grain, Inc., 75 F. Supp.2d 1037 (D. Neb. 1999) (unregistered buyer in Kansas took subject to the creditor's perfected security interest in the debtor's corn grown in Nebraska and properly noted on the master lists of the Nebraska central registry).

[38] 7 U.S.C. § 1631(e)(2). Consolidated Nutrition, L.C. v. IBP, Inc., 2003 S.D. 107, 669 N.W.2d 126, 51 U.C.C. Rep. Serv. 2d 329 (S.D. 2003) (registered buyer took free of the security interest in the debtor's hogs because at the time of the sales the secured party had neither filed an effective financing statement nor sent a written notice to the buyer concerning the security interest); Battle Creek State Bank v. Preusker, 253 Neb. 502, 571 N.W.2d 294 (Neb.1997) (although the bank's failure to list milk on the effective financing statement resulted in the purchaser of the milk taking free of the security interest, this protection did not extend to the unsecured creditors to whom the proceeds from the milk sales were transferred because the creditors did not qualify as buyers of farm products in ordinary course).

[39] 7 U.S.C. § 1631(e)(3)(B).

[40] *See* U.C.C. § 1-103(a)(3).

[41] 7 U.S.C. § 1631(c)(2)(e).

[42] *Id.* § 1631(f).

[43] The commission agent in Food Services of Am. v. Royal Heights, Inc., 123 Wash. 2d 779, 871 P.2d 590, 23 U.C.C. Rep. Serv. 2d 949 (1994), claimed priority in the proceeds of its sale of the debtor's apple crop made free of the competing bank's prior-perfected security interest. The court denied priority to the commission agent because of its failure to comply with Article 9's perfection requirements. The federal statute's protection extended to protect the commission agent as a seller but not as a competing secured party. *See also* Consolidated Nutrition, L.C. v. IBP, Inc., 2003 S.D. 107, 669 N.W.2d 126, 51 U.C.C. Rep. Serv. 2d 329 (S.D. 2003) (an application of proceeds to a pre-existing claim that the buyer had with the seller was governed by state law and not by the provision of the Food Security Act because the buyer in this context was acting as a lender and receiving the goods in satisfaction of a pre-existing claim rather than buying them).

a perfected security interest in farm products and a buyer in the ordinary course of business. The act thus constitutes a trap for the unwary. By using the term "central filing system" and referring to the secured party's filing as an "effective financing statement," it creates the impression that it supplants Article 9's filing requirements.[44] Needless confusion is generated by duplicating terms used in Article 9 but assigning them different meanings.[45]

The mechanisms established by the act also pose workability concerns. The provisions imposing fines on debtors that sell to buyers that are not on a list submitted to a secured party pursuant to a covenant in a security agreement may not provide a sufficient deterrent for farmers facing financial ruin, especially as the fines are collected by the government rather than being applied to the secured debt. Moreover, the advance-notice approach creates an incentive for a secured lender to send notification to all potential buyers. Rather than limiting notification to the buyers listed by the debtor, the secured party might be inclined to notify any other potential buyer in a relevant geographic area as a hedge against an off-list sale by the debtor. The incentive to over-notify imposes transactional costs on both secured lenders and potential buyers, which may be blitzed with notifications. Because the act does not stipulate a uniform format for notices, buyers must be prepared to assimilate information that will arrive in a variety of formats.

---

[44] For example, the bankruptcy court in *In re* Duffin, 1999 WL 33486712 (Bankr. D. Id. 1999), erroneously held that the central registry provided a separate and single index for all claims of creditors of interests in farm products in Idaho, so that filing had to be made in that registry in order to perfect a security interest in farm products. Therefore, even though the secured party had filed a U.C.C. financing statement describing the collateral as all of the debtor's crops, because the "effective financing statement" of the central registry described only the debtor's wheat crop, the court held in error that the secured party was not perfected in the debtor's potato crops and was subordinate to the trustee in bankruptcy.

[45] The language in the federal Act does not state the requirements that a buyer act in good faith and without knowledge that the sale to it violates the interests of third parties in order to qualify as a buyer of farm products in ordinary course. 7 U.S.C. § 1631(c)(1). *See* Lisco State Bank v. McCombs Ranches, Inc., 752 F. Supp. 329, 13 U.C.C. Rep. Serv. 2d 927 (D. Neb. 1990).

Chapter 13
CREDITORS WITH LIENS ARISING BY OPERATION OF LAW

SYNOPSIS

§ 13.01 POSSESSORY LIENS THAT ARISE BY OPERATION OF LAW — § 9-333

Article 9 provides priority over even perfected secured parties for liens that arise by operation of law in favor of certain persons that provide services or materials with respect to goods.[1] It refers to such liens as "possessory liens," which is an apt description in that only those liens whose effectiveness depends upon possession of the goods by the provider qualify for priority.[2]

Article 9 does not apply to a possessory lien except to the extent section 9-333 governs priorities between a possessory lienor and a secured party.[3] The classic example of a possessory lien is one that arises when repair work is conducted on goods, such as a car.[4] The common law of most states gives the garage that does the repair work an artisan's lien[5] on the car so long as it retains possession. In other words, the garage can sell the car at foreclosure if the owner fails to pay the repair bill. The lien will have priority over even a perfected Article 9 security interest because the following elements are present: (1) the services or materials are furnished

---

[1] U.C.C. § 9-333.

[2] A nonpossessory lien may qualify as an agricultural lien, discussed in § 13.02 *infra*.

[3] U.C.C. § 9-109(d)(2).

[4] Schleimer v. Arrowhead Garage, Inc., 260 N.Y.S.2d 271, 2 U.C.C. Rep. Serv. 753 (Civ. Ct. 1965).

[5] The term "mechanic's lien" generally refers to liens arising by operation of law in favor of persons who provide services or materials to improve land. An architect, who is an artisan, might have the benefit of a mechanic's lien, while a mechanic who repairs a car might have the benefit of an artisan's lien. Go figure!

in the ordinary course of the provider's business; (2) the effectiveness of the lien depends upon retention of possession by the provider; and (3) the lien arises by operation of a statutory or common-law rule.[6] The key point with regard to the last element is that the lien must not be consensual and it must not result from a judicial or quasi-judicial proceeding. Thus, the provider must be neither an Article 9 secured party nor a lien creditor.

The rationale for the priority granted for possessory liens is akin to the rationale that undergirds the special priority granted purchase-money security interests.[7] If a car is in need of repair, for example, its value as collateral will have been reduced. Because the services and materials supplied by the garage restore the car's value, it is only fair that the garage obtain priority in the car for the purpose of recovering its repair bill. The remaining value of the car — the value that was present before the repairs were done — is still available to the secured party.[8]

States provide liens for a wide array of interests. Some liens are rooted in the common law; others arise by statute. In addition to artisan's liens, there are carriers' liens, logger's liens, innkeeper's liens, and even plastic fabricator's liens. The original drafters indicated that the Code's priority rule was designed to favor "liens securing claims arising from work intended to enhance or preserve the value of the collateral."[9] Even storage liens have been held to be within the scope of the rule when storage has preserved the value of the goods.[10]

As indicated above, a lien must be possessory in nature to fall within the priority rule of Article 9. It does not benefit a person that never acquires possession of the goods[11] or one that voluntarily surrenders possession.[12] Reacquiring possession of the goods after they have been surrendered will also leave the lienholder unprotected.[13] By contrast, involuntary relinquishment of possession, such as by a secured party's replevy[14] of the

---

[6] U.C.C. § 9-333.

[7] For discussion of the policy underlying purchase-money secured party priority, see § 10.04 *supra*.

[8] A secured party must be careful or this value could be lost. If the car is sold at the garage's foreclosure sale, the purchaser will take free of the secured party's interest. *See* § 18.02[E] *infra* (junior liens destroyed through foreclosure). Whether the secured party is entitled to share in any surplus (*i.e.*, amount in excess of the repair bill) received at the sale turns on the state law governing the foreclosure. Because of these risks, the secured party may simply choose to pay the repair bill prior to foreclosure and add the amount to the balance of the secured obligation.

[9] U.C.C. § 9-310, Comment 1 (1962 Official Text).

[10] Central Trust Co., N.A. v. Dan's Marina, 858 S.W.2d 211, 23 U.C.C. Rep. Serv. 2d 308 (Ky. Ct. App. 1993).

[11] Circle 76 Fertilizer, Inc. v. Nelson, 365 N.W.2d 460, 41 U.C.C. Rep. Serv. 1079 (Neb. 1985) (supplier of fertilizer with statutory lien never had possession of debtor's crops).

[12] Forrest Cate Ford, Inc. v. Fryar, 465 S.W.2d 882, 8 U.C.C. Rep. Serv. 239 (Tenn. Ct. App. 1970).

[13] Balzer Mach. Co. v. Klineline Sand & Gravel Co., 271 Or. 596, 533 P.2d 321, 16 U.C.C. Rep. Serv. 1160 (1975).

[14] Replevin is discussed in § 18.01[B] *infra*.

property, will not defeat a lienholder's priority.[15] One court has properly held that a statutory lienholder that temporarily surrenders possession to a subcontractor for purposes of doing a portion of the repair work does not jeopardize its priority.[16] This is consistent with the constructive possession doctrine available to secured parties with possessory security interests.[17]

In some instances, a state statute may entitle a lienholder to file a notice of its lien and return the property to the debtor rather than retain possession.[18] If this option is pursued, the lienholder does not enjoy the benefit of Article 9's priority rule. The secured party does not necessarily prevail, however. The statutory lien is then entirely beyond the scope of Article 9[19] and the court must determine priority without reference to section 9-333. A court could apply Article 9's residual priority rule — section 9-201(a) — and award priority to the secured party, or it could resolve the priority dispute under law other than Article 9.[20]

If a possessory lien arises from the common law, it has priority over even a perfected security interest.[21] The same is true of statutory liens with one exception — a possessory lien created by a statute that expressly subordinates the lien to an Article 9 security interest loses the priority that otherwise would be available.[22] In the absence of express subordination, a statute creating a possessory lien might still have been construed under pre-Code case law as subordinate to security interests. If the subordination of the lien is based on case law rather than the express provisions of the statute, however, Article 9 "provides a rule of interpretation that the possessory lien takes priority, even if the statute has been construed judicially to make the possessory lien subordinate."[23]

Most jurisdictions have enacted forfeiture statutes under which a governmental entity can seize property. Sometimes the seized property is subject to a perfected security interest. Although the government's interest appears to be analogous to a possessory lien, the claim of the governmental entity that seizes the goods does not fit within the parameters of the Code's priority rule because the seizure does not preserve or enhance the value of the

[15] Finch v. Miller, 271 Or. 271, 531 P.2d 892 (1975).
[16] Beverly Bank of Chicago v. Little, 527 So. 2d 706, 7 U.C.C. Rep. Serv. 2d 1272 (Ala. 1988).
[17] See § 6.03[B] supra.
[18] See, e.g., Kan. Stat. Ann. § 58-201.
[19] U.C.C. § 9-109(d)(2). See § 1.07[B] supra.
[20] See § 14.04 infra. See also Church Bros. Body Serv., Inc. v. Merchants Nat'l Bank & Trust Co. of Indianapolis, 559 N.E.2d 328, 13 U.C.C. Rep. Serv. 2d 537 (Ind. Ct. App. 1990) (pre-Code law applied to resolve priority dispute between security interest and nonpossessory artisan's lien).
[21] Charter One Auto Fin. v. Inkas Coffee Distrib. Realty, 2005 WL 1097097, 57 U.C.C. Rep. Serv. 2d 672 (Conn. Super. Ct. 2005) (storage company's common-law possessory lien for storage fees on an automobile had priority over the prior interest of the secured party that had perfected by notation on the certificate of title).
[22] Affiliated Bank v. Evans Tool & Mfg. Co., Inc., 229 Ill. App. 3d 464, 593 N.E.2d 145, 19 U.C.C. Rep. Serv. 2d 928 (1992); In re S.M. Acquisition Co., 296 B.R. 452, 51 U.C.C. Rep. Serv. 2d 867 (Bankr. N.D. Ill. 2003).
[23] U.C.C. § 9-333, Comment 2.

goods. Resolution of the dispute in these cases falls outside the scope of Article 9.[24]

§ 13.02 AGRICULTURAL LIENS — §§ 9-317, 9-322(a)(1)

Article 9 also governs certain aspects of "agricultural liens."[25] An agricultural lien is a nonpossessory statutory[26] lien on farm products[27] that is not a security interest (*i.e.*, is not consensual) and that secures payment to a person that in ordinary course of business furnishes goods or services, or leases real property, to assist with a debtor's farming operation.[28] Examples include a landlord's lien for unpaid rent on crops raised on the demised premises, a commercial harvester's lien for services rendered on crops left in the farmer's possession, and a feeder's lien for services rendered on livestock that remain on a rancher's land. Such liens arise by operation of law other than Article 9, but once created they are swept into Article 9 for perfection, priority, and enforcement purposes.[29] In other words, once an agricultural lien becomes effective, it is afforded the same treatment as an Article 9 security interest. "Effectiveness" of an agricultural lien is the equivalent of "attachment" of a security interest.[30]

Because agricultural liens are by definition nonpossessory, perfection is accomplished by filing a financing statement.[31] Many of the priority rules contain specific provisions dealing with agricultural liens, inevitably affording them the same treatment as ordinary security interests.[32] For example, section 9-317(a) provides that an unperfected security interest or agricultural lien is subordinate to the rights of a lien creditor, and section 9-317(b) allows a buyer that gives value and takes delivery of goods without knowledge of a security interest or agricultural lien to take free of the interest or lien if it is unperfected at the time of delivery.[33] Similarly,

---

[24] *Compare* State v. One 1976 Pontiac Firebird, 402 A.2d 254, 26 U.C.C. Rep. Serv. 1306 (N.J. Super. Ct. 1979) (state statute made seizure subject to prior security interest) *with* United States v. One 1969 Plymouth Fury Auto., 476 F.2d 960, 12 U.C.C. Rep. Serv. 1228 (5th Cir. 1973) (forfeiture to government held superior to security interest because statute did not provide for subordination).

[25] U.C.C. § 9-109(a)(2). *See* § 1.07[B] *supra*.

[26] Unlike possessory liens (discussed in the preceding section), Article 9 does not apply to nonpossessory liens on farm products that arise pursuant to a common-law rule.

[27] U.C.C. § 9-102(a)(34), discussed in § 1.04[A][2] *supra*.

[28] U.C.C. § 9-102(a)(5).

[29] The term "secured party" includes a person that holds an agricultural lien. U.C.C. § 9-102(72)(B).

[30] *Compare* U.C.C. § 9-308(a) (security interest is perfected when it *attaches* and all applicable requirements of § 9-310 are satisfied) *with* § 9-308(b) (agricultural lien is perfected when it becomes *effective* and all applicable requirements of § 9-310 are satisfied).

[31] U.C.C. § 9-310(a).

[32] U.C.C. § 9-322(g) provides an exception to the rule that agricultural liens are to be afforded the same treatment as Article 9 security interests for priority purposes — a perfected agricultural lien will take priority over a conflicting security interest if the statute creating the lien so provides.

[33] Buyers of farm products may take priority over even perfected security interests under the federal Food Security Act, 7 U.S.C. § 1631. *See* Chapter 12 *supra*.

section 9-322(a)(1) provides that "conflicting security interests and agricultural liens rank according to priority in time of filing or perfection." If, for example, a bank takes a security interest in a farmer's crops and files its financing statement on November 5, it will be subordinate to a commercial harvester with a statutorily-created agricultural lien on the same crops who filed on November 1.

There is a trap for the unwary built into the perfection rules for agricultural liens. As a rule, Article 9 designates a central office in the state of the debtor's location as the place to file a financing statement to perfect a security interest.[34] With an agricultural lien, however, the place of filing is a central office in the state where the farm products subject to the lien are located.[35] For example, suppose Farmer, who lives in Iowa, rents crop land in Missouri from Landlord, who acquires by statute a lien on Farmer's crops as security for unpaid rent. To perfect its agricultural lien, Landlord must file centrally in Missouri. If Bank takes a security interest in the crops, it will perfect by filing in Iowa. If either Landlord or Bank limits its search for conflicting interests to the office in which it files its own financing statement, it will not locate a financing statement filed by the other.

§ 13.03 FEDERAL TAX LIENS

The Tax Lien Act of 1966 grants to the federal government a lien on all property belonging to a taxpayer that neglects or refuses to pay taxes following a demand for payment.[36] The lien arises if the following events have occurred: (1) the government has made a valid tax assessment; (2) notice has been given to the taxpayer stating the amount owed and demanding that it be paid; and (3) the taxpayer has failed to make payment within ten days following the demand.[37] Once created, the lien relates back to the date on which the assessment was made,[38] and its scope is exceptionally broad, attaching to all existing and after-acquired real and personal property in which the taxpayer has an interest.[39] The lien is a "secret lien," meaning that the Internal Revenue Service need not give any public notice in order for it to arise and be enforced. It continues in effect until the tax is paid or a ten-year limitation period has expired.[40]

Because the lien is secret, third parties that are unaware of it and acquire an interest in the taxpayer's property — including Article 9 secured parties

[34] See § 5.05 supra.

[35] U.C.C. § 9-302.

[36] I.R.C. § 6321. The best analysis of these issues is Michelle Cecil, "Bankruptcy: Tax Issues Affecting Insolvent and Bankrupt Debtors," which comprises Ch. 158 of Business Organizations with Tax Planning (Matthew Bender, 1996).

[37] I.R.C. §§ 6303(a), 6321, 6331(a).

[38] I.R.C. § 6322.

[39] Treas. Reg. § 301.6321-1.

[40] I.R.C. § 6322.

— are potentially at risk. To reduce the level of risk, the tax laws encourage the government to file a public notice of its lien[41] by providing that the lien is invalid as against certain interests that arise before the filing is made. The protected parties are purchasers, judgment lien creditors, mechanic's lienors and, most importantly for our purposes, holders of security interests.[42]

Federal law defines "security interest" to include only interests that have been properly perfected under state law.[43] Thus, under Article 9, it is appropriate to speak in terms of perfected and unperfected security interests, but for tax-law purposes the holder of an unperfected Article 9 security interest does not have a "security interest" at all and has no protection against even an unfiled tax lien. Only secured parties that have perfected prior to the government's filing have any hope of prevailing in a priority contest with the IRS.

Even if a secured party has properly perfected before notice of the federal tax lien is filed, it will not prevail over the government unless its security interest is *choate*.[44] A security interest is choate if the identity of the secured party, the property to which the interest attaches, and the amount of the debt can all be accurately established. For a secured party with a single loan and a security interest in a readily identifiable asset, choateness is not a problem. For example, if the secured party has a security interest in the debtor's car and has properly perfected by having its lien noted on the certificate of title, the fact that the car was subject to a hidden federal tax lien at the time of perfection is irrelevant. All that matters is that the secured party perfected its interest before the government filed its tax-lien notice. The secured party will have no difficulty proving the elements necessary to show choateness.

The choateness doctrine is most troublesome when a secured party is attempting to enforce a lien on after-acquired property or on collateral securing future advances. In *Rice Investment Co. v. United States*,[45] for example, a secured party with a properly perfected security interest in the debtor's inventory, including after-acquired inventory, lost a priority battle with the government because it was unable to establish that the inventory it was claiming was in existence and owned by the debtor at the time the government filed its notice of tax lien. Similarly, in *Texas Oil & Gas Corp. v. United States*,[46] the court held that a secured party's perfected security

---

[41] In the case of personal property, the filing must be made in a single office located in the taxpayer's state of residence. I.R.C. § 6323(f)(1)(A)(ii), (2)(B).

[42] I.R.C. § 6323(a). Planned Furniture Promotions, Inc. v. Benjamin S. Youngblood, Inc., 2005 WL 1073635, 57 U.C.C. Rep. Serv. 2d 678 (M.D. Ga. 2005) (perfected security interest had priority over a subsequently-filed tax lien).

[43] I.R.C. § 6323(h)(1).

[44] Choateness is a judicially-created doctrine. The seminal case under the Tax Lien Act of 1966 is *United States v. McDermott*, 507 U.S. 447, 113 S. Ct. 1526, 123 L. Ed. 2d 128 (1993).

[45] 625 F.2d 565 (5th Cir. 1980).

[46] 466 F.2d 1040 (5th Cir. 1972), *cert. denied*, 410 U.S. 929, 93 S. Ct. 1367, 35 L. Ed. 2d 591 (1973).

interest was inchoate because its future-advances clause rendered the amount of the indebtedness uncertain as of the time the government's notice was filed.

The Tax Lien Act contains two important exceptions to the choateness doctrine. The first exception,[47] which applies only to security agreements that contain future advances clauses, allows a secured party to obtain priority for its advances over a filed tax lien if certain conditions are met. To obtain priority for amounts advanced before the tax-lien notice is filed, the secured party need only be perfected. To obtain priority for a subsequent advance, there are three requirements: (1) the advance must be made before the 46th day following the tax-lien filing; (2) the collateral must have been covered by the terms of a written[48] security agreement entered into before the tax-lien filing; and (3) the advance must be protected under state law against a creditor with a judgment lien arising out of an unsecured obligation. The period during which the secured party can obtain priority for future advances terminates early if the secured party acquires knowledge or actual notice of the tax-lien filing.

This provision can best be understood by contrasting it with the Article 9 provision dealing with priority for future advances as against a lien creditor.[49] That provision was drafted with the Tax Lien Act in mind and, because of its provisions, the third requirement for priority over the government (that future advances made before the 46th day after tax-lien filing must be protected under state law from a judgment lien creditor) is always satisfied. Specifically, Article 9 provides that a secured party has priority over a person that becomes a lien creditor while the security interest is perfected for: (1) all advances made before the person becomes a lien creditor; (2) all advances made within 45 days following the date on which the person becomes a lien creditor, irrespective of the secured party's knowledge of the person's interest; (3) all advances made more than 45 days following the date on which the person becomes a lien creditor if the secured party lacks knowledge of the person's lien at the time of the advance; and (4) all advances made pursuant to a commitment entered into without knowledge of the person's lien.

A few examples will help to illustrate the differences between the treatment of future advances under the U.C.C. and under the Tax Lien Act. Suppose SP has a perfected security interest in D's equipment, which is collateral for a $10,000 loan. The security agreement contains a future-advances clause. On May 1, the government files its tax-lien notice. On May 31, SP, which has neither actual notice[50] nor knowledge of the

[47] I.R.C. § 6323(d).

[48] Although the statute uses the term "written," it is subject to the Electronic Signatures in Global and National Commerce Act (E-Sign), 15 U.S.C. § 7001 et seq., meaning that its provisions are satisfied if there is an equivalent electronic record.

[49] U.C.C. § 9-323(b).

[50] The Internal Revenue Code does not define the term, but actual notice obviously means less than actual knowledge and more than either constructive or inquiry notice. For example,

government's filing, lends D an additional $10,000. SP will have priority over the government for both the original loan and the advance.[51] If SP had made the advance on June 30, more than 45 days after the tax-lien filing, the government would have had priority as to the advance (but not the original loan). The fact that SP was still without actual notice or knowledge when it made the advance on June 30 would be irrelevant. The period of protection for future advances never exceeds 45 days, and actual notice or knowledge shortens it. The only way for a secured party making a series of future advances to be perfectly safe is to check for tax-lien filings every 45 days.

Article 9 operates somewhat differently. Again, assume SP has a perfected security interest in D's equipment as security for a $10,000 loan and the security agreement has a future-advances clause. On May 1, L, an erstwhile unsecured creditor that has obtained a judgment against D, has the sheriff levy on the equipment. On May 31, SP, which does not have knowledge[52] of the levy, makes an advance. SP will have priority over L for both the original loan and the advance. The result would be the same if SP had knowledge of the levy, because Article 9 protects all advances made during the 45-day period without regard to knowledge. Even if the advance was made on June 30, SP would have priority if it still lacked knowledge of the levy. In short, the tax laws protect future advances for 45 days at most and perhaps for a shorter period; Article 9 protects such advances for at least 45 days and perhaps longer.[53]

The second exception to the choateness doctrine applies to after-acquired property clauses.[54] The exception applies to "commercial transactions financing agreements,"[55] meaning agreements entered into by lenders to make loans to taxpayers secured by "commercial financing security."[56]

---

suppose a secured party does not know that the government has a tax lien but learns from a reliable source that the government has padlocked the debtor's plant. This information ought to constitute actual notice, and a future advance made after acquiring such information will be subordinate to the tax lien. *Cf.* U.C.C. § 1-202(a) (defining notice).

[51] Without I.R.C. § 6323(d), the secured party would have priority as to its original loan (it was perfected before the tax-lien notice was filed), but its security interest would be inchoate with respect to the advance.

[52] Article 9 does not use the term "actual notice."

[53] The discussion of this area would not be complete without a reference to U.C.C. § 9-323, which provides a "forty-five day or less" rule for future advances made after a buyer or lessee not in ordinary course of business purchases the collateral. U.C.C. §§ 9-323(d), (e) (buyer); 9-323(f), (g) (lessee). *See* § 11.03[A][3] *supra*. *See also* § 9-323(a), which provides for unlimited priority for future advances against another secured party. *See* § 10.02 *supra*.

[54] I.R.C. § 6323(c). This provision also applies to a limited class of obligatory future-advances clauses.

[55] I.R.C. § 6323(c)(1)(A)(i). The provision also applies to real property construction or improvement financing agreements and to obligatory disbursement agreements. I.R.C. § 6323(c)(1)(A)(ii), (iii). Discussion of these agreements is beyond the scope of this book.

[56] I.R.C. § 6323(c)(2)(A). The lender must make the loan in ordinary course of business and the taxpayer must acquire the commercial financing security in ordinary course of business. This section of the Tax Lien Act also applies to certain agreements to purchase commercial financing security (other than inventory) from the taxpayer. This is roughly analogous to, although somewhat broader than, Article 9's coverage of sales of certain intangibles.

Commercial financing security in turn means paper of a kind ordinarily arising in commercial transactions, accounts receivable, mortgages on real property, and inventory. If a secured party has a written security agreement with the taxpayer that covers commercial-financing security, including after-acquired assets, and its security interest is protected under state law from a judgment lien arising out of an unsecured obligation (meaning that it is properly perfected before the government files its notice), it will have priority over the government as to commercial-financing security acquired by the taxpayer before the 46th day following tax-lien filing.[57] As with the future-advances exception discussed above, the period during which the secured party can obtain priority for after-acquired property terminates early if the secured party acquires knowledge or actual notice of the tax-lien filing.

As with the exception for future advances, the only sure way for a secured party to protect itself is by checking for tax-lien filings every 45 days. If such a filing is discovered during a search (or otherwise comes to the attention of the secured party), the secured party should move immediately to repossess its collateral. If it allows the debtor to retain the collateral beyond the protected period (45 days or less), it will later have to prove what collateral was in the debtor's hands when the period ended or it will face the inchoateness problem described in connection with the *Rice Investment Co.* case.

---

[57] Old Nat'l Bank v. RH Elec. Sys., Inc., 2005 WL 435479, 56 U.C.C. Rep. Serv. 2d 468 (S.D. Ind. 2005) (by filing tax liens in November 1999 and March 2000, the U.S. had priority over the bank's claim to after-acquired accounts that arose between August and November 2000); American Inv. Fin. v. U.S., 364 F. Supp.2d 1321, 57 U.C.C. Rep. Serv. 2d 94 (D. Utah 2005) (IRS liens had priority over the lender's security interest in health-care-insurance receivables for services that were performed outside the 45-day safe harbor provision, even though the contracts that gave rise to the receivables pre-dated the tax liens).

Chapter 14

PURCHASERS (OTHER THAN SECURED PARTIES) AND LIEN CREDITORS VERSUS UNPERFECTED SECURED PARTIES

SYNOPSIS

§ 14.01 ARTICLE 9's RESIDUAL PRIORITY RULE — § 9-201(a)

Article 9 contains a residual rule that renders a security interest — even one that is unperfected — effective against the debtor, purchasers from the debtor, and creditors of the debtor.[1] This rule is subject to numerous exceptions that subordinate unperfected security interests to the rights of competing claimants, and the ensuing sections of this chapter examine those exceptions. If there is no exception, however, the residual rule becomes the rule of decision.[2]

---

[1] U.C.C. § 9-201(a).

[2] Richard McCluhan Assocs., Inc. v. Shari Candies, Inc., 2005 WL 2130214, 57 U.C.C. Rep. Serv. 2d 988 (Minn. Ct. App. 2005) (unpublished) (perfected secured party in the debtor's assets had priority over a general creditor that continued to provide services on account despite the debtor's financial distress; equitable principles could not alter the priority because the secured creditor did not have any role in inducing the extension of further services).

§ 14.02 LIEN CREDITORS

[A] General Rule — § 9-317(a)(2)

Article 9 includes rules that establish priority between a secured party and a lien creditor.[3] The term "lien creditor" means "(A) a creditor that has acquired a lien on the property involved by attachment, levy, or the like; (B) an assignee for benefit of creditors from the time of the assignment; (C) a trustee in bankruptcy from the date of the filing of the petition; or (D) a receiver in equity from the time of appointment."[4] "Lien creditor" is misleading[5] because Article 9 also refers to parties with liens that do not fall within the term's definition. A secured party's security interest is a lien, for example, but it is consensual in nature and therefore secured parties are not Article 9 lien creditors. A creditor may also have a lien arising by operation of a common-law or statutory rule,[6] but again such creditors are not lien creditors. The common element among parties that qualify as lien creditors is that their liens arise as the result of a judicial or quasi-judicial proceeding. The most important lien creditor, the trustee in bankruptcy, is covered extensively in Chapter 16.[7]

Next in order of importance is an initially unsecured creditor that acquires lien-creditor status through levy or a similar process. Suppose, for example, Seller sells hard drives to Debtor, a computer manufacturer, on unsecured credit. This transaction is governed by Article 2 of the U.C.C. Because it is a sale, Debtor acquires title to the drives.[8] Calling it an unsecured sale on credit tells us that Seller chose to convey title without retaining any property interest in the drives. In effect, Seller traded the drives for a legally enforceable promise to pay the contract price. If Debtor fails to pay the price as it becomes due, Seller cannot repossess the drives.[9] Instead, Seller must file suit against Debtor claiming breach of contract. After recovering a judgment, Seller is entitled to use the state's debt-collection procedures. These procedures are called the "execution" process.

Missouri's execution process is typical and is used here for illustrative purposes. Seller's judgment entitles it to apply to the court clerk for a writ of execution,[10] which is an order directing the sheriff to levy on Debtor's

---

[3] U.C.C. § 9-317(a)(2).

[4] U.C.C. § 9-102(a)(52).

[5] The term was labeled "gibberish" by one scholar. Mellinkoff, *The Language of the Uniform Commercial Code*, 77 Yale L.J. 185 (1967).

[6] *See* Chapter 13 *supra*.

[7] *See* § 16.01[C] *infra*.

[8] *See* U.C.C. §§ 2-106(1) ("sale" means passing title from seller to buyer for a price); 2-401(2) (unless otherwise agreed, title passes to buyer on physical delivery of goods).

[9] U.C.C. § 2-702 creates a limited exception to this rule. Seller can reclaim the drives *in specie* if Debtor was insolvent on the delivery date and Seller demands their return within ten days thereafter (or a longer reasonable time if Debtor misrepresented its solvency in writing during the three months preceding delivery).

[10] Rule 76.01, Mo. R. Civ. P.

assets. In effect, the sheriff acts as Seller's agent for purposes of satisfying the judgment. "Levy" means to take into legal custody and, in the case of tangible goods capable of being moved, requires physical seizure by the sheriff.[11] Note that a writ of execution allows levy on *any* of the debtor's assets.[12] The drives may be subjected to levy, but Seller has no more (or less) right to have the sheriff levy on them than it has to have the sheriff levy on any other particular asset, including real estate. The act of levy confers on the sheriff a power of sale,[13] and any proceeds derived from the execution sale will (after paying the sheriff's expenses) go to Seller in full or partial satisfaction of the judgment. The act of levy also creates a lien in favor of Seller and converts Seller into an Article 9 lien creditor.[14]

Under the "first-in-time, first-in-right" rule, a lien on assets acquired by levy gives the lien creditor priority over persons that acquire property interests in those assets subsequent to their seizure by the sheriff, but it does not give priority over existing property interests. The U.C.C. contains an exception to this rule, providing that an unperfected security interest is subordinate to the rights of a subsequent lien creditor.[15] The practical effect of granting priority to the lien creditor is that an unperfected security interest in the collateral will be extinguished by the sheriff's execution sale.[16] Had the security interest been perfected prior to the sheriff's levy, the secured party would have had priority, and thus its security interest would have remained enforceable against the collateral in the hands of the execution-sale purchaser.

In certain cases, Article 9 gives a secured party priority even though it did not have a perfected security interest at the time a competing claimant became a lien creditor.[17] A secured party will prevail if, before the claimant

---

[11] Rule 76.06, Mo. R. Civ. P. Different procedures are prescribed for levy on other types of assets. If an asset is in the custody or under the control of a third person, levy requires that the person be served with a writ of garnishment. Rule 90.01 *et seq.*, Mo. R. Civ. P.

[12] Certain assets can be claimed by a judgment debtor as exempt, meaning that they can be placed beyond the reach of an executing creditor. *See generally* Mo. Rev. Stat. § 513.430 (list of exemptions), Rule 76.075, Mo. R. Civ. P. (procedure for claiming exemptions). Each state has its own list of exempt property.

[13] The procedures to be employed at an execution sale are set forth in Rule 76.18, Mo. R. Civ. P.

[14] Rule 76.07, Mo. R. Civ. P. In limited circumstances, levy may proceed from an attachment rather than an execution. Rule 85.0 *et seq.*, Mo. R. Civ. P. Attachment, an ancillary process used in conjunction with a creditor's suit for a money judgment, permits levy prior to judgment. Assets subjected to an attachment levy are held *in custodia legis* pending the outcome of the litigation. If the creditor recovers a money judgment, the assets are sold at an execution sale. For purposes of Article 9, the creditor becomes a lien creditor at the moment of levy.

[15] U.C.C. § 9-317(a)(2)(A). *See* Citibank, N.A. v. Prime Motor Inns Ltd. Partnership, 98 N.Y.2d 743, 750 N.Y.S.2d 818, 780 N.E.2d 503, 49 U.C.C. Rep. Serv. 2d 934 (2002) (because the bank levied upon a $500,000 lawsuit settlement by initiating a turnover proceeding shortly before the secured creditor filed its financing statement, the bank had priority).

[16] It is axiomatic that junior interests are eliminated by foreclosure sales, including execution sales and Article 9 foreclosure sales. *See* § 18.02[E] *infra.* Any excess from the execution sale is a proceed to which the junior interests attach automatically. *See* § 2.03[B] *supra.*

[17] U.C.C. § 9-317(a)(2)(B).

becomes a lien creditor, the secured party satisfies one of the conditions of section 9-203(b)(3) and also files a financing statement covering the collateral. For example, a secured party that has the debtor authenticate a security agreement[18] and files a financing statement will have priority over a subsequent lien creditor even though perfection cannot not occur until the secured party later extends value to the debtor.[19] By contrast, the secured party would have lost if it had merely filed the financing statement before the lien creditor's interest arose. The purpose of this provision is to treat the initial advance of value by the secured party the same as any subsequent advance.[20]

[B]   Purchase-Money Security Interest — § 9-317(e)

Article 9 includes an exception to the general rule that allows a secured party to prevail even though it perfects after a lien creditor's interest attaches to the goods that serve as the secured party's collateral. Section 9-317(e) provides:

> [I]f a person files a financing statement with respect to a purchase-money security interest before or within 20 days after the debtor receives delivery of the collateral, the security interest takes priority over the rights of a buyer, lessee, or lien creditor which arise between the time the security interest attaches and the time of filing.[21]

This provision operates only in favor of a purchase-money secured party.[22] Its primary rationale is to facilitate secured sales[23] by allowing buyers to take delivery without sellers first having to file financing statements.[24] If a lien creditor's interest arises shortly after delivery, a diligent secured party should not suffer a loss of priority because it has a twenty-day grace period during which to perfect and still attain priority.[25] A lien creditor

---

[18] U.C.C. § 9-203(b)(3)(A).

[19] U.C.C. §§ 9-308(a), 9-203(b)(1).

[20] U.C.C. § 9-317, Comment 4. A secured party's rights in future advances as against a lien creditor are discussed in § 13.03 *supra* and § 14.02[C] *infra*.

[21] This provision is subject to §§ 9-320 and 9-321. U.C.C. § 9-317(e).

[22] *See* § 1.05 *supra*. Purchase-money security interests exist only with respect to goods and associated software, if any. *See* § 10.04[A] *supra*.

[23] Although the rule was adopted to protect sellers, it applies to all purchase-money secured parties.

[24] *In re* Moore, 7 U.C.C. Rep. Serv. 578 (Bankr. C.D. Me. 1969) (provisions concerned only with allowing retroactive priority during the applicable grace period); *In re* Estergaard, 2006 WL 936173, 59 U.C.C. Rep. Serv. 2d 660 (Bankr. D. Colo. 2006) (because § 9-317(e) applies to financing statements, and because the Colorado certificate of title act (unlike the acts in some other states) does not permit perfection by notation on the certificate of title to relate back to the creation of the lien, the secured party was not perfected when the debtor filed for bankruptcy between the time of the purchase of the car and the filing of the certificate of title noting the security interest).

[25] Secured sellers do not ordinarily file financing statements before goods have been deliv-

is not prejudiced unduly because it does not rely upon the absence of a filed financing statement in attaching its lien to property in the debtor's possession. [26]

This purchase-money exception is comparable to the noninventory purchase-money exception to the "first-to-file-or-perfect" priority rule that governs conflicting security interests in the same collateral. [27] The latter exception protects a purchase-money secured party that perfects during the grace period from a prior-perfected secured party with an after-acquired security interest in the same collateral, as well as a secured party whose interest attaches during the grace period and which perfects before the purchase-money secured party perfects.

[C] Future Advances — § 9-323(b)

Although this chapter deals generally with the rights of unperfected secured parties, it bears noting briefly that Article 9 also contains a provision that governs priority between a perfected security interest that extends to future advances pursuant to the terms of the security agreement [28] and the interest of a lien creditor. Under this provision, the lien creditor takes subject to the security interest only to the extent that it secures advances made (1) before the lien creditor's interest arises, (2) within 45 days after the lien creditor's interest arises, even if the secured party knows of that interest at the time it makes the advance, (3) more than 45 days after the lien creditor's interest arises, if made without knowledge of that interest, or (4) pursuant to a commitment entered into at any time, so long as the commitment was made without knowledge of the lien creditor's interest. [29] The absolute protection afforded the secured party for the initial 45-day period was included to protect security interests against liens arising under the Federal Tax Lien Act of 1966, and the future-advances rule is discussed more fully in that context. [30]

---

ered. Thus, the Code selects the buyer's receipt of possession as the triggering date for the grace period even though attachment of the security interest may have occurred earlier. *See, e.g.,* U.C.C. §§ 2-501(1) (buyer obtains rights in goods — a "special property interest" — upon their identification to a contract for sale); 1-204(4) (value includes any consideration sufficient to support a simple contract). A filing before the end of the grace period defeats any lien creditor whose rights arise between the time of attachment and the time of filing.

[26] Compliance with a certificate-of-title statute "for obtaining priority over the rights of a lien creditor is equivalent to the filing of a financing statement under this article." U.C.C. § 9-311(b). As a result, a party that takes a purchase-money security interest in an automobile and properly perfects by compliance with the certificate-of-title statute will attain relation-back priority under section 9-317(e). Some state certificate-of-title laws expand the grace period by giving secured parties 25 or even 30 days following attachment in which to perfect and still obtain relation-back priority.

[27] *See* § 10.04[A] *supra.*

[28] Future advances clauses are discussed generally in § 3.03 *supra.*

[29] U.C.C. § 9-323(b).

[30] *See* § 13.03 *supra.*

§ 14.03 OTHER PURCHASERS

[A] General Rules — § 9-317(b)–(d)

Section 9-317(b) states that, except as provided in the exception dealing with purchase-money security interests,[31] "a buyer, other than a secured party, of tangible chattel paper, documents, goods, instruments, or a certificated security takes free of a security interest or agricultural lien if the buyer gives value and receives delivery of the collateral without knowledge of the security interest or agricultural lien and before it is perfected."[32] Although the provision seems somewhat unwieldy, it is crafted to correlate with other Article 9 priority provisions. Careful dissection of the language readily reveals the focus of the priorities it covers.

Section 9-317(b) covers conflicts over goods, instruments, documents, tangible chattel paper, and security certificates. Because a buyer under this provision can prevail only by taking delivery of the property, the section can apply only in cases in which delivery is possible. Accordingly, the section is limited to goods and to forms of indispensable paper. Section 9-317(d) deals with buyers of intangibles (*i.e.*, collateral incapable of being delivered).[33] Section 9-317(c) provides a similar rule for lessees of goods that receive delivery.

A person that qualifies as a buyer of goods in ordinary course of business and buys from the debtor that created the security interest takes free of that interest without regard to either perfection or the buyer's knowledge of the security interest.[34] In addition, certain buyers of instruments, documents and chattel paper are entitled to priority over even a perfected secured party.[35] Section 9-317(b) thus addresses the rights of a buyer not protected under other provisions: (1) a buyer of goods that does not buy in ordinary course of business; (2) a buyer of goods in ordinary course of business whose seller did not create the security interest; or (3) a buyer of an instrument, document, tangible chattel paper, or certificated security not entitled to priority over a perfected secured party.

---

[31] *See* U.C.C. § 9-317(e) and § 14.02[B] *supra*.

[32] Buyers of tangible chattel paper and promissory notes are secured parties if their transaction of purchase is governed by Article 9. Thus, U.C.C. § 9-317(b) applies only if the transaction of purchase is not excluded from the scope of Article 9. *See* U.C.C. § 9-109(d)(4)-(7), discussed in § 1.07[F][1] *supra*. *See also* U.C.C. § 1-201(b)(35) (definition of security interest includes interest of "buyer of accounts, chattel paper, a payment intangible, and a promissory note *in a transaction that is subject to Article 9*" [emphasis supplied]); § 10.01 note 18.

[33] In 1972, all securities were represented by certificates, U.C.C. § 8-102(1) (1962 Official Text), and qualified as instruments for purposes of Article 9, U.C.C. § 9-105(1)(I) (1972 Official Text). Securities were removed to the category "investment property" in 1994, and "certificated securities" became a subcategory. Certificated securities are indispensable paper; other types of investment property are intangibles. Article 9 continues to recognize this distinction. *See* U.C.C. §§ 9-317(b) (section dealing with buyers that receive delivery includes certificated securities); 9-317(d) (section dealing with buyers that do not receive delivery includes investment property other than certificated securities). *See generally* § 1.04[E] *supra*.

[34] U.C.C. § 9-320(a).

[35] *See* § 11.03[C], [D] *supra*.

To prevail under section 9-317(b), a buyer must both give value and receive delivery of the collateral without knowledge of a security interest and before it is perfected.[36] A buyer that qualifies is a type of bona-fide purchaser for value — albeit one that does not meet all the requirements set forth in other sections for priority over perfected security interests. Such buyers are presumed to rely on the Code's filing system and are protected from secured parties that fail to give notice in that system.[37]

Section 9-317(d) includes a comparable provision that applies to buyers of accounts, electronic chattel paper, general intangibles, and investment property other than certificated securities. Because these types of property are intangible, the requirement that the buyer take delivery in order to prevail is deleted as irrelevant. Otherwise, the requirements for the buyer to prevail are identical to the requirements in section 9-317(b): The buyer cannot be a secured party[38] and must give value without knowledge of the security interest and before it is perfected.

Section 9-317 also deals with the rights of lessees of goods and licensees of general intangibles (other than lessees and licensees in ordinary course of business).[39] The rights of lessees and licensees are similar to the rights of buyers. A lessee of goods takes free of a security interest or agricultural lien[40] if the lessee gives value and takes delivery before perfection and without knowledge of the interest or lien.[41] A licensee of a general intangible must give value before the security interest is perfected and need only lack knowledge at the time value is given to obtain priority.[42] This provision

---

[36] Chase Manhattan Bank, N.A. v. J & L General Contractors, Inc., 832 S.W.2d 204, 18 U.C.C. Rep. Serv. 2d 1286 (Tex. Ct. App. 1992) (purchaser was buyer not in ordinary course that gave value and received delivery of goods with no knowledge of creditor's security interest); Case Credit Corp. v. Barry Equip. Co., Inc., 2005 WL 705113 (Mass. Super. Ct. 2005) (court rejected buyer's argument that the security interest itself became ineffectual when the perfection by the financing statement lapsed; material issue of fact presented as to whether the buyer had knowledge of the security interest at the time that it received possession of the collateral).

[37] The only method of perfection contemplated by this section is filing a financing statement. If the secured party perfected by possession or control, the buyer could not take delivery and therefore could not prevail. Further, the Code has separate rules protecting consumer buyers of consumer goods from purchase-money secured parties that rely on automatic perfection, U.C.C. § 9-320(b), and protecting buyers that rely on clean certificates of title from secured parties that perfect as to goods covered by certificates of title. U.C.C. § 9-337(1).

[38] In the case of accounts, electronic chattel paper, and general intangibles that qualify as payment intangibles, the buyer will be a secured party unless the transaction of purchase is excluded from the scope of Article 9. See discussion in note 32 supra.

[39] As might be expected, a lessee or licensee in ordinary course of business takes free of a perfected security interest created by the lessor or licensor even if the lessee or licensee knows of its existence. U.C.C. §§ 9-321(c) (lessee), 9-321(b) (licensee). See also §§ 9-321(a) (defining licensee in ordinary course of business), 2A-103(1)(o) (defining lessee in ordinary course of business). See also § 11.03 supra.

[40] Agricultural liens are effective only as to farm products, U.C.C. § 9-102(a)(5), and thus lessees are unlikely.

[41] U.C.C. § 9-317(c).

[42] U.C.C. § 9-317(d).

is of particular importance in that most software, a general intangible under Article 9,[43] is licensed rather than sold.

[B]   Purchase-Money Security Interests — § 9-317(e)

As is the case with lien creditors,[44] there is a purchase-money exception to the general rule that protects secured parties from buyers and lessees whose rights arise between the time the security interest attaches and the time the secured party perfects by filing.[45] For example, suppose Seller sells a computer (for business use) to Buyer on credit and retains a purchase-money security interest in it. If Buyer resells the computer to Purchaser, who gives value and takes delivery before Seller files a financing statement, Purchaser will nevertheless take subject to Seller's interest if the filing occurs during the grace period. Unlike lien creditors, buyers and lessees generally rely on the filing system, and to avoid the harsh effects of the relation-back rule, they must ask appropriate questions of, and receive truthful answers from, their vendors.

[C]   Future Advances — § 9-323(d)–(g)

As is the case with lien creditors,[46] Article 9 includes provisions that govern priority between a perfected security interest that extends to future advances pursuant to the terms of the security agreement and the interests of buyers and lessees. A buyer or lessee of goods takes free of the security interest to the extent that the secured party makes advances either with knowledge of the purchase or more than 45 days after it occurs, unless the advance is made pursuant to a commitment entered into without knowledge of the purchase and before the expiration of the 45-day period.[47] A buyer in ordinary course of business that takes free of a security interest under Section 9-320, and a lessee in ordinary course of business that takes free under Section 9-321, are not subject to future advances. A secured party's right to priority in future advances as against a buyer or lessee is discussed in greater detail elsewhere in this book.[48]

§ 14.04   CLAIMANTS NOT EXPRESSLY GOVERNED BY ARTICLE 9

Article 9 contains rules that explicitly govern priority contests between a secured party and a purchaser, a lien creditor, another secured party, and certain persons with liens that arise by operation of law. This list by no means exhausts the types of persons that may claim a competing

---

[43] U.C.C. § 9-102(a)(42). *See also* § 9-102(a)(75) (defining software).

[44] *See* § 14.02[B] *supra.*

[45] U.C.C. § 9-317(e).

[46] *See* § 14.02[C] *supra.*

[47] U.C.C. § 9-323(d), (e) (buyers), and § 9-323(f), (g) (lessees).

[48] *See* § 11.03[A][3] *supra.*

interest. If the adverse claimant does not fall within one of the articulated categories, the court must decide between resolving the contest under the Code's residual priority rule[49] or resolving it by application of rules derived from the common law or equity.[50] If the residual priority rule is applied, the secured party prevails regardless of perfection. The outcome is less certain when non-Code rules are applied.

For example, suppose Finance Company, which has a security interest in Debtor's inventory, permits Debtor to retain cash proceeds from the sale of inventory and to commingle those proceeds with other funds in its general operating account, which is maintained at Bank. Suppose further that Debtor owes money to Bank and is in default on its obligation. Under the common law, Bank has a right of "setoff" — a right to seize the funds in the account and apply them to reduce the outstanding indebtedness to Bank. Who will have priority if Bank seizes funds in which Finance Company claims an interest, either as identifiable proceeds of its inventory collateral[51] or by virtue of a direct security interest in the deposit account itself?[52]

Finance Company will, of course, assert the residual priority rule. In deciding whether to apply that rule as the rule of decision, the court must first determine whether the express provisions of Article 9 *preclude* its application. Assume that the security interest is a proceeds interest. Article 9 excludes a right of setoff from its scope.[53] If this excludes from coverage every aspect of a contest involving the exercise of setoff, then the residual rule is inapplicable. Most courts have interpreted the exclusion narrowly, however, to mean simply that a bank need not enter into a security agreement with its depositor to have a right of setoff.[54] In other words, the exclusion merely affirms that Bank's right of setoff arises under the

---

[49] U.C.C. § 9-201(a), discussed in § 14.01 *supra*.

[50] *See* U.C.C. § 1-103(b) (unless preempted, common-law and equitable rules applicable).

[51] U.C.C. § 9-315(a)(2). *See generally* William H. Henning, *Article 9's Treatment of Commingled Cash Proceeds in Noninsolvency Cases*, 35 Ark. L. Rev. 191 (Winter 1982).

Setoff is only one method by which a depositary bank can gain control of deposited funds. An advantage of setoff is that it is a self-help remedy that can be implemented without the cooperation of the debtor (depositor). If the debtor will cooperate, the bank will be better off having the funds in the account paid to it voluntarily. When cash proceeds in a deposit account are paid to a transferee, the transferee takes free of any security interest in the proceeds unless the transfer is a fraudulent conveyance or is in some other respect a collusive attempt to defraud the secured party. U.C.C. § 9-332. Further, if the funds are paid by check the transferee may qualify as a holder in due course and thereby defeat the security interest. U.C.C. § 9-331. The rights of holders in due course are discussed in § 11.03[D] *supra*.

[52] A security interest cannot be taken in a deposit account in a consumer transaction. U.C.C. § 9-109(d)(13) (narrowing exclusion from Article 9 to assignments of deposit accounts in consumer transactions). Even in a consumer transaction, a secured party can attempt to trace proceeds into a deposit account. *Id.*

[53] U.C.C. § 9-109(d)(10).

[54] *See, e.g.,* Citizens Nat'l Bank of Whitley Cty. v. Mid-States Dev. Co., 177 Ind. App. 548, 380 N.E.2d 1243, 3 A.L.R.4th 987, 24 U.C.C. Rep. Serv. 1321 (1978); Insley Mfg. Corp. v. Draper Bank & Trust, 717 P.2d 1341, 1 U.C.C. Rep. Serv. 2d 961 (Utah 1986).

common law and is not a security interest under Article 9. Courts that interpret the exclusion narrowly grant priority to the secured party under the residual rule. A few courts have interpreted the exclusion broadly to remove all issues involving setoff, including priority issues, from the scope of Article 9.[55]

Perhaps the best discussion of the issues can be found in *National Acceptance Co. of Virginia v. Virginia Capital Bank,*[56] where a federal district court was called upon to resolve a dispute under Virginia law. Because Virginia's courts had not ruled on the proper interpretation of the exclusion for rights of setoff, the district court gave alternative analyses. Under a narrow interpretation, the party claiming a security interest in the deposited funds would prevail under Article 9's residual rule. Under a broad interpretation, resolution would turn on non-Code law. The court found that the non-Code law of Virginia follows the majority rule that a bank exercising setoff is subordinate to an adverse claimant if it knows or has reason to know of the claimant's interest.[57] Because the evidence indicated that the bank had (at a minimum) notice of the secured party's interest, the court concluded that the secured party would prevail under either a narrow or broad interpretation.

Assume now that the interest of the secured party in the funds on deposit in the general operating account is a nonproceeds interest in a deposit account. A security interest in a deposit account must be perfected by control.[58] In the case of a deposit account maintained at a bank that is not the secured party, this requires the secured party to obtain a control agreement or to become the customer with respect to the account.[59] If the secured party perfects by a control agreement, it is vulnerable to the maintaining bank's exercise of set-off[60] unless the control agreement provides for subordination of the set-off right.[61] If the secured party becomes the customer with respect to the account, it has priority over the maintaining bank's right of set-off.[62]

A bank exercising setoff is but one example of a third party whose rights may not be expressly governed by the provisions of Article 9. In each such instance, the court must decide whether to confer priority on the secured

---

[55] *See, e.g.*, State Bank of Rose Creek v. First Bank of Austin, 320 N.W.2d 723, 33 U.C.C. Rep. Serv. 1755 (Minn. 1982).

[56] 498 F. Supp. 1078, 30 U.C.C. Rep. Serv. 1145 (E.D. Va. 1980).

[57] The majority rule is sometimes referred to as the "legal" rule. Under the minority (or "equitable") rule, a third-party claimant has priority even if the bank exercising setoff lacks knowledge or notice.

[58] U.C.C. §§ 9-312(b)(1), 9-314(a), 9-104. Control of deposit accounts is discussed generally in § 6.04[B] *supra*.

[59] U.C.C. § 9-104(2), (3).

[60] U.C.C. § 9-340(a).

[61] Parties can alter the Code's normal priority rules through a subordination agreement. U.C.C. § 9-339.

[62] U.C.C. § 9-340(c).

party through application of the residual rule or to decide the case based on the non-Code law of the state.

Chapter 15

FIXTURES, ACCESSIONS AND COMMINGLED GOODS

SYNOPSIS

§ 15.01   FIXTURES DEFINED — § 9-102(a)(41)

The U.C.C. defines "fixtures" as goods that have become so related to a particular parcel of land that an interest in them arises under real estate law.[1] Thus, although Article 9 establishes a complex system of perfection and priority for security interests in fixtures, it leaves the basic definition

---

[1] U.C.C. § 9-102(a)(41).

of "fixtures" to non-Code law. Under real estate law, a "fixture" is an item of personalty that is so affixed to land (or to a structure on land) that a purchaser of the land[2] would believe that title to the item would pass with a deed to the land. By virtue of this affixation, however, a fixture does not lose its separate identity such that it becomes merged into the realty for all purposes. As a result, a creditor may obtain an Article 9 security interest in a fixture (either prior to or after its affixation),[3] and a fixture may be removed from the realty and sold as goods at an Article 9 foreclosure sale.[4] In other words, a fixture has attributes associated with both realty and personalty.

Courts use a facts-and-circumstances test to determine whether a particular asset qualifies as a fixture, typically focusing upon three elements: (1) the intent of the annexor,[5] (2) the degree of physical affixation to the realty, and (3) the degree to which the asset is adapted to the particular characteristics of the real estate.[6] The first factor — the intent of the annexor — is important in disputes between a secured party and the party that owned the land at the time of affixation,[7] but courts largely ignore this factor in disputes between a secured party and a subsequent purchaser of the land. In deciding whether to buy or lend against the land, a purchaser typically will have relied upon the appearance that the fixture was part of the land, and the reasonable expectations of the purchaser outweigh the hidden intentions of the annexor. Accordingly, in most disputes involving whether a good constitutes a fixture, the issue turns on the degree of affixation and adaptation. A good that is plugged into the wall is "affixed" to the land, but a court is not likely characterize that good as a fixture. If a couple of screws connect a good to the land to keep it from vibrating, it may or may not be a fixture. If the good is so extensively attached to or embedded in the land that it cannot be removed without intensive labor, the good is almost certainly a fixture. Adaptation comes into play if the physical connection between the good and the land is slight, but the good has been specially designed to fit into a particular area.[8] For example, drapes that are loosely attached but are specifically designed for a particular room may qualify as fixtures.[9]

---

[2] Under both the Code and real estate law, the term "purchase" includes any voluntary transaction that creates or transfers an interest in property. As a result, the term "purchaser" of the land would include both buyers and mortgagees. *See* U.C.C. §§ 1-201(b)(29), 1-201(b)(30).

[3] To acquire a security interest in an item that is a fixture, or might become a fixture, the secured party must satisfy the basic requirements for attachment in section 9-203.

[4] *See* § 15.04 *infra*.

[5] The "annexor" is the person affixing the asset to the land.

[6] *See, e.g., In re* MBA Poultry, L.L.C., 291 F.3d 528, 47 U.C.C. Rep. Serv. 2d 1488 (8th Cir. 2002) (stainless steel superstructure in bird-processing plant satisfied all three criteria).

[7] If the asset would not be a fixture in a contest between the annexor and the owner of the land, it should not be a fixture if the secured party is asserting its rights against the owner.

[8] *See, e.g., In re* Sand & Sage Farm & Ranch, Inc., 266 B.R. 507, 45 U.C.C. Rep. Serv. 2d 910 (Bankr. D. Kan. 2001) (pivot irrigation system constituted fixture; need for system in semi-arid conditions of western Kansas demonstrated relation between goods and use of land).

[9] *See, e.g.,* Sears, Roebuck & Co. v. Seven Palms Motor Inn, 530 S.W.2d 695 (Mo. 1975). The concept of adaptation is sometimes called "constructive annexation."

Certain goods become so embedded in land that they lose their individual identity and become part of the land for all purposes. Many houses, for example, are technically movable[10] in that they can be lifted from their foundations; nevertheless, courts typically characterize a house as pure real estate and not as a fixture.[11] Likewise, real estate law considers most ordinary building materials that have been incorporated into a structure — such as mortar, paint, or lumber — to be pure realty. Real estate law does not treat such materials as fixtures because they are unlikely to retain their physical integrity or their value if removed from the land.

Conceptually, some ordinary building materials might qualify as fixtures under non-Code law, but policy suggests that they should not be subject to an Article 9 security interest. For example, bricks used to build a house might have significant value if removed from the house, but no Article 9 secured party should be allowed to remove the bricks because doing so would destroy the economic value of the house. Although removing a fixture often requires the secured party to inflict some physical damage to the land and often decreases the land's fair market value, it would be wasteful to allow a secured party to disassemble a structure piecemeal and thereby destroy its capacity to carry out the basic functions for which it was designed. Accordingly, Article 9 precludes parties from taking a security interest in ordinary building materials that have been incorporated into an improvement, regardless of their classification under real estate law.[12] The distinction is more theoretical than practical. Ordinary building materials that are so incorporated will almost certainly be classified as pure realty under non-Code state law.[13]

§ 15.02 FIXTURE FILINGS — § 9-102(a)(40)

A secured party may take a security interest in a fixture, but a buyer of the land would expect to become the owner of the fixture and a mortgagee would expect the fixture to serve as collateral for a mortgage loan. Because of the potential conflict between a secured party with an interest in the fixture as personalty and one or more parties with an interest in the fixture as realty, the filing system should provide for notice of a fixture interest to be placed in the chain of title to the land. Article 9 facilitates this notice through the concept of a "fixture filing." A fixture filing is a financing statement that covers goods that "are or are to become fixtures" and that satisfies both the general requirements for the sufficiency of a financing statement and the specific requirements for the sufficiency of a real-estate

---

[10] "Goods" are "all things that are movable when the security interest attaches," and specifically includes fixtures. U.C.C. § 9-102(a)(44).

[11] Smaller structures such as sheds may qualify as goods.

[12] U.C.C. § 9-334(a).

[13] An unpaid supplier of building materials typically acquires a mechanic's lien, giving it a right to foreclose on the land (as opposed to any specific materials). The creation and enforcement of mechanics' liens varies from state to state and is thus beyond the scope of this book.

related financing statement.[14] To be sufficient as a fixture filing,[15] the statement must:

- indicate that it covers goods that are fixtures or are to become fixtures,[16]

- indicate that it is to be filed in the real property records,[17]

- provide a description of the real property to which the collateral is related,[18] and

- if the debtor does not have an interest of record in the real property, provide the name of a record owner of the land.[19]

As one might expect, the Code dictates that fixture filings be made in the office in which a mortgage on the underlying land would be recorded.[20] In other words, to serve as a fixture filing, an ordinary financing statement must be adapted to serve the functions of the real estate recording system.[21] To do so, the filing officer must have the name of at least one record owner of the land. Many (but not all) priority contests turn on whether the secured party has made a timely fixture filing.

---

[14] U.C.C. § 9-102(a)(40) (" 'Fixture filing' means the filing of a financing statement covering goods that are or are to become fixtures and satisfying Section 9-502(a) and (b).").

[15] Allied Mut. Ins. Co. v. Midplains Waste Management, L.L.C., 612 N.W.2d 488, 42 U.C.C. Rep. Serv. 2d 296 (Neb. 2000) (financing statement ineffective as fixture filing because it did not include required information).

[16] U.C.C. § 9-502(b)(1).

[17] U.C.C. § 9-502(b)(3). Because most jurisdictions provide for local (e.g., county, district, parish or town) recording of real estate interests, the secured party will typically file a fixture filing in the recording office in the locality where the relevant land (i.e., the land to which the goods are or are to be affixed) is located. U.C.C. § 9-501(a)(1)(B).

Article 9 contains special provisions allowing a security interest in the real estate-related assets of a transmitting utility to be perfected by a single, central filing that has the effect of a fixture filing and that remains effective until a termination statement is filed. The rationale is that many utilities span large parts of a state and that the normal fixture filing rules would require filings in multiple counties. See U.C.C. §§ 9-102(a)(80) (defining "transmitting utility"); 9-501(b) (central filing operates as a fixture filing); 9-515(f) (duration of filing).

[18] U.C.C. § 9-502(b)(3). The description of the land is sufficient for purposes of a fixture filing if it would be sufficient to give constructive notice to subsequent purchasers of the land if used in a recorded mortgage.

[19] U.C.C. § 9-502(b)(4). Often, the debtor that creates an Article 9 security interest in the fixture will also be the record owner of the land. Sometimes, however, this will not be the case. For example, a party granting a security interest in fixtures may be a tenant in possession of the land under an unrecorded lease, or may be purchasing the land under an unrecorded installment land contract.

[20] U.C.C. § 9-501(a)(1)(B). If the fixture filing is in proper form and is presented for filing with the proper fees, the secured party is perfected even if the filing officer mistakenly files it in the chattel records. U.C.C. §§ 9-516(a), 9-517.

[21] A recorded mortgage can serve as a fixture filing if the mortgage sufficiently describes the goods, if the goods are or are to become fixtures to the land described in the mortgage, and if the mortgage contains all the information necessary for a valid financing statement (other than an instruction directing that it be filed in the land records). U.C.C. § 9-502(c). If a mortgage serves as a valid fixture filing, it remains effective until the secured debt is released or satisfied of record. U.C.C. § 9-515(g).

If a secured party takes a security interest in goods that it expects to become fixtures, prudence dictates that the secured party make dual filings — *i.e.*, both a fixture filing and a financing statement sufficient to perfect a security interest in the goods in their nonaffixed form. This "belt and suspenders" approach protects the secured party against the risk that the debtor never affixes the goods or that a court later holds that the goods did not qualify as fixtures.

§ 15.03 PRIORITIES IN FIXTURES

[A] The Code's Residual Rule — § 9-334(c)

Article 9's residual priority rule for fixtures is section 9-334(c), which provides that "a security interest in fixtures is subordinate to the conflicting interest of an encumbrancer[22] or owner of the related real property other than the debtor." Thus, in contrast to the Code's general residual priority rule,[23] the residual rule for fixtures is that the secured party loses to conflicting real estate interests. The potential reach of this rule is limited by numerous exceptions that, if satisfied, permit a security interest in fixtures to take priority over a conflicting real estate interest.

[B] The Purchase-Money Priority Exception — § 9-334(d)

Article 9 provides special priority status for certain parties holding purchase-money security interests. As discussed in Chapter 10, a secured party that takes a purchase-money security interest in noninventory collateral (and perfects within 20 days after the debtor takes possession) will take priority over a secured party holding a prior-perfected security interest in that collateral by virtue of an after-acquired property clause.[24] Section 9-334(d) provides a comparable priority rule for purchase-money security interests in fixtures. Section 9-334(d) provides:

> Except as otherwise provided in subsection (h), a perfected security interest in fixtures has priority over a conflicting interest of an encumbrancer or owner of the real property if the debtor has an interest of record in or is in possession of the real property and: (1) the security interest is a purchase-money security interest; (2) the interest of the encumbrancer or owner arises before the goods become fixtures; and (3) the security interest is perfected by a fixture filing before the goods become fixtures or within 20 days thereafter.[25]

---

[22] An "encumbrance" is "a right, other than an ownership interest, in real property." The term includes a mortgage or other lien on real property. U.C.C. § 9-102(a)(32).

[23] Under the Code's general residual priority rule, the secured party wins unless another provision dictates a contrary result. U.C.C. § 9-201(a).

[24] U.C.C. § 9-324(a).

[25] U.C.C. § 9-334(d).

For example, suppose Bank holds a recorded mortgage on Grocer's land and building. On July 31, Secured Party sells Grocer a walk-in freezer on credit, taking back a purchase-money security interest in the freezer. On August 1, Grocer installs the freezer in its store, thereby rendering it a fixture and giving Bank an interest it by virtue of its mortgage. On August 9, Secured Party makes a proper fixture filing covering the freezer. On these facts, Secured Party's security interest has priority over Bank's interest in the freezer under its mortgage. This result makes good policy sense; granting purchase-money priority to Secured Party facilitates commerce by encouraging credit sales and has no deleterious effect on Bank. At the time Bank took its mortgage, there was no freezer affixed to the land; accordingly, Bank cannot reasonably have expected to take priority with respect to the freezer (or any other subsequently attached fixtures obtained using purchase-money credit).[26]

It may not be entirely logical to require any form of perfection — much less a fixture filing — to enable a purchase-money creditor like Secured Party to prevail over Bank in this example if Bank has made no future advances after affixation. Nevertheless, for purchase-money priority, Article 9 requires a fixture filing within the grace period. As a policy matter, the requirement provides the secured party with an incentive to act promptly to place its interest on the land records, thus providing a more complete set of records for persons that might subsequently rely upon them.

Note carefully that section 9-334(d) does not provide priority over real estate interests that arise *after an asset becomes a fixture.* For example, suppose that on July 31, Secured Party sells Grocer a walk-in freezer on credit and takes back a purchase-money security interest. On August 1, Grocer installs the freezer in its store, thereby rendering it a fixture. On August 5, Grocer borrows $100,000 from Bank and grants Bank a mortgage on the land, which Bank records that same day. On August 9 — within 20 days after the freezer became a fixture — Secured Party makes a proper fixture filing. On these facts, Secured Party cannot claim purchase-money priority in the freezer, and Bank takes priority under the residual priority rule of section 9-334(c). Viewed from the perspective of third parties searching the land records, this result is sensible. If Bank had performed a title search on August 5, prior to taking its mortgage interest, the search would not have revealed a fixture filing covering the freezer. As a result, a reasonable person in Bank's position would have concluded that the freezer (which was already affixed to the land) was unencumbered.[27]

---

[26] It is possible, of course, that Secured Party's removal of the freezer might cause physical damage to the land, and this risk threatens the Bank's security as mortgagee. Section 9-604(d) ameliorates the risk by requiring that Secured Party "promptly reimburse any encumbrancer or owner of the real property, other than the debtor, for the cost of repair of any physical injury caused by the removal."

[27] A buyer or mortgagee may not actually rely on fixtures in a particular case, but Article 9 predicates its priority rules upon the assumption that a typical buyer or mortgagee will so rely.

Note also that the purchase-money priority exception applies only if the debtor has an interest of record in the land or is in possession of it. This means that a secured party cannot rely upon purchase-money priority if its security interest is created by someone other than an owner or lessee of the land. For example, suppose Secured Party sells a furnace on credit to Contractor. Contractor is doing remodeling work on Owner's building, which is subject to a previously recorded mortgage in favor of Bank. Even if Secured Party takes a purchase-money security interest and makes a fixture filing within 20 days after the furnace becomes a fixture, Secured Party will not obtain priority over Bank, because Contractor had neither a record interest in nor possession of the land.[28]

[C] The "First-to-File-or-Record" Exception — § 9-334(e)(1)

A party holding a security interest in fixtures can also claim priority over persons that have a conflicting interest in the land under section 9-334(e)(1)'s "first-to-file-or-record" exception to the residual priority rule. Under this exception, a party that takes a security interest in fixtures and perfects by making a fixture filing takes priority over the interest of an owner or encumbrancer whose interest is recorded after the fixture filing.[29] This exception applies to both purchase-money and nonpurchase-money security interests, as demonstrated by the following examples:

- On August 1, Secured Party sells Grocer a walk-in freezer, taking a security interest to secure the purchase price. That same day, Secured Party makes a fixture filing properly covering the freezer. Grocer installs the freezer in its store on August 2, rendering it a fixture. On August 5, Grocer borrows $100,000 from Bank, which takes and records a mortgage on the land and store. Because Bank recorded its mortgage after Secured Party's fixture filing, Secured Party's security interest in the freezer will take priority over Bank's interest in the freezer as mortgagee.

- On August 1, Merchant borrows $100,000 from Bank and grants Bank a security interest in all its personal property, now-owned or after-acquired, including fixtures located on Merchant's business premises. On August 5, Bank makes a fixture filing. On August 10, Merchant sells the premises to Buyer, who records her deed later that day. Because Bank made its fixture filing before Buyer recorded its deed to the premises, Buyer takes the premises subject to Bank's security interest in the fixtures.

- On August 1, Merchant borrows $100,000 from Bank and grants Bank a security interest in all of its personal property, now-owned or after-acquired, including fixtures located on Merchant's

---

[28] U.C.C. § 9-334(c). If Secured Party wants priority over Bank or Owner, it can obtain that party's consent to its security interest. U.C.C. § 9-334(f)(1).

[29] U.C.C. § 9-334(e)(1).

business premises. On August 5, Bank files a regular financing statement (but does not make a fixture filing). On August 10, Merchant sells the premises to Buyer, who records her deed later that day. Because Bank did not make a fixture filing before Buyer recorded its deed to the premises, Buyer takes the premises free and clear of Bank's security interest in the fixtures.

A secured party that makes a fixture filing before the conflicting real estate interest is recorded will not prevail if the holder of the conflicting interest is a successor to a person that would have had priority over the secured party. For example, suppose Bank holds a recorded mortgage on Grocer's land and building. On July 31, Secured Party sells Grocer a walk-in freezer on credit, taking back a purchase-money security interest in the freezer. On August 1, Grocer installs the freezer in its store, thereby rendering it a fixture. Secured Party fails to make a fixture filing, however, until October 1. On November 1, Bank conducts a proper foreclosure sale under Grocer's mortgage, and Buyer purchases the land at the sale. Buyer records a deed on November 2. In this case, although Secured Party made its fixture filing (October 1) before Buyer recorded its deed (November 2), this is irrelevant. At the time of the foreclosure sale, Bank had priority in the freezer under the Code's residual fixture priority rule, because Secured Party had failed to qualify for purchase-money priority by making a fixture filing within the 20-day grace period. Thus, Bank's foreclosure sale extinguished the Secured Party's subordinate interest in the freezer, and Buyer takes the freezer free of Secured Party's interest.

[D]   The Nonreliance-Creditor Exception — § 9-334(e)(3)

Article 9 requires a secured party claiming an interest in fixtures to make a fixture filing to obtain priority against persons that might be called "reliance creditors" — i.e., persons that typically rely on the real estate records in deciding whether to buy or lend against land. Other creditors — such as creditors that acquire a lien on land and/or fixtures by virtue of a judgment or an execution process[30] — are "nonreliance" creditors and are typically not protected by recording statutes.[31] Because these creditors typically do not rely upon the public records, it would be pointless to require a secured party to make a fixture filing to obtain priority over them. Any

[30] Creditors that acquire an interest in personalty by virtue of an execution process are called lien creditors in Article 9. *See* discussion in Chapter 14 *supra*. The concept is the same here, except that a creditor that levies upon the land (and, therefore, is deemed to have levied upon the fixtures as part of the land) is not strictly an Article 9 lien creditor (as the lien is attaching to realty, not personalty). It is possible, however, for such a creditor to have the sheriff levy on just the fixture and remove it from the land, at which point the creditor becomes an Article 9 lien creditor.

[31] *See* U.C.C. § 9-334 Comment 9. State real estate law is not unanimous on this point. Although most state recording acts do not protect judgment creditors, some do give such creditors priority over unrecorded interests. *See, e.g.*, Colo. Rev. Stat. Ann. § 38-35-109(1) (unrecorded instrument is invalid as "against *any person with any kind of rights* in or to such real property who first records") (emphasis added).

method of perfecting a security interest under Article 9 should be sufficient for this purpose. This principle finds expression in section 9-334(e)(3), which states that a party claiming a perfected security interest in fixtures has priority if "the conflicting interest is a lien on the real property obtained by legal or equitable proceedings after the security interest was perfected *by any method permitted by this article. . . ."* [32] The following examples demonstrate the application of the nonreliance creditor exception:

- On July 31, Secured Party sells a walk-in freezer to Grocer on credit, retaining a purchase-money security interest. On August 1, Grocer installs the freezer in its store premises, rendering it a fixture. Secured Party does not make a fixture filing, but does file an Article 9 financing statement on August 2 that is sufficient to perfect a security interest in Grocer's equipment. On October 1, Customer obtains a judgment against Grocer arising out of a slip-and-fall accident, and the judgment constitutes a lien against all of Grocer's real estate. Although Customer obtains a lien against the freezer by virtue of the judgment, this lien is subordinate to Secured Party's perfected security interest in the freezer.

- On July 31, Secured Party sells Tycoon a walk-in freezer on credit for use in his home, retaining a purchase-money security interest. On August 1, the freezer is installed in Tycoon's home, rendering it a fixture. Secured Party does not file a fixture filing or a financing statement covering the freezer. On October 1, Victim obtains a judgment against Tycoon for injuries sustained in an automobile accident caused by Tycoon's negligence, and the judgment constitutes a lien against Tycoon's home. Although Creditor obtains a lien against the freezer by virtue of the judgment, this lien is subordinate to Secured Party's security interest, which was automatically perfected upon attachment. [33]

The most feared nonreliance creditor is the trustee in bankruptcy. If a secured party fails to make a fixture filing and finds itself in a priority contest with the trustee, can it prevail if it has perfected using one of the Code's nonfixture methods? The drafters of the U.C.C. assumed that the answer was "yes," but the issue was open until 1984, when Congress amended the Bankruptcy Code to make clear that if a trustee is claiming an interest in fixtures, the trustee stands in the position of a lien creditor levying on personalty under state law, not in the position of a bona fide purchaser of real property. [34]

---

[32] U.C.C. § 9-334(e)(3) (emphasis added).

[33] U.C.C. § 9-309(1).

[34] *See* 11 U.S.C. § 544(a)(3). *See also* 11 U.S.C. § 547(e)(1) (trustee treated as lien creditor of personalty rather than bona-fide purchaser of real estate for preferential-transfer purposes).

[E] The Exception for "Readily Removable Collateral" — § 9-334(e)(2)

Article 9 contains an exception limited to security interests in fixtures that are readily removable and that are (1) "factory or office machines," (2) "equipment that is not primarily used or leased for use in the operation of the real property" to which the goods are affixed, or (3) "replacements of domestic appliances that are consumer goods."[35] A secured party may perfect a security interest in any of these goods by any method permitted by Article 9, including filing and automatic perfection. Under this exception, no fixture filing is necessary — ordinary perfection is sufficient even against reliance creditors. To qualify for protection under this section, the secured party must perfect the security interest before the goods are affixed to the land.

The rationale for the exception rests in the reasonable contextual expectations of commercial parties. For example, suppose Secured Party sells a photocopier to Debtor on credit, retaining a purchase-money security interest. Debtor installs the photocopier into a recessed area in one wall of Debtor's office building to save office space. Unaware of Debtor's plan, Secured Party merely files an ordinary financing statement covering the copier and does not make a fixture filing. Shortly thereafter, Debtor obtains a loan from Bank and grants Bank a mortgage on its office building. Given the photocopier's readily removable character, Bank likely would not expect it to be a fixture and thus would not likely rely upon the presence of the photocopier in deciding whether to make the mortgage loan. Nevertheless, a court might later conclude that the combination of affixation by a wall plug and adaptation to a particular feature of the building[36] renders the copier a fixture. By virtue of the "readily removable" exception, Secured Party in this example will have priority in the photocopier over Bank.

For domestic appliances that are consumer goods, the exception requires that the collateral be a replacement, not an original. This limitation serves to protect a lender (typically a construction lender) that may have relied on having a lien on the original appliances when it provided financing to the debtor. Such a lender should realize that appliances eventually break down. A provision requiring a purchase-money secured party to make a fixture filing to obtain priority for an interest in a replacement appliance would drive up the transaction costs for what are routine sales (usually perfected automatically) and thus would serve no useful notice function.[37]

---

[35] U.C.C. § 9-334(e)(2).

[36] Adaptation is discussed in § 15.01 *supra*.

[37] U.C.C. § 9-334 Comment 8.

[F]   Special Rules for Construction Mortgages — § 9-334(h)

Article 9 provides a special priority rule designed to protect a construction lender's interest in fixtures under a construction mortgage:[38]

> Except as otherwise provided [in sections 9-334(e) and (f)], a security interest in fixtures is subordinate to a construction mortgage if a record of the mortgage is recorded before the goods become fixtures and the goods become fixtures before the completion of the construction. A mortgage has this priority to the same extent as a construction mortgage to the extent that it is given to refinance a construction mortgage.[39]

This provision effectively precludes the operation of the purchase-money priority exception against construction lenders. For example, suppose Debtor is building an office building financed by a construction loan from First Bank, which has recorded a mortgage. On August 1, Secured Party sells Debtor 50 sets of cabinets for wall-mounted installation in the offices, retaining a purchase-money security interest in the cabinets. On August 2, the cabinets are installed and become fixtures. On August 3, Secured Party makes a fixture filing describing the cabinets. Without the special rule on construction mortgages, Secured Party would take priority over Bank under the purchase-money priority exception.[40] Under section 9-334(h), however, Secured Party's security interest in the cabinets is subordinate to First Bank's mortgage.[41]

Why this preference for a construction lender? Recall that the purchase-money priority exception rests upon the assumption that a mortgagee whose interest arose before goods became fixtures will not have relied upon the goods in deciding whether to lend money. This assumption is not valid for a construction mortgagee, however, which typically knows of the construction plans from the outset and makes its decision to lend assuming that the fixtures will become part of the structure.[42] Consequently, a construction mortgagee is a reliance creditor from the outset. The priority accruing to a construction mortgagee passes to a permanent (or "take-out") lender to which the mortgage is assigned when construction is complete.

---

[38] Under Article 9, "[a] mortgage is a construction mortgage to the extent that it secures an obligation incurred for the construction of an improvement on land, including the acquisition cost of the land, if a recorded record of the mortgage so indicates." U.C.C. § 9-334(h).

[39] U.C.C. § 9-334(h).

[40] *See* § 15.03[B] *supra*.

[41] In this example, state law might also permit Secured Party to claim a mechanic's lien against the land if Debtor does not pay for the cabinets. The relative priority of a mechanic's lien and a construction mortgage is not governed by Article 9, and is beyond the scope of this book.

[42] In many circumstances, a construction lender will have factored the cost of fixtures into the amount of its construction loan and thus expects to finance the fixtures. As a result, enabling the debtor to grant purchase-money priority in the fixtures to a competing secured party would allow the debtor to "double finance" the fixtures.

If a construction lender or permanent lender acquires an interest in fixtures placed on the land after construction is complete (typically through an after-acquired fixtures clause in a mortgage), the rationale for this provision no longer applies. The priority for construction mortgages thus applies only to goods that become fixtures before construction is completed. For example, if Secured Party sells Debtor 50 units of cabinets that Debtor installs six months after construction is complete, and if the cabinets become fixtures upon installation, Secured Party can acquire priority over a properly recorded construction mortgage or permanent take-out mortgage by making a proper fixture filing during the 20-day grace period.

There are two other situations that are less significant but nevertheless deserve brief mention. First, if a construction lender or permanent takeout lender consents in writing to a security interest or disclaims an interest in fixtures, or if it gives a debtor consent to remove fixtures, the secured party acquires priority over the mortgage with respect to those fixtures.[43] Second, if a construction mortgagee fails to record its mortgage before the goods become fixtures — not likely, but possible if the construction lender is careless — it subjects itself to the risk of losing priority under the "first-to-file-or-record" exception to the residual priority rule.[44]

[G] Exception for Manufactured Homes — § 9-335(e)(4)

Article 9 contains a special priority rule addressing the potential conflict between a party that finances a debtor's purchase of a "manufactured home"[45] and a party holding a lien upon the land to which the home becomes attached. In most states, mobile homes are covered by certificate-of-title statutes. In those states, a secured party must perfect its security interest in a mobile home (assuming that the mobile home is not inventory in the debtor's hands) by having it noted upon the home's certificate of title. Under section 9-334(e)(4), a security interest in a manufactured home that is created in a "manufactured home transaction"[46] takes priority over the interest of an owner or encumbrancer of the land to which the home is attached, provided that the secured party properly perfects under the certificate-of-title statute. For example, suppose Debtor purchases a manufactured home on credit from Seller and grants Seller a purchase-money security interest in the home. Seller properly perfects by having its security interest noted on the certificate of title covering the home. The home is then affixed to land that Debtor is purchasing from Vendor on an installment land contract. Seller's security interest has priority over the claim of Vendor under the contract for deed.[47] Prudent title examiners in certificate-of-title

---

[43] U.C.C. § 9-334(f); *see* § 15.03[H] *infra*.

[44] *See* § 15.03[C] *supra*.

[45] The definition of "manufactured home" in section 9-102(a)(53) includes a typical mobile home or prefabricated home that is movable in one or more sections. *See* § 1.04[A] *supra*.

[46] A "manufactured home transaction" is either a transaction that creates a purchase-money security interest in a manufactured home or a transaction in which a manufactured home is the primary collateral. U.C.C. § 9-102(a)(54).

[47] Conseco Fin. Servicing Corp. v. Old Nat'l Bank, 754 N.E.2d 997, 45 U.C.C. Rep. Serv. 2d 652 (Ind. Ct. App. 2001).

states should check the records of the state agency that issues certificates of title if there is a manufactured home on the land.

[H]   Exception Based on Consent or Right of Removal — § 9-334(f)

Two additional exceptions to the residual priority rule for fixtures merit brief mention. The first exception is based on consent. If an encumbrancer or owner that would otherwise have priority over a secured party with respect to fixtures either consents to the security interest or disclaims an interest in the fixtures, the secured party acquires priority.[48] This is merely a particular application of the general rule that parties may enter into subordination agreements altering the priorities created by the U.C.C.'s normal priority rules.[49]

The final exception arises primarily in the case of fixtures attached to leased land. A majority of jurisdictions have adopted what is sometimes called the "trade fixture" doctrine. Under this doctrine, goods affixed to leased business premises generally are treated as personalty as between the lessor and the lessee. As a result, the lessee may remove the goods at the conclusion of the lease term unless the lease expressly provides to the contrary. Further, most jurisdictions have expanded this doctrine to include goods affixed by lessees of residential property. Article 9 incorporates this concept, giving a secured party with an interest in fixtures priority over the conflicting claim of an encumbrancer or owner of the land if "the debtor has a right to remove the goods as against the encumbrancer or owner," regardless of whether the secured party's interest in the fixtures is perfected.[50] The Code provides that the Article 9 secured party's priority continues "for a reasonable time" if the debtor's right to remove the goods terminates.[51] This provision is important in those jurisdictions where the lessee's right to remove fixtures terminates upon expiration of the lease (or expiration of the period during which the lessee is a holdover tenant), as it affords the secured party priority for a reasonable time so that it can repossess the fixtures.[52]

§ 15.04   SECURED PARTY'S RIGHT TO REMOVE FIXTURES AFTER DEFAULT — § 9-604(c), (d)

Section 9-604 sets forth a secured party's rights with respect to fixtures after default. Not surprisingly, a secured party may not repossess fixtures

---

[48] U.C.C. § 9-334(f)(1). The consent or disclaimer must appear in an authenticated record.

[49] U.C.C. § 9-339.

[50] U.C.C. § 9-334(f)(2). The rationale does not apply to parties that buy the land from, or become mortgagees of, the lessor.

[51] U.C.C. § 9-334(g).

[52] If a debtor no longer has access to the premises, a secured party would be well-advised to use judicial repossession rather than attempting to repossess by self-help. *See* discussion in Chapter 17 *infra*.

if it lacks priority against an owner or encumbrancer of the land.[53] In other words, if the secured party is not first in line, it cannot repossess at all. Thus, unless the subordinate secured party obtains the consent of all parties having priority, its security interest is worthless and it must rely for protection on any rights it may have under the state's laws governing mechanics' liens.

Even if a secured party has first priority, section 9-604(d) constrains the secured party's repossession and enforcement rights to protect owners and encumbrancers from unjustified harm due to the removal of fixtures. In some circumstances, removal of a fixture will cause physical injury to the underlying land. Section 9-604(d) provides that a secured party repossessing fixtures must "promptly reimburse any encumbrancer or owner of the real property, other than the debtor, for the cost of repair of any physical injury caused by the removal."[54] While the repossessing secured party must compensate for physical injury, it "need not reimburse the encumbrancer or owner for any diminution in value of the real property caused by the absence of the goods removed or by any necessity of replacing them."[55] For example, suppose Secured Party has a perfected security interest in Grocer's walk-in freezer, which constitutes a fixture. Secured Party has priority over Bank, which holds a mortgage upon Grocer's store. Secured Party removes the fixture and sells it following Grocer's default. In the process of removing the freezer, Secured Party does $400 in physical damage to the store by tearing down a wall to gain access to the freezer. Further, Secured Party's removal of the freezer reduces the fair market value of the store by $4,000 (the cost to obtain and install a replacement freezer). Secured Party must reimburse Bank for the $400 in physical damage to the store premises, but need not pay any sum to reimburse the Bank for the reduction in the fair market value of the premises.

The rationale for this result should be apparent. Article 9 typically grants secured parties priority as to fixtures if an adverse encumbrancer or owner has not relied on the presence of the fixtures. In this example, the fact that removal of the freezer reduced the fair market value of the premises by $4,000 should not seriously interfere with Bank's reasonable expectations, as Bank likely did not rely upon having priority in the freezer. If Secured Party causes physical injury to the land in removing the freezer, however, there is a direct and substantial interference with the Bank's expectations regarding the physical integrity of the mortgaged premises, and Secured Party should have to compensate Bank for this interference.[56] In addition to granting an owner or encumbrancer a right of reimbursement, the Code also provides that the owner or encumbrancer may refuse permission to

---

[53] U.C.C. § 9-604(c).

[54] U.C.C. § 9-604(d).

[55] Id.

[56] If removal of a fixture would cause such massive harm as to be wasteful, a court might find that the goods are ordinary building materials and therefore no security interest continues to attach to them. See § 15.01 supra.

remove a fixture until the secured party gives adequate security for the performance of this obligation.[57]

In some circumstances, an encumbrancer of land may foreclose its lien and force a sale of the land even though a secured party has priority with respect to fixtures. In this instance, the secured party retains the right to remove the fixtures, but can it leave the fixtures in place and instead claim an interest in the proceeds from the sale of the land? For example, suppose Bank holds a mortgage on Debtor's land and Secured Party has a perfected security interest in Debtor's fixtures that gives Secured Party priority over Bank. Debtor then defaults to Bank, which forecloses on Debtor's land, selling it to Buyer. Can Secured Party claim first priority in the sale proceeds? A leading case interpreting the 1972 text of Article 9, *Maplewood Bank & Trust v. Sears, Roebuck & Co.*,[58] held that the answer was no. The court held that a secured party's right to priority in fixtures was limited to their removal and that a secured party had no claim against the land itself — and thus no claim to the proceeds of the foreclosure sale. Instead, a secured party's priority in fixtures continued against the foreclosure-sale buyer.

Section 9-604(b) overrules the *Maplewood* case[59] by providing that a party with a security interest in fixtures may choose to enforce its interest either under Article 9's enforcement provisions or under applicable state real estate law. If the secured party enforces its interest under real estate law, none of Article 9's enforcement provisions apply to its actions.[60] Thus, in the above hypothetical, if real estate law permitted Secured Party to join in Bank's foreclosure action and enforce its interest in that proceeding, Secured Party could claim first priority against the foreclosure-sale proceeds.[61]

§ 15.05 ACCESSIONS — § 9-335

[A] Nature of the Interest

Accessions are analogous to fixtures, except that an accession is an item of personalty that is attached to another item of personalty rather than to real estate. Accessions are "goods that are physically united with other

---

[57] U.C.C. § 9-604(d). In *Berger v. Alexopoulos*, 280 A.D.2d 505, 721 N.Y.S.2d 81, 44 U.C.C. Rep. Serv. 2d 307 (2001), the owner of real property demanded rent and liability insurance as a condition to the secured party's removal of fixtures installed by the tenant/debtor. Because the owner was entitled only to compensation for any damages resulting from the removal, the court held that the owner's refusal to surrender the collateral constituted conversion.

[58] 625 A.2d 537 (N.J. App. 1993).

[59] *See* U.C.C. § 9-604, Comment 3.

[60] U.C.C. § 9-604(b)(2).

[61] If state law does not permit Secured Party to join in Bank's foreclosure action, then the purchaser at the Bank's foreclosure sale takes title to the fixture subject to Secured Party's security interest, which Secured Party may enforce pursuant to Article 9. U.C.C. § 9-604(b)(1).

goods in such a manner that the identity of the original goods is not lost."[62] In other words, an accession retains its identity and can be removed from the goods to which it is attached and sold separately. This distinguishes it from a "commingled good," which arises if an item of personalty becomes so intertwined into a larger whole (also personalty) that it loses its separate identity.

Section 9-102(a)(1)'s definition of "accessions" differs somewhat from the common-law definition. At common law, an asset did not become an accession until it was so intertwined with the whole that, although retaining its separate identity, its removal would cause substantial harm to the whole.[63] One should note carefully that section 9-102(a)(1)'s definition applies only to a dispute governed by section 9-335, *i.e.*, a priority contest between a secured party claiming an interest in an accession and a third party claiming an interest in the whole. If the issue is simply whether a security agreement is sufficiently broad to grant the secured party an interest in a particular item that is somehow connected with a larger whole, the common-law definition of accessions governs.

For example, if Secured Party has a security interest in Debtor's car, its interest extends to the motor because the motor, being integral to the functioning of the car, qualifies as a common-law accession. The security interest might not extend to Debtor's cellular phone installed in the car; the cellular phone likely would not constitute an accession, as its removal would not cause substantial harm to the car as a whole or compromise its operability. Thus, if Secured Party repossessed the car following Debtor's default and failed to remove the cellular phone and return it to Debtor, Secured Party likely would be liable for conversion. As a result, a well-drafted security agreement will contain language that extends the security interest to all accessions and accessories, whenever acquired.

[B] Priorities

Section 9-335 resolves the priority dispute that arises if a secured party has a security interest in an accession (as defined by the Code) and a third party claims a competing interest in the whole. Under section 9-335(c), this priority dispute is resolved by the Code's ordinary priority rules, as demonstrated by the following examples:

- Debtor grants Bank a security interest in a new computer hard drive to be installed in Debtor's business computer. The computer is already subject to a perfected security interest in favor of Finance Company. If Bank's interest is a purchase-money security interest (*i.e.*, if Debtor acquired the hard drive with money advanced by the Bank), Bank will take priority as to the hard drive over Finance Company's interest in the entire computer so

---

[62] U.C.C. § 9-102(a)(1).

[63] *See generally* R. Brown, The Law of Personal Property §§ 6.1-6.7 (W. Raushenbush 3d ed. 1975).

long as Bank perfects its interest within the 20-day grace period after Debtor received possession of the hard drive.[64] If Bank fails to perfect its interest within this grace period, or if Bank's interest is not a purchase-money interest, Finance Company will take priority as to the installed hard drive based upon its prior-perfected security interest in the whole computer.[65]

- After installing the hard drive, Debtor sells the computer to Buyer. If Bank has perfected its security interest in the hard drive before the sale to Buyer, Bank's security interest in the hard drive will remain effective against Buyer. If, however, Buyer gave value and took possession of the computer without knowledge of Bank's security interest and before it was perfected, Buyer will take the computer free of Bank's interest in the hard drive.[66]

Section 9-335 provides a special priority rule for accessions to goods covered by certificate-of-title statutes. Under section 9-335(d), a security interest in an accession is subordinate to a security interest in the whole that is perfected under a certificate-of-title statute.[67] Thus, suppose Debtor asks Seller to finance a new stereo system for its car and agrees to grant a purchase-money security interest in the system. GMAC has a security interest in the car that is perfected by notation upon the car's certificate of title. Under section 9-335(d), GMAC has priority over Seller with respect to the stereo system, notwithstanding Article 9's traditional priority for a purchase-money secured party.[68]

§ 15.06　COMMINGLED GOODS — § 9-336

[A]　Rights

Section 9-336 governs the effectiveness of a security interest in goods that have been "commingled," or "physically united with other goods in such a manner that [the goods'] identity is lost in a product or mass."[69] If a secured party's collateral becomes so commingled, the secured party's interest

---

[64] U.C.C. § 9-324(e). If Debtor's computer constituted consumer goods, Bank's purchase-money security interest would be automatically perfected upon attachment. U.C.C. § 9-309(1).

[65] U.C.C. § 9-322(a)(1).

[66] U.C.C. § 9-317(b). If the security interest in the hard drive was a purchase-money security interest, however, Bank would have a 20-day grace period in which to perfect its security interest and obtain relation-back priority over an intervening third party such as Buyer. U.C.C. § 9-317(e).

[67] U.C.C. § 9-335(d) ("A security interest in an accession is subordinate to a security interest in the whole which is perfected by compliance with the requirements of a certificate-of-title statute under Section 9-311(d).").

[68] Seller could obtain priority over GMAC with respect to the stereo system if Seller and GMAC entered into a subordination agreement. U.C.C. § 9-339.

[69] U.C.C. § 9-336(a).

attaches to the resulting product or mass.[70] Furthermore, if the secured party properly perfected its security interest in the goods prior to commingling, its resulting security interest in the product or mass is likewise perfected.[71] For example, suppose Bank has a security interest in Debtor's flour, and Debtor later combines the flour with eggs, water and sugar to make a cake. The flour loses its identity in the process of baking the cake, but this does not completely eliminate Bank's security interest. If Bank perfected its security interest in the flour and can prove that the flour went into the cake, it can claim a perfected security interest in the cake.[72]

Determining whether a security interest arises in a product or mass is not always easy. For example, suppose Supplier sells Debtor cattle feed on secured credit and Bank has a security interest in Debtor's cattle. If all the feed has been consumed when Debtor defaults, can Supplier argue that it has an interest in the cattle as a "product or mass" under section 9-336? Case law has generally refused to allow feed suppliers to assert claims against cattle in these circumstances.[73] The theory behind these cases, however — that there is nothing left of the feed after the cattle have eaten it — seems a bit strained. The feed has clearly been converted into meat, and there is no logical reason why section 9-336 should not apply. Nevertheless, a prudent feed supplier that wants an interest in the cattle as well as the feed should so specify in its security agreement.

[B] Priorities

Most priority problems involving commingled goods can be resolved fairly easily. With respect to the conflicting rights of lien creditors and buyers, section 9-336 incorporates the Code's standard priority rules. Thus, a perfected security interest in a product or mass will have priority over the interest of a lien creditor or a buyer not in ordinary course of business, but a buyer in ordinary course will take free of the security interest.[74]

Any two or more conflicting perfected[75] security interests that arise solely under section 9-336 rank equally in priority "in proportion to the value of the collateral at the time it became commingled goods."[76] For example,

---

[70] U.C.C. § 9-336(c).

[71] U.C.C. § 9-336(d).

[72] Of course, if a Debtor is a baker and Bank has a blanket lien upon all of Debtor's inventory, now-owned and after-acquired, then Bank's security interest would attach directly to the cake anyway. Section 9-336 would only be necessary in the circumstance where Bank did not have any other basis under its security agreement for asserting an interest in the completed cake.

[73] *See, e.g.*, First Nat'l Bank of Brush v. Bostron, 39 Colo. Ct. App. 107, 564 P.2d 964, 21 U.C.C. Rep. Serv. 1475 (1977); Farmers Coop. Elevator Co. v. Union State Bank, 409 N.W.2d 178, 4 U.C.C. Rep. Serv. 2d 1 (Iowa 1987); *In re* McDougall, 60 B.R. 635, 1 U.C.C. Rep. Serv. 2d 563 (Bankr. W.D. Pa. 1986); *In re* Pelton, 171 B.R. 641 (Bankr. W.D. Wis. 1994). The cases have also considered and rejected the argument that the cattle are "proceeds" of the feed.

[74] U.C.C. § 9-336(e).

[75] Not surprisingly, a perfected security interest in commingled goods takes priority over a conflicting unperfected security interest in the same goods. U.C.C. § 9-336(f)(1).

[76] U.C.C. § 9-336(f)(2).

suppose Bank has a perfected security interest in Debtor's flour (worth $100) and Finance Company has a perfected security interest in Debtor's eggs (worth $200). Debtor commingles the flour and eggs to make cakes. Suppose further that after Debtor's default, the cakes are sold for only $150. From this $150, Bank would receive $50 and Finance Company $100.[77]

Note, however, that this priority rule applies only if the conflicting security interests both arise under section 9-336. Section 9-336's priority rule will not apply if one secured party claims a direct security interest in the commingled product or mass; in that case, the Code's standard priority rules apply. For example, suppose Bank has a perfected security interest in Debtor's flour and Finance Company has a perfected security interest in all of Debtor's now-owned and after-acquired inventory. Debtor commingles the flour with other ingredients to make cakes. If Finance Company filed a financing statement covering the inventory before Bank filed a financing statement covering the flour, then Finance Company will have priority in the cakes under the first-to-file-or-perfect rule. Likewise, if Bank filed against the flour before Finance Company filed against the inventory, Bank will enjoy priority in the cakes to the extent of its security interest.[78]

---

[77] If there are multiple parties holding conflicting security interests in a single input, then section 9-336 treats those parties as a single secured party for purposes of establishing their collective share, and then the Code's normal priority rules determine how to distribute that collective share among them. See U.C.C. § 9-336 Comment 6. For example, suppose that Bank has a perfected first-priority security interest in Debtor's eggs (worth $200) to secure a debt of $150, Finance Company has a perfected second-priority security interest in the same eggs to secure a debt of $250, and First Savings has a perfected security interest in Debtor's flour (worth $400) to secure a debt of $500. Debtor commingles the eggs and flour to make cakes, which sell for $750. Debtor then defaults to all three parties. For purposes of section 9-336, Bank and Finance Company will be treated like a single secured party whose interest has equal priority with that of First Savings in proportion to the value of their respective inputs. Thus, First Savings would be entitled to collect $500 of the sale proceeds, and Bank and Finance Company will collectively have priority with respect to the other $250. As between Bank and Finance Company, priority with respect to that $250 will be based upon first-to-file-or-perfect; thus, Bank will collect $150 of the proceeds in satisfaction of its debt, and Finance Company will receive the remaining $100. See U.C.C. § 9-336 Comment 6, Example 5.

[78] U.C.C. § 9-336 Comment 7.

Chapter 16

BANKRUPTCY

SYNOPSIS

§ 16.01 BACKGROUND

[A] Introduction

When a debtor files for bankruptcy protection, the secured party's ability to enforce its security interest becomes subject to the substantive and procedural limitations imposed by federal bankruptcy law. Although Article 9 is "state" law, most current decisions interpreting and applying Article 9 arise in the federal bankruptcy courts. Accordingly, a thorough understanding of the law of secured transactions requires a basic understanding of bankruptcy law.

A variety of policies and concerns motivate our system of federal bankruptcy law. One concern is that, outside of bankruptcy, a debtor's financial distress can trigger a "race to the courthouse" by its creditors, with each creditor attempting to maximize its recovery before recovery efforts exhaust the debtor's assets. Such a "race" has the potential to force the distressed but possibly solvent debtor into insolvency, when time, planning, and some "breathing space" might have enabled the debtor to recover a sound financial position. Thus, one of the primary objectives of bankruptcy law is to provide a comprehensive system of debt collection that can help either avoid or mitigate the adverse consequences of the "race to the courthouse."

In bankruptcy an insolvent debtor's financial affairs are administered in a collective proceeding rather than through the ad hoc collection efforts of individual creditors.[1] Within this collective proceeding, there is a strong emphasis upon the equitable (as distinct from equal) treatment of all creditors; bankruptcy law generally treats similarly situated creditors in a similar fashion, and discourages attempts by creditors to "opt out" of the collective process.[2] Current bankruptcy law provides more, however, than just a collective debt collection system. Bankruptcy also provides insolvent debtors with the opportunity to obtain a "fresh start" or to "reorganize" their financial affairs. Individual debtors may choose to liquidate their pre-bankruptcy assets and thereby obtain an order discharging their pre-bankruptcy debts. In contrast, individual and business debtors may retain their assets and attempt to restructure and repay some or all of their pre-bankruptcy debts in a reorganization proceeding.

This variety of objectives is manifested in Title 11 of the United States Code, commonly known as the Bankruptcy Code. Enacted by Congress in 1978 and revised on several subsequent occasions (most recently by the

---

[1] Elizabeth Warren, *Bankruptcy Policy*, 54 U. Chi. L. Rev. 775 (1987).

[2] This objective explains, for example, the Bankruptcy Code provision allowing the bankruptcy trustee to avoid (*i.e.*, set aside or recover) certain transfers by the debtor prior to bankruptcy that had the effect of preferring certain creditors over other, similarly situated creditors (these transfers are called "preferences"). 11 U.S.C. § 547; *see* § 16.04[E] *infra*.

Bankruptcy Abuse Prevention and Consumer Protection Act of 2005, or "BAPCPA"), the Code divides bankruptcy law into separate "Chapters." Three of these Chapters (1, 3, and 5) contain general provisions that apply in all types of bankruptcy cases. The remaining Chapters govern the specific types of bankruptcy cases. Chapter 7 establishes the rules governing the liquidation of individual or business debtors.[3] Chapter 11 governs the attempt by a business debtor to implement a plan for restructuring its pre-bankruptcy debts and rehabilitating its business.[4] Chapter 12 establishes a procedure whereby farmers may restructure and repay pre-bankruptcy debts using post-bankruptcy earnings.[5] Chapter 13 sets forth the rules that govern how an individual wage-earner may restructure its pre-bankruptcy debts and repay them using post-bankruptcy disposable income.[6] This book does not discuss the procedure that governs proceedings under each Chapter of the Code; instead, this book generally will focus only upon those aspects of bankruptcy law that have significant consequences for Article 9 secured transactions and the behavior of debtors and secured parties.[7]

[B] The Bankruptcy Estate

The filing of a bankruptcy petition creates a bankruptcy estate.[8] Subject to limited statutory exceptions, all of the interests in property (whether legal or equitable) owned by the debtor at the moment of the bankruptcy petition become part of the bankruptcy estate.[9]

In a Chapter 7 case, the debtor essentially gives up all of its nonexempt property in exchange for a fresh start and a discharge of its debts. Thus, the Chapter 7 debtor generally does not retain possession and control of property of the estate. Instead, the bankruptcy trustee distributes the estate's property in one of three ways: first, the trustee abandons any overencumbered property (*i.e.*, property that secures a debt in excess of its value) or otherwise worthless property;[10] second, the trustee abandons any exempt property (*i.e.*, property that the debtor can retain free of creditor claims under applicable state or federal exemptions);[11] third, the trustee

---

[3] 11 U.S.C. §§ 701-728.

[4] *Id.* §§ 1101-1146. Although the majority of Chapter 11 cases involve debtors that are corporations, partnerships, or other business entities, the Supreme Court has held that individual debtors can use the provisions of Chapter 11. Toibb v. Radloff, 501 U.S. 157 (1991).

[5] 11 U.S.C. §§ 1201-1231.

[6] *Id.* §§ 1301-1330.

[7] For further discussion of the general procedures of bankruptcy, *see generally* Michael J. Herbert, *Understanding Bankruptcy* (1995).

[8] 11 U.S.C. § 541(a).

[9] *Id.* § 541(a)(1).

[10] *Id.* § 554(a). When the trustee abandons property of the estate, title to that property is vested back into the debtor. Any creditor with a security interest in that property may then enforce that security interest, but only after first obtaining relief from the automatic stay as discussed in § 16.03[B] *infra*.

[11] 11 U.S.C. § 554(a).

liquidates the remaining property and distributes the proceeds to pay persons holding valid claims against the debtor and administrative expenses.[12]

In contrast, in reorganization cases under Chapters 11, 12, and 13, property of the estate generally remains in control of the bankrupt debtor. In these Chapters, the bankrupt debtor typically retains its pre-bankruptcy assets and attempts to repay the claims of creditors using assets obtained and income generated after the bankruptcy petition. Thus, the reorganizing debtor remains in possession of property of the estate, and may continue to use that property in its reorganization efforts (subject to the supervision of the bankruptcy court).[13]

As noted above, the bankruptcy estate includes all legal or equitable interests in property owned by the debtor at the time the debtor files a bankruptcy petition. If a secured party repossesses property from the debtor and completes an Article 9 disposition of the property before the debtor files a bankruptcy petition, the property does not enter the bankruptcy estate — ownership will have passed to the foreclosure sale purchaser[14] and Article 9 provides no right of post-sale redemption.[15] If the secured party has repossessed property of the debtor prior to the bankruptcy petition but has not yet completed an Article 9 disposition, the debtor's rights in the property have not yet been extinguished.[16] In this situation, the proper view is that the repossessed property does become property of the bankruptcy estate, and that the secured party is obligated to turn the property over to the trustee.[17]

---

[12] *Id.* § 726.

[13] *Id.* §§ 1107(a), 1203(a), 1303.

[14] U.C.C. § 9-617(a)(1).

[15] U.C.C. § 9-623(c). There is a limited possibility that the trustee/DIP may be able to set aside the pre-bankruptcy foreclosure sale as a fraudulent transfer, in which case the property would become part of the bankruptcy estate. This possibility is discussed in § 16.04[F][3] *infra.*

[16] U.C.C. § 9-617(a)(1).

[17] 11 U.S.C. § 542(a); *see also* U.S. v. Whiting Pools, Inc., 462 U.S. 198, 209 (1983) ("[T]he reorganization estate includes property of the debtor that has been seized by a creditor prior to the filing of a petition for reorganization."); *In re* Moffett, 356 F.3d 518, 52 U.C.C. Rep. Serv. 2d 539 (4th Cir. 2004) (vehicle that had been repossessed but not sold became part of bankruptcy estate); *In re* Estis, 311 B.R. 592, 54 U.C.C. Rep. Serv. 2d 198 (Bankr. D. Kan. 2004) (same).

The U.S. Court of Appeals for the Eleventh Circuit raised some question about this issue, at least as applied to repossessed vehicles, in its decisions in *In re Kalter,* 292 F.3d 1350 (11th Cir. 2002) (interpreting Florida law) and *In re Lewis,* 137 F.3d 1280 (11th Cir. 1998) (interpreting Alabama law). In each of those cases, the secured party had not yet disposed of the repossessed vehicle prior to the bankruptcy petition, but had applied for a title certificate to permit the secured party to demonstrate a clear title to a potential purchaser. In each case, the court treated the secured party's conduct as having terminated the debtor's title to the vehicle, and held that the debtor's unexercised right of redemption was merely an intangible interest insufficient to make the vehicle part of the bankruptcy estate.

The *Kalter* and *Lewis* decisions (both of which arose under pre-revision Article 9) are poorly reasoned and patently incorrect. Furthermore, section 9-619(c) of revised Article 9 provides that "a transfer of the record or legal title to collateral to a secured party" in anticipation of

[C] The Bankruptcy Trustee

The central figure in bankruptcy cases is the trustee. The trustee is the official representative of the bankruptcy estate.[18] In a Chapter 7 case, a trustee is always appointed. The Chapter 7 trustee collects and manages the property in the bankruptcy estate, investigates the bankrupt's financial affairs, sets aside improper pre-bankruptcy transfers by the debtor, liquidates the property of the estate, and distributes the proceeds to those creditors entitled to payment under the Code's distributive scheme.[19] In reorganization cases, however, the role of the trustee differs. As in Chapter 7 cases, a trustee is always appointed in Chapter 12 and 13 cases, but that trustee does not collect and manage the property of the estate. Instead, the Chapter 12 or Chapter 13 trustee investigates the bankrupt debtor's financial affairs, sets aside improper pre-bankruptcy transfers by the debtor, and collects all of the debtor's post-bankruptcy disposable net income. The trustee then uses this income to pay the claims of creditors in accordance with the debtor's court-approved plan of reorganization.[20] Trustees are not appointed as a matter of course in Chapter 11 cases.[21] In the typical Chapter 11 case, the Code authorizes the bankrupt debtor (called the "debtor-in-possession" or "DIP") to carry out the powers of a Chapter 11 trustee.[22]

In any bankruptcy case, the trustee (or the DIP) presents the primary potential threat to the Article 9 secured party and its ability to enforce its security interest. In all cases, the trustee/DIP examines the claims of creditors and can enforce any legal claims that the estate might have against creditors or other third parties. Pursuant to its avoiding powers, the trustee/DIP may invalidate certain pre-bankruptcy transfers, including unperfected security interests,[23] fraudulent transfers,[24] and security interests or other transfers that had the effect of preferring the Article 9 secured party over other pre-bankruptcy creditors.[25]

---

an Article 9 sale is "not of itself a disposition of collateral" and thus would not extinguish the debtor's equitable interest in the vehicle. U.C.C. § 9-619(c). Following the enactment of section 9-619(c), it is doubtful that any court would continue to follow the unfortunate decisions in *Kalter* and *Lewis*.

[18] 11 U.S.C. § 323(a).

[19] *Id.* § 704.

[20] *Id.* §§ 1202(b); 1302(b).

[21] A trustee may be appointed upon request of any party in interest for cause (including the debtor's dishonesty, fraud, or incompetence), or if the court concludes that appointment of a trustee is otherwise necessary to protect the estate or the interests of creditors or other interest holders (such as stockholders of a bankrupt corporation). *Id.* § 1104(a).

[22] *Id.* § 1107(a). The powers of the Chapter 11 trustee are listed in § 1106(a) and are similar to the powers provided to trustees in the other bankruptcy chapters.

[23] *Id.* § 544(a). *See* § 16.04[B] *infra*.

[24] 11 U.S.C. §§ 544(b), 548. *See* § 16.04[F] *infra*.

[25] 11 U.C.C. § 547. *See* § 16.04[E] *infra*.

§ 16.02 CONTRASTING SECURED AND UNSECURED CLAIMS

[A] What Is a Claim?

Bankruptcy is a collective process in which the court resolves "claims" arising under nonbankruptcy law against financially distressed debtors. The Bankruptcy Code defines the term "claim" very broadly to incorporate any "right to payment, whether or not . . . reduced to judgment, liquidated, unliquidated, fixed, contingent, matured, unmatured, disputed, undisputed, legal, equitable, secured, or unsecured."[26] Likewise, the Code broadly defines "creditor" to include any individual or entity that holds "a claim against the debtor" that arose prior to filing of the bankruptcy petition.[27] By defining the terms "claim" and "creditor" so broadly, the Code makes it possible for the bankruptcy process to address and resolve all of the debtor's legal obligations arising out of its pre-bankruptcy activities.[28]

[B] The Allowance of Claims

To make distributions to creditors, bankruptcy must identify those creditors holding valid claims against the debtor. Not surprisingly, bankruptcy law does not honor all pre-bankruptcy claims; instead, policy concerns justify the disallowance of some claims. Sometimes the rationale for disallowing a claim rests upon nonbankruptcy law. For example, claims that are not enforceable under nonbankruptcy law — such as a "debt" evidenced by a forged promissory note — are not enforced in bankruptcy, lest such claimants receive better treatment in bankruptcy courts than they would outside of bankruptcy.[29] In other cases, the rationale for disallowance is based on concerns of sound bankruptcy policy, such as the disallowance of claims for unmatured interest.[30]

---

[26] 11 U.S.C. § 101(5)(A).

[27] *Id.* § 101(10).

[28] S. Rep. No. 989, 95th Cong., 2d Sess. 22.

[29] 11 U.S.C. § 502(b)(1).

[30] *Id.* § 502(b)(2). For example, suppose that Creditor asserted an otherwise valid claim for $1,000 for goods shipped to Debtor on open account, and Creditor's terms included an 18% interest charge on past due accounts. Section 502 would allow the claim in the amount of $1,000, plus any interest that had accrued up to the date of the bankruptcy petition, but section 502(b)(2) would disallow the claim to the extent of any interest that otherwise would have accrued under nonbankruptcy law after the petition date.

The Bankruptcy Code denies unmatured interest on unsecured claims as a matter of administrative convenience. Debtors typically do not have the assets to pay 100% of the principal balance of unsecured claims — much less any interest on those claims. By disallowing claims for unmatured interest, the Bankruptcy Code avoids the accrual of interest (and the inconvenience of recomputing claim balances) as the case proceeds. Vanston Bondholders' Protective Comm. v. Green, 329 U.S. 156 (1946); *In re* Brooks, 323 F.3d 675 (8th Cir. 2003); *In re* Hanna, 872 F.2d 829 (8th Cir. 1989).

Notwithstanding section 502(b)(2), creditors holding oversecured claims (claims secured by property with a value exceeding the balance of the debt) can collect post-petition interest as

Thus, Bankruptcy Code section 502 distinguishes between *allowed claims* and *disallowed claims*. Under section 502(a), claims are deemed "allowed" unless the trustee, the debtor, or some other party in interest raises a valid objection to the claim.[31] Once a proper party raises an objection to the claim, the court must conduct a hearing and determine the amount of the creditor's allowed claim.[32]

[C] Secured Claims, Unsecured Claims, and Valuation

The Bankruptcy Code further separates claims into two primary categories — *secured claims* and *unsecured claims*. As a starting point, bankruptcy takes secured creditors as it finds them on the petition date — a security interest that is enforceable under nonbankruptcy law will also be respected in bankruptcy.[33] A creditor with a valid lien (such as a mortgage or Article 9 security interest) upon certain of the debtor's assets is treated as the holder of a *secured claim* against those assets and retains its pre-bankruptcy priority for any distribution from those assets.[34] If Bank holds a valid Article 9 security interest in Chapter 7 Debtor's inventory (worth $100,000) to secure a debt of $40,000, Bank will be repaid its $40,000 from the proceeds of the inventory before any administrative expenses or general creditors will be paid.[35] In contrast, the holders of *unsecured claims* — general creditors without any pre-bankruptcy lien against specific assets of the debtor — receive payment only on a pro rata basis to the extent that assets remain after payment of secured claims and the expenses of bankruptcy administration.[36]

In some cases, however, a creditor will hold an *undersecured* claim — a claim that is secured by a lien upon assets of the debtor that have a value less than the total balance of the creditor's allowed claim. For example, suppose Bank holds a valid Article 9 security interest in Chapter 7 Debtor's

---

part of their allowed claim, up to but not beyond the value of the collateral. 11 U.S.C. § 506(a)(1), (b). Interest on secured claims is discussed in further detail in § 16.03[B][1][a][ii] *infra*.

[31] 11 U.S.C. § 502(a) (claims deemed allowed unless party in interest objects).

[32] *Id.* § 502(b) (if objection is filed, court must determine amount of allowed claim after notice and hearing). Section 502(b) elaborates the circumstances upon which the court must disallow a creditor's claim; its full reach is beyond the scope of this book.

[33] This general statement is subject to two caveats regarding its scope. First, while the secured party's lien itself is respected, the bankruptcy petition stays the secured party's nonbankruptcy remedies to enforce that lien (such as foreclosure) during the pendency of bankruptcy, as discussed in § 16.03[A] *infra*. Second, in certain circumstances the Code gives the trustee or the debtor the power to avoid a creditor's security interest, either in whole or in part, in order to advance one or more of the Code's underlying policy objectives. Section 16.04 discusses these "avoiding powers."

[34] 11 U.S.C. § 506(a)(1).

[35] The trustee could, however, first deduct the "reasonable, necessary costs and expenses" of preserving and disposing of the inventory to the extent those costs and expenses provided a benefit to Bank. *Id.* § 506(c).

[36] *Id.* §§ 726(a), 507(b).

inventory (worth $40,000) to secure a debt of $100,000. Outside of bankruptcy, the creditor would be deemed to hold one legal claim against the debtor in the amount of $100,000. The Bankruptcy Code, however, "bifurcates" the claim of an undersecured creditor such as Bank. Section 506(a)(1) treats Bank's claim as if it were *two separate claims* — a secured claim equal to the value of the collateral, and an unsecured claim to the extent of the deficiency balance of Bank's claim. [37] In this example, Bank would thus have a secured claim of $40,000 and an unsecured claim of $60,000. [38]

Few issues have generated more controversy in bankruptcy than the proper method for determining the value of a secured party's collateral. An item of collateral might bring different prices if sold in different contexts. For example, a car sold at a foreclosure sale on the courthouse steps might bring a $10,000 sale price. The same car might bring a price of $11,000 if sold in a dealer auction, or a price of $13,000 if sold on a retail auto sales lot. Which price reflects the car's "value" for purposes of bankruptcy valuation?

Section 506(a)(1) does not specify one particular measure of value for all collateral valuations. Instead, section 506(a)(1) provides a flexible, case-by-case standard, under which the court should determine the value of collateral "in light of the purpose of the valuation and of the proposed disposition or use of such property. . . ."[39] This standard suggests that the

---

[37] Section 506(a)(1) literally states that an allowed claim secured by a valid lien on certain property is secured to the extent of "the value of such creditor's interest in the estate's interest in such property." *Id.* § 506(a)(1). In interpreting this section, the Supreme Court has equated the quoted language with "the value of the collateral." United Savings Ass'n of Texas v. Timbers of Inwood Forest Assocs., Ltd., 484 U.S. 365 (1988).

[38] In this hypothetical, the most likely scenario is that the Chapter 7 trustee will abandon the property to Bank, which will conduct an Article 9 sale of the inventory and apply the proceeds to Bank's debt. The unsecured portion of the Bank's claim (the portion remaining after Bank sells the inventory) will be discharged in bankruptcy following any pro rata distribution to unsecured creditors.

In limited circumstances, Chapter 7 debtors may attempt to retain an overencumbered asset (such as a house or a valuable piece of art or jewelry). For example, suppose that a Chapter 7 debtor owns a home worth $60,000 that is subject to a mortgage held by Bank securing a debt of $70,000. Debtor wishes to retain possession of her home because she fears that after bankruptcy she will be unable to obtain credit to purchase another home. Thus, Debtor continues making her monthly mortgage payments to avoid losing her home (although she is not paying any of her other debts). Under section 506(a)(1), Bank would have a secured claim for $60,000 and an unsecured claim of $10,000; further, Debtor's liability for the unsecured claim will be discharged. Bank's mortgage lien, however, will survive bankruptcy unaffected. Thus, if Debtor wants to avoid foreclosure of the lien following bankruptcy, Debtor will have to repay the entire mortgage balance, not just the $60,000 secured portion of Bank's claim. Dewsnup v. Timm, 502 U.S. 410 (1992).

In Chapter 11 cases only, the Code gives the undersecured creditor an option: it can (i) allow its claim to be bifurcated under section 506(a)(1) or (ii) elect to have its entire claim treated as secured under section 1111(b), even though section 506(a)(1) would otherwise bifurcate its claim. 11 U.S.C. § 1111(b). In the example given in the text, if Bank exercises its section 1111(b) election, Bank would have a secured claim for $100,000 and no unsecured claim at all. As a result of this election, Bank would have no right to receive any pro rata distributions to unsecured creditors.

[39] *Id.* § 506(a).

court's determination of the collateral's "market value" is a function of both the debtor's proposed use of the collateral and the procedural context of the bankruptcy case.[40] For example, if a secured party is seeking relief from the automatic stay to be permitted to foreclose on the collateral, section 506(a)(1) suggests that the court should value the collateral using the price the collateral would bring in a commercially reasonable foreclosure sale.[41] By contrast, if a Chapter 11 debtor proposes to retain the collateral under its plan, a court evaluating the debtor's plan should value the collateral based on its "replacement value" — *i.e.*, the price that it would cost the debtor to purchase similar collateral in a market transaction.[42]

As part of the Bankruptcy Abuse Prevention and Consumer Protection Act of 2005 ("BAPCPA"), Congress added a new section 506(a)(2), which mandates valuation based on "replacement value" as to individual Chapter 7 and Chapter 13 debtors. Section 506(a)(2) provides as follows:

> If the debtor is an individual in a case under chapter 7 or 13, [the value of] personal property securing an allowed claim shall be determined based on the replacement value of such property as of the date of the filing of the petition without deduction for costs of sale or marketing. With respect to property acquired for personal, family, or household purposes, replacement value shall mean the price a retail merchant would charge for property of that kind considering the age and condition of the property at the time value is determined.[43]

§ 16.03 THE AUTOMATIC STAY

[A] Nature and Scope

Outside of bankruptcy, creditors can resort to their ordinary collection remedies upon the debtor's default. The filing of a bankruptcy petition, however, automatically triggers the stay authorized by section 362(a), which enjoins creditors from exercising their ordinary remedies to enforce or collect debts that arose prior to the bankruptcy petition.[44] Under section 362(a), the filing of a bankruptcy petition means that a creditor legally may not engage in any of the following customary collection activities: filing suit to collect a pre-bankruptcy debt;[45] prosecuting a previously filed suit to

---

[40] For a thoughtful treatment of valuation issues in bankruptcy, *see* Robert M. Lawless & Stephen P. Ferris, *Economics and the Rhetoric of Valuation*, 5 J. Bankr. L. & Prac. 3 (1995).

[41] *See infra* § 16.03[B] (valuation in context of motions for relief from automatic stay).

[42] *Cf.* Associates Commercial Corp. v. Rash, 520 U.S. 953 (1997) (replacement value measure appropriate in context of Chapter 13 debtor's proposal to retain collateral over objection of secured party).

[43] 11 U.S.C. § 506(a)(2). For further discussion of the impact of section 506(a)(2) in the Chapter 7 context, see *infra* § 16.08 (valuation in context of Chapter 7 debtor's redemption of collateral).

[44] 11 U.S.C. § 362(a). The stay is self-executing; it arises automatically upon the filing of the bankruptcy petition, without any action by the debtor or the bankruptcy court.

[45] *Id.* § 362(a)(1).

collect a pre-bankruptcy debt;[46] enforcing a judgment obtained prior to bankruptcy;[47] attaching, levying upon, or repossessing property of the bankruptcy estate;[48] obtaining, perfecting, or enforcing a lien or security interest in property of the debtor or the bankruptcy estate;[49] or taking any other action "to collect, assess, or recover" a pre-bankruptcy debt (including setting off a mutual debt owed to the debtor).[50] Section 362(a) defines the scope of the stay in such broad and sweeping terms that dunning letters, phone calls to the debtor, and even polite requests for payment must stop once the debtor files its bankruptcy petition. Once the debtor files a bankruptcy petition, creditors "may continue to breathe, eat and sleep and are free to dream about the debtor,"[51] but cannot do anything else with regard to the debtor unless that action falls within the limited and exclusive set of exceptions specified in section 362(b).[52]

What happens when a creditor violates the automatic stay? Generally speaking, the debtor is unaffected; creditor actions taken in violation of the automatic stay are void.[53] A creditor cannot argue that its actions should be given effect because it lacked notice or knowledge of the debtor's bankruptcy filing; actions that violate the stay are void even if the creditor honestly was unaware of the bankruptcy filing. Furthermore, creditors that knowingly violate the stay face potentially serious financial consequences. Under section 362(h), an individual that suffers injury as a result of a

---

[46] *Id.*

[47] *Id.* § 362(a)(2).

[48] *Id.* § 362(a)(3).

[49] *Id.* § 362(a)(4), (5).

[50] *Id.* § 362(a)(6), (7). The Supreme Court has held, however, that while a bank may not effect a setoff of the debtor's bank account without obtaining relief from the stay, a bank can place an "administrative freeze" on a debtor's bank account — thereby preventing any disbursements from the account — without violating the stay. Citizens Bank of Md. v. Strumpf, 516 U.S. 16 (1995).

[51] 1 David G. Epstein, Steve H. Nickles & James J. White, *Bankruptcy,* § 3-1, at 79 (West Prac. ed. 1992).

[52] Section 362(b) allows the commencement or continuation of certain actions to establish or enforce the debtor's noncommercial obligations. *See* 11 U.S.C. §§ 362(b)(1) (criminal proceedings against debtor); 362(b)(2) (actions to establish paternity or orders for alimony, maintenance or support); 362(b)(4) (actions by governmental units to enforce police or regulatory power); 362(b)(9) (governmental tax audits and issuance of tax deficiency notices). Section 362(b)(10) permits a landlord of nonresidential land to repossess the land from the debtor if the lease has expired. Finally, section 362(b)(3) permits a secured party to perfect a lien against property of the estate (such as by filing an Article 9 financing statement) after the petition date — notwithstanding the stay prohibitions in section 362(a)(4)-(5) — in two limited circumstances that will be discussed in conjunction with the trustee's avoiding powers in § 16.04[B] and § 16.04[E] *infra.*

[53] Easley v. Pettibone Michigan Corp., 990 F.2d 905 (6th Cir. 1993) (post-petition filing of lawsuit against debtor); *In re* Schwartz, 954 F.2d 569 (9th Cir. 1992) (post-petition IRS tax assessment); *In re* Ward, 837 F.2d 124 (3d Cir. 1988) (post-petition sheriff's foreclosure sale); *In re* Mitchell, 279 B.R. 839 (9th Cir. Bankr. 2002) (post-petition foreclosure of debtor's residence); *In re* Prine, 222 B.R. 610 (Bankr. N.D. Iowa 1997) (post-petition notation of secured party's lien on title certificate); *In re* Servico, Inc., 144 B.R. 933 (Bankr. S.D. Fla. 1992) (post-petition tax sale).

willful violation of the stay can recover actual damages (including costs and attorneys' fees).[54] In addition, section 362(h) authorizes the award of punitive damages for willful stay violations that involve egregious or outrageous conduct.[55] Unless the bankruptcy court terminates or modifies the effectiveness of the stay, it remains in effect until the bankruptcy case is closed or dismissed, or until the debtor receives its discharge, whichever first occurs.[56] Further, the stay remains in effect to enjoin actions against any asset that is property of the bankruptcy estate for as long as that asset remains a part of the bankruptcy estate.[57]

By halting all external collection efforts, the stay essentially forces creditors to resolve their claims against the debtor through the collective bankruptcy process, under the supervision of the bankruptcy court. The injunctive nature of the stay thus helps to promote the key objectives of the bankruptcy process: to provide the debtor with a "breathing spell" during which the debtor can arrange a plan for its reorganization or its

---

[54] 11 U.S.C. § 362(h). On its face, section 362(h) limits the availability of damages to an "individual" injured by a willful stay violation. The majority of circuit courts has interpreted this provision literally and has refused to award damages or fees to corporate debtors. *In re* Spookyworld, Inc., 346 F.3d 1 (1st Cir. 2003); *In re* Just Brakes Corp. Sys., Inc., 108 F.3d 881 (8th Cir. 1997); Jove Engineering, Inc. v. I.R.S., 92 F.3d 1539 (11th Cir. 1996); *In re* Goodman, 991 F.2d 613 (9th Cir. 1993); *In re* Chateaugay Corp., 920 F.2d 183 (2d Cir. 1990). A few courts, however, have held that section 362(h)'s reference to "individual" debtors was likely a drafting error by Congress and have awarded damages or fees to corporate debtors. *In re* Atlantic Business & Community Corp., 901 F.2d 325 (3d Cir. 1990); Budget Serv. Co. v. Better Homes of Va., Inc., 804 F.2d 289 (4th Cir. 1986).

Courts have also disagreed as to whether the trustee can recover damages and fees under section 362(h). *Compare In re* Pace, 67 F.3d 187 (9th Cir. 1995) (no; trustee not an "individual") *with In re* Garofalo's Finer Foods, Inc., 186 B.R. 414 (N.D. Ill. 1995) (yes; trustee is an "individual"). Even if the trustee cannot recover damages and fees under section 362(h), however, the court retains discretion to award the trustee costs and attorneys' fees under its power to sanction contempt as articulated in 11 U.S.C. § 105(a). *In re* Pace, 67 F.3d 187 (9th Cir. 1995); *In re* Lickman 297 B.R. 162 (Bankr. M.D. Fla. 2003).

[55] *See, e.g., In re* Wagner, 74 B.R. 898 (Bankr. E.D. Pa. 1987) (secured party burst into debtor's home, extinguished lights, held finger to debtor's head and threatened to "blow [debtor's] brains out" unless debtor repaid debt). Such egregious examples are easy, but some bankruptcy courts have also awarded punitive damages for creditor activity that posed no such physical threats. *See, e.g., In re* Shade, 261 B.R. 213 (Bankr. C.D. Ill. 2001) (secured party representative accosted debtor in courthouse following initial meeting of creditors and repeatedly demanded payment of secured party's claim, reducing debtor to tears; court awarded $9,000 in punitive damages); *In re* Cepero, 226 B.R. 595 (Bankr. S.D. Ohio 1998) (secured party disposed of repossessed automobile after receiving repeated phone calls advising that debtor had filed bankruptcy petition and requesting return of the automobile; court awarded $12,000 in punitive damages); *In re* Miller, 200 B.R. 415 (Bankr. M.D. Fla. 1996) (creditor continued sending dunning letters and phone calls to couple following Chapter 7 petition in effort to collect $770 claim; court awarded $10,000 in punitive damages).

[56] 11 U.S.C. § 362(c)(2).

[57] *Id.* § 362(c)(1). During the case, property of the estate remains in the estate unless it is liquidated, abandoned under section 554, or the debtor can and does claim the property as exempt under section 522. In reorganization cases, confirmation of a plan of reorganization vests title to property of the estate in the reorganized debtor. *Id.* §§ 1141(b) (Chapter 11); 1227(b) (Chapter 12); 1327(b) (Chapter 13).

orderly liquidation without undue pressure or harassment from creditors,[58] and to preserve the assets of the bankruptcy estate for equitable distribution to similarly situated creditors.[59]

[B]　Relief from Stay

In adopting a broad, self-executing stay, Congress recognized that there would be situations in which a creditor's interest in carrying out an otherwise stayed action (*e.g.*, repossession and foreclosure of collateral) would outweigh the interests of the estate or the debtor in having the stay remain in effect. Congress thus provided a mechanism to allow the court, at the request of an affected creditor, to grant relief from the automatic stay to permit that creditor to act in a manner otherwise forbidden by section 362(a).[60] The Bankruptcy Code sets forth two standards for relief from the stay that are relevant to Article 9 secured parties: section 361(d)(1), which entitles a creditor to relief for "cause," and section 362(d)(2), which entitles a creditor to relief if the debtor has no equity in the collateral and the collateral is not necessary for the debtor's effective reorganization.[61]

[1]　Relief for "Cause" — 11 U.S.C. § 362(d)(1)

Section 362(d)(1) provides that the court shall grant a creditor relief from the stay if that creditor demonstrates "cause, including the lack of adequate protection of an interest in property" held by that creditor.[62]

[a]　Lack of adequate protection

The most frequently litigated ground in lifting the automatic stay for "cause" involves an allegation by a creditor that its interest in the debtor's property is not being "adequately protected." Because an unsecured creditor

---

[58] H.R. Rep. No. 595, 95th Cong., 1st Sess. 340.

[59] *In re* Richardson Builders, Inc., 123 B.R. 736, 738 (Bankr. W.D. Va. 1990).

[60] Section 362(d) specifies four types of relief that the bankruptcy court might order. First, the court could *terminate* the stay, permitting a creditor to begin or resume its collection efforts, but without validating any prior actions taken in violation of the stay. Second, the court could *annul* the stay, thereby validating any prior actions taken in violation of the stay. Third, the court could *modify* the stay, permitting a creditor to take a particular action but otherwise leaving the stay in place with respect to other actions (*e.g.*, allowing the creditor to reduce an unliquidated claim to judgment in state court, but not allowing any execution upon that judgment). Fourth, the court could *condition* the continued effectiveness of the stay upon some action by the trustee or the debtor (*e.g.*, allowing the stay to remain in effect upon the condition that the debtor file its reorganization plan within 30 days).

[61] 11 U.S.C. § 362(d). Section 362(d) also provides two other grounds for relief from stay applicable to real estate mortgagees. Section 362(d)(3) permits relief from the stay to certain real estate mortgagees in cases involving "single asset real estate." Section 362(d)(4) permits relief from stay to real estate mortgagees in cases in which the debtor's petition is part of a scheme to hinder, delay, or defraud creditors that involves either transfer of the mortgaged property without the mortgagee's consent or repetitive bankruptcy petitions.

[62] *Id.* § 362(d)(1).

has no interest in any specific assets of the debtor, relief for lack of adequate protection is limited to creditors with valid and enforceable interests in specific assets of the debtor under nonbankruptcy law (such as Article 9 secured parties).

[i] Preserving the value of the secured party's encumbrance

Outside of bankruptcy, a secured party could repossess its collateral from the debtor after default, liquidate the collateral in compliance with applicable law, recover the collateral's value as of the date of the sale, and apply that amount to the underlying debt. By preventing the creditor from repossessing and selling the collateral — and by allowing the trustee or DIP to retain and use the collateral[63] — the stay imposes upon the secured party a risk that its collateral may depreciate during the pendency of the bankruptcy case. This depreciation could result from ordinary fluctuations in the value of the collateral,[64] from use of the collateral that physically exhausts the collateral's economic value,[65] or from damage to or destruction of the collateral in an uninsured casualty. This risk of depreciation during bankruptcy poses a serious threat to the secured party. For example, assume that Bank holds a valid lien upon Debtor's car to secure a $5,000 debt. Debtor files a Chapter 11 petition, and on the petition date, the car's value is $5,000. During the Debtor's bankruptcy, however, the debtor's continued operation of the car will cause it to depreciate (for the sake of this example, assume that this depreciation can be measured at $150 per month). This depreciation would be of no consequence if Debtor could repay Bank the full $5,000 balance of the debt — but as Debtor is insolvent, full repayment is unlikely. Indeed, Debtor theoretically could remain in Chapter 11 for twelve months, fail to reorganize successfully, and then convert to a Chapter 7 liquidation. During that twelve months, the car would depreciate in value by $1,800 — by which time the car would bring a sale price of only $3,200. Debtor's post-petition use of the car thus creates a threat that Bank — which could have recovered its claim in full but for the automatic stay — will instead recover only a portion of its original secured claim. In this circumstance, Debtor's use of the car means that Bank's security interest in the car is not adequately protected.

Congress provided a mechanism for a secured party such as Bank to protect itself from the risk of depreciation during the pendency of bankruptcy. Because "cause" for relief from the stay includes "lack of adequate protection," Bank can request that the bankruptcy court terminate the stay

---

[63] Under section 363(d), the trustee generally may use property of the estate in the ordinary course of business, without notice or hearing. The debtor in possession in a Chapter 11 case, or the debtor in a Chapter 12 or 13 case, also has the powers of a trustee under section 363(d). *Id.* §§ 1107(a), 1203, 1303.

[64] For example, inventory might decrease in value due to functional or stylistic obsolescence.

[65] For example, by driving a car 2,000 miles per month during the pendency of the bankruptcy, Debtor would exhaust some portion of the car's useful life.

and allow Bank to foreclose on its security interest immediately, or condition any continuation of the stay upon Debtor's providing "adequate protection" of Bank's security interest.[66] Once Bank makes this request,[67] Debtor must either provide Bank with adequate protection of its security interest or surrender the collateral to the secured party; if Debtor does neither, the bankruptcy court must lift the stay and permit Bank to pursue its nonbankruptcy remedies.

The trustee/DIP enjoys some flexibility under the Bankruptcy Code in how to provide adequate protection of a secured party's interest. The trustee/DIP can provide adequate protection by any action that eliminates the risk that continuation of the stay will impose a depreciation loss upon the secured party.[68] As a result, it is perhaps easiest to think of adequate protection as being similar to "insurance" against depreciation in the collateral. To provide adequate protection of a secured party's interest in collateral, the trustee/DIP must ensure that the value of the secured party's collateral (either the original collateral or some substitute collateral) is preserved or that the secured party is compensated for any depreciation that occurs. Section 361 provides an illustrative list of the ways in which the trustee/DIP might provide adequate protection:

- *Cash payments.* If the estate has sufficient unencumbered funds, the trustee/DIP can make cash payments to the secured party in an amount necessary to offset the expected depreciation in the collateral's value. The secured party would apply these payments to reduce the debt, thereby maintaining the value of the collateral relative to the underlying debt.[69]

- *Replacement lien.* If the estate has equity in another asset and the equity in that asset exceeds the anticipated depreciation of the collateral, the trustee can grant the secured party a lien upon that other asset.[70]

- *The "Indubitable Equivalent."* The trustee can provide any other form of relief that will provide the secured party with the "indubitable equivalent" of its interest in the collateral.[71]

---

[66] Although section 363(d) authorizes the trustee to use a secured party's collateral in the ordinary course of business, section 363(e) provides that, upon the secured party's request, the court may prohibit or condition the trustee's use of the collateral "as is necessary to provide adequate protection" of the secured party's interest in the collateral.

[67] This request is typically made by way of a pleading filed with the bankruptcy court and entitled either "Motion to Lift Stay" or "Motion for Adequate Protection."

[68] Thus, for example, if the debtor has allowed casualty insurance upon the collateral to lapse, adequate protection requires that the trustee/DIP insure the collateral up to its then-current value, and failure to do so justifies relief from the automatic stay. *In re* Jones, 189 B.R. 13 (Bankr. E.D. Okla. 1995); *In re* Hancock, 126 B.R. 270 (Bankr. E.D. Tex. 1991); *In re* Scott Segal Farms, Inc., 31 B.R. 377 (Bankr. S.D. Fla. 1983).

[69] 11 U.S.C. § 361(1).

[70] *Id.* § 361(2).

[71] *Id.* § 361(3).

Although the term "indubitable equivalent" is vague,[72] it definitely includes the existence of an "equity cushion," meaning any surplus value (*i.e.*, equity) in the collateral over and above the balance of the debt. For example, assume that Bank holds a security interest in Debtor's car to secure repayment of a debt in the amount of $5,000. If Debtor's car had a value of $9,000 on the petition date, Bank would have a $4,000 equity cushion (the car's excess value relative to the $5,000 debt). Even if Debtor remained in bankruptcy for a full year, and the car depreciated by $150/month throughout that period, Bank would still remain fully secured; thus, as of the petition date, Debtor's use of the car does not seriously threaten the Bank's security interest in the car.[73] Under those circumstances, the court properly should refuse to grant Bank relief from the stay, because the equity cushion provides adequate protection for Bank's security interest.[74]

[ii] The problem of lost opportunity costs

When the debtor files for bankruptcy, it typically ceases making payments on its debts. The consequence is that any creditor holding a claim against the debtor is not collecting the interest that would otherwise accrue under the pre-bankruptcy agreement and applicable nonbankruptcy law. Outside of bankruptcy, of course, a secured party could repossess its collateral following default, liquidate the collateral, apply the proceeds to the debt, and then reinvest those proceeds in some alternative investment opportunity that would produce a return — *e.g.*, it could re-loan the proceeds to a solvent borrower capable of paying interest. By preventing the secured party from pursuing this course of action, the stay imposes a lost opportunity cost upon the secured party. Further, as discussed earlier,

---

[72] The phrase "indubitable equivalent" comes from an opinion by Judge Learned Hand in *In re* Murel Holding Corp., 75 F.2d 941 (2d Cir. 1935), where Judge Hand used the term "most indubitable equivalence" in attempting to explain the parameters of the term "adequate protection" as it was used under the Bankruptcy Act of 1898.

[73] This statement assumes that the debtor continues to maintain adequate insurance on the car to protect against a casualty loss. If the debtor failed to maintain adequate insurance on the car, the secured party would lack adequate protection and could obtain relief from the automatic stay. *See, e.g., In re* Paradise Boat Leasing Corp., 2 B.R. 482 (Bankr. D.V.I. 1979).

[74] *In re* Mellor, 734 F.2d 1396 (9th Cir. 1984); *In re* Colonial Ctr., Inc., 156 B.R. 452 (Bankr. E.D. Pa. 1993); *In re* Shaw Industries, Inc., 300 B.R. 861 (Bankr. W.D. Pa. 2003); *In re* Steffens, 275 B.R. 570 (Bankr. D. Colo. 2002). Over time, of course, depreciation of the collateral would eventually consume the equity cushion. Once the equity cushion is consumed and the secured party is no longer oversecured, the secured party could again request adequate protection of its interest. Thereafter, the trustee would have to provide adequate protection sufficient to satisfy sections 361-363.

Occasionally, creditors have tried to argue that the debtor must adequately protect the equity cushion itself — *i.e.*, that the court must preserve the equity cushion at its bargained-for size. One could argue that, as an economic matter, the creditor that bargained for the security of an equity cushion may have agreed to accept a lower interest rate or may have made other concessions in return, such that protection of the equity cushion is necessary to provide the creditor with the assurance of its bargain. Courts, however, have generally rejected arguments that the trustee/DIP must provide adequate protection of the equity cushion itself. *See, e.g., In re* Hanna, 912 F.2d 945 (8th Cir. 1990); *In re* Senior Care Properties, Inc., 137 B.R. 527 (Bankr. N.D. Fla. 1992); *In re* Lane, 108 B.R. 6 (Bankr. D. Mass. 1989).

bankruptcy law generally compounds this burden by disallowing claims for unmatured interest.[75]

For some secured creditors, Bankruptcy Code section 506(b) partially mitigates this effect of the automatic stay. Section 506(b) provides that an *oversecured* creditor — *i.e.*, a creditor with collateral that has a value exceeding the balance of its allowed claim — may collect interest upon its secured claim, up to (but not beyond) the total value of the collateral.[76] But what about undersecured creditors? On the one hand, section 506(b) by its terms includes only oversecured creditors; thus, one can argue, by negative implication, that Congress did not intend for undersecured creditors to receive interest upon their secured claims.[77] On the other hand, outside of bankruptcy, an undersecured creditor could have used its state law security interest to liquidate the collateral following default and reinvest the proceeds in some alternative interest-bearing investment. Thus, one could also argue that the creditor's right to immediate foreclosure upon default is an "interest in property" that is not adequately protected unless the creditor receives interest upon the secured portion of its claim during the pendency of the stay. During the 1980s, this debate generated a significant body of case law regarding whether "adequate protection" required the trustee to pay post-petition interest on undersecured claims. A significant number of bankruptcy court decisions held that adequate protection did require the payment of post-petition interest.[78]

When the issue finally reached the Supreme Court in *United Savings Ass'n of Texas v. Timbers of Inwood Forest Associates, Ltd.*,[79] the Court concluded that undersecured creditors were *not* entitled to interest during the pendency of the stay under the guise of "adequate protection." Writing for a unanimous Court, Justice Scalia found section 506(b) determinative:

> Since [section 506(b)] permits postpetition interest to be paid only out of the "security cushion," the undersecured creditor, who has no such cushion, falls within the general rule disallowing postpetition interest. If the Code had meant to give the undersecured creditor, who is thus denied interest on his claim, interest on the value of his collateral, surely [section 506(b)] is where that disposition would have been set forth, and not obscured within the "adequate protection" provision of § 362(d)(1).[80]

---

[75] *See* § 16.02[B] *supra*.

[76] 11 U.S.C. § 506(b). If the trustee/debtor does not pay this interest to the oversecured creditor during the pendency of the bankruptcy stay, the unpaid interest accrues and is added to the creditor's secured claim.

[77] Justice Scalia relied upon this argument in rejecting the undersecured creditor's right to collect interest under the guise of "adequate protection" in United Savings Ass'n of Texas v. Timbers of Inwood Forest Assocs., Ltd., 484 U.S. 365 (1988), discussed below.

[78] *See, e.g., In re* American Mariner Indus., Inc., 734 F.2d 426 (9th Cir. 1984) (collecting cases).

[79] 484 U.S. 365 (1988).

[80] *Timbers*, 484 U.S. at 372–73 (citations omitted).

Commentators have criticized the *Timbers* decision both for its economic premises[81] and its method of statutory interpretation,[82] but the Court's subsequent bankruptcy decisions have never questioned *Timbers*. Accordingly, *Timbers* stands for the proposition that the trustee/DIP must provide "adequate protection" only in cases where the risk of depreciation in the value of the collateral poses a threat to the secured party's overall secured position.

[b] Other cause for relief

Section 362(d)(1) does not limit "cause" for relief from the automatic stay only to those circumstances presenting lack of adequate protection. Instead, the bankruptcy court has the discretion to grant relief from the stay in other circumstances where the harm caused by the stay outweighs the benefit to the estate and the debtor from continuing the stay's effectiveness. Thus, courts have terminated the stay upon concluding that a debtor had filed its bankruptcy petition in bad faith or in a clear attempt to abuse the bankruptcy process. An illustrative example is *In re Dixie Broadcasting, Inc.*,[83] where the debtor had entered into a contract to sell a radio station but later reneged when it received a better offer from another prospective purchaser. When the contract vendee sued for specific performance, the debtor filed a Chapter 11 petition to prevent the state court from ordering specific performance. The court granted the vendee's motion to lift the stay, and the Eleventh Circuit affirmed, stating that "[t]he Bankruptcy Code is not intended to insulate financially secure sellers or buyers from the bargains they strike."[84] Likewise, courts have lifted the stay against pending litigation based upon the conclusion that the litigation would be more appropriately resolved in a forum other than the bankruptcy court.[85]

---

[81] Douglas G. Baird, *The Elements of Bankruptcy* 204 (rev. ed. 1993) ("[o]ne can look at *Timbers* as essentially requiring Bank to make a forced, interest-free loan for the duration of the bankruptcy"); David Gray Carlson, *Adequate Protection Payments and the Surrender of Cash Collateral in Chapter 11 Reorganizations*, 15 Cardozo L. Rev. 1357, 1359 (1994) (*Timbers* "denies that time exists").

[82] Justice Scalia's statement that there is no express statutory authority for the payment of interest to undersecured creditors is dubious in light of the "indubitable equivalent" language of section 361(3). In economic terms, part of the "indubitable equivalent" of a secured party's interest in collateral is the interest that the secured party could earn upon liquidation of the collateral and reinvestment of the proceeds.

[83] 871 F.2d 1023 (11th Cir.), *cert. denied,* 493 U.S. 853 (1989).

[84] *Id.* at 1028.

[85] For example, the Fourth Circuit has suggested that the court can consider lifting the stay where the issues involved in pending litigation involve only state law such that the expertise of the bankruptcy court is unnecessary, and where modifying the stay to permit litigation to proceed in state court would promote judicial economy. *In re* Robbins, 964 F.2d 342 (4th Cir. 1992). *See also In re* MacDonald, 755 F.2d 715 (9th Cir. 1985) (bankruptcy court lifted stay to permit pursuit of state court spousal-support modification, in deference to state court expertise regarding family law matters); Garland Coal & Mining Co. v. United Mine Workers of Am., 778 F.2d 1297 (8th Cir. 1985) (bankruptcy courts ordinarily should lift stay to allow resolution of labor disputes through arbitration).

[2]   Relief under 11 U.S.C. § 362(d)(2)

Under section 362(d)(2), a secured party can obtain relief from the stay in order to repossess and foreclose upon its collateral if "the debtor does not have an equity" in the collateral and the collateral "is not necessary to an effective reorganization."[86] If these grounds for relief are present, then relief from the stay is both necessary and appropriate; under such circumstances, neither the debtor nor general creditors will benefit if the collateral remains property of the estate.

[a]   Does debtor have equity in the collateral?

For purposes of section 362(d)(2), the debtor has no "equity" in an asset if the sum of all encumbrances on that asset exceeds the value of the asset.[87] To make this determination, of course, the bankruptcy court must determine the value of the collateral. The Bankruptcy Code does not specify a particular method of appraisal. Typically, the interested parties (usually the party seeking relief from stay and the trustee/DIP) present evidence regarding the value of the collateral, sometimes in the form of expert testimony. The bankruptcy court considers this evidence and makes a determination of the collateral's value "in light of the purpose of the valuation and of the collateral's proposed disposition or use,"[88] with the burden of persuasion placed upon the party seeking relief from the stay.[89] If the court's valuation reflects that the debtor does have equity in the collateral, the secured party's motion for relief from the stay under section 362(d)(2) must be denied — as it should be, because the purpose of the stay is to protect that equity for the benefit of general creditors and the debtor's potential reorganization.

Section 506(a)(1) requires the court to value the collateral "in light of the purpose of the valuation and of the collateral's proposed disposition or use." The proper interpretation of this language has generated significant litigation in the bankruptcy courts, with significant disagreement among different courts. Perhaps the best example of the divergent judicial views has involved the valuation of vehicles. For example, suppose Debtor owns an automobile subject to a properly perfected security interest in favor of Bank, securing Debtor's obligation to Bank in the amount of $10,000. Debtor files a Chapter 13 petition and wants to retain the automobile. This particular make and model of automobile has a "bluebook" retail value of $12,000 and a "bluebook" wholesale value of $9,900. In the context of a motion to lift the stay, should the court value Debtor's automobile at its

---

[86] 11 U.S.C. § 362(d)(2). In a liquidation proceeding under Chapter 7, the debtor is not contemplating any reorganization; thus, only the first ground (lack of equity) is relevant.

[87] *In re* Indian Palms Assocs., Ltd., 61 F.3d 197 (3d Cir. 1995); *In re* Sutton, 904 F.2d 327 (5th Cir. 1990); Stewart v. Gurley, 745 F.2d 1194 (9th Cir.1984); *In re* Hurst, 212 B.R. 890 (Bankr. W.D. Tenn. 1997).

[88] 11 U.S.C. § 506(a)(1).

[89] 11 U.S.C. § 362(g)(1); *In re* Dandridge, 221 B.R. 741 (Bankr. W.D. Tenn. 1998); *In re* Food Barn Stores, Inc., 159 B.R. 264 (Bankr. W.D. Mo. 1993).

retail value (leaving Debtor with equity in the automobile) or at its wholesale value (leaving Debtor with no equity)?[90]

Prior to 1997, courts generally followed one of three approaches to this question. A significant number of courts argued that if a debtor proposed to retain an automobile as a part of its reorganization, the court should value the auto at its "going concern" or "retail" value.[91] Many other courts argued that the court should value the automobile at its "wholesale" or "liquidation" value, on the theory that such a valuation more readily reflects the amount that a secured party like Bank would obtain if it foreclosed upon the automobile.[92] Yet other courts took a third, intermediate approach, holding that courts should value the automobile at the average of its retail and wholesale values.[93]

In 1997, the U.S. Supreme Court addressed this issue in *Associates Commercial Corp. v. Rash*.[94] In *Rash*, the debtor proposed to retain a tractor-trailer truck to use in his Chapter 13 reorganization efforts. The Fifth Circuit affirmed the bankruptcy court's valuation of the truck at its "net foreclosure value" (*i.e.*, its liquidation value) rather than its "going concern" value.[95] By an 8-1 margin, the Supreme Court reversed and remanded, holding that where the debtor proposed to retain the collateral in a Chapter 13 case, section 506(a) required the court to value the collateral at its "replacement value" — that is, "the price a willing buyer in the debtor's trade, business, or situation would pay to obtain like property from a willing seller."[96] Justice Ginsburg's opinion suggests that this replace-ment-value measure is appropriate based upon the risks presented to the secured party when the debtor proposes to retain the collateral:

> When a debtor surrenders the property, a creditor obtains it immediately, and is free to sell it and reinvest the proceeds. . . . If a debtor keeps the property and continues to use it, the creditor obtains at once neither the property nor its value and is exposed to double risks: The debtor may again default and the property may deteriorate from extended use. Adjustments in the interest rate and secured creditor demands for more "adequate protection" do not

---

[90] It is more accurate to ask "which measure should be the *starting point*" for the court's valuation. Obviously, if the auto is in below-average condition and in need of repair, the court should reduce the value of the auto below its "bluebook" value accordingly. In contrast, if the auto has low mileage and is generally in excellent condition, the court should increase the value of the auto above its "bluebook" value.

[91] *E.g.*, *In re* Trimble, 50 F.3d 530 (8th Cir. 1995) (value of automobile properly based upon retail value, without deduction for costs of sale).

[92] *E.g.*, *In re* Mitchell, 954 F.2d 557 (9th Cir.), *cert. denied*, 506 U.S. 908 (1992).

[93] *E.g.*, *In re* Hoskins, 102 F.3d 311 (7th Cir. 1996).

[94] 520 U.S. 953 (1997).

[95] *Rash*, 90 F.3d 1036, 1044 (5th Cir. en banc 1996) ("[T]he creditor's interest is in the nature of a security interest, giving the creditor the right to repossess and sell the collateral and nothing more. . . . [T]he valuation should start with what the creditor could realize by exercising that right.").

[96] *Rash*, 520 U.S. at 960.

fully offset these risks. Of prime significance, the replacement-value standard accurately gauges the debtor's "use" of the property. . . . The debtor in this case elected to use the collateral to generate an income stream. That actual use, rather than a foreclosure sale that will not take place, is the proper guide under a prescription hinged to the property's "disposition or use."[97]

Just as soon as the Supreme Court "clarified" this issue by adopting the replacement-value standard, however, the Court immediately confused it again in a footnote, stating "[w]hether replacement value is the equivalent of retail value, wholesale value, or some other value will depend on the type of debtor and the nature of the property."[98]

The Court's point is a legitimate one — although some debtors could only obtain a replacement vehicle through a retail dealer, other debtors could acquire a replacement vehicle at a wholesale price (such as through a private auto auction). For this latter type of debtor, "replacement value" should mean wholesale value.[99] Furthermore, the Court also noted that even where retail value is the appropriate starting point for valuation, the court could make an appropriate downward adjustment to the value to account for the fact that the typical retail price would include some items — like warranties and reconditioning expenses — that "the debtor does not receive when he retains his vehicle."[100]

Courts struggled to interpret the Supreme Court's footnote and (perhaps unsurprisingly) continued to reach different results. In the aftermath of *Rash*, many courts concluded that the "starting point" for valuing vehicles is the midpoint between the retail and wholesale bluebook values.[101] A number of decisions, however, rejected this view as inconsistent with *Rash's* admonition that valuation must occur on a case-by-case basis.[102] Many of these decisions have instead concluded that where the debtor proposes to retain the vehicle, the "replacement value" generally means retail bluebook value, with a downward adjustment for items such as warranty or reconditioning costs.[103]

---

[97] *Id.* at 963 (citations and footnotes omitted).

[98] *Id.* at 965 n.6.

[99] *In re* Oglesby, 221 B.R. 515 (Bankr. D. Colo. 1998).

[100] *Rash*, 520 U.S. at 965 n.6.

[101] *In re* Marquez, 270 B.R. 761 (Bankr. D. Ariz. 2001); *In re* Oglesby, 221 B.R. 515 (Bankr. D. Colo. 1998); *In re* Younger, 216 B.R. 649 (Bankr. W.D. Okla. 1998); *In re* Franklin, 213 B.R. 781 (Bankr. N.D. Fla. 1997).

[102] Evabank v. Baxter, 278 B.R. 867 (N.D. Ala. 2002); *In re* Gonzalez, 295 B.R. 584 (Bankr. N.D. Ill. 2003).

[103] Most courts have calculated the downward adjustment based upon the specific facts of the case. *See, e.g., In re* Gonzalez, 295 B.R. 584 (Bankr. N.D. Ill. 2003); *In re* Dziendziel, 295 B.R. 184 (Bankr. W.D.N.Y. 2003). Others have simply made a percentage deduction. *See, e.g., In re* Renzelman, 227 B.R. 740 (Bankr. W.D. Mo. 1998) (five percent reduction appropriate to account for warranties, reconditioning, cleaning, detailing, dealer preparation, and other services not provided when debtor simply retains its vehicle).

In 2005, BAPCPA added section 506(a)(2), quoted earlier in § 16.02[C], which applies in cases involving individual debtors in Chapter 7 or Chapter 13.[104] Under section 506(a)(2), the property of these debtors must be valued at its replacement value as of the petition date, without deduction for costs of sale or marketing.[105] If the individual Chapter 7 or 13 debtor acquired the property for personal, family, or household purposes, "replacement value" means the price that a retail merchant would charge for property in like condition.[106]

[b]   Is the collateral necessary for debtor's reorganization?

If the court's valuation reflects that the debtor has no equity in the collateral, the court must grant relief from the stay, unless the debtor can prove that the collateral is "necessary for an effective reorganization" of the debtor.[107] To carry the burden of persuasion on this point,[108] the debtor must prove two things. First, the debtor must prove that the particular item of collateral is "necessary" to the debtor's reorganization effort. Courts have not read the term "necessary" too literally, however, as is reflected in *In re Fields*.[109] In the *Fields* case, the secured party sought relief from the stay against certain of the debtor's assets, arguing that because the debtor had other assets it could use to reorganize, the secured party's collateral was not "necessary" to the debtor's reorganization. The court properly rejected this argument. Consider, for example, a debtor in the commercial airline business which owns airplanes, each financed with a different lender. No one plane is really *necessary*, under a literal reading of that term, but how many planes would have to be lost to stay litigation before the court finally had to draw the line and deny such motions because the remaining planes were necessary? Applying such a reading to "necessary" would reward impatient creditors while punishing creditors that exercised self-restraint and did not immediately seek relief from the stay. This approach would only encourage a post-petition race to seek stay relief, in direct conflict with clear bankruptcy policy that discourages such *pre*-petition races.[110]

---

[104] *See supra* text accompanying note 43.

[105] 11 U.S.C. § 506(a)(2). In cases involving Chapter 11 debtors, Chapter 12 debtors, or Chapter 7 debtors other than individuals, valuation would continue to follow the case-by-case, context-driven approach suggested in section 506(a)(1).

[106] *Id.*

[107] *Id.* § 362(d)(2). Obviously, Chapter 7 cases contemplate liquidation of the debtor's property rather than reorganization of the debtor's financial affairs. Accordingly, in a Chapter 7 case, the court should grant a motion for relief from the stay if the debtor has no equity in the property.

[108] *Id.* § 362(g)(2) (party opposing relief from stay has burden of proof on all issues other than issue of debtor's equity in property); *In re* Food Barn Stores, Inc., 159 B.R. 264 (Bankr. W.D. Mo. 1993).

[109] 127 B.R. 150 (Bankr. W.D. Tex. 1991).

[110] *Id.* at 152.

Instead, the court must consider the particular asset's necessity in light of the kind of debtor involved and the kind of reorganization that the debtor contemplates.[111] For example, assume that Waters' Edge, Inc. sells clothing in its own stores and by mail order, and that it is attempting to reorganize in Chapter 11. If Waters' Edge contemplates a reorganization plan whereby it will continue to sell its merchandise in its own retail stores, a court would consider the debtor's trade fixtures (clothing racks, display shelving, counters, cash registers, etc.) to be "necessary" to the debtor's contemplated reorganization. If Waters' Edge plans to close its retail stores and sell only by mail order, however, the court would be more likely to consider the trade fixtures as unnecessary to the debtor's reorganization.

Second, the debtor must prove that an "effective reorganization" is possible. As the Supreme Court noted in the *Timbers* decision, this requirement means that "there must be a 'reasonable possibility of a successful reorganization within a reasonable time.' "[112] If the debtor cannot prove that it is likely to reorganize successfully or within a reasonable period of time, the court should lift the stay — further reorganization efforts by the debtor under those circumstances will waste estate resources that could otherwise go to satisfy the claims of creditors. As a practical matter, the debtor's burden of proof on this point becomes progressively harder for the debtor to meet the longer it remains in bankruptcy. As one court has explained:

> [I]n the initial stages of a Chapter 11 proceeding, the debtor should be granted significant leeway in attempting to establish that successful reorganization is a reasonable possibility. However, as the case progresses, so too does the debtor's burden of proving that successful reorganization may be reasonably expected. . . . [T]he test should be viewed as a continuum with the scales tipping in favor of the debtor in the early stages and the burden of proof becoming greater in the later stages.[113]

[3] Procedural Issues and Burden of Proof

The bankruptcy court does not order relief from the stay *sua sponte*; a secured party seeking relief from the stay must file a motion with the bankruptcy court requesting that the court lift the stay. Under section 362(e)(1), the court must act upon the motion within 30 days; if not, the moving party automatically receives the requested relief. Typically, during this 30-day period, the court conducts a preliminary hearing, after which it either (a) enters an order granting or denying the requested relief, or (b) continues the stay temporarily, pending a later final hearing and determination of the motion.[114] If the court continues the stay pending a final

---

[111] *Id.* at 154.

[112] *Timbers*, 484 U.S. at 376 (quoting the Fifth Circuit's *en banc* opinion in the *Timbers* case). Although the quoted statement was dicta in the *Timbers* case, bankruptcy courts, in subsequent cases, have followed this standard uniformly.

[113] *In re* Ashgrove Apts. of DeKalb Cty., Ltd., 121 B.R. 752, 756 (Bankr. S.D. Ohio 1990).

[114] 11 U.S.C. § 362(e)(1).

hearing, the court must conclude that final hearing within 30 days of the preliminary hearing, unless the court extends that 30-day period with the consent of the parties or based upon "compelling circumstances."[115]

In the 2005 amendments, Congress placed specific additional constraints upon the ability of most individual debtors to delay a final determination of a secured party's motion for relief from stay. If the debtor is an individual and the case is a Chapter 7, 11, or 13 case, the stay terminates 60 days after the secured party's motion, unless the court renders a final determination of the motion within that 60-day period or unless the 60-day period is extended by the secured party's consent or by the court — but the court may only extend this 60-day period "for such *specific* time as the court finds is required for good cause," and the court must make specific factual findings justifying the extension.[116]

The moving party bears the burden of persuasion on the issue of the debtor's equity in the property.[117] Accordingly, a secured party seeking relief from the stay under section 362(d)(2) bears the burden of persuasion as to the value of the collateral. The party opposing relief from the stay (typically the trustee/DIP) bears the burden of persuasion on all other issues, including the existence of adequate protection (or other "cause") and the debtor's prospects for reorganization within a reasonable time.[118] In exceptional circumstances, the court can order relief from the stay without notice if the party seeking relief would be "irreparably damaged" by the delay occasioned by notice and a hearing.[119]

§ 16.04   THE TRUSTEE'S AVOIDANCE POWERS

[A]   Background

As discussed previously, the bankruptcy process seeks to facilitate the debtor's fresh financial start while simultaneously preserving the value of estate property and providing for the equitable treatment of similarly situated creditors. Debtors typically file for bankruptcy protection following a period of financial difficulty. During this period, some creditors may have patiently "worked with" the debtor, extending payment deadlines in an attempt to alleviate the debtor's adverse financial circumstances. Other creditors, however, may have begun exercising their state law collection remedies — reducing their claims to judgment or levying upon the debtor's assets — or may have attempted to negotiate security arrangements with the debtor in exchange for their continued forbearance. As a result of these pre-bankruptcy actions, creditors who were once similarly situated may no

---

[115] *Id.*

[116] *Id.* § 362(e)(2) (emphasis added).

[117] *Id.* § 362(g)(1); *In re* Dandridge, 221 B.R. 741 (Bankr. W.D. Tenn. 1998); *In re* Food Barn Stores, Inc., 159 B.R. 264 (Bankr. W.D. Mo. 1993).

[118] 11 U.S.C. § 362(g)(2); *In re* Food Barn Stores, Inc., 159 B.R. 264 (Bankr. W.D. Mo. 1993).

[119] 11 U.S.C. § 362(f).

longer be in similar positions on the petition date. In addition, such pre-bankruptcy actions may cause a significant depletion of the debtor's property, thereby compromising the Bankruptcy Code's objective of preserving the estate for the benefit of the debtor's reorganization and equitable distribution to creditors.

To combat this problem, the Bankruptcy Code authorizes a series of *avoiding powers* — causes of action that allow the bankruptcy trustee (or the debtor in reorganization proceedings)[120] to avoid, or nullify, certain inequitable or illegitimate dispositions of property by the debtor or obligations incurred by the debtor during some period of time prior to bankruptcy or during bankruptcy. The avoiding powers include:

- the "strong-arm" power to avoid unperfected security interests and other transfers made or obligations incurred by the debtor that could have been avoided by judgment lien creditors (or bona fide purchasers in the case of land) under state law;[121]

- the power to avoid transfers made or obligations incurred by the debtor that could have been avoided by an actual unsecured creditor under applicable nonbankruptcy law;[122]

- the power to avoid preferential transfers that occurred within 90 days prior to bankruptcy (or within one year, if the preferred creditor was an "insider");[123]

- the power to avoid fraudulent transfers made or obligations incurred within two years prior to bankruptcy;[124]

- the power to avoid certain statutory liens against the debtor's property;[125]

---

[120] In a Chapter 11 or Chapter 12 case, the debtor in possession receives the powers of a trustee, including the avoiding powers. 11 U.S.C. §§ 1107(a), 1203.

The Code does not expressly delegate the avoiding powers to a Chapter 13 debtor. *Id.* § 1303. The legislative history, however, suggests that "[§ 1303] does not imply that the debtor does not also possess other powers concurrently with the trustee," 124 Cong. Rec. 32,409 (floor statement of Rep. Edwards), and a number of courts have concluded that a Chapter 13 debtor can exercise the avoiding powers. *See, e.g., In re* Fitzgerald, 237 B.R. 252 (Bankr. D. Conn. 1999); *In re* Hernandez, 150 B.R. 29 (Bankr. S.D. Tex. 1993); *In re* Pinkstaff, 121 B.R. 596 (Bankr. D. Or. 1990); *In re* Robinson, 80 B.R. 455 (Bankr. N.D. Ill. 1987). The trend in recent decisions, however, suggests a growing doubt that a Chapter 13 debtor can exercise the avoiding powers. *See, e.g., In re* Stangel, 219 F.3d 498 (5th Cir. 2000); *In re* Hansen, 332 B.R. 8 (10th Cir. Bankr. 2005); *In re* Merrifield, 214 B.R. 362 (8th Cir. Bankr. 1997); *In re* Richardson, 311 B.R. 302 (Bankr. S.D. Fla. 2004); *In re* Montoya, 285 B.R. 490 (Bankr. D.N.M. 2002); *In re* Miller, 251 B.R. 770 (Bankr. D. Mass. 2000).

[121] 11 U.S.C. § 544(a).

[122] *Id.* § 544(b)(1).

[123] *Id.* § 547.

[124] *Id.* § 548.

[125] *Id.* § 545.

- the power to avoid unauthorized post-petition transfers of property of the estate;[126] and

- the power to avoid certain rights of setoff against the debtor.[127]

The trustee's avoiding powers generally enable the trustee to preserve the estate by ameliorating the harm caused by actions of creditors or the debtor just prior to or in anticipation of bankruptcy. Further, the avoiding powers allow the trustee to negate some advantages obtained by creditors prior to or in anticipation of bankruptcy, thereby ostensibly ensuring equitable treatment of otherwise similarly situated creditors.

Despite the seeming breadth of the trustee's avoidance powers, however, they do not enable the trustee to set aside all pre-bankruptcy transfers made or obligations incurred by the debtor. Not all transfers prior to bankruptcy result in an unjustified depletion of the estate or inequitable recovery by one or more creditors. Unlimited avoidance powers would threaten the security of credit transactions generally; the risk that a trustee could invalidate all pre-bankruptcy transactions with a bankrupt debtor could cause creditors to overreact by refusing to extend future credit to debtors in financial distress, or by extending credit upon terms that are far more unfavorable to debtors. To prevent these potential adverse effects upon credit transactions generally, Congress focused the avoiding powers only upon those transactions it considered to be nefarious — transactions that would inappropriately diminish the bankruptcy estate and/or result in unequal or inequitable distribution to creditors. The following sections discuss these avoiding powers in turn.

---

[126] *Id.* § 549(a). The purpose of section 549 is the preservation of the estate; once the debtor is in bankruptcy, estate property can be transferred only as authorized by the express terms of the Bankruptcy Code or by the order of the bankruptcy court. The trustee's power to avoid unauthorized post-petition transfers of estate property is subject to certain exceptions (listed in §§ 549(b) and 549(c)) that are beyond the scope of this book.

[127] Generally speaking, a creditor can offset a mutual debt it owes to the debtor if each party's debt arose prior to the petition date and the creditor would have a right of setoff under nonbankruptcy law (such as a bank's right to exercise a setoff against the debtor's funds on deposit with the bank). The trustee can prevent a creditor from exercising its setoff right, however, to the extent any of the following is true: (1) the creditor holds a disallowed claim; (2) the creditor acquired its claim from a third party after the petition date; (3) the creditor acquired its claim from a third party during the 90 days prior to bankruptcy and while the debtor was insolvent; or (4) the creditor incurred its debt during the 90 days prior to bankruptcy, while the debtor was insolvent, for the purpose of acquiring a right to setoff. 11 U.S.C. § 553(a). For example, if Bank had accepted $15,000 of deposits by Debtor during the week prior to Debtor's bankruptcy, while Debtor was insolvent, Bank could not use those deposits to offset Debtor's $15,000 unsecured debt to Bank. *In re* United Sciences of Am., Inc., 893 F.2d 720 (5th Cir. 1990). In addition, the trustee can set aside any setoff that a creditor exercised during the 90 days prior to bankruptcy to the extent that the setoff had the effect of improving the creditor's position. 11 U.S.C. § 553(b).

[B]   Strong-Arm Power — 11 U.S.C. § 544(a)

[1]   The Trustee as Hypothetical Lien Creditor vs. the Unperfected Secured Party

Section 544(a)(1) provides that the trustee can avoid any transfer made or obligation incurred by the debtor that a judgment lien creditor could have avoided under nonbankruptcy law as of the date of the bankruptcy petition.[128] This "strong-arm" power primarily allows the trustee to avoid security interests that are unperfected as of the petition date,[129] by means

---

[128] 11 U.S.C. § 544(a)(1). In addition to granting the trustee the status of hypothetical judgment lien creditor, section 544(a) grants the trustee the status of two other hypothetical persons. Section 544(a)(2) endows the trustee with the powers of a hypothetical creditor that obtained an execution upon the debtor that was returned unsatisfied. Section 544(a)(2) only has significance in those states where an unsatisfied execution confers special rights of avoidance upon the execution creditor, and thus this section is rarely used.

Section 544(a)(3) bestows upon the trustee the status of a hypothetical bona fide purchaser of the debtor's land (other than fixtures). Section 544(a)(3) would thus permit the trustee to avoid an unrecorded mortgage against the debtor's land. Giving the trustee the status of a bona fide purchaser is necessary to achieve this result because, under most state recording statutes, unrecorded mortgages are effective against judgment lien creditors; thus, the trustee could not avoid an unrecorded mortgage under section 544(a)(1). Because section 544(a)(2) is rarely used and section 544(a)(3) deals with land, the text focuses exclusively upon section 544(a)(1) and the trustee as a hypothetical judgment lien creditor.

Nevertheless, because interests in fixtures can arise under both Article 9 and real estate law, one must take care not to overstate the trustee's strong-arm rights with respect to fixtures. For example, consider the transaction in *In re Gregory*, 316 B.R. 82, 55 U.C.C. Rep. Serv. 2d 96 (Bankr. W.D. Mich. 2004). A Chapter 7 debtor had granted a mortgage on its land; the mortgage also covered "all fixtures now or hereafter a part of the property," including a manufactured home installed on the land and constituting a fixture under Michigan law. The mortgage was properly recorded in the county land records, but the mortgage lender did not have its encumbrance noted on the manufactured home's certificate of title. After the debtor's Chapter 7 petition, the trustee raised a strong-arm challenge to the mortgagee's lien on the manufactured home. The trustee argued that because the mortgagee failed to perfect its interest in the home by having its lien noted on the title certificate, the trustee could avoid the mortgagee's "unperfected" lien on the manufactured home under section 544(a)(1). The court rejected this argument, noting that the mortgage lender did not take an Article 9 security interest in fixtures, but instead took a valid mortgage lien (which attached to the manufactured home because the home was a fixture) and properly perfected that mortgage lien by recording the mortgage on the land records.

[129] If a secured party perfected its security interest by filing a financing statement and that statement is still effective on the petition date, the trustee cannot avoid the secured party's interest using the strong-arm clause — even if the financing statement subsequently lapses during the bankruptcy case. Under U.C.C. § 9-515(c), the lapse of a financing statement causes retroactive loss of perfection for the secured party only against a "purchaser of the collateral for value." By contrast, lapse of a financing statement causes only a prospective loss of priority against lien creditors. Thus, the trustee — who only has the status of a lien creditor — could not retroactively invalidate the secured party's perfection on the petition date under the strong-arm clause and U.C.C. § 9-515(c).

In situations that a secured party is relying upon temporary perfection, perfection might lapse if the secured party failed to take steps to maintain it after the period of temporary perfection lapses. Temporary perfection rules create the possibility that a secured creditor's interest could be perfected as of the petition date and later lapse after the petition date. In

of a two-step process involving the combined effect of the Bankruptcy Code and Article 9.

For example, suppose that Bank possesses a security interest in Debtor's inventory (worth $100,000) to secure a debt of $100,000, but that Bank failed to file a financing statement covering the inventory. If Debtor files for bankruptcy, section 544(a)(1) arms the trustee with all of the rights and powers of a judgment lien creditor as of the petition date (Step 1) — thereby allowing the trustee to assert any rights that such a creditor could have asserted under nonbankruptcy law. In turn, U.C.C. section 9-317(a) provides that a lien creditor takes priority over an unperfected security interest. Therefore, the trustee/DIP can assert its status as a lien creditor under state law to avoid Bank's unperfected security interest (Step 2). The consequences of this avoidance are twofold. First, the trustee can liquidate the inventory and use the proceeds to pay administrative expenses and unsecured creditors, rather than having to abandon the inventory to Bank or sell it and distribute the proceeds to Bank in reduction of Bank's claim against Debtor. Second, while Debtor's underlying obligation to Bank remains enforceable, Bank's claim is treated as unsecured, significantly reducing Bank's recovery on its claim.

Note that section 544(a)(1) clothes the trustee with the status of a judgment lien creditor *even if no such creditor actually existed on the petition date*. The trustee has the status of the "hypothetical lien creditor," regardless of whether any of the debtor's actual creditors had acquired judgment liens prior to bankruptcy. To illustrate, suppose that in the above hypothetical none of Debtor's general creditors had reduced their claims to judgment and levied upon Debtor's assets prior to bankruptcy. Outside of bankruptcy, Bank's unperfected security interest would still have had priority over the claims of Debtor's other creditors, and Bank would have recovered its claim in full.[130] The Debtor's bankruptcy filing, however,

---

such a case, courts have held that the trustee could use its strong-arm power to avoid the secured party's security interest after it lapses, even if that interest technically was perfected on the petition date. For example, suppose that Secured Party held an automatically-perfected purchase-money security interest in Debtor's television (which was a consumer good), and that 5 days prior to the petition date Debtor had exchanged the television for a piece of equipment used in the Debtor's business. On the petition date, Secured Party's proceeds interest in the equipment is temporarily perfected under U.C.C. § 9-315(c), but that perfection will lapse on the 21st day following the exchange unless Secured Party takes sufficient steps to perfect its interest in the equipment as proceeds. U.C.C. § 9-315(d). If Secured Party fails to file a financing statement or otherwise perfect its interest in the equipment within that period, its perfection will lapse, and a number of decisions have held that the trustee can avoid the security interest under the strong-arm clause. *See, e.g., In re* Reliance Equities, Inc., 966 F.2d 1338, 17 U.C.C. Rep. Serv. 2d 1316 (10th Cir. 1992); *In re* Schwinn Cycling and Fitness, Inc., 313 B.R. 473 (D. Colo. 2004).

[130] Recall that unperfected security interests are effective even against general creditors of the debtor. U.C.C. § 9-201(a).

In the early stages of the most recent Article 9 revision process, Professor James J. White proposed that the drafters abolish the rule that judgment lien creditors prevail over unperfected security interests. Instead, White suggested that the Code's residual priority rule should apply to make an unperfected security interest valid even against lien creditors. White's

permits the trustee to assert the status of a lien creditor, thereby enabling the trustee to avoid Bank's unperfected security interest.[131]

Why should bankruptcy law allow the trustee/DIP to assert rights in bankruptcy that no general creditor could have asserted outside of bankruptcy? There are two plausible justifications for this result. The first is that unperfected security interests are really "secret liens" that create the potential for abuse by the debtor and reliance by third parties. This explanation is not terribly satisfying. Unperfected security interests constitute "secret liens" outside of bankruptcy, but they are still enforceable against general creditors under nonbankruptcy law.[132] The second justification is that the strong-arm power serves a preventive function that helps to facilitate bankruptcy law's underlying objectives. Outside of bankruptcy, a debtor's general unsecured creditors could race to reduce their claims to judgment and levy upon property subject to an unperfected security interest — thereby taking priority over unperfected secured parties and other general creditors. Practically speaking, each individual creditor must participate in this race; those who delay or do not participate at all may be left with a worthless judgment against the debtor. This sort of "race" by unsecured creditors, however, may produce consequences that bankruptcy law wants to avoid. The pressure of creditor collection activity may make it difficult or impossible for the marginal debtor to carry out its business or financial affairs. Indeed, collection activity by unsecured creditors might force the debtor into bankruptcy prematurely, when informal negotiations with creditors instead might have enabled the debtor to restructure its debts and avoid bankruptcy altogether. By enabling the trustee (as a representative of the debtor's general creditors) to assert the status of a judgment lien creditor if the debtor does go bankrupt, section 544(a)(1) ostensibly encourages the debtor's general creditors not to engage in this counterproductive collection race — thereby (hopefully) maximizing the debtor's ability to sort out its financial affairs and avoid a needless bankruptcy.[133]

---

thesis was that lien creditors are not typically reliance creditors (and thus are not harmed by the "secret lien" nature of an unperfected security interest), and that litigation by trustees to avoid unperfected security interests was a waste of judicial resources. James J. White, *Revising Article 9 to Reduce Wasteful Litigation*, 26 Loy. L.A. L. Rev. 823 (1993). Despite Professor White's suggestion, however, revised Article 9 retained the rule that an unperfected security interest is subordinate to the interest of a lien creditor. U.C.C. § 9-317(a)(1).

[131] *In re* Merritt Dredging Co., Inc., 839 F.2d 203, 5 U.C.C. Rep. Serv. 2d 900 (4th Cir.), *cert. denied,* 487 U.S. 1236 (1988); *In re* Kors, Inc., 819 F.2d 19 (2d Cir. 1987); *In re* Pasteurized Eggs Corp., 296 B.R. 283, 51 U.C.C. Rep. Serv. 2d 274 (D.N.H. 2003); *In re* Hurst, 308 B.R. 298, 53 U.C.C. Rep. Serv. 2d 342 (Bankr. S.D. Ohio 2004); *In re* Morgan, 291 B.R. 795, 50 U.C.C. Rep. Serv. 2d 596 (Bankr. E.D. Tenn. 2003); *In re* Advance Insulation & Supply, Inc., 176 B.R. 390, 3 U.C.C. Rep. Serv. 2d 1957 (Bankr. D. Md. 1994), *aff'd,* 176 B.R. 401 (D. Md. 1995). *But see In re* Lynum, 246 B.R. 537, 42 U.C.C. Rep. Serv. 2d 619 (Bankr. E.D. Ky. 2000) (while bankruptcy trustee could avoid senior but unperfected security interest, trustee could not avoid properly perfected security interest held by junior creditor).

[132] U.C.C. § 9-201(a).

[133] One might describe this as the optimistic or "the glass is half-full" theory of creditor behavior. Many critics of the strong-arm power instead adopt the pessimistic "the glass is half-

Note that section 544(a) allows the trustee/DIP to exercise the strong-arm power to avoid an unperfected security interest without regard to any knowledge that the trustee, the debtor, or any creditor might have about that security interest.[134] In this regard, section 544(a) treats the trustee/DIP as having "a pure heart and an empty head." For example, suppose that Bank held an unrecorded mortgage on Debtor's land, but that the trustee knew of the Bank's mortgage. The trustee's knowledge of Bank's unrecorded interest would *not* deprive it of the ability to assert its strong-arm powers under section 544(a). Section 544(a) makes the trustee's knowledge irrelevant; the strong-arm power bestows the status of a lien creditor without knowledge of Bank's security interest, *even if no such creditor actually existed as of the petition date*. Because such a bona fide purchaser of the land would have prevailed over Bank's unrecorded mortgage, the trustee/DIP can avoid Bank's mortgage despite its actual knowledge.

[2] Relation-Back Priority — 11 U.S.C. § 546(b)

The strong-arm power creates a potential statutory trap for certain creditors that might otherwise rely upon the existence of relation-back priority rules that arise under nonbankruptcy law. For example, suppose that Debtor purchases a drill press from Seller, which takes a purchase-money security interest (PMSI) in the press. Knowing that it has the benefit of a 20-day grace period in which to perfect its PMSI and still prevail against intervening lien creditors,[135] Seller does not file its financing statement immediately. The day after the sale, Debtor files a bankruptcy petition. Two days later, and still within the applicable state-law grace period, Seller files its financing statement in the appropriate filing office. As between Trustee and Seller, what is the status of Seller's security interest?

If one looked solely at the language of section 544(a)(1), Trustee would be able to avoid Seller's security interest on the ground that Seller had not perfected that interest prior to Debtor's bankruptcy filing. Outside of bankruptcy, however, Seller's PMSI would have taken priority over the claim of an intervening lien creditor, because Seller perfected its PMSI by filing within the grace period specified in U.C.C. section 9-317(e). Given the

---

empty" theory of creditor behavior, arguing that it is simply naive to think that section 544(a)(1) will discourage unsecured creditors from undertaking collection activity in anticipation of bankruptcy. The pessimists may have the better of the argument here — after all, if the debtor has not yet filed for bankruptcy, what's to say the debtor *actually will* file for bankruptcy? An unsecured creditor that can win the race to the courthouse improves its likelihood of a full recovery, and if no bankruptcy ever ensues, that creditor improves its position vis-a-vis general creditors and unperfected secured creditors. As a result, unsecured creditors without crystal balls or psychic abilities will often choose to engage in this race anyway, notwithstanding the rationale of section 544(a)(1).

[134] *In re* Kitchin Equip. Co., 960 F.2d 1242, 17 U.C.C. Rep. Serv. 2d 322 (4th Cir. 1992); McEvoy v. Ron Watkins, Inc., 105 B.R. 362 (N.D. Tex. 1987); *In re* Chama, Inc., 265 B.R. 662 (Bankr. D. Del. 2000); *In re* Williams, 124 B.R. 311 (Bankr. C.D. Cal. 1991).

[135] U.C.C. § 9-317(e).

rationale of the strong-arm clause, Trustee logically should stand in the same position as a lien creditor would have stood under nonbankruptcy law. To accomplish this result, Congress limited the trustee's strong-arm power in section 546(b) — thereby making the power subject to any provisions of nonbankruptcy law (such as Article 9's grace period for perfecting PMSIs) that permit relation-back priority over intervening third parties.[136] Because Seller perfected its PMSI within the grace period specified in Article 9, Trustee cannot avoid Seller's PMSI under the strong-arm clause.

Full understanding of this example requires additional consideration of section 362 and the effect of the automatic stay. As discussed previously,[137] the filing of the bankruptcy petition operates to stay "any act to . . . perfect . . . any lien against property of the estate."[138] On its face, this would seem to prevent Seller's post-petition financing statement from having any legal effect to perfect Seller's PMSI. Section 362(b)(3) provides an exception in this particular circumstance, however, allowing a creditor to undertake "any act to perfect . . . an interest in property to the extent that the trustee's rights and powers are subject to perfection under section 546(b). . . ."[139] This exception permits a secured party in Seller's position to file its financing statement without violating the automatic stay. Note, however, that this exception only protects the secured party if it acts to perfect its interest within the applicable state-law grace period.[140] Further, the exception applies only to permit the secured party's *perfection* of the interest; the stay remains effective to prevent any action to *enforce* the lien, unless the court orders relief from the stay.

[C] Subrogation to State-Law Avoidance Powers of an Unsecured Creditor — 11 U.S.C. § 544(b)(1)

Section 544(b)(1) authorizes the trustee to avoid "any transfer of an interest of the debtor in property or any obligation incurred by the debtor that is voidable under applicable law by a creditor holding an unsecured claim. . . ."[141] This provision allows the trustee to assert any state-law

---

[136] 11 U.S.C. § 546(b)(1)(A) (the avoiding powers are subject to "any generally applicable law that permits perfection of an interest in property to be effective against an entity that acquires rights in such property before the date of perfection"). Note that section 546(b) does not itself authorize relation-back priority for any secured party, but only recognizes and incorporates provisions of nonbankruptcy law that provide for relation-back priority over third parties who claim intervening interests.

[137] *See* § 16.03[A] *supra*.

[138] 11 U.S.C. § 362(a)(4).

[139] *Id.* § 362(b)(3).

[140] *In re* Continental Country Club, Inc., 64 B.R. 177 (Bankr. M.D. Fla. 1986). In the example in the text, Debtor filed its petition the day after taking possession of the drill press. Thus, to qualify for the protection of section 546(b)(1)(A) and not violate the automatic stay, Seller must file its financing statement within nineteen days of the bankruptcy petition. U.C.C. § 9-317(e). Any filing by Seller after that period elapses would violate the automatic stay and would not perfect Seller's security interest, which Trustee could then avoid under section 544(a)(1).

[141] 11 U.S.C. § 544(b)(1).

avoidance claim that one of the debtor's *actual* unsecured creditors could have asserted. Unlike the strong-arm clause, section 544(b)(1) does not endow the trustee with the status of a "hypothetical" creditor. To assert an avoidance claim under section 544(b)(1), the trustee must identify an actual, honest-to-goodness unsecured creditor of the debtor that could have asserted the power to avoid the particular transfer under state law. If the trustee can identify such a creditor, section 544(b)(1) subrogates the trustee to the rights of that creditor and permits the trustee to assert this claim on behalf of the estate.[142]

As a practical matter, nonbankruptcy law rarely grants unsecured creditors the power to set aside transfers by the debtor, and thus section 544(b)(1) is of limited use to the trustee/DIP. There are two primary circumstances under which trustees/DIPs have asserted section 544(b)(1) avoidance claims. The first involves transfers that are fraudulent under applicable state fraudulent transfer law; these transfers are treated in greater detail in conjunction with the discussion of Bankruptcy Code section 548.[143] The second involves bulk sale transfers that did not comply with applicable state law governing bulk sales. In a jurisdiction in which U.C.C. Article 6 still governs bulk sales,[144] section 544(b)(1) allows the trustee to set aside a bulk sale under Article 6 if it can identify a particular creditor that did not receive notice of the bulk sale.[145]

[D] Power to Avoid Statutory Liens

"Statutory liens" are liens that arise as a matter of nonbankruptcy law "solely by force of a statute on specified circumstances or conditions."[146] Often, statutory liens reflect a legislative judgment that particular types of creditors (such as mechanics who service automobiles) deserve special protection from the risk of nonpayment. Generally speaking, bankruptcy law respects statutory liens arising under nonbankruptcy law, and the trustee/DIP cannot avoid statutory liens that validly arose prior to the petition date.

Section 545, however, allows the trustee/DIP to avoid a statutory lien against an asset of the debtor in three limited circumstances. First, section 545(1) permits the trustee/DIP to avoid a statutory lien against any asset where that lien took effect only because the debtor became insolvent or filed for bankruptcy.[147] This provision is necessary to preserve the efficacy of

---

[142] The trustee may avoid the transfer under section 544(b)(1) in its entirety, regardless of the size of the actual unsecured creditor's claim. *In re* Acequia, Inc., 34 F.3d 800 (9th Cir. 1994); *In re* Agricultural Research & Tech. Group, Inc., 916 F.2d 528 (9th Cir. 1990); *In re* DLC, Ltd., 295 B.R. 593 (8th Cir. Bankr. 2003).

[143] *See* § 16.04[F][4] *infra.*

[144] The National Conference of Commissioners on Uniform State Laws has repealed Article 6 from the official version of the U.C.C. Nevertheless, Article 6 has not yet been repealed by all of the states that originally enacted it.

[145] *In re* Villa Roel, Inc., 57 B.R. 835, 42 U.C.C. Rep. Serv. 1396 (Bankr. D.D.C. 1985).

[146] 11 U.S.C. § 101(53). *See* Chapter 13 *supra.*

[147] 11 U.S.C. § 545(1).

federal bankruptcy law; otherwise, states could establish statutory "insolvency" liens that would circumvent the Bankruptcy Code's priority scheme for distribution to creditors. Second, section 545(2) permits the trustee/DIP to avoid a statutory lien against any asset if that statutory lien could not have been enforced against a bona fide purchaser of the asset outside of bankruptcy.[148] For example, section 545(2) would allow the trustee to avoid a federal tax lien against a debtor's assets if the IRS had not filed a notice of tax lien filing as of the petition date.[149] This allows the trustee/DIP to avoid secret statutory liens to the same extent as they would be avoidable by an innocent purchaser under nonbankruptcy law. Finally, sections 545(3) and 545(4) permit the trustee/DIP to avoid any common law or statutory landlord's lien for unpaid rent.[150] A pertinent example involves a landlord's statutory lien on farm products for unpaid rent on leased crop land. This lien is an agricultural lien governed by Article 9 once it arises,[151] but it is not consensual in nature and accordingly is subject to avoidance under sections 545(3) and 545(4).[152]

[E] Power to Avoid Preferential Transfers — 11 U.S.C. § 547

[1] Background

Suppose that Debtor has two creditors, A and B, to which Debtor owes $100 each. Suppose further that Debtor has only $100 in assets, and uses those assets to make full payment to A before declaring bankruptcy. A receives payment in full, B receives nothing. One might say that the Debtor has chosen to "prefer" A to B, or that A has received a "preferential" payment. Outside of bankruptcy, commercial law generally does not care about preferential transfers, and essentially leaves creditors like A and B to their own wiles and efforts. If Debtor pays A in full (whether voluntarily or in response to A's demands) and pays B nothing, that is B's problem; B could have prevented this result by pursuing its remedies more promptly or by being more insistent in its collection efforts.

Bankruptcy law does care about such transfers, however, because one of the goals of bankruptcy is to provide a collective debt-resolution process that distributes Debtor's assets in a way that treats similarly situated creditors in similar fashion. In the above example, before the payment, A and B were similarly situated general creditors; in a Chapter 7 liquidation, each creditor would have received $50 on its claim. By choosing to pay A

---

[148] *Id.* § 545(2).

[149] *In re* J.B. Winchells, Inc., 106 B.R. 384 (Bankr. E.D. Pa. 1989).

[150] 11 U.S.C. § 545(3), (4). Note carefully that section 545 does not authorize the trustee to avoid a lien for rent for which the lienor contractually bargained — such a lien is a security interest, not a statutory lien. Dallas v. S.A.G., Inc., 836 F.2d 1307 (11th Cir. 1988).

[151] Agricultural liens are discussed in § 13.02 *supra.*

[152] *See, e.g., In re* Harrell, 55 B.R. 203 (Bankr. E.D.N.C. 1985).

in full and B nothing, Debtor circumvents bankruptcy's distributive scheme to the detriment of B.

While the foregoing example involves a purposeful attempt to prefer one creditor over another, transfers can have preferential effect regardless of the debtor's motive or the impetus for the transfer. For example, suppose that the payment of $100 to A had occurred involuntarily as a result of an execution sale upon Debtor's property. The payment still has precisely the same effect as a voluntary payment by Debtor; if the execution had never occurred, both A and B would have received $50 in a Chapter 7 liquidation. Unless bankruptcy law provided a mechanism to deal with such transfers, creditors would have a significant incentive to engage in "last-minute" or "eve-of-insolvency" collection activities — *i.e.*, to reduce their unsecured claims to judgment and execute upon those claims before other creditors could act. Such collection activity has the potential for triggering the "race to the courthouse" that bankruptcy law seeks to avoid (or at least mitigate) in the first place. Thus, to discourage the piecemeal dismemberment of the debtor's assets and to facilitate equitable distribution to each class of similarly situated creditors, Congress provided the trustee with the power to avoid certain preferential transfers that occur just prior to the filing of a bankruptcy petition.

[2] Proving the Elements of a Preference

The trustee can avoid any transfer (whether or not voluntary) of an interest in the debtor's property if the transfer meets all of the following characteristics specified in section 547(b):

- *The transfer must have been made to a creditor or must have benefitted a creditor.*[153] Preference law is concerned only with pre-bankruptcy actions that enable creditors to collect their pre-bankruptcy claims (*e.g.*, the debtor repays a loan to a creditor) or render those claims more secure (*e.g.*, the debtor grants a creditor a security interest in certain assets to secure a previously unsecured obligation). If the transfer does not benefit a creditor (*e.g.*, the debtor makes a gift of valuable property to a friend), preference law does not apply to that transfer.[154]

- *The transfer must have been made on account of an antecedent debt, i.e., a liability that the debtor incurred before the debtor made the transfer.*[155] Again, preference law focuses only upon those transfers that enable a creditor to collect a pre-existing debt or render a pre-existing debt more secure. Thus, if Debtor grants Bank a security interest in a car to secure a simultaneous[156]

---

[153] 11 U.S.C. § 547(b)(1).

[154] In some cases, gift transfers by the debtor prior to bankruptcy may be avoidable as fraudulent transfers under section 548. *See* § 16.04[F][2] *infra*.

[155] 11 U.S.C. § 547(b)(2).

[156] As a practical matter, a truly simultaneous transfer is unlikely. Even when Buyer pays

$2,000 loan to Debtor by Bank, there is no preference; Bank is not engaging in activity intended to collect or secure an obligation previously incurred by Debtor. In contrast, if Debtor grants Bank a security interest in a car to secure an otherwise unsecured $2,000 loan made by Bank to Debtor two months earlier, Debtor has transferred an interest in its property on account of an antecedent debt.

- *The debtor must have been insolvent when the transfer took place.*[157] Preference law is not concerned with avoiding transfers that occurred when the debtor was solvent; if a debtor is solvent, it can repay all of its obligations, and thus any transfer by the debtor could not have had the effect of preferring the recipient to the detriment of other creditors. Section 547(f) provides that in any action to avoid a preferential transfer, the debtor is presumed to have been insolvent during the 90 days prior to the filing of the bankruptcy petition.[158]

- *The transfer must have taken place within 90 days prior to the filing of the bankruptcy petition (or within one year prior to the petition, in the case of a transfer to an "insider").*[159] Preference law focuses upon transfers of the debtor's property in anticipation of the debtor's bankruptcy. Preference law aims to prevent creditors from "opting out" of the collective bankruptcy process by trying to collect or secure their pre-bankruptcy claims during the debtor's "slide into bankruptcy."[160] Congress could have adopted a subjective standard that focused upon the creditor's state of mind (*i.e.*, was the creditor trying to "opt out"?), but this would have been very difficult to apply. Instead, Congress opted

---

cash to Seller to purchase goods over the counter, Buyer's payment typically occurs at least a few seconds after Buyer's obligation to pay for the goods arises. Technically speaking, even a delay of one second between the arising of Buyer's obligation and Buyer's transfer would mean that the transfer occurred on account of an antecedent debt — a result that would stretch the trustee's preference avoiding power well past the bounds of reason. As a practical matter, courts have not interpreted the term "antecedent" so restrictively as to set aside payments made in cash sales. Furthermore, as discussed *infra* § 16.04[E][4][a], section 547(c)(1) provides an exception that prevents the trustee from recovering transfers such as cash sales that involve "substantially contemporaneous" exchanges for new value. Thus, in many cases, section 547(c)(1) would mitigate the effect of a court's decision to adopt an overly technical interpretation of section 547(b)(2).

[157] 11 U.S.C. § 547(b)(3). The Bankruptcy Code applies a "balance sheet" test for insolvency — the debtor is "insolvent" if the sum of its debts exceed the value of its assets. *Id.* § 101(32).

[158] *Id.* § 547(f). This presumption is motivated primarily by efficiency. In most bankruptcy cases, the debtor will have been insolvent for some time prior to filing its bankruptcy petition, and thus it would serve no real purpose to force the trustee to spend the time and resources necessary to reconstruct the debtor's records to prove that the debtor was insolvent at the time of the allegedly preferential transfer. As a consequence of this presumption, the recipient of the allegedly preferential transfer bears the burden of coming forward with evidence to demonstrate that the debtor was solvent at the time of the transfer.

[159] *Id.* § 547(b)(4).

[160] H.R. Rep. No. 595, 95th Cong., 1st Sess. 177–78.

for a bright-line preference period — the 90 days immediately prior to the bankruptcy petition. Transfers that occur within this period are conclusively suspect as potential preferences, even if the creditor had no idea of the debtor's financial difficulties. In contrast, the trustee cannot reach transfers that occurred more than 90 days prior to bankruptcy, even if the benefitted creditor fully expected the debtor to seek bankruptcy protection in the near future. Note carefully that the Code expands the preference period to one year if the transferee is an "insider."[161] Because "insiders" have a close relationship with the debtor, they could possess inside information about the debtor's financial circumstances, or could exercise control over the debtor's financial decisions (such as when to seek bankruptcy protection). To prevent insiders from using this information or control to manipulate the timing of preferential transfers,[162] the Bankruptcy Code expands the preference period to one year for transfers that benefit insiders.

- *Finally, the transfer must have actually improved the creditor's position.*[163] Preference law works on the "no harm, no foul" principle; it does not care about transfers that result in the creditor recovering no more than it would have recovered if instead it had been paid only through a liquidation of the debtor's assets. Section 547(b) only reaches those transfers that enabled the recipient to recover more than the recipient would have recovered through liquidation alone. To apply section 547(b), the court must determine what amount the creditor would have received in a Chapter 7 liquidation case *if the alleged preferential transfer had not been made.* If the creditor actually received more than that "hypothetical liquidation" amount, then the transfer had the effect of improving the creditor's position. The following three variations on a common hypothetical demonstrate the proper application of section 547(b):

---

[161] 11 U.S.C. § 101(31) provides a list of characteristics that make a transferee an "insider." Generally speaking, an "insider" can be a relative, an officer or director of a corporation, a partner of a partnership — in other words, someone who has a sufficiently close relationship with the debtor that they can be presumed to be in a position to possess information about the debtor's financial condition, or to possess control over the debtor's financial decisionmaking.

Note, however, that if the trustee attempts to recover an allegedly preferential transfer from an insider, and that transfer occurred more than 90 days prior to the petition date, the trustee is *not* entitled to the presumption that the debtor was insolvent at the time of the transfer. The presumption of insolvency in section 547(f) is strictly limited to the 90 days immediately prior to the petition date.

[162] For example, suppose that X is president and sole shareholder of Debtor, and that X had loaned $10,000 to Debtor. As an insider, X is in a position to cause Debtor to repay its debt to X, and is also in a position to cause Debtor not to file bankruptcy until 91 days later — after the general preference period would have passed.

[163] 11 U.S.C. § 547(b)(5).

- Debtor makes full repayment of a $10,000 unsecured loan from Bank and files its bankruptcy petition 20 days later. If Debtor had not made the repayment, Bank would have received only a partial distribution on its claim in a Chapter 7 liquidation.[164] By receiving payment in full prior to bankruptcy, Bank has improved its position to the detriment of Debtor's other general creditors.

- Debtor makes full repayment of a $10,000 loan secured by Debtor's inventory, which has a value of $30,000. Because Bank held a fully secured claim, Bank would have received full payment on its claim in a Chapter 7 liquidation case anyway; its receipt of the repayment did not improve Bank's position. For this reason, courts have held that the trustee cannot avoid a payment to a fully secured creditor as a preference.[165]

- Debtor makes full repayment of a $10,000 loan secured by Debtor's inventory, which has a value of $5,000. At the time it received payment, Bank held an undersecured claim. Had Bank not received the payment and had Debtor filed a Chapter 7 petition, section 506(a)(1) would have bifurcated Bank's claim into a secured claim of $5,000 and an unsecured claim of $5,000. In that hypothetical Chapter 7 liquidation, Bank would have received full payment of its secured claim, but less than full payment on its unsecured claim; therefore, Debtor's payment to Bank improved its position and can be avoided as a preference.[166]

---

[164] This statement assumes that Debtor is insolvent at the time of the bankruptcy petition. [Note, however, that insolvency is *not* a condition precedent to the filing of a voluntary petition in bankruptcy.] If Debtor is insolvent, by definition it has insufficient assets to pay its creditors and thus general unsecured creditors will receive less than full payment in a Chapter 7 liquidation under the Bankruptcy Code's distributive scheme. *In re* Keplinger, 284 B.R. 344 (N.D.N.Y. 2002); *In re* Milwaukee Cheese Wisconsin, Inc., 164 B.R. 297 (Bankr. E.D. Wis. 1993); *In re* Lease-A-Fleet, Inc., 141 B.R. 853 (Bankr. E.D. Pa. 1992).

[165] *In re* EDC, Inc., 930 F.2d 1275 (7th Cir. 1991); Braniff Airways, Inc. v. Exxon Co., U.S.A., 814 F.2d 1030 (5th Cir. 1987); *In re* Pineview Care Center, Inc., 142 B.R. 677 (Bankr. D.N.J. 1992), *aff'd*, 152 B.R. 703 (D.N.J. 1993). The statement in the text assumes that the trustee has no legitimate basis upon which to avoid Bank's security interest. If the trustee can avoid Bank's security interest under any of the avoiding powers, then Bank will be treated as an unsecured creditor and the $10,000 payment in full will have improved Bank's position. *In re* Adams, 102 B.R. 271, 10 U.C.C. Rep. Serv. 2d 1014 (Bankr. M.D. Ga. 1989).

[166] *In re* Smith's Home Furnishings, Inc., 265 F.3d 959 (9th Cir. 2001); *In re* Air Conditioning, Inc. of Stuart, 845 F.2d 293 (11th Cir.), *cert. denied*, 488 U.S. 993 (1988); *In re* Telesphere Communications, Inc., 229 B.R. 173 (Bankr. N.D. Ill. 1999); *see also* 4 Collier on Bankruptcy ¶ 547.08, at 547–47 to 547–48 ("[p]ayments to a partially secured creditor from property not covered by its lien . . . have a preferential effect, because in a chapter 7 liquidation, that creditor would receive a distribution for its lien in addition to the payments already received"). In this example, the only way that Bank could prove that it had not been made better off would be for Bank to demonstrate that it applied the payments to reduce the secured, rather than the unsecured, portion of its claim. Vern Countryman, *The Concept of a Voidable Preference in Bankruptcy*, 38 Vand. L. Rev. 713, 744 (1985).

[3] Determining When the Transfer Occurred

A transfer cannot constitute a preference unless it occurred on account of an antecedent debt and within the applicable preference period. Given these standards, the trustee must establish the date on which a transfer took place to establish that the transfer satisfies section 547(b). To determine the effective date of pre-petition transfers, section 547(e) provides rules that establish the date a transfer is deemed to have occurred for purposes of preference law. For example, section 547(e) deems any allegedly preferential payment to have been made when the payment legally took effect between the parties under nonbankruptcy law.[167] Thus, a $10,000 payment to Bank by Debtor on December 4 would be deemed to have occurred on December 4 for purposes of section 547(b).[168]

The granting of a security interest by the debtor can also constitute a preferential transfer. Suppose Debtor grants a security interest in its equipment to Bank one month prior to bankruptcy to secure a previously unsecured debt owed to Bank. As a result, Debtor has improved Bank's position as compared to other general creditors — Bank would now receive full payment to the extent of the equipment's value, whereas general creditors would receive only pro rata distributions from unencumbered assets.

When the allegedly preferential transfer is the debtor's granting of a security interest, section 547(e) provides an intricate timing rule that "dates" the security interest for purposes of section 547 based upon when that security interest was "perfected." Section 547 deems a security interest to have been granted when it legally took effect between the parties under nonbankruptcy law (*e.g.*, for a security interest in personal property, when that interest attached under U.C.C. section 9-203), *but only if the secured party perfected*[169] *that security interest at that time or within thirty*[170] *days*

Courts have disagreed over the proper amount that the trustee should recover from Bank in this example. Some courts have suggested that the trustee should be able to avoid the transfer only to the extent that it was preferential. Levit v. Ingersoll Rand Fin. Corp., 874 F.2d 1186 (7th Cir. 1989) (dicta). Under this view, the trustee could not recover the $5,000 portion of the payment allocable to Bank's secured claim, as Bank would have received that $5,000 anyway in a Chapter 7 liquidation. The actual language of section 547, however, does not support this view. Section 547 does not authorize the trustee to avoid transfers to the extent that they are preferential; instead, it authorizes the trustee to "avoid any transfer" that is preferential in effect. Taken literally, section 547 thus authorizes the trustee to avoid the entire $10,000 payment from Bank. In that case, however, Bank's secured and unsecured claims are revived; Bank would then hold a $5,000 secured claim and a $5,000 unsecured claim.

[167] 11 U.S.C. § 547(e)(2)(A).

[168] One caveat is appropriate here. If a debtor makes a payment to a creditor using a check, the Supreme Court has held that transfer (for purposes of section 547(b)) does not occur when the debtor delivers the check to the creditor, but only when the check is *actually paid* by the drawee bank. Barnhill v. Johnson, 503 U.S. 393 (1992).

[169] A transfer of an interest in personal property or fixtures is "perfected" for purposes of preference law "when a creditor on a simple contract cannot acquire a judicial lien that is superior to the interest of the transferee." 11 U.S.C. § 547(e)(1)(B). Under Article 9, of course, a lien creditor cannot acquire rights superior to the holder of a validly perfected Article 9

thereafter.[171] If the creditor delays in perfecting the security interest for more than thirty days following attachment, the security interest will be deemed to have been granted on the date that the creditor actually perfected that interest.[172] If the creditor has not perfected its security interest by the later of the petition date or the end of the thirty-day period following attachment, the security interest will be deemed to have been granted on the date of the bankruptcy petition.[173]

The following example demonstrates section 547(e)'s timing rule. Suppose Debtor borrowed $20,000 from Bank on June 1, and simultaneously granted Bank a security interest in certain equipment to secure repayment of this debt. Debtor then filed for bankruptcy on July 10. Under section 547(e):

- If Bank filed a proper financing statement in the correct office on or before July 1, the security interest will be deemed to have been granted on June 1 — meaning that the creation of the security interest was not a transfer on account of an antecedent debt, and thus that the trustee cannot avoid the security interest as a preference.

- If Bank did not file its financing statement until July 5, the security interest will be deemed to have been granted on that date. Because the debt arose on June 1, the security interest

---

security interest. U.C.C. § 9-317(a)(2). Thus, if a security interest was validly perfected under Article 9, it is "perfected" for purposes of section 547. *See, e.g., In re* North, 310 B.R. 152, 53 U.C.C. Rep. Serv. 2d 635 (Bankr. D. Ariz. 2004) (secured party applied for certificate of title reflecting secured party's interest more than 90 days prior to bankruptcy, but title certificate was actually issued less than 90 days prior to bankruptcy; because filing of proper application was sufficient for perfection under state law, court held that transfer of security interest did not occur within the preference period).

[170] 11 U.S.C. § 547(e)(2)(A). Prior to BAPCPA, section 547(e)(2)(A) provided only a 10-day period. This created substantial problems because the 10-day period did not match the 20-day grace period available to purchase-money secured parties under Article 9 (and the 30-day grace period available in some states to creditors taking a security interest in titled vehicles). *See, e.g.,* Fidelity Financial Services, Inc. v. Fink, 522 U.S. 211 (1998) (lender's security interest in automobile avoidable as a preference where lender delayed in perfection for 21 days after security interest attached, even though applicable law allowed lender 30 days in which to perfect and obtain relation-back priority over intervening judicial liens). Section 547(e)(2)(A)'s expansion of the period to 30 days should resolve these problems, as 30 days is equal to or longer than virtually all relation-back priority rules applicable under state law.

[171] 11 U.S.C. § 547(e)(2)(A). If the debtor files for bankruptcy before this period elapses, the secured party can still act to perfect its security interest for purposes of section 547 without violating the automatic stay, as long as the secured party acts before the end of the applicable period. 11 U.S.C. §§ 362(b)(3), 547(e)(2)(A). Thus, if Debtor granted Bank a nonpurchase-money security interest on June 1 and filed a bankruptcy petition on June 3, Bank could file its financing statement (and thereby perfect its security interest for purposes of section 547), up to and including July 1, without violating the automatic stay. Caution: *This timing rule is relevant only for purposes of section 547.* In the above example, Bank's security interest would still have been unperfected under Article 9 as of the petition date, and thus the trustee could avoid that security interest under the strong-arm power. *See* § 16.04[B][1] *infra; In re* Planned Protective Servs., Inc., 130 B.R. 94 (Bankr. C.D. Cal. 1991).

[172] 11 U.S.C. § 547(e)(2)(B).

[173] *Id.* § 547(e)(2)(C).

would then be considered a transfer on account of an antecedent debt for purposes of section 547(b).

- If Bank never filed its financing statement or took possession of the collateral, the security interest will be deemed to have been granted on July 10 (the petition date), and thus would be a transfer on account of an antecedent debt.

The rationale for this timing provision lies in the fact that delayed perfection of a security interest creates an ostensible-ownership or "secret-lien" problem. As explained previously, this secret-lien problem can operate to mislead the debtor's creditors or other third parties into believing that encumbered assets are not encumbered.[174] Further, because an unperfected security interest is not effective against lien creditors such as the trustee, one might characterize delayed perfection of a security interest prior to bankruptcy as a last-minute attempt by a creditor to improve its position in anticipation of bankruptcy.[175]

Section 547(e) provides another timing rule that applies primarily in cases of security interests covering after-acquired property. Suppose that on June 1, Debtor borrows $100,000 from Bank, which takes and properly perfects a security interest in all ten of Debtor's machines under a security agreement that also covers after-acquired equipment. Suppose further that Debtor files for bankruptcy on December 1, that Debtor had acquired two additional machines on November 1, that the value of all 12 machines is $80,000, and that Debtor still owes Bank $100,000. The trustee cannot avoid Bank's security interest in the original ten machines as a preference. Because the security interest in those ten machines is deemed to have been granted on June 1 (when the security interest was perfected), two of the necessary elements of a preference are missing — the debtor did not create the security interest in the original ten machines on account of an antecedent debt, nor did the debtor create this interest within the 90-day avoidance period. Preference law, however, treats the security interest in the two after-acquired machines differently. Under section 547(e)(3), the security interest in those two machines is deemed to have been granted on November 1, when Debtor acquired the machines.[176] As a result, the security interest in the two machines acquired on November 1 is an avoidable preference: there was a transfer of a security interest in Debtor's property (the two machines), to a creditor (Bank), on account of an antecedent debt (a transfer deemed to have occurred on November 1, on account of a debt that arose on June 1), within the 90 days prior to bankruptcy (30 days prior to the bankruptcy filing on December 1), and while Debtor was insolvent (recall that Debtor is presumed to have been insolvent during the 90 days prior to bankruptcy). Finally, the transfer made Bank better off by reducing

---

[174] 1 David G. Epstein, Steve H. Nickles, & James J. White, *Bankruptcy,* § 6-11, at 542 (West Pract. ed. 1992).

[175] *Id.*

[176] 11 U.S.C. § 547(e)(3) ("For purposes of this section, a transfer is not made until the debtor has acquired rights in the property transferred.").

Bank's unsecured claim. With the transfer, the Bank has a security interest in twelve machines (worth $80,000) to secure a $100,000 claim; without the transfer, the Bank would have had a security interest in only ten machines (worth less than $80,000, assuming the two additional machines have some economic value) to secure a $100,000 claim.

It should be apparent that section 547(e)(3) places the trustee in a better position than a lien creditor would occupy outside of bankruptcy under Article 9. Outside of bankruptcy, a lien creditor could not avoid a properly perfected security interest against after-acquired collateral.[177] Upon reflection, however, this provision makes sense in light of the objectives of preference law. In this example, Debtor took funds that would have been unencumbered property of the estate and used them to purchase goods that improved the position of a partially unsecured creditor (*i.e.*, that rendered the creditor less undersecured) just prior to bankruptcy. In substance, this action had the same effect as if Debtor had taken the same dollars and instead used them to pay an unsecured creditor — which would have been an obvious preference.

[4] Exceptions to the Trustee's Preference Avoidance Power

Section 547(b) casts a broad net designed to catch all transfers that have a preferential effect. Because Congress drafted it so broadly, section 547(b) also catches a variety of legitimate transfers that are technically preferences but really bestow no improper advantage upon creditors who receive them. As discussed earlier, Congress did not want to authorize the avoidance of such benign transfers, out of concern for the impact that such a broad preference rule could have upon commercial transactions generally. To protect these benign transfers from the trustee's preference avoiding powers, Congress provided a series of exceptions in section 547(c).

[a] Substantially contemporaneous exchanges for new value

Suppose that on June 1, Debtor purchases a machine from Seller, paying with a check. The following day, Seller presents the check for payment to the drawee bank and the bank pays the check. If Debtor goes bankrupt two weeks later, can Trustee recover the funds paid to Seller? Because payment by check is technically a credit transaction, the transfer of Debtor's funds to Seller does not occur until the drawee bank actually paid the check on June 2 — meaning that the Seller received a payment on account of an antecedent debt (the debt incurred on June 1)! As a result, the transfer meets the standard for a preference under section 547(b).[178] This transfer,

---

[177] U.C.C. § 9-317(a)(2).

[178] Until the drawee bank pays the check, Seller has essentially extended credit to Debtor. Accordingly, there is a transfer of Debtor's property (payment of the check), to a creditor (Seller), on account of an antecedent debt (the check was paid on June 2 on account of a debt incurred on June 1), during the 90-day avoidance period (during which Debtor is presumed

however, does not bestow any illegitimate advantage upon Seller, and there is no good reason to permit the trustee to avoid the transfer. Seller's acceptance of payment by check was a reasonable alternative to cash payment, given the significant amount of day-to-day commerce transacted by check. Further, Debtor received new value (the machine) in exchange for the transfer, and thus the transaction did not diminish the Debtor's estate to the detriment of other creditors.[179] Allowing the trustee to recover the funds paid to Seller would give Debtor's other creditors a windfall at Seller's expense. To prevent this result, Congress provided that the trustee cannot avoid a transfer that was "intended by the debtor and the creditor . . . to be a contemporaneous exchange for new value given to the debtor," as long as the transfer was "in fact a substantially contemporaneous exchange."[180]

Although the legislative history of section 547(c)(1) suggests that Congress was primarily concerned with the "payment by check" scenario, the language of section 547(c)(1) is not so limited. For example, suppose that while shopping in a rural area 45 miles from home, Debtor locates and decides to purchase a rare antique vase for $5,000. Seller is only willing to accept cash or check, so Debtor calls Bank (where Debtor is a favored customer) and asks Bank for a $5,000 loan to be immediately deposited into Debtor's account to cover Debtor's check to Seller. Bank agrees to make the loan so long as Debtor will grant Bank a security interest in Debtor's equipment; Bank and Debtor agree that Debtor will come to the Bank when Debtor returns later that day to sign the necessary documents to reflect Bank's security interest. Later that day, Debtor indeed signs a security agreement with Bank and Bank properly perfects its security interest by filing. If Debtor files for bankruptcy one week later, Trustee cannot avoid Bank's security interest. Although Debtor's obligation to Bank arose before Bank's security interest attached (and therefore was an antecedent debt), the parties intended the security interest to be a contemporaneous exchange for new value (the $5,000 loan) given to Debtor by Bank, and the transfer was in fact *substantially* contemporaneous. Under the circumstances

---

to have been insolvent), and the transfer enabled Seller to receive payment in full (better treatment than it would have received as an unsecured creditor in a Chapter 7 liquidation).

[179] "New value" is defined to include money, money's worth in goods, services, or new credit, and the release of an otherwise unavoidable lien against the debtor's property. 11 U.S.C. § 547(a)(2); *In re* Robinson Bros. Drilling, Inc., 877 F.2d 32 (10th Cir. 1989) (even though satisfaction of debt was not new value, release of lien against debtor's assets was new value). "New value" does not include satisfaction of an antecedent unsecured debt. *In re* Chase & Sanborn Corp., 904 F.2d 588 (11th Cir. 1990) (such an argument would render section 547 a "tautological nullity"); *In re* Jotan, Inc., 264 B.R. 735 (Bankr. M.D. Fla. 2001). Further, "new value" does not include the mere substitution of a new unsecured obligation in place of the original obligation, *In re* Wellington Constr. Corp., 82 B.R. 424 (Bankr. N.D. Miss. 1987), or mere forbearance in the collection of a debt. *In re* Air Conditioning, Inc. of Stuart, 845 F.2d 293 (11th Cir.), *cert. denied*, 488 U.S. 993 (1988); In re RDM Sports Group, Inc., 250 B.R. 805 (Bankr. N.D. Ga. 2000).

[180] 11 U.S.C. § 547(c)(1).

surrounding this transaction,[181] the delay of a few hours does not justify allowing the trustee to recover a windfall at Bank's expense.

Note carefully that section 547(c)(1) requires that the parties must have intended that the transfer constitute a contemporaneous exchange for new value. If this intent is not present at the time the debtor's obligation arises, the subsequent transfer does not qualify for the protection of section 547(c)(1), no matter how small the delay.[182]

A secured party might attempt to use section 547(c)(1) in a case involving delayed perfection of a security interest, but such an argument will undoubtedly fail. For example, suppose that on June 1, Debtor borrows $10,000 from Bank, which takes a security interest in Debtor's equipment. Suppose further that Debtor files a bankruptcy petition on July 15. If Bank perfected its security interest on or before July 1, section 547(e) will deem the security interest to have been granted to Bank on June 1. Accordingly, a court likely would conclude that the security interest was not granted on account of an antecedent debt, and the trustee thus could not avoid the transfer anyway.[183] In contrast, if Bank did not perfect its security interest until after July 1, section 547(c)(1) will not save the Bank's lien, because a delay of more than 30 days would almost certainly preclude a conclusion that the transfer was in fact substantially contemporaneous.[184]

[b] "Ordinary-course" payments

A wide variety of pre-petition payments — such as utility payments, payment on installment debt, and timely payments for inventory or equipment purchased on open account — constitute preferences under the standard set forth in section 547(b), even though these transfers are so

---

[181] Case law clearly establishes that contemporaneity is a question of fact that courts must determine on the merits of each case. Thus, drawing clear lines is hazardous; nevertheless, courts generally have concluded that delays of one week or less have satisfied section 547(c)(1)'s "substantially contemporaneous" requirement. Dean v. Davis, 242 U.S. 438 (1917) (mortgage executed to secure loan made one week earlier considered substantially contemporaneous); *In re* Quade, 108 B.R. 681 (Bankr. N.D. Iowa 1989) (substitution of collateral substantially contemporaneous even though substitution delayed by six days).

[182] *In re* Jolly N, Inc., 122 B.R. 897 (Bankr. D. N.J. 1991). This "intent" requirement derives from the Supreme Court's decision in National City Bank of N.Y. v. Hotchkiss, 231 U.S. 50 (1913). *Hotchkiss* involved a Bank that made an unsecured loan to Debtor but later that day demanded collateral. Debtor complied with Bank's request by pledging valuable securities. In Debtor's subsequent bankruptcy, the Court affirmed the trial court's conclusion that the pledge was a preferential transfer.

[183] Theoretically, the court might take a strict or literal interpretation of "antecedent" and conclude that the momentary delay between the loan and the signing of the security agreement rendered the debt "antecedent." In that case, the Bank would have to rely upon section 547(c)(1) to save its security interest from avoidance.

[184] As discussed *supra* note 170, prior to 2005, section 547(e)(2)(A)'s timing rule provided only a 10-day period. Even with this shorter period, the substantial weight of case authority held that a delay in perfection greater than 10 days prevented a conclusion that the security interest was protected as a substantially contemporaneous transfer. *In re* Holder, 892 F.2d 29 (4th Cir. 1989); *In re* Lopez, 265 B.R. 570 (Bankr. N.D. Ohio 2001); *In re* Petrewsky, 147 B.R. 27 (Bankr. S.D. Ohio 1992).

routine that they occur millions of times daily in ordinary commerce. Congress felt that widespread avoidance of such routine payments would be too disruptive of daily commercial activity, even if many such payments clearly benefit the recipients as compared to other unpaid creditors. Further, Congress worried that widespread avoidance of such routine payments could discourage a financially distressed debtor's primary creditors from extending further credit — thereby exacerbating the debtor's financial difficulties and perhaps even increasing the likelihood of the debtor's bankruptcy.[185]

To avoid such effects, Congress enacted section 547(c)(2), which provides an exception for "ordinary course" payments. Prior to 2005, section 547(c)(2) provided that the trustee could not recover any payment that met all three of the following standards: (a) the payment was on account of a debt incurred in the ordinary course of business or financial affairs of both the debtor and the transferee; (b) the payment itself was made in the ordinary course of business or financial affairs of both the debtor and the transferee; and (c) the payment itself was made in accordance with ordinary business terms. This standard produced a great deal of litigation, particularly involving the question of untimely or erratic payments — *i.e.*, are a debtor's monthly debt payments made "in the ordinary course" if they are not consistently made on a timely basis?[186]

Based upon concerns that former section 547(c)(2) placed too high a burden upon creditors seeking to retain ordinary course payments, Congress amended section 547(c)(2) in 2005. Section 547(c)(2) now provides that the trustee cannot recover any transfer in payment of a debt incurred by the debtor in the ordinary course of business or financial affairs of the debtor and the transferee, so long as *either* (A) the payment was made in the ordinary course of business or financial affairs of the debtor and the transferee or (B) the payment was made according to ordinary business terms.[187]

If the debtor incurred the debt or the creditor extended the credit under atypical circumstances, section 547(c)(2) cannot protect payments on that debt.[188] Likewise, section 547(c)(2) is unlikely to protect payments that are

---

[185] Vern Countryman, *The Concept of a Voidable Preference in Bankruptcy*, 38 Vand. L. Rev. 713 (1985).

[186] Many courts held that a late payment could be an "ordinary course" payment if late payments were the standard course of dealing between the parties. *See, e.g., In re* Tolona Pizza Prods. Corp., 3 F.3d 1029, 1032 (7th Cir. 1993). Other courts held that payments are outside the "ordinary course" if the debtor pays in an inconsistent rather than timely fashion. *In re* Xonics Imaging, Inc., 837 F.2d 763 (7th Cir. 1988); *In re* Cook United, Inc., 117 B.R. 884 (Bankr. N.D. Ohio 1990).

[187] 11 U.S.C. § 547(c)(2).

[188] *In re* Energy Co-op, Inc., 832 F.2d 997, 5 U.C.C. Rep. Serv. 2d 99 (7th Cir. 1987) (payment made to settle breach of contract claim not made in ordinary course); Industrial & Municipal Eng'g, Inc., 127 B.R. 848 (Bankr. C.D. Ill. 1990) (payment made to settle lawsuit not made in ordinary course).

Prior to 1984, section 547(c)(2) provided that payments could not qualify for protection unless

made involuntarily via levy or garnishment,[189] nor will it protect payments that are unusually large relative to the regular periodic payment amount.[190]

By its terms, the "ordinary-course" exception is limited to payments; the granting of a security interest could not qualify for protection from avoidance under section 547(c)(2), even if the debtor and creditor routinely enter into security agreements in the ordinary course of their financial dealings.[191]

[c] Security interests granted in conjunction with enabling loans

The typical PMSI transaction does not result in an illegitimate preferential transfer to a creditor; after all, the granting of a PMSI enables the debtor to acquire additional property, thereby expanding the size of the debtor's estate. The timing of certain enabling loan transactions, however, can result in security interests that technically satisfy each element for a preferential transfer under section 547(b).[192] For example, suppose that on June 1, Debtor borrows $40,000 from Bank to purchase a new drill press that Debtor plans to acquire later in June when Debtor expands its operations. Contemporaneously with the loan, Debtor signs a security agreement and financing statement describing the drill press, and Bank files the financing statement. Debtor purchases the drill press on June 19, and then files for bankruptcy protection on August 1. Under these circumstances, Bank's purchase money security interest (PMSI) is a transfer that satisfies each element of section 547(b): it is a transfer to a creditor (Bank),

---

they were made within 45 days of the date that the debt arose. Under that provision, payments on long-term debt could not qualify for ordinary course protection. In 1984, Congress removed the 45-day limitation, and this triggered a debate in the courts regarding whether payments on long-term debt could qualify for protection as ordinary course transfers. In *Union Bank v. Wolas*, 502 U.S. 151 (1991), however, the Supreme Court held that payments on long-term debt can qualify for protection under section 547(c)(2).

[189] WJM, Inc. v. Massachusetts Dept. of Public Welfare, 840 F.2d 996 (1st Cir. 1988). If the debtor makes a payment without judicial process in response to creditor demands for payment, however, the debtor's payment is still within the "ordinary course" if the creditor's collection effort (*e.g.*, dunning letters or phone calls) is not unusual. *See, e.g.*, In re L. Bee Furniture Co., 203 B.R. 778 (Bankr. M.D. Fla. 1996).

[190] *In re* Healthco Int'l, Inc., 132 F.3d 104 (1st Cir. 1997); *In re* McElroy, 228 B.R. 791 (Bankr. M.D. Fla. 1999); *In re* Roemig, 123 B.R. 405 (Bankr. D.N.M. 1991).

[191] *In re* Blackburn, 90 B.R. 569 (Bankr. M.D. Ga. 1987).

[192] Students should not assume that all enabling loan transactions will need to be saved by section 547(c)(3). In fact, most purchase-money secured transactions will not even run afoul of section 547(b) in the first place. For example, suppose that Consumer buys a TV set from Retailer under an installment contract by which Retailer retains a purchase-money security interest. In this situation, Consumer would not be granting the purchase-money security interest on account of an antecedent debt, but on account of a contemporaneous debt. As a result, the trustee could not avoid the security interest under section 547(b), and Retailer would not have to rely upon the section 547(c)(3) exception. As explained in the text, section 547(c)(3) primarily protects the enabling lender in cases where attachment is delayed after the purchase-money debt arises.

on account of an antecedent debt (the PMSI does not attach until June 19 when Debtor acquires rights in the drill press, whereas Debtor incurred the debt on June 1), during the 90 days prior to bankruptcy, while Debtor is presumed to have been insolvent, and the PMSI makes Bank better off than it would have been as an unsecured creditor in a Chapter 7 liquidation. But there is no defensible reason for preference law to allow Trustee to avoid Bank's PMSI; Bank did not take the PMSI to secure an existing obligation, but instead took the PMSI in exchange for credit that enabled Debtor to acquire a valuable asset. Allowing Trustee to avoid Bank's PMSI would bestow a windfall upon the Debtor's other creditors to the detriment of Bank, solely because attachment was delayed until Debtor acquired the drill press.

To prevent this result, section 547(c)(3) provides that the trustee/DIP cannot avoid a security interest to the extent that it:

- secures new value given at or after the signing of a written[193] security agreement describing the collateral;

- secures new value given by or on behalf of the secured party;

- secures new value given to enable the debtor to acquire the collateral, as long as it was in fact used by the debtor to acquire the collateral; and

- was perfected on or before 30 days after the debtor took possession of the collateral.[194]

Note carefully that section 547(c)(3) does not protect PMSIs from avoidance in all cases. Delayed perfection of a PMSI could also result in the security interest being avoidable as a preference. Returning to the above example, suppose that Debtor had purchased the drill press on June 19, but Bank had not filed its financing statement to perfect its PMSI until July 25 (more than 30 days after Debtor took possession of the drill press). Because of this excessive delay in perfection, Bank's PMSI would not qualify for protection under section 547(c)(3) and trustee could avoid the PMSI as a preference.[195]

---

[193] Although the Code uses the term "written," it is subject to the Electronic Signatures in Global and National Commerce Act (E-Sign), 15 U.S.C. Section 7001 et seq. Under E-Sign, a writing requirement imposed by law such as the Bankruptcy Code may, if parties agree, be satisfied by a record in electronic form.

[194] 11 U.S.C. § 547(c)(3).

[195] In this example, Bank might then attempt to argue that the PMSI should be treated as a contemporaneous exchange for new value under section 547(c)(1). Such an argument, however, will almost certainly fail. Most courts have concluded that section 547(c)(1) does not apply to purchase-money or "enabling loan" transactions. In re Locklin, 101 F.3d 435 (5th Cir. 1996); In re Tressler, 771 F.2d 791 (3d Cir. 1985). Likewise, as discussed supra note 184 and accompanying text, a delay in perfection beyond the 30-day period provided in section 547(e)(2)(A) would likely defeat any argument that the PMSI was a substantially contemporaneous transfer for new value. In re Holder, 892 F.2d 29 (4th Cir. 1989).

[d] Transfers ameliorating an earlier preference

Suppose that Debtor is a financially distressed baker seeking additional flour from Supplier. Supplier refuses to consider supplying any more flour to Debtor unless Debtor pays 50% of its existing account balance. In response to this statement, Debtor pays $6,000 to Supplier in satisfaction of 50% of its account balance. Four days later, Supplier agrees to and does ship Debtor an additional $2,500 worth of flour. Debtor cannot extract itself from financial difficulty, however, and files for bankruptcy three weeks later. Debtor's payment to Supplier constitutes a preference under section 547(b); Supplier cannot claim the payment was a contemporaneous exchange for new value or an ordinary course transfer. Nevertheless, Supplier subsequently ameliorated the effect of this payment by extending new credit that enabled Debtor to acquire additional assets. Thus, if Trustee could recover the full $6,000 payment from Supplier, Trustee and other general creditors would receive a windfall at Supplier's expense. Furthermore, such a result would discourage creditors such as Supplier from extending additional unsecured credit to distressed debtors, which in turn could compromise the ability of debtors to resolve their financial affairs and avoid bankruptcy.[196]

To account for such "post-preference" extensions of new value, section 547(c)(4) provides that the trustee cannot recover an otherwise preferential transfer to the extent that, after the transfer, the preferred creditor gave new value to or for the benefit of the debtor (A) not secured by an otherwise unavoidable security interest; and (B) on account of which new value the debtor did not make an otherwise unavoidable transfer to or for the benefit of the creditor.[197] The language of section 547(c)(4) is not a model of clarity, but the idea behind it is simple: the trustee should not be able to avoid a preferential transfer to the extent that the benefitted creditor subsequently extends new value or credit that ameliorates the effect of the earlier preference. In the above example, Supplier's extension of $2,500 of unsecured credit ameliorated the effect of the earlier $6,000 preferential payment; thus, trustee can only recover $3,500 from Supplier.[198] Likewise, if Debtor pays $10,000 owed to its lawyer on the 80th day prior to Debtor's bankruptcy petition, Trustee cannot recover this payment if Debtor's lawyer provided an additional $10,000 worth of services (for which the Debtor has not paid) between the time of the payment and the time of the bankruptcy petition.[199]

---

[196] *In re* New York City Shoes, Inc., 880 F.2d 679 (3d Cir. 1989); *In re* IRFM, Inc., 144 B.R. 886 (Bankr. C.D. Cal. 1992), *aff'd*, 52 F.3d 228 (9th Cir. 1995).

[197] 11 U.S.C. § 547(c)(4); *In re* Micro Innovations Corp., 185 F.3d 329 (5th Cir. 1999).

[198] What if Supplier had shipped the flour before Debtor had repaid half of its account balance? The net effect of this transaction on Debtor's balance sheet would have been the same; in this situation, however, the advance of new credit would not ameliorate a prior preference, and thus, section 547(c)(4) would not protect Supplier. *In re* McLaughlin, 183 B.R. 171, 26 U.C.C. Rep. Serv. 2d 1110 (Bankr. W.D. Wis. 1995).

[199] *In re* Sounds Distributing, Inc., 80 B.R. 749 (Bankr. W.D. Pa. 1987).

In contrast, if Supplier in the earlier hypothetical had taken a purchase-money security interest when it sold Debtor the $2,500 of additional flour, Supplier's extension of new credit would have been fully secured, and would not have ameliorated the preferential effect of the earlier $6,000 payment. In those circumstances, section 547(c)(4) would not protect Supplier, and the trustee could avoid the $6,000 payment in full.[200]

[e] Floating liens in inventory and receivables

In a floating lien transaction covering inventory or accounts, the parties understand that the secured party will advance credit to the debtor as the debtor acquires inventory or generates accounts — and that the debtor will correspondingly repay some or all of that credit as the debtor sells inventory or collects accounts. This process of borrowing and repaying continues on a revolving basis, with the secured party possessing a lien upon whatever collateral the debtor owns at any point in time. As the debtor acquires new inventory or generates new accounts, they are added to the "pool" of collateral over which the secured party's lien "floats."

Section 547(e)(3)'s timing rule, however, presents a problem to secured parties with floating liens upon inventory and/or accounts. Under section 547(e)(3), the "transfer" of a security interest in any particular item of collateral does not occur until the debtor acquires rights in that item of collateral. For purposes of preference law, therefore, each time the debtor acquires a new item of inventory, the debtor's inventory lender receives a "transfer" of a security interest in that item of inventory. Because the security interest in this new item of inventory secures the balance of the debtor's previously incurred loan, the transfer occurs on account of an "antecedent" debt. As a result, the security interest in any item of inventory acquired during the 90 days prior to bankruptcy qualifies as a preferential transfer under section 547(b), unless the secured party was already fully secured at the time the debtor acquired that item of inventory.

This timing problem is exacerbated by the fact that, for many debtors, their inventory or accounts "turn over" (*i.e.*, their inventory is sold or their accounts are collected, and replaced with new inventory or new accounts) every 90 days, if not more frequently. For example, suppose that Debtor files for bankruptcy protection on June 1, owing Bank $100,000 secured by a floating lien upon Debtor's inventory (worth $80,000). Further, suppose that each item of Debtor's inventory as of the petition date has been acquired during the previous 30 days. Under these circumstances, Bank's security interest in Debtor's entire inventory technically constitutes a preference under section 547(b). Unless bankruptcy law provides some measure of protection for floating liens, the trustee could avoid Bank's entire floating lien!

Allowing the trustee to avoid Bank's entire floating lien, however, would be counterproductive. Floating liens generally provide a convenient and

---

[200] 11 U.S.C. § 547(c)(4)(A); *In re* Micro Innovations Corp., 185 F.3d 329 (5th Cir. 1999); *In re* Toyota of Jefferson, Inc., 14 F.3d 1088 (5th Cir. 1994).

efficient means for businesses such as Debtor to finance business inventory or receivables, and do not inherently offend any policies underlying preference law. Thus, to protect floating liens in inventory or accounts from blanket avoidance because of section 547(e)(3)'s timing rule, section 547(c)(5) provides an exception for certain perfected security interests in inventory and accounts.[201]

This exception for floating liens is not absolute, however, because purchases of new inventory can in fact create an illegitimate preferential benefit. For example, an undersecured creditor with a floating lien may bring pressure on the debtor to acquire additional collateral to bolster the creditor's overall secured position. To the extent that the debtor acquires this additional collateral with assets that would otherwise have remained available for payment to general creditors, the acquisition of the additional collateral bestows an illegitimate preferential benefit upon the creditor. Thus, section 547(c)(5) permits the trustee to avoid a floating lien in inventory or accounts to the extent that the "transfers" (*i.e.*, the attachment of the secured party's lien when the debtor acquires additional inventory or receivables) resulted in an improvement of the creditor's overall secured position to the detriment of unsecured creditors during the last 90 days prior to bankruptcy (or one year, in the case of an insider creditor).

To determine the amount that the trustee can avoid, section 547(c)(5) applies a "net improvement" test that requires the following calculations:

- Step One: Determine the debtor's outstanding loan balance on the 90th day prior to the debtor's bankruptcy filing[202] and the value of the collateral on that same day.

- Step Two: Determine the debtor's outstanding loan balance on the petition date and the value of the collateral on that same date.

- Step Three: Compare the creditor's overall secured position (*i.e.*, the value of its collateral less the outstanding loan balance) on the 90th day prior to bankruptcy with the creditor's overall position on the petition date.

If the creditor held a fully secured claim on the 90th day prior to bankruptcy, the creditor's overall secured position cannot be improved to the detriment of unsecured creditors, and the trustee cannot avoid the creditor's floating lien to any extent. But if the creditor was undersecured on the 90th day prior to bankruptcy, and that shortfall has been reduced by the petition

---

[201] Section 547(a)(1) defines the terms "inventory" and "receivable" more broadly than the corresponding Article 9 categories "inventory" and "account." For purposes of section 547, "inventory" includes farm products held for sale or lease, and "receivable" includes any right to payment (thus including Article 9 chattel paper, payment intangibles and rights to payment under instruments).

[202] 11 U.S.C. § 547(c)(5)(A)(i). If the creditor is an insider, the relevant date would be the date one year prior to debtor's bankruptcy. *Id.* § 547(c)(5)(A)(ii). If the creditor's first extension of credit to the debtor occurred within 90 days prior to bankruptcy, the relevant date would be the date of the creditor's first extension of credit to the debtor. *Id.* § 547(c)(5)(B).

date, the debtor's acquisition of additional inventory or receivables has improved the creditor's position and trustee can avoid the creditor's floating lien to the extent of the improvement.[203]

The improvement in position must arise "to the prejudice of other creditors holding unsecured claims."[204] This means that the debtor must have used otherwise unencumbered assets to acquire additional collateral that improved the creditor's position. If the creditor's position is improved because the debtor's inventory simply appreciated in value, this improvement did not reduce the value of the debtor's estate to the prejudice of unsecured creditors, and the trustee cannot avoid the creditor's lien on account of that improvement.

To make the necessary calculations under section 547(c)(5), the court must determine the appropriate value of the collateral as of the relevant measuring dates. The trustee and the creditor will often disagree, however, on the proper valuation of the collateral. Because there is no avoidable improvement in position if the creditor held a fully secured claim on the 90th day prior to bankruptcy, the trustee will seek to value the collateral at its lowest possible value (*e.g.*, its liquidation or foreclosure sale value). In contrast, the creditor will seek to value the collateral at its highest possible value (*e.g.*, the retail value of inventory or the face amount of receivables). As with valuation in other contexts, courts have developed no hard and fast rules for the appropriate valuation of inventory for purposes of section 547(c)(5); instead, courts conduct this valuation on a case-by-case basis, taking into account the likely manner of the use or disposition of the collateral. For example, in *In re Clark Pipe and Supply Co., Inc.*,[205] the evidence reflected that the debtor was in the process of liquidating its assets throughout the 90-day period prior to bankruptcy. Based upon this evidence, the Fifth Circuit concluded that the inventory properly was valued at its liquidation value.[206] In contrast, if a Chapter 11 debtor is seeking to operate and reorganize its retail department store operations, the court might more properly value the debtor's inventory using a "going concern" or "replacement value" measure.[207]

[f] Statutory liens

If a creditor obtains a valid statutory lien under nonbankruptcy law during the 90 days immediately prior to bankruptcy, the attachment of that

---

[203] *In re* Wesley Indus., Inc., 30 F.3d 1438 (11th Cir. 1994); *In re* Ebbler Furniture and Appliances, Inc., 804 F.2d 87 (7th Cir. 1986).

[204] 11 U.S.C. § 547(c)(5).

[205] 893 F.2d 693 (5th Cir. 1990).

[206] *In re* Clark Pipe & Supply Co., 893 F.2d 693 (5th Cir. 1990) (appropriate measure of collateral value is net amount creditor could have received if/when it could have repossessed and sold inventory).

[207] Although the Supreme Court's decision in Associates Commercial Corp. v. Rash, discussed in § 16.03[B][2][a] *supra*, focused on the valuation of vehicles in Chapter 13, the Court's interpretation of section 506(a) suggests that a replacement-value approach would be required when a debtor was seeking to use the collateral in its reorganization efforts.

lien satisfies the standards for a preferential transfer in section 547(b). The trustee/DIP cannot use section 547 to avoid a statutory lien, however; section 547(c)(6) provides that section 545 is the exclusive statutory authority by which the trustee/DIP can avoid a statutory lien.[208]

[g] Consumer transfers

If the debtor is an individual with primarily consumer debts, section 547(c)(8) provides that the trustee cannot recover any transfer in which the total value of the property transferred was less than $600.[209] If the value of the property transferred is $600 or more, however, section 547(c)(8) does not protect the creditor to any extent.[210]

[h] Nonconsumer transfers

If the debtor is an individual whose debts are not primarily consumer debts, section 547(c)(9) provides that the trustee cannot recover any transfer in which the total value of the property transferred was less than $5,000.[211] If the value of the property transferred is $5,000 or more, however, section 547(c)(9) does not protect the creditor to any extent.[212]

[F] Power to Avoid Fraudulent Transfers

[1] Intentionally Fraudulent Transfers — 11 U.S.C. § 548(a)(1)(A)

Sometimes debtors deliberately seek to frustrate the legitimate collection efforts of their creditors by giving property (or transferring it for nominal consideration) to friends or relatives. Since the Statute of 13 Elizabeth in 1570, the common law has allowed creditors harmed by intentionally fraudulent transfers to invalidate such transfers. Today, both the Uniform Fraudulent Conveyance Act (UFCA) and the Uniform Fraudulent Transfer Act (UFTA) contain provisions that permit creditors to avoid transfers made by the debtor with the intent to hinder, delay, or defraud creditors.[213]

---

[208] 11 U.S.C. § 547(c)(6). See § 16.04[D] *supra.*

[209] *Id.* § 547(c)(8). A number of courts have concluded that multiple transfers to the same creditor can be aggregated and avoided if the total of those transfers exceeds $600. *See, e.g., In re* Hailes, 77 F.3d 873 (5th Cir. 1996); *In re* Djerf, 188 B.R. 586 (Bankr. D. Minn. 1995); *In re* Alarcon, 186 B.R. 135 (Bankr. D.N.M. 1995).

[210] Creditors have attempted to argue that § 547(c)(8) should protect the transfer to the extent of $600, but courts have rejected these arguments. *In re* Via, 107 B.R. 91 (Bankr. W.D. Va. 1989); *In re* Vickery, 63 B.R. 222 (Bankr. E.D. Tenn. 1986).

[211] 11 U.S.C. § 547(c)(9).

[212] Because section 547(c)(9) was enacted in 2005, case authority interpreting section 547(c)(9) has yet to develop; however, because sections 547(c)(9) and 547(c)(8) have parallel structures, cases interpreting section 547(c)(8) may prove useful in guiding interpretation of section 547(c)(9).

[213] UFCA § 7, UFTA § 4(a)(1). The UFTA is the more recent of the two model fraudulent transfer statutes, and was designed to modernize and replace the UFCA.

Because these transfers also operate to disadvantage an insolvent debtor's unsecured creditors, section 548(a)(1)(A) of the Bankruptcy Code permits the trustee/DIP to bring an action to avoid intentionally fraudulent transfers made by the debtor within the two-year period prior to bankruptcy.[214]

[2] Constructively Fraudulent Transfers — 11 U.S.C. § 548(a)(1)(B)

More frequently, a financially distressed debtor makes a transfer by gift or for insufficient consideration without any specific intent to hinder, delay, or defraud creditors. The debtor's pure motives, however, provide cold comfort to creditors for whom the transfer has the same effect — assets that might have satisfied creditor claims have instead gone to other parties for less than fair market value, thereby depleting the assets available for unpaid creditors. In recognition of the fact that such transfers tend to have the same impact as intentionally fraudulent transfers, the common law has long deemed such transfers by insolvent debtors to be avoidable as *constructively* fraudulent transfers. Both the UFCA and the UFTA allow creditors to avoid constructively fraudulent transfers,[215] and the Bankruptcy Code provides a similar rule in section 548(a)(1)(B). This section permits the trustee/DIP to avoid any transfer of the debtor's property or any obligation incurred by the debtor, if

- the transfer was made or the obligation was incurred within two years prior to the debtor's bankruptcy;
- the debtor received less than a "reasonably equivalent value" in exchange; and
- the debtor
  - was insolvent at the time the transfer was made or obligation was incurred, or was rendered insolvent as a result;
  - was engaging in business or a transaction with "unreasonably small capital";
  - intended to incur or expected to incur debts beyond its ability to repay; or
  - made the transfer or incurred the obligation to or for the benefit of an insider under an employment contract and not in the ordinary course of business.[216]

Thus, if Debtor sells its equipment (worth $100,000) to Buyer for a price of $50,000, thereby rendering Debtor insolvent, and Debtor files for bankruptcy within two years of the sale, Trustee can establish that the transfer was constructively fraudulent under section 548(a)(1)(B). Trustee could

---

[214] 11 U.S.C. § 548(a)(1)(A).

[215] UFCA § 4, UFTA § 4(a)(2).

[216] 11 U.S.C. § 548(a)(1)(B).

thus recover the equipment from Buyer, even if Buyer had acted in good faith and without knowledge that the transfer was fraudulent.[217]

Because of the harshness of this result for Buyer, the Bankruptcy Code does provide some protection for good faith purchasers and their subsequent transferees. If Buyer did purchase the equipment in good faith, Buyer would receive a lien upon the equipment to secure repayment of the $50,000 that Buyer paid to Debtor.[218] Further, if Buyer has already conveyed the equipment to Third Party by the time that Trustee discovers the fraudulent sale to Buyer, Trustee cannot recover the equipment from Third Party if Third Party took the property for value, in good faith, and without knowledge of the fact that Buyer's purchase from Debtor violated section 548(a).[219]

Generally, section 548(a)(1)(b) presents few significant threats to the typical secured party (except in the context of a pre-bankruptcy foreclosure sale, which will be discussed shortly). The trustee cannot avoid pre-petition payments by the debtor on the debt as constructively fraudulent transfers, because the debtor receives equivalent value (*i.e.*, *pro tanto* satisfaction of the debt) in exchange for the payments.[220] Likewise, because section 548 defines "value" to include "securing . . . [an] antecedent debt,"[221] the trustee/DIP cannot use section 548 to avoid a security interest just because the debtor granted that interest to secure a previously unsecured obligation of the debtor.[222] If the debtor granted a security interest in its property to secure the debt of an unrelated person, however, the debtor would not have received any value in exchange. Under those circumstances, the trustee could avoid the security interest as a fraudulent transfer if the debtor was insolvent at the time or was rendered insolvent as a result of granting the security interest.[223]

---

[217] *Id.* § 550(a)(1).

[218] *Id.* § 548(c) ("a transferee . . . that takes for value and in good faith has a lien . . . to the extent that such transferee . . . gave value to the debtor in exchange for such transfer. . . ."); Stratton v. Equitable Bank, N.A., 104 B.R. 713, 11 U.C.C. Rep. Serv. 2d 149 (D. Md. 1989), *aff'd*, 912 F.2d 464 (4th Cir. 1990).

[219] 11 U.S.C. § 550(b).

[220] Section 548(d)(2)(A) expressly defines "value" to include "satisfaction . . . of a present or antecedent debt."

[221] 11 U.S.C. § 548(d)(2)(A).

[222] *In re* Anand, 210 B.R. 456 (Bankr. N.D. Ill. 1997); *In re* Countdown of Conn., Inc., 115 B.R. 18 (Bankr. D. Conn. 1990).

[223] For purposes of determining whether the debtor is insolvent under section 548(a)(2), the court must take into account both the debtor's fixed liabilities and its contingent liabilities. In valuing the debtor's contingent liabilities (*e.g.*, the debtor's liability upon a guaranty of another's obligation), the court must take into account the probability that the contingency will occur. Covey v. Commercial Nat'l Bank of Peoria, 960 F.2d 657 (7th Cir. 1992). Thus, if Debtor grants a security interest in its equipment to Bank to secure the obligation of Third Party, the court, in valuing the contingent liability created by Debtor's granting of the security interest, must take into account the likelihood of default by Third Party.

[3] Pre-bankruptcy Foreclosure Sales as Fraudulent Transfers

A trustee might attempt to invoke section 548 to set aside a pre-bankruptcy foreclosure sale as a constructively fraudulent transfer. As discussed in Chapter 18, foreclosure sales sometimes bring notoriously low prices. Because foreclosure sales often occur quickly and with less advertising than arms-length sales, foreclosure sales often yield few bidders and sometimes result in bargain prices.

For example, suppose that after default by Debtor, Bank repossesses Debtor's inventory pursuant to its security agreement and conducts a public sale at which Buyer purchases all of the inventory for a total price of $50,000. Suppose further that the inventory had a wholesale value of $90,000 if bought and sold in the ordinary course of business. If Debtor then files for bankruptcy three months later, Trustee might attempt to invalidate the foreclosure sale as a constructively fraudulent transfer. Nevertheless, there are countervailing policy concerns that could justify a contrary result. To the extent trustees can collaterally attack foreclosure sales based upon low sale prices, this could have the undesirable effect of discouraging or "chilling" bidding at foreclosure sales — which in turn could generally depress foreclosure sale prices. [224]

Assuming that Debtor was insolvent at the time of the foreclosure sale, [225] the foreclosure sale seems to fit the standard established in section 548(a)(1)(B). There is a transfer of Debtor's property (the sale of the inventory), while Debtor was insolvent, and Debtor appears to have received less than "reasonably equivalent value" in exchange — Debtor received $50,000 (satisfaction of debt) in exchange for inventory that had a significantly higher market value. Further, there are good reasons that bankruptcy law *should* want to set aside such a sale; if Trustee can recover the sale and liquidate the inventory at its fair wholesale value, Trustee could capture $40,000 of additional value for the benefit of general creditors.

The question of whether the trustee can avoid a pre-bankruptcy foreclosure sale that generated a price below fair market value raged through bankruptcy courts until the Supreme Court purported to resolve the debate in *BFP v. Resolution Trust Corporation*. [226] The foreclosure sale at issue in *BFP* involved the debtor's house, which had an alleged fair market value of $725,000 but which sold at a pre-bankruptcy foreclosure for only $433,000.

---

[224] This same "chilling effect" explains the rationale behind Article 9's rather strong finality rules that permit collateral attack against Article 9 foreclosure sales in only very limited circumstances. *See* § 18.02[E] *infra*.

[225] The trustee bears the burden of proving that the transfer was fraudulent, *In re* Colonial Realty Co., 226 B.R. 513 (Bankr. D. Conn. 1998), and thus must prove that the debtor was insolvent at the time of the transfer or was rendered insolvent as a result. *In re* North Am. Dealer Group, Inc., 62 B.R. 423 (Bankr. E.D.N.Y. 1986). Section 548 does not provide a presumption of insolvency similar to the one that exists in preference actions under section 547.

[226] 511 U.S. 531 (1994).

The trustee argued that the sale was constructively fraudulent because it yielded only 57% of the home's fair market value.[227] The purchaser argued, however, that the purchase price received at a regularly conducted, noncollusive foreclosure sale should be deemed "reasonably equivalent value."[228] Unlike the UFTA, which contains express language adopting such a conclusive presumption,[229] section 548(a)(1)(B) contains no language purporting to define the term "reasonably equivalent value," nor does it establish any presumption regarding its meaning. Nevertheless, the purchaser urged the Court to conclude that this conclusive presumption was implicit in section 548(a)(1)(B).

In a 5-4 decision, the Court concluded that the trustee cannot use section 548 to set aside a regularly conducted, noncollusive foreclosure sale of land — regardless of the fact that the sale generated a price far below an ordinary market sale price.[230] Justice Scalia concluded that the term "reasonably equivalent value" as used in section 548(a)(1)(B) did not mean "fair market value" in the context of a foreclosure sale:

> The language [of § 548(a)(1)(B)] requires judicial inquiry into whether the foreclosed property was sold for a price that approximated its worth at the time of sale. An appraiser's reconstruction of "fair market value" could show what similar property would be worth if it did not have to be sold within the time and manner strictures of state-prescribed foreclosure. But property that must be sold within those strictures is simply worth less. No one would pay as much to own such property as he would pay to own real estate that could be sold at leisure and pursuant to normal marketing techniques.[231]

---

[227] The trustee's argument relied upon a rule that derived from the opinion in Durrett v. Washington Nat'l Ins. Co., 621 F.2d 201 (5th Cir. 1980), in which the court suggested that any sale for less than 70% of the property's fair market value was presumptively constructively fraudulent. Prior to *BFP*, a significant number of bankruptcy courts had adopted this rule of thumb, which became known as the *"Durrett"* rule. *See, e.g.*, In re Littleton, 888 F.2d 90 (11th Cir. 1989). *See also* William H. Henning, *An Analysis of* Durrett *and Its Impact on Rea and Personal Property Foreclosures: Some Proposed Modifications*, 63 N.C. L. Rev. 257 (198' .

[228] Prior to *BFP*, two Circuits adopted the rule advocated by the purchaser. *In re* Winshall Settlor's Trust, 758 F.2d 1136 (6th Cir. 1985); *In re* Madrid, 21 B.R. 424 (9th Cir. Bankr. 1982), *aff'd on other grounds*, 725 F.2d 1197 (9th Cir.), *cert. denied*, 469 U.S. 833 (1984).

[229] UFTA § 3(b) ("[A] person gives reasonably equivalent value if the person acquires an interest of the debtor in an asset pursuant to a regularly conducted, noncollusive foreclosure sale or execution of a power of sale for the acquisition or disposition of the interest of the debtor upon default under a mortgage, deed of trust, or security agreement."). The UFCA uses the term "fair consideration" instead of "reasonably equivalent value," UFCA § 3, and its definition of "fair consideration" contains no presumption comparable to the one found in UFTA § 3(b).

[230] *BFP*, 511 U.S. at 545.

[231] *Id.* at 538–39. Commentators have strongly criticized Scalia's statement that property being sold at foreclosure is "worth less" than it would be if sold at arms-length, on the ground that Scalia is conflating the terms "value" and "price." The fact that a foreclosure sale brings a lower price does not mean that the property is actually intrinsically worth less. Robert M. Lawless & Stephen P. Ferris, *Economics and the Rhetoric of Valuation*, 5 J. Bankr. L. & Prac. 3 (1995).

In an opinion ringing with strong federalist undercurrents, Justice Scalia concluded that state foreclosure and fraudulent transfer laws have never authorized the setting aside of a foreclosure sale solely because the sale generated an inadequate price. Given this long history of state laws designed to promote finality in foreclosure sales, Justice Scalia concluded that the words "reasonably equivalent value" in section 548(a)(1)(B) do not reflect a clear legislative intent to displace state foreclosure law and permit bankruptcy trustees to set aside foreclosure sales based solely upon low sale prices.[232] Accordingly, the majority concluded that "a fair and proper price, or a 'reasonably equivalent value,' for foreclosed property, is the price in fact received at the foreclosure sale, so long as all the requirements of the State's foreclosure law have been complied with."[233]

Thus, the trustee/DIP cannot use section 548(a)(1)(B) to attack a pre-bankruptcy foreclosure sale of land *unless there is some irregularity in the conduct of the sale*.[234] The Court explicitly limited the *BFP* decision to private foreclosures of land, purporting to leave open the question of whether section 548(a)(1)(B) applies to other forced sales (such as tax sales or Article 9 sales).[235] Despite this limitation, however, it is almost certain that the Court would reach the same result if faced with a trustee's attempt to use section 548(a)(1)(B) to avoid a pre-bankruptcy foreclosure of personal property. If the secured party complied with all of the requirements of U.C.C. Article 9 and conducted a commercially reasonable sale at which the buyer purchased in good faith, the debtor could not set aside the sale, regardless of the sale price.[236] Accordingly, the rationale of *BFP* would suggest that the trustee could not set aside the foreclosure sale under section 548(a)(1)(B). In contrast, if the secured party failed to comply with the requirements of Article 9 and conducted a commercially unreasonable sale, a bankruptcy court might permit the trustee to assert section 548(a)(1)(B) if the sale resulted in a manifestly low price relative to the collateral's fair market value.[237]

[4] Avoiding Fraudulent Transfers under State Law — 11 U.S.C. § 544(b)(1)

Section 544(b)(1) allows the trustee to set aside any transfers of the debtor's property that an actual unsecured creditor could have avoided

---

[232] *BFP*, 511 U.S. at 538–45.

[233] *Id.* at 545.

[234] *Id.* at 545–46 ("Any irregularity in the conduct of the sale that would permit judicial invalidation of the sale under applicable state law deprives the sale price of its conclusive force under [§ 548(a)(1)(B)], and the transfer may be avoided if the price received was not reasonably equivalent to the property's actual value at the time of the sale.").

[235] *Id.* at 537 n.3.

[236] U.C.C. § 9-617(b). *See* § 18.02[E] *infra.*

[237] Even this conclusion is subject to doubt, however, as Article 9 typically does not allow the debtor to invalidate even a commercially unreasonable sale. *See* U.C.C. § 9-617(b) (good faith transferee at Article 9 foreclosure sale receives debtor's rights in collateral even if secured party fails to comply with Article 9 sale requirements).

under state law.[238] As discussed earlier, state fraudulent transfer laws (either the UFTA, the UFCA, or some statutory descendant of the Statute of 13 Elizabeth) uniformly permit unsecured creditors to set aside both intentionally and constructively fraudulent transfers. Thus, assuming that the trustee can identify an actual unsecured creditor of the debtor who is capable of asserting a state law fraudulent transfer claim, the trustee could use section 544(b) to assert that claim on behalf of the estate.

Because the applicable standards for establishing a fraudulent transfer are essentially the same under both section 548(a) and most applicable state fraudulent transfer laws, the trustee will choose to proceed under section 544(b) only if the transfer occurred more than two years prior to bankruptcy (and thus outside the two-year reach-back period of section 548). State law may provide aggrieved creditors with a longer reach-back period for avoiding fraudulent transfers. For example, the UFTA generally allows creditors a period of 4 years in which to seek avoidance of a fraudulent transfer.[239]

§ 16.05   THE TRUSTEE'S RIGHT TO ASSERT THE DEBTOR'S DEFENSES — 11 U.S.C. § 558

Under section 558, the trustee can assert on behalf of the estate "any defense available to the debtor as against any entity other than the estate."[240] Although section 558 technically is not an avoiding power, the trustee can use it to similar effect. First, the trustee can use section 558 to reduce or eliminate a creditor's security for its claim to the extent that the debtor had a valid defense to the claim. For example, suppose that Bank claimed a pre-petition security interest against all of Debtor's inventory but that Debtor did not properly authenticate the security agreement. Under section 558, the trustee could assert that Bank failed to satisfy the requirements for attachment and thus acquired no valid security interest in Debtor's inventory.

Alternatively, the trustee may use section 558 to attack the enforceability of the creditor's underlying claim. For example, suppose that Shark claims a security interest in Debtor's jewelry to secure a debt incurred when Shark made Debtor a loan at usurious interest rates. If the jurisdiction's usury law would have permitted Debtor to avoid the obligation to repay some or all of the principal or interest of this loan, the trustee may assert that usury law as a defense to Shark's claim, thereby reducing the debt and the lien which secures it.[241]

In asserting the debtor's defenses under section 558, the trustee stands no better or no worse than the debtor stood as of the bankruptcy petition

---

[238] *See* § 16.04[C] *supra*.

[239] UFTA § 9(a), (b).

[240] 11 U.S.C. § 558.

[241] *In re* McCorhill Publishing, Inc., 86 B.R. 783, 8 U.C.C. Rep. Serv. 2d 203 (Bankr. S.D.N.Y. 1988).

date. Any attempted waiver of defenses by the debtor after the bankruptcy petition is filed has no legal effect; section 558 makes clear that the debtor's attempted post-petition waiver of defenses "does not bind the estate."[242] In contrast, if the debtor had waived the defense in question prior to the petition date and the waiver was enforceable under nonbankruptcy law, the trustee would be bound by the waiver and could not assert that defense under section 558.[243]

§ 16.06 SECURITY INTERESTS IN AFTER-ACQUIRED PROPERTY — 11 U.S.C. § 552

[A] The General Rule Cutting Off Liens Against After-Acquired Property — 11 U.S.C. § 552(a)

Businesses commonly finance their activities by loans secured by floating liens that cover all presently-owned and after-acquired collateral of a particular type, such as inventory and/or accounts receivable. Outside of bankruptcy, the debtor cannot avoid an enforceable and properly perfected floating lien; each time the debtor acquires new assets of the type covered by the floating lien, the floating lien automatically attaches to those assets, and will continue to cover all new assets of that type until the debtor satisfies the underlying obligation.

While the operation of a floating lien outside of bankruptcy is a straightforward matter, its operation after bankruptcy ensues is more complicated. If a floating lien continued to attach to property acquired by the debtor after the bankruptcy petition date, this could significantly compromise the debtor's ability to reorganize its financial affairs. For example, suppose Bank holds a perfected floating lien upon Debtor's inventory and accounts. Debtor needs additional credit to reorganize successfully, but Bank does not wish to provide further financing to Debtor. Finance Company is willing to provide Debtor with a credit line, but only if Finance Company can be assured of a first priority lien upon Debtor's new inventory and accounts. Thus, if Bank's floating lien survived Debtor's bankruptcy filing, it could seriously compromise Debtor's ability to obtain the financing necessary to reorganize. For debtors to obtain a fresh start, Congress concluded that debtors needed the ability to negotiate for post-petition credit to be secured by assets acquired post-petition, without being limited by the terms of pre-petition agreements creating floating liens.[244] Congress accomplished this objective by enacting section 552(a), which provides that "property acquired by the estate or by the debtor after the commencement of the case [*i.e.*, the petition date] is not subject to any lien resulting from any security agreement entered into by the debtor before the commencement of the case."[245]

---

[242] 11 U.S.C. § 558.

[243] *In re* Wey, 827 F.2d 140 (7th Cir. 1987).

[244] *In re* Bumper Sales, Inc., 907 F.2d 1430, 11 U.C.C. Rep. Serv. 2d 1044 (4th Cir. 1990); *In re* Photo Promotion Assocs., Inc., 53 B.R. 759 (Bankr. S.D.N.Y. 1985).

[245] 11 U.S.C. § 552(a).

Note that section 552(a) has no effect on the creditor's security interest to the extent it had attached to property acquired by the debtor *prior to the petition date*; section 552(a) only cuts off the *prospective effect* of a creditor's floating lien as of the petition date. A useful way to recall the effect of section 552(a) is to analogize it to the chalk line that police draw around the body of an accident or murder victim. Bankruptcy declares Debtor "dead" in a financial sense, and section 552(a) draws a chalk line around Debtor's "body" (*i.e.*, Debtor's pre-petition property). If Bank has a validly perfected and otherwise unavoidable security interest against any of the property within that chalk line (such as Debtor's pre-petition inventory), Bank maintains its security interest in that property, notwithstanding Debtor's bankruptcy. But if the reorganizing Debtor acquires new inventory after the petition date, section 552(a) provides that Bank's security interest does not attach to that new inventory — even if Bank's pre-petition security agreement contained an after-acquired property clause that would have been enforceable outside of bankruptcy. The new inventory would remain "outside the chalk line," and Debtor could use it freely in its reorganization efforts.

[B]   Proceeds of Pre-petition Collateral — 11 U.S.C. § 552(b)(1)

One must take care to distinguish between (a) after-acquired property of the debtor and (b) proceeds of pre-petition collateral that the debtor receives post-petition. Although the debtor's after-acquired property is not subject to any pre-petition security interest, the same is not true with respect to proceeds of pre-petition collateral. For example, suppose that on the petition date, Debtor owns 100 units of inventory subject to Bank's validly perfected pre-petition security interest. Suppose further that two weeks after bankruptcy, Debtor sells those 100 units for a total of $10,000. Outside of bankruptcy, Bank would have a validly perfected security interest in the $10,000, because it is identifiable proceeds of collateral in which Bank had a perfected security interest.[246] Moreover, sound policy suggests that Bank should maintain its security interest in the $10,000 despite Debtor's bankruptcy. Bank's pre-petition security interest in the 100 units of inventory — which is not affected by section 552(a) — is worthless if Debtor can liquidate those units of inventory and use the proceeds without regard to Bank's lien. To provide meaningful protection for Bank's security interest in pre-petition collateral, bankruptcy must protect not only Bank's interest in the collateral, but also the proceeds of that collateral.

To provide this protection, Congress enacted section 552(b)(1), which provides that if a pre-petition security interest encumbers both pre-petition collateral and its proceeds, any proceeds of that pre-petition collateral remain subject to the security interest *even if the debtor receives them after the petition date*.[247] In the above example, Bank's pre-petition security

---

[246] U.C.C. § 9-315(a), (c), (d).

[247] 11 U.S.C. § 552(b)(1); *In re Bumper Sales, Inc.*, 907 F.2d 1430, 11 U.C.C. Rep. Serv.

interest had validly attached to Debtor's pre-petition inventory, and Bank's security interest in that inventory automatically continued into identifiable proceeds.[248] Bank thus would continue to hold an enforceable security interest in the $10,000 of inventory proceeds, notwithstanding section 552(a).

Now consider a more complicated scenario in which Debtor files for bankruptcy holding 100 units of inventory, subject to Bank's validly perfected pre-petition floating lien. Two weeks after the petition date, Debtor sells all 100 units of inventory for $10,000, and uses that cash to purchase 100 new units of inventory from suppliers. Bank cannot claim a direct security interest in the new inventory by virtue of the after-acquired property clause in its pre-petition security agreement; as discussed above, section 552(a) cuts off the prospective effect of that clause. The new inventory, however, constitutes identifiable second-generation proceeds of the pre-petition inventory.[249] Can Bank successfully claim a security interest in the new inventory as proceeds of the pre-petition inventory under section 552(b)? As the Fourth Circuit noted in *In re Bumper Sales, Inc.*,[250] the answer is yes. In *Bumper Sales*, the secured party held a validly perfected pre-petition floating lien against the debtor's inventory and accounts. The debtor continued operating in bankruptcy for nearly six months before the secured party asked the court for adequate protection of its security interest. During that period, the debtor's inventory and accounts turned over at least twice, so that by the time of the secured party's motion, all of the debtor's existing inventory and accounts had been received or generated after the petition date. Accordingly, the debtor argued that section 552(a) had extinguished the secured party's lien altogether. The Fourth Circuit disagreed, holding that the new inventory was identifiable second-generation proceeds of the pre-petition inventory and thus that the secured party's lien remained effective under section 552(b)(1).[251]

There is a practical lesson lurking in the *Bumper Sales* case — a prudent secured party should not count on being as lucky as the secured creditor

---

2d 1044 (4th Cir. 1990). The language of section 552(b)(1) covers not only "proceeds" of pre-petition collateral, but also "profits," "products," or "offspring" of pre-petition collateral. Smith v. Dairymen, Inc., 790 F.2d 1107, 1 U.C.C. Rep. Serv. 2d 543 (4th Cir. 1986) (creditor with pre-petition lien upon cows and milk entitled to lien upon post-petition milk); In re Wobig, 73 B.R. 292 (Bankr. D. Neb. 1987) (creditor with pre-petition lien upon sows and offspring entitled to lien upon feeder pigs born after bankruptcy petition). Section 552(b)(2) provides similar protection for post-petition "rents" of pre-petition collateral. Note, however, that a secured party will not have an automatic security interest in an asset that is not a proceed. Proceeds are discussed in § 2.03 *supra*.

[248] Recall that proceeds coverage is automatic under Article 9 unless the security agreement provides otherwise. U.C.C. §§ 9-203(f), 9-315(a). *See* § 2.04[B] *supra*.

[249] Recall that proceeds of proceeds constitute "proceeds," U.C.C. § 9-102(a)(64), and thus, the security interest in the original collateral continues in such proceeds so long as they are "identifiable," *i.e.*, so long as they can be traced precisely to the original collateral. *Id.* § 9-315(a), (b).

[250] 907 F.2d 1430, 11 U.C.C. Rep. Serv. 2d 1044 (4th Cir. 1990).

[251] *Bumper Sales*, 907 F.2d at 1439; *see also In re* Package Design & Supply Co., Inc., 217 B.R. 422 (Bankr. W.D.N.Y. 1998); *In re* Sherwood Ford, Inc., 125 B.R. 957 (Bankr. D. Md. 1991).

in that case. That secured party failed to act prudently to protect its secured position, but ended up being protected anyway. Why was the secured party so lucky? Even under Article 9, a secured party only obtains a security interest in *identifiable* (*i.e.*, traceable) proceeds.[252] Because the debtor in the case stipulated that it had acquired all of the post-petition inventory using the proceeds of pre-petition inventory and accounts, the secured party did not have to trace the post-petition inventory precisely back to the pre-petition inventory. As a result, the Fourth Circuit had no choice but to conclude that the new inventory was identifiable proceeds of the pre-petition inventory.

Most secured parties cannot count on such good fortune. If the *Bumper Sales* debtor had commingled any of the proceeds of pre-petition inventory with other operating funds, and had then used those commingled funds to purchase new inventory during bankruptcy, the secured party would have had a difficult (and perhaps impossible) tracing burden — and thus might have lost its security interest altogether under section 552(a)! Rather than rely upon such uncommon good luck, the secured party in *Bumper Sales* should have filed a motion for adequate protection as soon as the debtor filed its bankruptcy petition. This motion should have sought an order requiring the debtor to sequester all proceeds of the secured party's collateral in a separate account containing only proceeds — thus enabling the secured party to trace the proceeds of its collateral with ease and preserving the secured party's ability to invoke the protection of section 552(b)(1). Alternatively, the motion should have asked the court to condition debtor's use of the proceeds — allowing such use only if the debtor granted the secured party a replacement lien upon post-petition inventory and accounts.

§ 16.07   THE DEBTOR'S RIGHT TO CLAIM EXEMPT PROPERTY

[A]   Generally

The common law generally permits a creditor to enforce a judgment against any assets of the debtor that the creditor can locate. This general rule, however, is subject in every jurisdiction to constitutional or statutory *exemption* provisions, which allow an individual debtor to declare certain assets (or a portion of the debtor's equity in certain assets) to be exempt from seizure and sale by creditors. The goal of exemption laws is to avoid leaving an individual debtor destitute as a result of creditor collection activity. By providing the financially distressed debtor with some minimum amount of assets free of creditor claims, exemption laws enable the debtor to gain the financial foothold necessary to make a fresh financial start.[253]

---

[252] U.C.C. § 9-315(a)-(b).

[253] William J. Woodward, *Exemptions, Opting Out, and Bankruptcy Reform*, 43 Ohio St. L.J. 335 (1982).

Bankruptcy law also incorporates the idea of exemptions for individual debtors. Section 522(d) provides a list of exemptions accorded to an individual debtor as a matter of bankruptcy law. These include, *inter alia*, $20,200 of equity in the debtor's residence, $3,225 of equity in one motor vehicle, $525 of equity in each item of the debtor's household goods (up to a total of $10,775), $1,350 of equity in the debtor's jewelry, and $2,025 of equity in the debtor's professional books or tools.[254] Under section 522(b), an individual debtor may declare certain assets as exempt from the claims of creditors pursuant to the foregoing federal exemptions[255] or may choose instead the exemptions available in the debtor's jurisdiction under nonbankruptcy law,[256] unless the debtor is located in a state that has opted to require debtors to rely only upon nonbankruptcy exemption laws.[257] In that case, the debtor has no option and is limited to whatever exemptions are provided under nonbankruptcy law.

Exemptions do not arise automatically; instead, the debtor must file with the court a list of the property that it claims as exempt.[258] The trustee and any creditor may then object and challenge any particular claim of exemption. Absent timely objection,[259] the property is exempted as claimed.[260] If there is a timely objection, the court must determine whether the debtor is entitled to the claimed exemption, with the objecting party bearing the burden of persuasion.[261] If the debtor is entitled to exempt an asset in its entirety (for example, the state's exemption law entitles the debtor to claim $2,000 of equity in one vehicle, and the debtor's car is worth only $1,500), the asset is returned to the debtor. If the asset is only partially exempt, the estate is entitled to the nonexempt portion of the asset; the trustee thus retains possession of the asset, and the debtor instead receives payment equal to the value of the exemption out of the proceeds of the asset.[262]

---

[254] 11 U.S.C. § 522(d). These amounts are effective as of April 1, 2007, and they are automatically adjusted at three-year intervals based upon the Consumer Price Index. *Id.* § 104(b).

[255] *Id.* § 522(b)(1).

[256] *Id.* § 522(b)(2).

[257] Most states have opted out of the federal bankruptcy exemptions contained in section 522(d). Consequently, in most states, debtors may claim the same exemptions in bankruptcy that they could have claimed outside of bankruptcy.

[258] 11 U.S.C. § 522(*l*). In a voluntary bankruptcy case, the debtor must file its list of claimed exemptions along with the petition or within 15 days thereafter. Bankr. Rules 1007, 4003(a).

[259] Generally, the trustee or any creditor must file any objection within 30 days after the initial meeting of creditors, unless the court grants additional time for objections. Bankr. Rule 4003(b).

[260] The Supreme Court has held that a Chapter 7 trustee could not contest the validity of a debtor's claimed exemption after the 30-day objection period had expired, even if debtor had no colorable basis for claiming the exemption. Taylor v. Freeland & Kronz, 503 U.S. 638 (1992).

[261] Bankr. Rule 4003(c).

[262] *In re* Salzer, 52 F.3d 708 (7th Cir. 1995), *cert. denied*, 516 U.S. 1177 (1996); *In re* Hyman, 123 B.R. 342 (9th Cir. Bankr. 1991), *aff'd*, 967 F.2d 1316 (9th Cir. 1992).

[B] The Debtor's Power to Avoid Liens Against Exempt Property

Suppose that Debtor's automobile is subject to three liens: a voluntary security interest granted to Bank to secure a $5,000 loan, a mechanic's lien held by Garage for unpaid repairs totaling $2,000, and an execution lien for a $10,000 judgment in favor of Plaintiff. If the applicable exemption law permits Debtor to exempt $4,000 of equity in one vehicle, to what extent do these liens affect Debtor's ability to claim the car as exempt property?

Outside of bankruptcy, a debtor's ability to claim exemptions would be of no concern to a voluntary secured creditor like Bank. Exemptions generally are not effective against the holder of a valid security interest; as a practical matter, the granting of a consensual security interest in an asset is tantamount to a waiver of the right to assert the exemption against the secured party. The same is true in bankruptcy; as long as a security interest is valid and not otherwise avoidable in bankruptcy, the debtor's exemption rights are generally subordinate to the secured party's interest.[263] The same principle holds true for statutory lienholders like Garage: statutory liens generally take priority over the debtor's exemptions, on the theory that the debtor's assertion of the exemption would compromise the legislature's decision to accord special protection to the statutory lienholder. In contrast, judicial liens arise through execution, levy, or the like — the very processes against which exemptions seek to protect debtors.[264]

If Plaintiff can freely enforce its execution lien without regard to Debtor's ability to claim an exemption in its car, this would compromise Debtor's ability to obtain a fresh start. The Code thus provides debtors with a mechanism to preserve exemptions, despite the actions of judicial lien creditors. Under section 522(f)(1)(A), the debtor can avoid a judicial lien against an asset "to the extent that such lien impairs an exemption to which the debtor would have been entitled"[265] — in other words, to the extent that the debtor would have been entitled to claim the asset as exempt under applicable exemption law *but for the effect of the judicial lien*.[266] Accordingly, Debtor in the above example cannot avoid the liens of either Bank or Garage, regardless of the car's value. Debtor can avoid Plaintiff's execution lien

---

[263] 11 U.S.C. § 522(c)(2); H.R. Rep. No. 595, 95th Cong., 1st Sess. 361 (1977). This means, of course, that if the lien is so large that there is no equity in the property, the debtor effectively loses the exemption altogether.

[264] *See* § 14.02 *supra*.

[265] 11 U.S.C. § 522(f)(1)(A). By its language, section 522(f)(1) allows the debtor to avoid "the fixing . . . [of a lien upon] an interest of the debtor in property." The Supreme Court has interpreted this language to mean that a debtor can avoid an exemption-impairing judicial lien against an asset that the debtor owned *before the judicial lien arose*, but not a judicial lien that arose before the debtor owned the asset or simultaneously with debtor's acquisition of the asset. Farrey v. Sanderfoot, 500 U.S. 291 (1991) (in divorce settlement, debtor received ex-wife's share of family home, subject to judicial lien in favor of ex-wife to secure debtor's monetary payment obligations; debtor could not avoid ex-wife's lien because it arose simultaneously to his acquisition of ex-wife's share of the home).

[266] Owen v. Owen, 500 U.S. 305 (1991).

under section 522(f)(1)(A), however, to the extent that Plaintiff's lien impairs Debtor's ability to claim an exemption in the car. If the car is worth $11,000 or less, enforcement of Plaintiff's execution lien against the car would completely impair Debtor's ability to claim an exemption in the car; Debtor could thus avoid Plaintiff's lien altogether.[267] If the car was worth $12,000, Debtor could not avoid Plaintiff's lien altogether, but could avoid the lien to the extent of the Debtor's exempt portion of the equity in the car. The lien would remain effective, however, against the nonexempt portion of Debtor's equity in the car ($1,000).

The Code provides one significant exception to the general rule that exemptions are not effective to defeat the rights of a secured party. Under section 522(f)(1)(B), the debtor may avoid a *nonpossessory, nonpurchase-money* security interest to the extent it would impair the debtor's ability to claim an exemption in any of the following assets belonging to the debtor or a dependent:

- household furnishings, household goods, clothes, appliances, books, animals, crops, musical instruments, or jewelry, so long as these assets are held for personal, family, or household use;

- implements, professional books, or tools of the trade; or

- professionally prescribed health aids.[268]

Section 522(f)(1)(B) permits the debtor to avoid exemption-impairing liens against these types of assets *even if the debtor had earlier signed a waiver of its exemptions.*[269] Congress allowed the debtor to avoid nonpossessory, nonpurchase-money liens against these kinds of assets out of concern for potential creditor overreaching. Congress feared that creditors lending money to consumer debtors were taking security interests in household goods and requiring debtors to waive the right to claim those goods as

---

[267] Under section 522(f)(2), a lien "impairs" an exemption to the extent that the value of the property is less than the sum of (a) the lien, (b) all other unavoidable liens on the asset, and (c) the allowed amount of the exemption. In this example, the value of the car is $11,000, and the sum of (a), (b), and (c) is $21,000. The lien thus "impairs" the exemption to the full $10,000 extent of the lien, and is fully avoidable under section 522(f)(1)(A).

[268] 11 U.S.C. § 522(f)(1)(B). Courts have disagreed as to whether a debtor may use section 522(f)(1)(B) to avoid an exemption-impairing lien on livestock such as dairy cattle. *Compare In re* Patterson, 825 F.2d 1140 (7th Cir. 1987) (dairy cattle are "animals," do not constitute "tools of the trade," and lien in animals cannot be avoided unless animals held for personal, household, or family purposes) *with In re* Parrotte, 22 F.3d 472 (2d Cir. 1994) (livestock constituted tools of debtor's trade) *and In re* Heape, 886 F.2d 280 (10th Cir. 1989) (same). The debtor cannot avoid a security interest in household furnishings if the debtor acquired them primarily for business or commercial purposes. *See, e.g., In re* Reid, 757 F.2d 230 (10th Cir. 1985) (paintings acquired by debtor in satisfaction of business debt and pledged as collateral for business loan).

Although section 522(f)(1)(B) allows the debtor to avoid the identified exemption-impairing liens, section 522(f)(3) imposes a further maximum dollar limit with respect to certain items. Under section 522(f)(3), a debtor who takes the applicable state law exemptions cannot avoid a lien against implements, professional books, tools of the trade, farm animals, or crops, to the extent that the value of such items exceeds $5,475.

[269] 11 U.S.C. § 522(f)(1)(B).

exempt. Although these types of assets generally have high replacement costs, they tend to have significantly smaller resale or forced sale values, and thus creditors are not likely to repossess these assets except as a last resort. Accordingly, Congress feared that creditors would use threats of repossession as a means of coercing unknowing debtors into making payments they could not otherwise afford to make.[270] By allowing the debtor to preserve his or her exemption in these assets, despite a waiver of exemptions, section 522(f)(1)(B) prevents this sort of creditor overreaching.[271]

The debtor may not use section 522(f)(1)(B) to avoid an exemption-impairing possessory security interest. According to the courts, whether the security interest is "nonpossessory" for purposes of section 522(f)(1)(B) depends upon the intent of the parties at the time the security interest attached. If the parties structured the transaction as a pledge, with the secured party holding the collateral, the security interest is not avoidable under section 522(f)(1)(B) even if it impairs the debtor's right to claim that item as exempt. In contrast, if the debtor retained possession prior to default, the security interest is nonpossessory, even if the secured party rightfully took possession of the collateral prior to bankruptcy to enforce its lien.[272] Likewise, to the extent that a lien qualifies as a purchase-money security interest under state law, the debtor may not use section 522(f)(1)(B) to avoid the lien.[273] This limitation reflects the solicitude that commercial law typically provides to purchase-money creditors.

Section 522(f)(1)(B) has generated a significant amount of litigation regarding whether the purchase-money character of a security interest survives the debtor's refinancing of the debt. For example, suppose Debtor purchases a television set from Seller, who retains a purchase-money security interest to secure the set's purchase price of $800, and that Seller subsequently assigns its interest to Finance Company. Suppose further that nine months later, after paying off one-half of the price of the set, Debtor signs a new promissory note to Finance Company in the amount of $1,000 — representing both the refinancing of the $400 balance of the original contract and a new loan to Debtor of $600. Debtor then goes bankrupt without repaying anything to Finance Company, seeks to retain the television set as exempt, and further seeks to avoid Finance Company's security interest as an exemption-impairing lien. A significant minority of courts have held that Debtor's refinancing of the original debt "transforms" the purchase-money security interest into a nonpurchase-money security

---

[270] H.R. Rep. No. 595, 95th Cong., 1st Sess. 127.

[271] 11 U.S.C. § 522(f)(1)(B) is not the only federal law that prevents such creditor behavior. Federal Trade Commission and Federal Reserve Board regulations prohibit nonpurchase-money security interests in a consumer's household goods. *See, e.g.*, 16 C.F.R. § 444.2(4) (FTC); 12 C.F.R. § 227.13(d) (FRB).

[272] *In re* Vann, 177 B.R. 704 (D. Kan. 1995); *In re* Schultz, 101 B.R. 68 (Bankr. N.D. Iowa 1989).

[273] 11 U.S.C. § 522(f)(2); U.C.C. § 9-103.

interest avoidable under section 522(f)(1)(B).[274] Most of these courts have reasoned that refinancing a purchase-money debt extinguishes the original debt and replaces it with a new obligation secured by a lien that cannot qualify as a PMSI, because the debtor already owned the collateral at the time of the refinancing.[275] In contrast, the majority of courts have adopted the view that Debtor's refinancing does not *automatically* destroy the purchase-money character of Finance Company's lien.[276] The majority view is preferable, as it looks to solve this question by reference to economic substance rather than form. As one bankruptcy court explained:

> Though in form the original note is canceled, its balance is absorbed into the refinancing loan. To the extent of that balance, the purchase-money security interest taken under the original note likewise survives because what is owed on the original note is not eliminated, it is merely transferred to, and increased in amount by, another obligation. The refinancing changes the character of neither the balance due under the first loan nor the security interest taken under it.[277]

Under this view, Finance Co.'s security interest would have a dual status: it would be a PMSI to the extent that it secures the unpaid balance attributable to the television set ($400), and a nonpurchase-money security interest to the extent of the remaining loan balance ($600). Debtor thus could not avoid Finance Co.'s lien to the extent that the lien secures the remaining $400 balance attributable to the television, but Debtor could use section 522(f)(1)(B) to avoid the lien to the extent it secures the remaining loan balance.[278]

---

[274] This is often called the "transformation rule." *See In re* Matthews, 724 F.2d 798, 37 U.C.C. Rep. Serv. 1332 (9th Cir. 1984).

[275] A few courts have reasoned, incorrectly, that a security interest cannot constitute a PMSI under Article 9 if it secures more than the purchase price. *E.g., In re* Jones, 5 B.R. 655, 30 U.C.C. Rep. Serv. 1697 (Bankr. M.D.N.C. 1980); *In re* Scott, 5 B.R. 37, 29 U.C.C. Rep. Serv. 1038 (Bankr. M.D. Pa. 1980). This interpretation, however, is at odds with the language of Article 9 — which provides that a security interest is a PMSI "to the extent that" it secures the purchase price or an enabling loan, U.C.C. § 9-103(b) — and has been rejected by most courts. *E.g.,* Geist v. Converse Cty. Bank, 79 B.R. 939, 5 U.C.C. Rep. Serv. 2d 1267 (D. Wyo. 1987); *In re* Conn, 16 B.R. 454, 33 U.C.C. Rep. Serv. 701 (Bankr. W.D. Ky. 1982). This issue is discussed in detail in § 1.05 *supra.*

[276] *E.g.,* Pristas v. Landaus of Plymouth, Inc., 742 F.2d 797, 39 U.C.C. Rep. Serv. 1 (3d Cir. 1984); *In re* K & P Logging, Inc. 272 B.R. 867 (Bankr. D.S.C. 2001); *In re* McAllister, 267 B.R. 614 (Bankr. N.D. Iowa 2001). Note that Article 9 generally provides that a purchase-money security interest does not lose its status as a purchase-money security interest merely because "the purchase-money obligation has been renewed, refinanced, consolidated, or restructured." U.C.C. § 9-103(f)(3). By its terms, however, section 9-103(f)(3) does not apply to consumer-goods transactions — thus leaving the possibility that a court might still apply the "transformation rule" discussed in the text when a debtor refinances a purchase-money obligation secured by consumer goods.

[277] *In re* Conn, 16 B.R. 454, 33 U.C.C. Rep. Serv. 701 (Bankr. W.D. Ky. 1982).

[278] *In re* Parsley, 104 B.R. 72, 10 U.C.C. Rep. Serv. 2d 1398 (Bankr. S.D. Ind. 1988). Note that a creditor such as Finance Co. must prove the extent to which its security interest qualifies for purchase-money status, and the creditor's failure to meet this burden would enable the debtor to avoid the security interest altogether under section 522(f)(2). Geist v. Converse County Bank, 79 B.R. 939, 5 U.C.C. Rep. Serv. 2d 1267 (D. Wyo. 1987).

In 1994, Congress amended section 522 by adding subsection 522(f)(3), which places a further limitation upon the debtor's power to avoid exemption-impairing liens under section 522(f)(1). Under section 522(f)(3), a debtor who claims exemptions under nonbankruptcy law cannot avoid the fixing of a nonpossessory, nonpurchase-money security interest in implements, professional books, tools of the trade, farm animals or crops, to the extent that the value of such items exceeds $5,475. [279]

§ 16.08   THE CHAPTER 7 DEBTOR'S RIGHT OF REDEMPTION — 11 U.S.C. § 722

A debtor suffering from financial distress may wish to retain possession of certain important but encumbered assets (for example, the debtor's automobile). Outside of bankruptcy, however, a debtor in default can redeem the collateral and avoid foreclosure of a valid security interest only by paying the full amount of the debt (plus accrued but unpaid interest and reasonable costs of collection). [280] This may render it impossible for the debtor to retain possession of encumbered property, especially property in which the debtor has no equity.

In a Chapter 7 liquidation case, however, bankruptcy law gives certain debtors the ability to redeem the collateral from a lien at a bargain price — the amount of the creditor's allowed secured claim. In the case of an undersecured claim, this enables the debtor to redeem the collateral by paying the value of the collateral rather than the full balance of the debt. Section 722 provides the debtor with this right of redemption under the following circumstances:

- *The creditor's lien must secure a dischargeable consumer debt.* The debtor may not use section 722 to redeem collateral that secures a business indebtedness. [281] The debt must be one that is *capable of being discharged*; the debtor may exercise its right of redemption under section 722 even if a creditor later successfully challenges the debtor's right to discharge. [282]

- *The collateral sought to be redeemed must be tangible personal property intended primarily for personal, family or household use.* The asset sought to be redeemed must be "consumer goods" as defined by U.C.C. Article 9. [283]

---

[279] 11 U.S.C. § 522(f)(3).

[280] U.C.C. § 9-623(b).

[281] *In re* Runski, 102 F.3d 744 (4th Cir. 1996); *In re* Pipes, 78 B.R. 981 (Bankr. W.D. Mo. 1987).

[282] 11 U.S.C. § 523(a) provides a list of certain debts — for example, liability for child-support obligations, liability for willful or malicious injury, or liability for death or personal injury caused by drunk driving — that the debtor cannot discharge in bankruptcy.

[283] U.C.C. § 9-102(a)(23). *See also In re* Runski, 102 F.3d 744 (4th Cir. 1996); *In re* Pipes, 78 B.R. 981 (Bankr. W.D. Mo. 1987).

- *The collateral sought to be redeemed must be exempted under section 522, or must have been abandoned by the trustee under section 554.* To the extent that the debtor has equity in an asset and that equity could benefit the estate, bankruptcy law should not permit redemption; in that case, the equity in that asset should remain with the estate for the benefit of general creditors. If the debtor has no equity in the collateral, however, the trustee likely will consider the collateral to be burdensome to the estate and abandon the collateral under section 554. In that case, the debtor can redeem the collateral by paying the amount of the secured claim to its holder. Alternatively, if the debtor has equity in the collateral but that equity is entirely exempt from general creditors, the estate has no interest in the collateral and redemption is also permitted.[284] If there is no applicable exemption law covering the asset and the trustee has not abandoned it, the debtor cannot redeem it.[285]

- *The debtor must have filed a timely statement of its intention to redeem the collateral.* The debtor must file this statement with the clerk of the bankruptcy court within 30 days following the petition date or, if the initial meeting of creditors[286] takes place during that 30 days, by the date of such meeting.[287]

- *The debtor must actually complete the redemption within 45 days after the initial meeting of creditors.*[288] Section 722 requires the debtor to make a lump-sum payment to the creditor equal to the amount of the creditor's allowed secured claim.[289]

Before the debtor may exercise its redemption right under section 722, the court must value the creditor's secured claim under section 506(a). Valuations for redemption purposes typically involve two principal issues, both of which are resolved by section 506(a)(2) (adopted in 2005 as part of BAPCPA). The first issue is the timing (*i.e.*, the effective date) of the valuation — should the collateral be valued as of the petition date or the date on which the debtor actually redeems the collateral (by which time the collateral's value might have either appreciated or, perhaps more likely,

---

[284] *In re* Fitzgerald, 20 B.R. 27 (Bankr. N.D.N.Y. 1982).

[285] *In re* Zaicek, 29 B.R. 31 (Bankr. W.D. Ky. 1983).

[286] In every bankruptcy case, there is an initial meeting of creditors conducted pursuant to 11 U.S.C. § 341. At this meeting, the trustee and creditors may question the debtor under oath about the debtor's assets and financial affairs. *Id.* § 343.

[287] *Id.* § 521(a)(2)(A).

[288] *Id.* § 521(a)(2)(B), 521(a)(6).

[289] *Id.* § 722 (payment must be "in full"); *In re* Edwards, 901 F.2d 1383 (7th Cir. 1990); *In re* Bell, 700 F.2d 1053 (6th Cir. 1983). If the debtor wants to retain possession of the collateral and make installment payments to the creditor, the debtor has other alternatives for doing so, including (a) reaffirmation of the debt under section 524(c), *infra* § 16.09, and (b) filing a Chapter 13 petition and providing for installment payments to the creditor as part of the Chapter 13 plan. *See In re* Tucker, 158 B.R. 150 (Bankr. W.D. Mo. 1993) (debtor must redeem in lump-sum rather than installments).

depreciated)? Section 506(a)(2) provides that in a Chapter 7 or 13 case involving an individual debtor, the collateral is to be valued as of the petition date and not the redemption date.[290] The rationale for this choice is that outside of bankruptcy, the creditor could have repossessed the collateral and resold it under Article 9 with little delay and without the consequence of the automatic stay. Thus, a petition-date valuation would more closely approximate the creditor's alternative foreclosure remedy.

The second issue concerns the measure of value that courts should use for redemption purposes. Section 506(a)(2) resolves this issue by stating that collateral must be redeemed based upon its "replacement value," meaning "the price a retail merchant would charge for property of that kind considering the age and condition of the property."[291] This prevents a consumer debtor from redeeming the car at a price lower than the consumer debtor would have been required to pay in the retail market for a comparable replacement vehicle.

§ 16.09   REAFFIRMATION BY THE DEBTOR — 11 U.S.C. § 524(c)

[A]   Reaffirmation Agreements

Where redemption is not feasible, the Bankruptcy Code provides the debtor with another option for retaining encumbered property — reaffirmation of the debt. Under limited circumstances, section 524(c) allows a debtor in bankruptcy to make a contract with a creditor under which it agrees to repay a debt to the creditor, even though bankruptcy would otherwise discharge that debt. For example, suppose that Debtor owes Bank $5,000, secured by a consensual lien on Debtor's car. The car is worth only $4,000, and the Chapter 7 trustee has abandoned the car to Debtor. Debtor needs the car to get to and from work and desperately wants to retain possession of it. Unfortunately, Debtor does not have $4,000 in cash with which to redeem the car from Bank's lien under section 722, nor can Debtor likely obtain credit to acquire a comparable car. Bank is willing, however, to allow Debtor to retain possession of the car if the Debtor will reaffirm its obligation to Bank (*i.e.*, if Debtor promises to resume and continue making monthly payments on the full $5,000 balance of the debt). To the extent that section 524(c) permits Debtor to enter into a reaffirmation agreement with Bank, Debtor has an additional alternative for retaining possession of encumbered collateral.[292]

Although the Bankruptcy Code permits reaffirmation agreements, it does not encourage them. Discharge of indebtedness is one of the primary

---

[290] 11 U.S.C. § 506(a)(2).

[291] *Id.*

[292] Reaffirmation under section 524 is not limited to secured debts; theoretically, a debtor could choose to reaffirm an unsecured debt. In this text, discussion of reaffirmation is limited to its application to secured debts.

benefits that bankruptcy provides the individual debtor, and reaffirming a dischargeable debt often may not be in a debtor's best economic interest. Indeed, Congress feared that many reaffirmations were not economically sensible and resulted from threats or overreaching by creditors (*e.g.*, "Reaffirm this debt or we'll make sure that you never get credit from us or anybody else again.").[293] In an attempt to reduce the frequency of unwarranted reaffirmations, Congress provided a series of prerequisites in section 524(c) that a creditor must satisfy before it may legally enforce a reaffirmation agreement:

- *The debtor and creditor must have entered into the reaffirmation agreement before discharge.*[294] Section 524(a) generally operates to enjoin any act "to collect, recover, or offset" a discharged debt.[295] This injunction prevents the enforcement of any reaffirmation agreement entered into after discharge. Further, this injunction also reaches surreptitious attempts by creditors to obtain repayment or reaffirmation outside the scope of section 524(c). For example, suppose Debtor owed Bank a debt of $1,000 discharged in bankruptcy in 1994, and that Debtor approached Bank in 1997 to seek a $2,000 loan. In order to obtain repayment of the previously discharged debt, Bank agrees to loan Debtor $2,000, but only if Debtor will sign a promissory note for $3,000. Bank's actions violate section 524(a), and Bank could not enforce the promissory note to collect the additional $1,000.[296]

- *The debtor must not have validly rescinded the reaffirmation agreement.* Bankruptcy law permits the debtor to change its mind and rescind a reaffirmation agreement, but only if the debtor acts to rescind in prompt fashion. To rescind effectively, the debtor must give notice of rescission before the *later* of (a) the debtor's discharge or (b) the passage of more than 60 days after entering the reaffirmation agreement.[297] The rationale for this debtor opt-out provision is that a "cooling-off" period will allow debtors to reconsider and avoid the consequences of an imprudent decision to reaffirm a pre-petition debt, especially in those cases where the decision to reaffirm may have resulted from significant pressure by a creditor.

- *At or before the time the debtor signs the agreement, the debtor must have received the disclosures described in section 524(k).* Section 524(k) requires lengthy disclosures intended to advise the debtor of (among other things) the amount of the reaffirmed debt, the pertinent credit terms, the debtor's right to rescind the

---

[293] H.R. Rep. No. 595, 95th Cong., 1st Sess. 162–64 (1977).

[294] 11 U.S.C. § 524(c)(1).

[295] *Id.* § 524(a)(2).

[296] Van Meter v. American State Bank, 89 B.R. 32 (W.D. Ark. 1988); *In re* Smurzynski, 72 B.R. 368 (Bankr. N.D. Ill. 1987).

[297] 11 U.S.C. § 524(c)(4).

agreement, and the fact that the debtor is not required to enter into a reaffirmation agreement.[298]

• *The reaffirmation agreement must have been filed with the bankruptcy court.*[299]

• *If the debtor was not represented by an attorney at the time the agreement was negotiated, the bankruptcy court must have approved the agreement.* Where the debtor enters a reaffirmation agreement without legal advice, there is a justifiable concern that the debtor may not have fully understood the consequences of the agreement. By requiring approval of reaffirmation agreements entered into by uncounseled debtors, the Bankruptcy Code provides such debtors with protection from imprudent reaffirmation agreements. Where the debtor acts without legal advice, the Code provides several procedural safeguards before a creditor can enforce a reaffirmation agreement. *First*, the debtor must appear in person at a hearing, at which the court must (a) inform the debtor that it is not required to enter into a reaffirmation agreement and (b) explain the legal effect and consequences of entering into and defaulting under a reaffirmation agreement.[300] *Second*, the court cannot enforce the agreement unless the court determines that the agreement is in the "best interest of the debtor" and will not pose "undue hardship" to the debtor or a dependent.[301]

• *If the debtor was represented by an attorney at the time the agreement was negotiated, that attorney must have filed the required affidavit with the bankruptcy court.* The attorney's affidavit must declare that the debtor entered into the reaffirmation agreement voluntarily and with full information, that the agreement does not impose an undue hardship upon the debtor or a dependent, and that the attorney fully advised the debtor of the consequences of entering into and defaulting under a reaffirmation agreement.[302] The rationale for this provision is that if the debtor entered into the agreement with the advice of a competent attorney, the agreement probably reflects the debtor's best

---

[298] *Id.* § 524(k).

[299] *Id.* § 524(c)(3).

[300] *Id.* § 524(d)(1).

[301] *Id.* §§ 524(c)(6)(A), 524(d)(2). This determination is not required, however, if the debtor is seeking to reaffirm a consumer debt secured by real estate. *Id.* §§ 524(c)(6)(B), 524(d)(2). Courts have occasionally expressed significant doubt about the debtor's ability to make the payments specified in the reaffirmation agreement as grounds for disapproving the agreement as not being in the debtor's best interest. *In re* Bryant, 43 B.R. 189 (Bankr. E.D. Mich. 1984).

[302] 11 U.S.C. § 524(c)(3)(A)-(C).

interests and thus should be freely enforced without the need for court approval.[303]

- *Finally, the agreement must be enforceable under applicable nonbankruptcy law.*[304] Under the common law, of course, the debtor's promise to pay a discharged debt does not require additional consideration; the original promise to pay constitutes sufficient "moral consideration" to enforce the reaffirmation. Nevertheless, nonbankruptcy law may provide the debtor with other defenses to the enforcement of the reaffirmation agreement, such as unconscionability, fraud, or duress.

Whereas redemption under section 722 is nonconsensual, reaffirmation under section 524(c) obviously requires an agreement between the debtor and the secured creditor.[305] Neither party can legally compel the other to accept reaffirmation. Thus, it is important to appreciate the circumstances under which a debtor is likely to reaffirm a secured debt. For example, consider the hypothetical introduced at the beginning of this section, in which Debtor wishes to retain possession of its car but does not have the $4,000 cash necessary to redeem the vehicle. If Debtor is in Chapter 7 liquidation, Bank (which holds an undersecured claim) has little incentive to cooperate with Debtor's desire to retain possession of the car — unless Debtor is willing to negotiate an agreement that will make Bank better off than Bank would be if it repossessed and sold the car. If Debtor simply surrendered the car, Bank would receive $4,000 (less expenses of sale) from the car, but little or nothing on its unsecured deficiency claim. Here, each party has an incentive to reaffirm: reaffirmation is Debtor's only feasible means of maintaining a suitable car, and Bank's only means of obtaining a larger recovery than it would receive if Debtor simply surrendered the collateral.[306]

---

[303] This requirement was added in 1984. Prior to 1984, the court had to approve *all* reaffirmation agreements, regardless of whether the debtor had the benefit of counsel. One might argue that a sophisticated debtor who enters a reaffirmation agreement with the advice of counsel should be held to the agreement regardless of whether the agreement meets the other requirements of section 524(c). Courts have rejected this argument, however. *See In re* Getzoff, 180 B.R. 572 (9th Cir. Bankr. 1995).

[304] 11 U.S.C. § 524(c).

[305] If the debtor wishes to reaffirm a secured debt in order to retain the collateral, section 521 requires the debtor to file a statement of its intent with the clerk of the bankruptcy court within 30 days following the petition date (or, if the initial meeting of creditors takes place during that 30 days, by the date of such meeting). *Id.* § 521(a)(2)(A). Further, section 521 obligates the debtor to carry out its intent and enter into a reaffirmation agreement within 30 days following its statement of intent. *Id.* § 521(a)(2)(B).

[306] Again, the comment in the text presumes that Debtor is in a Chapter 7 liquidation proceeding. While reaffirmation is not limited to Chapter 7, debtors in Chapter 11, 12, or 13 cases do not need reaffirmation to retain possession of collateral; those Chapters permit a debtor to retain possession of collateral while repaying undersecured pre-petition claims under a reorganization plan. *See, e.g., In re* Moffett, 356 F.3d 518, 52 U.C.C. Rep. Serv. 2d 539 (4th Cir. 2004) (even though Chapter 13 debtor's reorganization plan did not include a lump-sum payment of debt secured by car, section 1322(b) permitted debtor to restructure timing of her payments to protect her right of redemption).

[B]   Retention of Collateral Without Either Redemption or Reaffirmation

Continuing with the previous hypothetical, what if Debtor can neither redeem the car nor negotiate an acceptable reaffirmation agreement with Bank? Does Debtor have any other alternative for retaining possession of the car? If Debtor was in default at the time of its petition, the answer is no. But if Debtor was not in default at the time of its petition, the answer has not been as clear. Some have argued that if Debtor keeps making its monthly payments in a timely fashion and Bank keeps accepting them, Debtor can retain possession of the car without having to redeem it or enter into a reaffirmation agreement — a practice often called a "ride-through." Courts have split on whether the Bankruptcy Code permits this practice.

[1]   The Law Prior to BAPCPA

Analysis of the "ride-through" issue begins with former section 521(2). This section provided as follows:

> [I]f an individual debtor's schedule of assets and liabilities includes consumer debts which are secured by property of the estate —
>
> > (A) within thirty days after the date of the filing of a petition under Chapter 7 . . . the debtor shall file with the clerk a statement of his intention with respect to the retention or surrender of such property and, if applicable, specifying that such property is claimed as exempt, that the debtor intends to redeem such property, or that the debtor intends to reaffirm debts secured by such property;
> >
> > (B) within forty-five days after the filing of the notice of intent under this section . . . the debtor shall perform his intention with respect to such property . . .; and
> >
> > (C) nothing in subparagraphs (A) and (B) of this paragraph shall alter the debtor's or the trustee's rights with regard to such property . . . .

One of the leading cases addressing the "ride-through" issue is *In re Edwards*.[307] In the *Edwards* case, a Chapter 7 debtor attempted to retain possession of two cars without either redemption or reaffirmation. The creditor argued that under section 521(2), the debtor had only three choices — redeem the cars, surrender them, or reaffirm the debts. Thus, the creditor moved to compel the debtor to exercise one of these choices, and the bankruptcy court granted this motion. The Seventh Circuit affirmed the bankruptcy court's order, holding that section 521(2) did not permit a Chapter 7 debtor to retain possession of collateral without either redeeming it or reaffirming the underlying debt.[308] In reaching this result, the

---

[307] 901 F.2d 1383 (7th Cir. 1990).

[308] *Edwards*, 901 F.2d at 1386.

Edwards court expressed the view that retention of possession without redemption or reaffirmation imposed unjustified financial risks upon the creditor — who could end up (if the debtor later defaulted) with depreciated collateral and no personal recourse against the debtor.[309]

In contrast to *Edwards* is the Fourth Circuit's decision in *In re Belanger*.[310] The debtors were current in repaying a debt secured by their mobile home at the time they filed a Chapter 7 bankruptcy petition. The debtors neither reaffirmed the debt nor redeemed the home, but simply continued making timely monthly payments to the creditor during the Chapter 7 proceeding. As in *Edwards*, the creditor argued that section 521(2) limited the Chapter 7 debtor to either redemption, reaffirmation, or surrender of the collateral. The Fourth Circuit disagreed and allowed the debtors to retain possession of the home as long as they continued making timely installment payments under the original contract.[311] The *Belanger* court noted that nothing in the language of section 521(2) required the debtor "to choose redemption, reaffirmation or surrender of the property to the exclusion of all other alternatives";[312] thus, this section did not foreclose the possibility that the debtors could simply keep the original contract alive despite their Chapter 7 petition. The court also expressed concern that the *Edwards* approach would force the debtors to redeem or accept the creditor's terms of reaffirmation, thus giving the creditor too much bargaining leverage in reaffirmation negotiations.[313]

Obviously, the *Belanger* result provides the Chapter 7 debtor who was not in default on the petition date with little incentive to reaffirm a secured debt.[314] Under *Belanger*, such a debtor can retain possession of the

---

[309] *Id.* ("[Section 521(2)] speaks strongly against permitting debtors to improve their position dramatically against secured creditors by relieving them of personal liability. When a debtor is relieved of personal liability on loans secured by collateral, the debtor has little or no incentive to insure or maintain the property in which a creditor retains a security interest. The value of the collateral may fall below the level of the loan, leaving the creditor undersecured and driving up future costs of credit."). The First, Fifth, and Eleventh Circuits have also adopted this view. *In re* Burr, 160 F.3d 843 (1st Cir. 1998); *In re* Johnson, 89 F.3d 249 (5th Cir. 1996); *In re* Taylor, 3 F.3d 1512 (11th Cir. 1993).

[310] 962 F.2d 345 (4th Cir. 1992).

[311] *Belanger*, 962 F.2d at 347. The Second, Ninth, and Tenth Circuits have reached a similar conclusion. *In re* Boodrow, 126 F.3d 43 (2d Cir. 1997), *cert. denied*, 118 S. Ct. 1055 (1998); *In re* Parker, 139 F.3d 668 (9th Cir.), *cert. denied*, 119 S. Ct. 592 (1998); Lowry Fed. Credit Union v. West, 882 F.2d 1543 (10th Cir. 1989).

[312] *Belanger*, 962 F.2d at 347–48. The Fourth Circuit cited two justifications for this conclusion. First, it argued that the language "if applicable" in section 521(2)(A) meant that the debtor only had to specify either redemption, reaffirmation, or surrender *when the debtor was in default*; under this view, a debtor that was not in default would still have the ability to retain the collateral as long as it tendered timely performance. Second, the court held that section 521(2)(C) demonstrated that section 521(2) was "procedural" in nature and did not affect the debtor's substantive rights under its contract (including the right to retain possession of the collateral as long as the debtor was not in default).

[313] *Id.* at 348. The *Belanger* court also rejected the creditor's argument that "a debtor who wishes to retain the collateral and make installment payments as they come due should resort to Chapter 13. . . ." *Id.* at 349.

[314] One scholar has criticized the *Belanger* result as illogical and inequitable because it

collateral and obtain a discharge of the debt as long as the debtor continues making timely payments and does not violate the terms of its security agreement.[315] The creditor's lien survives the discharge, of course, and will sufficiently protect the creditor to the extent that the collateral maintains its value.[316] The debtor's discharge, however, will protect the debtor from liability in the event the collateral depreciates to a value below the remaining balance of the debt.

[2]   The Law After BAPCPA

At first blush, it appears that Congress intended for BAPCPA (enacted in 2005) to abolish the "ride-through" practice. It remains uncertain, however, that the amendments will actually have that effect.

Revised section 521(a)(2) is essentially identical to old section 521(2), although it does reduce the time for the debtor to perform its statement of intention from 45 days to 30 days.[317] Congress's apparent intention to abolish the "ride-through" practice is reflected by new section 362(h)(1), which provides that if the debtor fails to file its statement of intention or perform its intention on a timely basis, the automatic stay is lifted.[318] Some commentators have concluded that the addition of section 362(h)(1) abolishes "ride-through,"[319] but future case law may prove this conclusion to be unjustified. The lifting of the automatic stay would clearly permit the secured party to proceed to foreclose on the collateral — but only if the debtor is in default.[320] Thus, in jurisdictions that followed the *Belanger*

---

treats a creditor whose debtor is in default more favorably than a creditor whose debtor is current. Ned W. Waxman, *Redemption or Reaffirmation: The Debtor's Exclusive Means of Retaining Possession of Collateral in Chapter 7*, 56 U. Pitt. L. Rev. 187, 202 (1994) ("[I]f both debtors desire to retain the collateral and neither has sufficient funds to redeem, then the debtor who is current would be able to retain the collateral without reaffirming, while the debtor in default would be required to reaffirm the debt in order to keep the collateral. Thus, the creditor whose debtor is current will no longer have recourse to the personal liability of that debtor, while the creditor whose debtor was in default will have recourse after the reaffirmation.").

[315] What if the debtor's bankruptcy filing itself constitutes a default under the security agreement? Does this provision (often called an *ipso facto* clause) allow the creditor to declare a default and thus avoid the result in *Belanger*? The likely answer is no; the majority of courts have refused to enforce *ipso facto* clauses in bankruptcy. *E.g.*, Riggs Nat'l Bank v. Perry, 729 F.2d 982 (4th Cir. 1984); *In re* Nikokyrakis, 109 B.R. 260 (Bankr. N.D. Ohio 1989).

[316] Dewsnup v. Timm, 502 U.S. 410 (1992).

[317] 11 U.S.C. § 502(a)(2)(A)-(C).

[318] *Id.* § 362(h)(1). The trustee can file a motion seeking turnover of the collateral on the ground that it is "of consequential value or benefit to the estate." If the court agrees after notice and a hearing, the court can order the debtor to turn the collateral over to the trustee and, if so, the automatic stay remains intact. *Id.* § 362(h)(2).

[319] *See, e.g.*, Philip R. Principe, *Did BAPCPA Eliminate the "Fourth Option" for Individual Debtors' Secured Personal Property?*, 24 Am. Bankr. Inst. J. 6, 48–49 (Oct. 2005).

[320] Section 521(d) provides that in this situation, nothing in the Bankruptcy Code "shall prevent or limit the operation" of an *ipso facto* clause making bankruptcy an event of default under the debtor's security agreement. Nevertheless, if the debtor was not otherwise in default on the petition date, and the secured party has continued to accept monthly payments post-

analysis, even revised section 521(a)(2) may still permit a "ride-through" as long as the debtor is not in default, continues to meet its repayment schedule promptly, and the secured party accepts the debtor's installment payments.[321]

petition, a court might well conclude that the creditor had waived its ability to claim a default based upon an *ipso facto* clause. *See, e.g.,* 4 Collier on Bankruptcy ¶ 521.10[5], at 521–59 (15th ed. Supp. 2005).

[321] The 2005 bankruptcy amendments also added new section 521(a)(6), which provides that a Chapter 7 debtor cannot retain possession of purchase-money collateral unless the debtor, within 45 days following the first meeting of creditors, either enters into a reaffirmation agreement of the purchase-money debt or redeems the collateral. 11 U.S.C. § 521(a)(6). If the debtor fails to do so, the automatic stay is lifted "and the creditor may take whatever action as to such property is permitted by applicable nonbankruptcy law. . . ." *Id.* While some commentators have cited section 521(a)(6) as further support for the view that the 2005 bankruptcy amendments have abolished "ride-through," *see* Principe, *supra* note 314, this result is not entirely clear. If the debtor was not in default prior to bankruptcy and has continued to make timely installment payments that the secured party has accepted, a court following the *Belanger* analysis may yet conclude that "applicable nonbankruptcy law" would not permit the secured party to foreclose on the collateral.

Part V

DEFAULT

Chapter 17

DEFAULT AND ITS CONSEQUENCES

§ 17.01 IMPORTANCE OF THE CONCEPT OF DEFAULT

A security interest becomes enforceable when it has attached to the debtor's rights in the collateral.[1] Enforceability means that upon "default,"[2] the secured party legally may pursue the remedies set forth in the security agreement and in Article 9.[3] The existence of a default is thus critical to the availability of those remedies.[4]

---

[1] U.C.C. § 9-203(a).

[2] "Default" typically will involve an action or failure to act by the obligor on the debt, such as a failure to make timely payment on the debt. In some cases, however, the obligor on the debt is not the owner of the collateral (or the "debtor," as Article 9 defines the term). In those cases, a default may involve an action or failure to act by the debtor, such as a sale of the collateral in violation of the security agreement. In most cases, the obligor and the debtor are the same person. Thus, for ease of reading, the text often uses the customary term "debtor's default" or "default by the debtor" rather than the more cumbersome "default by the debtor or obligor."

[3] U.C.C. § 9-601(a).

[4] Any secured party that wrongfully repossesses collateral, whether intentionally or in the mistaken belief that a default has occurred, potentially faces significant liability. *See, e.g.,* Ansley v. Conseco Fin. Serv. Corp., 2002 WL 31955217, 49 U.C.C. Rep. Serv. 2d 955 (Mich. Ct. App. 2002) (creditor liable in conversion where creditor provided no proof that it held security interest in mobile home or that debtor was in default on payment obligations); Corbin v. Regions Bank, 574 S.E.2d 616, 49 U.C.C. Rep. Serv. 2d 1328 (Ga. Ct. App. 2002) (when debtor was unable to make payments on purchase of used truck due to physical disability, but had secured credit disability insurance in favor of creditor, jury could find that existence of credit insurance claim meant that debtor had not defaulted). Repossession in the absence of default typically constitutes a conversion that entitles the debtor to a credit equivalent to

405

The U.C.C. does not define "default," leaving that to the agreement of the parties and to the common law. Most of the cases holding the debtor in default as a matter of common law involve a failure to make a payment when due.[5] While an occasional case holds that some other event constitutes a common-law default,[6] the secured party cannot prudently rely solely upon the common law for sufficient protection. Thus, every well-drafted security agreement contains a section setting forth the various events (often called "events of default") that will constitute a default under the agreement. The parties should tailor the list of events of default to fit the context of their transaction, but common events of default include the following:

- Failure to make a payment when due;

- Breach of any obligation imposed upon the debtor under another contract between the debtor and the secured party;

- Materially false representations made by the debtor in financial statements or other information furnished to the secured party in connection with any transaction between the parties;

- Breach of any warranty made by the debtor to the secured party, such as a warranty that the debtor has unencumbered title to the collateral;

- Breach of any promise made to the secured party by the debtor, such as a promise to use the collateral in a certain manner, keep the collateral in a certain location, insure the collateral, or permit inspection of the collateral or of the debtor's records;

- Sale or other disposition of the collateral without the secured party's written consent (except for ordinary-course sales of inventory);

- Creation of a competing lien on the collateral, whether the lien arises voluntarily as a result of the debtor's agreement (*i.e.*, a competing security interest) or involuntarily as a result of a rule of law (*e.g.*, an artisan's lien, tax lien, or judgment lien);

- Death or bankruptcy of the debtor;[7]

- Dissolution, termination, insolvency, or failure of the debtor's business; or an assignment for the benefit of creditors or other state debtor's relief proceeding;

---

the fair market value of the collateral at the time of the repossession. Further, as conversion is an intentional tort, wrongful repossession also exposes the secured party to the risk of punitive damages. Damages for wrongful repossession are discussed in § 19.01[B].

[5] *See, e.g.*, Cofield v. Randolph Cty. Comm'n, 90 F.3d 468, 30 U.C.C. Rep. Serv. 2d 374 (11th Cir. 1996); Nationsbank v. Clegg, 29 U.C.C. Rep. Serv. 2d 1366 (Tenn. App. 1996).

[6] *See, e.g.*, Bentley v. Textile Banking Co., 26 A.D. 2d 112, 271 N.Y.S.2d 417 (App. Div. 1966) (debtor's bankruptcy constituted default).

[7] Note that while security agreements customarily specify that the debtor's bankruptcy constitutes a default, these "ipso facto" clauses are generally not enforceable in bankruptcy. *See* Michael J. Herbert, Understanding Bankruptcy §§ 9.03[F], 9.04[D] (1996).

- Theft, loss, or substantial damage to or destruction of the collateral;

- Failure to account properly for proceeds of the collateral; and

- Any event that causes the secured party to feel insecure, such as a decline in the debtor's business fortunes or a depletion in the value of the collateral.[8]

The preceding list is not exclusive, and a secured party may define other events as a default depending upon the nature of the transaction.[9] In many commercial financing arrangements, for example, the secured party will require the debtor to maintain at all times collateral valued at a stipulated level in relation to the loan (the loan-to-value ratio),[10] and failure to maintain the necessary ratio will constitute an event of default. For another example, suppose Secured Party sells goods to Debtor on credit, retaining a purchase-money security interest in them. If the goods prove to be defective, in breach of warranty, Debtor may unilaterally reduce its payments, relying upon an Article 2 provision that permits a buyer to notify a seller of breach and then deduct all or part of the damages from that portion of the price that is still due.[11] Secured Party, of course, will insist that Debtor's payment obligation is independent of its warranty obligation; a clause making any attempt at setoff an event of default, regardless of motivation, will achieve this result.

This chapter does not attempt to list all of the events that might constitute a default. A competent transactional attorney must have a solid understanding of the transaction at issue and a good imagination to anticipate foreseeable risks and draft a document that protects the secured party against those risks. The security agreement should include as a default anything that foreseeably could impair the debtor's ability to pay or the secured party's interest in the collateral.

[A] Waiver of Default

The fact that a default occurs does not mean that the secured party *must* foreclose on its collateral. In some instances, the security agreement may

---

[8] The secured party may declare a default and accelerate the maturity of the debt on grounds of insecurity only if the agreement so provides and the secured party "in good faith believes that the prospect of payment or performance is impaired," with the debtor bearing the burden to show the secured party's lack of good faith. U.C.C. § 1-309. For further discussion, *see* § 17.01[B] *infra*.

[9] State statutes sometimes limit the permissible events of default in consumer contracts, and a secured party's remedies under Article 9 are subject to such statutes. U.C.C. § 9-201(b), (c). For example, Mo. Rev. Stat. § 408.552 provides that in certain credit transactions, primarily consumer in nature, an agreement concerning default "is enforceable only to the extent that: (1) The borrower fails to make a payment as required by agreement; or (2) The lender's prospect of payment, performance, or ability to realize upon the collateral is significantly impaired; the burden of establishing significant impairment is on the lender."

[10] *See* § 3.04[B] *supra*.

[11] U.C.C. § 2-717.

grant the secured party a remedy that is not as drastic as foreclosure. For example, if the debtor fails to keep the collateral insured, the security agreement may provide that the secured party may purchase insurance and add its cost to the principal balance of the obligation.[12] Even in the event of a default in payment, the secured party typically will attempt to work with the debtor to resolve the problem without having to resort to foreclosure. For example, suppose the debtor makes a late payment. Rather than declaring a default and accelerating the loan, the secured party may admonish the debtor, extend the time for the debtor to make the payment, or just do nothing. After all, foreclosure is an expensive process that often leaves a deficiency unpaid, and (if carried out improperly) can expose the secured party to liability. In short, the secured party may choose to waive the default.

This attitude of leniency and compromise is one that courts should encourage, but in fact numerous court decisions have held that waiver of a default may compromise the secured party's ability to enforce its rights in the event of a future default. The problem typically arises when a secured party that has waived a default on prior occasions becomes fed up with the debtor's behavior and decides to accelerate the maturity of the indebtedness and foreclose its security interest. If the debtor attempts to resist foreclosure by arguing that the secured party's prior conduct has waived its enforcement rights, the secured party may attempt to rely upon an "anti-waiver clause" (assuming its security agreement contained such a clause). An anti-waiver clause — which is a boilerplate provision contained in most security agreements — typically provides roughly as follows:

> All rights, powers, and remedies of Secured Party hereunder or under any other obligation are cumulative and not alternative and shall not be exhausted by any single assertion thereof. The failure of Secured Party to exercise any such right, power or remedy will not be deemed a waiver thereof nor preclude any further or additional exercise of such right, power or remedy, now or in the future, upon any obligation of Debtor. The waiver of any default hereunder shall not be a waiver of any subsequent default.

Parties asserting anti-waiver clauses have met with mixed success in court decisions. For example, suppose Debtor makes one late payment which Secured Party accepts. Suppose further that Debtor is late making its payment the following month, at which time Secured Party refuses the payment, accelerates the debt, and repossesses the collateral. Debtor may argue that the waiver in the first instance operated also as a waiver in the second instance, thereby obligating Secured Party to accept the untimely payment rather than declare a default. Based upon the weight of authority, with just one prior waiver, a court probably will not accept Debtor's

---

[12] A secured party in possession of the collateral has the right to purchase insurance and add it to the debt, even without a clause in the security agreement authorizing it to do so. *See* U.C.C. § 9-207(b)(1).

argument.[13] If Secured Party has accepted late payments from Debtor on several previous occasions, however, Debtor's argument becomes much stronger.[14]

Numerous courts have concluded that an established pattern of accepting late payments results in "waiver by estoppel" — in other words, the secured party is estopped from insisting upon the strict terms of the agreement (*i.e.*, timely payment) in the future. In most of these cases, courts concluded that the inclusion of an anti-waiver clause in the security agreement did not preclude this result. Many courts following the waiver-by-estoppel approach have borrowed the "course of performance" concept from Article 2.[15] For example, the secured party in *Moe v. John Deere Co.*[16] accepted a series of late payments and then declared a default without notifying the debtor that it had decided to enforce all future payment due dates in a strict fashion. The court held that the secured party had engaged in a course of performance that estopped it from insisting on timely payment or relying on the anti-waiver provision in the security agreement. The court noted that the secured party could revoke its waiver[17] by notifying the debtor that it would insist upon timely payments in the future.

While the waiver-by-estoppel argument has some appeal in consumer cases, it loses some of its force in commercial contracts.[18] After all, a commercial debtor is probably well aware of the fact that it is making its payments late, and may well be relying on the fact that it is more trouble for the secured party to foreclose on the loan than it is to continue to accept late payments. As a result, a number of decisions have refused to apply the waiver doctrine in the commercial context, especially if the security agreement contained an anti-waiver provision.[19]

As discussed previously,[20] any repossession without the existence of a default constitutes a conversion. Thus, a secured party that repossesses the

---

[13] *See, e.g.*, Ash v. Peoples Bank of Greensboro, 500 So. 2d 5, 3 U.C.C. Rep. Serv. 2d 426 (Ala. 1986).

[14] Note that the text does not suggest that the debtor would certainly prevail if the secured party had accepted multiple late payments. While cases frequently find waiver based upon acceptance of multiple late payments, courts in numerous decisions have refused to find waiver despite the secured party's acceptance of multiple late payments. *See, e.g.,* McGrady v. Nissan Motor Acceptance Corp., 40 F. Supp. 2d 1323, 41 U.C.C. Rep. Serv. 2d 986 (M.D. Ala. 1998) (court enforced anti-waiver clause in consumer transaction even though creditor had accepted eleven delinquent payments).

[15] U.C.C. § 2-208. Waiver by estoppel can also be predicated upon a course of dealing established during past loan transactions between the parties. *See, e.g.*, J.R. Hale Contracting Co. v. United N.M. Bank, 799 P.2d 581, 13 U.C.C. Rep. Serv. 2d 53 (N.M. 1990).

[16] 516 N.W.2d 332, 25 U.C.C. Rep. Serv. 2d 997 (S.D. 1994). *See also* Mercedes-Benz Credit Corp. v. Morgan, 850 S.W.2d 297, 20 U.C.C. Rep. Serv. 2d 705 (Ark. 1993); Nevada Nat'l Bank v. Huff, 582 P.2d 364, 24 U.C.C. Rep. Serv. 1044 (Nev. 1978).

[17] U.C.C. § 2-209(5) permits revocation of a waiver affecting an executory portion of a contract unless revocation would be unjust because of reliance on the waiver.

[18] *See, e.g.*, B.P.G. Autoland Jeep-Eagle, Inc. v. Chrysler Credit Corp., 799 F. Supp. 1250, 19 U.C.C. Rep. Serv. 2d 649 (D. Mass. 1992).

[19] *See, e.g.*, Lewis v. Nat'l City Bank, 814 F. Supp. 696, 21 U.C.C. Rep. Serv. 2d 380 (N.D. Ill. 1993), *aff'd*, 23 F.3d 410 (7th Cir. 1994).

[20] *See* note 4 *supra*.

collateral, only to have the debtor successfully raise the defense of waiver by estoppel, is liable for conversion. If the facts indicate that the creditor has simply tired of accepting late payments and chosen to accelerate the debt, however, courts have shown the creditor more leniency than in cases of knowing conversion. For example, the court in *Cobb v. Midwest Recovery Bureau Co.*[21] held that the secured party's repossession was wrongful because it had failed to notify the debtor that it would insist on timely payments in the future; however, the court refused to allow punitive damages. Courts have not been equally forgiving when the secured party pursues its default remedies following an express waiver of default. For example, in *Alaska Statebank v. Fairco*,[22] the secured party told the defaulting debtor that it would not foreclose until after the holidays. When it later reneged and repossessed its collateral — effectively shutting down the debtor's business before it could reap the benefits of the holiday season — the court approved an award of punitive damages.

[B] Acceleration Clauses and Insecurity Clauses

If default occurs, the secured party may legally invoke the remedies provided in Article 9 as well as any remedies included in the security agreement. The agreement typically will contain an acceleration clause which, when invoked, renders the entire outstanding debt presently due and payable. The secured party will then repossess the collateral and proceed with foreclosure.[23]

If the secured party accelerates the maturity of the debt following one of the standard events of default, such as nonpayment or failure to protect the collateral, there is relatively little controversy. For example, suppose Secured Party accelerates the maturity of the debt after Debtor misses two monthly payments and fails to keep the collateral insured. Debtor may attempt to argue that acceleration is improper because Debtor's net worth is easily sufficient to ensure that Secured Party will eventually collect full payment of the debt. Nevertheless, if the security agreement provides that nonpayment and failure to insure are events of default, Debtor's argument will almost certainly fail.[24]

---

[21] 295 N.W.2d 232, 28 U.C.C. Rep. Serv. 941 (Minn. 1980).

[22] 674 P.2d 288, 37 U.C.C. Rep. Serv. 1782 (Alaska 1983).

[23] The secured party need not accelerate in order to foreclose, but if it fails to accelerate, it cannot retain from the foreclosure sale any proceeds in excess of the amount due and unpaid at that time. Thus, it is exceptionally rare for a secured party to foreclose without first accelerating the maturity of the debt.

[24] Although the Code imposes a general obligation of good faith in the enforcement of a security agreement, *see* U.C.C. § 1-304, this does not mean that a secured party can pursue its remedies only when its likelihood of payment or its security is threatened. The weight of authority holds that the specific provisions of section 1-309 — which require likelihood of nonpayment or a threat to the creditor's security before the creditor may accelerate "at will" or for "insecurity" — do not apply following a traditional objective event of default defined in the security agreement. *See, e.g.*, Bowen v. Danna, 637 S.W.2d 560, 34 U.C.C. Rep. Serv. 1095 (Ark. 1982); *but see* Brown v. AVEMCO Inv. Corp., 603 F.2d 1367 (9th Cir. 1979)

Problems can arise, however, if the secured party accelerates[25] based upon an "insecurity clause" — *i.e.*, a clause that entitles the secured party to accelerate either "at will" or when it "deems itself insecure." The U.C.C. permits acceleration based upon an insecurity clause only if the secured party "in good faith believes that the prospect of payment or performance is impaired."[26] Even though the debtor bears the burden of establishing lack of good faith,[27] numerous lenders have incurred liability under this standard. Much of the litigation in these cases has turned on whether a lender's good faith is evaluated using a subjective or an objective standard. The Code's original definition of good faith invoked a purely subjective test — whether the secured party is honest in its belief that its prospect of payment or performance is impaired.[28] Under the purely subjective good-faith standard, an honest lender invoking an insecurity clause would be immune from liability, even if most lenders would not have accelerated under the same circumstances. Indeed, under the subjective standard, some courts treated secured parties as acting in good faith even though they relied upon incorrect information and further inquiry would have revealed the true facts.[29] Over the past 15 years, however, the Uniform Commercial Code revision process has resulted in a systematic redefinition of "good faith" to include both "honesty in fact" and "the observance of reasonable commercial standards of fair dealing."[30] Under this approach, a lender's decision to invoke an insecurity clause will also be evaluated based upon whether a reasonable secured party might have chosen to act similarly based upon the same circumstances.[31] Generally speaking, lenders have

---

(acceleration of debt and repossession and sale of plane, based upon debtor's lease and sale of plane, lacked good faith when plane's purchasers were prepared to redeem the plane and thus secured party had no reason to believe its prospect of payment was impaired).

Although the general duty of good faith applies, it is unlikely that a secured party would be held to have violated that duty by accelerating due to an event that the parties agreed would constitute a default. Acceleration based upon such a default would be permissible unless the court concluded that the secured party was using the event of default as a pretext and was, in truth, accelerating the loan due to personal animus or some other illegitimate reason. *See* R. Wilson Freyermuth, *Enforcement of Acceleration Provisions and the Rhetoric of Good Faith*, 1998 B.Y.U. L. Rev. 1035.

[25] Although most of the cases involve attempts to accelerate, the problems described in this section also arise when the secured party requires that the debtor provide additional collateral pursuant to a clause that allows it to demand so at will or when it deems itself insecure. U.C.C. § 1-309.

[26] U.C.C. § 1-309.

[27] U.C.C. § 1-309. The effect is to create a presumption of good faith in the secured party's favor.

[28] U.C.C. § 1-201(19) (1972 text).

[29] *See, e.g.*, Van Horn v. Van De Wol, Inc., 6 Wash. App. 959, 497 P.2d 252, 10 U.C.C. Rep. Serv. 1143 (Wash. App. 1972) (negligence in failing to investigate further is irrelevant to determination of good faith).

[30] U.C.C. § 1-201(b)(20).

[31] Even under the Code's original subjective definition of good faith, numerous courts held that a lender's decision to invoke an insecurity clause lacked good faith under circumstances where a reasonable lender would not have taken such action. For example, in *Sheppard Federal Credit Union v. Palmer*, 408 F.2d 1369, 6 U.C.C. Rep. Serv. 30 (5th Cir. 1969), the secured

not fared well in litigation and an entire field of "lender liability" cases has developed in which courts have imposed substantial damages for conduct that may well have been subjectively honest. [32] While many of these cases involved unsecured loans, their analysis of the problems associated with acceleration is relevant to enforcement of secured loans as well.

§ 17.02 REMEDIES AVAILABLE UPON DEFAULT

[A] Types of Remedies

Provided that the debtor is in default, the secured party can avail itself of a variety of remedies. Because Article 9 sets forth the core remedies, the security agreement need not reiterate them, although the typical security agreement does precisely that. The Code's remedial scheme permits the secured party to take possession of the collateral — through self-help if it can be done without breach of the peace, otherwise through judicial action — and then dispose of it in an attempt to satisfy the underlying obligation. [33] This process is the right of *foreclosure*.

Most security agreements establish remedies that go well beyond what the Code provides. The most important remedy not provided by operation of law, as discussed in the preceding section, is the right to accelerate the debt. In addition, most well-drafted security agreements will provide for some or all of the following remedies:

- The right to require the debtor to provide additional collateral; [34]

- The right to recover attorneys' fees and costs of collection;

- The right to remedy a default (*e.g.*, purchasing insurance for uninsured collateral or paying off a competing lien) and add the cost of doing so to the principal balance of the debt;

---

party — a credit union located on an Air Force base — accelerated and repossessed a vehicle because the debtor (an officer) was leaving the Air Force. The secured party accelerated even though every indication suggested that the debtor would quickly find other suitable employment, and the debtor in fact did obtain other employment. The court, citing Professor Gilmore's authoritative treatise *Security Interests in Personal Property*, held that the secured party had acted in bad faith because it did not have an objective basis for believing that its debt was insecure. *See also* Blaine v. General Motors Acceptance Corp., 82 Misc. 2d 653, 370 N.Y.S.2d 323, 17 U.C.C. Rep. Serv. 641 (Co. Ct. 1975) (applying objective standard to uphold creditor's acceleration for insecurity where creditor acted following debtor's arrest for drug transportation, based upon threat of forfeiture of collateral); Clayton v. Crossroads Equip. Co., 655 P.2d 1125, 34 U.C.C. Rep. Serv. 1448 (Utah 1982) (applying objective standard to impose liability on accelerating creditor, even though creditor had received information indicating that debtor's financial condition had deteriorated).

[32] The seminal case in this area is K.M.C. Co. v. Irving Trust Co., 757 F.2d 752 (6th Cir. 1985), in which the creditor refused to extend the debtor additional credit under an outstanding line of credit.

[33] If the collateral is intangible and not capable of repossession, Article 9 provides alternative methods for realizing upon its value. Foreclosure on intangible assets is discussed in § 18.03 *infra*.

[34] When this right is linked to an insecurity clause, the provisions of U.C.C. § 1-309 are applicable. *See* discussion in § 17.01[B] *supra*.

- The right to require that the debtor assemble the collateral and make it available to the secured party at a place designated by the secured party (so long as it is reasonably convenient to the debtor);[35] and

- The right of the secured party to use collateral other than consumer goods pending its disposition.[36]

The security agreement may specify additional remedies depending upon the context of the transaction or the law of the jurisdiction. In Missouri, for example, a secured party may include a clause in its security agreement allowing it to sell collateral upon fifteen days' notice following its replevy[37] by the sheriff even though the court has not rendered a final judgment awarding possession to the secured party.[38]

A secured party need not pursue its remedies as an Article 9 secured party at all. It can instead ignore its collateral, sue to obtain an *in personam* judgment on the debt, and then use the ordinary judicial procedures available to any judgment creditor within the jurisdiction.[39] In other words, the secured party can obtain a writ of execution pursuant to which the sheriff can levy on and sell any nonexempt assets of the debtor, real or personal. These assets can include, but are not limited to, the collateral.[40] There is a potential advantage for the secured party in following this procedure. Because the sheriff conducts the sale following procedures

---

[35] U.C.C. § 9-609(c) explicitly authorizes this remedy, but only if the security agreement so specifies. The value of this remedy lies in its *in terrorem* effect, although at least one court has issued a mandatory injunction requiring that the debtor comply with a mandatory-assembly clause. *See* Clark Equip. Co. v. Armstrong Equip. Co., 431 F.2d 54, 7 U.C.C. Rep. Serv. 1249 (5th Cir. 1970), *cert. denied*, 402 U.S. 909 (1971).

[36] U.C.C. § 9-207(b)(4) sanctions this remedy. A secured party in possession of collateral has a statutory right to use or operate it for the purpose of preserving its value, even if this is not included in the security agreement. But if the secured party wishes to use the collateral to produce revenue — such as by leasing it to generate rent — the security agreement must permit this remedy or the secured party must get a court order authorizing such use. For a case in which the secured party leased an aircraft to produce significant revenue pending disposition, *see* Contrail Leasing Partners, Ltd. v. Consolidated Airways, Inc., 742 F.2d 1095, 39 U.C.C. Rep. Serv. 9 (7th Cir. 1984). *See also In re* MJK Clearing, Inc., 286 B.R. 862, 48 U.C.C. Rep. Serv. 2d 1244 (Bankr. D. Minn. 2002) (security agreement gave pledgee right to commingle money given as collateral or to repledge it in other transactions).

[37] Replevin is a judicial action in which the collateral is seized by the sheriff and then the court determines which party has the superior right of possession. If the debtor is in default, the secured party is statutorily entitled to possession [U.C.C. § 9-609(a)] and will ultimately obtain a judgment of possession from the court. The debtor, however, must have the opportunity to answer, and if the debtor does so, the issue must proceed to trial. In the meantime, the sheriff holds the asset *in custodia legis.*

[38] *See* B-W Acceptance Corp. v. Alexander, 494 S.W.2d 75 (Mo. 1973).

[39] U.C.C. § 9-601(a)(1) permits the secured party to reduce its claim to judgment, foreclose, or otherwise enforce the security agreement by any available judicial procedure. *See, e.g.*, Financial Pacific Leasing, L.L.C. v. Freeman, 108 Wash. App. 1052, 46 U.C.C. Rep. Serv. 2d 610 (2001) (contrary to debtor's assertion, secured party was not required to make effort to repossess collateral before bringing claim for judgment).

[40] *See* § 14.02 *supra.*

approved under non-Code state law, the secured party is insulated from liability if there is some defect in the sale process.[41] Further, the secured party does not lose its Article 9 priority by proceeding in this fashion, as any lien on the collateral created by the levy relates back to the date on which the secured party perfected its security interest (or, if earlier, the date on which it filed its financing statement).[42]

There are serious drawbacks, however, to suing on the debt without first proceeding to repossess and foreclose on the collateral. Unless the secured party has some basis for pre-judgment attachment,[43] the secured party will have to wait until final judgment before it can obtain a writ of execution. During this interim period, the collateral — which is still in the hands of the debtor — may diminish in value or disappear, threatening the secured party's prospects for eventual recovery. Further, because most sheriff's sales are auction sales for ready cash, they typically bring very low prices — perhaps much lower than a secured party might obtain in an ordinary course, arms-length private sale. This latter disadvantage is offset by the fact that the secured party can bid at the sheriff's sale[44] — and, because the amount bid by the purchaser at the sheriff's sale will be applied to reduce the judgment debt (after the costs of the sheriff's sale are paid), the secured party can bid up to the amount of its judgment without producing any cash. In other words, if the judgment is for $10,000 and the secured party is the successful bidder at $7,000, its judgment will be reduced in the court records to $3,000. The secured party then becomes the owner of the asset and can resell it in a more favorable market without having to worry about the Code's procedural requirements for foreclosure sales.[45]

---

[41] *See, e.g.,* Dakota Bank & Trust Co. v. Reed, 402 N.W.2d 887, 3 U.C.C. Rep. Serv. 2d 1976 (N.D. 1987). By contrast, if the secured party conducts an Article 9 foreclosure sale, the secured party faces liability if it conducts a commercially unreasonable sale that causes injury to the debtor. U.C.C. §§ 9-610(b), 9-625(b).

[42] U.C.C. § 9-601(e). Conceptually, the sheriff's levy and sale is a foreclosure of the original security interest. U.C.C. § 9-601(f). In most states, levy creates a lien that runs in favor of the judgment creditor. *See* § 14.02 *supra.* In the case of a secured party, this lien is not important unless the secured party failed to perfect its security interest. The fact that the sheriff's sale is a foreclosure of the original security interest offers protection against a claim that the levy and sale amount to a preferential transfer that is avoidable in bankruptcy. *See* discussion of preferential transfers in § 16.04[E] *supra.*

[43] Although the grounds for attachment vary from state to state, the secured party typically must allege some type of fraud or evasion of process to obtain prejudgment attachment. A writ of attachment, when issued, orders the sheriff to seize assets of the debtor (including the collateral) and to hold them pending the outcome of the litigation. If the secured party ultimately obtains a judgment, the assets can be sold under a writ of execution.

[44] U.C.C. § 9-601(f). Similarly, the secured party can bid at its own foreclosure sale if the sale is conducted by public auction. *See* § 18.02[C] *infra.*

[45] Sometimes a judgment creditor may acquire the property at an execution sale via credit bid and then later sell the property at a profit. When this occurs, the judgment debtor may attempt to set aside the execution sale based upon the inadequacy of the sale price. Generally speaking, however, courts will not set aside an execution sale based upon inadequacy of the sale price alone, absent some irregularity in the execution sale procedure. *See, e.g.,* Miebach v. Colasurdo, 102 Wash. 2d 170, 685 P.2d 1074 (1974). Likewise, the Uniform Fraudulent Transfer Act provides that a below-market-value execution sale price will not render the execution sale a fraudulent conveyance if the sale was "regularly conducted and noncollusive." UFTA §§ 3(b), 4(a)(2).

The Code creates one additional remedy worth a brief mention. If the secured party has taken a security interest in both real and personal property as part of the same transaction,[46] it may be convenient to sell them together. Indeed, it may be financially advantageous to sell a business that owns the real property on which it operates as a going concern rather than in a piecemeal fashion. In such cases, the Code provides that "a secured party may proceed . . . as to both the personal property and the real property in accordance with the rights with respect to the real property, in which case the other provisions of [Article 9, Part 6] do not apply."[47] This means that the secured party can sell the personal property as a part of the real property foreclosure, in which case it need not also comply with the procedural rules governing Article 9 foreclosure sales. Alternatively, the secured party can proceed under Article 9 with respect to the personal property without prejudicing any rights that it has with respect to the real property.[48]

[B] Cumulation of Remedies

Article 9 provides that the remedies available to the secured party — those available under the Code, the security agreement, and non-Code state law — are cumulative.[49] The secured party thus may exercise the various remedies simultaneously and need not make an election among them. The secured party can sue to obtain an *in personam* judgment without losing its right to repossess the collateral at a later date and commence an Article 9 foreclosure.[50] It can go through the Article 9 foreclosure process and then sue to obtain a judgment for any remaining deficiency.[51] It can first pursue guarantors and then proceed against the collateral, or vice-versa.[52] It can exercise its common-law right of setoff against a bank account of the debtor and later proceed against the rest of its collateral.[53] Perhaps the most

---

[46] This is commonly the case in commercial mortgage loans.

[47] U.C.C. § 9-604(a)(2).

[48] U.C.C. § 9-604(a)(1); *In re* Kearns, 314 B.R. 819, 544 U.C.C. Rep. Serv. 2d 958 (Bankr. 9th Cir. 2004) (secured creditor did not forfeit its mortgage lien on the borrowers' real property by foreclosing on its security interest in the borrowers' automobile that secured the same loan).

[49] U.C.C. § 9-601(c).

[50] *See, e.g.,* Avco Fin. Servs. of Billings One, Inc. v. Christiaens, 201 Mont. 117, 652 P.2d 220, 34 U.C.C. Rep. Serv. 1445 (1982); Fleming v. Carroll Publishing Co., 621 A.2d 829, 20 U.C.C. Rep. Serv. 2d 1141 (D.C. App. 1993).

[51] The secured party's right to a deficiency judgment may be precluded or limited because of its misconduct during the foreclosure process. This topic is discussed in § 19.02 *infra.*

[52] If the secured party is going to defer action against guarantors, it should advise them that, by doing so, it is not abandoning its rights against them. Although such notice ought not be necessary under the doctrine of cumulative remedies, courts are solicitous of guarantors. Failure to give notice exposes a secured party to the argument that it abandoned its rights against a guarantor. *Cf.* ESL Fed. Credit Union v. Bovee, 2005 WL 1083669, 56 U.C.C. Rep. Serv. 2d 517 (N.Y. Sup. Ct. 2005) (denying summary judgment against guarantor where secured creditor returned repossessed vehicle and released its security interest upon debtor's cure of default, without obtaining guarantor's consent).

[53] *See, e.g.,* Jensen v. State Bank of Allison, 518 F.2d 1, 17 U.C.C. Rep. Serv. 286 (8th Cir. 1975).

extreme instance of the application of the cumulative remedies doctrine *is Kennedy v. Bank of Ephraim*,[54] in which the secured party held as collateral a certificate of deposit that it had issued to the debtor. Rather than cashing out the certificate, the secured party sued the debtor for an *in personam* judgment and then proceeded to levy against real estate owned by the debtor. The court held that the secured party was free to follow this rather unusual course under the cumulative-remedies doctrine.

The doctrine has some limitations. A few states have special consumer legislation that requires the secured party to make an election of remedies.[55] In addition, a few courts have held that a secured party may not simultaneously pursue two remedies against the debtor. The leading case to this effect is *Ayares-Eisenberg Perrine Datsun, Inc. v. Sun Bank of Miami*,[56] in which the court concluded that simultaneously maintaining an action for an *in personam* judgment and foreclosing against the collateral amounted to harassment of the debtor. Although Article 9 does not entirely displace common-law limitations on harassment of debtors,[57] it is difficult to understand why it is harassment for a secured party to do simultaneously what it could legitimately do sequentially, and a contrary (and appropriate) result was reached in *Glamorgan Coal Corp. v. Bowen*.[58] After all, the secured party has an obligation to proceed in good faith, and compliance with this duty should provide sufficient protection against debtor harassment.

In some circumstances, to protect the rights of another creditor, a court may require a secured party to exhaust the value of specific collateral before proceeding against other assets. This concept — called *equitable marshaling* — arises when there are two potential assets available for satisfaction of competing creditors' claims but only one of the creditors has access to both funds. For example, suppose both First Bank and Second Bank have perfected security interests in Debtor's equipment, with First Bank having priority. First Bank also has a mortgage on Debtor's real estate, but Second Bank does not. Under the doctrine of marshaling, a court may require First Bank to foreclose against the real estate before it can enforce its interest in the equipment, thereby maximizing Second Bank's chances of being repaid out of the proceeds of the equipment.[59] The marshaling doctrine is designed to protect competing creditors, and it cannot be used by the debtor or guarantors to undercut the cumulative-remedies doctrine. In other words,

---

[54] 594 P.2d 881, 26 U.C.C. Rep. Serv. 558 (Utah 1979).

[55] *See, e.g.*, California's Unruh Act, Cal. Civ. Code § 1801 *et seq.* (West 1985), pursuant to which parties enforcing retail installment sales contracts must make a binding election to pursue either the collateral or an *in personam* judgment.

[56] 455 So. 2d 525, 39 U.C.C. Rep. Serv. 360 (Fla. App. 1984).

[57] U.C.C. § 1-103(b) ("Unless displaced by the particular provisions of [the Uniform Commercial Code], the principles of law and equity . . . supplement its provisions.").

[58] 742 F. Supp. 308, 13 U.C.C. Rep. Serv. 2d 596 (W.D. Va. 1990).

[59] One of the leading cases on equitable marshaling is Shedoudy v. Surgical Supply Co., 100 Cal. App. 3d 730, 161 Cal. Rptr. 164, 28 U.C.C. Rep. Serv. 1181 (1980).

a guarantor cannot insist that a secured party proceed against the collateral before attempting to enforce the guaranty.

Chapter 18

THE FORECLOSURE PROCESS

§ 18.01   REPOSSESSION — § 9-609

Once default occurs,[1] a secured party may take possession of the

---

[1] As discussed in Chapter 17, a secured party's ability to repossess and sell collateral depends upon the existence of a default. Absent default, repossession and disposition of the collateral

collateral,[2] dispose of it,[3] and apply the proceeds of that disposition to the balance of the debt.[4] In an effort to facilitate this objective, Article 9 permits a secured party to "require the debtor to assemble the collateral and make it available to the secured party at a place to be designated by the secured party which is reasonably convenient to both parties."[5] Frequently, however, the debtor does not cooperate and voluntarily relinquish the collateral to the secured party. In such cases, the secured party must choose between using the judicial process to recover possession of the collateral or trying to recover possession by "self-help" (*i.e.*, outside the judicial process). Article 9 permits the secured party to use "self-help" to repossess the collateral, if it can do so without "breach of the peace."[6] If the secured party cannot repossess the collateral without breaching the peace, it may not use self-help and must instead repossess by judicial action.[7]

---

constitutes conversion. *See, e.g.*, Ansley v. Conseco Fin. Serv. Corp., 2002 WL 31955217, 49 U.C.C. Rep. Serv. 2d 955 (Mich. Ct. App. 2002) (creditor liable in conversion where it provided no proof that it held security interest in mobile home or that debtor was in default on payment obligations); Corbin v. Regions Bank, 574 S.E.2d 616, 49 U.C.C. Rep. Serv. 2d 1328 (Ga. Ct. App. 2002) (if debtor unable to make payments on purchase of used truck due to physical disability, but debtor had secured credit disability insurance in favor of creditor, jury could find that existence of credit insurance claim meant that debtor had not defaulted).

[2] U.C.C. § 9-609(a)(1).

[3] U.C.C. § 9-610(a).

[4] U.C.C. § 9-615(a).

[5] U.C.C. § 9-609(c).

[6] U.C.C. § 9-609(b). A secured party that breaches the peace during an attempted self-help repossession exposes itself to considerable liability, including the possibility of punitive damages. For example, in *Big Three Motors, Inc. v. Rutherford*, 432 So. 2d 483, 36 U.C.C. Rep. Serv. 338 (Ala. 1983), the secured party's agents forced the debtor's car off the highway and insisted that she return to their office, where they seized her car. Not surprisingly, the jury treated the seizure as a conversion and assessed significant punitive damages. The scope of a secured party's liability for conversion and/or failure to satisfy its obligations under Article 9 is discussed further in Chapter 19.

Few repossessions are as dramatic as the one in *Rutherford*, but every self-help repossession carries with it the possibility that a breach of the peace could result in liability. Furthermore, a secured party cannot avoid potential liability merely by hiring an independent contractor to repossess the collateral. Virtually all courts have held that repossession is a nondelegable duty and that the secured party is liable if an independent contractor breaches the peace in carrying out the repossession. *See, e.g.*, Mbank, El Paso, N.A. v. Sanchez, 836 S.W.2d 151, 17 U.C.C. Rep. Serv. 2d 1358 (Tex. 1992) (secured party liable for both actual damages caused by independent contractor and for punitive damages); Henderson v. Security Nat'l Bank, 72 Cal. App. 3d 764, 140 Cal. Rptr. 388, 22 U.C.C. Rep. Serv. 846 (1977) (secured party liable for actual but not punitive damages).

[7] Louisiana does not permit a secured party to exercise self-help repossession under any circumstances. La. Stat. Ann. tit. 10, § 9-609. The Wisconsin Consumer Act provides that a merchant may not "take possession of collateral . . . by means other than legal process" unless the debtor surrenders the collateral. Wis. Stat. Ann. § 425.206(1)(a). *See* Whitford and Laufer, *The Impact of Denying Self-Help Repossession of Automobiles: A Case Study of the Wisconsin Consumer Act*, 1975 Wis. L. Rev. 607. According to the empirical study of Whitford and Laufer, the enactment of this statute did result in a "modest" increase in car loan interest rates and the size of required down payments. *Id.* at 638.

[A] Self-Help

The theoretical justification for permitting self-help repossession is economic efficiency. There are financial costs for a secured party in recovering possession of its collateral by way of judicial action. These include the costs of filing a civil action — including attorney fees, if the secured party proceeds with the assistance of counsel — as well as the "lost opportunity" costs the secured party suffers because the judicial process delays it in enforcing its security interest. If the secured party incurs these costs but is unable to recover them from either the obligor or the collateral,[8] it may simply "pass along" that cost to all borrowers in the form of higher interest rates. Theoretically, then, the availability of peaceful self-help repossession — which would permit the secured party to repossess and sell its collateral without incurring these costs — should reduce the cost of borrowing.

Attempts to exercise self-help repossession, however, sometimes trigger objections that present the risk of confrontation and violence. Because violent confrontation poses the risk of injury to the debtor, the secured party, and possibly even innocent bystanders, Article 9 attempts to avoid these potential social costs by permitting the secured party to use self-help only if it will not constitute a "breach of the peace."

[1] "Breach of the Peace"

Article 9 does not define the term "breach of the peace," but the Code drafters were well aware of its meaning based on pre-Code case law.[9] The issue of whether a secured party has breached the peace is necessarily dependent upon the factual context of the particular dispute. Nevertheless, one can extract some general guidelines from repeatedly recurring situations in the case law.

If the debtor is present and consents to the repossession, the secured party is free to proceed by self-help.[10] Likewise, if the debtor is not present

---

[8] Most security agreements provide that the debtor is personally liable for the secured party's costs of repossession and enforcement, and that the collateral also secures the repayment of any such expenses incurred by the secured party. Article 9 permits the secured party to recover the reasonable expenses of repossession and disposition out of the proceeds of the disposition (including attorney fees where the security agreement so provides). U.C.C. § 9-615(a)(1). Nevertheless, disposition of the collateral may not generate sufficient proceeds to allow the secured party to recover the expenses of disposition, and the obligor may lack sufficient nonexempt assets with which to satisfy its liability for those expenses.

[9] See, e.g., Girard v. Anderson, 219 Iowa 142, 257 N.W. 400 (1934) (leading pre-Code case holding that secured party's unauthorized entry into debtor's business premises to repossess collateral amounted to breach of the peace).

[10] See, e.g., McGrady v. Nissan Motor Acceptance Corp., 40 F. Supp. 2d 1323, 41 U.C.C. Rep. Serv. 2d 986 (M.D. Ala. 1998) (no breach of peace based simply on debtor's allegation that she felt under duress and was crying when she nevertheless consented to repossession).

A secured party is probably on safe ground if someone other than the debtor consents to the repossession. See, e.g., Cottam v. Heppner, 777 P.2d 468, 9 U.C.C. Rep. Serv. 2d 805 (Utah 1989) (third-party's consent to removal of debtor's cattle from third-party's corral upheld). It would be unwise, however, to enter a closed area to remove collateral based on the consent

and the secured party is repossessing the collateral from a public location — for example, if the collateral is an automobile and the secured party is repossessing it from a public street or a parking lot — the repossession does not breach the peace. If the debtor is present and protests the secured party's attempt to repossess the collateral, however, the prudent secured party will cease its self-help efforts. The weight of authority establishes that if the secured party continues with its self-help repossession after the debtor has raised an objection, it has breached the peace, *even if actual violence does not result.*[11] Courts have interpreted the "breach of the peace" standard to forbid self-help in circumstances where there is a reasonable possibility that violence may result, and have concluded that the debtor's protest is sufficient to alert the secured party as to the risk of violence if the secured party continues to use self-help.

By raising a timely objection, the debtor effectively can force the secured party to use the judicial process to repossess the collateral. Although this adds to the cost of repossession and creates some delay in the secured party's enforcement of its remedies, most judicial actions to repossess collateral are fairly routine and the costs are not excessive. Furthermore, the secured party may recover the costs of judicial repossession following the disposition of the collateral (including the secured party's attorneys' fees, if the security agreement obligates the debtor to pay such fees).[12] As a result, cases taking a broad view of "breach of the peace" reflect an implicit conclusion that the societal benefit of requiring judicial process in the face of the debtor's protest — *i.e.,* the avoidance of violent confrontation and the risk of potential injury — outweighs the additional costs of collection.

Some decisions have upheld a secured party's use of self-help repossession, even in the face of a debtor's protest, when no violence actually resulted. For example, in *Chrysler Credit Corp. v. Koontz,*[13] the secured party sent its "repo" agent to the debtor's home, where the agent proceeded to take possession of a car in the debtor's front yard. The debtor came racing out of the house in his underwear, shouting "Don't take it," but the agent ignored the debtor and took the car. The court reasoned that, even though

---

of a small child or someone obviously lacking in mental capacity because of potential exposure to civil or even criminal liability. Society has recognized a strong interest in protecting these classes of individuals from dealings with strangers.

[11] *See, e.g.,* Morris v. First Nat'l Bank & Trust Co. of Ravenna, 21 Ohio St. 2d 25, 254 N.E.2d 683, 7 U.C.C. Rep. Serv. 131 (Ohio 1970); Dixon v. Ford Motor Credit Co., 72 Ill. App. 3d 903, 391 N.E.2d 493 (Ill. Ct. App. 1970); Hester v. Bandy, 627 So. 2d 833, 24 U.C.C. Rep. Serv. 2d 1344 (Miss. 1993).

As a practical matter, most of these decisions have involved an objection by a debtor who was present at the time of the attempted repossession. By contrast, can a debtor "pre-empt" a creditor's self-help repossession effort by sending a letter stating the debtor's objection to any such efforts? The likely answer is no. *See* Valentino v. Glendale Nissan, Inc., 740 N.E.2d 538, 43 U.C.C. Rep. Serv. 2d 680 (Ill. Ct. App. 2000) (letter sent in advance indicating debtor objected to car's repossession; no breach of peace when secured party nevertheless repossessed car in debtor's absence).

[12] U.C.C. § 9-615(a)(1).

[13] 277 Ill. App. 3d 1078, 661 N.E.2d 1171, 29 U.C.C. Rep. Serv. 2d 1 (Ill. Ct. App. 1996).

actual violence is not necessary to establish a breach of the peace, there must be some language or conduct that brings home to the repossessor the fact that violence is imminent. The court thus held that no breach of the peace occurred because the debtor had not held a weapon, clenched his fists, or even argued toe-to-toe with the repossessor.

Decisions such as *Koontz* reflect poor commercial policy. Assessing the volatility of a debtor's protest is difficult — particularly after the fact, when the parties and other witnesses may have different perceptions about "how vehemently" the debtor protested. The debtor's protests alone should have alerted the agent to the possibility of violence. Further, to the extent courts expect judicial decisions to influence future conduct, the holding in *Koontz* encourages the very behavior that the "breach of the peace" standard seeks to avoid. Based on this decision, an attorney advising a client who is in default and fears repossession would have to suggest that the client express himself vehemently — perhaps even threatening physical violence — to stop the repossession. This approach, however, would simply exacerbate the risk of violence and increase the likelihood that self-help repossession would result in injury to the debtor or bystanders. Although the *Koontz* court stressed the efficiency of self-help, efficiency is an insufficient rationale for a decision that increases the risk that repossessions will turn violent.

The facts of *Koontz* also raise a question of whether a secured party can enter upon the debtor's premises to repossess the collateral. The Restatement (Second) of Torts provides that "[o]ne is privileged to enter land in the possession of another, at a reasonable time and in a reasonable manner, for the purpose of removing a chattel to the immediate possession of which the actor is entitled. . . ."[14] Consistent with this principle, most courts have held that the secured party has a limited privilege against trespass liability and can make minimally intrusive incursions onto the debtor's land to repossess collateral.[15] For example, numerous decisions allow the secured party to go onto the debtor's driveway or yard to remove an asset in plain sight.[16] Most courts, however, have refused to extend the privilege

---

[14] Restatement (Second) of Torts § 198.

[15] A prudent secured party must nevertheless exercise great care in entering onto the debtor's land. For example, in Trash v. Credit Acceptance Corp., 821 So. 2d 968, 48 U.C.C. Rep. Serv. 2d 1224 (Ala. 2001), agents of the secured party repossessed a car from the debtor's driveway by placing clear dishwashing soap on the driveway to provide a lubricant to drag the car from the driveway into the street. The agents then left the scene without removing the fluid from the driveway or warning the debtor of its presence. The court held that the secured party breached the peace by creating a hazard that posed a substantial risk of injury (which actually resulted when the debtor slipped on the liquid and injured his back).

[16] *See, e.g.*, Callaway v. Whittenton, 892 So. 2d 852, 52 U.C.C. Rep. Serv. 2d 525 (Ala. 2003) (secured party entitled to enter debtor's front yard to repossess debtor's vehicle); Giles v. First Va. Credit Serv., Inc., 2002 WL 377949, 46 U.C.C. Rep. Serv. 2d 913 (N.C. Ct. App. 2002) (no breach of peace due to removal of automobile from debtor's driveway without entry to any enclosed area); Oaklawn Bank v. Baldwin, 709 S.W.2d 91, 1 U.C.C. Rep. Serv. 2d 596 (Ark. 1986) (removing car from debtor's driveway did not breach peace); Raffa v. Dania Bank, 321 So. 2d 83, 18 U.C.C. Rep. Serv. 263 (Fla. Dist. Ct. App. 1975) (car partially under carport in debtor's driveway removed without breach of the peace). Comment d to section 198 of the Restatement (Second) of Torts suggests that a secured party must make demand upon the

to assets located in an enclosed space — such as the debtor's home or garage — where the debtor presumably has a greater expectation of privacy from unwanted intrusions. Several decisions permitting the removal of assets from the debtor's land stress that the repossession occurred without the secured party's entering any "gates, doors or other barricades."[17] A secured party that chooses to enter a restricted space risks the assessment of punitive damages and, in extreme cases, criminal sanctions for trespass or for breaking and entering.[18] For example, in *Bloomquist v. First Nat'l Bank of Elk River*,[19] the secured party removed a pane of glass and entered the debtor's place of business to remove collateral. The court held that this was a breach of the peace and sustained an award of punitive damages.

When repossessing collateral from land owned by a third person, the secured party should exercise caution, even if the collateral is in plain sight. Even though the debtor may have impliedly consented to minimal intrusions onto the debtor's own land, no comparable basis supports a conclusion that a third party has done so. Although the cases in this area are mixed, the action is risky;[20] as a result, a prudent secured party should obtain the third party's consent to enter upon the land before effecting a repossession.

Another common theme in the cases is the use of trickery to effect the repossession. Several decisions have held that bringing along a uniformed off-duty police officer to make it appear that the secured party is carrying out the repossession under color of law amounts to "constructive force" and thus breaches the peace.[21] These cases rest upon the rationale that the debtor has the right to protest (and thus require the secured party to repossess by judicial process) and that the presence of a police officer

---

debtor for turnover of the collateral before entering onto the debtor's premises to effect a repossession: "[o]rdinarily a demand on the possessor, either to deliver the chattel at the border of the land or to permit the actor to go on the land and get it, is required before an entry can reasonably be made." In most cases, however, a prudent secured party will send a written notice to the debtor following the debtor's default, notifying the debtor that a default exists and demanding that the debtor turn over the collateral.

[17] *See, e.g.*, Oaklawn Bank v. Baldwin, 709 S.W.2d 91, 1 U.C.C. Rep. Serv. 2d 596 (Ark. 1986); Ragde v. Peoples Bank, 53 Wash. App. 173, 767 P.2d 949, 7 U.C.C. Rep. Serv. 2d 1314 (1989). When the collateral is located in an open garage, most courts have supported the repossessing creditor. *See, e.g.*, Pierce v. Leasing Int'l, Inc., 142 Ga. App. 371, 235 S.E.2d 752, 22 U.C.C. Rep. Serv. 269 (1977).

[18] For further discussion of remedies for creditor misconduct, *see* § 19.01[B] *infra*.

[19] 378 N.W.2d 81, 42 U.C.C. Rep. Serv. 37 (Minn. Ct. App. 1985).

[20] *See, e.g.*, Census Fed. Credit Union v. Wann, 403 N.E.2d 348, 28 U.C.C. Rep. Serv. 1207 (Ind. Ct. App. 1980) (removal from apartment building's parking lot did not breach peace); Salisbury Livestock Co. v. Colorado Central Credit Union, 793 P.2d 470, 12 U.C.C. Rep. Serv. 2d 894 (Wyo. 1990) (court reversed directed verdict in favor of secured party and remanded for trial, holding that reasonable juror could conclude that removal of collateral from land of third party breached the peace).

[21] *See, e.g.*, Walker v. Walthall, 588 P.2d 863, 25 U.C.C. Rep. Serv. 918 (Ariz. Ct. App. 1978); First & Farmers Bank of Somerset v. Henderson, 763 S.W.2d 137, 7 U.C.C. Rep. Serv. 2d 1305 (Ky. Ct. App. 1988); Stone Machinery Co. v. Kessler, 463 P.2d 651, 7 U.C.C. Rep. Serv. 135 (Wash. Ct. App. 1970).

discourages the debtor from asserting this right — after all, most persons are strongly disinclined to resist the efforts of a police officer apparently acting within his or her authority. Yet courts occasionally have upheld other types of trickery. For example, in *Thompson v. Ford Motor Credit Co.*,[22] the court upheld the secured party's repossession from a parking garage, even though the secured party falsely told the garage operator that it had the debtor's express permission to take the car. The court suggested that no breach of the peace occurred because the trickery did not prevent the debtor from asserting a legal right nor did it increase the risk that the repossession would turn violent.

The reader should take the foregoing comments for what they are — mere generalizations. The cases tend to be extremely fact-specific and colorful, and authority can be found on both sides of almost every issue.[23] In the face of this uncertainty, a creditor might be tempted to provide in the security agreement its own definition of "breach of the peace." After all, the Code generally permits the parties to specify the standards by which the fulfillment of their rights and duties are to be measured as long as those standards are "not manifestly unreasonable."[24] Nevertheless, given the strong policy in favor of deterring violence, the Code makes clear that a security agreement may not authorize a secured party to engage in conduct that would otherwise constitute a breach of the peace.[25]

[2] Disabling the Collateral

If the collateral is large or heavy equipment, repossession and storage prior to disposition may be prohibitively expensive. Accordingly, after default, Article 9 allows a secured party to "render equipment unusable and dispose of collateral on a debtor's premises."[26] For example, this provision would allow a secured party with a security interest in a machine to remove key components — thereby preventing the debtor from using the machine prior to disposition — and to sell the machine in place on the debtor's premises.

This provision is of limited use, and secured parties rarely rely upon it. First, if the secured party removes a part from the collateral but leaves the debtor in possession, the debtor may be able to replace the part and continue using the collateral. Second, selling the collateral on the debtor's premises makes little sense without the debtor's cooperation, because the buyer will have to take possession of the collateral from the debtor — and will likely have to resort to judicial process if the debtor is not cooperative. This complication will likely drive down the price that a buyer would pay for the collateral.

---

[22] 550 F.2d 256, 21 U.C.C. Rep. Serv. 907 (5th Cir. 1977).

[23] For a comprehensive discussion of case law on the subject, *see* Jean Braucher, *The Repo Code: A Study of Adjustment to Uncertainty in Commercial Law*, 74 Wash. U.L.Q. 549 (1997).

[24] U.C.C. § 9-603(a).

[25] U.C.C. § 9-603(b).

[26] U.C.C. § 9-609(a)(2).

[B] Judicial Action

If a debtor does not surrender the collateral and the secured party cannot peacefully repossess it, the secured party must resort to a judicial action to recover possession. An action in replevin[27] typically commences with the secured party filing a petition asking that the court find that its right to possession is superior to that of the debtor.[28] The secured party typically also asks for a writ of replevin, which is a court order directing the sheriff to take possession of the collateral. Because the sheriff handles the repossession under color of law, the risk of a violent confrontation is dramatically reduced; if violence does result, the sheriff is the appropriate person to deal with it. In many jurisdictions, the sheriff turns the property over to the secured party for safekeeping while the action is pending; in others, the sheriff retains possession of the property during the pendency of the action. Once the secured party obtains a final judgment awarding it permanent possession of the collateral,[29] it is free to proceed with its Article 9 disposition.

Because replevin requires the involvement of a public official, replevin actions involve state action and thus must satisfy the Constitution's mandate that deprivation of property requires due process of law. In a series of cases that began with *Fuentes v. Shevin*[30] and culminated with *North Georgia Finishing, Inc. v. Di-Chem, Inc.*,[31] the Supreme Court defined the type of notice and hearing necessary to satisfy the due process standard. In *Fuentes*, the Court held that, in consumer transactions, a public official could not seize assets of the debtor unless the debtor received notice and an opportunity for a pre-seizure hearing for the purpose of contesting the validity of the creditor's claim. The most important of the cases is *Mitchell v. W.T. Grant Co.*,[32] in which the Court backed off somewhat from its holding in *Fuentes*. The *Mitchell* decision allows seizure without prior notice and an opportunity for a pre-seizure hearing, so long as the replevin process contains the following safeguards:

- the writ of replevin must be signed by a judge rather than a clerk;
- the creditor must file an affidavit in support of its petition that contains specific factual allegations supporting its claim for possession;

---

[27] In some jurisdictions, replevin has been superseded by a statutory cause of action called "claim and delivery."

[28] The secured party's right to possession must be predicated upon a default. *See* U.C.C. § 9-609 and the discussion of default in Chapter 17 *supra*. *See also* Christie's Inc. v. Davis, 2002 WL 31730992, 49 U.C.C. Rep. Serv. 2d 684 (S.D.N.Y. 2002) (debtor's default and secured party's immediate right to foreclose entitled secured party to replevin, despite debtor's speculation that secured party would act in a commercially unreasonable manner in disposing of collateral).

[29] Originally, a replevin action resulted only in a judgment for possession of the collateral, but many modern versions allow for an alternative judgment for the value of the collateral.

[30] 407 U.S. 67, *reh'g denied*, 409 U.S. 902 (1972).

[31] 419 U.S. 601 (1975) (extending the holding in *Mitchell*, note 32 *infra*, to nonconsumer transactions).

[32] 416 U.S. 600 (1974).

- the debtor must have a right to a hearing soon after the seizure for the purpose of showing that it will probably prevail on the merits and that, therefore, the writ should be dissolved and the property returned;

- the debtor must have an alternative right to regain possession by posting a bond; and

- the creditor must post a bond indemnifying the debtor against loss.

If these procedures are in place, the court may issue a writ of replevin on an *ex parte* basis.

Replevin involves costs that a secured party can avoid using self-help repossession.[33] In addition to costs and attorney's fees, the secured party must post a bond to indemnify the debtor for its damages in the event the secured party's action proves wrongful.[34] There are also delays associated with replevin, because the debtor must receive time to answer the petition. In most cases, however, the costs and delays are minimal because the debtor fails to answer the petition and the secured party obtains a default judgment.

§ 18.02   DISPOSITION OF COLLATERAL — §§ 9-610 TO 9-615

Once a secured party has possession of collateral, through self-help or judicial action, it can proceed with its foreclosure.[35] This usually means the secured party will dispose of the collateral by sale, following procedures set forth in Article 9.[36] While disposition can consist of a lease of goods or a license of a general intangible rather than a sale,[37] virtually all secured

---

[33] The secured party can include in its security agreement a clause allowing it to add to the indebtedness its attorney's fees and legal expenses (to the extent that such clauses are generally permitted under state law). U.C.C. § 9-615(a)(1).

[34] The typical case involving damages is one in which the debtor convinces the court that there has been no default and thus that the repossession was wrongful.

[35] The correct view is that the secured party's repossession does not cause the debtor's title to pass to the secured creditor; title remains in the debtor until the secured party disposes of the collateral, U.C.C. § 9-617(a)(1), or satisfies the procedures to accept the collateral in full or partial satisfaction of the secured obligation (strict foreclosure), U.C.C. § 9-622(a)(2). *See, e.g.,* Motors Acceptance Corp. v. Rozier, 597 S.E.2d 367, 54 U.C.C. Rep. Serv. 2d 31 (Ga. 2004). In a blatant misinterpretation of state law and Article 9, federal courts in the Eleventh Circuit have held that where the secured party had repossessed (but not sold) the collateral prior to the debtor's bankruptcy, the collateral was no longer property of the bankruptcy estate. *See, e.g., In re* Kalter, 292 F.3d 1350, 48 U.C.C. Rep. Serv. 2d 411 (11th Cir. 2002) (interpreting Florida law); *In re* Lewis, 137 F.3d 1280, 35 U.C.C. Rep. Serv. 2d 740 (11th Cir. 1998) (interpreting Alabama law). To the extent these decisions indicate that mere repossession terminates the debtor's title to the collateral, they are inconsistent with section 9-617(a)(1) and 9-622(a)(2), and thus plainly incorrect.

[36] The alternative is strict foreclosure (retention of title to the collateral by the secured party in lieu of sale), discussed in § 18.04 *infra.*

[37] *See, e.g.,* Canadian Community Bank v. Ascher Findley Co., 229 Cal. App. 3d 1139, 280

parties hold foreclosure sales. A foreclosure sale of goods is subject to the provisions of Article 2, and Article 2A is applicable if the disposition is by lease.[38]

Before exploring the specific procedures outlined in Article 9, it is important to understand their underlying philosophy. The drafters hoped that Article 9 dispositions would produce higher prices than those typically obtained in real estate foreclosures. They were keenly aware that the procedures traditionally governing real estate foreclosures tend to produce prices below fair market value. Specifically, real estate foreclosures are almost invariably conducted by auction rather than by placement with a qualified broker. Further, bidders must typically pay cash when the hammer falls, which reduces the pool of potential buyers. Lastly, many states grant the debtor a right to redeem the land after the foreclosure sale, which further discourages potential bidders.

Article 9, by contrast, does not permit post-disposition redemption,[39] and its procedures governing disposition are deliberately flexible. The secured party can dispose of the collateral by auction or by any other commercially reasonable method, and can do so for cash or on credit.[40] Article 9 does not require a secured party to obtain an asset's fair market value, but by requiring the secured party to dispose of the asset in a commercially reasonable manner, it encourages the adoption of procedures designed to achieve that goal.

[A] The Standard of Commercial Reasonableness

Section 9-610(b) requires that every aspect of a secured party's disposition of collateral — including the manner, method, time, place and other terms — be "commercially reasonable."[41] The advantage of this flexible standard

---

Cal. Rptr. 521, 14 U.C.C. Rep. Serv. 2d 958 (1991). Another variant, involving neither sale nor lease, arises if the collateral is a certificate of deposit issued by the secured party. The secured party can simply cancel the CD and retain its proceeds in satisfaction of the debt, a procedure that is akin to exercising the common law right of setoff. Because the CD is worth a fixed amount of money, a sale is not needed to maximize its market value. *See, e.g.*, Smith v. Mark Twain Nat'l Bank, 805 F.2d 278, 2 U.C.C. Rep. Serv. 2d 1059 (8th Cir. 1986). Similarly, if insured collateral is totally destroyed by the debtor, the secured party should be free simply to convey title to the insurer in exchange for a settlement check.

[38] U.C.C. § 9-610, Comment 11. Article 9 provides that a sale or other disposition by the secured party "includes the warranties relating to title, possession, quiet enjoyment, and the like which by operation of law accompany a voluntary disposition" of such goods, unless the secured party effectively disclaims such warranties. U.C.C. § 9-610(d). The secured party may disclaim any such warranties by means of "a record evidencing the contract for disposition and including an express disclaimer or modification" of the warranties. U.C.C. § 9-610(e). A record will constitute a sufficient disclaimer if it indicates "[t]here is no warranty relating to title, possession, quiet enjoyment, or the like" or uses similar language. U.C.C. § 9-610(f).

[39] Article 9 does provide a pre-disposition right of redemption. *See* U.C.C. § 9-623, discussed in § 18.05 *infra*.

[40] U.C.C. § 9-610(b). This provision also allows a secured party to dispose of the collateral as a unit or to break it down into parcels that are disposed of separately.

[41] Although Article 9 does not permit a contractual waiver of a secured party's duty to

is that it encourages secured parties to adopt procedures designed to bring a fair price for the collateral.[42] The disadvantage — at least from a creditor's perspective — is that it allows courts to use 20/20 hindsight to second-guess virtually every step that a creditor has taken in disposing of collateral. Courts have examined whether the secured party chose an adequate method of disposition given the nature of the collateral, whether the secured party properly advertised the disposition, whether the secured party conducted the disposition at a reasonable time (both in absolute terms and in relation to the date on which the advertising appeared), and whether the terms of the disposition were reasonable.

[1] Duty to Publicize

One of the most important elements of a commercially reasonable disposition — and one not mentioned directly in the Code — is the duty to publicize it adequately. Compliance with this duty requires the secured party to ensure that (a) advertisement of the disposition is sufficient to reach the proper audience for the collateral involved, (b) there is sufficient time following the advertising for potential buyers to respond before the disposition occurs, (c) the advertising contains adequate and accurate information about the collateral and the disposition, and (d) the collateral is available for inspection by potential buyers prior to the disposition.

The most important of these issues is whether the advertising was sufficient to reach potential buyers for the type of asset involved. With highly specialized collateral, targeted advertising may be needed — perhaps even in publications or trade magazines that have a nationwide circulation. For example, *Contrail Leasing Partners, Ltd. v. Consolidated Airways, Inc.*[43] involved the foreclosure sale of a corporate jet. The court held that the secured party's advertising, which consisted of one small ad in a trade publication, was not commercially reasonable. The court suggested that the secured party should have run a more conspicuous ad and should have placed that ad in additional trade journals to expose the collateral to buyers likely to be interested in a corporate jet. This approach suggests that a

---

dispose of collateral in a commercially reasonable fashion, U.C.C. § 9-602(7), it does permit the parties to agree as to the standards measuring the fulfillment of that obligation if those standards are not manifestly unreasonable. U.C.C. § 9-603(a). *See* HSBC Bank USA v. Economy Steel, Inc., 747 N.Y.S.2d 661, 48 U.C.C. Rep. Serv. 2d 1494 (App. Div. 2002) (debtor precluded from complaining that sale was commercially unreasonable when parties had agreed that specified auctioneer would sell collateral); *but see* Baird Credit Corp. v. Seher, 2003 WL 1720029, 50 U.C.C. Rep. Serv. 2d 591 (N.D. Ill. 2003) (although security agreement gave creditor sole option to decide whether to liquidate collateral on default, creditor's discretion controlled by duty of good faith).

[42] *See, e.g.,* R & J of Tennessee, Inc. v. Blankenship-Melton Real Estate, Inc., 166 S.W.3d 195, 55 U.C.C. Rep. Serv. 2d 278 (Tenn. Ct. App. 2004) (sale of truck, tractor, and mobile home not commercially reasonable when secured party waited over seven months to conduct the sale, allowed debtor to use the collateral during this period, did not advertise the sale in a newspaper, did not use the services of an appraiser or experienced auctioneer, and was the only bidder at the sale).

[43] 742 F.2d 1095, 39 U.C.C. Rep. Serv. 9 (7th Cir. 1983).

secured party must explore the potential market so that its advertising will be effective,[44] and a prudent secured party disposing of specialized collateral might well consult a broker or dealer of such goods to help design its approach to advertising.

Advertising must do more than merely reach the proper audience. It must accurately describe the collateral,[45] and it must give correct information regarding the mechanics of the disposition.[46] A number of courts have also held that the advertising must give sufficient information to allow prospective buyers to inspect the collateral prior to the disposition.[47]

[2] Disposition Within a Reasonable Time

For most transactions, the Code does not specify the time period within which a secured party must dispose of collateral after default, other than to state that the time of the disposition must be commercially reasonable. In other words, a secured party must not act precipitously and dispose of the collateral before its advertising has had time to be effective, nor can it delay so long that the collateral depreciates significantly in value. The cases exploring this issue are highly fact-specific.[48] For example, courts obviously allow a longer time period if the collateral is a motor vehicle than if it is perishable foodstuffs. The conduct of a secured party during this time period is also relevant. A creditor that is "sitting on its hands" will evoke less sympathy than one that takes time to fix the collateral to enhance its value or to conduct a widespread advertising campaign in an attempt to attract additional bidders.

Prior to the enactment of revised Article 9, some decisions penalized secured parties for unreasonable delay in disposition using a doctrine

---

[44] *See also, e.g.*, Chavers v. Frazier, 93 B.R. 366 (Bankr. M.D. Tenn. 1989) (sale of jet plane commercially unreasonable due to advertising that ran too briefly and used text that suggested a distress sale); Key Bank of Maine v. Dunbar, 28 U.C.C. Rep. Serv. 2d 398 (E.D. Pa. 1995) (failure to take time necessary to explore and reach potential market for boat rendered sale commercially unreasonable); Smith v. Daniels, 634 S.W.2d 276, 34 U.C.C. Rep. Serv. 355 (Tenn. Ct. App. 1982) (advertising in county paper and calling local dealers was unreasonable for amusement equipment which was normally sold by advertising in major cities, in trade magazines, and by sending flyers to dealers).

[45] *See, e.g.*, ROC-Century Assoc. v. Giunta, 658 A.2d 223, 27 U.C.C. Rep. Serv. 2d 1091 (Me. 1995) (sale of partnership interest unreasonable because advertising mischaracterized nature of rights being sold).

[46] *See, e.g.*, Weiss v. Northwest Acceptance Corp., 274 Or. 343, 546 P.2d 1065, 19 U.C.C. Rep. Serv. 348 (1976) (advertising inaccurately stated that cash would be required).

[47] *See, e.g.*, Kobuk Eng'g & Contracting Servs., Inc. v. Superior Tank & Constr. Co.-Alaska, Inc., 568 P.2d 1007, 22 U.C.C. Rep. Serv. 854 (Alaska 1977); Connex Press, Inc. v. Int'l Airmotive, Inc., 436 F. Supp. 51, 22 U.C.C. Rep. Serv. 1310 (D.D.C. 1977).

[48] For example, even if a foreclosure sale results in a reduced sale price due in part to a secured party's delay in the foreclosure, other factors may justify a conclusion that the secured party's conduct was commercially reasonable. *See, e.g.*, Layne v. Bank One, Ky., N.A., 395 F.3d 271, 55 U.C.C. Rep. Serv. 2d 704 (6th Cir. 2005) (secured party's sale of stock that declined significantly in value when "tech bubble" burst in 2001 nevertheless commercially reasonable, despite delay, where debtors were negotiating with secured party to provide additional collateral to avoid sale).

known as "constructive strict foreclosure." Strict foreclosure is a voluntary mechanism initiated by a secured party that intends to retain the collateral — including any equity to which the debtor (or a junior secured party) might otherwise be entitled — in lieu of a normal foreclosure disposition of the collateral. [49] Although Article 9 has always required that the secured party give effective notice of its intent to pursue strict foreclosure, some courts nevertheless treated the secured party's unreasonable delay in disposing of the collateral as being the "constructive" equivalent of notice of the secured party's intent to retain the collateral. [50] Revised Article 9 abolishes the doctrine of constructive strict foreclosure. [51] Instead, it makes clear that unreasonable delay in disposition renders the secured party liable for any damages caused by the delay. [52]

There is one situation in which Article 9 provides a specific time period for the disposition of collateral. If the collateral is consumer goods and the debtor has repaid 60% of the loan (or, in a purchase-money transaction, 60% of the cash price), [53] it is likely that the debtor has built up some equity in the collateral. In such cases, Article 9 does not allow the secured party to initiate a strict foreclosure. [54] Instead, it requires the secured party to dispose of the collateral within 90 days after taking possession, unless "the debtor and all secondary obligors have agreed [to a longer period] in an agreement to that effect entered into and authenticated after default." [55]

---

[49] If there is equity in the collateral, the debtor or junior secured party can object to strict foreclosure and force a disposition. If there is no timely objection, title to the collateral is vested in the secured party. Generally speaking, strict foreclosure results in the full satisfaction of the debtor's obligation, even if the value of the collateral is less than the outstanding balance of that obligation, but Article 9 does permit the secured party and the debtor to agree to a stipulated deficiency amount and thereby use strict foreclosure in partial satisfaction of the debtor's obligation (except in consumer transactions). U.C.C. § 9-620(a). Strict foreclosure is discussed in greater detail in § 18.04 *infra*.

[50] *See, e.g.,* Haufler v. Ardinger, 28 U.C.C. Rep. Serv. 893 (Mass. Ct. App. 1979).

[51] U.C.C. § 9-620(b). *See also* § 9-620 Comment 5. For further discussion of strict foreclosure under revised Article 9, *see* § 18.04 *infra*.

[52] U.C.C. § 9-625(b).

[53] Article 9 differentiates between purchase-money and other transactions. U.C.C. § 9-620(e). In a typical nonpurchase-money transaction, the debtor takes out a loan against consumer goods that he or she already owns, and determining whether 60% of the principal amount of the loan has been repaid is a straightforward matter. In a purchase-money transaction, the 60%-rule is applied to the "cash price," and that price is not necessarily the amount financed. It is, instead, the amount that the seller would have charged if the asset had been sold for cash rather than on credit. If, for example, the seller's price for a car is $20,000 and the buyer makes a $2,000 down payment and finances $18,000 (with the seller or with a lender), the secured party may not use strict foreclosure after the debtor has paid a total of $12,000 (60% of the cash price of $20,000). The debtor gets credit for the down payment, and thus the rule is triggered when the debtor has reduced the principal by an additional $10,000.

[54] *See* § 18.04 *infra*.

[55] U.C.C. § 9-620(f)(2). The section permits waiver of the 90-day period by agreement to accommodate circumstances in which a disposition within 90 days might actually be commercially unreasonable. For example, suppose that Secured Party repossesses a pleasure boat from Debtor in Wisconsin on December 1. It would make little sense for Secured Party to sell the boat in Wisconsin during the dead of winter or to spend the funds necessary move the boat to Florida where it might sell during that 90-day period. In such a case, the parties could agree that the Secured Party could simply wait until spring to sell the boat.

[3]   The Method of Disposition: Public versus Private

A secured party can dispose of the collateral at either a public or private disposition so long as the method chosen is commercially reasonable.[56] The distinction between public and private dispositions is relevant to the following issues: (1) whether the method chosen is commercially reasonable; (2) what information the required notice should contain; and (3) whether the secured party may purchase the collateral. This section discusses the first issue.[57]

As a rule, a public disposition means a disposition by auction sale and a private disposition refers to any other type of disposition. Although the Code does not define the term "public disposition," the comments to section 9-610 provide that a "public disposition" is "one at which the price is determined after the public has had a meaningful opportunity for competitive bidding."[58] This suggests that the auction must be open to the general public. This issue has arisen in a number of cases involving "dealers' auctions," which are auctions open only to those that deal in assets of that type. The typical dealer's auction involves automobiles. Most courts have concluded that such dispositions are private because they are not open to the general public,[59] but this result is debatable. By holding that the disposition is private, the courts prevent the secured party from bidding.[60]

---

[56] U.C.C. § 9-610(b).

[57] Notice is discussed in § 18.02[B] *infra*, and a secured party's right to buy at its own sale is discussed in § 18.02[C] *infra*.

[58] U.C.C. § 9-610 Comment 7.

[59] *See, e.g.*, John Derry Motors, Inc. v. Steinbronn, 383 N.W.2d 553, 42 U.C.C. Rep. Serv. 1855 (Iowa 1986) (auction limited to automobile dealers); Morrell Employees Credit Union v. Uselton, 28 U.C.C. Rep. Serv. 269 (Tenn. Ct. App. 1979) (auction limited to credit union members). *See also* Restatement of Security § 48 Comment c, indicating that a public sale must be open to the public.

The cases that find such dispositions to be private generally turn on whether the notice sent to the debtor was sufficient. Typically, a secured party will have sent a notice that states the date of the auction but not the time and place. This would be sufficient for a private disposition, but not for a public disposition. U.C.C. § 9-613(1)(E). Because the debtor likely will not be eligible to bid at an auction limited to dealers, it may be that a private-sale type of notice is sufficient, and thus the decisions can be explained as an attempt by the courts to protect secured parties that have sent such notices. Nevertheless, on balance, commercial policy would better serve debtor's interests if it characterized dealers' auctions as public dispositions. Requiring that a secured party state the date and time of an auction in its notice is not particularly burdensome.

[60] A secured party cannot purchase the collateral at a private disposition unless the collateral is of a type customarily sold in a "recognized market" or is of a type for which there exist "widely distributed standard price quotations." U.C.C. § 9-610(c)(2). Comment 9 to section 9-610 defines a "recognized market" as "one in which the items sold are fungible and prices are not subject to individual negotiation." Because a dealer's auction is not a "recognized market," the secured party cannot bid at a dealer's auction if that auction is a private disposition. *See, e.g.*, Vornado PS, L.L.C. v. Primestone Investment Partners, L.P., 821 A.2d 296, 49 U.C.C. Rep. Serv. 2d 1348 (Del. Ct. Ch. 2002) (decision to conduct public disposition not commercially unreasonable because secured party was one of most interested and able potential buyers of collateral, and private disposition would have eliminated secured party as potential buyer).

If the auction is competitive, the debtor is better served by letting the secured party bid against other prospective buyers.[61] The hallmark of a public disposition should be its competitive nature, not whether the public is invited.

At some auctions, very few parties — sometimes, only the secured party — show up to bid. As a result, the lack of competitive bidding may result in the collateral being disposed of for a fraction of its value. Because the price received upon disposition provides the basis to establish the amount of any deficiency, an obligor may attempt to argue that a low price demonstrates that the disposition was not commercially reasonable. The paucity of bidders and/or a low price, standing alone, should *not* lead to the conclusion that a disposition was commercially unreasonable. Instead, the proper inquiry is whether the *procedures* adopted by the secured party were reasonably designed to result in a competitive auction. A paucity of bidders and/or a low price may serve as a "red flag" that justifies further investigation of the circumstances surrounding the auction. For example, the fact that the secured party was the only bidder may suggest inadequate advertising, that an auction was not a commercially reasonable method of disposition, or that the time selected for the auction was not commercially reasonable. Although courts should be suspicious in such cases and investigate such auctions with care, the facts may indicate that the secured party acted in all respects in a commercially reasonable manner and that the lack of bidders was happenstance. In such a case, the court should not penalize the secured party for going ahead with the auction.[62] Nevertheless, a secured party whose auction attracts disappointingly few bidders should consider abandoning the effort and starting over with a private disposition. In so doing, the secured party should take care to re-notify all parties entitled to notice and to tailor its advertising to its newly selected method.[63]

Although a secured party should be permitted significant latitude in choosing the method of disposition, its range of discretion has limits. *United States v. Willis*[64] is a classic case disapproving of a public disposition. The secured party in the case was aware of two offers to purchase the collateral privately but chose to go ahead with an auction that produced only one-fifth the amount expressed in the private offers. The court properly held that the secured party's decision to dispose of the collateral at auction was

---

[61] A debtor might also argue that a disposition by dealer's auction ought not be approved because it resulted in a wholesale price being paid for the collateral rather than a retail price. This issue is discussed in § 18.02[A][5] *infra*.

[62] *See, e.g.*, *In re* Zsa Zsa, Ltd., 352 F. Supp. 665, 11 U.C.C. Rep. Serv. 1116 (S.D.N.Y. 1972), *aff'd*, 475 F.2d 1393 (2d Cir. 1973) (secured party did not bid, but sale at 10% of market value to sole bidder upheld). *See also* U.C.C. § 9-627(a) (fact that secured party could have obtained better price by disposition at different time or in different manner is not, by itself, sufficient to establish that disposition was commercially unreasonable).

[63] *See, e.g.*, Gateway Aviation, Inc. v. Cessna Aircraft Co., 577 S.W.2d 860, 25 U.C.C. Rep. Serv. 901 (Mo. Ct. App. 1978) (debtor entitled to notice of private disposition when secured party shifted to that method, even though notice of abandoned public disposition had been sent). *See also* §§ 18.02[B][2] and [3] *infra*.

[64] 593 F.2d 247, 25 U.C.C. Rep. Serv. 1178 (6th Cir. 1979).

commercially unreasonable.[65] The comments to section 9-610 support the result in *Willis*, stating that section 9-610 "encourages private dispositions on the assumption that they frequently will result in higher realization on collateral for the benefit of all concerned."[66]

Of course, the arguments set forth above apply equally if the results of a private disposition prove disappointing. This fact may suggest that the collateral was of a type that should have been disposed of at auction. For example, in some parts of the country, livestock may bring higher prices at auctions than in private dispositions.

[4]   Is There a Duty to "Fix Up" the Collateral?

A secured party is under a duty to use reasonable care in the "custody and preservation of collateral" in its possession.[67] Is there, however, a duty to "fix up" the collateral so that it will command a higher price? Certainly, policy reasons support imposing at least minimal responsibilities on the secured party. For example, a car dealer that is going to sell a repossessed car from its lot at retail should at least clean the car so that it is attractive to customers. Perhaps the dealer should even have to send the car to its body shop (if it has one) to knock out minor collision damage, or to its service department for a minor tune-up so that the car runs smoothly. Of course, the decision whether to commit major resources to repairing an item should be solely within the discretion of the secured party.

Article 9 does not expressly impose even a minimal duty to "fix up" collateral, but instead leaves such decisions to the discretion of a secured party.[68] A few decisions, however, have relied on the general concept of

---

[65] *See also* United States v. Terrey, 554 F.2d 685, 21 U.C.C. Rep. Serv. 1488 (5th Cir. 1977) (sale of assets of electric sign-manufacturing enterprise at auction was commercially unreasonable). However, the debtor cannot dictate the secured party's method of disposition. For example, the debtor in *U.S. Bancorp Equipment Finance, Inc. v. Ameriquest Holdings LLC*, 2004 WL 2801601, 55 U.C.C. Rep. Serv. 2d 423 (D. Minn. 2004) had purchased commercial aircraft via secured financing and leased those aircraft to commercial airlines. The debtor went into default after the economic impact of the 9/11 tragedy resulted in the cancellation of these leases. The debtor argued that the secured party's auction sale of the planes was commercially unreasonable because the secured party refused to follow the debtor's suggestion of leasing the planes to foreign carriers. The court rejected this argument, noting that nothing in Article 9 required the secured party to agree to lease the planes to foreign carriers.

[66] U.C.C. § 9-610 Comment 2. *See, e.g.,* Automotive Fin. Corp. v. Smart Auto Ctr., Inc., 334 F.3d 685, 51 U.C.C. Rep. Serv. 2d 297 (7th Cir. 2003) (because odometer and title problems on vehicles from Canada would have required them to be sold "mileage unknown," which would likely have produced low auction prices, secured party's private disposition to dealer who had experience in handling Canadian vehicles with unknown mileage was commercially reasonable).

[67] U.C.C. § 9-207(a). This provision is equally applicable to possessory security interests in the absence of default.

[68] Article 9 states explicitly that the secured party can dispose of the collateral in its existing condition or after any commercially reasonable preparation or processing. U.C.C. § 9-610(a). Further, the Code states that the secured party "may" make use of the collateral for the purpose of preserving its value. U.C.C. § 9-207(b)(4).

commercial reasonableness in imposing a minimal fix-up duty.[69] These decisions establish sound policy, as a court should not ratify a secured party's decision to drag a filthy car straight to the auction block without a detour through the carwash.

[5] Price as an Indicator of Commercial Unreasonableness

A low price may suggest that a secured party did not properly advertise the disposition, that its method of disposition was unreasonable, or that it conducted the disposition at an unreasonable time. A low price standing alone, however — uncoupled from any of these procedural flaws — is not sufficient to invalidate a disposition.[70] The standard of commercial reasonableness requires that the secured party adopt procedures *designed* — not *guaranteed* — to produce a reasonable price. Nevertheless, low prices cause courts to scrutinize closely the secured party's disposition efforts.[71]

Suppose a secured party chooses to sell the collateral at wholesale. Can the debtor successfully claim that the sale was commercially unreasonable because the secured party made no attempt to obtain a retail price?[72] The

[69] *See, e.g.,* Weiss v. Northwest Acceptance Corp., 274 Or. 343, 546 P.2d 1065, 19 U.C.C. Rep. Serv. 348 (1976). *But see* C.I.T. Corp. v. Duncan Grading & Constr., Inc., 739 F.2d 359, 38 U.C.C. Rep. Serv. 1821 (8th Cir. 1984) (secured party not under duty to clean up construction equipment prior to sale). The Code, to some extent, discourages secured parties from fixing up their collateral. After all, if a decision to invest in the collateral is not commercially reasonable, the secured party will be unable to recoup its investment from the proceeds of disposition. *See* U.C.C. § 9-615(a)(1). Courts have somewhat ameliorated this constraint by showing general leniency in allowing secured parties to recover the expenses of preparing collateral for disposition. *See* discussion in § 18.02[D] *infra*.

[70] The Code explicitly states that the fact that the secured party could have obtained a better price by following other procedures is not *of itself* sufficient to hold that a disposition was commercially unreasonable. U.C.C. § 9-627(a). *See also* General Elec. Capital Corp. v. Stelmach Constr. Co., 2001 WL 969052, 45 U.C.C. Rep. Serv. 2d 675 (D. Kan. 2001) (sales price substantially below valuation of debtor's expert did not render sale commercially unreasonable where secured party followed reasonable sale procedures directed toward enhancing sale price); *In re* Zsa Zsa, Ltd., 352 F. Supp. 665, 11 U.C.C. Rep. Serv. 1116 (S.D.N.Y. 1972), *aff'd*, 475 F.2d 1393 (2d Cir. 1973) (sale at 10% of market value to sole bidder upheld). *But see* F.D.I.C. v. Herald Square Fabrics Corp., 81 A.D.2d 168, 439 N.Y.S.2d 944, 32 U.C.C. Rep. Serv. 558 (N.Y. Sup. Ct. 1981) (low price alone proved commercial unreasonableness of sale).

[71] *See, e.g.,* Coxall v. Clover Commercial Corp., 4 Misc. 3d 654, 781 N.Y.S.2d 567, 54 U.C.C. Rep. Serv. 2d 5 (N.Y. City Civ. Ct. 2004) (foreclosure sale brought a price only 18.5% of car's original purchase price four months earlier; court noted that "marked discrepancies between the disposal and sale prices signal a need for closer scrutiny, especially where . . . the possibilities for self-dealing are substantial. . . ."); SNCB Corp. Fin., Ltd. v. Shuster, 877 F. Supp. 820, 26 U.C.C. Rep. Serv. 2d 953 (S.D.N.Y. 1994) (low price caused court to scrutinize procedures closely, but sale was upheld as commercially reasonable). *See also* § 9-610 Comment 10.

[72] *Compare In re* Estate of Sagmiller, 615 N.W.2d 567, 44 U.C.C. Rep. Serv. 2d 309 (N.D. 2000) (use of dealer-only auction sale was commercially reasonable) *with* Action Management, Inc. v. Gross, 44 U.C.C. Rep. Serv. 2d 623 (Pa. Ct. Com. Pl. 2001) (sale at wholesale auction in absence of any prior attempts to sell vehicle held commercially unreasonable).

court in *Ford Motor Credit Co. v. Jackson*[73] answered this question in the affirmative. In *Jackson*, the secured party — a dealership that owned both retail and wholesale outlets — held a truck as collateral and chose to sell it at wholesale. The court noted that the truck needed no fixing up to prepare it for retail sale, and that the secured party received only about one-half the price it would have obtained through a retail sale. These factors persuaded the court that the decision to sell at wholesale rendered the foreclosure commercially unreasonable.

Despite their superficial appeal, decisions like *Jackson* are incorrect. First, they are contrary to the express language of the Code. Article 9 provides that "[a] disposition of collateral is made in a commercially reasonable manner if the disposition is made: (1) in the usual manner on any recognized market; (2) at the price current in any recognized market at the time of the disposition; or (3) *otherwise in conformity with reasonable commercial practices among dealers in the type of property that was the subject of the disposition.*"[74] Further, the fact that the secured party may have obtained a higher price at a retail sale does not mean that the retail price is more "fair" or "reasonable." Retail sales often involve higher costs (*e.g.*, retail sales commissions), and the price received at a retail sale reflects those increased costs. Further, by selling at retail, the secured party may lose a sale that it otherwise would have made (*i.e.*, the secured party might have sold another unit from its own inventory to the same customer). Judge Posner gave perhaps the best analysis of the issue in *Contrail Leasing Partners, Ltd. v. Consolidated Airways, Inc.*,[75] when he stated:

> Although retail prices tend to be higher than wholesale prices, this is because it costs more to sell at retail. Not only can there be, therefor, no presumption that the net gains to the seller are different at the two levels, but economic theory implies that returns at the two levels will tend toward equality, since until they are equalized dealers will have incentives to enter at the level where the higher returns are being earned and by entering will bid those returns down.[76]

[B] Notice of Disposition

Unless they receive notice of a proposed disposition, persons with an interest in the collateral may be unable to protect their interests. Sufficient prior notice of a disposition may permit such a person to find financing to redeem the collateral,[77] to seek injunctive relief if there is any valid basis to challenge the secured party's conduct,[78] or to attract additional bidders

---

[73] 466 N.E.2d 330, 39 U.C.C. Rep. Serv. 743 (Ill. Ct. App. 1984).

[74] U.C.C. § 9-627(b) (emphasis added).

[75] 742 F.2d 1095, 39 U.C.C. Rep. Serv. 9 (7th Cir. 1983).

[76] 742 F.2d at 1101, 39 U.C.C. Rep. Serv. at 17.

[77] U.C.C. § 9-623.

[78] Any person entitled to notice may want to police the disposition to make certain that it is carried out in a commercially reasonable manner. Injunctive relief in furtherance of this goal may be obtained under U.C.C. § 9-625(a). *See* discussion of pre-disposition remedies in Chapter 19 *infra*.

to the disposition in an attempt to maximize the price (and thus limit the size of any deficiency). To ensure that affected persons have an adequate opportunity to protect their interests from foreclosure, Article 9 provides a structure that generally requires the foreclosing secured party to give notice, prior to disposition, to certain persons most likely to be affected by that disposition.

The most common issues arising with respect to notice are: (1) which persons are entitled to notice; (2) the amount of notice required prior to disposition; (3) the contents of the notice; and (4) the circumstances under which notice is excused altogether. The following subsections discuss these issues in turn.

[1] Persons Entitled to Notice

Article 9 requires that a secured party give pre-disposition notice to the "debtor" and "any secondary obligor."[79] In this context, note the distinction between the terms "debtor" and "obligor." The Code defines the term "obligor" to include the person that "owes payment or other performance of the obligation" being secured.[80] A "debtor" is "a person having an interest, other than a security interest or other lien, in the collateral, whether or not the person is an obligor."[81] The term "secondary obligor" describes a person that is a surety for the secured obligation.[82] Thus, by its terms, Article 9 requires a secured party to notify the person who supplied the collateral (the "debtor") and any surety for the debt (the "secondary obligor"), but it does not require the secured party to notify the primary obligor unless that person is also a debtor.

For example, suppose Henning borrows $1,000 from Bank, Lawrence grants a security interest in his automobile to secure Henning's obligation (but does not co-sign Henning's promissory note or otherwise guarantee the obligation), and Freyermuth agrees to be a surety for the obligation. If Henning defaults and Bank repossesses the car from Lawrence, to whom must Bank give pre-disposition notice? Under section 9-611(b), Bank must give notice to Lawrence (the debtor) and Freyermuth (a secondary obligor), but has no obligation to notify Henning, who is the primary obligor but not a debtor.[83]

The Code's rationale in this circumstance is that notice to Lawrence (who, as debtor, will have a strong incentive to police the disposition to protect his equity in the collateral) and Freyermuth (who, as secondary obligor, will have a strong incentive to police the disposition to minimize the amount of his liability) should be sufficient to protect Henning — who, after all,

---

[79] U.C.C. § 9-611(c)(1), (2).

[80] U.C.C. § 9-102(a)(59).

[81] U.C.C. § 9-102(a)(28)(A).

[82] U.C.C. § 9-102(a)(71) (" 'Secondary obligor' means an obligor to the extent that: (A) the obligor's obligation is secondary; or (B) the obligor has a right of recourse with respect to an obligation secured by collateral against the debtor, another obligor, or property of either.").

[83] See U.C.C. § 9-611 Comment 3.

must pay the full amount of the obligation to Bank (absent misconduct by the Bank). Nevertheless, for prudential reasons, Bank will probably give Henning notice of the disposition anyway, either out of courtesy or in hope that Henning may make additional efforts to satisfy the debt prior to the disposition.

A secured party should make certain that each entitled person is sent a copy of the notice.[84] If, for example, the debtors are husband and wife, the secured party should send a separate notice to each. If the notice is sent to "Mr. and Mrs." and the couple has separated, the secured party's notice to the debtor that no longer lives at the address may be insufficient.[85] The problem is not that the notice was sent to the wrong address — the secured party may rely on the debtor's original address if it has not received notice of a different address[86] — but rather that the secured party cannot depend upon the debtor still living at the address to forward the information to the other debtor.

If the collateral is consumer goods, a secured party does not have to send notice to anyone other than the debtor and any secondary obligor. For all other types of collateral, however, a foreclosing secured party may have to provide notice to other persons. Junior secured parties, for example, have a significant interest in obtaining notice of a senior secured party's disposition, as it will extinguish the junior security interest.[87] Further, a junior secured party has an interest in generating a surplus at the disposition given that the Code allows it to share in that surplus.[88] Alternatively, a junior might want to redeem the collateral by paying off the senior and adding its expenditure to the principal obligation.[89]

---

[84] Under U.C.C. § 1-202(f), notice to an organization is effective "from the time it is brought to the attention of the individual conducting that transaction and, in any event, from the time it would have been brought to the individual's attention if the organization had exercised due diligence." "Organization" is broadly defined to include any legal person other than an individual, U.C.C. § 1-201(b)(25), and the term "person" includes essentially all forms of business entities. U.C.C. § 1-201(b)(27).

[85] *See, e.g.*, Huntington Nat'l Bank of Wash. Court House v. Stockwell, 10 Ohio App. 3d 30, 460 N.E.2d 303, 37 U.C.C. Rep. Serv. 1799 (Ct. App. 1983). If the couple resides together, most courts have found that notice to one spouse is notice to the other. In *In re* De Pasquale, 166 B.R. 663, 23 U.C.C. Rep. Serv. 2d 1022 (Bankr. N.D. Ill. 1994), the court justified this result on the basis that the other spouse was aware of the notice.

[86] Comment 6 to section 9-611 provides that Article 9 "leaves to judicial resolution, based upon the facts of each case, the question whether the requirement of 'reasonable notification' requires a 'second try,' *i.e.*, whether a secured party who sends notification and learns that the debtor did not receive it must attempt to locate the debtor and send another notification."

[87] U.C.C. § 9-617(a)(3). The title of the buyer at the foreclosure sale is discussed in § 18.02[E] *infra*.

[88] The junior must notify the senior in a record that it wants to share in the surplus before distribution of the proceeds of sale is complete. U.C.C. § 9-615(a)(3). *See* discussion at § 18.02[D] *infra*. In addition, notification to the senior will entitle the junior to damages if the senior's sale is commercially unreasonable and would, if properly conducted, have generated a surplus. U.C.C. § 9-625(b).

[89] A competing secured party (junior or senior) may avoid a foreclosure sale by redeeming the collateral. U.C.C. § 9-623.

In this regard, Article 9 requires the foreclosing secured party to search the Article 9 filing records and provide notice to any other secured party or lienholder that, as of ten days prior to the date of the notice, holds an interest in the same collateral that is perfected either by filing or by notation on a certificate of title.[90] The drafters imposed this search duty on the foreclosing secured party because "[m]any of the problems arising from dispositions of collateral encumbered by multiple security interests can be ameliorated or solved by informing all secured parties of an intended disposition and affording them the opportunity to work with one another."[91] Article 9 provides a "safe-harbor" rule to help the foreclosing secured party satisfy its search obligations.[92]

Furthermore, Article 9 requires a foreclosing secured party to send notice to any other secured party or lienholder (such as the holder of a judgment lien) that has previously advised the foreclosing secured party, by an authenticated notification, that it claims an interest in the collateral.[93] Although the drafters intended this notification provision primarily to benefit junior interests, a senior secured party that learns that a junior has acquired an interest in its collateral may wish to take advantage of the provision.[94] By advising the junior of its interest, the senior gains some protection if the debtor defaults to the junior and the junior commences foreclosure proceedings. Although the disposition will not extinguish the senior's interest,[95] the senior will want to know of the disposition.[96] This

---

[90] U.C.C. § 9-611(c)(3)(B), (C).

[91] U.C.C. § 9-611, Comment 4.

[92] U.C.C. § 9-611(e). To qualify for this safe harbor, a foreclosing secured party should file a "request for information" with the filing officer, seeking information about all financing statements indexed under the debtor's name. The request must be filed not less than 20 days nor more than 30 days prior to the notification date. The notification date is the earlier of the date the secured party sends notice to the debtor and any secondary obligor or obtains waivers from such persons. U.C.C. § 9-611(a). After filing its request, the foreclosing secured party should receive from the filing officer copies of all effective financing statements indexed under the name of the debtor. The foreclosing secured party may then provide the necessary notification to any secured party that has filed a financing statement describing the collateral. If the foreclosing secured party provides notice to every person revealed by a timely request for information, or if it files a timely request but does not receive a response from the filing officer, it is deemed to have satisfied the "search-and-notify" obligation imposed by § 9-611(c)(3)(B).

[93] U.C.C. § 9-611(c)(3)(A). This provision would provide a judgment lienholder with a means to take steps to ensure the receipt of notice of a senior creditor's disposition of the collateral; typically, the existence of a judgment lien against personal property would not appear in the public filing records (and thus the "search-and-notify" obligation would not protect the typical judgment lienholder).

[94] In most such cases, the senior will have the option of declaring a default and proceeding to foreclose on the collateral. Most security agreements make the creation of a competing security interest an event of default.

[95] See discussion in § 18.02[D] infra. Even if the buyer at a foreclosure sale is a buyer in ordinary course of business (which will likely be the case if the secured party is a seller that puts the collateral back into its inventory for resale), the buyer cannot take advantage of U.C.C. § 9-320(a) because the senior's security interest will not have been created by the buyer's immediate seller (the junior secured party). Accordingly, the buyer at the foreclosure sale is

will permit the senior to redeem the collateral from the junior prior to disposition or to take steps to have the foreclosure buyer redeem the collateral to avoid repossession by the senior. Another option (though seldom exercised) is for the senior to repossess the collateral from the junior before the junior's disposition.[97] As between the two secured parties, the senior has the superior possessory interest if default has occurred; by taking over the process and conducting its own disposition, the senior gains a significant level of protection.

There is a party not mentioned in the Code that must also be given notice of a disposition by sale. If the United States government has filed a notice of tax lien more than 30 days before a foreclosure sale, its lien will survive the sale — even if that lien is junior to the secured party's interest — unless the secured party provides proper notice at least 25 days prior to the sale.[98]

In limited circumstances a person may be a debtor, secondary obligor, or other person entitled to notice, and yet may be unknown to (and undiscoverable by) the foreclosing secured party. For example, suppose Freyermuth holds a perfected security interest in Henning's equipment and repossesses it following default. Unknown to Freyermuth, however, Henning had sold the equipment two days earlier to Lawrence, who had not yet taken delivery of the equipment. Further, and also unknown to Freyermuth, Lawrence had granted a security interest in the equipment to Bank, which filed a financing statement covering the collateral and naming Lawrence as debtor. Technically, Lawrence is now a debtor with respect to the collateral (even though Lawrence is not an obligor) — but requiring Freyermuth to notify Lawrence and Bank of the sale would pose an impossible search burden upon Freyermuth. In this context, Article 9 excuses Freyermuth from providing notice to either Lawrence or Bank; notice to Henning alone is legally sufficient.[99]

---

at risk of having the collateral repossessed from it by the senior if the debtor is in default to the senior. Because the buyer may then have to redeem the collateral to protect its interest, it should pay no more at the junior's sale than the fair market value of the collateral less the amount of the senior's debt. Also, the buyer at the junior's sale should notify the senior of its interest to prevent the senior from making post-sale advances to the debtor that would increase the senior's interest in the collateral. *See* U.C.C. § 9-323(d). Nothing the buyer can do will prevent the secured party from obtaining priority for advances made pursuant to a commitment entered into without knowledge of the buyer's interest. *See* U.C.C. § 9-323(e). A secured party's priority rights against a buyer with respect to future advances is discussed generally in § 11.03[A][3] *supra*.

[96] The fact that the senior's interest survives foreclosure is of little good if its collateral has been sold to a third party that then disappears with it.

[97] *See, e.g.*, American Heritage & Trust Co. v. O. & E., Inc., 40 Colo. Ct. App. 306, 576 P.2d 566, 23 U.C.C. Rep. Serv. 1034 (1978).

[98] 26 U.S.C. § 7425(b). The government has a post-sale right of redemption for real property, but not for personalty. *See* 26 U.S.C. § 7425(d). Tax liens are discussed generally in Chapter 13 *supra*.

[99] U.C.C. § 9-605(1), (2). If Freyermuth became aware of the transfer to Lawrence prior to the sale, and also became aware of Lawrence's address (or some other means of communicating with Lawrence), Freyermuth would then have to notify both Lawrence and Bank.

[2] Amount of Notice Necessary

Section 9-611(b) requires that a secured party send a "reasonable authenticated notification" of the disposition.[100] This means that the secured party must send the notice so that a party receiving it in due course will have a reasonable opportunity, prior to disposition, to exercise its redemption rights or take other steps reasonably calculated to protect its interests.[101] Article 9 provides the foreclosing secured party with an express "safe harbor" in nonconsumer transactions if the secured party sends the notice no later than 10 days prior to the disposition.[102] This does not suggest that the secured party *must* give notice 10 days prior to disposition. At least one court has approved of a notice that gave the debtor only three business days prior to a sale,[103] and the comments to section 9-612 clearly indicate that the 10-day provision is a "safe harbor" and not a "minimum requirement."[104] A notice period of less than 10 days is dangerous, however; even a notice sent a week before the disposition has occasionally been attacked because a weekend or holiday cut down on the amount of time available to the recipient to protect its interest.[105]

A careful secured party should never encounter a problem. Although a debtor or secondary obligor cannot waive the right to notice prior to default, a security agreement can establish the standards by which to measure the secured party's fulfillment of its duties if the standards selected are not "manifestly unreasonable."[106] Further, should a secured party or the debtor find a buyer willing to pay a fair price but not willing to wait for the agreed-upon time to expire, the debtor can facilitate a sale by waiving its right to notice.[107]

The Code does not require that an entitled person *receive* the notice, only that the secured party send it. This distinction is consistent with the Code's definition of "notify," which states that "[a] person 'notifies' or 'gives' a notice or notification to another person by taking such steps as may be reasonably required to inform the other person in ordinary course *whether or not the other person actually comes to know of it.*"[108] Thus, in most cases the

[100] U.C.C. § 9-611(b).

[101] U.C.C. § 9-612 Comment 2.

[102] U.C.C. § 9-612(b).

[103] *See, e.g.*, Citizens State Bank v. Sparks, 202 Neb. 661, 276 N.W.2d 661, 26 U.C.C. Rep. Serv. 589 (1979).

[104] U.C.C. § 9-612 Comment 3.

[105] *See, e.g.*, Levers v. Rio King Land & Inv. Co., 93 Nev. 95, 560 P.2d 917, 21 U.C.C. Rep. Serv. 344 (1977).

[106] U.C.C. § 9-603(a). A security agreement that specifies that notice will be deemed sufficient if it is sent a certain number of days before the disposition should insulate the secured party as long as it subsequently complies with the terms of the agreement.

[107] The right to notice may be waived after default in an authenticated record. *See* U.C.C. § 9-624(a) and the discussion in § 18.02[B][4] *infra*. A secured party that wants to facilitate an early disposition should obtain waivers of the right to redemption as well as the right to pre-disposition notice. *See* § 18.05 *infra*.

[108] U.C.C. § 1-202(d) (emphasis added). *See also* McGrady v. Nissan Motor Acceptance Corp.,

secured party need only place the notice in the mail, properly addressed and with proper postage, to comply with the Code's requirements. Several caveats, however, are in order. If a secured party knows that an entitled person has moved and is aware of the new address, some courts have held that the secured party must send a notice to that address.[109] If the secured party knows that an entitled person has moved but does not have the new address, some courts have imposed a duty to take minimal steps to locate and notify the entitled person, such as looking in a city directory or contacting a known relative or business associate of the person.[110]

[3] Form and Content of Notice

Article 9 requires a secured party to send an "authenticated" notification,[111] which effectively requires that it send notice in a "record" — i.e., either as a writing or as information that is "stored in an electronic or other medium and is retrievable in perceivable form."[112] An oral notification will not suffice.[113]

As discussed earlier, reasonable notification allows the recipient to protect its interest by redeeming the collateral, attending the disposition (or causing others to attend) and bidding the price up to a fair level, or policing the disposition to make certain that it comports with the requirement of commercial reasonableness. Prior versions of Article 9 provided minimal guidance regarding the contents of a "reasonable" notification. Revised Article 9 addressed this shortcoming by providing the secured party with a "safe harbor" rule applicable to most foreclosures. Except in the case of a consumer-goods transaction,[114] a secured party's notice is sufficient if it

---

40 F. Supp. 2d 1323, 41 U.C.C. Rep. Serv. 2d 986 (M.D. Ala. 1998) (no evidence that notice containing proper name and address had been sent improperly, despite not being received by debtor).

[109] *See, e.g., In re* Carter, 511 F.2d 1203, 16 U.C.C. Rep. Serv. 874 (9th Cir. 1975). Out of caution, the secured party should also send a notice to the address specified in the agreement.

[110] *See, e.g.,* Mallicoat v. Volunteer Fin. & Loan Corp., 57 Tenn. App. 106, 415 S.W.2d 347, 3 U.C.C. Rep. Serv. 1035 (1966) (secured party that received notice back from post office marked "undeliverable" had duty to try to locate debtor). The comments to section 9-611 suggest that a secured party that sends a notification and later learns that the intended recipient did not receive it *may* have to attempt to locate the person and send another notice. *See* U.C.C. § 9-611, Comment 6 (leaving to "judicial resolution" whether requirement of reasonable notification requires "second try" by secured party).

[111] U.C.C. § 9-611(c).

[112] U.C.C. § 9-102(a)(69).

[113] *See* U.C.C. § 9-611 Comment 5. As a matter of policy, one can question why oral notice should not be sufficient if such notice is commercially reasonable under the particular circumstances. As a matter of prudence, however, any secured party should send a writing because the secured party will ordinarily bear the burden of proving compliance with the notice requirement, *see, e.g.,* Boatmen's Bank v. Dahmer, 716 S.W.2d 876, 2 U.C.C. Rep. Serv. 2d 754 (Mo. Ct. App. 1986), and a writing greatly simplifies that task.

[114] U.C.C. § 9-102(a)(24). Recall that revised Article 9 distinguishes between a "consumer transaction" and a "consumer-goods transaction." For a discussion of the distinction, *see* § 1.04[A][1] *infra.*

- describes the debtor and the secured party;
- describes the collateral that is the subject of the intended disposition;
- states the method of the intended disposition;
- states that the debtor is entitled to an accounting of the unpaid indebtedness and states the charge, if any, for such an accounting; and
- states the time and place of a public disposition or the time after which the secured party may dispose of the collateral privately.[115]

A secured party does not have to provide the notification in the exact words that appear in the statute.[116] Furthermore, a court may conclude that a secured party's notification is "reasonable" under the circumstances, even if it lacks one or more of the elements listed in the "safe-harbor" provision.[117] Nevertheless, a secured party would be wise to track the suggested language closely.

In a consumer-goods transaction, the above five elements are *mandatory*.[118] Furthermore, a notice in a consumer-goods transaction must also include

- a description of any liability that the recipient may have for a deficiency judgment following disposition;
- a telephone number from which the recipient may obtain information about the amount that must be paid to redeem the collateral; and
- a telephone number or mailing address from which the recipient may obtain information concerning the disposition of the collateral and the obligation secured.[119]

Again, although no particular phrasing is required, a prudent secured party should track the language of the statute as closely as possible. For convenience, the revisions also provide a suggested "safe-harbor" form, written in "plain English," that (if complied with) satisfies the reasonable-notification requirement.[120]

---

[115] U.C.C. § 9-613(1).

[116] *See* U.C.C. § 9-613(4) ("A particular phrasing of the notification is not required.").

[117] U.C.C. § 9-613(2). For convenience, Article 9 also provides a suggested form that, if complied with, satisfies the reasonable-notification requirement. U.C.C. § 9-613(5).

[118] *See, e.g.,* Coxall v. Clover Commercial Corp., 4 Misc. 3d 654, 781 N.Y.S.2d 567, 54 U.C.C. Rep. Serv. 2d 5 (N.Y. City Civ. Ct. 2004) (letters to debtor insufficient because they did not indicate debtor had the right to an accounting or the charge, if any, for an accounting).

[119] U.C.C. § 9-614(1). *See also In re* Downing, 286 B.R. 900, 49 U.C.C. Rep. Serv. 2d 983 (Bankr. W.D. Mo. 2002) (notice that provided "You are notified that [secured party] intends to sell the vehicle as allowed under state law, but no sooner than 10 days after the date of this letter" held insufficient, because it failed to notify debtor that secured party intended private disposition, that debtor had right to accounting, and that debtor would be liable for any deficiency following disposition).

[120] U.C.C. § 9-614(3).

Secured parties should take special care to comply with these requirements. Although a creditor could argue that less-than-perfect compliance does not render a notice unreasonable,[121] courts have shown a willingness to construe the statutory requirements strictly. For example, in *Gateway Aviation, Inc. v. Cessna Aircraft Co.*,[122] the secured party sent proper notice of an auction, but withdrew the collateral when the bidding proved disappointing and instead sought a private buyer. The secured party later found a person who purchased the collateral for several thousand dollars more than the top bid at the auction. In an action for a deficiency, the court held that the private disposition was defective because the secured party had failed properly to notify the debtor.[123]

A secured party may include additional information in its notification, beyond the stated requirements of the Code, if the additional information is not seriously misleading.[124] For example, a notice may be defective if the secured party overstates the amount of the debt and thereby discourages the debtor from exercising its redemption right.[125] If the notice contains errors in required or additional information that are not misleading or prejudicial to the debtor, however, courts should be careful not to penalize the secured party, especially in transactions not involving consumers. Article 9 holds the secured party to a slightly higher standard with regard to consumer-goods transactions. Errors in the information required by section 9-614(1) render the notice defective. Assuming that the secured party has used the "safe-harbor" form specified in section 9-614(3), errors in additional information that the secured party chooses to provide will not render the notice defective unless that information is misleading with respect to the recipient's rights under Article 9.[126]

[4]   When Notice Is Excused

A secured party need not give pre-disposition notice if: (1) the collateral is perishable; (2) the collateral threatens to decline speedily in value; 3)

---

[121] *See* U.C.C. § 9-613(2) (finder of fact may conclude that a notification is reasonable under the circumstances, even if it lacks some of the information specified in the "safe harbor" provision).

[122] 577 S.W.2d 860, 25 U.C.C. Rep. Serv. 901 (Mo. Ct. App. 1978).

[123] Although harsh, the result in *Gateway Aviation* can be justified. The debtor should have had an opportunity to police the private disposition to make certain that it was conducted fairly; further, with additional notice of the private disposition, the debtor might have come up with the money to redeem the collateral after the date of the auction but before the private disposition actually occurred.

[124] U.C.C. § 9-613(3)(B).

[125] *See, e.g.*, Wilmington Trust Co. v. Conner, 415 A.2d 773, 28 U.C.C. Rep. Serv. 900 (Del. 1980); Travis v. Boulevard Bank, 880 F. Supp. 1226, 28 U.C.C. Rep. Serv. 2d 410 (N.D. Ill. 1995). Whether the notice must advise the debtor of redemption rights is discussed in § 18.05 *infra*.

[126] U.C.C. § 9-614(5). Overly rigorous policing of the foreclosure process (in this and other contexts) by the courts could have the unintended effect of causing more secured parties to have their collateral sold through a judicial proceeding. This approach could have the perverse effect of reducing the amounts realized through foreclosure, thereby increasing the deficiencies borne by debtors.

the collateral is of a type customarily sold on a recognized market; or (4) there is an effective waiver of the right to notice.[127]

The rationale for the first exception is obvious. If the collateral is a crop of harvested tomatoes sitting in a truck in the heat of summer when repossession occurs, the secured party should not have to give notice. The collateral is perishable and the debtor will suffer positive harm if the secured party waits until it has complied with a notice requirement. Cases involving truly perishable assets are rare, however, and secured parties have had little success in attempting to use this provision. Several reported cases involve cattle — which must be fed and watered or they will perish — and the courts are nearly uniform in holding that a secured party disposing of cattle must give notice.[128] This result is appropriate because nothing intrinsic about the cattle makes them perishable — they simply require care, and the secured party has the statutory responsibility to provide that care following repossession.[129]

The most common examples of collateral that threatens to decline speedily in value are stocks and commodities. In *Moutray v. Perry State Bank*,[130] the secured party failed to send notice prior to disposition of the debtor's milo crop, but the court held that notice was excused because the evidence showed that the market for milo was likely to drop precipitously. In contrast, in *Chittenden Trust Co. v. Andre Noel Sports*,[131] the secured party failed to give notice prior to its disposition of high-fashion ski and sports apparel. The court properly refused to excuse the failure because the ski season had ended long before the disposition had occurred. Had repossession occurred just before the end of the season, however, the secured party might have prevailed by convincing the court that such seasonal goods had to be disposed of immediately to obtain a fair price.

Courts have limited the third exception — collateral customarily sold on a recognized market — to assets that are sold without negotiation.[132] If, for example, the collateral consists of shares of a commonly traded stock, there is no plausible rationale for requiring notice.[133] If the debtor has the money to redeem the stock, the same money will buy an equivalent number of shares on the market. Furthermore, the debtor does not need to police the sale of a commonly traded stock for fairness. If the secured party sells the stock for its prevailing market price, the sale is, by definition,

---

[127] U.C.C. §§ 9-611(d), 9-624(a).

[128] *See, e.g.*, Boatmen's Bank of Nev. v. Dahmer, 716 S.W.2d 876, 2 U.C.C. Rep. Serv. 2d 754 (Mo. Ct. App. 1986). *Cf.* City Bank & Trust Co. v. Van Andel, 220 Neb. 152, 368 N.W.2d 789, 41 U.C.C. Rep. Serv. 282 (1985) (whether cattle were perishable was question of fact for jury).

[129] U.C.C. § 9-207(a).

[130] 748 S.W.2d 749, 7 U.C.C. Rep. Serv. 2d 1340 (Mo. Ct. App. 1988).

[131] 159 Vt. 307, 621 A.2d 215, 20 U.C.C. Rep. Serv. 2d 710 (1992).

[132] U.C.C. § 9-610 Comment 9.

[133] *See, e.g.*, Finch v. Auburn Nat'l Bank of Auburn, 646 So. 2d 64, 25 U.C.C. Rep. Serv. 2d 1300 (Ala. Ct. App. 1995) (notice not required for stock traded on Midwest Stock Exchange).

commercially reasonable; if it is not sold for that price, the secured party's misconduct sticks out like a sore thumb.[134]

In a number of cases, a secured party has tried to use this exception when it failed to give notice in connection with the disposition of a used car or similar asset that has a "bluebook" price quotation. The courts have almost uniformly rejected such arguments[135] — and appropriately so, because bluebook quotes simply provide a starting point for negotiating a price. With other assets, the issue is murkier. For example, even with a prevailing market price for cattle, they may be sold at auction by competitive bidding in a particular area. In such cases, whether the collateral falls within the exception is an issue of fact for the jury.[136]

Finally, a person entitled to notice can waive the requirement after default by an authenticated agreement.[137] An entitled person may not waive the notice requirement in advance,[138] but allowing waiver once default occurs makes sense. If the secured party finds a potential buyer that is willing to pay a reasonable price for the collateral but is unwilling to wait while the secured party notifies the debtor and a commercially reasonable time passes, it may be in everyone's interest to waive the notice requirement so that the secured party can proceed with the disposition. After default, there should be little concern that a waiver is the product of overreaching by the secured party.

[C] Whether Secured Party Can Purchase at Disposition

A secured party is free to purchase the collateral at a public disposition, but may not do so at a private disposition unless it is of a type customarily sold on a "recognized market" or is the subject of "widely distributed standard price quotations."[139] This distinction between public and private dispositions is sound. A public disposition features competitive bidding,[140] and as a matter of policy and fairness the secured party should be able to join the competition. The debtor and other interested persons can only benefit from the participation of an extra bidder. In contrast, private dispositions provide too great an opportunity and temptation for secured

---

[134] The same rationale underlies the policy permitting the secured party to buy such assets at a private disposition. U.C.C. § 9-610(c)(2). *See* discussion in § 18.02[C] *infra.*

[135] *See, e.g.*, Beneficial Fin. Co. of Black Hawk Cty. v. Reed, 212 N.W.2d 454, 13 U.C.C. Rep. Serv. 974 (Iowa 1973). This phrase ("type sold on a recognized market") is discussed further in the context of the secured party's right to purchase the collateral at a private disposition. *See* discussion in § 18.02[C] *infra.*

[136] *See, e.g.*, Havins v. First Nat'l Bank of Paducah, 919 S.W.2d 177, 29 U.C.C. Rep. Serv. 2d 1053 (Tex. Ct. App. 1996) (cattle auction); Aspen Enters., Inc. v. Bodge, 37 Cal. App. 4th 1811, 44 Cal. Rptr. 2d 763, 27 U.C.C. Rep. Serv. 2d 681 (1995) (used tires).

[137] U.C.C. § 9-624(a).

[138] U.C.C. § 9-602(7).

[139] U.C.C. § 9-610(c).

[140] Whether auctions that are not open qualify as public dispositions so that a secured party can compete is discussed in § 18.02[A][3] *supra.*

parties to purchase the collateral and then later resell it for their own account at a higher price. If the collateral is something like a commonly traded stock or a commodity that sells without negotiation on a recognized market, however, there is no reason to prevent the secured party from buying at a private disposition. If the secured party pays less than the prevailing price, the debtor can easily prove that the transaction was not commercially reasonable.[141]

The more difficult problem involves the meaning of the phrase "widely distributed standard price quotations." Because the Code uses the companion phrase "customarily sold on a recognized market" to describe one of the situations in which notice is excused, the additional phrase "widely distributed standard price quotations" — which the Code does not use in the notice context — arguably refers to something other than a disposition on a recognized market. But what? The most obvious example would be the used-car type of situation, where the asset is the subject of "bluebook" price quotations. Several decisions suggest the secured party should not be allowed to purchase such assets privately because the bluebook price is only the starting point for negotiations; the actual price paid depends upon the individual characteristics of the particular asset.[142] A few decisions, however, rule to the contrary.[143]

Although the language of the Code invites courts to allow a secured party to purchase "bluebook" assets privately, policy considerations dictate otherwise. Such an interpretation would allow a secured party to "cherry pick" — i.e., to buy those assets that are in better-than-average condition for their bluebook price and then resell them at a higher price. Because the price at the foreclosure disposition establishes the amount of the debtor's deficiency, such a result would be patently unfair. Courts should discourage this type of activity, even if it means effectively collapsing the definition of "standard price quotations" into that used for "recognized markets."

[D] Application of Proceeds of Disposition

Article 9 establishes a four-step process to govern the manner in which the foreclosing secured party must distribute the proceeds of its disposition of the collateral. First, the secured party may reimburse itself for the reasonable expenses incurred to repossess and dispose of the collateral.[144]

---

[141] See § 18.02[B][4] supra.

[142] See, e.g., Northern Commercial Co. v. Cobb, 778 P.2d 205, 10 U.C.C. Rep. Serv. 2d 197 (Alaska 1989) (construction equipment did not fit within exception even though there were nationally published retail and wholesale prices available); M.P. Crum Co. v. First Southwest Savings & Loan Ass'n, 704 S.W.2d 925, 1 U.C.C. Rep. Serv. 2d 332 (Tex. Ct. App. 1986) (disposition of home mortgages).

[143] See, e.g., Dischner v. United Bank Alaska, 631 P.2d 107, 33 U.C.C. Rep. Serv. 796 (Alaska 1981). Cf. L.C. Arthur Trucking, Inc. v. Evans, 13 U.C.C. Rep. Serv. 2d 623 (Va. Cir. Ct. 1990) (tractor-trailer was of type customarily sold in recognized market).

[144] U.C.C. § 9-615(a)(1). These expenses include: the cost of repossession; the cost of holding

The secured party may also recover its attorney's fees and other legal expenses from the proceeds of the collateral, if the security agreement so provides and the law of the jurisdiction does not otherwise preclude such recovery.[145] Second, the foreclosing secured party applies the proceeds to the balance of the secured indebtedness being foreclosed upon.[146] Third, if there remain additional proceeds, the foreclosing secured party must apply them to the claims of junior secured parties or other junior lienholders that have provided the foreclosing secured party with a timely demand for payment.[147] Fourth, the secured party must turn over any remaining surplus to the debtor.[148]

If the proceeds of a secured party's disposition are insufficient to satisfy the secured obligation, the obligor is liable for any deficiency.[149] Generally, the amount of the deficiency is measured by the difference between the amount of the secured obligation and the net proceeds received upon disposition (i.e., the disposition price less expenses of sale). If the secured party's disposition of the collateral was commercially reasonable, the price received on disposition establishes the amount of the deficiency even if the price was less than the collateral's actual fair market value. While Article 9's requirements are designed to produce a disposition that will generate a fair price for the collateral, compliance with those requirements does not guarantee that the secured party will receive such a price. By itself, a low price is not sufficient to establish that the disposition was unreasonable so as to affect the secured party's ability to obtain a deficiency.[150]

There is one situation, however, in which a low disposition price may result in a limitation on a secured party's deficiency judgment. This situation arises if the secured party, a person related to the secured party, or a secondary obligor acquires the collateral at the disposition for a price

---

or storing the collateral pending disposition; the cost of preparing the collateral for disposition, including any commercially reasonable expenses incurred in fixing the collateral so that it commands a higher price (see discussion in § 18.02[A][4] supra); and the cost of conducting the disposition, including any reasonable auctioneer's charges. Courts have also allowed the secured party to recover expenses incurred in paying off other liens to clear the title to the collateral prior to disposition. See, e.g., Contrail Leasing Partners, Ltd. v. Consolidated Airways, Inc., 742 F.2d 1095, 39 U.C.C. Rep. Serv. 9 (7th Cir. 1983).

[145] U.C.C. § 9-615(a)(1).

[146] U.C.C. § 9-615(a)(2).

[147] U.C.C. § 9-615(a)(3). To be entitled to payment, any subordinate party must make an authenticated demand before the foreclosing secured party has completed distribution of the proceeds. If the foreclosing secured party requests reasonable proof of the junior's claimant's interest and the junior claimant fails to provide it, the foreclosing secured party can ignore the demand. U.C.C. § 9-615(b).

[148] U.C.C. § 9-615(d)(1). The requirement assumes that the security interest secures an indebtedness. If the secured party is a buyer of accounts, chattel paper, payment intangibles or promissory notes, it owns the equity and need not account to the debtor for it.

[149] U.C.C. § 9-615(d)(2).

[150] See § 18.02[A][5] supra. A secured party's liability for failing to dispose of collateral in a commercially reasonable manner, and the effect of such a disposition on a secured party's ability to recover a deficiency judgment, is addressed in §§ 19.01[B][2] and 19.02 infra.

that is "significantly below" the price that the secured party would have received in a commercially reasonable sale to an unrelated third party. In such a case, section 9-615(f) provides that a surplus or deficiency will be calculated based on the price that the secured party would have received in such a sale, rather than the price it actually received.[151] As the comments indicate, this section tries to address the risk that a secured party might acquire the collateral at foreclosure for a bargain price and thereby capture an unjustifiable share of the debtor's equity in the collateral or inflate the amount of the obligor's deficiency.[152]

As noted above, section 9-615 authorizes the foreclosing secured party to apply proceeds to the claims of junior lienholders that have made a timely and effective demand for the distribution of surplus proceeds. Occasionally, courts have become confused regarding the proper distribution of proceeds under a disposition conducted by a *junior* secured party when a *senior* secured party asserts a claim to them. Suppose Henning owns equipment subject to two security interests held by Lawrence and Freyermuth, respectively, with Lawrence holding the senior interest. Henning defaults to Freyermuth, and Freyermuth repossesses the equipment and conducts an auction sale. Does Lawrence have a superior claim to the proceeds from the auction?

The correct answer is no. When a secured party takes a security interest in an asset owned by the debtor, its interest in the asset is limited. The debtor retains its property interest in the collateral and, in a nonpossessory security arrangement, the right of possession. Should default and repossession occur, the debtor retains a right of redemption. Most importantly, the debtor has a right to any equity that it has built up in the collateral — a right that is vindicated in foreclosure proceedings by the secured party's duty to turn over to the debtor any surplus proceeds. Thus, when a junior secured party like Freyermuth acquires an interest in collateral already subject to a senior's lien, the junior's security interest technically does not interfere with the existing rights of the senior. Conceptually, the junior's interest is best understood as attaching only to the debtor's equity in the collateral. Even if the senior's security agreement makes it an event of default for the debtor to alienate that equity, the debtor has the *power* to do so.[153] Thus, although Freyermuth has a right to repossess the equipment and foreclose upon it, all he can dispose of is his right to Henning's equity (and Henning's title and right to possession). As a result, the person who purchases the equipment at the foreclosure takes it subject to Lawrence's senior security interest, and is at risk of having Lawrence repossess the

---

[151] U.C.C. § 9-615(f).

[152] U.C.C. § 9-615 Comment 6 ("[This section] recognizes that when the foreclosing secured party or a related party is the transferee of the collateral, the secured party sometimes lacks the incentive to maximize the proceeds of the disposition. As a consequence, the disposition may comply with the procedural requirements of [Article 9] . . . but nevertheless fetch a low price.").

[153] U.C.C. § 9-401(b).

equipment if Henning also defaults to Lawrence.[154] This means, conceptually, that the proceeds of Freyermuth's disposition are not "proceeds" of Lawrence's security interest, because the disposition did not transfer the rights to which Lawrence's security interest attached.[155] As a result, Article 9 does not entitle Lawrence to participate in the distribution of the proceeds of Freyermuth's disposition.[156] To reach them, Lawrence must employ an extra-Code process such as garnishment.

Not every court has understood this point. According to some courts, Freyermuth's failure to turn the proceeds over to Lawrence upon demand would constitute a conversion.[157] The decisions are incorrect; requiring the foreclosing junior to turn over the proceeds of its disposition to the senior is inconsistent with both the derivative rights principle that provides a conceptual underpinning for Article 9 and the express language of section 9-615(a) — which does not provide for application of proceeds of disposition to the claims of senior secured parties. In the above hypothetical, Lawrence's security interest remains intact and he can continue to look to the equipment for satisfaction.

Article 9 places an additional duty upon a foreclosing secured party in a consumer-goods transaction.[158] If disposition produces a surplus to which the debtor is entitled, the secured party must provide the debtor with a written explanation of how the secured party calculated that surplus. Likewise, if the disposition leaves a deficiency for which a consumer obligor is liable, the secured party must provide the obligor with a written explanation of how the secured party calculated the deficiency.[159] The

---

[154] *See* related discussion in § 18.02[B][1] *supra*. Because the Code authorizes the junior's disposition, the buyer is not a converter. It becomes liable for conversion, however, if it later resists the senior's proper demand to turn over possession. Because security agreements often define repossession as an event of default, the prospect of the debtor's default to the senior is high.

[155] *See, e.g.,* Consolidated Equip. Sales, Inc. v. First State Bank & Trust Co. of Guthrie, 627 P.2d 432, 31 U.C.C. Rep. Serv. 677 (Okla. 1981); Delaware Truck Sales, Inc. v. Wilson, 618 A.2d 303, 20 U.C.C. Rep. Serv. 2d 1420 (N.J. 1993).

[156] *See, e.g.,* Continental Bank of Buffalo Grove, N.A. v. Krebs, 184 Ill. App. 3d 693, 540 N.E.2d 1023, 10 U.C.C. Rep. Serv. 2d 246 (1989) (relying on U.C.C. § 9-311 to hold that senior secured party is not entitled to proceeds of junior's disposition).

[157] *See, e.g.,* Consolidated Equip. Sales, Inc. v. First State Bank & Trust Co. of Guthrie, 627 P.2d 432, 31 U.C.C. Rep. Serv. 677 (Okla. 1981); Delaware Truck Sales, Inc. v. Wilson, 618 A.2d 303, 20 U.C.C. Rep. Serv. 2d 1420 (N.J. 1993).

[158] For a definition of the term "consumer-goods transaction" and how that term differs from the term "consumer transaction," *see* § 1.04[A] *supra*.

[159] U.C.C. § 9-616(b). The "explanation" must be a writing that states the amount of the surplus or deficiency, explains how the secured party calculated it, states whether "future debits, credits, charges . . . and expenses may affect the amount of the surplus or deficiency," and provides a phone number or mailing address from which the recipient could obtain additional information about the transaction. U.C.C. § 9-616(a)(1). Further, section 9-616(c) requires that the explanation is sufficient only if it includes the following information in the following order: the aggregate amount of the secured obligation(s); the amount of proceeds of the disposition; the aggregate amount of the secured obligation(s) after the application of the proceeds; the amount and types of expenses of repossession and disposition; the amounts

secured party must provide the explanation at or before the time when it accounts for any surplus or makes its first written demand for payment of the deficiency.[160]

[E] Property Rights of Transferee at Disposition

If a secured party disposes of collateral after default to a transferee that pays value, the disposition transfers the debtor's rights in the collateral to the transferee,[161] thereby extinguishing the right of redemption (which exists only until the time of disposition).[162] The disposition also discharges both the security interest being foreclosed and any subordinate liens or security interests.[163] This discharge is an application of the doctrine of derivative rights, pursuant to which a transferee acquires whatever rights were held by its transferor. If a senior secured party transfers collateral to a buyer at foreclosure, the buyer acquires the senior's rights and this results in the discharge of junior liens.[164] The buyer, however, takes subject to any liens that are senior to the interest of the foreclosing secured party. A foreclosure buyer thus should pay no more than the fair market value of the collateral (if unencumbered) less the balance of any debts secured by senior liens.[165]

Generally speaking, a transferee for value at a foreclosure disposition acquires these rights even if the secured party has breached the peace in its repossession efforts, conducted a commercially unreasonable disposition, or failed to give all necessary notices. In other words, the secured party's failure to comply with its responsibilities under Article 9 does not give the debtor a basis for collateral attack of the disposition through judicial proceedings. The debtor's remedy is against the foreclosing secured party, not the transferee.[166] This rule promotes the finality of rights acquired through foreclosure — and thereby (hopefully) encourages widespread participation in foreclosure dispositions.

---

of credits (if any) to which any obligor is known to be entitled; and the amount of the surplus or deficiency. No particular phrasing is required, and an explanation substantially complying with the requirements is sufficient even if it contains minor errors that are not seriously misleading. U.C.C. § 9-616(d).

[160] U.C.C. § 9-616(b)(1)(A). A debtor or consumer obligor does not have to wait until the secured party makes a written demand for payment to receive an explanation of how the secured party calculated the surplus or deficiency. Instead, section 9-616 authorizes the debtor or consumer obligor, after disposition of the collateral, to make an authenticated request to receive an explanation. Within 14 days after such a request, the secured party must provide an explanation or a record waiving its right to pursue a deficiency judgment. § 9-616(b)(1)(B), (2).

[161] U.C.C. § 9-617(a)(1).

[162] U.C.C. § 9-623(b).

[163] U.C.C. § 9-617(a)(2), (3).

[164] The junior secured party's right to notice of the disposition so that it can protect its interests is discussed in § 18.02[B][1] *supra*, and the junior's right to participate in the distribution of the proceeds is discussed in § 18.02[D] *supra*.

[165] *See* note 95 *supra*.

[166] Chapter 19 provides further discussion of the remedies for creditor misbehavior.

Under limited circumstances, however, Article 9 permits an adversely-affected person to seek judicial invalidation of a secured party's disposition of collateral. Section 9-617(b) provides that the transferee does not acquire "clear title" (*i.e.*, the debtor's rights in the collateral, free of the interest foreclosed and subordinate interests) if the transferee did not act in "good faith."[167] "Good faith" means both honesty in fact and the observance of reasonable commercial standards of fair dealing.[168] A transferee that lacks good faith takes the collateral subject to the debtor's rights in it as well as the security interest of the foreclosing party and all other security interests or liens.[169] Thus, if the transferee lacks good faith, a person with redemption rights may still redeem the collateral by satisfying the debt.[170]

A transferee lacks good faith if it knows of defects in the disposition or acts in collusion with secured party or other bidders.[171] Suppose Debtor owes Secured Party $9,500, secured by a security interest in Debtor's car. Secured Party repossesses Debtor's car following default and schedules an auction. Lawrence wants to purchase the car for $10,000, but lacks the cash needed to participate in the auction. Lawrence approaches Secured Party, and they agree that if Secured Party purchases the car at the auction, Secured Party will in turn sell the car to Lawrence for $10,000 and will extend him $8,000 in credit to complete the purchase. Secured Party conducts the auction and purchases the car for a high bid of $9,000. In this circumstance, by virtue of Secured Party's collusion with Lawrence, the disposition did not extinguish Debtor's interest in the car. Debtor could bring an action against Secured Party and either redeem the car by satisfying the debt or require Secured Party to conduct a new disposition.[172]

Because recent U.C.C. revisions have expanded the duty of "good faith" beyond its original and purely subjective "honesty in fact" definition, there is a risk that this expansion may have an unintended chilling effect upon prospective bidders. Under former law, buyers at auctions had no duty to investigate the secured party's compliance with the requirements of Article 9 or to inquire into the circumstances surrounding the disposition.[173] This made sense because the Code's duty of good faith then required only "honesty in fact."[174] But if good faith now incorporates "the observance of reasonable commercial standards of fair dealing,"[175] must an auction buyer

---

[167] U.C.C. § 9-617(b).

[168] U.C.C. § 1-201(b)(20).

[169] U.C.C. § 9-617(c).

[170] U.C.C. § 9-623(b).

[171] U.C.C. § 9-617 Comment 3.

[172] Injunctive relief to force a secured party to conduct a commercially reasonable disposition is available under U.C.C. § 9-625(a). A properly conducted second disposition would not excuse the secured party from any liability that it might have incurred as a result of its first disposition.

[173] U.C.C. § 9-504 Comment 4 (1972 text).

[174] U.C.C. § 1-201(19) (1972 text).

[175] U.C.C. § 1-201(b)(20).

conduct an inquiry into the character of the disposition? It is doubtful that the drafters so intended, and such an inquiry could easily discourage bidding, leading to lower auction prices and correspondingly higher deficiency judgments. Nevertheless, courts have often demonstrated a willingness to apply the duty of "good faith" in sweeping terms when presented with compelling facts.

Even unsecured parties (or in the event of an insolvent debtor, a trustee in bankruptcy as the debtor's representative) may be able to set aside a disposition if it constitutes a fraudulent conveyance.[176] In such a case, the court will typically order that restitution of the purchase price be made to the buyer as a condition to granting relief.[177]

§ 18.03   FORECLOSURE ON INTANGIBLE ASSETS — § 9-607

If a foreclosure involves collateral representing rights to payment (such as accounts or chattel paper), a secured party may choose to take steps that are unnecessary in foreclosing against other kinds of assets.[178] The secured party must first choose whether to sell the collateral as a package to a factor[179] or attempt to collect from the various account debtors and obligors on instruments.[180] If the secured party sells the collateral to a factor *en*

---

[176] If the trustee sets aside the disposition and is then able to avoid the security interest, it can make a distribution to unsecured creditors. *See, e.g.*, Sheffield Progressive, Inc. v. Kingston Tool Co., 10 Mass. App. Ct. 47, 405 N.E.2d 985, 29 U.C.C. Rep. Serv. 292 (1980). *Cf.* Bezanson v. Fleet Bank-NH, 29 F.3d 16, 24 U.C.C. Rep. Serv. 2d 399 (1st Cir. 1994) (facts suggested fraudulent conveyance but debtor's action was brought against secured party for holding commercially unreasonable disposition that failed to produce surplus). The subject of fraudulent conveyances in bankruptcy is discussed in detail in § 16.04[F] *supra*.

[177] If the secured party is joined in the action, the court should order that it make the restitutionary payment. If it is not joined, the party setting aside the disposition should be entitled to restitution from the secured party for the payment made to the buyer.

A foreclosing secured party might also have liability to the buyer based upon breach of a warranty. Under Article 9, a foreclosure disposition includes any warranty of title or quiet enjoyment that is implied by other law governing the transaction, unless the secured party disclaims the warranty as provided by the other law or by section 9-610(e) and (f). *See* U.C.C. §§ 2-312 (warranty of title in sale of goods), 2A-211 (warranty against interference in lease of goods). The secured party may also be liable for breach of an express warranty made in connection with the disposition (U.C.C. §§ 2-313, 2A-210), and for breach of an implied warranty of merchantability if it is a merchant with respect to goods of that kind (U.C.C. §§ 2-314, 2A-212).

[178] Full treatment of this topic is beyond the scope of this book. The text provides only a basic summary of Article 9's guidelines.

[179] The term "factor" describes a person that buys payment rights, whether at foreclosure or otherwise. *See* § 3.04[A] *supra*. After making its purchase, the factor will proceed to collect from the individual account debtors or obligors on promissory notes. Having bought the assets outright, the factor will not be under a duty to remit any surplus to the debtor. Any surplus value should have been realized through the secured party's commercially reasonable disposition to the factor.

[180] U.C.C. § 9-102(a)(3). The term "account debtor" does not include a person obligated on a negotiable instrument, even if the instrument is part of chattel paper. *Id.*

masse, the normal provisions governing Article 9 foreclosures govern the sale. If instead the secured party chooses collection, it will have to notify each account debtor and obligor to make payment to it;[181] further, the secured party will then have to collect in a commercially reasonable manner. This means that the secured party must exercise reasonable judgment in deciding whether to expend resources in pursuit of financially strapped account debtors and obligors, and it must act reasonably in compromising claims against account debtors and obligors who assert defenses or counterclaims that might have been valid if the debtor had attempted to collect.[182]

If a secured party is a buyer of accounts, chattel paper, payment intangibles, or promissory notes, it ordinarily need not worry about collecting them in a commercially reasonable manner because the debtor will not be liable for any deficiency and the secured party need not account for any surplus.[183] But if the secured party has a right of recourse or charge-back against the debtor in the event it cannot collect, its collection efforts must be commercially reasonable.[184] If a secured party takes an unconditional

---

[181] Article 9 permits a secured party, at any time after default, to notify account debtors of the assignment and to direct them to make payment to the secured party. U.C.C. § 9-607(a)(1). Article 9 also permits the secured party to give notice to account debtors, even prior to default, that the right to payment has been assigned and that the payment should be made payment to the secured party. U.C.C. § 9-406(a). After receiving notice of such an assignment, the account debtor thereafter may discharge its obligation only by payment to the secured party. Certain notification-financing arrangements follow this pattern; in those transactions, because the secured party will already have notified the account debtors to make payment to it, the secured party need provide no further notification following the debtor's default.

Articles 3 and 4 govern the mechanics of collection and the obligations of parties to a negotiable instrument. A secured party will have an easier time of collection if it is a holder, and as a matter of prudence it will have the debtor indorse the instrument to it when the security interest first attaches. Having the status of holder is a necessary first step for the secured party to later assert that it is a "holder in due course" entitled to collect the instrument free from claims and defenses.

Although a secured party may, after default, notify the obligor on an instrument to make payment to it, U.C.C. § 9-607(a)(1), this in no way vitiates any obligation that the party seeking to enforce the instrument may have to present it for payment or to surrender it when payment is received. Because an obligor on a negotiable instrument that constitutes part of chattel paper is not an account debtor, the rules of Article 3 govern collection of the note.

[182] The most common example would be a breach of warranty claim against the debtor. For example, suppose Henning purchased equipment on account from Seller/Debtor, which assigned the account to Bank. Bank will take the account subject to any claim Henning might have that the equipment breached any express or implied warranties of quality or fitness unless Henning has entered into an enforceable agreement not to assert claims against any assignee of Seller/Debtor. U.C.C. § 9-404(a). In attempting to collect the account from Henning, Bank may enforce Henning's agreement to waive claims and defenses to defeat any breach of warranty claim, provided that Bank took its assignment of the account for value, in good faith, and without notice of any such claim. U.C.C. § 9-403(a).

[183] If an assignee buys accounts, chattel paper, payment intangibles or promissory notes outright, there is no underlying obligation; thus, concepts like deficiency and surplus are inapt, and the debtor is neither entitled to a surplus nor is the obligor liable for any deficiency unless the security agreement provides otherwise. U.C.C. § 9-608(b), Comment 3.

[184] U.C.C. § 9-607(c).

assignment of payment rights, its contract with the debtor will typically give it a right of recourse in the event an account debtor or obligor asserts a contract defense or counterclaim. In such situations, the secured party must take care that it can defend any compromise it makes with an account debtor or obligor as a commercially reasonable exercise of judgment.

With certain general intangibles, a secured party may need the consent of a third party to effectively transfer the debtor's rights by foreclosure. For example, the right to be a franchisee is a valuable right and, if the secured party wants to sell the debtor's rights as a franchisee, the buyer will ordinarily have to meet with the franchisor's approval.[185]

§ 18.04 STRICT FORECLOSURE — §§ 9-620 TO 9-622

Strict foreclosure is an Article 9 remedy that can, in appropriate circumstances, benefit both the secured party and the debtor. A strict foreclosure is essentially a trade under which the secured party acquires the debtor's rights in the collateral without having to go through the normal disposition processes (with the procedural hassles that accompany those processes and the potential liability for failing to comply with them).[186] In exchange, the underlying obligation of the debtor (or some portion of that obligation) is extinguished.[187] The secured party is then free to do as it wishes with the

---

[185] Some franchise agreements preclude assignment entirely, and similar problems arise with government licenses. Under Article 9, the fact that a franchise or license agreement prohibits the debtor from creating a security interest in the franchise or license (or makes such a transfer an event of default) does not prevent the security interest from having legal effect. U.C.C. § 9-408(a). Likewise, the fact that a statute or other rule of law purports to prohibit or restrict the debtor from creating a security interest in a license or permit, or requires government consent for such a transfer, does not prevent the security interest from taking effect. U.C.C. § 9-408(c).

Nevertheless, Article 9 does recognize limitations upon a secured party's ability to enforce a security interest in a license or franchise. U.C.C. § 9-408(d)(6). For example, suppose Henning purchases a license for business software from Macrosoft, which license is nontransferable by its terms without the prior consent of Macrosoft. Henning later grants a security interest in all of his assets to Bank. Bank obtains a security interest in the software, despite the no-transfer provision in the license; nevertheless, Bank cannot enforce the security interest against the software without the prior consent of Macrosoft. Thus, Bank is unable to enforce its security interest against Henning's computers (without risking liability to Macrosoft for conversion) without first removing the software from those computers.

[186] The normal processes are discussed in § 18.02 *supra.*

[187] In this regard, strict foreclosure under Article 9 is analogous to the mortgagor's execution and delivery of a "deed in lieu of foreclosure" under the law of real estate mortgages.

Under Article 9 as originally promulgated, strict foreclosure resulted in the *complete* satisfaction of the debtor's obligation; the Code did not authorize strict foreclosure in *partial* satisfaction of the debt. *See* U.C.C. § 9-505(2) (1972 text) (secured party may retain collateral "in satisfaction of the obligation); U.C.C. § 9-505 Comment 1 (1972 text) (strict foreclosure involves "abandoning any claim for a deficiency"). This position was subject to criticism on the ground that the parties should be free to stipulate to a "fair price" for the collateral in lieu of foreclosure — and thereby stipulate to a deficiency if the stipulation occurs after default. Revised Article 9 permits partial strict foreclosure in nonconsumer transactions. U.C.C. § 9-620(a), (g).

collateral, without regard to the provisions that govern Article 9 dispositions.

A secured party initiates a strict foreclosure by making a "proposal," which the Code defines as an "a record authenticated by a secured party which includes the terms on which the secured party is willing to accept collateral in full or partial satisfaction of the obligation it secures."[188] The secured party must provide notice of the proposal to all persons who would have been entitled to notice prior to a disposition.[189] The decision to seek strict foreclosure rests with the secured party; the debtor cannot force the secured party to use the procedure.

If a secured party receives a timely authenticated notice of objection from any recipient of its proposal, or from any other person holding a subordinate interest in the collateral, the secured party cannot use strict foreclosure.[190] A person entitled to notice of the secured party's proposal must notify the secured party of an objection within 20 days after notice of the proposal was sent to the objecting person.[191] Any other person (such as a creditor that holds a subordinate judgment lien, but that has not sent the secured party an authenticated notice of its interest in the collateral) may notify the secured party of an objection within 20 days of the last notification given by the secured party or, if no notifications are given, before the debtor consents to the proposal.

For example, suppose Henning owns an automobile subject to a first priority security interest in favor of Freyermuth, a second priority security interest in favor of Lawrence, and a judgment lien in favor of Bruno. On February 1, Henning defaults to Freyermuth. On February 2, Freyermuth proposes in an authenticated record to accept the car in full satisfaction of Henning's obligation, sending notification of the proposal to Henning. Freyermuth sends notice of the proposal to Lawrence on February 5. Henning may object to Freyermuth's proposal until February 22. Lawrence and Bruno may object to the proposal until February 25. Even if Henning

---

[188] U.C.C. § 9-102(a)(66). Courts have required that the notice clearly indicate the creditor's intention to retain the collateral in satisfaction of the debt. *See, e.g.*, Ainslie v. Inman, 577 S.E.2d 246, 49 U.C.C. Rep. Serv. 2d 1319 (Va. 2003) (letter notifying debtor that creditor was "taking possession of and foreclosing upon" collateral insufficient notice that creditor intended to retain collateral in full satisfaction of debt); Hansford v. Burns, 241 Ga. App. 407, 40 U.C.C. Rep. Serv. 2d 592 (1999) (letter indicating creditor was "taking back the collateral" insufficient to indicate proposal to retain collateral in satisfaction of debt).

[189] U.C.C. § 9-621(a). The question of which persons are entitled to receive notice prior to disposition is discussed in § 18.02[B][1] *supra. See also, e.g.*, digiGAN, Inc. v. iValidate, Inc., 2004 WL 203010, 52 U.C.C. Rep. Serv. 2d 1022 (S.D.N.Y. 2004) (secured party's failure to send strict foreclosure proposal to person to whom debtor had already sold the collateral did not defeat effectiveness of secured party's proposal when buyer had not provided secured party with an authenticated notification of its claim of interest in the collateral). Note that a secured party need only notify a secondary obligor if the secured party is proposing partial strict foreclosure. U.C.C. § 9-621(b).

[190] U.C.C. § 9-620(a)(2).

[191] U.C.C. § 9-620(d)(1).

and Lawrence consent to the proposal, Freyermuth may not use strict foreclosure if Bruno provides a timely objection.

If a secured party does not receive a timely objection to its proposal, the debtor's rights in the collateral become vested in the secured party, and the secured party's interest is extinguished (along with any subordinate security interests or liens).[192] Further, the debt is discharged to the extent specified in the proposal. Thus, following a partial strict foreclosure, the secured party may seek to recover the stipulated deficiency from any obligor via judicial action.[193]

Obviously, a debtor should object to a strict foreclosure proposal if it believes that a normal disposition would generate a surplus. Because a successful strict foreclosure will also extinguish the lien of a junior secured party or lienholder, the holder of a junior interest should also object if a normal disposition could reasonably produce a surplus over the balance of the lien being foreclosed.

The Code precludes a secured party from initiating strict foreclosure in certain cases involving consumer goods. The provision presumes that if the debtor has repaid 60% of the loan in a nonpurchase-money transaction or 60% of the cash price in a purchase-money transaction, the debtor likely has acquired sufficient equity to justify disposition of the collateral to preserve that equity for the debtor's benefit.[194] A debtor that believes that this assumption is false and would prefer a strict foreclosure may waive this compulsory-disposition requirement after default.[195]

As originally promulgated, Article 9 required a secured party to have possession of the collateral before it could propose strict foreclosure.[196] Because no convincing rationale justified this requirement, Article 9 now permits the secured party to propose strict foreclosure even prior to taking possession.[197] If the collateral is consumer goods, however, a debtor may not give effective consent to a secured party's proposal while the collateral remains in the debtor's possession.[198]

The Code imposes upon the secured party a duty of good faith in the enforcement of any of its remedies.[199] Accordingly, the duty applies to a

---

[192] U.C.C. § 9-622(a). Strict foreclosure extinguishes subordinate interests even if the secured party fails to comply with its notification requirements. U.C.C. § 9-622(b). Any person that was entitled to notification, but did not receive it, may recover any damages caused by the secured party's noncompliance. U.C.C. § 9-625(b).

[193] U.C.C. § 9-622(a)(1). Partial strict foreclosure is not available in consumer transactions. U.C.C. § 9-620(g). Further, the comments make clear that a secured party's proposal of partial strict foreclosure must specify the amount of the secured obligation to be satisfied, or at least a means of calculating that amount. See U.C.C. § 9-620 Comment 4. Finally, a debtor may not be deemed to have consented to partial strict foreclosure by silence; instead, the debtor must accept the proposal in a record authenticated after default. U.C.C. § 9-620(c)(1).

[194] U.C.C. § 9-620(e). See also discussion in § 18.02[B][2] supra.

[195] U.C.C. § 9-624(b).

[196] U.C.C. § 9-505(2) (1972 text).

[197] U.C.C. § 9-620 Comment 7.

[198] U.C.C. § 9-620(a)(3).

[199] U.C.C. § 1-304.

secured party's proposal of strict foreclosure. For example, suppose Henning owes Freyermuth $1,000, secured by a security interest in a $50,000 corporate bond. Freyermuth proposes to accept the bond in full satisfaction of Henning's obligation, hoping that Henning will inadvertently fail to object on a timely basis. Under these circumstances, Freyermuth's proposal lacks good faith and is not effective. [200]

§ 18.05 REDEMPTION — § 9-623

Under section 9-623, a right of redemption extends to "[the] debtor, any secondary obligor, or any other secured party or lienholder." [201] This includes both senior or subordinate security interests as well as judicial and other liens. [202]

The U.C.C. does not allow post-disposition redemption, [203] and therefore the redeeming person must exercise its right before the secured party has disposed of the collateral, entered into a contract for its disposition, or acquired the debtor's rights by strict foreclosure. [204] To redeem, the person must tender "fulfillment of all obligations secured by the collateral" (including expenses reasonably incurred by the secured party in repossessing the collateral and preparing it for disposition) [205] and, to the extent provided in the agreement and not prohibited by law, the secured party's reasonable attorney's fees and legal expenses. [206] The fact that the redeeming person must satisfy the entire indebtedness plus costs makes the redemption provision of limited usefulness to debtors in financial distress. The reality is that the right is more helpful to other secured parties than it is to debtors.

One of the major purposes underlying the Code's notice requirements is protection of the right of redemption. While commercial debtors and other secured parties are likely to realize that a foreclosure disposition will terminate their redemption rights, consumer debtors are less likely to be

---

[200] U.C.C. § 9-620 Comment 11. The comments make clear, however, that determinations about the existence of "good faith" are contextual and that the mere existence of equity in the collateral does not mean that a secured party's proposal lacks good faith. *Id.* ("[I]n the normal case proposals and acceptances should not be second-guessed on the basis of the 'value' of the collateral involved. Disputes about valuation or even a clear excess of collateral value over the amount of obligations satisfied do not necessarily demonstrate the absence of good faith.").

[201] U.C.C. § 9-623(a).

[202] U.C.C. § 9-623 Comment 2.

[203] The right to set aside a bad-faith disposition and then redeem the collateral is discussed in § 18.02[E] *supra.*

[204] U.C.C. § 9-623(c). *See, e.g.,* South Bay Bank N.A. v. Oates, 2001 WL 1297486, 47 U.C.C. Rep. Serv. 2d 422 (Cal. Ct. App. 2001) (junior secured party cannot redeem collateral after senior secured party has retained collateral in satisfaction of obligation).

[205] U.C.C. § 9-623(b)(1). *See, e.g.,* Automotive Fin. Corp. v. Smart Auto Ctr., Inc., 334 F.3d 685, 51 U.C.C. Rep. Serv. 2d 297 (7th Cir. 2003) (because exercise of redemption right requires full payment of all monetary obligations due, secured party did not have to return possession of collateral based upon debtor's offer to enter new agreement extending time for payment).

[206] U.C.C. § 9-623(b)(2).

aware of this. Accordingly, the secured party in a consumer-goods transaction must include in the pre-disposition notification a telephone number from which the recipient may obtain information from the secured party regarding the amount necessary to redeem the collateral.[207] Even if not required to do so, many secured parties routinely advise debtors of their redemption rights, but doing so can create a trap for the careless creditor. In several cases, secured parties have provided inaccurate redemption information, and courts have responded by concluding that the inaccuracy rendered the entire notice invalid. In *Moore v. Fidelity Financial Services, Inc.,*[208] for example, the secured party sent the debtor a notice of private disposition that properly indicated the date *after which* the collateral would be sold. Unfortunately for the secured party, the notice went on to state that the collateral could be redeemed *until the specified date.* The correct rule is that the debtor can redeem until the disposition has actually occurred or the secured party has entered into a contract to dispose of the collateral; thus, the court felt that the notice could have misled the debtor into believing that he had less time to redeem than he actually had. This type of careful scrutiny by courts is understandable, as inaccurate information regarding redemption may have the effect of discouraging entitled persons from seeking redemption. As a result, a creditor that chooses (or is required) to advise entitled persons of the right of redemption must be sure to do so in an accurate manner.[209]

Generally speaking, a person with a right of redemption may waive that right after default in an authenticated agreement.[210] The only reason for doing so would be to facilitate an early disposition of the collateral, and a secured party seeking a waiver of the right of redemption should make certain that the waiver also covers the debtor's right to be notified of the disposition.[211] Article 9 does not permit waiver of the right to redemption in a consumer-goods transaction.[212]

---

[207] U.C.C. § 9-614(1).

[208] 869 F. Supp. 557, 25 U.C.C. Rep. Serv. 2d 1306 (N.D. Ill. 1994).

[209] *See also* DiDominico v. First Nat'l Bank of Md., 57 Md. App. 62, 468 A.2d 1046, 37 U.C.C. Rep. Serv. 1427 (1984) (notice inaccurately informed debtor that redemption was limited to fifteen days).

[210] The right of redemption cannot be waived prior to default. *See* U.C.C. § 9-602(11). *See also* Data Security, Inc. v. Plessman, 1 Neb. App. 659, 510 N.W.2d 361, 23 U.C.C. Rep. Serv. 2d 989 (1993).

[211] The right to notice may also be waived after default in an authenticated agreement. *See* U.C.C. § 9-624(a), (b). A secured party that wants to consummate a quick disposition should seek a waiver of both the right to notice and the right to redemption.

[212] U.C.C. § 9-624(c).

Chapter 19

THE CONSEQUENCES OF CREDITOR MISBEHAVIOR

SYNOPSIS

§ 19.01 OVERVIEW

Chapter 18 dealt primarily with the rights and duties of secured parties during the foreclosure process. Chapter 19 focuses on the consequences that may befall a secured party that fails to conform its conduct to the Code's requirements. Creditor misbehavior takes many forms, among them:

- Repossessing collateral even though there has not been an event of default;

- Repossessing collateral in a manner that constitutes a breach of the peace;[1]

- Failing to take one or more of the many steps necessary to ensure a commercially reasonable disposition of the collateral;[2]

- Failing to give proper notice of disposition (sometimes characterized as an aspect of commercial reasonableness);[3]

---

[1] See § 18.01[A][1] *supra.*
[2] See § 18.02[A] *supra.*
[3] See § 18.02[B] *supra.*

- Buying improperly at a private disposition;[4]

- Failing to allow redemption;[5]

- Failing to use reasonable care to preserve collateral in its possession;[6]

- Failing to file a termination statement or relinquish control when required by the Code;[7] and

- Failing to respond to the debtor's request for a statement confirming the balance of the indebtedness or identifying the collateral.[8]

The most common complaints allege a failure to effect a commercially reasonable disposition and/or a failure to give proper notice. If a secured party fails to conform its conduct to the Code's requirements, Article 9 provides a variety of pre-disposition and post-disposition remedies to aggrieved persons.[9]

[A] Pre-Disposition Remedies

If a secured party is about to conduct a sale in a commercially unreasonable manner—for example, if it gave notice of its intention to sell the collateral at an auction sale at 2:00 a.m. on a Sunday morning—the debtor, a secondary obligor, or a junior lienholder might wish to seek a court order requiring the secured party to conduct the sale in a reasonable manner. If a secured party plans to proceed in a manner that is inconsistent with the Code's duties of good faith and commercial reasonableness, it is vital for there to be an appropriate remedy. This remedy will be of particular importance when it is applied before the secured party can complete an unreasonable disposition. Section 9-625(a) therefore provides that "[i]f it is established that a secured party is not proceeding in accordance with [Article 9], a court may order or restrain collection, enforcement, or disposition of collateral on appropriate terms and conditions."[10] An injunctive pre-disposition remedy may be useful in the following situations:

- If a secured party is planning a commercially unreasonable disposition—such as a public auction of an asset that is so specialized

---

[4] *See* § 18.02[C] *supra.*

[5] *See* § 18.05 *supra.*

[6] *See* § 19.01[B][3] *infra.*

[7] *See* § 19.01[B][4] *infra.*

[8] *See* § 19.01[B][5] *infra.*

[9] Article 9 does not expressly limit the persons who may sue for relief for a secured party's failure to comply with Part 6 of Article 9, but in the typical situation, only the debtor, an obligor, or a junior lienholder would actually suffer harm as a result of the secured party's conduct. *See, e.g., Robertson v. Horton Bros. Recovery, Inc.,* 2005 WL 736681, 56 U.C.C. Rep. Serv. 2d 925 (D. Del. 2005) (family members of debtor who did not demonstrate that they helped debtor purchase her car or that they held a property interest in the car did not have standing to pursue claim for damages allegedly suffered due to secured party's attempted repossession of the car).

[10] U.C.C. § 9-625(a).

that only a private sale will suffice—a court may issue a mandatory injunction requiring the secured party to conduct the sale in accordance with terms and conditions dictated by the judge;

- If a secured party has failed to give proper notice prior to an anticipated disposition, a court can issue a temporary restraining order prohibiting disposition for a time that is sufficient to allow an aggrieved party either to redeem or to prepare to protect its interests; and

- If a secured party's repossession is wrongful because there is no default, the debtor should be able to recover the collateral through a replevin action.

In the first two situations,[11] the question arises whether the party seeking relief must demonstrate the presence of the normal equitable requirements for obtaining injunctive relief—most notably the requirement of showing irreparable injury if the relief is not granted.[12] Because most secured parties are financially solvent (and thus capable of paying any damages awarded), the cases are rare in which the party seeking relief can make such a showing. Although the courts have split on the point, some authority supports the proposition that the party seeking relief need not meet the normal conditions for obtaining injunctive relief if the relief is authorized by statute.[13] Because of the importance that the drafters placed on the pre-disposition remedies and the limited intrusiveness of those remedies, the better-reasoned position is that the Code displaces the conditions normally found in equity.[14]

If there has been a default and the complaint is that the secured party breached the peace in repossessing the collateral, replevin should not be available[15]—the secured party still has the superior possessory interest, even if it gained possession in an inappropriate manner. Returning the collateral to the debtor will not cure the default, and the secured party could simply repossess it again. In such a circumstance, damages are sufficient to compensate the debtor for any injury it suffers.

---

[11] With regard to the third situation, the laws governing replevin actions typically specify the type of showing that the party seeking relief must make and the security it must provide.

[12] *See generally* Dan B. Dobbs, The Law of Remedies § 2.9(2), at 228 (2d Pract. ed. 1993). The other common requirements are that the party seeking relief post security for any harm caused by the court's order and demonstrate a probability of success on the merits.

[13] *Id.* § 2.10, at 244-46 (tendency is for courts to view statutory authorization of injunctive relief as substitute for irreparable injury rule).

[14] *See* U.C.C. § 1-103(b) (unless displaced by particular Code provisions, Code is supplemented by principles of law and equity).

[15] *See, e.g.,* Clark v. Associates Commercial Corp., 820 F. Supp. 562, 21 U.C.C. Rep. Serv. 2d 860 (D. Kan. 1993) (temporary restraining order pending replevin inappropriate where debtor was in default but repossession breached the peace).

[B] Monetary Damages

What theories support a monetary recovery if a secured party engages in creditor misconduct? As a practical matter, the answer depends upon the type of misconduct involved.

[1] Wrongful Repossession

Section 9-625(b) provides that the secured party is liable for damages "in the amount of any loss caused by a failure to comply with this Article."[16] This language authorizes the court to award damages in an amount sufficient to place the injured party in the position that it would have occupied had no violation occurred.

Section 9-625(b)'s provision for damages, however, does not displace the injured party's remedies under tort law. If a secured party repossesses collateral in the mistaken belief that the debtor has defaulted, the debtor may choose to seek recovery of the goods *in specie* and sue for the tort of trespass to chattels. In such an action, the debtor may recover possession of the collateral, as well as damages for any harm done to the collateral and for the loss of its use while the collateral was in the secured party's possession.[17] Alternatively, if the debtor does not want the collateral returned *in specie*, the debtor may allow the secured party to retain it and instead assert a claim for the intentional tort of conversion.[18] The standard measure of damages for conversion is the fair market value of the asset at the time of the conversion.[19] For example, suppose Freyermuth holds a security interest in Henning's automobile to secure a personal loan to Henning in the amount of $10,000. Because he wrongfully (but in good faith) believes Henning is in default, Freyermuth repossesses the car and conducts a commercially reasonable sale at which Lawrence purchases the car for $8,000—$3,000 less than its actual fair market value of $11,000. Henning could sue to set aside the foreclosure sale and recover the automobile from Lawrence,[20] and could also sue Freyermuth for damages for any harm done to the automobile and for the loss of the automobile's

---

[16] U.C.C. § 9-625(b).

[17] *See* Restatement (Second) of Torts § 222 Comment a.

[18] *See, e.g.*, Warren v. Ford Motor Credit Co., 693 F.2d 1373, 35 U.C.C. Rep. Serv. 306 (11th Cir. 1982); Chen v. Profit Sharing Plan of Donald H. Bohne, DDS, P.A., 456 S.E.2d 237 (Ga. App. 1995). Similarly, a subordinate creditor that takes possession of property in which a secured party has a superior security interest following default is also liable in conversion if the subordinate creditor refuses to turn over the collateral to the senior secured party. *See, e.g.*, Fleet Capital Corp. v. Yamaha Motor Corp., U.S.A., 2002 U.S. Dist. LEXIS 18115, 48 U.C.C. Rep. Serv. 2d 1137 (S.D.N.Y. 2002); Guaranty State Bank & Trust Co. v. Van Diest Supply Co., 55 P.3d 357, 48 U.C.C. Rep. Serv. 2d 1197 (Kan. Ct. App. 2002).

[19] *See, e.g.*, Fleet Capital Corp. v. Yamaha Motor Corp., U.S.A., 48 U.C.C. Rep. Serv. 2d 1137 (S.D.N.Y. 2002); Chemlease Worldwide, Inc. v. Brace, Inc., 338 N.W.2d 428, 37 U.C.C. Rep. Serv. 647 (Minn. 1983); Restatement (Second) of Torts § 222A Comment c (providing for recovery of "full value" of converted asset).

[20] If there is no default, a secured party cannot pass the debtor's rights in the collateral to a transferee. U.C.C. § 9-617(a).

use following repossession (*e.g.*, the amount required to lease a comparable vehicle during the period Henning was out of possession). Alternatively, Henning could simply choose to sue Freyermuth for damages for conversion, and could recover damages from Freyermuth in the amount of $1,000—the $11,000 fair market value of the automobile[21] less the $10,000 balance owed to Freyermuth.[22]

Even though conversion is an intentional tort, courts typically refuse to allow a jury to impose punitive damages if a secured party has acted in the mistaken but good faith belief that a default has occurred.[23] Although the standards vary somewhat from state to state, an award of punitive damages typically requires some type of egregious conduct by the secured party—either actual malicious conduct, or what courts have often called "constructive malice." Constructive malice typically consists of conduct that is reckless or grossly negligent. A case that comes close to the line *is Mitchell v. Ford Motor Credit Co.*,[24] in which the court approved an award of punitive damages following a wrongful repossession. The court concluded that the secured party was guilty of gross negligence because its records were in such a shambles that such incidents were bound to occur.

A debtor that claims wrongful repossession because the secured party committed a breach of the peace does not have a right to return of the goods *in specie*;[25] in such cases, the debtor may recover only monetary damages. In determining the theoretical basis for assessing damages, most courts simply treat the situation as analogous to a wrongful repossession without default and hold the secured party liable in conversion.[26] This is entirely appropriate and has the advantage of providing a uniform approach to all aspects of wrongful repossession. Courts may award punitive damages in cases of egregious conduct by the secured party.

A related situation occurs when a secured party refuses to accept a tender of the proper amount necessary to redeem the collateral.[27] In this situation, courts have appropriately recognized a cause of action for conversion because the secured party winds up in the same position it would have

---

[21] While the $8,000 price received by Freyermuth at the otherwise commercially reasonable sale would be some evidence of the car's fair market value, it is not conclusive in that regard. *See* § 18.02 *supra.*

[22] In contrast, if the fair market value of the car had been only $9,000, Henning could raise the claim for conversion as a counterclaim to Freyermuth's suit for a deficiency judgment. *See* § 19.02 *infra.*

[23] *See, e.g.*, Oaklawn Bank v. Baldwin, 709 S.W.2d 91, 1 U.C.C. Rep. Serv. 2d 596 (Ark. 1986).

[24] 688 P.2d 42, 38 U.C.C. Rep. Serv. 1812 (Okla. 1984).

[25] *See, e.g.*, Clark v. Associates Commercial Corp., 820 F. Supp. 562, 21 U.C.C. Rep. Serv. 2d 860 (D. Kan. 1993).

[26] *See, e.g.*, Kinetics Tech. Int'l Corp. v. Fourth Nat'l Bank of Tulsa, 705 F.2d 396, 36 U.C.C. Rep. Serv. 292 (10th Cir. 1983); Henderson v. Security Nat'l Bank, 72 Cal. App. 3d 764, 140 Cal. Rptr. 388, 22 U.C.C. Rep. Serv. 846 (1977). *But see* Nez v. Forney, 783 P.2d 471, 10 U.C.C. Rep. Serv. 2d 289 (N.M. 1989) (debtor's action for wrongful repossession sounded in contract).

[27] Redemption is discussed in § 18.05 *supra.*

occupied had it repossessed in the absence of a default. Similarly, damages based upon conversion are appropriate if a secured party miscalculates the amount necessary to redeem and demands an amount larger than the outstanding balance of the secured obligation.[28]

Depending upon the nature of a secured party's conduct, liability may accrue for torts other than conversion, and the secured party may even face criminal sanctions in extreme cases. The cases are replete with instances of overbearing creditors that have wrongfully entered another's property or roughed up someone who resisted repossession. On the civil side, this conduct may constitute trespass, assault, battery, or intentional infliction of emotional distress, or perhaps a violation of the federal Fair Debt Collection Practices Act.[29] On the criminal side, the secured party may be guilty of trespass, breach of the peace, assault, or battery. A debtor injured by a wrongful repossession could seek to recover damages under section 9-625(b), and could recover the amount necessary to place the debtor in the position it would have occupied had no violation occurred.[30] Section 9-625(b) does not preclude the debtor from claiming a different measure of damages under tort law, however.[31]

For example, suppose Freyermuth holds a security interest in Henning's car and repossesses the car following Henning's default—but does so by self-help despite Henning's strong verbal objection and attempted physical resistance, thereby breaching the peace under the law of the jurisdiction. Assume that this conduct enables Freyermuth to obtain possession of the car one month sooner than he would have obtained it in a judicial proceeding. At the time of the repossession, Henning owes Freyermuth $10,000 and the car's fair market value is $15,000. Freyermuth proceeds to conduct a commercially reasonable foreclosure sale at which Lawrence purchases the car for $10,000. On what theories can Henning recover damages, and in what amount?

If Henning chooses to proceed under section 9-625, the appropriate measure of damages will be the amount reasonably calculated to put Henning in the position he would have occupied had Freyermuth complied with Article 9 and sought judicial repossession—i.e., Henning would have had possession and use of the car for another month. Thus, under section 9-625, Henning could recover the value of one month's use of the car, which may be no more than a few hundred dollars. As a result, on these facts Henning should instead raise a conversion claim, upon which he could recover

---

[28] *See, e.g.*, Owens v. Automobile Recovery Bureau, Inc., 544 S.W.2d 26, 20 U.C.C. Rep. Serv. 820 (Mo. Ct. App. 1976).

[29] The FDCPA provides that a debt collector may not use "unfair or unconscionable means" to collect a debt, including taking or threatening to repossess by self-help if "(A) there is no present right to possession of the property claimed as collateral through an enforceable security interest; (B) there is no present intention to take possession of the property; or (C) the property is exempt by law from such dispossession or disablement." 15 U.S.C. § 1692f(6).

[30] *See* U.C.C. § 1-305(a); *see also* U.C.C. § 9-625, Comment 3.

[31] U.C.C. § 9-625, Comment 3. *See also* U.C.C. § 1-103(b) (unless specifically displaced, principles of law and equity supplement the Code's provisions).

damages in the amount of $5,000 (the car's fair market value less the balance of the debt owed to Freyermuth). In contrast, if the fair market value of the car had been only $10,000 at the time of repossession, Henning might instead choose to proceed under section 9-625(b). Under either approach, the court could award punitive damages, if appropriate, for Freyermuth's decision to proceed with self-help despite Henning's verbal objection and attempted physical resistance.[32]

[2] Wrongful Disposition of the Collateral

If an aggrieved person seeks damages on account of a secured party's conduct in disposing of collateral, section 9-625(b) authorizes the aggrieved person to recover the damages that flow from the secured party's conduct.[33] In measuring the aggrieved person's damages, one must look to the Code's general damages provision, which states that the remedies provided by the Code "must be liberally administered to the end that the aggrieved party may be put in as good a position as if the other party had fully performed but neither consequential or special damages nor penal damages may be had except as specifically provided in [the Uniform Commercial Code] or by other rule of law."[34] If the aggrieved person seeks damages under this provision, recovery of consequential damages (such as damages for emotional distress) is limited by the high foreseeability standards of general contract law. Furthermore, the aggrieved party typically cannot recover punitive damages unless it can state a tort claim for trespass, conversion, intentional infliction of emotional distress, or the like.

As noted above, the fact that section 9-625(b)'s damages provision sounds in contract does not mean that it displaces the availability of conversion (or another tort theory) as an alternative remedy. There are sound policy reasons for permitting recovery using a conversion measure in certain situations, especially in cases where the misconduct involves a failure to give proper notice to the debtor. Debtors rarely redeem collateral or take steps to protect their interests at foreclosure sales; thus, a failure to give notice is not likely to have an impact on the price received at the sale. Allowing only section 9-625(b) as a basis for recovery would yield no damages in such circumstances. Such a result would provide secured parties with relatively little incentive to make systematic efforts to comply with their obligations under Article 9.[35] Allowing debtors the alternative remedy of conversion, however, presents secured parties with the more meaningful

---

[32] The Code does not generally permit punitive damages, but it permits a court to award punitive damages if another rule of law (such as the law of conversion) so authorizes. U.C.C. § 1-305(a). The comments to § 9-625 make clear that underlying principles of tort law, such as the law of conversion, supplement the remedies provided in section 9-625. U.C.C. § 9-625, Comment 3.

[33] U.C.C. § 9-625(b).

[34] U.C.C. § 1-305(a). *See also* § 9-625, Comment 3.

[35] Even if it does not lead to measurable damages, failure to give notice can have a profound effect on the secured party's right to a deficiency judgment. *See* discussion in § 19.02 *infra*.

risk that a court might award damages and thus may have a more significant *in terrorem* effect. [36]

The difference between damages based upon conversion and damages based upon the Code's remedial provision is illustrated neatly by the facts of *Schrock v. Citizens Valley Bank*, [37] in which the secured party conducted an auction sale in a commercially unreasonable manner. The auction produced only $143,000, but expert testimony indicated that a commercially reasonable auction would have produced $170,000—roughly 85% of the collateral's $200,000 fair market value. Using the Code's remedial provision, the court should place the debtor "in as good a position as if the [secured] party had fully performed," and full performance in this context means a commercially reasonable auction. Thus, assuming that the debt in *Schrock* was $150,000, the Code's remedial scheme would entitle the debtor to recover damages of $20,000—the surplus that would have been produced by a commercially reasonable sale. In conversion, however, the debtor could recover damages of $50,000—the fair market value of the collateral less the balance of the secured debt. [38]

[3] Failure to Use Reasonable Care Regarding Collateral in Secured Party's Possession

Article 9 obligates a secured party to use reasonable care in the custody and preservation of collateral in its possession. [39] If the secured party fails to satisfy this obligation, an aggrieved person may recover damages for "any loss" caused by such failure. [40]

[4] Failure to File or Send Termination Statement

The Code permits a debtor to demand that a secured party provide a termination statement terminating the effectiveness of a financing statement if there remains no outstanding obligation and no commitment by the secured party to make subsequent advances, incur obligations, or otherwise give value to be secured by the collateral described in that financing statement. [41] If the collateral is consumer goods, the Code obligates the secured party to file such a termination statement within one month after satisfaction of the secured obligation, even if the debtor does not request

---

[36] *But see* Kennedy v. Fournie, 898 S.W.2d 672, 26 U.C.C. Rep. Serv. 2d 640 (Mo. Ct. App. 1995) (debtor was not entitled to conversion damages for failure to give proper notice because secured party was entitled to possession and debtor made no attempt to redeem the collateral).

[37] 621 P.2d 96, 30 U.C.C. Rep. Serv. 1169 (Or. Ct. App. 1980).

[38] The effect of such misconduct on a secured party's claim for a deficiency is discussed in § 19.02 *infra*.

[39] U.C.C. § 9-207(a). The debtor and secured party may define in the security agreement what constitutes "reasonable care," unless the standards are "manifestly unreasonable." U.C.C. § 9-603(a).

[40] U.C.C. § 9-625(b).

[41] U.C.C. § 9-513(c) (20 days following receipt of authenticated demand). Termination statements are discussed generally in § 5.06[c] *supra*.

a termination statement.[42] If the secured party fails to satisfy its obligation in a timely fashion, the secured party is liable for any loss caused by its failure, *plus* a minimum statutory penalty in the amount of $500.[43]

[5] Failure to Provide Statement of Account or List of Collateral

Article 9 permits a debtor to request that the secured party issue a statement setting forth or confirming the outstanding balance of the debtor's unpaid obligation to the secured party. In addition, Article 9 permits the debtor to request that the secured party approve or correct a list of the secured party's collateral.[44] Such statements are of some use to the debtor in obtaining subsequent financing or in refinancing the secured obligations, as future secured parties likely will seek to confirm the extent of encumbrances against the debtor's assets.[45] Article 9 obligates the secured party to respond to the debtor's request within 14 days;[46] if it fails to comply, the secured party is liable for any resulting loss, which may include (for example) the debtor's inability to obtain alternative financing or the increased costs of such financing.[47] Furthermore, in the event the secured party fails to comply with such a request without reasonable cause, it is also liable for statutory damages of $500 (in addition to actual damages).[48]

---

[42] U.C.C. § 9-513(a).

[43] U.C.C. § 9-625(e)(4). Similarly, a secured party that fails to relinquish control as required by U.C.C. § 9-208 or § 9-209 is liable for any loss caused plus the minimum statutory penalty. U.C.C. § 9-625(e)(1), (2).

[44] U.C.C. § 9-210(b).

[45] The impact of the Code's first-to-file-or-perfect rule for conflicting security interests in the same collateral (as explained in Chapter 10) may render these statements of somewhat limited use to future secured parties. For example, suppose Bank is considering a loan to Debtor secured by all of Debtor's equipment (which has a value of $50,000). In investigating Debtor's creditworthiness, Bank discovers an existing filed financing statement in favor of Finance Company, covering the Debtor's equipment. Bank requires Debtor to ask Finance Company to confirm the balance of the secured obligations under § 9-210, and Finance Company confirms that the balance of the debt is only $500. As explained in Chapter 10, Bank cannot assume that it can safely make the loan based upon the confirmation that Debtor has $49,500 of equity in the equipment. If Bank made the loan to Debtor, nothing would prevent Finance Company from later making another loan to Debtor secured by the Debtor's equipment (as long as its financing statement covering equipment remained effective to perfect that interest). Under § 9-322(a)(1), Finance Company would have first priority as to the equipment to the full extent of those additional loans. As a result, Bank cannot ensure its desired priority if it relies solely upon Finance Company's confirmation to the debtor of the balance of the secured obligations.

[46] U.C.C. § 9-210(b).

[47] U.C.C. § 9-625(b).

[48] U.C.C. § 9-625(f). If the secured party never claimed any interest in the collateral or the obligations referenced in the request, it has reasonable cause for its failure to comply. *Id.*

§ 19.02 SECURED PARTY'S RIGHT TO DEFICIENCY JUDGMENT

Claims of creditor misconduct commonly arise when a secured party conducts a foreclosure that fails to satisfy the secured obligation and thereafter seeks a judgment for the remaining deficiency. The secured party's right to recover a deficiency arises from section 9-615(d), which provides that "the secured party shall account to and pay a debtor for any surplus" and that "the obligor is liable for any deficiency."[49] The secured party's failure to observe Article 9's disposition rules, however, renders the secured party liable for any resulting loss under section 9-625(b). To what extent does the secured party's failure to observe Article 9's disposition rules affect its right to collect its deficiency judgment?

To understand Article 9's treatment of this question, it is first necessary to consider the way courts approached the question prior to the effective date of revised Article 9 in July 2001. A hypothetical should prove useful. Suppose Debtor owes Bank $225,000 secured by a security interest in Debtor's equipment. Debtor defaults, and Bank conducts a commercially unreasonable auction sale that yields a price of $150,000. Further, suppose that a reasonable auction sale would have produced a price of $175,000, and that the equipment could have sold for as much as $185,000 if it could have been sold in an arms-length transaction (*i.e.*, not in the context of a foreclosure auction). Finally, suppose Bank attempts to sue Debtor to collect a deficiency judgment of $75,000, and Debtor objects that Bank's sale was commercially unreasonable.

Prior to revised Article 9, courts took one of three approaches to such a dispute. The first approach, sometimes called the "set-off" approach, was based on a straightforward reading of the text of the prior version of Article 9—the secured party could recover the amount of the deficiency reduced by any actual losses attributable to its misconduct. Courts following this approach would calculate independently the amount due to each party and then "net out" the results, leaving a judgment in favor of one of the litigants.[50] Under this approach, a secured party's misbehavior neither barred a deficiency nor created a presumption of harm. The secured party bore the burden of proving the facts that supported its claim, and the obligor carried the burden of proving that the misconduct had caused it to suffer a loss. In the above hypothetical, Bank would have a claim for a $75,000 deficiency—calculated as its debt ($225,000) less the proceeds of its sale ($150,000). In turn, if Debtor raised a counterclaim based upon Article 9's remedial provision, Debtor would recover damages of $25,000—the amount that Bank would have received had it conducted a commercially reasonable sale ($175,000) less the actual sale proceeds ($150,000). When the claims are netted out, the Bank would recover a judgment for $50,000. If Debtor

---

[49] U.C.C. § 9-615(d). If the issue of a deficiency arises following a secured party's collection or enforcement of rights to payment, § 9-608(a)(4) provides a similar rule.

[50] *See, e.g.*, Boender v. Chicago N. Clubhouse Ass'n, Inc., 608 N.E.2d 207, 20 U.C.C. Rep. Serv. 2d 687 (Ill. Ct. App. 1992).

instead raises a counterclaim based on the tort theory of conversion,[51] it would be entitled to recover damages of $35,000—the collateral's fair market value ($185,000) less the amount actually received ($150,000). Thus, after netting the claims, Bank would recover a deficiency judgment for $40,000.[52]

While the "set-off" approach was both straightforward and consistent with the text of prior Article 9, very few courts adopted it. Many state courts instead adopted the "absolute bar" rule, under which a secured party that violated its obligations in disposing of the collateral *could not recover a deficiency judgment regardless of the collateral's actual value.* Applying the "absolute bar" approach to the above hypothetical, once Debtor proved that Bank's sale was commercially unreasonable, Debtor would be entitled to summary judgment against Bank on Bank's action for a deficiency judgment—even though a commercially reasonable sale would have produced a bona fide deficiency of $50,000![53]

Some courts took a third approach, rejecting the "absolute bar" rule because (a) it had no support in the text of Article 9, (b) it created undeserved windfalls for debtors in cases such as the above hypothetical, and (c) such a punitive sanction was disproportionate given the relatively nebulous "commercially reasonable" standard that Article 9 imposes on secured parties.[54] These courts adopted a rule known as the "rebuttable

---

[51] *See* discussion in § 19.02[B] *infra.*

[52] If the value of Debtor's counterclaim exceeded the value of Bank's claim, using whatever measure the court deemed appropriate, Debtor would be entitled to an affirmative recovery.

[53] *See, e.g., In re* Kelaidis, 276 B.R. 266, 47 U.C.C. Rep. Serv. 2d 823 (10th Cir. Bankr. 2002) (noting Utah courts' consistent application of absolute bar rule). For a compilation of cases applying the absolute bar rule, see Robert M. Lloyd, *The Absolute Bar Rule in UCC Foreclosure Cases: A Prescription for Waste,* 40 UCLA L. Rev. 695 (1993).

Proponents of the "absolute bar" rule cited two primary justifications for the rule. First, the rule is very simple and courts can apply it easily; courts do not have to make difficult factual judgments about what sale price the secured party might have obtained at a commercially reasonable sale. Second, the rule has a significant *in terrorem* effect upon secured parties, for whom it provides a clear message: comply with Article 9's obligations or lose your right to a deficiency judgment altogether.

[54] *See, e.g.,* Baragas v. Coupland State Bank, 2001 Tex. App. LEXIS 7885, 46 U.C.C. Rep. Serv. 2d 565 (Tex. Ct. App. 2001) (despite failure to give proper notice of public auction, court upheld deficiency judgment against guarantors because most of sale proceeds had derived from private sales with proper notice, guarantors did not show that public sale was commercially unreasonable, and barring deficiency would give guarantors windfall).

In the hypothetical in the text, for example, Bank will expect a significant deficiency (somewhere around $50,000). Bank thus has a significant incentive to conduct a sale that will preserve its right to enforce that deficiency. But Bank will be hard-pressed to know exactly when it has done "enough" to make its sale "commercially reasonable." For example, how many advertisements should it run? Three? Six? Twelve? On the one hand, we presumably want Bank to run an additional advertisement if it will attract more bidders and produce a higher sale price. On the other hand, because Bank will add these expenses of sale to the balance of the debt, U.C.C. § 9-615(a)(1), such expenses will increase Debtor's deficiency if they do not actually produce a higher sale price.

The problem is that Bank has no way to know exactly when an additional advertisement

presumption" rule. Under this rule, once an obligor demonstrated that the secured party violated Article 9's requirements in disposing of the collateral, the court drew a presumption that the collateral's value equaled the outstanding debt.[55] In other words, the court established a presumption that a proper disposition would have generated sale proceeds exactly sufficient to satisfy the debt. Effectively, this presumption placed upon the secured party the burden of going forward with evidence to the contrary— *i.e.*, to recover a deficiency, the secured party had to produce evidence that even a sale in full compliance with Article 9's requirements would still have resulted in a deficiency based upon the actual value of the collateral. If the secured party could not rebut the presumption, it could not recover a deficiency judgment. If the secured party did successfully rebut the presumption, it could recover a deficiency unless the obligor successfully refuted the secured party's evidence. The obligor bore the ultimate burden of persuasion on the issue of loss.

In the above hypothetical, the "rebuttable presumption" rule would have given Debtor the benefit of a presumption that the collateral was worth $225,000 (the full amount of the debt). Bank would have to produce evidence to rebut the presumption and demonstrate that a commercially reasonable auction still would have resulted in a deficiency. Thus, assuming Bank produced sufficient credible evidence that a commercially reasonable sale would have produced a price of $175,000, Bank could recover a deficiency judgment in the amount of $50,000.[56]

Based upon widespread criticism of the absolute bar rule, revised Article 9 has expressly adopted the rebuttable presumption rule *for all nonconsumer transactions*. If a secured party seeks a deficiency judgment, it does not have to establish compliance with the Code's requirements as part of its prima facie case.[57] If the debtor or a secondary obligor raises the secured party's noncompliance as an issue, the secured party must prove that the disposition complied with the Code's requirements.[58] If the secured party

---

will (or will not) produce more bidders, and thus the absolute bar rule may in fact encourage secured parties to run extra (and potentially ineffective) advertisements—thereby driving up deficiency judgments—just to protect its right to collect a deficiency judgment (*i.e.*, to protect against the risk that a court might say, after the fact, "you should've run more advertisements"). Thus, some have argued that the absolute bar rule, although a boon to the individual entitled to raise it, was not in the best interests of debtors as a class. *See* Robert M. Lloyd, *The Absolute Bar Rule in UCC Foreclosure Cases: A Prescription for Waste*, 40 UCLA L. Rev. 695 (1993).

[55] *Cf.* Lease Resolution Corp. v. Aut-A-Wash, Inc., 59 Mass. App. 1107, 52 U.C.C. Rep. Serv. 2d 534 (2003) (unpublished) (rebuttable presumption approach inapplicable where evidence showed that secured party gave proper notice and complied with all other provisions of Article 9).

[56] If the court instead proceeded upon a conversion theory, the secured party would have to produce evidence tending to prove that the fair market value of the collateral was less than the amount of the debt. Thus, if Bank produced sufficient credible evidence that the fair market value of the collateral was only $185,000, Bank could recover a $40,000 deficiency judgment.

[57] U.C.C. § 9-626(a)(1).

[58] U.C.C. § 9-626(a)(2).

fails to carry this burden, then a presumption arises that a disposition in compliance with the Code's requirements would have produced a price sufficient to satisfy the outstanding debt.[59] The secured party may not recover a deficiency unless it proves that a disposition in compliance with the Code's requirements would have produced a price less than the balance of the debt. If the secured party carries this burden, it may recover a judgment equal to the amount of the secured obligation less the amount that would have been received in a commercially reasonable disposition.[60]

In *consumer transactions*, however, Article 9 does not provide a specific rule to govern the consequences of a secured party's noncompliance. Section 9-626(b) provides that Article 9 "is intended to leave to the court the determination of the proper rules in consumer transactions" and permits courts in consumer transactions "to apply established approaches."[61] As a result, in consumer transactions, courts retain the discretion to choose to apply any of the three approaches taken by courts under the previous version of Article 9—including the "absolute bar" rule. Not surprisingly, some courts in states that had applied the "absolute bar" rule prior to revised Article 9 have continued to apply that rule in consumer transactions.[62]

§ 19.03   THE CONSUMER PENALTY—§ 9-625(c)

Article 9 contains a provision that is sometimes called the "consumer penalty." If a secured party fails to comply with Article 9 in disposing of consumer goods, the Code permits the debtor or a secondary obligor to recover "in any event an amount not less than the credit service charge plus 10 percent of the principal amount of the debt or the time price differential plus 10 percent of the cash price."[63] Because this provision is appended onto Article 9's basic damages provision and establishes an amount recoverable "in any event," one should read the consumer penalty as a substitute for ordinary monetary damages. If the consumer cannot establish loss in the ordinary manner, or if the amount of that loss is less than the consumer penalty, the consumer may recover the penalty *rather than* ordinary damages. In other words, the section functions to a certain

---

[59] U.C.C. § 9-626(a)(4).

[60] U.C.C. § 9-626(a)(3).

[61] U.C.C. § 9-626(b).

[62] *See, e.g.,* Coxall v. Clover Commercial Corp., 4 Misc. 3d 654, 781 N.Y.S.2d 567, 54 U.C.C. Rep. Serv. 2d 5 (N.Y. City Civ. Ct. 2004); *In re* Downing, 286 B.R. 900, 49 U.C.C. Rep. Serv. 2d 983 (Bankr. W.D. Mo. 2002).

[63] U.C.C. § 9-625(c)(2); *see, e.g.,* Coxall v. Clover Commercial Corp., 4 Misc. 3d 654, 781 N.Y.S.2d 567, 54 U.C.C. Rep. Serv. 2d 5 (N.Y. City Civ. Ct. 2004) (consumer debtor entitled to statutory damage recovery of $1,846.24). Other aggrieved parties (such as a junior secured party) may recover damages under section 9-625(b), but may not rely upon the consumer penalty.

extent as a liquidated damages provision;[64] the consumer could not recover both actual damages and the full amount of the consumer penalty.[65]

Calculating the amount of the consumer penalty can be tricky because there are two basic formulas. Understanding which formula to use requires an appreciation for the difference between a *credit service charge* (which is the equivalent of interest on a loan) and a *time-price differential*. At the time the Code was first adopted, several jurisdictions had statutes or constitutional provisions establishing restrictive usury laws. For example, suppose that a state's law allowed for a maximum interest rate of 10%. If a debtor went to a bank to borrow money to buy a car, the bank could not charge interest at a higher rate. Though these restrictions were popular in many states, they had a negative impact upon some sectors of the economy in those states. For example, if a national automotive concern that sold cars to consumers on secured credit could not obtain a competitive interest rate in a particular state, it might choose to do business in another state. Recognizing this economic reality, some courts came up with the fiction of the time-price differential. In a state with a 10% usury limit, if a seller was willing to sell an asset for $10,000 today but had to be repaid $11,500 in installments over the course of a year, these courts reasoned that the $1,500 difference was not "interest" and therefore was not subject to the usury laws. It was, instead, a "time-price differential." In other words, the time-price differential was simply a means to avoid the impact of the usury laws.

The following hypothetical situations illustrate the differences in the formulas contained in the consumer penalty. Suppose Henning, a consumer, decides to purchase a car priced at $25,000. He intends to pay $5,000 down and finance $20,000, and has a choice of having Dealer or Bank handle the financing. If Henning borrows $20,000 from Bank to be repaid over four years and the total interest Bank will receive over the life of the loan is $4,000, the consumer penalty that Bank must pay if it engages in misconduct will be $6,000—the sum of $2,000 (ten percent of the principal amount of the debt) and $4,000 (the credit service charge). If he had decided to finance the $20,000 with Dealer and had agreed to repay a total of $24,000 over four years, the consumer penalty would be $4,000 (the time-price differential) plus ten percent of the cash price. But would the "cash price" be the cash amount that Henning had to pay Dealer to buy the car without any financing ($25,000), or the amount financed ($20,000)? It is tempting to say that $20,000 is the proper amount, because this equates the penalties for sellers and lenders. The problem is that the Code also uses the term "cash price" in its strict foreclosure provision[66] and, in that context, it

---

[64] Indeed, the provision appears to serve both a punitive and a liquidated damages function, concepts that are antithetical in normal contract law. The term "consumer penalty" is thus something of a misnomer.

[65] Chisolm v. TranSouth Fin. Corp., 194 F.R.D. 538, 42 U.C.C. Rep. Serv. 2d 332 (E.D. Va. 2000) (actual damages or statutory damages are recoverable, but not both).

[66] U.C.C. § 9-620(e).

almost certainly means the full price that would have been paid on the date of sale (in the example, $25,000).[67]

After grasping the basic formula, one may apply the consumer penalty as the drafters envisioned it in a relatively straightforward fashion. For example, suppose that in the above hypothetical, Henning chose to finance the car from Bank. Suppose further that Bank conducts a commercially unreasonable sale, bringing a price of $8,000 and leaving a deficiency of $8,000. As discussed above, Bank would incur a $6,000 penalty because of its misconduct. If Bank cannot overcome the presumption that the car was worth the same amount as the debt, Bank cannot recover a deficiency judgment. Should Henning also be allowed to obtain a judgment for the $6,000 consumer penalty? The answer should be no. The effect of the presumption is to establish the loss flowing from the misconduct; on our facts, the loss is presumed to be $8,000. Because the consumer penalty is an alternative to damages, allowing Henning to recover it would violate the spirit of the Code.[68]

In this regard, it is important to remember that Article 9 permits courts to adopt the absolute bar rule to prohibit a deficiency judgment if a secured party has conducted a commercially unreasonable disposition in a consumer transaction. Can a consumer debtor avoid a deficiency judgment entirely under the absolute bar rule and also recover the consumer penalty? The answer should be no, as this would appear to add a penalty on top of a penalty. The debtor should be required to elect between the absolute bar rule and the result that would be reached by netting out the deficiency against the consumer penalty.[69] Unfortunately, a few decisions, such as *Wilmington Trust Co. v. Conner*,[70] have permitted consumer debtors to apply both the absolute bar rule and the consumer penalty. Even more unfortunately, the drafters of revised Article 9 expressly refused to reject cases like *Conner*—the comments to section 9-625 merely state that the Code "leaves the treatment of statutory damages as it was under former Article 9."[71] Although the drafters presumably did not intend this language

---

[67] Because the purpose of the limitation on strict foreclosure is to protect the debtor's equity, whereas the purpose of the consumer penalty is (at least in part) to penalize creditor misbehavior, one might argue that it is appropriate to assign different meanings to the same term in these different contexts. This argument is subject to criticism, however—the consumer penalty also serves to protect the equity of consumer debtors generally, by encouraging creditors to conduct reasonable sales.

[68] If Bank's unreasonable sale produced a price of $11,000, leaving a deficiency of $5,000, and Bank could not overcome the presumption, Henning would have a choice of taking the presumed $5,000 in damages (wiping out the deficiency) or the $6,000 consumer penalty. Obviously, Henning would select the consumer penalty, but the court should net this out against the full deficiency. In other words, Henning should recover $1,000.

[69] For a case that gets the issue right, *see* First City Bank-Farmers Branch v. Guex, 659 S.W.2d 734, 37 U.C.C. Rep. Serv. 1008 (Tex. Ct. App. 1983).

[70] 415 A.2d 773, 28 U.C.C. Rep. Serv. 900 (Del. 1980). *See also, e.g.,* Coxall v. Clover Commercial Corp., 4 Misc. 3d 654, 781 N.Y.S.2d 567, 54 U.C.C. Rep. Serv. 2d 5 (N.Y. City Civ. Ct. 2004); *In re* Angel, 142 B.R. 194 (Bankr. S.D. Ohio 1992).

[71] U.C.C. § 9-625, Comment 4.

to reflect their approval of cases like *Conner*, some courts may use the comments to justify allowing debtors in consumer-goods transactions to recover both actual damages and the consumer penalty (or to assert the benefit of the absolute bar rule and still recover the consumer penalty).

Table of Cases

[References are to page and footnote numbers.]

[References are to page and footnote numbers.]

[References are to page and footnote numbers.]

[References are to page and footnote numbers.]

[References are to page and footnote numbers.]

[References are to page and footnote numbers.]

[References are to page and footnote numbers.]

X

Y

Z

Table of Statutes

[References are to page and footnote numbers.]

[References are to page and footnote numbers.]

[References are to page and footnote numbers.]

[References are to page and footnote numbers.]

[References are to page and footnote numbers.]

[References are to page and footnote numbers.]

[References are to page and footnote numbers.]

[References are to page and footnote numbers.]

[References are to page and footnote numbers.]

[References are to page and footnote numbers.]

[References are to page and footnote numbers.]

[References are to page and footnote numbers.]

INDEX

[References are to page numbers.]

[References are to page numbers.]

[References are to page numbers.]

[References are to page numbers.]

[References are to page numbers.]

[References are to page numbers.]

MULTISTATE TRANSACTIONS—Cont.

Understanding priorities . . . 228

N

NOTICE

Disposition of collateral (See COLLATERAL, DISPOSITION OF)

Filing, perfection by (See FILING, PERFECTION BY)

O

ONGOING FINANCING RELATIONSHIPS

After-acquired property

 Exceptions . . . 102

 General applicability . . . 99

Facilitating clauses generally . . . 97

Future advances . . . 103

Inventory and accounts

 Factoring of . . . 106

 Financing against . . . 108

 Floor planning inventory . . . 110

P

PAYMENT INTANGIBLES

Sales of

 Generally . . . 49

 Automatic perfection . . . 186

PERFECTION

Generally . . . 113

Alternative methods of

 Generally . . . 116

 Control . . . 119

 Delivery . . . 119

 Financing statement, filing of . . . 117

 Perfection under federal law . . . 118

 Possession . . . 117

 State certificate-of-title statute . . . 118

 Temporary perfection . . . 117

Automatic (See AUTOMATIC PERFECTION)

Continuity of . . . 120

Occurrence . . . 119

Purpose . . . 115

POSSESSION, PERFECTION BY

Generally . . . 155

POSSESSION, PERFECTION BY—Cont.

Concept of

 Generally . . . 169

 Agents and bailees, possession by . . . 170

 Secured party, possession by . . . 169

 Symbolic or constructive delivery 172

History . . . 155

Perfection by control

 Deposit accounts . . . 177

 Electronic chattel paper . . . 177

 Electronic documents . . . 177

 Investment property . . . 173

 Letter-of-credit rights . . . 177

Possession under Article 9 . . . 157

Possessory security arrangements

 Generally . . . 158

 Goods in storage or manufacture

  Generally . . . 161

  Field warehousing . . . 164

  Terminal warehousing . . . 161

 Goods in transit . . . 167

 Valuables and indispensable paper, pledges of . . . 159

PROCEEDS

Enforceability of security interests . . . 93

Secured parties (See SECURED PARTIES)

PROCEEDS, PERFECTION OF

Continuous perfection

 Generally . . . 197

 Identifiable cash proceeds . . . 197

 Same filing office

  Basic rule . . . 199

  "Cash-phase" rule . . . 200

  Timely general perfection . . . 201

Grace period of temporary perfection . . 195

PROPERTY

Collateral

 Classifications of . . . 42

 Property rights of transferee . . . 451

Investment property (See INVESTMENT PROPERTY)

PURCHASERS OTHER THAN SECURED PARTIES

Generally . . . 295

Article 9's residual priority rule . . . 295

[References are to page numbers.]

[References are to page numbers.]